D0680605

FOREWORD BY C. PETER WAGNER

THE
KINGDOM
AND THE
POWER

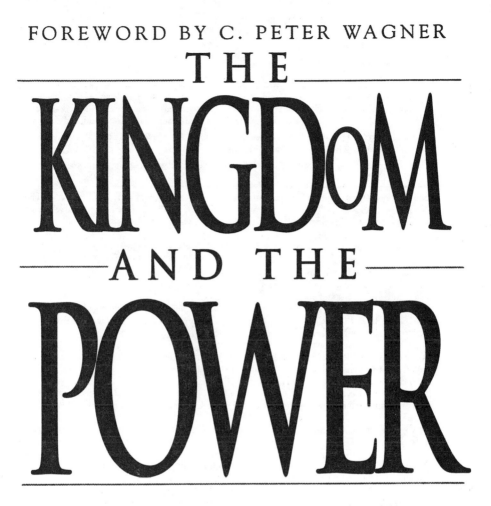

FOREWORD BY C. PETER WAGNER

THE
KINGDoM
AND THE
POWER

Are Healing and the Spiritual Gifts Used by Jesus
and the Early Church Meant for the Church Today?

A Biblical Look at How to Bring the Gospel to the World with Power

J.I. PACKER, JEFF NIEHAUS, WAYNE GRUDEM,
S.M. BURGESS, DAVID LEWIS AND JOHN WHITE
EDITED BY GARY S. GREIG AND KEVIN N. SPRINGER

Regal Books
A Division of Gospel Light
Ventura, California, U.S.A.

Published by Regal Books
A Division of Gospel Light
Ventura, California, U.S.A.
Printed in U.S.A.

Regal Books is a ministry of Gospel Light, an evangelical Christian publisher dedicated to serving the local church. We believe God's vision for Gospel Light is to provide church leaders with biblical, user-friendly materials that will help them evangelize, disciple and minister to children, youth and families.

It is our prayer that this Regal Book will help you discover biblical truth for your own life and help you meet the needs of others. May God richly bless you.

For a free catalog of resources from Regal Books/Gospel Light please contact your Christian supplier or call 1-800-4-GOSPEL.

Library of Congress Catloging-in-Publication Data
The kingdom and the power : are the healing and the spiritual gifts used by Jesus and the early church meant for the church today? / edited by Gary S. Greig, and Kevin N. Springer.
    p. cm.
Includes bibliographical references and index.
ISBN 0-8307-1634-3
    1. Miracles. 2. Spiritual healing. 3. Holy Spirit.
4. Evangelicalism. I: Greig, Gary S. II. Springer, Kevin.
BT97.2.P65 1993   93-31682
231.7'3—dc20   CIP

Rights for publishing this book in other languages are contracted by Gospel Literature International (GLINT). GLINT also provides technical help for the adaptation, translation and publishing of Bible study resources and books in scores of languages worldwide. For further information, contact GLINT, P.O. Box 4060, Ontario, CA 91761-1003, U.S.A., or the publisher.

We dedicate this book to
JOHN WIMBER
who has fearlessly pioneered effective
biblical models of power evangelism,
healing, and gift-based ministry

CONTENTS

About the Authors   11
Foreword   15
    C. Peter Wagner
Introduction   17
    Gary S. Greig and Kevin N. Springer

I. EXEGETICAL AND THEOLOGICAL STUDIES

1. Old Testament Foundations: 41
   Signs and Wonders in Prophetic Ministry and the
   Substitutionary Atonement of Isaiah 53
       Jeffrey Niehaus, Gordon-Conwell Theological Seminary
       South Hamilton, Massachusetts

2. Should Christians Expect Miracles Today?   55
   Objections and Answers from the Bible
       Wayne Grudem, Trinity Evangelical Divinity School
       Deerfield, Illinois

3. A Biblical View of the Relationship of Sin   111
   and the Fruits of Sin: Sickness, Demonization,
   Death, Natural Calamity
       Peter H. Davids, Langley Vineyard Christian Fellowship
       Langley, British Columbia, Canada

4. The Purpose of Signs and Wonders in the New Testament: 133
   What Terms for Miraculous Power Denote and Their
   Relationship to the Gospel
   Gary S. Greig, Gospel Light Publications
   Ventura, California
   Fuller Theological Seminary
   Pasadena, California

5. Following Christ's Example: 175
   A Biblical View of Discipleship
   Don Williams, Vineyard Christian Fellowship
   La Jolla, California

6. Power Ministry in the Epistles: 197
   A Reply to the Evangelical Cessationist Position
   Walter R. Bodine
   Dallas, Texas

7. The Empowered Christian Life 207
   James I. Packer, Regent College
   Vancouver, British Columbia, Canada

II. PASTORAL REFLECTIONS

8. A Pastor's View of Praying for the Sick 219
   and Overcoming the Evil One in the Power of the Spirit
   Roger Barrier, Casas Adobes Baptist Church
   Tucson, Arizona

9. Healing and Deliverance—Because of the Cross: 245
   Seeing the Power of the Gospel at Work Through
   Prayer for Healing and Deliverance
   Lloyd D. Fretz, Missionary Church, Canada East
   Kitchener, Ontario, Canada

10. Coming Out of the Hangar: 257
    Confessions of an Evangelical Deist
    Kirk Bottomly, Emmanuel Presbyterian Church
    Thousand Oaks, California

III. Related Studies

11. Proclaiming the Gospel with Miraculous Gifts   277
    in the Postbiblical Early Church
    Stanley M. Burgess, Southwest Missouri State Univeristy
    Springfield, Missouri

12. Revival and the Spirit's Power: 289
    A Psychiatric View of Behavioral Phenomena
    Associated with Healing and Gift-based Ministry
    John White
    Cloverdale, British Columbia, Canada

13. A Social Anthropologist's Analysis of   321
    Contemporary Healing
    David C. Lewis, The University of Cambridge
    Cambridge, England

14. Communicating and Ministering the Power of   345
    the Gospel Cross-culturally:
    The Power of God for Christians Who Ride Two Horses
    Charles H. and Marguerite G. Kraft
    Fuller Theological Seminary
    Pasadena, California
    Biola University
    La Mirada, California

Appendices

Appendix 1:   359
Power Evangelism and the New Testament Evidence

Appendix 2:   393
John 14:12—The Commission to All Believers to Do the
Miraculous Works of Jesus

Appendix 3:   399
Matthew 28:18-20—The Great Commission and
Jesus' Commands to Preach and Heal

Appendix 4:   **405**
Spiritual Gifts—A Wonder-Working God
Versus a Wonder-Working Church?

Appendix 5:   **413**
Spiritual Warfare—A Biblical View of Demons
and God-Directed Weapons

Appendix 6:   **421**
Models of Prayer for Healing and Related Phenomena

Appendix 7:   **437**
The Sufficiency of Scripture and Distortion of
What Scripture Teaches About Itself

Abbreviations   **443**
Select Bibliography   **445**
Subject Index   **451**
Scripture Index   **457**

ABOUT THE AUTHORS

Gary S. Greig is senior editor of Gospel Light Publications, Ventura, California, U.S.A., and is Adjunct Assistant Professor of Hebrew, Fuller Theological Seminary, Pasadena, California. He received a B.A. (Archaeology and Egyptology, 1983) from the Hebrew University, Jerusalem, Israel, did graduate study in the School of Theology at Fuller Seminary (1982-1983), Pasadena, California, U.S.A., and received an M.A. and Ph.D. (Near Eastern Languages and Civilizations, 1990) from the University of Chicago, Oriental Institute. He has published articles in scholarly publications and journals and is an elder at Community Presbyterian Church (PCUSA), Ventura, California.

Kevin N. Springer is associate pastor of the Vineyard Christian Fellowship, Anaheim, California, U.S.A. He received an M.A. (Church History and Theology, 1976) from Ashland Theological Seminary, Ashland, Ohio, and did graduate work (Reformation History) at the University of Western Ontario, London, Ontario, Canada. He has authored numerous articles and books, including *Power Evangelism* (with John Wimber; HarperCollins), *Power Healing* (with John Wimber; HarperCollins), and *Power Encounters* (HarperCollins).

Roger Barrier is the senior pastor of the Casas Adobes Baptist Church in Tucson, Arizona, U.S.A., which is affiliated with the Southern Baptist Convention. During Roger's 18-year ministry, the church has grown from 200 to more than 6,000 members. He received a B.A. (Greek and Religion, 1972) from Baylor University, an M.Div. (1975) from Southwestern Baptist Seminary, and a D.Min. (1992) from Golden Gate Baptist Seminary, San Francisco, California.

Walter R. Bodine is currently engaged in independent scholarly work in biblical and ancient Near Eastern studies, focusing now on Sumerian and Assyriological studies. He received a Ph.D. (Biblical Hebrew and Old Testament, 1973) from Harvard University. He inaugurated and chaired the Linguistics and Biblical Hebrew unit of the Society of Biblical Literature from 1982-1991. He has published several scholarly works, including *Linguistics and Biblical Hebrew* (editor, Eisenbrauns, 1992), *The Greek Text of Judges: Recensional Developments* (Harvard Semitic Monographs, no. 23; Scholars Press, 1980), and *Discourse Analysis and Biblical Literature* (editor, Scholars Press, forthcoming).

Kirk Bottomly is associate pastor for Christian Education at Emmanuel Presbyterian Church (PCUSA), Thousand Oaks, California, U.S.A. He received Christ as a teenager through the ministry of The Navigators and was discipled by Campus Crusade for Christ. Before entering pastoral ministry he worked as a technical writer, product manager, and speech writer in the San Francisco business community and was an active lay leader in an Evangelical Covenant Church and a Presbyterian (PCUSA) church. He received an M.Div. (1990) from Princeton Theological Seminary, after having done additional graduate work at the University of California, Berkeley (English Literature), Berkeley, California, and at Tübingen University (Theology), Tübingen, Germany.

Stanley M. Burgess is Professor of Religious Studies at Southwest Missouri State University. He received a B.A. and M.A. from the University of Michigan and a Ph.D. from the University of Missouri-Columbia. He has written numerous scholarly articles on Church history and the history of Christianity as well as several scholarly books, including *The Spirit and the Church: Antiquity* (Hendrickson) and *The Holy Spirit: Eastern Christian Traditions* (Hendrickson).

Peter H. Davids is researcher and theological instructor on staff at the Langley Vineyard Christian Fellowship, Langley, British Columbia, Canada. Prior to this post, he was Professor of Biblical Studies and New Testament at Canadian Theological Seminary, Regina, Saskatchewan, Canada. He received a Ph.D. (New Testament, 1974) from the University of Manchester, England. He has written commentaries on the book of James (*New International Greek Testament Commentary*, Eerdmans) and 1 Peter (*New International Commentary on the New Testament*, Eerdmans), as well as numerous articles for scholarly journals.

Lloyd D. Fretz is District Superintendent of the Missionary Church, Canada East, and oversees more than 70 churches and 9 ethnic congregations throughout Eastern Canada. He and his wife, Marie, planted churches for 19 years and he has pastored 3 churches in 24 years. He and his wife frequently lead seminars and speak at conferences on renewal and spiritual warfare.

Wayne Grudem is Professor of Biblical and Systematic Theology at Trinity Evangelical Divinity School, Deerfield, Illinois, U.S.A., where he has taught since 1981. He received an M.Div. from Westminster Seminary, Philadelphia, and a Ph.D. (New Testament) from the University of Cambridge, Cambridge, England. He was ordained as a minister in the Baptist General Conference in 1974 and has published numerous scholarly articles and four books, including *The Gift of Prophecy in the New Testament and Today* (Crossway), *Recovering Biblical Manhood and Womanhood* (coedited with John Piper; Crossway), and his latest work, *Systematic Theology: An Introductory Course in the Doctrinal Teachings of the Whole Bible* (InterVarsity UK and Zondervan). He is a member of the Vineyard Christian Fellowship of Evanston, Illinois.

Charles H. Kraft is Professor of Anthropology and Intercultural Communication at the School of World Mission, Fuller Theological Seminary, Pasadena, California, U.S.A. He received a B.D. from Ashland Theological Seminary, Ashland, Ohio, and a Ph.D. (Anthropological Linguistics) from Hartford Seminary Foundation. He is ordained in the Brethren Church (Ashland, Ohio), served as a missionary in Nigeria, and taught African languages and linguistics at Michigan State University and the University of California at Los Angeles. He has published widely both in missiology and in African linguistics, and his books include *Christianity in Culture* (Orbis, 1979) and *Christianity with Power* (Servant, 1989). He and his wife, Marguerite Kraft, are members of Pasadena Covenant Church.

Marguerite G. Kraft is Associate Professor of Anthropology and Linguistics at the School of Intercultural Studies, Biola University. She received a Ph.D. (Intercultural Studies, 1990) and a D.Missiology from the School of World Mission, Fuller Theological Seminary. She and her husband, Charles Kraft, planted churches in northern Nigeria. She has also taught courses and lectured in Kenya, Philippines, Papua New Guinea, Micronesia, Thailand, India, and Taiwan. Her books include *Worldview and the Communication of the Gospel* (William Carey, 1978).

David C. Lewis is a cultural anthropologist and is currently a research associate of the Mongolia and Inner Asian Studies Unit at the University of Cambridge, Cambridge, England, where he received his Ph.D. (Anthropology). He also serves as a consultant anthropologist for several Christian mission organizations. He has conducted research projects at Nottingham University and the Oxford Hardy Research Centre (Religious Experience Research Project, 1984-1985). He has written numerous scholarly articles and books, including *Healing: Fiction, Fantasy or Fact?* (Hodder & Stoughton).

Jeffrey Niehaus is Associate Professor of Old Testament at Gordon-Conwell Theological Seminary in South Hamilton, Massachusetts, U.S.A. He received a Ph.D. (English and American Literature, 1975) from Harvard University and completed postgraduate work (Old Testament and Ancient Near Eastern studies, 1980-1982) at the University of Liverpool, England. He has published numerous articles in scholarly journals and several books including commentaries on Amos (Baker), Obadiah (Baker), and *The Sinai Theology* (Zondervan, 1993). He is an elder at Grace Fellowship, Christian and Missionary Alliance, Danvers, Massachusetts.

James I. Packer is Fangwoo Youtong Chee Professor of Theology at Regent College, Vancouver, British Columbia, Canada. He received a Ph.D. (Philosophy) from the University of Oxford, Oxford, England. He taught at Tyndale Hall and was warden of Latimer House, Oxford, and also served as associate principal of Trinity College, Bristol, England. As an Anglican theologian, Dr. Packer has played a major role in British and North American evangelicalism. He has written numerous books and scholarly articles, including the best-selling book, *Knowing God*.

John White is a psychiatrist and former missionary in Latin America who has a worldwide speaking and writing ministry. He completed medical studies at the University of Manchester, Manchester, England. He has written numerous books, including *Eros Defiled* (InterVarsity), *The Golden Cow* (InterVarsity), and *When the Spirit Comes with Power* (InterVarsity).

Don Williams is senior pastor of the Coast Vineyard Christian Fellowship in La Jolla, near San Diego, California, U.S.A. He received an M.Div. from Princeton Seminary, Princeton, New Jersey, and a Ph.D. (New Testament) from Columbia University. He has held teaching posts at Claremont College (Professor of Religion), Claremont, California, and at Fuller Theological Seminary (Adjunct Professor of New Testament), Pasadena, California. He was a pastor for many years at Hollywood Presbyterian Church and also pastored Mount Soledad Presbyterian Church in La Jolla near San Diego. He has written several books, including *Signs, Wonders and the Kingdom of God* (Servant).

FOREWORD

This book is overdue!

The signs and wonders controversy has occupied the attention of thoughtful Christians here in the United States and in several other parts of the world for more than a decade now, and it is time for resolution. *The Kingdom and the Power* will contribute greatly to transforming heat into light.

When the Pentecostal movement burst on the scene at the beginning of our century, the knee-jerk reaction of more traditional Christians was to write them off as a false cult along with Mormons and Jehovah's Witnesses. But that obviously carnal position could not be maintained, given the clear manifestations of the fruit of the Holy Spirit and the unprecedented numerical growth of the movement. After World War II, God raised up leaders such as Thomas Zimmerman of the Assemblies of God to mainstream Pentecostals into the National Association of Evangelicals and evangelicalism.

The price for this, however, was a gradual de-emphasizing of the signs, wonders and other miraculous ministries so outwardly characteristic of the first- and early second-generation Pentecostals. Evangelicals could live with the Pentecostals as long as they were polite enough not to raise issues such as speaking in tongues or power ministries in mixed company such as the Lausanne Committee for World Evangelization.

Just when things seemed to be settling down, the charismatic renewal came upon the scene in the early 1960s. Many Pentecostals regretted this because for one thing they did not know how to relate to Lutherans and Episcopalians who spoke in tongues as well as drank beer; and for another, they could not understand how God could baptize Roman Catholics in the Holy Spirit. To complicate matters more, the charismatics began giving signs and wonders and slaying in the Spirit the high profile that Pentecostals once did.

This upset traditional Christians so much that many church splits occurred through the 1960s and 1970s.

Partly because of the church splits, the boundaries between those who practiced signs and wonders and traditional evangelicals remained distinct enough to tolerate.

Until John Wimber came along.

John, who worked with me at the Fuller Evangelistic Association, had no background in either the Pentecostal or charismatic movements. He did not have a radical experience of "the baptism." He just started a local church and felt led to take the kind of ministry he read about in the Gospels and Acts literally. The fact that those in what later became the Anaheim Vineyard prayed for the sick did not particularly threaten traditional evangelicals. What really upset many of them was that some were being healed by the direct power of God!

In 1982, John began teaching MC510 "Signs, Wonders and Church Growth" at Fuller Theological Seminary, an institution regarded by some as representative of the very inner circle of traditional evangelicalism. Again, controversy was sparked not so much by John's teaching but by his "ministry times" when sick people were healed and demons were cast out right in the classroom. By then, two Fuller professors, Charles Kraft and I, had become overt proponents of Wimber's teaching and ministry models.

The most heated years of the Fuller controversy were 1985-1989. John and I were the ones who took most of the heat. It was painful, but neither of us felt that the Lord wanted us to be defensive or to answer the critics. Wimber's books, *Power Evangelism* (HarperCollins) and *Power Healing* (HarperCollins), and my book *How to Have a Healing Ministry in Any Church* (Regal) contain nothing of a polemical note.

Meanwhile, the critics have continued to campaign against power ministries in increasingly energetic and hostile tones. In my opinion, it is time for answers to be given, and both John Wimber and I are grateful we do not have to do it. A movement that some refer to as the "third wave," has produced increasing numbers of biblical scholars, theologians, and pastors who have examined the evidence on both sides. And they are prepared to offer a biblical resolution to the controversy, which has both theological integrity and pastoral sensitivity.

I want to thank my friends, Gary Greig and Kevin Springer, for giving leadership to the distinguished team of authors who have contributed to *The Kingdom and the Power*. For many, it will be the answer we have been waiting for.

C. Peter Wagner
Fuller Theological Seminary

Introduction

Gary S. Greig and Kevin N. Springer

Increasing millions of believers worldwide claim that God still works miraculously through His people today.[1] They claim that Christians should expect to preach the gospel and minister the gospel's power with all the gifts of the Spirit, including the miraculous gifts (prophecy, word of knowledge, word of wisdom, gifts of healing, working of miracles, distinguishing spirits, tongues, interpretation). The topics of the work of God's Spirit, healing, and ministry with miraculous spiritual gifts and their relationship to the gospel and evangelism have been flash points of division among Christians in the twentieth century with the emergence of the Pentecostal and charismatic movements and the emergence of what has been called the "third wave" movement.

The often divisive rhetoric surrounding the controversy suggests the need for a careful reexamination of the biblical evidence related to these topics. This book intends to encourage the reader to reexamine the basic issues in Scripture and draw his or her own conclusions regarding the implications for evangelism and ministry in the Church today.

In books, magazines, conferences, cassette tapes, and videos, many pastors and lay leaders are finding themselves confronted over and over with questions such as the following about healing ministry and ministry with all spiritual gifts, including the miraculous gifts.

- Can any church or liturgical tradition have a healing ministry and personal prayer ministry?
- Can any church or liturgical tradition help people find freedom in Christ from demonic oppression and related emotional and spiritual bondage?

• Can any church or liturgical tradition encourage lay ministry that utilizes all spiritual gifts?

• Is such ministry foreign to the gospel and the message of the Cross, or is it a natural, biblical extension of the power of the Cross to cleanse and redeem us from sin and sin's consequences?

• What does Scripture have to say about such issues?

Is ministry with all spiritual gifts and healing a biblical idea? Was such ministry just for the Early Church, and if so, where does Scripture teach such a notion? Why did the Church preserve instructions for healing prayer ministry in the canon of Scripture (Jas. 5:14-16)?

Do healing and gift-based ministry (meaning ministry with all spiritual gifts)[2] have any role in Scripture's view of preaching the gospel? Is the Church to follow the preaching and healing pattern of evangelism practiced by our Lord, the apostles and the Early Church?

THE PURPOSE OF THIS BOOK

Much has been written recently on these issues. Many voices among evangelicals have offered conflicting answers to such questions. Some of the literature seems to answer these questions with a partially affirmative or a wholly affirmative response,[3] and some of the literature seems to answer them with a partially negative or a wholly negative response.[4]

On one side of the controversy, healing and spiritual gifts have no necessary role in the proclamation of the gospel and the Word of God. They are not to receive so much attention that they usurp a church's focus on Christ and the gospel. Protestant cessationism represents the most extreme form of this viewpoint. Certain Protestant theologians from the Reformation era onward have popularized the view that the miraculous gifts of the Spirit mentioned in the New Testament ceased after the Apostolic Age, since they were neither necessary nor functional after the New Testament was completed.[5]

On the other side of the controversy, proponents point out that no scriptural passage clearly teaches that any gift of the Spirit should or would cease before the return of Christ.[6] According to this view, healing ministry and ministry with all spiritual gifts are more than just a nice idea, which may or may not be worthy of emphasis in a church's ministry repertoire. Healing and spiritual gifts are signs of God's kingdom and rule in Christ—symbols of His grace and His redeeming work through the Cross—which are as nonnegotiable now as they were in the Early Church.

Such questions as those articulated above have been raised in the recent literature and, in turn, gave rise to this book. The purpose of this book is to reexamine these questions in Scripture and their implications from a pastoral perspective. Scholars and church leaders from a broad range of evangelical, liturgical, and denominational backgrounds (including Covenant, Missionary Church, Southern Baptist, Anglican, Vineyard, Presbyterian, Christian and Missionary Alliance, United Methodist) have contributed 14 chapters discussing the issues from an exegetical and pastoral point of view as well as from church-historical, psychiatric, sociological, and missiological points of view.

The first seven chapters of this book explore the issues exegetically. Jeffrey Niehaus explores the relationship of signs, wonders, and miracles to the prophetic word in the Old Testament. This relationship is the foundation of the prophetic New Covenant ministry of word and deed in the New Testament Church. He also discusses the relationship of healing and spiritual gifts to the substitutionary atonement of Christ foretold in Isaiah 53. Wayne Grudem addresses the question of whether we should expect the Holy Spirit to work in miraculous ways in connection with the preaching of the gospel and the life of the Church today.

Peter Davids explores the relationship of sin to forgiveness, healing, and wholeness in Scripture and surveys the biblical evidence concerning sin and the fruit of sin—sickness, demonization, death, and natural calamity. He also examines Scripture's view of how, on the basis of the atoning power of the Cross, God works to reverse the fruit of sin. Gary Greig explores the nature and purpose of signs and wonders in the New Testament, showing how they function to encourage faith in Christ, to illustrate God's grace in the gospel, and to bring glory to Christ.

Don Williams investigates the biblical evidence for discipleship, showing how Jesus intended to pass on His ministry of word and deed to His disciples and, through them, to all believers. Walter Bodine traces the evidence for power ministry in the Epistles, showing that the New Testament evidence is not insignificant for ongoing regular ministry with all spiritual gifts that functioned in the Early Church. James Packer discusses the biblical evidence of God's power in the believer's life. He concludes that expecting supernatural demonstrations of God's power in evangelism and in the life of the Church is healthy and biblical, when it is within the only legitimate biblical "power scenario," which is power in weakness—humble, selfless dependence on God.

The next three chapters explore the pastoral implications of the issues. Roger Barrier, a Southern Baptist pastor, discusses the importance of praying for healing and deliverance from demons in the power of the Holy Spirit as one means a church can use to show Christ's love to those in need. Lloyd Fretz, District Supervisor of the Missionary Church, Canada East, recounts cases of seeing the power of the gospel bring true freedom in Christ through prayer for healing and deliverance from demonic influence. Kirk Bottomly, a Presbyterian (PCUSA) pastor, discusses the challenges and blessings of pursuing ministry with all spiritual gifts in one's own life and in the life of the local church. He underscores the need in evangelicalism for a return to biblical paradigms of faith, and a fundamental change from a deistic rationalistic worldview to a biblically based worldview of God's supernatural involvement in our lives, in our churches, and in our evangelism.

The final four chapters explore the issues from the perspective of church history, psychiatry, sociology, and missiology. Stanley Burgess discusses evidence of the continuity of all spiritual gifts in the life and evangelism of the postbiblical Early Church. John White offers a psychiatrist's analysis of the unusual reactions and manifestations (trembling, falling, weeping, etc.) accompanying past and contemporary revivals. David Lewis discusses the sociological, psychological, and medical aspects of reported cases of healing. He focuses on his own in-depth statistical analysis of 100 randomly selected cases out of a total pool of 1,890 cases of reported healings associated with prayer in Christ's name.

In their chapter, Charles Kraft and Marguerite Kraft discuss the problem of dual allegiance to Christ and to demonic power among Christian converts in Third World countries. They urge that biblical strategies be developed for cross-cultural ministry to communicate the gospel and to minister its power through prayer for healing and deliverance from demonic power.

Seven Appendices offer additional studies of the New Testament evidence and key passages related to power evangelism, Jesus' commissions to His disciples and the Church, spiritual gifts, spiritual warfare, models of prayer for healing and related phenomena, and what Scripture shows regarding its own sufficiency.

A FRESH OUTPOURING OF RENEWAL

Over the last decade, many evangelicals claim to have experienced a fresh outpouring of revival and renewal in the Holy Spirit across denominational lines. They do not identify themselves as Pentecostal or charismatic, though they affirm and support the same work of God's Spirit in those movements. Instead they have chosen to remain and work for renewal in their own denominational traditions. New denominational movements have also arisen out of the renewal such as the Vineyard Christian Fellowship under the leadership of John Wimber, one of the leading pioneers of the recent renewal movement among evangelicals.

The recent renewal has been called "the third wave of the Holy Spirit" by C. Peter Wagner. Anglican researcher and statistician, David Barrett, has estimated that 33 million believers worldwide are a part of the third wave movement.[7]

The third wave, Wagner says, is analogous to the first two waves of the Holy Spirit's work in the Pentecostal and charismatic movements. However, third wave proponents distinguish their theology and practice from that of Pentecostals and charismatics in certain ways.[8] Although third wave proponents are open to all the miraculous gifts and miraculous work of God, they generally understand the baptism of the Spirit not as a second blessing but as a part of conversion (1 Cor. 12:13; Eph. 1:13,14; Titus 3:5; John 3:3,5-8; Rom. 8:9; Gal. 3:26 and 4:6).

At the same time, the third wave acknowledge the need to be filled and empowered by the Holy Spirit more than once after conversion (Eph. 5:18; Acts 4:8,31; 7:55; 13:9,52). They do not focus on the gift of tongues above all other spiritual gifts as the evidence of being filled with the Spirit. (Indeed, some third wave leaders who minister with miraculous gifts such as healing and discerning of spirits do not speak in tongues.) Rather, they affirm the value of all spiritual gifts, whether miraculous or nonmiraculous. They emphasize the potential of all Christians, not just specially gifted persons, to minister healing and to minister with all the miraculous gifts (John 14:12; 1 Cor. 12:7; 14:1,5,12,13, 24,31; Matt. 7:7-11).[9] Third wave proponents also emphasize the biblical pattern of using spiritual gifts and healing not only in the life of the Church but also in evangelism (see below and see appendix 1).

Third wave proponents claim that the renewal has brought several positive elements to evangelicalism, including a greater understanding and openness to the work and power of the Holy Spirit taught in Scripture. Many evangelicals, some say, have begun to realize that biblical Christianity is much more than they had previously known. They have begun to move from an unbalanced emphasis based only on the proclaimed Word to a scripturally balanced emphasis based on both the proclaimed Word and ministry in God's power (Rom. 15:18,19; 1 Cor. 2:4,5; 4:20; 11:1; Gal. 3:5; 1 Thess. 1:5; Heb. 2:3,4; 1 Pet. 4:11; Jas. 5:13-16).

Proponents of third wave theology and practice claim to have attempted such a biblical balance—a balance between the fruit of the Spirit and the gifts of the Spirit, between the proclamation of the gospel and the works of healing and gift-based ministry, which are said to demonstrate the power of Christ in the gospel.

THE GOSPEL AND THE POWER OF THE CROSS

Throughout this book, and particularly in appendix 1, the contributors set forth the biblical evidence showing that healing ministry and miraculous spiritual gifts were the chief demonstration of the redeeming power of the Cross that accompanied the preaching of the gospel in the New Testament Church. The substitutionary atonement of Christ on the cross is the heart of the gospel. First Peter 2:24 makes this clear: "He himself bore our sins in his body on the tree, so that we might die to sins and live for righteousness; by his wounds you have been healed." Christ's atoning work on the cross is the center of gravity in New Testament faith (Matt. 20:28; Mark 10:45; John 12:27,31-33; Rom. 3:22-25; 5:8,9; 2 Cor. 5:21; Gal. 3:13; Col. 1:21,22; 1 Tim. 2:6; Heb. 2:14; 9:14,26-28; 10:10; 1 Pet. 1:18-21; 2:24; 3:18; 1 John 2:2; 3:5,8; Rev. 12:11).

The power of the Cross is first and foremost in the atonement and the forgiveness of all sin that the Cross provides (1 John 2:2). Scripture is also clear that the Cross provides the basis for all God's work in our lives to sanctify us and to restore us from the brokenness of sin (1 Pet. 2:24, "So that we might die to sins and live for righteousness; by his wounds you have been healed"; 2 Cor. 5:21, "In him we might become the righteousness of God"; Col. 1:22, "To present you holy in his sight"; 1 John 3:8, "The reason the Son of God appeared was to destroy the devil's work"). Just as Scripture suggests we may experience sanctification and the eradication of sin only in part in this life (Phil. 3:12,13; 1 John 1:9), so Scripture also seems clear that prior to the return of Christ, we will experience healing and spiritual gifts only in part (see below and compare 1 Cor. 13:9 with 1 Cor. 12:8-10; 13:8-12; 1 John 3:2; Rev. 22:4; and cf. Gal. 4:14; Phil. 2:27; 1 Tim. 5:23; 2 Tim. 4:20).

In their chapters, Dr. Niehaus and Dr. Davids discuss this "already-not yet" tension of the kingdom of God in relation to healing and spiritual gifts. Dr. Niehaus's chapter discusses the relationship of the substitutionary atonement of Christ and divine healing in the context of Isaiah 53. In a recent book, Professor Gordon Fee discussed in detail the biblical evidence concerning the relationship, showing that healing is made possible by the atonement of the Cross but is not necessarily guaranteed to be fully experienced by believers in this age:

Healing is provided for [in the atonement] because the atonement brought release from the...consequences of sin; nonetheless, since we have not yet received the redemption of our bodies, suffering and death are still our lot until the resurrection.[10]

The reader will find more detailed discussion of this issue in Dr. Fee's book and in Dr. Niehaus's and Dr. Davids' chapters.

The contributors to this book share the conviction that the cross of Christ is the solution to every problem men and women face (cf. 2 Pet. 1:3). We do not believe that healing and spiritual gifts are the solution to every problem nor that the Cross is limited to or equivalent to spiritual gifts and healing. Rather, Scripture is clear that the work of Christ on the cross to forgive our sins is the fountainhead from which all other blessings of the Christian faith flow, including healing and spiritual gifts.

Healing and spiritual gifts mean nothing by themselves, since demonic counterfeits are well-attested in non-Christian religions and cults, as Scripture itself suggests (Exod. 7:11,22; 8:7; Acts 8:9-11; 13:6ff.; 16:16; 19:13,18,19). But Scripture is clear that Christian healing and spiritual gifts are unique in that they show the superior power of the true and living God (Acts 8:9-11; 13:6ff.; 16:16; 19:13-19), they honor and glorify Christ, proclaiming Him Lord (1 Cor. 12:1-3; 1 John 4:2), they are accompanied by good fruit (Matt. 7:20; Gal. 5:22,23), and they encourage faith and growth in Christ (1 Cor. 14:12; Eph. 4:11; 1 Pet. 4:10,11).

Christ and His cross are everything, as Paul said in Philippians 1:21: "For to me, to live is Christ and to die is gain." One may preach (and indeed many have preached) the cross of Christ without healing ministry and still express the heart of the gospel, as Paul did at Athens (Acts 17:16-34). But it is the multifaceted grace and power of Christ's death on the cross, forgiving our sins, that make healing and spiritual gifts possible in the Christian life (Isa. 53:4-5; 1 Pet. 2:24; Acts 3:13-16; Gal. 3:5).

Furthermore, certain passages in the New Testament suggest that healing and spiritual gifts actually illustrate the grace, forgiveness, and atoning power of the Cross (Matt. 9:6; 11:4; Mark 2:10; Luke 4:18,19; 5:24; 7:22; Jas. 5:15,16; cf. Rom. 15:18,19; 1 Cor. 2:2-5 [and 2 Cor. 12:12]; 1 Thess. 1:5; see appendix 1, "Power Evangelism and the New Testament Evidence," and Dr. Greig's chapter). Is it simply coincidental in this regard that the Greek word *charisma* "spiritual gift" is derived from the same root as Greek *charis* "grace" and *charizomai* "forgive, pardon"?[11]

This is why Paul sought not only to preach the gospel boldly (Eph. 6:19,20) but also sought regularly to heal the sick and minister with signs and wonders and all spiritual gifts alongside his preaching (Rom. 15:18,19; 1 Cor. 2:4,5; 2 Cor. 12:12; 1 Thess. 1:5; cf. Acts 13:7-12; 14:3,9,10; 15:12; 16:16-18; 19:4-6,8-12; 20:7-10; 28:8,9). This is why in Philippians 3 Paul says in one breath, "I consider everything a loss compared to the surpassing greatness of *knowing Christ Jesus my Lord*" (Phil. 3:8) and in the next breath, "I want to know Christ *and the power of his resurrection*" (Phil. 3:10). The work of Christ on the cross is not equivalent to spiritual gifts and healing, but the forgiving power of His cross makes them possible and is illustrated and demonstrated through them in a unique way.

NEW TESTAMENT SCHOLARSHIP AND THE EVIDENCE

Many New Testament scholars, publishing over the last century in English, German, and French, seem to have concluded that, throughout the New Testament, the power and compassion of God in healing and gift-based ministry are integrally related to the proclamation of the gospel and the ministry of the Word of God. Many point out that in the New Testament's view such ministry is a sign of God's forgiveness and grace in the gospel.[12] The following quotations summarize research on the subject.

F. F. Bruce, the well-known evangelical British New Testament scholar, considered Jesus' healing ministry an integral part of the message Jesus preached:

> While the miracles served as signs, they were not performed in order to be signs. They were as much a part and parcel of Jesus's ministry as was his preaching—not...seals affixed to the document to certify its genuiness but an integral element in the very text of the document.[13]

A. Feuillet, a French New Testament scholar, points out that just as Jesus' preaching was regularly accompanied by healing and gift-based ministry, so was that of His disciples:

> In Mark ii.2 and iv.33 Jesus is seen "to proclaim the Word."...In Mk. xvi.19-20, once Jesus ascended to heaven, the apostles in their turn "proclaim the Word." And as the Word proclaimed by Jesus was accompanied by works of power, it was exactly the same according to Mark xvi.20 for the Word proclaimed by the apostles....What Jesus began to say (the Word) and to do (the miracles), all that is continued after the Ascension by the apostles.
>
> Moved by the Spirit, the apostles take up the call of Jesus for repentance ([Acts] ii.38, iii.26, v.31, xviii.30) and his announcement of the "Kingdom of God" ([Acts] viii.12, xix.8, xx.25, xxvi-

ii.31)....They bear witness to the resurrection of Jesus: cf. [Acts] i.22, ii.32, iii.15, iv.33, v.32, x.39, 41, xiii.31. They depend on the invocation of the Name of Jesus....It is for this Name that the apostles suffer ([Acts] v.21, xxi.13; cf. I Pet. iv.14); it is this Name that they preach ([Acts] iv.10-12, 17-18; v.28-40).

And the invocation of this Name puts into action the divine power kept by Jesus. The result is that, by this invocation, the apostles accomplish miraculous wonders like those of Jesus' public ministry, heal the sick, drive out demons and even raise the dead: [Acts] iii.1-10, viii.6-7, ix.32-43, xiv.8-18, xx.7-12...v.16...xix.12.[14]

The British New Testament scholar, Alan Richardson, points out that Jesus' healing ministry was a necessary concomitant of His preaching:

The working of miracles is a part of the proclamation of the Kingdom of God, not an end in itself. Similarly, the sin of Chorazin and Bethsaida [Lk. 10:13; Mat. 11:21] is spiritual blindness; they do not accept the preaching of the Kingdom of God or understand the miracles which were its inevitable concomitants....Can we interpret the remarkable connexion which this Q saying establishes between the miracles and repentance in any other way than by understanding the miracles as the necessary concomitants of the preaching of the Kingdom of God?[15]

Dr. Bertold Klappert, a German New Testament scholar, similarly describes the unity of word and deed in Jesus' proclamation:

The healings are part of Jesus' word and are not to be detached from his proclamation. According to Lk. 4:18, Jesus related the prophetic word of Isa. 61:1f. to his own mission. God sent him to bring good news to the poor and sight to the blind. This denotes the unity of word and deed in Jesus' proclamation....The proclamation of the kingdom of God takes place by means of Jesus' word, and Jesus' healings are the physical expression of his word.[16]

The German New Testament scholar, Professor Gerhard Friedrich of Tübingen, points out that the New Testament concept of preaching the gospel is more than verbally communicating the rational content of the gospel and that it includes demonstrating the power of the gospel through healing ministry:

Euaggelizesthai ["to preach the gospel"] is not just speaking and preaching; it is proclamation with full authority and power. Signs and wonders accompany the evangelical message. They belong together, for the Word is powerful and effective. The proclamation of the age of grace, of the rule of God, creates a healthy state in every respect. Bodily disorders are healed and man's relationship to God is set right (Mt. 4:23; 9:35; 11:5; Lk. 9:6; Acts 8:4-8; 10:36ff.; 14:8-18; 16:17ff.; Rom. 15:16-20; II Cor. 12:12; Gal. 3:5). Joy reigns where this Word is proclaimed (Acts 8:8). It brings *sotēria* ["salvation"] (I Cor. 15:1f.)...Hence, *euaggelizesthai* ["to preach the gospel"] is to offer salvation. It is the powerful proclamation the good news, the impartation of *sotēria* ["salvation"]. This would be missed if *euaggelizesthai* ["to preach the gospel"] were to take place in human fashion *en sophia logou* ["(merely) in the wisdom of words"] (I Cor. 1:17).[17]

The British scholar, D. S. Cairns, says the biblical evidence shows that the miraculous signs of Jesus' healing ministry were "integral parts of the revelation, and not adjuncts to it."[18] Christ, Cairns says, does miracles out of love and compassion for men and women, "because he cannot help working them."[19] The Dutch New Testament scholar, H. van der Loos, points out the same about the apostles' healing ministry:

> The miracles were therefore not works or signs which happened for the sake of the apostles, but originated in the point at issue, viz. the proclamation of salvation by Jesus Christ and the coming of His Kingdom. They did not accompany the preaching of the gospel as incidentals, but formed an integral part of it; in the healing, as a visible function of the Kingdom of God, something that could be experienced, God's will to heal the whole of man was manifested.[20]

E. Thurneysen points out that Jesus' healing ministry illustrated the gospel in that the healings are "signs which show the victory of Christ over sin and death and thereby confirm the power of his word."[21] Professor Walter Grundmann, a German scholar, similarly stresses that Jesus' healing ministry showed that He came to destroy the devil's work through sin (1 John 3:8):

> The miracles of Jesus are a part of the invading rule of God which

Jesus brings with his person in preaching and acting. They are the rule of God overcoming and pushing back the demonic-satanic sphere of influence.[22]

H. van der Loos points out that God's power manifested in Jesus' healing ministry shows that Jesus came to destroy sin and to begin to reverse the effects sin has brought upon mankind:

> This power presents itself in dual form, viz. as evidential power and as militant power. As evidential power it identifies Jesus as the Messiah-King and reveals His divine mission. As militant power it reveals Jesus as the adversary of all the forces of ruin. For Jesus has come to smash the forces of disease, sin and death, to dethrone Satan. This dual nature of the power function finds striking expression in Jesus' important pronouncement: "But if I cast out devils by the Spirit of God, then the Kingdom of God is come unto you," Mt. 12:28, and cf. Lk. 11:20.[23]

Professor Richardson affirms that "miracles of healing are, as it were, symbolic demonstrations of God's forgiveness in action."[24]

The German scholar, Professor Otfried Hofius, summarizes the New Testament evidence concerning the integral relationship of healing and gift-based ministry to the proclamation of the gospel and the Word of God:

> According to the witness of the Synoptic Gospels, Jesus sent out his disciples to preach and to perform miracles (Mat. 10:7f.; Mk. 3:14f.; Lk. 9:1f.; 10:9; cf. Mk. 6:7ff.; Lk. 9:6)....
>
> Similarly, Acts mentions many times the correlation of apostolic proclamation and apostolic miracle-working (2:2f.; 4:29f.; cf. 3:1ff.; 4:16,22; 5:12; 6:8; 8:5ff.; 9:32ff.; 15:12; 20:7ff.). The miracles are co-ordinated with the preaching—they are "accompanying signs," by which Christ confirms the word of the witnesses (Acts 14:3; cf. Mk. 16:20). As in the authoritative word (Acts 6:10) so in the signs is manifested the power of the Holy Spirit promised to the disciples (Acts 1:8)....
>
> For Paul, too, "word and deed," preaching and signs belong together; in both Christ is at work in the power of the Spirit (Rom. 15:18f.). Signs and wonders accompany the proclamation which takes place "in demonstration of the Spirit and

power" (I Cor. 2:4; cf. I Thes. 1:5)....To the hearers of the preaching also the Holy Spirit mediates miraculous powers (Gal. 3:5). That is why alongside the gifts of proclamation the charisma of healing and the power to perform miracles belong to the living gifts of the Spirit in the church (I Cor. 12:18ff., 28; cf. Jas. 5:14f.).

Finally Hebrews also bears witness that God confirms the preaching of salvation, which proclaims the dawn of the age of salvation, by signs and wonders (2:3ff.), which, as "powers of the world to come" (6:5), foreshadow the completion of salvation....

Preaching and miracles thus belong essentially together according to the New Testament. In both Jesus Christ proves himself to be the living Lord, present in his church in the Holy Spirit.[25]

EVANGELISM WITH OR WITHOUT USE OF HEALING AND MIRACULOUS GIFTS

Scholars such as those quoted above and cited in the footnotes unanimously agree that the New Testament's concept of evangelism included healing ministry and ministry with all spiritual gifts (see also appendix 1: "Power Evangelism and the New Testament Evidence"). But this conclusion does not suggest, on the other hand, that "any form of evangelism not accompanied by miracles [is] not...true evangelism"[26] or that such evangelism is "substandard."[27]

As was mentioned above, the fact that Paul preached the gospel without any signs and wonders at the Areopagus in Athens (Acts 17:16-34) is enough to show that biblical evangelism is not substandard "when no genuine sign or wonder is performed."[28] The obviously anointed ministry of such a great evangelist as Billy Graham is enough to show that evangelism unaccompanied by miraculous healing is not substandard. But Graham also affirms the use in the Church today of all spiritual gifts, including the miraculous gifts—healing, tongues, miraculous powers, and so on—because, according to him, they are biblical.[29]

And though evangelism unaccompanied by healing and miraculous gifts is anything but substandard, it does seem biblically abnormal to overlook or ignore, as some evangelicals do, the way Jesus, the apostles, and the Early Church evangelized with preaching accompanied by use of miraculous gifts and healing.

PURSUING A BIBLICAL VIEW OF GOD'S POWER

The Epistles contain more than 40 references to the power of God (Greek *dunamis*). Passages like Ephesians 6:10 command us to seek God's power in order to serve Him and live for Him: "Finally, be strong in the Lord and in his mighty power." Many other passages like the following show that God's power is central to proclaiming the gospel, ministering the Word of God, and growing spiritually:

> **Romans 15:18,19:** "I will not venture to speak of anything except what Christ has accomplished through me in leading the Gentiles to obey God by what I have said and done—by the *power of signs and miracles*, through the *power of the Spirit*. So from Jerusalem all the way around to Illyricum, I have fully proclaimed the gospel of Christ."
>
> **1 Corinthians 1:17,18:** "For Christ did not send me to baptize, but to preach the gospel—not with words of human wisdom, lest the cross of Christ *be emptied of its power*. For the message of the cross is foolishness to those who are perishing, but to us who are being saved it is the *power of God*."
>
> **1 Corinthians 2:4,5:** "My message and my preaching were not with wise and persuasive words, but with a demonstration of the *Spirit's power*, so that your faith might not rest on men's wisdom, but on *God's power*."
>
> **1 Corinthians 4:20:** "The kingdom of God is not a matter of talk but of *power*."
>
> **Ephesians 1:18-20:** "I pray also that the eyes of your heart may be enlightened in order that you may know the hope to which he has called you, the riches of his glorious inheritance in the saints, and his incomparably *great power* for us who believe. That *power* is like the working of his mighty strength, which he exerted in Christ when he raised him from the dead and seated him at his right hand in the heavenly realms."
>
> **Ephesians 3:16,17:** "I pray that out of his glorious riches he may strengthen you with *power through his Spirit* in your inner being, so that Christ may dwell in your hearts through faith."
>
> **Ephesians 6:10,11:** "Finally, be strong in the Lord and in his *mighty power*. Put on the full armor of God so that you can take your stand against the devil's schemes."

1 Thessalonians 1:5: "Our gospel came to you not simply with words, but also with *power*, with the Holy Spirit and with deep conviction."

As Christians, we face growing darkness in society today—the exponential disintegration of the family and the increase in sexual brokenness, rape, and violence; rising child abuse; increasing teenage violence and murder; the spread of gangs from urban to suburban areas; the rise of New-Age occultism, witchcraft, and satanic ritual practices; heightened spiritual battles and conflicts, which many pastors and their congregations attest to today. In the face of all this, we need God's power in the Church more than ever today—we need *all* God wants to give us to do *all* that He intends His Body to do in living for Christ and reaching our communities with the gospel.

Scholars who have studied the New Testament concept of God's power point out the complete and whole picture one sees of His power throughout the New Testament. No aspect of power is excluded from the whole pattern of God working in the Christian life. God's power through the cross of Christ makes possible miraculous healing as much as it does sanctification, endurance, and "suffering for the gospel, by the power of God" (Tim. 1:8).[30]

EXPERIENCING SPIRITUAL GIFTS
AND HEALING IN PART

As pointed out by the scholars quoted above, miraculous healing is the chief expression of God's power accompanying the proclamation of the gospel in the New Testament. The overall witness of the New Testament regarding God's attitude toward healing shows that God desires to heal. His Son healed the sick.[31] The apostles and Early Church laity healed the sick (Stephen, Philip, Ananias, the Corinthians, Galatians, Jewish Christian churches, etc.).[32] God gave the Church gifts of healing (1 Cor. 12:9). As well, He commands the Church to pray for the sick (Jas. 5:14-16).

However, such a whole view of God's power as one sees in Scripture does not overlook sanctification on the one hand (Rom. 8:4-16; 1 Cor. 6:11-19; Gal. 5:16—6:10) nor suffering, weakness, and prolonged and unresolved sickness on the other (Rom. 8:17; 2 Cor. 4:7-11; 12:7-10; Gal. 4:13-14; 2 Tim. 1:8; 3:12). Although God desires to heal, Scripture also makes it clear, as was mentioned above, that in some cases we may not experience complete healing in this age.[33] In this age, according to Paul, the Church will only experience spiritual gifts, including healing, "in part" (*ek merous*) until the second coming of Christ: "For we know in part and we prophesy in part" (1 Cor. 13:9; cf. 1 Cor. 1:6,7 and 13:8-10,12; 1 John 3:2; Rev. 22:4).[34]

John Wimber touches on the issue of our faith and God's faithfulness in such cases in his discussion of suffering, persecution, and martyrdom for the faith:

> The fact that we are living between the first and second comings of Christ, what George Ladd calls living between the "already and the not yet," provides the interpretive key for understanding why the physical healing that Christ secured for us at the cross is not always experienced today. His sovereignty, lordship, and kingdom are what bring healing. Our part is to pray "Thy kingdom come" and trust him for whatever healing comes from his gracious hand....We have no right to presume that unless God heals in every instance there is something wrong with our faith or his faithfulness.[35]

And though not all may experience immediate or complete healing in this age, Scripture does not allow us, on the other hand, to be complacent and capitulate in the face of illness. We are commanded, rather, to pray for healing (Jas. 5:14-16)—again and again (Jas. 5:17,18 and 1 Kings 18:43)—just as we are to pray for deliverance from persecution (cf. Acts 12:3-17; Rom. 15:31; 2 Cor. 1:8-11; 2 Thess. 3:2; 2 Tim. 3:11; 4:17):

> Jesus says very little about sickness; He cures it. He does not explain that sickness is health; He calls it by its proper name, and has compassion upon the sick person. There is nothing sentimental or artificial about Jesus; He draws no fine distinctions, and utters no sophistries about healthy people being really sick and sick people really healthy....Jesus does not distinguish rigidly between sicknesses of the body and of the soul; He takes them both as different expressions of one supreme ailment in humanity.[36]

Even in weakness, when we see no immediate answer to prayer, Christ's power can work in us and through us, sanctifying us, enabling us to endure all difficulties (2 Cor. 12:7-10):

> The contrast between the *weakness* of the incarnate Lord and the

living power of the Risen Christ is central to the theology of the early Church: "He was crucified through weakness, yet He liveth through the power of God" (2 Cor. xiii. 4)....The birth of Christ, "born of a woman, born under the Law" (Gal. iv. 4), and His human life "in the form of a servant" (Phil. ii. 7), as well as His death on the Cross, which appears to be defeat and weakness, are the means of the breaking through of God's victorious power.[37]

POWER IN WEAKNESS AND BIBLICAL BALANCE

The evidence presented by the contributors shows that miraculous healing and spiritual gifts are not ends in themselves, according to Scripture. They are tools to be used to encourage the Body of Christ toward holiness of life, effective witness to the lost, and endurance (1 Pet. 4:10,11). Michael Green describes the balance well:

> Much Western Christianity has concentrated too much on the Cross, symbolizing the suffering, weakness, and sorrow of our earthly existence. There is truth in that but not exhaustive truth.
>
> Charismatic Christianity, on the other hand, has concentrated too much on the Resurrection, on the transcendental power of the new life, its signs and wonders and excitement.
>
> A realistic Christianity will hold equally fast to *both*. And that is what you see in Paul, who claims, "The signs of a true apostle were performed among you in all patience, with signs and wonders and mighty works" (2 Cor. 12:12), but almost in the same breath confides, "I am content with weaknesses, insults, hardships, persecutions, and calamities; for when I am weak, then I am strong" (2 Cor. 12:10).
>
> Power in weakness. That is the place of signs and wonders in today's church in general and in evangelism in particular.[38]

Richard Foster has also emphasized such a balance and pointed out that healing and gift-based ministry is simply a normal and biblical part of a life of faith in Christ:

> Healing prayer is part of the normal Christian life. It should not be elevated above any other ministry in the community of faith, nor

should it be undervalued; rather, it should be kept in proper balance. It is simply a normal aspect of what it means to live under the reign of God.[39]

Although miracles and healings of all kinds and classes should be received gladly as a part of what it means to live in the kingdom of God, they merely come with the territory for those who walk in the light of God's grace. They should be expected as part of the normal Christian life....One of the greatest hindrances today to the free exercise of the healing ministry is the tendency to view certain aspects of it as some sort of "big deal." The religion of the "big deal" stands in opposition to the way of Christ. It is this spirit that can lead to the cruelest excesses....Healing prayer is simply a way of showing love to people. The healings, physical or otherwise, are the natural outflow of compassion.[40]

This book intends to help the reader reexamine what Scripture shows about God's power and the function of healing and gift-based ministry as a demonstration of the power of the gospel. This book also shares the thoughtful reflection of pastors and church leaders about the importance of ministering the power of the gospel through prayer for healing and ministry with the gifts of the Spirit in order to reach the lost for Christ and to bless and strengthen the Body of Christ. What is offered in this book does not pretend to answer every practical and theological question related to healing and gift-based ministry. The following chapters represent only a preliminary attempt to reexamine the scriptural evidence and address the most basic issues related to such ministry.

Notes

1. Three waves of renewal in this century (Pentecostal, charismatic and third wave) are growing at a rate of 19 million new members a year or 54,000 a day worldwide according to a 1988 article by Anglican scholar and statistician, Dr. David Barrett, "The Twentieth-Century Pentecostal/Charismatic Renew-

al in the Holy Spirit, with Its Goal of World Evangelization," *International Bulletin of Missionary Research* (July 1988): 1-10; id., *World Christian Encyclopedia* (Oxford, England: Oxford University Press, 1982), pp. 6, 14, 55, 65, 816, 835, 838; id. "Statistics, Global," in S. M. Burgess et al., eds., *Dictionary of Pentecostal and Charismatic Movements* (Grand Rapids, MI: Zondervan, 1988), pp. 810-830; id., *Cosmos, Chaos, and Gospel: A Chronology of World Evangelization from Creation to New Creation*, (Birmingham, AL: New Hope, 1987). Explosive Pentecostal growth in Latin America is also documented by C. Peter Wagner, *Spiritual Power and Church Growth*, (Wheaton. IL: Creation House, 1987). Anglican Canon, James Wong, of Singapore described a "new wave of the Holy Spirit" in world evangelization "with signs and wonders," which he suggested is unaffiliated with the Pentecostal and charismatic movements: James Wong, "Reaching the Unreached," *The Courier* (March-April, 1984), p. 6; cf. Michael Cassidy, *Bursting the Wineskins* (Wheaton, IL: Harold Shaw, 1983), p. 11f.; V. Synan, *In the Latter Days: the Outpouring of the Holy Spirit in the Twentieth Century* (Ann Arbor, MI: Servant, 1984), p. 137f.

2. The term "gift-based ministry" refers to ministry with *all* spiritual gifts, including the miraculous gifts, which, as scriptural examples from the Gospels, Acts, and the Epistles show, demonstrate God's presence and power in a dramatic way (prophecy, word of knowledge, word of wisdom, gifts of healing, working of miracles, distinguishing spirits, tongues, interpretation). The term does not exclude less overt spiritual gifts (service, teaching, evangelism, encouragement, contributing to the needs of others, leadership, mercy, administration, helps). Both the overt miraculous gifts and the less overt gifts of the Spirit are intertwined with one another in the New Testament lists of Romans 12, 1 Corinthians 12, and Ephesians 4, suggesting that God does not see one gift as more valuable or necessary than another.

3. John Wimber and Kevin Springer, *Power Healing* (San Francisco, CA: HarperSanFrancisco, 1987); id., *Power Evangelism*, 2nd revised and expanded ed. (San Francisco, CA: HarperSanFrancisco, 1992); Kevin Springer, ed., *Power Encounters Among Christians in the Western World* (San Francisco,CA: HarperSanFrancisco, 1988); C. Peter Wagner, *How to Have a Healing Ministry in Any Church* (Ventura, CA: Regal, 1988); id., *The Third Wave of the Holy Spirit* (Ann Arbor, MI: Servant, 1988); Charles H. Kraft, *Christianity with Power: Your Worldview and Your Experience of the Supernatural* (Ann Arbor, MI: Servant, 1989); Richard Foster, *Prayer: Finding the Heart's True Home* (San Francisco, CA: HarperSanFrancisco, 1992), chaps. 18-20 (pp. 203-242); Don Williams, *Signs, Wonders, and the Kingdom of God* (Ann Arbor, MI: Servant, 1989); Wayne Grudem, *The Gift of Prophecy in the New Testament and Today* (Westchester, IL: Crossway, 1988); John White, *When the Spirit Comes with Power: Signs and Wonders Among God's People* (Downers Grove, IL: InterVarsity Press, 1988); Ken Blue, *Authority to Heal* (Downers Grove, IL: InterVarsity Press, 1987); David Lewis, *Healing: Fiction, Fantasy or Fact? A Comprehensive Analysis of Healings and Associated Phenomena at John Wimber's Harrogate Conference* (London, England: Hodder & Stoughton, 1989); David Pytches, *Spiritual Gifts in the Local Church: How to Integrate Them into the Ministry of*

the *People of* God (Minneapolis, MN: Bethany House, 1985); George Mallone, *Those Controversial Gifts* (Downers Grove, IL: InterVarsity Press, 1983); Michael Green, *I Believe in the Holy Spirit* (Grand Rapids, MI: Eerdmans, 1985); Colin Brown, *That You May Believe: Miracles and Faith Then and Now* (Grand Rapids, MI: Eerdmans, 1985); Morton T. Kelsey, *Healing and Christianity* (New York: HarperCollins, 1976) (revised and expanded, *Psychology, Medicine, & Christian Healing*, HarperCollins, 1988); Francis MacNutt, *Healing* (Notre Dame, IN: Ave Maria Press, 1974); J. D. G. Dunn, *Jesus and the Spirit: A Study of the Religious and Charismatic Experience of Jesus and the First Christians as Reflected in the New Testament* (Philadelphia, PA: The Westminster Press, 1975); id., *Baptism in the Holy Spirit: A Re-examination of the New Testament Teaching on the Gift of the Spirit in Relation to Pentecostalism Today* (Studies in Biblical Theology, 2nd series, no. 15) (London, England: SCM Press, 1970).

4. D. A. Carson, J. Armstrong, and J. M. Boice in M. S. Horton, ed., *Power Religion: The Selling Out of the Evangelical Church?* (Chicago, IL: Moody Press, 1992); M. G. Moriarty, *The New Charismatics. A Concerned Voice Responds to Dangerous New Trends* (Grand Rapids, MI: Zondervan, 1992); J. F. MacArthur, *Charismatic Chaos* (Grand Rapids, MI: Zondervan, 1992); Phillip Jensen, et al., *The Briefing* 45/46 (April 24, 1990; St. Matthias Anglican Church, Sydney, Australia): 1ff.; D. A. Carson, *How Long , O Lord* (Grand Rapids, MI: Baker, 1990), pp. 123ff.; J. R. Coggins and P. G. Hiebert, eds., *Wonders and the Word* (Hillsboro, KS: Kindred Press, 1989); P. Masters, *The Healing Epidemic* (London, England: The Wakeman Trust, 1988); J. Woodhouse, P. Barrett, and J. Reid, in R. Doyle, ed., *Signs and Wonders and Evangelicals: A Response to the Teaching of John Wimber* (Homebush West, Australia: Lancer Books, 1987); Lewis Smedes, ed., *Ministry and the Miraculous* (Fuller Theological Seminary, 1987); Ben Patterson, "Cause for Concern," *Christianity Today* (August 8, 1986), p. 20; Donald Lewis, "John Wimber: Signs and Wonders?" *Channels* (Spring, 1986), p. 10; Dave Hunt and T. A. McMahon, *The Seduction of Christianity: Spiritual Discernment in the Last Days* (Eugene, OR: Harvest House, 1985); F. D. Bruner and W. Hordern, *The Holy Spirit—Shy Member of the Trinity* (Minneapolis, MN: Augsburg, 1984); F. D. Bruner, *A Theology of the Holy Spirit: The Pentecostal Experience and the New Testament Witness* (Grand Rapids, MI: Eerdmans, 1970).

5. E.g., Benjamin B. Warfield, *Miracles: Yesterday and Today, True and False* (Grand Rapids, MI: Eerdmans, 1953). Formerly published as *Counterfeit Miracles*, (Edinburgh, Scotland: The Banner of Truth Trust, 1918); R. B. Gaffin, *Perspectives on Pentecost*, (Presbyterian and Reformed, 1979); R. L. Reymond, *What About Continuing Revelations and Miracles in the Presbyterian Church Today?* (Presbyterian and Reformed, 1977); W. Chantry, *Signs of the Apostles: Observations on Pentecostalism Old and New* (Edinburgh, Scotland: The Banner of Truth Trust, 1976); N. Geisler, *Signs and Wonders* (Wheaton, IL: Tyndale House, 1988).

6. See appendix 4: "Spiritual Gifts" and Wayne Grudem's chapter in this book, objection number 21; see also Professor Gordon Fee's comments on 1 Corinthians 13:9,10 in his commentary, *The First Epistle to the Corinthians*, pp. 644-645,

n. 23; 646 and nn. 30-31; F. F. Bruce, *1 and 2 Corinthians*, (The New Century Bible, London, England: Marshall, Morgan and Scott, 1971), p. 122; Wayne Grudem, *The Gift of Prophecy in the New Testament and Today* (Westchester, IL: Crossway, 1988), pp. 233-243.

7. D. B. Barrett, "Statistics, Global," in Burgess et al., eds., *Dictionary of Pentecostal and Charismatic Movements*, pp. 812-813.

8. Third wave theology and practice have been largely articulated by John Wimber and Kevin Springer as well as C. Peter Wagner and Charles H. Kraft: John Wimber and Kevin Springer, *Power Evangelism*, 2nd revised and expanded ed. (San Francisco, CA: HarperSanFrancisco, 1992); id., *Power Healing* (San Francisco, CA: HarperSanFrancisco, 1987); Kevin Springer, ed., *Power Encounters Among Christians in the Western World* (San Francisco, CA: HarperSanFrancisco, 1988); id. *Power Points: Your Action Plan to Hear God's Voice, Believe God's Word, Seek the Father, Submit to Christ, Take up the Cross, Depend on the Holy Spirit, Fulfill the Great Commission* (San Francisco, CA: HarperSanFrancisco, 1991); C. Peter Wagner, *The Third Wave of the Holy Spirit* (Ann Arbor, MI: Servant, 1988); id., *How to Have a Healing Ministry in Any Church* (Ventura, CA: Regal, 1988); Charles H. Kraft, *Christianity with Power: Your Worldview and Your Experience of the Supernatural* (Ann Arbor, MI: Servant, 1989).

9. See Don Williams' chapter and Wimber and Springer, *Power Points*, pp. 156ff.

10. Gordon D. Fee, *The Disease of the Health and Wealth Gospels* (Costa Mesa, CA: The Word for Today, 1979), p. 19; see also Wimber and Springer, *Power Healing*, pp. 152-157 (and references cited there), which also discusses the relationship, coming to similar conclusions.

11. BAGD, pp. 876-879.

12. See references cited in notes below and also J. Becker, "Wunder und Christologie," *NTS* 16 (1969-70): 138-140; G. Delling, "Das Verständnis des Wunders im Neuen Testament," *ZSTh* 24 (1955): 265-280; J. Hempel, *Heilung als Symbol und Wirklichkeit im Biblischen Schrifttum* (Nachrichten der Gesellschaft der Wissenschaften zu Göttingen, Philosophisch-historische Klasse, 3) 1958; B. Klappert, "Die Wunder Jesu im Neuen Testament," *Das Ungewöhnliche, Aussaat-Bücherei* 45 (1969): 25ff.; G. Mensching, W. Vollborn, E. Lohse, and E. Käsemann, "Wunder," in K. Galling et al., eds., *Die Religion in Geschichte und Gegenwart* (3rd ed., 1957-1965), vol. 6, pp. 1831ff.; R. Renner, *Die Wunder Jesu in Theologie und Unterricht*, 1966; G. Siegmund, "Theologie des Wunders," *Theologische Revue* 58 (1962): 289ff.; R. E. Brown, *The Gospel According to John*, vol. 1 (1967), pp. 525-532 ("Signs and Works"); id., "The Gospel Miracles," *New Testament Essays* (1965), pp. 168-191; A. B. Bruce, *The Miraculous Elements in the Gospels*, 1886; R. H. Fuller, *Interpreting the Miracles*, 1963; A. de Groot, *The Bible on Miracles* (St. Norbert Abbey Series 19), 1966; J. Kallas, *The Significance of the Synoptic Miracles*, 1961; K. Tagawa, *Miracles et évangile: La pensée personnelle de l'évangéliste Marc* (Études d'histoire et de philosophie religieuses*, vol. 62 (Paris, France: Presses Universitaires de France, 1966), pp. 75-80; J. S. Lawton, *Miracles and Revelation*, 1959; H. van der Loos, *The Miracles of Jesus* (Supplements to Novum Testamentum, vol. 8) (Leiden,

Netherlands: E. J. Brill, 1965); L. Monden, *Le miracle, signe de salut*, Desclée, 1960.

13. F. F. Bruce, *The Hard Sayings of Jesus* (Downers Grove, IL: InterVarsity, 1983), pp. 96-97.

14. A. Feuillet, "Le 'Commencement' de l'Economie Chrétienne d'après Heb. ii.3-4, Mar. i.1 et Acts 1.1-2," *NTS* 24 (1978): 171-173: "En Marc ii.2 et iv.33 on voit Jésus 'proclamer la Parole'....En Mc. xvi.19-20, une fois Jésus monté au ciel, les apôtres à leur tour 'proclament la Parole.' Et comme la Parole proclamée par Jésus était accompagnée d'oeuvres de puissance, il en va exactement de même d'après Marc xvi.20 pour la Parole proclamée par les apôtres....ce que Jésus a commencé à dire (la Parole) et à faire (les miracles), tout cela est continué après l'Ascension par les apôtres....Mus par l'Esprit, les apôtres reprennent l'appel de Jésus à la repentance (ii. 38, iii.26, v.31, xviii.30) et son annonce du 'Royaume de Dieu' (viii.12, xix.8, xx.25, xxviii.31)....ils attestent la résurrection de Jésus....Ils s'appuient sur l'invocation du Nom de Jésus....C'est pour ce Nom que les apôtres souffrent (v.21, xxi.13; cf. I Pet. iv.14); c'est ce Nom qu'ils prêchent (iv.10-12, 17-18; v.28-40). Et l'invocation de ce Nom met en action la puissance divine détenue par Jésus. Il en résulte que, par cette invocation, les apôtres accomplissent des prodiges semblables à ceux du ministère public de Jésus, guérissent les malades, chassent les démons et même ressuscitent des morts: iii.1-10, viii.6-7, ix.32-43, xiv.8-18, xx.7-12...v.16...xix.12."

15. A. Richardson, *The Miracle-Stories of the Gospels* (London, England: SCM Press, 1941), pp. 44-45.

16. B. Klappert, in C. Brown, ed., *The New International Dictionary of New Testament Theology* [hereafter NIDNTT] (Grand Rapids, MI: Eerdmans, 1986), vol. 3, p. 1108.

17. G. Friedrich, in G. Kittel, ed., *Theological Dictionary of the New Testament* [hereafter TDNT] (Grand Rapids, MI: Eerdmans, 1964-74), vol. II, p. 720.

18. D. S. Cairns, *The Faith That Rebels. A Re-examination of the Miracles of Jesus* (London, England: 1929), p. 93.

19. Ibid., p. 29.

20. H. van der Loos, *The Miracles of Jesus*, p. 220.

21. "[Die heilungen] sind...Zeichen, die den Sieg des Christus über Sünde und Tod anzeigen und damit die Macht seines Wortes bekräftigen," E. Thurneysen, *Die Lehre von der Seelsorge* (Zürich, 1946), p. 230.

22. W. Grundmann, *TDNT*, vol. 2, p.303.

23. H. van der Loos, *The Miracles of Jesus*, pp. 252f.

24. A. Richardson, *The Miracle-Stories of the Gospels*, p. 61f.

25. O. Hofius, *NIDNTT*, vol. 2, pp. 632-633.

26. M. Horton, *Power Religion*, p. 348.

27. Carson in Horton, ed. *Power Religion*, p. 117.

28. Ibid.

29. Billy Graham, *The Holy Spirit: Activating God's Power in Your Life* (Dallas, TX: WORD, Inc., 1978), chapter 13.

30. G. W. H. Lampe, in C. F. D. Moule, ed., *Miracles. Cambridge Studies in Their Philosophy and History* (London, England: A. R. Mowbray & Co., 1965), p.

171: "By the divine power the gospel is preached, converts are made, the Church is established in unity and brotherhood, the opposing powers, whether human or demonic, are conquered, persecution, of which certainly, much has to be endured, is turned to good account for the furtherance of the gospel, and judgment overtakes the persecutors"; C. H. Powell, *The Biblical Concept of Power* (London, England: Epworth Press, 1963), pp. 78-79.

31. E.g., **Matthew** 4:23; 9:35,36; 10:1,7,8; 11:5; 12:15,18; 15:30; 19:2 (cf. **Mark** 10:1); 21:14 (cf. **Luke** 21:37); **Mark** 1:38,39; 2:2, 11; 3:14,15; 6:12,13; 10:1 (cf. Matt. 19:2); **Luke** 4:18; 5:17, 24; 6:6-11,17,18; 7:22; 9:1,2; 10:9,13; 13:10-13,22,32; 14:4,7ff.; 21:37 (cf. Matt. 21:14); 16:15-18,20; **John** 3:2; 7:14,15,21-23,31,38; 10:25,32,38; 12:37,49; 14:10,12; **Acts** 1:1; 2:22; 10:38.

32. E.g., **Acts** 3:6,12; 4:29,30; 5:12-16,20,21,28,42; 6:8,10; 8:4-7,12; 9:17,18 (cf. 22:13),34,35; 14:3,8-10,15ff.; 15:12,36; 18:5,11 (cf. 2 Cor. 12:12; 1 Cor. 2:4,5); 19:8-12; **Romans** 15:18,19; **1 Corinthians** 2:4,5; 11:1; 12:1-11,28-31; **2 Corinthians** 12:12; **Galatians** 3:5; **Philippians** 4:9; **1 Thessalonians** 1:5,6; **Hebrews** 2:3,4; 6:1,2; **James** 5:13-16.

33. In Ephesians 6:18, Paul commands us to "pray in the Spirit on all occasions with all kinds of prayers and requests" (cf. 1 Thess. 5:17; Col. 4:2). Yet, Paul was ill in Galatia for a long enough period that it "was a trial" to the Galatians (Gal. 4:14); Epaphroditus did not experience immediate healing from illness and almost died according to Philippians 2:27; Timothy had chronic illnesses involving his stomach, which were not completely healed according to 1 Timothy 5:23; and Paul had to leave Trophimus sick in Miletus, apparently seeing no healing in response to prayer (2 Tim. 4:20).

34. On experiencing healing of illness as a "gift of grace," experienced only in part in the Early Church according to the New Testament, see A. Oepke, *"iaomai," TDNT*, vol. 3, p. 214 (cf. 1 Cor. 12:9,28,29); on experiencing spiritual gifts in this age only "in part (*ek merous* 1 Cor. 13:9)," see Gordon D. Fee, *The First Epistle to the Corinthians* (NICNT, ed., F. F. Bruce; Grand Rapids, MI: Eerdmans, 1987), p. 644 and n. 21; J. Schneider, *TDNT*, vol. 4, p. 596.

35. J. Wimber, *Kingdom Suffering: Facing Difficulty and Trial in the Christian Life* (Ann Arbor, MI: Servant, 1988), pp. 27-28; cf. id., *Power Healing*, pp. 147-166 (chap. 8), 184.

36. Richardson, *Miracle-Stories of the Gospels*, p. 68, quoting the German historian of Christianity, A. von Harnack, *The Mission and Expansion of Christianity in the First Three Centuries* (2nd ed., London, England: 1908; originally published in German, 1902), vol. 2, pp. 121f.

37. Richardson, *Miracle-Stories of the Gospels*, p. 11; cf. Powell, *The Biblical Concept of Power*, p. 142.

38. M. Green, *Evangelism Through the Local Church* (Nashville, TN: Nelson, 1992), p. 408.

39. Foster, *Prayer: Finding the Heart's True Home*, p. 203.

40. Foster, "Introduction" in Wimber and Springer, *Power Healing*, p. xi.

I

EXEGETICAL AND
THEOLOGICAL STUDIES

1

OLD TESTAMENT FOUNDATIONS:

SIGNS AND WONDERS IN PROPHETIC MINISTRY AND THE SUBSTITUTIONARY ATONEMENT OF ISAIAH 53

JEFFREY NIEHAUS

When the Son of God came to earth, He brought what the Bible metaphorically calls the "water" of the Holy Spirit, who had been poured out on Him without measure. The Son's first advent was foretold by the prophet Isaiah, who foresaw the result of Christ's ministry. He said it would be a time when "the Spirit is poured upon us from on high, and the desert becomes a fertile field" (Isa. 32:15). Isaiah was a great poet as well as a prophet, and he spoke powerfully of the Messiah's life and work. What he said has come to pass, and both he and the other Old Testament prophets have much to teach us, not only about God and His Christ, but also about prophetic ministry—a Kingdom ministry of signs and wonders—both in the past and today.

SIGNS AND WONDERS—MOSES AND JESUS

We know from the Old Testament that God did signs and wonders to advance His kingdom. The phrase, "signs and wonders," first occurs in the Bible to describe the plagues that God, through His prophet Moses, brought upon Egypt (Exod. 7:3). But the miracles of God in the Old Testament are not only destructive; God also parted the Red Sea, held up the waters of the Jordan River, and brought His people safely across both. Such miracles were part of His plan of salvation for Israel.

The New Testament declares that Jesus also worked great miracles as part of God's plan of salvation for His people. Some of Jesus' signs and wonders showed God's power over nature, just as Moses had done. For instance, Jesus turned water to wine (John 2:1ff.), caused a fig tree to shrivel up (Mark 11:12-14,20-24), and stilled the stormy waters of the Sea of Galilee (Matt. 8:23-27). But most of Jesus' miracles involved the healing of diseases and bodily infirmities, and deliverance from evil spirits.

The ministries of Jesus and Moses have important things in common. Both were covenant mediators: Moses mediated the Old Covenant; Jesus mediated the New. Both Moses (Deut. 34:10) and Jesus (Acts 3:22) were prophets. And both did signs and wonders that were part of the advance of God's kingdom—His program of salvation for His people.

SIGNS AND WONDERS AND PROPHETIC MINISTRY

The great examples of Moses and Jesus show a connection between prophetic ministry and signs and wonders. This is not accidental. The Old Testament contains evidence that God has always intended to establish a relationship between prophetic ministry and miracles, including divine healing.

Signs and wonders are a well-documented part of what it meant to be a prophet—one who was called to speak and act on God's behalf—in the Old Testament.[1] The word "prophet," for example, first occurs in the Old Testament in the context of a healing—the healing of King Abimelech's wife and slave girls. Abraham told Abimelech, king of Gerar, that his wife, Sarah, was his sister (she was actually his half sister, Gen. 20:12). Abraham did this out of fear that someone would kill him and take his wife because she was so beautiful (Gen. 20:11; he had done the same in Egypt, Gen. 12:12ff.). Abimelech believed Abraham and took Sarah, but God warned Abimelech in a dream that he must not have another man's wife. God also "closed the wombs" of Abimelech's wife and slave girls as both a warning and a punishment (Gen. 20:18).

God then told Abimelech, "Now return the man's wife, for *he is a prophet*, and he will pray for you and *you will live*" (Gen. 20:7). God's statement makes a clear connection between Abraham's prophetic call and the power to heal. The same is affirmed at the end of the chapter: "Then Abraham prayed to God, and God healed Abimelech, his wife and his slave girls so they could have children again" (Gen. 20:17).

The connection between God's prophets and God's healing ministry stands out even more boldly in the cases of Elijah and Elisha. Both of them did healings and other miracles that look forward to the ministry of Christ. The first reported "healing" done by Elijah was a resurrection—the son of the widow of Zarephath (1 Kings 17:19-24). Elisha also raised someone from the dead—the son of a Shunammite woman (2 Kings 4:32-37). In each case, the prophet lay upon the dead body and prayed, and as he did so the boy came back to life. (Similarly, the apostle Paul brought the boy Eutychus back from the dead by lying on him, Acts 20:10).

Both Elijah (1 Kings 17:7-16) and Elisha (2 Kings 4:1-7,42-44) miraculously reproduced scant supplies of food, just as Jesus did with the loaves and fishes. And Elisha healed Naaman the Syrian of leprosy by commanding him to go and wash in the Jordan seven times (2 Kings 5:1-19), just as Jesus healed the blind man by commanding him to go and wash in the pool of Siloam (John 9:1-7). The parallels between the miracles of these Old Testament prophets and the miracles of Jesus (and Paul) are remarkable, and they have a purpose.

GOD'S REASONS FOR PERFORMING MIRACLES

What was that purpose? Or to put it another way: Why did God perform these miracles of healing and provision? He did them for at least three reasons: (1) God did them to show that He is God; (2) He did them for evangelistic purposes; and (3) He did them out of compassion for His people. More than one of these reasons might have been in operation at any given time.

First, God sometimes performed signs and wonders to show His people that He alone is God (e.g., Elijah on Mount Carmel, 1 Kings 18:16-39). Whatever else a sign or a wonder does, it always brings glory to God, who alone could do it.

Second, God also performed healings through His prophets so that non-Israelites could know Him as the true God. So the widow of Zarephath, a suburb of pagan Sidon (a Phoenician city on the Mediterranean coast), exclaimed when Elijah raised her son from the dead: "Now I know that you are a man of God and that the word of the Lord from your mouth is truth" (1 Kings 17:24). Naaman the Syrian was converted to the true God when the Lord healed him by the word of the prophet Elisha: "Now I know that there is no God in all the world except in Israel....[and I] will never again make burnt offerings and sacrifices to any other god but the Lord" (2 Kings 5:15,17).

These Old Testament examples show that God has always wanted to reach people of all nations and bring them to salvation. Through prophets such as Abraham, Elijah, and Elisha, He showed this desire by healing those who were not Hebrews and, at least in some cases, turning them to Himself. There can be no doubt that such healings were not only acts of mercy, but also acts of evangelism.

Third, God did and does signs and wonders out of compassion for His own people. God did many miracles through Moses, both to free and to provide for His people. Through Elisha, God healed the waters of Jericho so His people could drink it (2 Kings 2:19-22), miraculously reproduced oil for a wife of one of the prophets (2 Kings 4:1-7), and made a poisonous stew safe for His people to eat (2 Kings 4:38-41).[2]

God worked miracles of healing and provision through His prophets as part of His care for His own people, but also to show people that He alone is God—so they must turn to Him and be saved. Whatever signs or wonders God did, He always received glory for His Name, because He alone could do them. All of this foreshadows what God did through Jesus Christ, who showed God's compassion and provision for His own people, but also touched "foreigners" for God (e.g., a Roman, a Samaritan, a Syro-Phoenician), and always displayed His Father's glory and glorified His Father. In addition to being the Son of God, Jesus is also the greatest of all prophets.

THE OLD TESTAMENT AND DELIVERANCE MINISTRY

One way that God healed people through the ministry of Jesus involved a blatant disruption of the demonic realm. We know that "The reason the Son of God appeared was to destroy the devil's work" (1 John 3:8). Nowhere is such destruction more obvious than in the salvation of a sinner, when the Spirit of Christ brings a person out of the kingdom of darkness into the kingdom of God (Acts 26:18; Col. 1:13), and gives that person "the right to become [a child] of

God" (John 1:12). But it was also an obvious, dramatic thing when Jesus "destroyed the devil's work" by casting out demons.

The Old Testament does not say much directly about the demonic realm, but what it says is intriguing. From it we learn that the power behind pagan religion is demonic. Before Joshua led the Israelites into the Promised Land, Moses spoke in a prophetic poem (Deut. 32) about the sins that future generations of Israelites would commit. His words are a theological commentary on pagan worship:

> They sacrificed to demons, which are not God—
>> gods they had not known,
>> gods that recently appeared,
>> gods your fathers did not fear (Deut. 32:17).

Later in the history of Israel, we read the sad fulfillment of Moses' prophecy:

> They sacrificed their sons
>> and their daughters to demons.
> They shed innocent blood,
>> the blood of their sons and daughters,
>> whom they sacrificed to the idols of Canaan (Ps. 106:37,38).

The apostle Paul wrote about the same spiritual dynamic when he warned the church in Corinth: "Do I mean then that a sacrifice offered to an idol is anything, or that an idol is anything? No, but the sacrifices of pagans are offered to demons, not to God, and I do not want you to be participants with demons" (1 Cor. 10:19,20). The point in both Old and New Testaments is that the power behind idolatry is demonic.[3]

In addition to a theological analysis of idolatrous worship, the Old Testament gives us an account of an actual deliverance. In this case, the power of God became available to set King Saul free from demonic oppression.

One of the saddest accounts in the history of Israel is the story of Saul's disobedience toward God. The prophet Samuel, who originally anointed Saul king, put the king's rebellion in the strongest terms: "Rebellion is like the sin of witchcraft," and added, "Because you have rejected the word of the Lord, he has rejected you as king" (1 Sam. 15:23). As part of God's punishment of Saul, "an evil spirit from the Lord tormented him" (1 Sam. 16:14). This statement does not mean that the Lord commands hosts of evil spirits and sends them against hapless mortals. Rather, the Lord sometimes allows evil spirits to have their way with people who have rebelled against Him, and that is one form of divine judgment upon them.

A good example of such judgment occurs in 1 Kings 22:19-28, where God allows a lying spirit to speak through false prophets. As a result, the sinful King Ahab is led astray to campaign against the Aramaeans and is killed in the battle. In the case of Saul, God allowed the judgment of demonic affliction to be ameliorated at times by His servant David. David would play the harp in Saul's presence when the evil spirit attacked the king, and then "relief would come to Saul; he would feel better, and the evil spirit would leave him" (1 Sam. 16:23).

This is a case of deliverance (at least temporary deliverance) from demonic oppression, but it is not just deliverance by a shepherd boy. David had already been anointed by Samuel to succeed Saul, and when he was, "from that day on the Spirit of the Lord came upon David in power" (1 Sam. 16:13). Not only was David anointed by the Spirit; he was also a prophet, as we know from Peter's sermon on the day of Pentecost (Acts 2:30). It appears, then, that the David who delivered Saul was an anointed, prophetic figure, who of course not only became king of Israel, but also spoke prophetically of Christ on a number of occasions (e.g., Pss. 2,16,22,110).

OLD TESTAMENT HEALING
AND THE PROPHETIC

These examples of healing and deliverance through prophetic figures in the Old Testament make a clear point. God chose to do signs and wonders through anointed, prophetic figures. He did them through His prophet and covenant mediator Moses; He also did them through other prophets such as Elijah, Elisha, and David. The New Testament evidence is similar. God did signs and wonders not only through Jesus[4] (the Prophet and Mediator of the New Covenant), but also through Jesus' disciples during His earthly ministry, and then through the apostles and other Christians[5] as the Church age began.[6]

The parallel suggests that God has always intended Kingdom life in both Old and New Testaments to be prophetic—a life that includes signs and wonders. This may seem a bold statement, but other evidence supports it, including both the outpourings of God's Spirit and the prophecies of such outpourings in the Old Testament.

The Old Testament contains prophecies and yearnings for God's extension of His kingdom by signs and wonders—of which the Church age is a fulfillment. Moses first gave voice to this yearning during the wilderness wanderings of Israel. In Numbers 11:16, we read how God had the elders of Israel stand around the tent of meeting (the Tabernacle). God then "took of the Spirit that was on [Moses] and put the Spirit on the 70 elders. When the Spirit rested on them, they prophesied" (Num. 11:25). Two other men, Eldad and Medad, were also listed among the elders, but had not come to the tent. But God also let His Spirit rest on them, "and they prophesied in the camp" (Num. 11:26). Joshua, who was Moses' helper, was jealous for his great leader. He wanted Moses to be the sole prophet. He complained to Moses about what was happening. But Moses, having God's heart, replied, "Are you jealous for my sake? I wish that all the Lord's people were prophets, and that the Lord would put his Spirit on them" (Num. 11:29).

We know that Moses had God's point of view when he said this, because God later promised to fulfill Moses' wish in a prophecy well known not only to Pentecostals and charismatics but to Christians everywhere:

> And afterward,
>   I will pour out my Spirit on all people.
> Your sons and daughters will prophesy,
>   your old men will dream dreams,
>   your young men will see visions.
> Even on my servants, both men and women,
>   I will pour out my Spirit in those days
>   (Joel 2:28,29).

Peter quoted Joel's prophecy on the day of Pentecost (Acts 2:17ff.) to explain how it came to pass that believers in Christ could be proclaiming the wonders of God in various tongues, "as the Spirit enabled them" (Acts 2:4). The outpouring of the Spirit that began there continued as the Church grew and God continued to gift His people for the work of His kingdom. The gift of the Spirit for kingdom work is what Jesus promised just before He ascended: "You will receive power when the Holy Spirit comes on you; and you will be my witnesses" (Acts 1:8). In other words, they could not be Jesus' "witnesses" until the "power" of the Holy Spirit came upon them.

The Holy Spirit—the "Spirit of prophecy" (Rev. 19:10)—was necessary to enable God's people to advance His kingdom. That Spirit was necessary both in the Old Testament (as the prophets and their signs and wonders illustrate) and the New Testament. And, because Jesus Christ is "the same yesterday and today and forever" (Heb. 13:8), the same "Spirit of prophecy," which is the "testimony of Jesus" (Rev. 19:10) is necessary today to make God's people faithful testimonies or witnesses of Christ.

The examples of Old Testament outpourings of the Spirit and prophecies of such outpourings, taken all together, strongly indicate that God has always intended kingdom life, life under His rule and reign, in both Old and New Testaments to be prophetic.[7] On the basis of Rev. 19:10, we can now define the "prophetic" as that which is a "testimony of Jesus Christ." Old and New Testament evidence connects the prophetic with signs and wonders, and argues that such a prophetic lifestyle includes miraculous healings, deliverances, and other works of power. The democratization of the Spirit from Pentecost onward means that signs and wonders are to be a normal part of Kingdom life. So it appears in the Early Church. That is no doubt why God provided lengthy New Testament passages (Rom. 12:1-8; 1 Cor. 12—14; Eph. 4:7-13; 1 Thess. 5:19-22; 1 Pet. 4:10,11) to help His people manage His abundant spiritual gifts.

If such was the case in the Early Church, one natural and related question is: To what extent can signs and wonders be expected in our day? A full answer to that question lies outside the scope of this chapter. A starting place for an answer may well be some of Jesus' comments on what it means to follow Him (e.g., Matt. 10:25; Luke 6:40; John 14:12). One question that can be addressed (at least in a limited way) is that of divine healing. Old Testament prophets did not heal everyone who needed healing, nor did Jesus Himself. To what extent may we expect God to heal people today? The question needs to be addressed because it involves an Old Testament passage (Isa. 53), which has sometimes been misunderstood.

ISAIAH 53: THE SUBSTITUTIONARY ATONEMENT OF CHRIST AND DIVINE HEALING

A discussion of healing and the Old Testament would not be complete without a look at Isaiah 53. More than any other Old Testament passage, Isaiah 53 portrays the character, ministry, sufferings, death, and exaltation of the Messiah—as well as His gifting of the Church. On the basis of this chapter alone, Isaiah's book might well be called the "Gospel" of the Old Testament. Among other things, Isaiah's prophecy anticipates the healing ministry of the Messiah:

Surely he took up our infirmities
and carried our sorrows,
yet we considered him stricken by God,
smitten by him, and afflicted.
But he was pierced for our transgressions,
he was crushed for our iniquities;
the punishment that brought us peace was upon him,
and by his wounds we are healed (Isa. 53:4,5).

Jesus began to fulfill the prophecy in these verses when He started His healing ministry, as Matthew reports: "He drove out the spirits with a word and healed all the sick. This was to fulfill what was spoken through the prophet Isaiah: 'He took up our infirmities and carried our diseases'" (Matt. 8:16,17, citing Isa. 53:4a). Matthew applies Isaiah's words to what Jesus did in His earthly ministry. But, as Luke says of the Lord's works, these are "all that Jesus began [erxato] to do and to teach, until the day he was taken up to heaven" (Acts 1:1,2). Luke describes the works of Jesus as those that He "began" to do, because Jesus then went on to do similar works in and through the Early Church (1 Cor. 12:6; Gal. 3:5). And He is still doing them. Therefore, Isaiah's words leave room for an understanding that the ongoing ministry of the Messiah includes miraculous healing and deliverance such as Matthew describes.

That does not mean that healing is automatically available to every believer today, anymore than it was when Jesus walked the earth, or in the Early Church (cf. Gal. 4:14; Phil. 2:27; 1 Tim. 5:23; 2 Tim. 4:20). It also does not mean that healing is "in the atonement" in the same way that forgiveness of sin is. On this point, Isaiah 53:5 ("The punishment that brought us peace was upon him, and by his wounds we are healed") has been misunderstood.[8] Isaiah's references to "punishment" and "wounds" in this verse are a description of the suffering servant's substitutionary atonement (cf. Isa. 53:6-12). But the "peace" (Hebrew shalom, "wholeness") that comes as a result, and the "healing" brought by His wounds, are primarily the healing from sin (cf. Isa. 1:5,6) and the peace of the promised Spirit (cf. Isa. 48:16; John 14:26,27), whom we have within because of Christ's atoning work.

Healing of sickness is made possible through the atonement ("he took up our sicknesses [hōlāyēnû]" Isa. 53:4; cf. Matt. 8:16,17), inasmuch as forgiveness of sin makes healing possible (Ps. 103:3; Jas. 5:15,16; see also Peter H. Davids' chapter in this book on sin and the fruits of sin). But Scripture also makes it clear that the healing of disease mentioned in Isaiah 53 will only be experienced in part.[9] In 1 Corinthians 13, Paul says that in this age the Church will only experience spiritual gifts, which include healing, *"in part (ek merous)"* until the second coming of Christ: "For we know *in part* and we prophesy *in part"* (1 Cor. 13:9; cf. 1 Cor. 1:6,7 and 13:8-10,12; 1 John 3:2; Rev. 22:4).[10]

The apostle Peter applies Isaiah 53:5 to the forgiveness of sin. Peter says of Christ, "He himself bore our sins in his body on the tree, so that we might die to sins and live for righteousness; *by his wounds you have been healed"* (1 Pet. 2:24). Just as Isaiah portrays sin as disease (Isa. 1:5,6), so Peter uses Isaiah's words to inform us that the "healing" of Isaiah 53:5 is first and foremost a healing from *sin.* That is the healing we find in the atonement. In the same vein, Peter goes on to quote Isaiah 53:6: "For you were *like sheep going astray,* but now you have returned to the Shepherd and Overseer of your souls" (1 Pet. 2:25). The work of the atonement is to heal us from sin and to return stray sheep to God, as Peter's application of Isaiah 53:5,6 makes clear. It makes physical healing possible ("He took up our infirmities" Isa. 53:4 and Matt. 8:16,17) but does not necessarily guarantee it in this age to God's people.

That does not mean healing and the atonement are totally unrelated. Because of Christ's atonement, God has sent healings and many other gifts of the Holy Spirit to His Church. As Gordon Fee has observed, "Healing is provided for [in the atonement] because the atonement brought release from the...consequences of sin; nonetheless, since we have not yet received the redemption of our bodies, suffering and death are still our lot until the resurrection."[11]

OLD AND NEW TESTAMENTS AND HEALING TODAY

From the Old Testament we see that God combined spiritual words and deeds of power as He advanced His kingdom through His servants the prophets. So when Elijah had raised the widow of Zarephath's son to life she exclaimed, "Now I know that you are a man of God and that the word of the Lord from your mouth is the truth (1 Kings 17:24). For her it was an act of *power,* her son's resurrection, that confirmed the truth of God's *word* from the prophet's mouth.

In a similar way, Elisha's healing of Naaman the Syrian made the latter a believer in God (2 Kings 5:15,17).[12] God used not only words, but also power, to bring the lost to Himself, even in the Old Testament. He did the same in the New Testament. Jesus not only *preached* the "Gospel of the Kingdom"—He *demonstrated* it by miraculous healings, deliverances, and resurrections (Matt. 4:23; John 11:38-44). Jesus' teaching and His works of power were intimately related—so much so that the people at Capernaum exclaimed, "What is this *teaching?* With *authority* and *power* he gives orders to evil spirits and they come out!" (Luke 4:36).

The apostle Paul followed Christ's example. His words to the Romans are noteworthy. He tells them, "I will not venture to speak of anything except what Christ has accomplished through me in leading the Gentiles to obey God by what I have said and done—by the power of signs and wonders, through the power of the Spirit" (Rom. 15:18,19). Paul characterizes his twofold ministry ("what I have *said* and *done* ") by saying, "I have *fully proclaimed [plēroō* "fill, fulfill"[13]] the gospel of Christ" (Rom. 15:19). Paul's account seems to make it clear that a "full" gospel proclamation consists both of preaching/teaching the word and of attendant works of power—signs and wonders. That is just what the Old Testament evidence would lead us to expect, for that is just the way God worked through Old Testament prophets who foreshadowed the person and work of Christ.

That twofold ministry of words and works does not stop with the apostle Paul or with the New Testament Church. As one moves through the Old Testament, the evidence mounts that God has in mind the creation of a prophetic people, who will be gifted to advance His Kingdom by signs and wonders like the prophets of old.[14] Another way of saying this is that Jesus not only died on the cross for our sins; He rose and ascended on high and—with the Father—sent His Spirit to enter His people (John 14:17) and empower them (Rom. 8:9-14) for prophetic living.

After all, "The testimony of Jesus is the spirit of prophecy" (Rev. 19:10). Those who are living testimonies of Jesus Christ have the Spirit of prophecy within them. This does not mean that all of God's people will prophesy, or that they are "prophets" in the sense that Agabus was a prophet (Acts 11:27,28; 21:10-11). Rather, God will work through His people by that Spirit to do signs and wonders—even miraculous healings—on earth, just as He worked through His prophets in the Old Testament, and through His Son, and through the disciples/apostles and early Christians. It was, after all, Jesus (that perfect prophet) who said, "A student is not above his teacher, but everyone who is fully trained will be like his teacher" (Luke 6:40; cf. Matt. 10:25). Jesus' words are a calling on God's Church. The Church can embrace that calling with faith and expectation, because Jesus also promised, "He who believes in me will also do the works that I do [*ta erga ha egō poiō*]," and He added, "And greater works than these [*meizona toutōn*] will he do, because I go to the Father" (John 14:12, *RSV*).

Notes

1. The Hebrew word translated "prophet" (*nābî'*) appears to be a passive participle from a root related to Akkadian *nabû*, "to call." The sense seems to be that a prophet is someone called by God to be a spokesman for God (cf. Exod. 4:14-16). The Greek word (*prophetēs*), which normally translates the Hebrew, and from which our English word "prophet" comes, means, according to Henry George Liddell and Robert Scott, *A Greek-English Lexicon* (Oxford, England: Clarendon, 1968), p. 1540, *"one who speaks for a god and interprets his will to man...revealer of God's will, prophet."* However, it is clear from what prophets did in the Old Testament that they had far more than a speaking role.
2. Elisha also miraculously caused a lost axhead to float, thus relieving the anxiety of the man who had both borrowed and lost it (2 Kings 6:1-7); and by Elisha's word God struck an army of hostile Aramaeans blind, facilitated their capture, and then restored their sight—as a result they left off raiding Israel's territory (2 Kings 6:8-23).
3. Cf. C. Fred Dickason, *Angels, Elect and Evil* (Chicago, IL: Moody, 1975), p. 152.
4. Matthew 4:23; 9:35,36; 10:1,7,8; 11:5; 12:15,18; 14:14; 15:30; 19:2 (cf. Mark 10:1); 21:14 (cf. Luke 21:37); Mark 1:32-39; 2:2,11,12; 3:14,15; 6:12,13; 10:1 (cf. Matt. 19:2); Luke 4:18,31-36,40-44; 5:17,24; 6:6-11,17,18; 7:22; 9:1,2; 10:9,13; 13:10-13,22,32; 14:4,7ff.; 21:37 (cf. Matt. 21:14); John 2:23; 3:2; 7:14,15,21-23,31,38; 10:25,32,38; 12:37,42,49; 14:10,12; Acts 1:1; 2:22; 10:38.
5. Acts 3:6,12; 4:29,30; 5:12-16,20,21,28,42; 6:8,10; 8:4-7,12; 9:17,18 (cf. 22:13), 34,35; 14:3,8-10,15ff.; 15:12,36; 18:5,11 (cf. 2 Cor. 12:12; 1 Cor. 2:4,5); 19:8-12; Romans 15:18,19; 1 Corinthians 2:4,5; 11:1; 12:1-11,28-31; 14:24,25; 2 Corinthians 12:12; Galatians 3:5; Philippians 4:9; 1 Thessalonians 1:5,6; Hebrews 2:3,4.
6. As George Eldon Ladd, *The Gospel of the Kingdom* (Grand Rapids, MI: Eerdmans, 1959), p. 115, says of the disciples, "The Kingdom of God was at work among men not only in the person of our Lord but also through His disciples as they brought the word and the signs of the Kingdom to the cities of Galilee."
7. It is also clear, of course, that part of Christ's work was to send the Spirit to all believers, thus enabling them to live such a "prophetic" lifestyle far beyond what Old Testament believers normally could do (cf. John 7:37-39; 14:16-17).
8. See Gordon D. Fee, *The Disease of the Health and Wealth Gospels* (Costa Mesa, CA: The Word for Today, 1979).
9. In Ephesians 6:18, Paul commands us to "pray in the Spirit on all occasions with all kinds of prayers and requests" (cf. Col. 4:2; 1 Thess. 5:17). Yet, Paul was ill in Galatia for a long enough period that it "was a trial" to the Galatians (Gal. 4:14); Epaphroditus did not experience immediate healing from illness and almost died according to Philippians 2:27. Timothy had chronic illnesses involving his stomach, which were not completely healed according to 1 Timothy 5:23; and Paul had to leave Trophimus sick in Miletus, apparently seeing no healing in response to prayer (2 Tim. 4:20).
10. On experiencing healing of illness as a "gift of grace," (1 Cor. 12:9,28,29) expe-

rienced only in part in the Early Church according to the New Testament, see A. Oepke, *"iaomai," TDNT*, vol. 3, p. 214; on experiencing spiritual gifts in this age only "in part (*ek merous*, 1 Cor. 13:9)," see Gordon Fee, *The First Epistle to the Corinthians* (NICNT, ed., F. F. Bruce; Grand Rapids, MI: Eerdmans, 1987), p. 644 and n. 21; Schneider, *TDNT*, vol. 4, p. 596.

11. Fee, *The Disease of the Health and Wealth Gospels*, p. 19. Fee goes on to say, "While there are scores of texts that explicitly tell us that our sin has been overcome through Christ's death and resurrection, there is *no* text that explicitly says the same thing about healing, not even Isaiah 53 and its New Testament citations."

12. Naaman may well have appreciated that (in the words of one British New Testament scholar) "miracles of healing are...symbolic demonstrations of God's forgiveness in action." Cf. Alan Richardson, *The Miracle-Stories of the Gospels* (London, England: SCM Press, 1942), pp. 61ff.

13. The use of *pleroo* "bring [the gospel] to full expression" in Romans 15:19 cannot mean that Paul *finished* preaching the gospel, because he was still planning to visit Rome and preach the gospel further in Spain (Rom. 1:13,15; 15:23f.). Nor can it mean that he *said everything* there was to say about the gospel (J. Murray, *The Epistle to the Romans* [NICNT; Grand Rapids, MI: Eerdmans, 1968], p. 214). But, as G. Friedrich points out, it means that Paul proclaimed the gospel in the way he described in Romans 15:18,19, in word and deed, "by the power of signs and wonders, by the power of the Spirit": "Again, Romans 15:19...does not mean that Paul has concluded his missionary work, but that the gospel is fulfilled when it has taken full effect. In the preaching of Paul, Christ has shown Himself effective in word and sign and miracle (v. 18). Hence the Gospel has been brought to fulfilment from Jerusalem to Illyricum and Christ is named in the communities (v. 20)" (Friedrich, *TDNT*, vol. 2, p. 732).

14. God shows by signs and wonders in both Testaments that He has invaded our space with His kingdom. As Ladd, *The Gospel of the Kingdom*, pp.107, 115, has noted, "When Israel rejected the Kingdom, the blessings which should have been theirs were given to those who would accept them....The kingdom of God, as the redemptive activity and rule of God in Christ, created the Church and works through the Church in the world. As the disciples of the Lord went throughout the villages of Palestine, they proclaimed that in their mission, the kingdom of God had come near to these villages (Luke 10:9). They performed the signs of the Kingdom, healing the sick and casting out demons, thus delivering men from the satanic power (vv. 9, 17)....In the same way, the kingdom of God, the redemptive activity and power of God, is working in the world today through the Church of Jesus Christ."

2

SHOULD CHRISTIANS EXPECT MIRACLES TODAY?

OBJECTIONS AND ANSWERS FROM THE BIBLE

WAYNE GRUDEM

Should we expect the Holy Spirit to work in powerful, miraculous ways in connection with the preaching of the gospel and the life of the Church today? This has been the claim of John Wimber and the Vineyard movement, and of others within what is called the "third wave" of renewal by the Holy Spirit.[1] Similar claims have been made for years by Christians within the Pentecostal and charismatic movements. But other evangelicals have differed with this claim, and have raised several objections. In this chapter, I want to consider some of the most frequent objections and propose some answers from Scripture.

1. Doesn't Jesus say, "An evil and adulterous generation seeks for a sign, but no sign shall be given to it except the sign of Jonah" (Matt. 16:4)?[2] Doesn't this mean we should not seek miracles today—rather, we should look to "the sign of Jonah," which means the resurrection of Christ, and emphasize that when we talk about miracles?[3]

The mistake made in this objection is a failure to look at the context and find whom Jesus was talking to. In the context of Matthew 16, it is the *Pharisees and Sadducees* who came, "and *to test him* they asked him to show them a sign from heaven" (Matt. 16:1). Similarly, it was the *hostile scribes and Pharisees* who came in Matthew 12:38-45, the *Pharisees* who began to argue with him "*to test him*" in Mark 8:11-12, and skeptics who came "to test him" and seek a sign from heaven in Luke 11:16. (The only passage that doesn't specify that the comment was directed against hostile unbelievers is Luke 11:29, but the parallel passage in Matthew 12:38-42 does specify that it was specifically the scribes and Pharisees against whom this word was directed.)

So in every instance the rebuke for seeking signs is addressed to hostile unbelievers. Jesus is rebuking Jewish leaders who had hard hearts and were simply seeking a pretext for criticizing Him. *In no case are such rebukes addressed to genuine followers of Jesus* who sought a miracle for physical healing or deliverance for themselves or others, either out of compassion for others or out of a desire to advance the gospel and see God's name glorified. *These warning verses, taken in their original contexts, apply to unbelievers*, and therefore to use them to apply to genuine Christians is an illegitimate application. *No New Testament passages warn against the use of miracles by genuine Christians.*

It seems to me that the New Testament encourages us to believe God and seek answers to prayer in many ways, including miraculous answers to prayer. (See Acts 4:30; 1 Cor. 14:1; Gal. 3:5 [implicitly], see also the entire pattern of gospel proclamation plus miraculous demonstration in the evangelism carried on in Acts 3:6,12ff.; 4:29,30; 5:12-16,20,21,28,42; 6:8,10; 8:4-7,12; 9:17,18 [cf. 22:13],34,35; 14:3,8-10,15ff.; 15:12,36; 18:5,11 [cf. 2 Cor. 12:12; 1 Cor. 2:4,5]; 19:8-12; compare Hebrews 2:4; Jas. 5:13-18.)

2. Doesn't Jesus warn us that in the end times false Christs and false prophets will work miracles, and they will be so deceptive, they will "deceive if possible even the elect"? Therefore isn't it dangerous to follow people who work miracles today? Might we be deceived into following a false prophet?

This objection is based on Mark 13:22, which says, "False Christs and false prophets will arise and show signs and wonders, to lead astray, if possible, the elect." Some people might be concerned that false Christs will be so deceptive, they could not tell what was wrong anyway. In that case, it might be safer to stay away from any church where miracles are being done, just in case the church was deceptive and trying to lead people astray. People will reason:

> False Christs work miracles.
> Miracles are occurring in church A.
> Therefore I will stay away from church A
> just to be safe (I really couldn't discern
> the falsehood anyway).

However, we should remember the New Testament does not speak that way. Instead, Jesus gives a test for false prophets: "*You will know them by their fruits*" (Matt. 7:16). The New Testament does not say false Christs and false prophets are so deceptive that even Christians cannot identify them. And it does *not* say false Christs *will* lead astray the elect; it just says that is the *purpose* they will try to accomplish. The Greek phrase is *pros to apoplanan, ei dunaton, tous eklektous*, (literally) "for the purpose of leading astray, if possible, the elect" (Mark 13:22). But Satan's purpose in this will not be accomplished. Jesus promises us, "*You will know them* by their fruits" (Matt. 7:16), and He says, "My sheep hear my voice, and I know them, and they follow me" (John 10:27).

Peter gives many marks of doctrinal purity and life character that distinguish false prophets from true prophets (2 Pet. 2:1-22). John tells us that false prophets bring false doctrine about Jesus Christ, and their teaching is from the world, not the apostles. He then says, "By this *we know* the spirit of truth and the spirit of error" (1 John 4:6). This is much better counsel than giving a bare warning about miracles that will make people think they have no way of telling false Christs from the true.

False religions (e.g., Mormons, Jehovah's Witnesses, Muslims, Buddhists) teach false doctrine. Pharisees (ancient and modern) oppose, and do not further, the work of the Kingdom. False prophets bear evil fruit—"nor can a bad tree bear good fruit" (Matt. 7:18). But where Christian churches do not teach false doctrine, and further the work of the Kingdom, exalt Jesus Christ, and bear abundant good fruit in the lives of thousands of people, we should know that these qualities are not deceptive marks—they are the marks of true Christianity in the power of the Holy Spirit. They are not the marks of a false religion.

3. *If we say that miracles should accompany the gospel today, doesn't this cheapen the gospel? Wouldn't this show that we don't think the gospel itself is powerful enough to save sinners—rather, we think the gospel of Christ is weak and needs help from miracles?*

If this objection is correct, then the working of miracles must have cheapened the gospel when Peter preached the gospel[4] as well, and when Paul preached[5]—and even when Jesus preached.[6] Miracles must have detracted from the gospel when Stephen and Philip preached (Acts 6:8; 8:6-8), and when Christians at Corinth and in the churches of Galatia worked miracles (1 Cor. 12:28; Gal. 3:5). Did miracles cheapen the gospel in almost the whole of the preaching of the Early Church, and still the Church used them? Surely this is an incorrect conclusion about miracles.

If miracles did not detract from the gospel in the repeated patterns we see in the New Testament, and if the working of miracles was given by God in all those cases, then this objection is not valid, and we are right to seek God for the working of miracles along with evangelism today as well. The New Testament pattern is that present-day miracles attest to the gospel and enhance the power of its proclamation (Rom. 15:18,19); they demonstrate the power of the gospel, but they certainly do not weaken it.

4. *What do miracles prove anyway? Since there can be true miracles and false miracles, miracles alone can never prove anything. Therefore, how could a miracle ever be God's means for converting an unbeliever?*

This objection is stated well by James Montgomery Boice, who says,

> My point is that miracles alone prove nothing. They may be false and deceptive as well as true and instructive, and we are never told that they are God's means for converting unbelievers or that we should seek to perform them....The New Testament does not teach that evangelism is to be done by cultivating miracles.[7]

I can agree with the beginning of the first statement: miracles alone prove nothing, and they may be false and deceptive as well as true and instructive. But I cannot agree with Boice's conclusion: Therefore miracles are never said to be God's means for converting unbelievers. For that to be true, we would first have to assume that people can never distinguish true from false miracles. Then the bare *fact* of a miracle would have no value for evangelism, because any given miracle could be either evil or good, and we could never tell the difference. (This is what Boice seems to assume in order for his argument to work.)

In fact, the New Testament picture is different. People see Jesus' miracles and they *know* He comes from God, and they believe in Him (John 2:11,23; 3:2; 20:30,31; etc.). They decide correctly that His miracles are "true and instructive," not "false and deceptive." And so it is with the later evangelistic ministry of the Early Church, as we see in Acts and the Epistles.

So I fail to understand how Boice would explain the evangelistic activity of Jesus Himself. Or the evangelistic activity of Peter and Paul. Or the evangelistic activity of Stephen. Would he say regarding miracles in the ministry of these people that "we are never told that they are God's means for converting unbelievers"?

Certainly the apostle Paul would not agree with this. He says,

I will not venture to speak of anything except what Christ has worked through me to win obedience from the Gentiles, *by word and deed, by the power of signs and wonders, by the power of the Holy Spirit*, so that from Jerusalem and as far round as Illyr'icum I have fully preached the gospel of Christ (Rom. 15:18,19).

These verses describe the whole of Paul's evangelistic ministry. He says that the "power of signs and wonders" is one of the means God Himself used for converting unbelievers. Paul says that he did evangelism with miracles. It is hard for me to understand how Boice can say, "We are never told that they [miracles] are God's means for converting unbelievers" (p. 127).

Perhaps at this point Boice would modify his statement and say it was only Jesus and the apostles who worked miracles along with their evangelism. But that would not seem to help his argument, because if miracles were a means God used to bring about faith when Jesus and the apostles preached, then why could God not use miracles to bring about faith when we preach today? Is our preaching today more powerful than that of Jesus and the apostles? Did they need miracles to accompany their preaching but we do not, because our preaching is so much more powerful? Certainly that is an incorrect argument.

We must remember it is *God Himself* who "bore witness" to the gospel "by signs and wonders and various miracles and by gifts of the Holy Spirit distributed according to his own will" (Heb. 2:4), and we cannot say that He has an inappropriate view of the power of the gospel message.

5. *Weren't miracles mostly limited to the apostles? Of course we see a lot of miracles in the book of Acts, but wasn't that a special time when new Scripture was being written?*

Some have argued that miracles were restricted to the apostles, or to the apostles and those closely connected with them. Before considering their arguments, it is important to note a remarkable concentration of miracles in the lives of the apostles as special representatives of Christ. For example, God was pleased to allow extraordinary miracles to be done through both Peter and Paul. In the very early days of the Church,

> Many signs and wonders were done among the people by the hands of the apostles....And more than ever believers were added to the Lord, multitudes both of men and women, so that they even carried out the sick into the streets, and laid them on beds and pallets, that as Peter came by at least his shadow might fall on some of them. The people also gathered from the towns around Jerusalem, bringing the sick and those afflicted with unclean spirits, *and they were all healed* (Acts 5:12-16).

Similarly, when Paul was in Ephesus, "God did extraordinary miracles by the hands of Paul, so that handkerchiefs or aprons were carried away from his body to the sick, and diseases left them and the evil spirits came out of them" (Acts 19:11-12).[8] Another example is found in raising Tabitha from the dead. When she had died, the disciples at Joppa sent for Peter to come and pray for her to be raised from the dead (Acts 9:36-42). They apparently thought that God had given an unusual concentration of miraculous power to Peter (or to the apostles generally). And Paul's ministry generally was characterized by miraculous events, because he summarizes his ministry by telling the Romans of the things Christ has worked through him to win obedience from the Gentiles "by the power of signs and wonders, by the power of the Holy Spirit" (Rom. 15:19).

Nevertheless, the unusual concentration of miracles in the ministries of the apostles does not prove that *no miracles* were performed by others. As we have clearly seen, "working of miracles" (1 Cor. 12:10) and other miraculous gifts (1 Cor. 12:4-11 mentions several) were part of the ordinary function of the Corinthian church, and Paul knows that God "works miracles" in the churches of Galatia as well (Gal. 3:5).

In the larger context of the New Testament, it is clear that miracles were worked by others who were not apostles, such as Stephen (Acts 6:8), Philip (Acts 8:6,7), Ananias (Acts 9:17,18; 22:13), Christians in the several churches in Galatia (Gal. 3:5) and those with gifts of "miracles" in the Body of Christ generally (1 Cor. 12:10,28). Miracles as such cannot then be regarded as exclusively signs of an apostle. "Workers of miracles" and "healers" are actually *distinguished* from "apostles" in 1 Corinthians 12:28:

And God has appointed in the church first apostles, second prophets, third teachers, then workers of miracles, then healers.

Similar evidence is seen in Mark 16:17,18: Serious questions have been raised about the authenticity of this passage as part of Mark's Gospel.[9] The text is nonetheless very early[10] and bears witness to at least one strand of tradition within the Early Church, which the manuscript evidence suggests came to be widely accepted in the postbiblical Early Church.[11] This text reports Jesus as saying,

And these signs will accompany those who believe: in my name they will cast out demons; they will speak in new tongues; they will pick up serpents, and if they drink any deadly thing, it will not hurt them; they will lay their hands on the sick; and they will recover.

Here also the power to work miracles is assumed to be the common possession of Christians. Those who wrote and passed on this early tradition, and who thought it represented the genuine teaching of Jesus, were certainly not aware of any idea that miracles were to be limited to the apostles.[12]

The argument that many other Christians in the New Testament worked miracles is sometimes answered by the claim that it was only the apostles and *those closely associated with them* or *those on whom the apostles laid their hands* who could work miracles.[13] However, this really proves very little because the story of the New Testament Church is the story of what was done through the apostles and those closely associated with them. A similar argument might be made about evangelism or founding of churches:

In the New Testament, churches were only founded by the apostles or their close associates; therefore, we should not found churches today.

Or,

In the New Testament, missionary work in other countries was only done by the apostles or their close associates; therefore, we should not do missionary work in other countries today.

These analogies show the inadequacy of the argument: The New Testament primarily shows how the Church *should* seek to act, not how it *should not* seek to act.

But if *many* other Christians throughout the first century Church were working miracles by the power of the Holy Spirit, then the power to work miracles could not be a sign to distinguish the apostles from other Christians.[14]

6. Wasn't the purpose of miracles to authenticate new Scripture as it was being given? Since no more Scripture is being given today, doesn't it mean there will be no more miracles today?

If we consider the New Testament period, it is more accurate to say that miracles authenticated preaching *the gospel* rather than just giving new Scripture. For example, when Philip went to a city in Samaria,

> The multitudes with one accord gave heed to what was said by Philip, *when they heard him and saw the signs which he did.* For unclean spirits came out of many who were possessed, crying with a loud voice; and many who were paralyzed or lame were healed. So there was much joy in that city (Acts 8:6-8).

But Philip did not write any words of Scripture. The same was true in the life of Stephen (Acts 6:8).

Several other purposes are given for miracles in the New Testament. A second purpose is to bear witness that the kingdom of God has come and has begun to expand its beneficial results into people's lives. The results of Jesus' miracles show the characteristics of God's kingdom. Jesus said, "If it is by the Spirit of God that I cast out demons, then *the kingdom of God has come upon you*" (Matt. 12:28). His triumph over the destructive forces of Satan showed what God's kingdom was like. In this way, every miracle of healing or deliverance from demonic oppression advanced the Kingdom and helped fulfill Jesus' ministry, for He came with the Spirit of the Lord on Him "to preach good news to the poor....to proclaim release to the captives and recovering of sight to the blind, to set at liberty those who are oppressed" (Luke 4:18).

Similarly, Jesus gave His disciples "power and authority over all demons and to cure diseases, and he sent them out *to preach the kingdom of God* and to heal" (Luke 9:1,2). He commanded them, "Preach as you go, saying, 'The kingdom of heaven is at hand.' Heal the sick, raise the dead, cleanse lepers, cast out demons" (Matt. 10:7-8; compare Matt. 4:23; 9:35; Acts 8:6,7,12).

A third purpose of miracles is to help those who are in need. The two blind men near Jericho cried out, "Have mercy on us," and Jesus "in pity" healed them (Matt. 20:30,34). When Jesus saw a great crowd of people, "he had compassion on them, and healed their sick" (Matt. 14:14; see also Luke 7:13). Here miracles give evidence of Christ's compassion toward those in need.

A fourth purpose of miracles, related to the second, is to remove hindrances to people's ministries. As soon as Jesus had healed Peter's mother-in-law, "she rose and served him" (Matt. 8:15). When God had mercy on Epaphroditus and restored his health (whether through miraculous means or not, Paul attributes it to God's mercy in Philippians 2:27), Epaphroditus was then able to minister to Paul and complete his function as a messenger returning to the Philippian church (Phil. 2:25-30).

The text does not explicitly say that Tabitha (or Dorcas) resumed her "good works and acts of charity" (Acts 9:36) after the Lord through Peter raised her from the dead (Acts 9:40,41). But by mentioning her good works and those who bore witness to her selfless care for the needs of others (Acts 9:39), it suggests that she would resume a similar ministry of mercy when she was raised from the dead. Related to this category would be the fact that Paul expects people to be edified when miraculous gifts are used in the Church (1 Cor. 12:7; 14:4,12,26).

A fifth purpose for miracles (and one to which all the others contribute) is to bring glory to God. After Jesus healed a paralytic, the crowds "were afraid, and they glorified God, who had given such authority to men" (Matt. 9:8). Similarly, Jesus said that the man who had been blind from birth was blind "that the works of God might be made manifest in him" (John 9:3).

These multiple purposes for miracles show that we should not claim they were limited only to the time when new Scripture was being written.

7. Doesn't Paul say miracles were the "signs of an apostle" (2 Cor. 12:12) that were given to show the unique authority of the apostles? And doesn't that mean we should not expect such signs today?

This objection is based on 2 Corinthians 12:12, where Paul says, "The *signs of a true apostle* were performed among you in all patience, with signs and wonders and mighty works."[15] Some people say the "signs of an apostle" here are miracles, and this verse implies that only the apostles (and their close companions) had the authority to work miracles.[16] These people then argue that this means other people did *not* have the authority to work miracles. They say that the working of the miracles ceased when the apostles and their close associates died. Therefore, they conclude, no further miracles are to be expected today. (Those who hold this position are sometimes known as "cessationists," because they hold to the ceasing or "cessation" of miracles early in the history of the Church.)

This argument is unpersuasive, however, for several reasons:

A. *The word "sign" alone does not necessarily mean "miracle."* People who say 2 Corinthians 12:12 shows that miracles ceased usually *assume* that "signs of an apostle" in this verse means miracles, but they do not give any reasons to support their assumption. And, the assumption is open to serious objections (see below), and, if no arguments can be given in its favor, there is no reason we should accept it.

Among modern commentators on 2 Corinthians, I found only three who understand the phrase "signs of an apostle" in 2 Corinthians 12:12 to mean miracles.[17] None of these commentators gives any argument to support this view. By contrast, the majority of commentators understand "signs of an apostle" to have a much broader meaning, including the qualities of Paul's life and the character and results of his ministry.[18] Some of these commentators think that these life and ministry qualities were accompanied by miracles or included miracles as one component among many, but none understand the phrase to refer primarily or exclusively to miracles.

The meaning of the word "sign" in Greek (*sēmeion*) is consistent with this. Although the word often refers to miracles, it has a much broader range of meaning than just "miracle": *sēmeion* simply means "something which indicates or refers to something else." Many nonmiraculous things are called "signs." For example, Paul's *handwritten signature* is his "sign" (2 Thess. 3:17); *circumcision* is a "sign" of Abraham's imputed righteousness (Rom. 4:11); *Judas's kiss* is a "sign" to the Jewish leaders (Matt. 26:48); the *rainbow* is a "sign" of the covenant (Gen. 9:12, LXX); *eating unleavened bread* during Passover every year is a "sign" of the Lord's deliverance (Exod. 13:9, LXX); *Rahab's scarlet cord* is a "sign" that the spies told her to hang in her window (1 Clem. 12:7).

Therefore, we cannot just assume that the phrase "signs of an apostle" means "miracles." We must rather look to the context to see what sense the word "signs" has in Paul's argument at this point.

B. *The grammar of this verse requires that the "signs of an apostle" are something other than miracles.* At the end of 2 Corinthians 12:12, Paul uses a different phrase, which piles up terms in such a way that miracles are unmistakably in view: He says,

The *signs of a true apostle* were performed among you in all patience, with signs and wonders and mighty works.[19]

The last phrase, "with signs and wonders and mighty works," contains a collection of all three terms used for miracles, and similar collections of terms elsewhere clearly are used to refer to miracles (note "signs and wonders" in Acts 4:30; 5:12; 14:3; 15:12; Rom. 15:19; Heb. 2:4). But if this last phrase means "*with miracles*," then Paul is saying, in effect,

The *signs of a true apostle* were performed among you in all patience, *with miracles*.

This means that the "signs of an apostle" must be something different from miracles—the signs of an apostle were not themselves miracles, but they were done *with* miracles.

C. *Paul tells elsewhere in 2 Corinthians what the "signs of an apostle" are.* This is not the only verse in 2 Corinthians in which Paul is concerned to defend his apostleship. The main theme of chapters 10-13 is Paul's defense of his true apostolic authority in opposition to the false apostles who were troubling the Corinthian church. If we want to know, then, what "signs" Paul pointed to when he wanted to establish his genuine apostleship, we need only look at the things he mentions in 2 Corinthians 10—13. In several verses Paul tells what marked him as a true apostle:

1. Spiritual power in conflict with evil (10:3,4,8-11; 13:2-4,10).
2. Jealous care for the welfare of the churches (11:1-6).
3. True knowledge of Jesus and His gospel plan (11:6).
4. Self-support (selflessness) (11:7-11).
5. Not taking advantage of churches; not striking them physically (11:20,21).
6. Suffering and hardship endured for Christ (11:23-29).
7. Being caught up into heaven (12:1-6).
8. Contentment and faith to endure a thorn in the flesh (12:7-9).
9. Gaining strength out of weakness (12:10).

The first item may have implied miraculous power in conflict with evil, but even that is not stated. The important thing is that Paul pointed not to miracles but to *indications of his personal character and Christlike ministry* when he wanted to show what marked a true apostle in contrast to self-seeking pretenders to that office (cf. 2 Pet. 2:1,22).

Another evidence that the "signs of a true apostle" in 2 Corinthians 12:12 were all these things and not simply miracles is that Paul says, "The signs of a true apostle were performed among you *in all patience.*" Now it would make little sense to say that miracles were performed "in all patience," for many miracles happen quite quickly. But it would make sense to say that Paul's Christlike ministry, his selflessness, his contentment, and his endurance of hardship for the sake of the Corinthians were performed "in all patience."

D. *The New Testament never says that miracles proved someone to be an apostle.* We should note that nowhere in this list does Paul claim miracles to prove his genuine apostleship. No verse in the New Testament says that miracles distinguished the apostles from other Christians.[20] Miracles could not be used to distinguish apostles from nonapostles, because many people who were not apostles also worked miracles—Stephen (Acts 6:8), Philip (Acts 8:6,7), Ananias (Acts 9:17,18; 22:13), Christians in the churches in Galatia (Gal. 3:5), and those with gifts of "miracles" in the Body of Christ generally (1 Cor. 12:10, 28). "Workers of miracles" and "healers" are actually *distinguished* from "apostles" in 1 Corinthians 12:28: "And God has appointed in the church first *apostles*, second prophets, third teachers, then *workers of miracles*, then healers."

But the character traits Paul does mention—self-sacrifice for the churches, endurance of hardship and so on—clearly distinguish him from servants of Satan, false apostles who are *not Christians at all:* Their lives will not be marked by humility, but pride; not by selflessness, but selfishness; not by generosity, but greed; not by seeking the advantage of others, but by taking advantage of others; not by spiritual power in physical weakness, but by confidence in their natural strength; not by enduring suffering and hardship, but by seeking their own comfort and ease.

When Paul acted in a Christlike manner among them, his actions were "signs" that his claim to be an apostle was a true claim: thus, these things were "signs of a true apostle."[21] In this context, the "signs" that mark a true apostle need not be things that showed an absolute difference between him and other Christians, but rather things that showed his ministry to be genuine, in distinction from false ministries.

Therefore, here Paul is not telling the Corinthians how to distinguish an apostle from other Christians (he did that in 1 Cor. 9:1,2; 15:7-11; Gal. 1:1,11-24, mentioning seeing the risen Christ and being commissioned by Him as an apostle), but here he is telling how to recognize what a genuine, Christ-approved ministry is.

Why then does he add that all these signs of a true apostle were done among the Corinthians "*with* signs and wonders and mighty works"? He is simply adding one additional factor to all the previous marks of his genuine apostleship. Miracles, of course, had a significant function in confirming the truth of

Paul's message, and Paul here makes explicit what the Corinthians may or may not have assumed to be one of the many factors included in the phrase "signs of a true apostle": in addition to all these other signs of a true apostle, his ministry also showed miraculous demonstrations of God's power.[22]

E. *Those who use 2 Corinthians 12:12 to argue against miracles today fail to understand the context of this verse.* The argument that the "signs of an apostle" are miracles does not fit the purpose of the context. In 2 Corinthians 12:12, Paul is *not* attempting to prove that he is an apostle distinct from other Christians who are not apostles. Rather, he is attempting to prove that he is a true representative of Christ *distinct from* others who are "false apostles" (2 Cor. 11:33). It is clear that these people are not even Christians, for Paul says about them:

> For such men are false apostles, deceitful workmen, disguising themselves as apostles of Christ. And no wonder, for even Satan disguises himself as an angel of light. So it is not strange if *his servants* also *disguise themselves as servants of righteousness.* Their end will correspond to their deeds (2 Cor. 11:13-15).

These false apostles are *Satan's* "*servants*" who are disguising themselves as "servants of righteousness" (2 Cor. 11:14,15). In short, the contrast is not between apostles who could work miracles and ordinary Christians who could not, but between genuine *Christian* apostles through whom the Holy Spirit worked and *non-Christian* pretenders to the apostolic office, through whom the Holy Spirit did not work at all.

Therefore, those who use this passage to distinguish Paul from other Christians and who argue that miracles cannot be done through *Christians* today are taking the phrase "signs of an apostle" out of its context and using it in a way that Paul never intended. Paul is distinguishing himself from *non-Christians*, not distinguishing himself from *other Christians*.

8. Doesn't Hebrews 2:3 tell us that miracles were restricted to the apostles, "those who heard him"?

In Hebrews 2:3,4, the author says about the message of salvation,

> It was declared at first by the Lord, and it was attested to us by those who heard him, while God also bore witness[23] by signs and wonders and various miracles and by gifts of the Holy Spirit distributed according to his own will.

The miracles here are said to come through those who heard the Lord firsthand ("those who heard him"), so it is argued that we should not expect them to be done through others who were not firsthand witnesses to the Lord's teaching and ministry.[24]

But this argument attempts to draw more from the passage than is there. First, the phrase "those who heard him" (Heb. 2:3) is certainly not limited to the apostles, for many others heard Jesus as well (Luke 10:1ff.; John 6:60-70; 1 Cor. 15:6). But more importantly, this position is claiming something the text simply does not say: That the gospel message was confirmed by miracles when it was preached by those who heard Jesus says nothing at all about whether it would be confirmed by miracles when preached by others who did not hear Jesus.

Finally, this passage says the message was confirmed not only by "signs and wonders and various miracles" but also by "gifts of the Holy Spirit." If someone argues that this passage limits miracles to the apostles and their companions, then he or she must also argue that *gifts of the Holy Spirit* are likewise limited to the first-century Church. But few would argue that there are no gifts of the Holy Spirit today.

9. *When Paul says, "Jews demand signs and Greeks seek wisdom, but we preach Christ crucified, a stumbling block to Jews and folly to Gentiles" (1 Cor. 1:22,23), doesn't he warn us against seeking signs and say that we should just preach the gospel of Christ?*

Here Paul cannot be denying that he performed miracles in connection with proclaming the gospel. In Romans 15:18,19, a passage Paul wrote while in Corinth, he said,

> For I will not venture to speak of anything except what Christ has wrought through me *to win obedience from the Gentiles*, by *word and deed, by the power of signs and wonders*, by the power of the Holy Spirit, so that from Jerusalem and as far round as Illyr'icum I have fully preached the gospel of Christ.

And 2 Corinthians 12:12 affirms clearly that Paul did work "signs and wonders and mighty works" among them.

So 1 Corinthians 1:22-24 cannot mean that Paul was denying the validity of *wisdom* or the validity of *signs*, for through Christ he worked signs and he taught wisdom. Rather, here he is saying that *signs and wisdom do not themselves save people, but the gospel saves people*. Signs and the wisdom Jews and Greeks were seeking were not the signs and wisdom of Christ, but simply *signs to entertain* or to fuel their hostility and skepticism, and wisdom that was the *wisdom of the world* rather than the wisdom of God.

10. *When Paul talks about "power," doesn't he mean the power of the gospel to change lives? In fact, he says, "I am not ashamed of the gospel: it is the power of God for salvation to every one who has faith" (Rom. 1:16). Doesn't this mean it is wrong to use the term "power evangelism" to refer to God's power to work miracles in connection with evangelism?*

Examining just the Greek word *dunamis* "power, miracle," the term Paul most frequently uses for "power," we find a number of passages that speak of miracles. He says that his entire ministry has been characterized by the *"power of signs and wonders, by the power of the Holy Spirit"* (Rom. 15:19). This is an important verse because it gives a description of his entire gospel ministry up to that point. In 1 Corinthians, Paul talks about "the working of *miracles*" (1 Cor. 12:10), and says that God has put in the Church "workers of *miracles*" (1 Cor. 12:28), in both cases using *dunamis.*

Paul uses the same term to speak of the "signs and wonders and *mighty works*" (2 Cor. 12:12), which he did at Corinth. And he similarly uses *dunamis* "power" to speak of the fact that God "works *miracles*" among the Galatian churches (Gal. 3:5). These passages are all examples of Paul tying together the idea of power with evangelism and miracles. Of course, other passages show how "power" is connected with God's power to change lives at conversion, or power to endure suffering and so on, but to say Paul *only* uses "power" to refer to God's power to change lives is certainly not true.

This is also clear in Acts, where the key verse to the whole book is Acts 1:8:

But you shall receive *power* when the Holy Spirit has come upon you; and you shall be my witnesses in Jerusalem and in all Judea and Samar'ia and to the end of the earth.

The word here translated "power" (*dunamis*) occurs nine other times in Acts. In one case (4:33), it is unclear whether this "power" refers to powerful preaching that convicted the hearers or to miraculous signs that accompanied the preaching. But in the other eight examples (2:22; 3:12; 4:7; 6:8; 8:10 [in this verse referring to pagan miracle-working power],13; 10:38; 19:11) it refers to power to work miracles. This meaning of the term *dunamis* is further confirmed by its frequent use in Luke's Gospel to refer to miracle-working power.

Therefore, when Jesus promised the disciples in Acts 1:8 that they would receive "power" when the Holy Spirit came upon them, it seems that they would have understood it to mean at least the power of the Holy Spirit to work miracles that would attest to the truthfulness of the gospel. Because the context of the sentence talks about being witnesses for Jesus, they may have understood Him to mean they would also receive the power of the Holy Spirit to work through their preaching and bring conviction of sins and awaken faith in people's hearts.

The point is, we cannot separate these uses and say the only kind of power the New Testament talks about is power to preach the gospel, or to bring regeneration. The New Testament often uses "power" in referring to power to work miracles in connection with the preaching of the gospel or in the ongoing life of the Church.

11. I have heard stories of people who spoke in tongues and later found out that it was a demonic counterfeit—a demon was speaking through them and uttering blasphemies against Christ in an unknown language. Shouldn't this danger warn us not to speak in tongues today?

We should recognize at the outset that there may be some mistake in reasoning behind this objection because Paul expressed no concern with this problem, even in the city of Corinth where many had come from a background of pagan temple worship, and where Paul had clearly said, "What pagans sacrifice they offer to demons and not to God" (1 Cor. 10:20). Nonetheless, Paul says, "I want you all to speak in tongues" (1 Cor. 14:5). He gives no warning that they should beware of demonic counterfeits or think this would be a possibility when they use this gift.

The theological reason underlying Paul's encouragement at this point is that the Holy Spirit is working powerfully within the lives of believers. Paul says, "I want you to understand that no one speaking by the Spirit of God ever says 'Jesus be cursed!' and no one can say 'Jesus is Lord' except by the Holy Spirit" (1 Cor. 12:3). Here Paul reassures the Corinthians that if they are speaking by the Holy Spirit working within them, they will not say, "Jesus be cursed!"[25]

Coming as it does at the beginning of a discussion of spiritual gifts, 1 Corinthians 12:3 is intended to function as reassurance to the Corinthians who may have suspected some Christians who came from backgrounds of demon worship in the temples at Corinth. Might this demonic influence still affect their use of a spiritual gift? Paul lays down the ground rule that those who genuinely profess faith that "Jesus is Lord" are doing so by the Holy Spirit working within, and that no one speaking by the power of the Holy Spirit will ever speak blasphemy or curses against Jesus.[26]

This fear, then, is not one that seemed to trouble Paul. He simply encouraged believers to pray in tongues and said that if they did so they would be edifying themselves (1 Cor. 14:4).

What shall we say, then, about the stories of Christians who say they spoke in tongues for a time and then found there was a demon within them who was empowering this speech, and the demon was cast out?[27] These are just examples of cases where experience is to be subject to Scripture and tested by Scripture, and the teaching of Scripture should not be subject to experience. We must be careful that we not let such reports of experiences cause us to adopt a different position than Scripture itself on this issue.

Specifically, if 1 Corinthians 12—14 views tongues as a good gift from the Holy Spirit that is valuable for edification and for the good of the Church, and if Paul can say, "I want you all to speak in tongues" (1 Cor. 14:5), then interpretations of contemporary experiences that, in effect, say, "I want you all to be afraid of tongues," go contrary to the emphasis of the New Testament. (Note, for example, C. Fred Dickason's quotation of Kurt Koch: "Seeking this gift for ourselves can be a very dangerous experience."[28] This is just not the perspective Paul has in the New Testament.)[29]

An alternative explanation for the stories given by Dickason is that the demons who said they were "tongues spirits," and that they came in when some charismatics laid hands on the Christian in question, were lying. Satan "is a liar and the father of lies" (John 8:44), and he would love to have Christians afraid of as many of the Holy Spirit's gifts as possible.

The possibility of demonic counterfeit of every gift certainly exists in the lives of unbelievers (see Matt. 7:22). But in the lives of believers, especially when there is positive fruit in their lives and positive fruit from their gifts, 1 Corinthians 12:3; 1 John 4:4 and Matthew 7:16-20 tell us these are not counterfeit gifts but real gifts from God. We must remember that Satan and demons do not do good, they do evil; and they do not bring blessing, they bring destruction (John 10:10).

12. In 1 Corinthians 14:22 we read, "Tongues are a sign not for believers but for unbelievers, while prophecy is not for unbelievers but for believers." Doesn't Paul mean here that tongues are a sign of a covenant curse by God against the unbelieving Jews? And shouldn't that warn us not to use tongues today?

This objection is based on Paul's having just quoted Isaiah 28:11. "By men of strange lips and with an alien tongue the Lord will speak to this people," and concluding that tongues are a sign for unbelievers. Since the context of Isaiah 28:11 is one of judgment on rebellious Israel, some commentators have understood Paul to mean that tongues are always a sign of judgment on the Jews who rejected Christ. Thus, they are a sign of a "covenant curse" from God at one particular time in history, and should certainly not be used by us today.[30]

In order to evaluate this objection to tongues today, we need to look at the purpose of this passage. Paul is warning Christians not to speak in tongues in church *without interpretation*, and, in 1 Corinthians 14:20-25, he says that if they do so it would be acting and thinking like "children" (1 Cor. 14:20). It is in this context that he quotes a prophecy of judgment from Isaiah 28:11,12:

> In the law it is written, "By men of strange tongues and by the lips of foreigners will I speak to this people, and even then they will not listen to me, says the Lord" (1 Cor. 14:21).

In the context of Isaiah 28, God is warning the rebellious people of the northern kingdom of Israel that the next words they heard from Him would be words of foreigners they could not understand—the Assyrian army would come on them as agents of God's judgment. Now Paul is about to take this as a general principle—when God speaks to people in language they cannot understand, it is quite evidently a sign of God's judgment.

Paul rightly applies this to the situation of speaking in tongues *without interpretation* in the church service. He calls it a sign (that is, a sign of judgment) on unbelievers:

> Thus, tongues are not a sign for believers but for unbelievers, while prophecy is not for unbelievers but for believers. If, therefore, the whole church assembles and all speak in tongues, and outsiders or unbelievers enter, will they not say that you are mad? (1 Cor. 14:22,23).

Here Paul uses the word "sign" to mean "sign of God's attitude" (whether positive or negative). Tongues that are not understood by outsiders are certainly a negative sign—a sign of judgment. Therefore, Paul cautions the Corinthians *not* to give such a sign to outsiders who come in. He tells them if an outsider comes in and hears only unintelligible speech, he or she will certainly not be saved but will conclude that the Corinthians are mad, and the uninterpreted tongues will therefore function to him or her as a sign of God's judgment.

By contrast, Paul says that prophecy is a sign of God's attitude as well, but here a positive sign of God's blessing. This is why he can say that prophecy is a sign "for believers" (v. 22). And this is why he concludes his section by saying, "If all prophesy, and an unbeliever or outsider enters, he is convicted by all, he is called to account by all, the secrets of his heart are disclosed; and so, falling on his face, he will worship God and declare that God is really among you" (vv. 24,25). When this happens, believers will certainly realize that God is active among them to bring blessing, and prophecy will regularly function as a sign *for believers* of God's positive attitude for them.[31]

Regarding public use of tongues *with interpretation*, it should be noted in connection with this passage that Paul's reaction to this recognition of the sign function of tongues is not to forbid tongues in public worship, but to regulate the use of tongues so they will always be interpreted when spoken in public (1 Cor. 14:27,28). This is an appropriate response, for it is only *incomprehensible* tongues that have this negative function toward unbelievers, both in Isaiah 28:11 and in 1 Corinthians 14:23. But when a speech in tongues is interpreted, it is no longer incomprehensible and it no longer retains this ominous sign function.[32]

Therefore, it is important to realize that in 1 Corinthians 14:20-23 Paul is not talking about the function of tongues in general, but only about the negative result of one particular abuse of tongues, namely, the abuse of speaking in public without an interpreter (and probably more than one person speaking at a time [cf. 1 Cor. 14:23,27]) so that it all became a scene of unedifying confusion.

In the rest of this section, Paul has a positive attitude toward the proper public function of using tongues plus interpretation, or the proper private function of speaking in tongues (1 Cor. 12:10,11,21,22; 14:4,5,18,26-28,39). So to use Paul's discussion of an abuse of tongues in 14:20-23 as the basis for a general polemic against all other (acceptable) uses of tongues is contrary to the entire context in 1 Corinthians 12-14.

This crucial point, essential to understanding Paul's meaning here, is completely overlooked by some Reformed and dispensational interpreters of this passage. For example, the fact that Paul is talking not about tongues with interpretation but about uninterpreted tongues (which were not able to be understood by the hearers) is overlooked by O. Palmer Robertson,[33] and also by Zane Hodges.[34] Neither Robertson nor Hodges adequately takes into account that at Corinth any unbeliever who entered a church, whether Jew or Gentile, would not understand what was spoken in tongues. Paul repeatedly says that uninterpreted tongues could not be understood by the hearers at Corinth (see 1 Cor. 14:2,9,11,14,16,19,23,28). Paul's main concern in 1 Corinthians 14 is to contrast intelligible with unintelligible speech.

In this connection, Robertson argues that tongues were a "sign" of the transition between God's dealing with Israel and His dealing with all nations.[35] That might possibly be true in some contexts (such as Acts 2), but it is totally foreign to the context of 1 Corinthians 12-14, where Paul makes no mention of the Gentile inclusion or of judgment on the Jews—he contrasts not "Jews" and "Gentiles" but "believers" and "unbelievers." And because he does not specify Jewish unbelievers, while there were certainly Gentile unbelievers visiting the church at Corinth as well, we must understand "unbeliever" here as referring to unbelievers generally (both Jewish unbelievers and Gentile unbelievers). Paul is using Isaiah 28:11,12 not as a prediction about Jewish unbelievers, but as an example or illustration (with reference to unbelievers generally). Realizing this, Carson is right to conclude that Paul cannot be speaking here of tongues as a sign of a covenantal curse on unbelieving Jews.[36]

Moreover, neither Robertson, Gaffin nor MacArthur, all of whom use this "covenantal curse" interpretation to argue against tongues today, take into account that Paul's solution in this passage is not to forbid the use of tongues altogether, but to direct that tongues be used with interpretation, or used privately (1 Cor. 14:27,28).

13. Since Paul says that a person who speaks in tongues "edifies himself" (1 Cor. 14:4), isn't it better to avoid tongues and seek other gifts that edify the Church?

This objection wrongly assumes that we should never do things to edify ourselves. But certainly that is incorrect. We should read our Bibles daily, pray, seek to grow in holiness and so forth. As we grow in Christian maturity, we are better able to serve Christ and edify His Church.

This objection also makes the mistake of drawing a conclusion that is contrary to Paul's own conclusion in this very chapter. However much Paul warns against using tongues without interpretation *in church*, he certainly views it positively and encourages it *in private*. He says, "He who speaks in a tongue *edifies himself*, but he who prophesies edifies the church" (1 Cor. 14:4). What is Paul's conclusion? It is not (as some would argue) that Christians should decide not to use the gift or decide that it has no value when used privately. Rather, he says in 1 Corinthians 14, "What am I to do? I will pray with the spirit and I will pray with the mind also" (v. 15). And he says, "I thank God that I speak in tongues more than you all" (v. 18); "Now *I want you all to speak in tongues*, but even more to prophesy" (v. 5) and "Earnestly desire to prophesy, and do not forbid speaking in tongues" (v. 39).

How does speaking in tongues edify the speaker? According to 1

Corinthians 14:2, "One who speaks in a tongue speaks not to men but to God." This implies that the person speaking in tongues is offering prayer or praise to God—even though his or her mind does not understand what is being said (1 Cor. 14:14-17). Rather, the prayer or praise is coming from the speaker's own human spirit and communicating directly to God (1 Cor. 14:2). If this is so, then we would certainly expect edification to follow. Just as prayer and worship in general will edify us as we practice them, so this kind of prayer and worship edifies us too, according to Paul.

14. Doesn't Jude 9 warn us not to rebuke demons? Then why is it that people today think they can speak directly to demons and cast them out?

This objection is based on the following verse in Jude: "But when the archangel Michael, contending with the devil, disputed about the body of Moses, he did not presume to pronounce a reviling judgment upon him, but said, 'The Lord rebuke you'" (Jude 9). However, in context Jude is not talking about Christians in their encounters with demonic forces, but is pointing out the error of immoral and rebellious false teachers who "reject authority" in general and "slander celestial beings" (v. 8). On their own authority, they foolishly speak blasphemous words against heavenly beings, whether angelic or demonic.

The reference to Michael is simply to show that the greatest angelic creature, no matter how powerful, did not presume to go beyond the limits of the authority God had given him. The false teachers, however, have far overstepped their bounds and they show their foolishness when they "revile whatever they do not understand" (v. 10).

Therefore, the lesson of the verse is simply, Don't try to go beyond the authority God has given you! When Jude 9 is viewed in this way, the only question that arises for a Christian from this verse is, What authority has God given us over demonic forces? And the rest of the New Testament speaks clearly to this in several places. Not only Jesus, and not only His 12 disciples, but also the 70 disciples, Paul and Philip (who was not an apostle) are *given* authority over demons by the Lord Jesus. Jude 9, therefore, simply cannot mean it is wrong for human beings to rebuke or command demons, or that it is wrong for any but the apostles to do so. Both Peter and James encourage *all* Christians to "resist" the devil, and Paul encourages believers in general to put on spiritual armor and prepare for spiritual warfare.

The fact that Jesus gives all believers authority to rebuke demons and command them to leave is seen in several passages. During Jesus' earthly ministry, when He sent the 12 disciples ahead of Him to preach the kingdom of

God, He "gave them power...*over all demons*" (Luke 9:1). After the 70 had preached the kingdom of God in towns and villages, they returned with joy, saying, "Lord, even the demons are subject to us in your name!" (Luke 10:17), and Jesus told them, "I have given you authority...over all the power of the enemy" (Luke 10:19). When Philip, the evangelist, went down to Samaria to preach the gospel of Christ, "unclean spirits came out of many who had them" (Acts 8:7, author's translation). Paul used spiritual authority over demons to say to a spirit of divination in a soothsaying girl, "I charge you in the name of Jesus Christ to come out of her" (Acts 16:18).

Paul was aware of the spiritual authority he had, both in face-to-face encounters such as he had in Acts 16, and in his prayer life as well. He said, "For though we live in the world we are not carrying on a worldly war, for the weapons of our warfare are not worldly but have divine power to destroy strongholds" (2 Cor. 10:3,4). Moreover, he spoke at some length of the struggle Christians have against "the wiles of the devil" in his description of conflict "against the spiritual hosts of wickedness in the heavenly places" (see Eph. 6:10-18). James tells all his readers (in many churches) to "resist the devil and he will flee from you" (Jas. 4:7). Similarly, Peter tells his readers in many churches in Asia Minor, "Your adversary the devil prowls about like a roaring lion, seeking some one to devour. Resist him, firm in your faith" (1 Pet. 5:8,9).[37]

15. Why do people speak directly to demons today and command them to leave, rather than just praying and asking God to drive the demon away? Isn't it safer just to pray to God about this?

In a way, this is similar to asking why Christians should share the gospel with another person rather than simply praying and asking God to reveal the gospel to that person directly. Or why should we speak words of encouragement to a Christian who is discouraged rather than just praying and asking God Himself to encourage that person directly? Why should we speak a word of rebuke or gentle admonition to a Christian, whom we see involved in some kind of sin, rather than just praying and asking God to take care of the sin in that person's life?

The answer to all these questions is that in the kind of world God has created, He has given us an active role in carrying out His plans, especially His plans for advancing the Kingdom and building up the Church. In all of these cases, *our direct involvement and activity* is important *in addition to our prayers*. And so it seems to be in our dealing with demonic forces as well.

As a wise father who does not settle all of his children's disputes for them, but sometimes sends them back out to the playground to settle a dispute themselves, so our heavenly Father encourages us to enter directly into conflict with demonic forces, in the name of Christ and in the power of the Holy Spirit. Thereby He enables us to gain the joy of participating in eternally significant ministry and the joy of triumphing over the destructive power of Satan and his demons in people's lives. God could certainly deal with demonic attacks every time we prayed and asked Him to do so, and He no doubt sometimes does. But the New Testament pattern seems to be that God ordinarily expects Christians themselves to speak directly to the unclean spirits.

We see this pattern of speaking directly to demons first in the ministry of Jesus. He spoke to the demon troubling a man in the synagogue, saying, "Be silent, and come out of him!" (Mark 1:25). He commanded the demons in the Gadarene demoniac, "Come out of the man, you unclean spirit!" (Mark 5:8). When Jesus encountered a young boy severely afflicted by a demon, "He rebuked the unclean spirit, saying to it, 'You dumb and deaf spirit, I command you, come out of him, and never enter him again'" (Mark 9:25). This was Jesus' general pattern, for people said about Him, "What is this word? For with authority and power he commands the unclean spirits, and they come out" (Luke 4:36).

This pattern was then imitated by Jesus' 70 disciples, for they said, "Lord, even the demons are subject to us in your name!" (Luke 10:17). Paul also followed this pattern when he spoke directly to the demon in the soothsaying girl at Philippi, "In the name of Jesus Christ I command you to come out of her!"—as a result, we read that "at that moment the spirit left her" (Acts 16:18, NIV). So the question should not be, What seems safe to us? but rather, What example and pattern does the New Testament give to us? True safety would seem to be in following the pattern given us in God's Word.

16. *If we say that people can give prophecies today, doesn't this mean people can, in effect, add to the words of Scripture? And isn't this wrong, since the Bible is complete?*

No, the gift of prophecy today is not adding words to Scripture. This is because words spoken in prophecies today have less authority than Scripture, and must always be tested by Scripture. We can see this from examining the teaching of the New Testament itself on this gift.

We can begin with Paul's teaching on prophecy in the congregation:

Let two or three prophets speak, and let the others weigh what is said. If a revelation is made to another sitting by, let the first be

silent. For you can all prophesy one by one, so that all may learn
and all be encouraged (1 Cor. 14:29-31; cf. vv. 24,25).

Following this Scripture, we can define the gift of prophecy as follows:

Prophecy is reporting something that God spontaneously brings to
mind.

This is because Paul talks about a "revelation" being made to someone—
what we would call something God spontaneously brings to mind. Based on this
"revelation," the person gives a "prophecy" to the congregation—what we
might call a report of something God had just brought to mind.

But does this kind of prophecy equal "the word of God"? Certainly not in
the sense we usually use the phrase "the word of God," namely, to refer to the
words of the Bible, which have *absolute divine authority* and can never be wrong.
Instead, errors can be made in prophecies that are spoken. That is why Paul
says, "Let the others weigh what is said" (1 Cor. 14:29) and "Do not despise
prophesying, but *test everything*; hold fast what is good" (1 Thess. 5:20,21). He
could not have said these things if prophecies were the very words of God in the
sense Scripture is the very words of God. Therefore, prophecies must have had
much less authority than Scripture.

Paul knew that prophetically gifted people at Corinth were not speaking
the very words of God because he said, "Did the word of God come forth from
you?" (1 Cor. 14:36, literal translation), implying the answer, no. In Acts 21:4,
we read of the disciples at Tyre, "Through the Spirit they told Paul not to go on
to Jerusalem." This seems to be a reference to prophecy directed toward Paul,
but Paul disobeyed it! He never would have done this if this prophecy contained God's very words. Then in Acts 21:10,11, Agabus prophesied that the
Jews at Jerusalem would "bind [Paul] and deliver him into the hands of the
Gentiles," a prediction that was nearly correct but not quite. The Romans
bound Paul (v. 33), and the Jews, rather than delivering him voluntarily, tried
to kill him and he had to be rescued by force (v. 32). The prediction was not far
off, but it was an inaccuracy in detail that would have called into question the
validity of any Old Testament prophet.

God does not make mistakes, and He does not give us erroneous revelations. But we can make mistakes in several ways: (1) We may not perfectly
distinguish what is from God and what are our own thoughts. (2) We may mis-
understand what is from God. (3) We may not report it with complete accuracy—some of our own ideas and interpretations may be mixed in.[38]

That is why I think some charismatics make a mistake when they begin a prophecy with, "Thus says the Lord...," as if they never made a mistake and their prophecies were like the Bible—100 percent God's words with not the tiniest bit of impurity or imperfection. It would be much better to preface a prophecy with, "I think the Lord is telling me...," or, "I think God is putting on my heart that..." This will not hurt the effectiveness of anything that is really from the Lord; because if it is from Him, He will bring it home to the heart of the person for whom it is intended.[39]

The reason people sometimes preface their prophecies with "Thus says the Lord" is that they read the phrase over and over in the Old Testament prophets. But we must realize that the gift of prophecy today is different from the Old Testament prophecies we read in the Bible. Old Testament prophets such as Isaiah and Jeremiah had an amazing responsibility—they were able to speak and write words that had absolute divine authority. This was because God not only *revealed* things to them, He also *guaranteed that their report of that revelation was in the very words He wanted*—what the Bible later calls "God-breathed" words (2 Tim. 3:16).

Thus the Old Testament prophets could say, "Thus says the Lord," and the words that followed were the very words of God. The Old Testament prophets wrote their words as God's words in Scripture for all time (see Deut. 18:18-20; Jer. 1:9; Num. 22:38; Ezek. 2:7, etc.). Therefore, to disbelieve or disobey a prophet's words was to disbelieve or disobey God (Deut. 18:19; 1 Sam. 8:7; 1 Kings 20:36, etc.).

In the New Testament, people speak and write God's very words and have them recorded in Scripture. We are surprised, however, to find that Jesus no longer calls them "prophets" but uses a new term, "apostles." The apostles are the New Testament counterpart to the Old Testament prophets (see Gal. 1:8,9,11,12; 1 Cor. 2:13; 14:37; 2 Cor. 13:3; 1 Thess. 2:13; 4:8,15; 2 Pet. 3:2, etc.). The apostles and a few others authorized by them (such as Mark, Luke, and the author of Hebrews), had authority to write the words of New Testament Scripture—but not the thousands of ordinary Christians who had prophetic gifts in the Early churches (Acts 2:17,18; 21:4,9-11; Rom. 12:6; 1 Cor. 14:29-38; Eph. 4:11; 1 Thess. 5:20; 1 Tim. 4:14; 1 John 4:1-3).

In conclusion, prophecy today is *merely human words* reporting what God has brought to mind, while the prophecies that were written down in the Old Testament were men speaking *God's words* to report what God had brought to mind.

In addition to the verses we have considered so far, one other type of evidence suggests that New Testament congregational prophets spoke with less authority than New Testament apostles or Scripture: The problem of successors to the apostles is solved not by encouraging Christians to listen to the prophets but by pointing to the Scriptures.

So Paul, at the end of his life, emphasizes "rightly handling the word of truth" (2 Tim. 2:15), and the God-breathed character of Scripture for "teaching, for reproof, for correction, and for training in righteousness" (2 Tim. 3:16). Jude urges his readers to "contend for the faith which was once for all delivered to the saints" (Jude 3). Peter, at the end of his life, encourages his readers to "pay attention" to Scripture, which is like "a lamp shining in a dark place" (2 Pet. 1:19,20), and reminds them of the teaching of the apostle Paul "in all his letters" (2 Pet. 3:16). In no case do we read exhortations to "give heed to the prophets in your churches" or to "obey the words of the Lord through your prophets." Yet, certainly prophets were prophesying in many local congregations after the death of the apostles. It seems that they did not have authority equal to the apostles, and the authors of Scripture knew that.

17. But won't any new revelation today have to come in words from God that are perfect and inerrant and equal to the Bible in authority?

This objection is made, for example, by John MacArthur, who assumes that all revelation from God must be accompanied by inerrant reports of that revelation, as it was in the writing of Scripture. He says,

> God's revelation is complete for now. The canon of Scripture is closed...the close of the New Testament has been followed by the utter absence of new revelation in any form.[40]

He says there cannot be prophecy today because "every authentic prophetic revelation will be as true, reliable, and inerrant as Scripture itself."[41]

MacArthur does not realize the Bible itself talks about "revelation" from God that has other results. For example, whenever someone comes to know God personally in salvation, it is because that person has received a revelation from Christ. "No one knows the Father except the Son and any one to whom the Son chooses to *reveal* him" (Matt. 11:27). And whenever God gives people up to self-destruction because of their sin, God's wrath is revealed. "The wrath of God is *revealed* from heaven against all ungodliness and wickedness of men who by their wickedness suppress the truth" (Rom. 1:18).

Even today, whenever God convicts someone of sin, it is a form of revelation as well, because Paul says, "If in anything you are otherwise minded,

God will *reveal* that also to you" (Phil. 3:15). When God gives Christians deeper understanding of the Christian faith, that is a kind of revelation, because Paul prays that God "may give you a spirit of wisdom and of *revelation* in the knowledge of him" (Eph. 1:17).

But new Scripture does not result from any of this. When a new Christian tells how he or she came to know God, that testimony is not new Scripture. When someone tells of conviction of sin, or of deeper knowledge of God, that testimony is not new Scripture. Similarly, when God gives a spontaneous revelation that results in prophecy, this does not result in new Scripture. MacArthur's assumption is simply incorrect.

18. Doesn't the use of prophecy today deny the sufficiency of Scripture?

No, it does not, because prophecy should never function with the absolute authority of Scripture (see above). It should never challenge the unique role the Bible plays in our lives. Rather, it functions on a level something like the kind of authority we give to advice from a friend, or to a subjective "intuition" or "gut feeling" about what to do in a situation. We do not follow these in every case (for they may be wrong), but we do not ignore them either. Often they help us make the right decision. So it is with the gift of prophecy: God can use it to make us aware of things we would otherwise overlook, but He will never use it to add new doctrinal teachings or new moral commands to what is in the Bible.

People who make this objection about prophecy challenging "the sufficiency of Scripture" should be asked to define carefully what they mean by the phrase "the sufficiency of Scripture." This is often not done, and confusion enters into the discussion. To some people the phrase means, (1) Scripture tells us God's will so we should allow no subjective factors in guidance on decisions today. To others it means, (2) Scripture reveals God's words to us, so there can be no more revelation from God to us today. To still others it means, (3) the canon[42] is closed so no more words are to be added to Scripture.

But in theological studies generally, "the sufficiency of Scripture" has a somewhat different sense, one that follows from the fact that the canon is closed. It means, (4) Scripture now contains all the words of God He intends His people to have in the Church age, and, therefore, it now contains everything we need God to tell us for salvation, for right doctrine, and for knowing His will for us. It means, therefore, *we are not to add to the moral commands of Scripture* and demand that people obey new moral principles we have made up, going beyond Scripture. And it means *we are not to add to the doctrinal teachings of Scripture,* demanding that people believe new teachings we have made up. What God has told us is sufficient for knowing what He wants us to believe and do.

Sometimes in discussions about spiritual gifts today, people have in mind senses (1) or (2) above, and, therefore, by their definition the gift of prophecy today is not possible. But when people who allow for prophecy today say they believe in the sufficiency of Scripture, they usually mean sense (3) or (4), both of which are consistent with the continuation of prophecy today. Careful definition is needed before the discussion can proceed, or people will simply talk past one another.

Once we understand that we are talking about the sufficiency of Scripture in sense (4) above, we can then realize that the Bible does not tell us *everything*—a fact everyone will agree to! Why should we think it impossible that God would bring to our mind some information that is not in Scripture but that would be helpful in a situation? Prophecy today can often do this, bringing to mind more facts about a situation, facts we had forgotten or of which we were not aware. For example, Scripture tells me I should pray; it does not tell me that my missionary friend in Japan is in need of prayer right now.

A real-life example may help make this clear. When I was praying with friends recently a woman in the group said, "While we were praying I saw a picture in my mind of two angry faces talking, and it looked like fire was coming out of their mouths." Then another woman said, "I think one of the faces was me. I've been gossiping and spreading dissension by some things I've said to other people in this room." There was silence, then the woman who first saw the mental picture said, "I think the other face was me. I've been gossiping too!" A church elder who was present then read James 3:5, "So the tongue is a little member and boasts of great things. How great a forest is set ablaze by a small fire!" After that, a beautiful time of repentance and forgiveness took place, including tears.

Now that type of event does not challenge a true understanding of "the sufficiency of Scripture" at all. Scripture tells me gossip is wrong; it does not tell me two people in the room have been gossiping (cf. 1 Cor. 14:24,25). Scripture tells me to go to my brother if he has something against me; it does not tell me that Robert has been angry with me about something I said. In addition, out of all the verses in the Bible, God will sometimes use prophecy to bring to mind exactly the right Scripture passage for the situation at hand. This happened to me recently at a meeting for our church. I had awakened that morning with a passage from 2 Samuel on my mind, and when I read it without comment at the meeting, the Holy Spirit used it to bring conviction to our hearts and tears to our eyes.

What a rich blessing this is for the New Covenant Age (from Pentecost until Christ returns)! Here is a great privilege we have over believers in the time of the Old Testament, when only a few people had the gift of prophecy. On the day of Pentecost, Peter said that the New Covenant Age had begun, because Joel's prophecy was fulfilled:

And in the last days it shall be, God declares, that I will pour out my Spirit upon all flesh, and your sons and your daughters shall prophesy, and your young men shall see visions, and your old men shall dream dreams; yes, and on my menservants and my maid servants in those days I will pour out my Spirit; and they shall prophesy (Acts 2:17,18).

Peter does not say only the apostles would prophesy. He does not say only church leaders would see visions and dreams. He says the Holy Spirit is going to give these things to old and young, to men and women, to parents and children. That means all sorts of people in the Church.

And Peter does not say this will be limited to the first few years of the Church (as some would tell us). Joel was predicting the time of the New Covenant, the time of the full outpouring of the Holy Spirit on God's people. That is the age we still live in today—and these are the blessings we should yet expect from God today.

19. If we allow for prophecy and things such as hearing from the Lord today, aren't we in danger of being led astray by an overemphasis on subjective guidance? Haven't many Christian groups in the past made shipwreck of their faith by following such subjective guidance and using "The Lord told me" to justify all sorts of serious errors?

Yes, there is a danger of excessive reliance on subjective impressions for guidance, and that must be clearly guarded against. People who continually seek subjective "messages" from God to guide their lives must be cautioned that *subjective personal guidance is not a primary function of New Testament prophecy.* They need to place much more emphasis on Scripture and seeking God's sure wisdom written there.

I readily admit that many mistakes have been made in this area in the past. People have placed an unhealthy emphasis on subjective guidance, neglected the teachings of Scripture, and fallen into error. Usually this has been because they did not realize that prophecy in the Church age is *not* the word of God, and can frequently contain errors. But here the question must be, Are misunderstandings and abuses *necessary* for the gift of prophecy to function? If we are to argue that mistakes and abuses of a gift make the gift itself invalid, then we would have to reject Bible teaching too (for many Bible teachers have taught error and started cults), and church administration as well (for many church leaders have led people astray). The *abuse* of a gift does not mean we must prohibit the *proper use* of the gift, unless it can be shown that there cannot be proper use—that *all* use has to be abuse.

Many charismatic writers would agree with my cautions against focusing on prophecy for personal guidance, as the following quotations indicate:

Michael Harper (Church of England):

Prophecies which tell other people what they are to do—are to be regarded with great suspicion.[43]

Dennis and Rita Bennett (American Episcopalians):

We should also be careful of personal, directive prophecy, especially outside the ministry of a mature and submitted man of God. Unrestrained "personal prophecy" did much to undermine the movement of the Holy Spirit which began at the turn of the century....Christians are certainly given words for one another "in the Lord"...and such words can be most refreshing and helpful, but there must be a witness of the Spirit on the part of the person receiving the words, and extreme caution should be used in receiving any alleged directive or predictive prophecy. Never undertake any project simply because you were told to by presumed prophetic utterance or interpretation of tongues, or by a presumed word of wisdom, or knowledge. Never do something just because a friend comes to you and says: "The Lord told me to tell you to do thus and thus." If the Lord has instructions for you, He will give you a witness in your own heart, in which case the words coming from a friend...will be a confirmation to what God *has already been* showing you. Your guidance must also agree with Scripture.[44]

Donald Gee (Assemblies of God):

[There are] grave problems raised by the habit of giving and receiving personal "messages" of guidance through the gifts of the Spirit....The Bible gives a place for such direction from the Holy

Spirit....But it must be kept in proportion. An examination of the Scriptures will show us that as a matter of fact the early Christians did *not* continually receive such voices from heaven. In most cases they made their decisions by the use of what we often call "sanctified common-sense" and lived quite normal lives. Many of our errors where spiritual gifts are concerned arise when we want the extraordinary and exceptional to be made the frequent and habitual. Let all who develop excessive desire for "messages" through the gifts take warning from the wreckage of past generations as well as of contemporaries....The Holy Scriptures are a lamp unto our feet and a light unto our path.[45]

Donald Bridge (British charismatic pastor):

The illuminist constantly finds that 'God tells him' to do things....Illuminists are often very sincere, very dedicated, and possessed of a commitment to obey God that shames more cautious Christians. Nevertheless they are treading a dangerous path. Their ancestors have trodden it before, and always with disastrous results in the long run. Inner feelings and special promptings are by their very nature subjective. The Bible provides our objective guide.[46]

On the other hand, many cessationists (i.e., people who don't believe in miraculous gifts such as prophecy today) are skeptical of *any* element of subjectivity in the realm of guidance. This is the opposite mistake. The people who make this objection are often the ones who need this subjective process most in their own Christian lives. This gift requires waiting on the Lord, listening for Him, hearing His prompting in our hearts. For Christians who are completely evangelical, doctrinally sound, intellectual, "objective" believers, probably what is needed most is the strong balancing influence of a more vital "subjective" relationship with the Lord in everyday life. And these people are also the ones who have the least likelihood of being led into error, for they already place great emphasis on solid grounding in the Word of God.

20. Paul says that the Church is "built upon the foundation of the apostles and prophets" (Eph. 2:20). Doesn't this mean that prophets, like apostles, were only given for the foundational years of the Church when they needed new words from God, but that they don't exist today?

I think this verse does not talk about the ordinary prophets who functioned in the various churches at the time of the New Testament. Rather, I think this verse refers to the apostles (who were the foundation of the Church) and calls them "apostle-prophets." The reasons for this are as follows.

Sometimes in the New Testament the term "prophet" (Greek *prophētēs*) is used to refer to the apostles. This is in contexts where there is emphasis on an external spiritual influence (from the Holy Spirit) under which the apostles spoke. Two examples of this are found in Ephesians 2:20 and 3:5.

Here Paul cannot be speaking of all the prophets in local congregations at that time, for prophets are said to be the "foundation" of the Church—and not just individual churches but the Church generally. As well, they are said to be the group to whom the "mystery" was revealed that Gentiles should be included, having equal standing in the Church (Eph. 3:5,6). These things were not true of all the believers who had the gift of prophecy in local congregations in Corinth, Thessalonica, Rome, Tyre, Ephesus, etc. Certainly we cannot say that all of the believers who were converted and began to prophesy in local congregations decades after the Church had begun were the "foundation" of the Church universal. Nor can we say that they were the ones to whom God had revealed the fact of Gentile inclusion in the Church. But these things were true of the apostles in their foundational role in the Church, as God revealed to them the mystery of the Gentile inclusion (cf. Acts 10:9-36; 11:4-18; 15:6-18; Gal. 2:1,2,7-9).

This identification of the apostles as prophets in Ephesians 2:20 and 3:5 is made more clear by the grammatically legitimate translation "the apostles who are also prophets."[47] But in Ephesians 4:11, in a different context (where Paul is talking about gifts given to the Church generally), Paul uses a different construction to distinguish "apostles" from "prophets" and shows that he is referring in this case to two distinct groups.[48]

If someone takes another view of this verse, and thinks it refers to two groups, "apostles *and* prophets," it would not really affect my understanding of the gift of prophecy in New Testament generally. This is because, according to this understanding, Paul would be talking about a very small and restricted group of "prophets"—people who were like the apostles in that they were the foundation of the universal Church, and they received the revelation of the full inclusion of Gentiles in the Church. Ephesians 2:20 and 3:5 would then be talking about this specialized group. For information on the nature of the gift of prophecy in ordinary New Testament churches, however, we would have to look at verses where ordinary congregational prophets were discussed, such as 1 Corinthians 12-14, 1 Thessalonians 5:19-21, etc.

Another instance where an apostle is viewed as a prophet is the apostle John in the book of Revelation (cf. Rev. 1:1-3). The term "prophecy" is appropriate to this book because of its emphasis on revelation given by God. The book of Revelation is an example of a prophecy given through an apostle and therefore possessing absolute divine authority—it is part of Scripture.

21. When Paul says, "As for prophecies, they will pass away; as for tongues, they will cease; as for knowledge, it will pass away" (1 Cor. 13:8), doesn't he mean that prophecies and tongues would cease early in the history of the Church?

Some have argued that 1 Corinthians 13:8 means that Paul expected prophecy and tongues to cease early in the history of the Church. But does the passage really teach that? We must look at the larger context:

> Love never ends; *as for prophecies, they will pass away; as for tongues, they will cease; as for knowledge, it will pass away.* For our knowledge is imperfect and our prophecy is imperfect; but when the perfect comes, the imperfect will pass away. When I was a child, I spoke like a child, I thought like a child, I reasoned like a child; when I became a man, I gave up childish ways. For now we see in a mirror dimly, but then face to face. Now I know in part; then I shall understand fully, even as I have been fully understood. So faith, hope, love abide, these three; but the greatest of these is love (1 Cor. 13:8-13).

In verse 9, Paul gives the *reason* why prophecy and tongues will cease: he says, "Our prophecy is imperfect; but *when the perfect comes, the imperfect will pass away*" (1 Cor. 13:9,10). So he says that prophecy will pass away at a certain time, namely, "when the perfect comes."

But when is that? It has to be the time when the Lord returns. This is because it has to be the same time as indicated by the word "then" in verse 12: "Now we see in a mirror dimly, but then *face to face*. Now I know in part; then I shall understand fully, even as I have been fully understood." To see "face to face" is an Old Testament phrase for seeing God personally (see Gen. 32:30; Exod. 33:11; Deut. 34:10; Judg. 6:22; Ezek. 20:35—these are the only Old Testament occurrences of this Greek phrase or its Hebrew equivalent, and they all refer to seeing God). The time when I shall know "as I have been known" also must refer to the Lord's return (1 John 3:2; Rev. 22:4).

Some have argued that "when the perfect comes" refers to the time when the New Testament canon is complete. (The last New Testament book written, Revelation, was written in A.D. 90 at the latest, about 35 years after Paul wrote 1 Corinthians.) But would the Corinthians ever have understood that from what Paul wrote? Is there any mention of a collection of New Testament books or a New Testament canon anywhere in the context of 1 Corinthians 13? Such an idea is foreign to the context. Moreover, such a statement would not fit Paul's purpose in the argument. Would it be persuasive to argue as follows: We can be sure that love will never end, for we know that it will last more than 35 years? This would hardly be a convincing argument. The context requires rather that Paul be contrasting this age with the age to come, and saying that love will endure into eternity.

Dr. D. Martyn Lloyd-Jones observes that the view that connects "when the perfect comes" (1 Cor. 13:10) to the time of the completion of the New Testament encounters another difficulty. "It means that you and I, who have the Scriptures open before us, know much more than the apostle Paul of God's truth....It means that we are altogether superior...even to the apostles themselves, including the apostle Paul! It means that we are now in a position in which...'we know, even as also we are known' by God...indeed, there is only one word to describe such a view, it is nonsense."[49] John Calvin, referring to 1 Corinthians 13:8-13, says, "It is stupid of people to make the whole of this discussion apply to the intervening time."[50]

This means we have a clear biblical statement that Paul expected the gift of prophecy (and, by implication, probably all spiritual gifts[51]) to continue through the entire Church age and to function for the benefit of the Church until the Lord returns.[52]

22. Doesn't the Bible teach that the Holy Spirit will never call attention to Himself, but will always direct our attention to Christ? Then how can it be right to place so much emphasis on the work of the Holy Spirit today?

This objection is based on trying to force a false alternative, one not supported by Scripture. Of course the Holy Spirit *does* glorify Jesus (John 16:14) and bear witness to Jesus (John 15:26; Acts 5:32; 1 John 2:3; 4:2). But this does not mean He does not make His own actions and words known. The Bible has *hundreds* of verses talking about the work of the Holy Spirit, making His work known, and the Bible is itself spoken or inspired by the Holy Spirit. Matthew 28:19, "Make disciples...baptizing them in the name of the Father and of the Son and of the Holy Spirit," suggests that the Holy Spirit is to be given equal honor with the Father and the Son in the Church.

Moreover, the Holy Spirit frequently made Himself known by some phenomenon or event that indicated His activity, both in the Old Testament and in the New Testament. This was true when the Holy Spirit came upon the 70 elders with Moses and they prophesied (Num. 11:25,26), or when the Holy Spirit came upon the judges to enable them to do great works of power (Judg. 14:6,19; 15:14). People could *see* the effect of the Holy Spirit coming on someone in these cases. This was also true when the Holy Spirit came mightily upon Saul and he prophesied with a band of prophets (1 Sam. 10:6,10), and it was frequently true when the Holy Spirit empowered the Old Testament prophets to give public prophecies.

The Holy Spirit also made Himself known or evident in a visible way when he descended as a dove on Jesus (John 1:32), or came as a sound of a rushing wind and with visible tongues of fire on the disciples at Pentecost (Acts 2:2,3). In addition, when people had the Holy Spirit poured out on them and began to speak in tongues or praise God in a remarkable and spontaneous way (see Acts 2:4; 10:44-46; 19:6), the Holy Spirit certainly made His presence known as well. And Jesus promised that the Holy Spirit within us would be so powerful He would be like a river of living water flowing out from our inmost beings (see John 7:39): Certainly that simile suggests a kind of presence people would be aware of, a presence that would somehow be perceptible.

In the Church, and in the lives of individual believers, the Holy Spirit does not entirely conceal His work, but makes Himself known in various ways. In Acts 13:1,2, it is the Holy Spirit who gives direction in response to fasting and worship. Acts 15:28 suggests that the apostles and elders of the Jerusalem church sought the Spirit in their decisions to find out what "seemed good to the Holy Spirit." The Spirit also bears witness with our spirit that we are children of God (Rom. 8:16), and cries, "Abba, Father!" (Gal. 4:6). He provides a guarantee or a down payment of our future fellowship with Him in heaven (2 Cor. 1:22; 5:5), and reveals His desires to us so that we can be led by those desires and follow them (Rom. 8:4-16; Gal. 5:16-25). He gives gifts that manifest His presence (1 Cor. 12:7-11). And from time to time He works miraculous signs and wonders and miracles that strongly attest to the presence of God in preaching the gospel (Heb. 2:4; cf. 1 Cor. 2:4; Rom. 15:19; 1 Thess. 1:5).

It seems more accurate, therefore, to say that although the Holy Spirit *does* glorify Jesus, He also frequently calls attention to His work and gives recognizable evidences that make His presence known. Indeed, it seems that one of His primary purposes in the New Covenant Age is to *manifest* the presence of God, to give indications that make the presence of God known. And when the Holy Spirit works in various ways that can be perceived by believers and unbelievers, this encourages people's faith that God is near and that He is working to fulfill His purposes in the Church and to bring blessing to His people.

23. How do we know that spiritual gifts today aren't just demonic counterfeits designed to lead people astray?

Certainly false miracles are mentioned in the Bible—but when we examine them we find they are never worked by genuine believers. Pharaoh's magicians were able to work some false miracles (Exod. 7:11,22; 8:7), even though they soon had to admit that God's power was greater (Exod. 8:19). Simon the sorcerer in the city of Samaria amazed people with his magic (Acts 8:9-11), even though the miracles done through Philip were much greater (Acts 8:13). In Philippi, Paul encountered a slave girl "who had a spirit of divination and brought her owners much gain by soothsaying" (Acts 16:16), but Paul rebuked the spirit and it came out of her (Acts 16:18).

We find further evidence in the Epistles. Paul says that when the man of sin comes it "will be with all power and with pretended signs and wonders, and with all wicked deception for those who are to perish" (2 Thess. 2:9,10), but those who follow them and are deceived do so "because they refused to love the truth and so be saved" (2 Thess. 2:10). This indicates that those who work false miracles in the end times by the power of Satan will not speak the truth but will preach a false gospel.

Finally, Revelation 13 indicates that a second beast will rise "out of the earth," one that has "all the authority of the first beast" and "works great signs, even making fire come down from heaven to earth in the sight of men; and by the signs which it is allowed to work in the presence of the beast, it deceives those who dwell on the earth" (Rev. 13:11-14). But once again a false gospel accompanies these miracles. This power is exercised in connection with the first beast who utters "haughty and blasphemous words,...it opened its mouth to utter blasphemies against God, blaspheming his name and his dwelling" (Rev. 13:5,6).

Two conclusions become clear from this brief survey of false miracles in Scripture. (1) The power of God is greater than the power of Satan to work miraculous signs, and God's people triumph in confrontations of power with those who work evil. In connection with this, John assures believers that "he who is in you is greater than he who is in the world" (1 John 4:4).[53] (2) The identity of these workers of false miracles is always known through their denial of the gospel.

There is no indication anywhere in Scripture that genuine Christians with the

Holy Spirit in them will work false miracles. In fact, in Corinth, a city filled with idolatry and demon worship (see 1 Cor. 10:20), Paul could say to the Corinthian believers, many of whom had come out of that kind of pagan background, "no one can say 'Jesus is Lord' except by the Holy Spirit" (1 Cor. 12:3). Here he gives them reassurance that those who make a genuine profession of faith in Jesus as Lord *do* in fact have the Holy Spirit in them. It is significant that he immediately proceeds to a discussion of spiritual gifts possessed by *"each"* true believer (1 Cor. 12:7). And he could do this in a culture where the danger of demonic counterfeit was just as real as it is for us today.

This should reassure us that if we see miracles being worked by those who make a genuine profession of faith (1 Cor. 12:3), who believe in the incarnation and deity of Christ (1 John 4:2), and who show the fruit of the Holy Spirit in their lives and bear fruit in their ministry (Matt. 7:20; cf. John 15:5; Gal. 5:22,23), we should not be suspicious that they are false miracles. Instead, we should be thankful to God that the Holy Spirit is working, even in those who may not hold exactly the same convictions we do on every point of doctrine.[54] Indeed, if God waited to work miracles only through those who were perfect in both doctrine and conduct of life, certainly no miracles would be worked until Christ's return.

24. *Doesn't John's Gospel show us that miracles lead to inferior faith and to the rejection of the gospel?*

This objection is argued quite clearly by D. A. Carson, based on his understanding of several verses in John.[55] I can respond to his argument with the following questions.

A. *Did Jesus rebuke the official at Capernaum for seeking his son's healing?* In John 4:48, where Jesus says, "Unless you see signs and wonders you will not believe,"[56] Carson calls this a "firm reproach"[57] (his commentary calls it a "sweeping rebuke").[58]

But there is certainly room to doubt whether this is any kind of reproach at all—there is no explicit indication of reproach in the context. John 4:53 shows that this "sign" (miracle) led to faith for the official: "He himself believed, and all his household." John continues his theme of emphasizing the value of miracles (which he calls "signs") in the next sentence. "This was now the second *sign* that Jesus did when he had come from Judea to Galilee" (John 4:54).[59]

B. *Did Jesus' miracles lead to inferior faith?* In John 10:37,38, Jesus says, "If I am not doing the works of my Father, then do not believe me; but if I do them, even though you do not believe me, believe the works, that you may know and understand that the Father is in me and I am in the Father."[60] Carson says of this passage that Jesus sees faith that is based on miracles "as of inferior quality, but certainly better than unbelief."[61]

But this is a misleading way to express it. Jesus does not see this "faith" as saving faith at all, for it is the kind of belief possessed by those who will not believe in Him ("even though *you do not believe me*"; Greek *kan emoi mē pisteuē te*). Rather, He is asking that they at least have some *intellectual acknowledgment* that God is working through Jesus: "That you may know and understand that the Father is in me and I am in the Father" (John 10:38). This *knowledge that* a fact is true is certainly not saving faith. Therefore, Carson's conclusion here that genuine faith occasioned by miracles is of inferior quality is not a correct one— this text does not talk about saving faith at all.

C. *Did Jesus' miracles lead to spurious faith?* Carson says, "Not all faith triggered by Jesus' signs proves valid: some of it is spurious ([Jn.] 2:23-25; cf. 8:30-31)."[62]

But the verses Carson cites do not prove that the faith of some people who believed was "spurious." John 2:23 simply says "Many *believed in his name* when they saw the signs which he did"—the verse says nothing about "spurious" faith.[63] Similarly, John 8:30 says, "As he spoke thus, *many believed in him*." It says nothing about signs and wonders in this passage, nor does it say anything about people having spurious faith as a result of signs and wonders. I fail to understand how Carson can use these two passages—neither of which says anyone had spurious faith, and both of which report many believed in Christ—to say some people have spurious faith triggered by signs and wonders. The passages do not prove that.

D. *Did raising Lazarus lead to rejection and anger?* In John 11, 12, regarding raising Lazarus from the dead, Carson notes that some religious leaders became angry as a result of this miracle. "The religious leaders are convinced that Jesus is actually performing miracles whose reality they cannot deny, but that does not foster faith: rather it fuels their rejection and anger."[64]

At this point I agree with Carson, that the miracles performed by Jesus led to rejection and anger in the religious leaders. However, I differ with any suggestion that John is warning us against miracles in the story of Lazarus. It is true that the religious leaders became more hostile, but that simply makes their *unbelief* more culpable. In the very context of John 11, John is showing that because of Jesus' miracles many people "believed in him" (John 11:45; cf. 12:10,11). The miracles *should have* led to faith for the Pharisees as well, but instead they became more hostile in their hardness of heart. John does not use this fact to show the harmful effect of miracles, but rather the amazingly hard hearts of the Pharisees.

The contemporary application should be clear. Miracles will always engender faith in some and hostile opposition in others—especially religious leaders who are jealous because of their loss of power and influence when genuine miracles are occurring and people are coming to faith outside of their influence.

E. *Did Jesus give a negative evaluation to Thomas's faith because Thomas saw Jesus after His resurrection?* Finally, Carson mentions the time when Thomas saw Jesus after His resurrection and then believed in Him. Carson's conclusion is that "the same relatively negative evaluation is given" to the value of seeing the miracle of the Resurrection, showing the superiority of faith that does not rest on miracles. Carson says, "Better than the kind of faith that insists on seeing Jesus' signs first hand is the faith that rests on the reports of the unique signs of Jesus (20:29-31)."[65]

But I do not think he has reasoned correctly from the redemptive-historical context of the verse. The contrast in the passage is not between seeing miracles and not seeing miracles. Rather, the contrast is between seeing Jesus in the flesh and not seeing Jesus in the flesh. Jesus does not say, "Have you believed because you have seen *a miracle?* Blessed are those who have not seen a miracle and yet believed." Rather, Jesus says, "Have you believed because you have seen *me?* Blessed are those who have not seen and yet believe" (John 20:29). There is a redemptive-historical reason for this: Jesus is ascending to heaven, and will no longer be on earth to be seen. The passage does not at all imply that *miracles* will cease, but that *Jesus will be absent.*

Any other conclusion than this not only is contrary to the words in the verse itself, but also to the larger context of the lives of the apostles in the Early Church. If those who saw Jesus with their own eyes had inferior faith, then the apostles and all other eyewitnesses of the Resurrection would have inferior faith! Surely this is incorrect. Moreover, it would mean all those who believed as a result of the signs and wonders done frequently by the apostles, and especially by Paul throughout his ministry, would have inferior faith—almost the entire first-century Church would have inferior faith! That is hardly the point of any passage in Acts, nor is there any hint of that kind of reasoning in either the Gospels or Acts.

When Carson speaks of "the same relatively negative evaluation"[66] given to the role of miracles in encouraging faith, his conclusion is inconsistent with the fact that it is *God Himself* who does these miracles. "While God *also bore witness* by signs and wonders and various miracles and by gifts of the Holy Spirit distributed according to his own will" (Heb. 2:4). Should it not give us pause to place a "negative evaluation" on what God Himself does to bear witness to the truth of His Word?

F. *Important verses in John not mentioned by Carson.* Finally, several more positive verses about miracles in John are not mentioned by Carson. At the bottom of page 100 (*Power Religion*) Carson has one brief sentence indicating that "Jesus' signs display His glory, at least to His disciples (John 2:11)"; and in the middle of page 101 he has a concessive sentence in which he admits that "some do believe because they see Jesus' works (e.g., 11:45)."[67] But these two sentences are tossed off in passing, while his overall picture is that John views signs in a negative way.

Why does Carson entirely omit consideration of many other passages that view signs very positively in John's Gospel? This theme runs through the whole Gospel, beginning at John 2:11 when Jesus has changed the water to wine. "This, the first of his *signs,* Jesus did at Cana in Galilee, *and manifested his glory;* and his disciples *believed* in him." This theme continues to the end of the Gospel where John says, "Jesus did *many other signs in the presence of the disciples*" (John 20:30), which he did not record, but he did record these in order that people might *believe.* "But *these are written* that you may *believe* that Jesus is the Christ, the Son of God, and that *believing* you may have life in his name" (John 20:31). From beginning to end, this Gospel shows people coming to faith because of the signs they see Jesus do.

Carson fails to mention the verses in which John shows time and again how the miraculous *signs* Jesus did brought about faith in those who saw these signs. For example, "When he was in Jerusalem at the Passover feast, *many believed in his name when they saw the signs which he did*" (John 2:23, a verse Carson surprisingly uses to speak of spurious faith). In the next chapter, Nicodemus comes and says, "We know that you are a teacher come from God; for no one can do these *signs* that you do, unless God is with him" (John 3:2). The reader could hardly miss the point John is trying to make: John wants his readers to draw the same conclusions from these signs that Nicodemus has drawn.

When Jesus healed the official's son, "He himself believed, and all his household. This was now the second *sign* that Jesus did" (John 4:53,54).

Later, John says, "a multitude followed him, because they saw the *signs* which he did on those who were diseased" (John 6:2). John's point is certainly that he wants his readers likewise to follow Jesus. Similarly, "When the people saw the *sign* which he had done, they said, 'This is indeed the prophet who is to come into the world!'" (John 6:14). John wants his readers to draw the same conclusion.

Similarly, at the feast of Tabernacles, "Many of the people believed in him; they said, 'When the Christ appears, will he do more *signs* than this man has done?'" (John 7:31). John even reports a division among the Pharisees, when some of them begin to say, "How can a man who is a sinner do such *signs?*" (John 9:16).

The Pharisees are troubled, because they are forced to admit, "This man performs many *signs*" (John 11:47), and they realize that if He continues to do miracles in this way, soon everyone will follow Jesus. "If we let him go on thus, every one will believe in him" (John 11:48). Once again, John is showing the extremely positive role that Jesus' miracles (or signs) had in engendering faith in those who saw Him.

When Jesus raised Lazarus, many came to faith. "On account of him many of the Jews were going away and believing in Jesus," (John 12:11). At the triumphal entry into Jerusalem, "The reason why the crowd went to meet him was that they heard he had done this *sign*" (John 12:18), but the Pharisees were dismayed, saying to one another, "You see that you can do nothing; look, the world has gone after him" (John 12:19).

It would be hard for John to be any more explicit in showing that the amazing signs Jesus did brought great multitudes of people to follow Him and believe in Him. Nonetheless, John continues to remind us that the Pharisees remain hostile in their unbelief, and are all the more culpable for that unbelief because they had seen these very miracles. "Though he had done so many *signs* before them, yet they did not believe in him" (John 12:37).

Finally, after the entire Gospel has shown how Jesus' miracles brought about faith in Him, John tells us that he recorded these "signs" for a specific purpose. "That you may believe that Jesus is the Christ, the Son of God, and that believing you may have life in his name" (John 20:31). The overwhelming evaluation of the role of signs regarding faith in John's Gospel is a positive one, not a negative one, and I am surprised that Carson's evaluation does not represent it that way, but ignores so much of the data that is there.

25. Isn't it wrong to place emphasis on present miracles? In the Bible, when "signs" and "wonders" are mentioned, it is usually in the context of calling people to look back to God's great works in the past, such as the Exodus or the resurrection of Christ. We should call people to remember those past great "signs," not to trust God for present "signs and wonders" today.

This objection has been stated well by D. A. Carson and James Montgomery Boice, following an argument by John Woodhouse, an Australian scholar. Carson places such emphasis on believing past miracles that he calls into question the value of present miracles to encourage faith. He says one of the major purposes of signs and wonders in Scripture is "to call the people of God back to those foundation events, to encourage them to remember God's saving acts in history."[68] Regarding Old Testament signs and wonders, he says, "Unbelief in Israel is nothing other than the reprehensible forgetting of all the wonders God performed at the Exodus." And in the Gospel of John, "John's readers are called to reflect on the signs that he reports...especially Jesus' resurrection, and thereby believe. The mandate to believe here rests on John's reports of God's past, redemptive-historical signs, not on testimonies of present on-going ones."[69]

Boice argues in a similar way, quoting with approval the following statement of John Woodhouse:

Faith involves remembering the signs and wonders by which God redeemed His people...unbelief is precisely a failure to remember those wonders...a consequence of this is the fact that *a desire for further signs and wonders is sinful and unbelieving.*[70]

But if it is sinful and unbelieving to have "a desire for further signs and wonders" after the death and resurrection of Christ, then it is hard to explain the activity of the Early Church. (1) The Christians in Jerusalem prayed that God would give them the ability to speak the Word with all boldness and that while they spoke, God would stretch out His hand "to heal," and that "signs and wonders" would be performed "through the name of your holy servant Jesus" (Acts 4:30). They certainly demonstrated an eager desire for further signs and wonders. Was their desire for "further signs and wonders" after the Resurrection "sinful and unbelieving"? (2) Similarly, the ministry of Peter and Paul in the New Testament was characterized by miraculous deeds. Shall we say that Peter and Paul were "sinful and unbelieving" in their prayers for further miracles after the Resurrection? (3) In addition, people in the church of Corinth and in other churches who had gifts of miracles and healing and prophecy (Rom. 12:6; 1 Cor. 12:7-11,28-30; 14:1-40; Gal. 3:5; 1 Thess. 5:20; Heb. 2:4) certainly were right to *desire* (zēloō "desire, exert oneself earnestly [for]," 1 Cor. 12:31; 14:1) that those gifts be operative in the life of the Church.

Boice and Woodhouse have adopted an incorrect line of reasoning. Because we are to remember God's great redemptive deeds in the past should not *discourage* us from praying for miraculous events to occur today, but rather should *encourage* us to pray that God would still work in miraculous ways today.

This is exactly the point of James 5:16-18: "Elijah was a man of like nature with ourselves" and then *encourages us* to pray with the *same kind of faith that Elijah had*, reminding us that "the prayer of a righteous man has great power in its effects." This is specifically set in a context of prayer for healing (Jas. 5:14-16).

In Carson's argument, he has only told half the story. He says belief based on reports of signs and wonders that God did in the past (such as the Exodus and the Resurrection) is to be a belief that God did signs and wonders in the past. But this is just a tautology: Belief that God has acted in the past is belief that God has acted in the past. What Carson fails to note in this section is what happens in the New Testament Church. The apostles not only say that Jesus in His earthly ministry was "attested to you by God with mighty works and wonders and signs which God did through him in your midst" (Acts 2:22), but they *also* perform *present signs and wonders* when proclaiming the gospel. Scriptural faith surely is not to be restricted to a belief that God has acted in the past. It must also include a belief that God will act in the present in our lives.

So I fail to see the force of Carson's argument, if it is intended to discourage the use of signs and wonders today. He is just saying that biblical reports of the past are to be believed as reports of the past. But any implication that we should discourage *present* signs and wonders is setting up a false alternative. When Carson says that in John, "The mandate to believe here rests on John's reports of God's past, redemptive-historical signs, not on testimonies of present on-going ones,"[71] this is because John is writing *a Gospel*—a story of what happened in Jesus' life. Of course, he does not present any people who come to faith *after* Jesus returned to heaven, because John's Gospel ends at that point. To find people who come to believe because of miracles that occur *after* the life of Jesus, we should not search the Gospel of John. For that we need to look to Acts and the Epistles—and they do show *present, ongoing miracles* in connection with the proclamation of the gospel.

26. Weren't miracles in the Bible always successful, instantaneous, and irreversible? If Jesus were here today, He would be emptying hospitals by healing everyone in them. The miracles claimed today are nothing like the miracles in the Bible.

This objection has recently been expressed well by Norman Geisler.[72] Geisler first formulates a much more restrictive definition of "miracle" than is usually found in discussions of miracles,[73] and then he uses that definition to argue against the possibility of contemporary miracles. Geisler says, "miracles (1) are always successful, (2) are immediate, (3) have no relapses, and (4) give confirmation of God's messenger" (pp. 28-30, *Signs and Wonders*). He finds support for this thesis largely in the ministry of Jesus, but when he passes beyond the life of Jesus and attempts to show that others who had the power to work miracles were never unsuccessful, his thesis is much less convincing. Regarding the demon-possessed boy, whom the disciples could not set free from the demon (Matt. 17:14-21), Geisler says, "the disciples simply forgot for the moment to faithfully exercise the power that Jesus had already given them."[74]

But this is an unpersuasive argument. Geisler says that the power to work miracles was always successful, and when the Bible talks about some who were not successful (and who contradict his thesis) he simply says they "forgot." Jesus, however, gives a different reason than Geisler does. "Because of your little faith" (Matt. 17:20). Lesser faith resulted in lesser power to work miracles.

Regarding Paul's failure to heal Epaphroditus (Phil. 2:27), Geisler is forced to make the dubious claim that perhaps Paul never attempted to heal Epaphroditus (though he had come to him in prison and was so ill he almost died), or that "Paul no longer possessed the gift of healing at this time" (p. 150). He employs the same claim to explain the fact that Paul left Trophimus ill at Miletus (2 Tim. 4:20). In these instances, Geisler goes well beyond the usual cessationist claim that miracles ended with the death of the apostles—he is claiming that miracles ceased in the life of the greatest apostle before his first Roman imprisonment. That is simply an unconvincing argument with respect to the apostle whose ministry was repeatedly characterized "by the power of signs and wonders, by the power of the Holy Spirit" (Rom. 15:19), and who could say with triumph in his last epistle, "I have fought the good fight, I have finished the race, *I have kept the faith*" (2 Tim. 4:7).

Geisler's description of miracles does not fit the case of the blind man of Bethsaida upon whom Jesus laid His hands. At first, the man did not see clearly but said he saw men who "look like trees, walking." After Jesus laid His hands on him a second time, the man "saw everything clearly" (Mark 8:24,25). Geisler responds that it was Jesus' intention to heal in two stages, in order to teach the disciples by using an object lesson about the gradual growth of their spiritual lives (pp. 153-154). Though the text says nothing to this effect, it may have been true. Even so, it disproves Geisler's thesis, for if it was Jesus' intention to heal in two stages then, it may also be His intention to heal people in two stages today—or in three or four or more stages. Once Geisler admits that it may be God's intention to work a miracle in stages, in order to accomplish His own purposes, then Geisler's entire claim that miracles must be immediate and complete is lost.[75]

Instead of accepting Geisler's definition, it seems better to conclude that even those whom God gifts with the ability to perform miracles from time to time may not be able to perform them whenever they wish, for the Holy Spirit continually is distributing them to each person "as he wills" (1 Cor. 12:11; the word "distributes" is a present participle in Greek, indicating a continuing activity of the Holy Spirit).

Moreover, there seems no reason to exclude (as Geisler apparently wants to do) unusual or remarkable answers to prayer from the category of "miracle," thus making the definition extremely restrictive. If God answers persistent prayer, for instance, for a physical healing for which there is no known medical explanation, and does so only after several months or years of prayer, yet does so in such a way that it seems quite clearly to be in response to prayer so that people are amazed and glorify God, there seems no reason to deny that a miracle has occurred simply because the earlier prayers were not answered immediately. Finally, Geisler fails to recognize that several New Testament texts indicate that spiritual gifts, whether miraculous or nonmiraculous in nature, may vary in strength or degree of intensity.

Paul says that if we have the gift of prophecy, we should use it *"in proportion to our faith"* (Rom. 12:6), indicating that the gift can be more or less strongly developed in different people, or in the same person over a period of time. This is why Paul can remind Timothy, "Do not neglect the gift you have" (1 Tim. 4:14), and can say, "I remind you to *rekindle* the gift of God that is within you" (2 Tim. 1:6).

It was possible for Timothy to allow his gift to weaken, apparently through infrequent use, and Paul reminds him to stir it up by using it and thereby strengthening it. This should not be surprising, for we realize it to be true in regard to a wide variety of gifts that increase in strength and effectiveness as they are used, whether evangelism, teaching, encouraging, administration, or faith. Apollos had a strong gift of preaching and teaching, for we read that he was "mighty (or "powerful," Greek *dunatos*) in the Scriptures" (Acts 18:24, NASB). And Paul apparently had a frequently used and effective gift of speaking in tongues because he says, "I thank God that I speak in tongues more than you all" (1 Cor. 14:18).[76]

All of these texts indicate that *spiritual gifts may vary in strength.* If we think of any gift, whether teaching or evangelism on the one hand, or prophecy or healing on the other, we should realize that within any congregation there will likely be people who are strong in the use of that gift, perhaps through long use and experience. As well, there will be others who are moderately strong in that gift, and others who probably have the gift but are just beginning to use it or have simply been given less effectiveness in its use through the sovereign distribution of the Holy Spirit.

27. Isn't it really impossible to define a miracle anyway? And if we can't define a miracle, how can we know what one is—and why do we spend so much time talking about something we can't even explain precisely?

I admit that philosophers have argued for a long time about what a miracle is. But many of them have started off on the wrong path because they assumed God was distant and not usually involved in the world. They assumed the world just operated "automatically" apart from God, by some rules they called "natural laws."

If we start instead with the idea that Christ "continually carries along all things by his word of power" (Heb. 1:3, my translation),[77] that in Christ "all things hold together" (Col. 1:17), and that God "accomplishes all things according to the counsel of his will" (Eph. 1:11), then we will have a much more accurate picture of God's *continual* involvement in everything that happens in the world. Then a definition more consistent with biblical patterns would be the following:

> A miracle is a less common kind of God's activity in which He arouses people's awe and wonder and bears witness to Himself.

This definition is based on an understanding of God's providence whereby God is continually involved in preserving, controlling, and governing all things.[78] If we understand providence in this way, we will naturally avoid some other common explanations or definitions of miracles.

For example, one definition of miracle is "a direct intervention of God in the world." But this definition assumes a deistic view of God's relationship to the world, in which the world continues on its own and God only intervenes in it occasionally. This is certainly not the biblical view, according to which God makes the rain to fall (Matt. 5:45), causes the grass to grow (Ps. 104:14) and continually carries along all things by His word of power (Heb. 1:3).

Another definition of miracle is "a more direct activity of God in the world." But to talk about a "more direct" working of God suggests that His ordinary providential activity is somehow not "direct," and again hints at a sort of deistic removal of God from the world.

Another definition of miracle is "God working in the world without using means to bring about the results He wishes." Yet to speak of God working "without means" leaves us with very few if any miracles in the Bible, for it is hard to think of a miracle that came about with no means at all. In the healing of people, for example, some of the physical properties of the sick person's body were doubtless involved as part of the healing. When Jesus multiplied the loaves and fishes, He used the original five loaves and two fishes that were there. When He changed water to wine, He used water and made it become wine. This definition seems to be inadequate.

Yet another definition of miracle is "an exception to a natural law" or "God acting contrary to the laws of nature." But the phrase "laws of nature" in popular understanding implies that certain qualities are inherent in the things that exist, "laws of nature" that operate independently of God. Further, "laws of nature" implies that God must intervene or "break" these laws in order for a miracle to occur. Once again, this definition does not adequately account for the biblical teaching on providence.

Another definition of miracle is "an event impossible to explain by natural causes." This definition is inadequate because: (1) it does not include God as the one who brings about the miracle; (2) it assumes God does not *use* some natural causes when He works in an unusual or amazing way, and thus it assumes again that God only occasionally intervenes in the world; and (3) it will result in a significant minimizing of actual miracles, and an increase in skepticism. This is so because when God works in answer to prayer, the result is often amazing to those who prayed, but it is not absolutely *impossible* to explain by natural causes, especially for a skeptic who simply refuses to see God's hand at work.

Therefore, the original definition given above, where a miracle is simply a *less common* way of God's working in the world, seems to be preferable and more consistent with the biblical doctrine of God's providence. This definition does not say a miracle is a *different kind* of working by God, but only that it is a less common way of God's working, and it is done to arouse people's surprise, awe or amazement in such a way that God bears witness to Himself.[19]

Now, if we accept the definition that a miracle is "a less common kind of God's activity in which He arouses people's awe and wonder and bears witness to Himself," then we may ask what kinds of things should be considered miracles. Of course, we are right to consider the incarnation of Jesus as God-man, and Jesus' resurrection from the dead, as the central and most important miracles in all history. The events of the Exodus, such as the parting of the Red Sea and the fall of Jericho were remarkable miracles. When Jesus healed people, cleansed lepers, and cast out demons, those were certainly miracles as well (see Matt. 11:4,5; Luke 4:36-41; John 2:23; 4:54; 6:2; 20:30,31).

But can we consider unusual answers to prayer to be miracles? Apparently so, if they are remarkable enough to arouse people's awe and wonder and cause them to acknowledge God's power at work: The answer to Elijah's prayer that God would send fire from heaven was a miracle (1 Kings 18:24,36-38), as were the answers to his prayers that the widow's dead son would come back to life (1 Kings 17:21) or that the rain would stop and later start again (1 Kings 17:1; 18:42-45 with Jas. 5:17,18).

In the New Testament, the release of Peter from prison in answer to the prayers of the Church was certainly a miracle (Acts 12:5-17; note also Paul's prayer for Publius's father in Acts 28:8). But there must have been many miracles not nearly as dramatic as those, because Jesus healed many hundreds of people, "*any that were sick with various diseases*" (Luke 4:40). Paul healed "*the rest of the people on the island who had diseases*" (Acts 28:9).

On the other hand, Christians see answers to prayer every day, and we should not water down our definition of miracle so much that every answer to prayer is called a miracle. But when an answer to prayer is so remarkable that people involved in it are amazed and acknowledge God's power at work in an unusual way, then it seems appropriate to call it a miracle.[80] This is consistent with our definition, and seems supported by the biblical evidence that works of God that aroused people's awe and wonder were called miracles (Greek *dunamis*).[81]

But whether we adopt a broad or narrow definition of miracle, all should agree that if God really does work in answer to our prayers, whether in common or uncommon ways, it is important that we recognize this and give thanks to Him. As well, we should not ignore the answered prayer or go to great lengths to devise possible "natural causes" to explain away what God has in fact done. Although we must be careful not to exaggerate in reporting details of answers to prayer, we must also avoid the opposite error of failing to glorify and thank God for what He has done.

28. Isn't it dangerous for churches to allow for miraculous spiritual gifts today?

To say that the use of many spiritual gifts today is "dangerous" is not an adequate criticism, because some things that are *right* are dangerous, at least in some sense. Missionary work is dangerous. Driving a car is dangerous. If we define "dangerous" to mean "something might go wrong," then we can criticize *anything* that anybody might do as "dangerous," and it just becomes an all-purpose criticism when we have no specific abuse to point to.

A better approach regarding the use of miracles and spiritual gifts is to ask, Is it in accordance with Scripture? and Have adequate steps been taken to guard against the dangers of abuse? I think that many responsible charismatic leaders have taken considerable care, using extensive teaching and writing, to guard against abuse and avoid the mistakes of previous generations; both the mistakes involved in abusing the gifts, and the mistake of forbidding some gifts altogether.[82]

Notes

1. See John Wimber, *Power Evangelism* (San Francisco, CA: HarperSanFrancisco, 1986); *Power Healing* (San Francisco, CA: HarperSanFrancisco, 1987); *Power Points* (San Francisco, CA: HarperSanFrancisco, 1991); C. Peter Wagner, *The Third Wave of the Holy Spirit* (Ann Arbor, MI: Servant, 1988); John White, *When the Spirit Comes with Power* (Downers Grove, IL: InterVarsity, 1988).
2. All Scripture quotations in this chapter are taken from the RSV unless otherwise noted.
3. This objection is made by D. A. Carson, "The Purpose of Signs and Wonders in the New Testament," in *Power Religion: The Selling Out of the Evangelical Church?*, edited by Michael Scott Horton (Chicago, IL: Moody, 1992), pp. 89-118; see esp. p. 97.
4. Acts 3:6, 12ff.; 5:12-16,20,21,28,42; 9:34,35; 10:44-46.
5. Acts 14:3,8-10,15ff.; 15:12,36; 16:13,14,16-18; 18:5,11 (cf. 2 Cor. 12:12; 1 Cor. 2:4,5); 19:8-12; Rom. 15:18,19; 1 Cor. 1:6,7; 2:4,5; 2 Cor. 12:12; 1 Thess. 1:5.
6. Matt. 4:23; 9:35,36; (cf. 10:1,7,8); 11:5; 12:15,18; 15:30; 19:2 (cf. Mark 10:1); 21:14 (cf. Luke 21:37); Mark 1: 38,39; 2:2,11; 3:14,15; 6:12,13; 10:1 (cf. Matt. 19:2); Luke 4:18; 5:17,24; 6:6-11,17,18; 7:22; (cf. 9:1,2; 10:9,13); 13:10-13,22,32; 14:4,7ff.; 21:37 (cf. Matt. 21:14); 16:15-18,20; John 3:2; 7:14,15,21-23,31,38; 10:25,32,38; 12:37,49; 14:10.
7. James Montgomery Boice, "A Better Way: The Power of the Word and Spirit," in Horton, ed., *Power Religion*, pp. 127-128.
8. In neither case should these events be thought of as some kind of "magic" that came automatically through Peter's shadow or handkerchiefs Paul had touched. But rather as an indication that the Holy Spirit was pleased to give such a full and remarkable empowering to the ministry of these men that on occasion He extended His work beyond their individual bodily presence even to things they came near or touched.
9. The manuscript evidence and considerations of style suggest that these verses were not originally part of the Gospel that Mark wrote.
10. It is included in several manuscripts of Tatian's *Diatessaron* (A.D. 170), and is quoted by Irenaeus (died A.D. 202) and Tertullian (died A.D. 220).
11. Though it is not found in many of the earliest and best Greek manuscripts, the longer ending of Mark 16:9-20 is nevertheless found in a majority of the extant Greek manuscripts of the New Testament (K. Aland and B. Aland,

The Text of the New Testament. An Introduction to the Critical Editions [Grand Rapids, MI and Leiden, Netherlands: Eerdmans and E. J. Brill, 1989], p. 292-293; W. L. Lane, Commentary on the Gospel of Mark, NICNT [Grand Rapids, MI: Eerdmans, 1974], pp. 603-604).

12. I am grateful to Professor Harold Hoehner of Dallas Theological Seminary for suggesting to me the arguments given here regarding 1 Corinthians 12:28 and Mark 16:17,18 (though he may disagree with my conclusion in this section).

13. See Walter J. Chantry, Signs of the Apostles: Observations on Pentecostalism Old and New (Edinburgh, Scotland: Banner of Truth, 1976), pp. 19-21.

14. See question 7, below, on the phrase "signs of an apostle" in 2 Corinthians 12:12.

15. The word "true" is not actually in the Greek text, which simply says, "the signs of an apostle." The RSV (which is quoted here) and NASB have added "true" to give the sense: Paul is contrasting his ministry with that of the false apostles.

16. See Chantry, Signs of the Apostles, especially pages 17-21; B. B. Warfield, Counterfeit Miracles (London, England: Banner of Truth, 1972; first published 1918); Norman Geisler, Signs and Wonders (Wheaton, IL: Tyndale House, 1988).

17. Colin Kruse, The Second Epistle of Paul to the Corinthians, TNTC (Leicester, England: InterVarsity Press, and Grand Rapids, MI: Eerdmans, 1987), p. 209; Jean Héring, The Second Epistle of Saint Paul to the Corinthians, trans. by A. W. Heathcote and P. J. Allcock (London, England: Epworth, 1967), pp. 95-96; and Murray Harris, "2 Corinthians," EBC, vol. 10, p. 398. Harris notes an alternative view where the "signs" are the changed lives of the Corinthians and the Christlike character of Paul.

18. The most extensive discussion in support of this view is found in Ralph P. Martin, II Corinthians, WBC (Dallas, TX: WORD, 1986), pp. 434-438; see also Philip E. Hughes, Paul's Second Epistle to the Corinthians, NIC (Grand Rapids, MI: Eerdmans, 1962), pp. 456-458 (following Chrysostom and Calvin); Alfred Plummer, A Critical and Exegetical Commentary on the Second Epistle of St. Paul to the Corinthians, ICC (Edinburgh, Scotland: T. & T. Clark, 1915), p. 359; R. V. G. Tasker, 2 Corinthians, TNTC (London, England: Tyndale Press, 1958), p. 180; Charles Hodge, An Exposition of 1 and 2 Corinthians (Wilmington, DE: Sovereign Grace, 1972 [reprint]), pp. 359-360; John Calvin, The Second Epistle of Paul the Apostle to the Corinthians, trans. by T. A. Smail, edited by D. W. Torrance and T. F. Torrance (Edinburgh, Scotland: Oliver and Boyd, and Grand Rapids, MI: Eerdmans, 1964), pp. 163-164; see also J. B. Lightfoot, The Epistle of St. Paul to the Galatians (Grand Rapids, MI: Zondervan, 1957), p. 99.

19. The grammar of the Greek text forces us to this distinction, since "the signs of an apostle" is in the nominative case, while "signs and wonders and mighty works" is in the dative, and cannot therefore be simply a restatement of "signs of an apostle" in apposition to it: Nouns in apposition in Greek must be in the same case. (The NIV ignores the grammar here and translates the two phrases as if they were in apposition; the RSV and NASB are more precise.)

20. Some interpreters assume that the false apostles were working miracles and

claiming revelations from God, so that Paul would have to claim greater miracles and revelations. But this is an assumption unsupported by evidence in the
text. Nothing in 2 Corinthians says that the false apostles claimed miracles or
revelations.

21. It is as if today a former pastor wrote to a church that had been taken over by
an unbelieving pastor. He might say, "The signs of a true pastor were done
among you." In such a case, he would point to his own character and conduct—not because these distinguished him from other Christians in the congregation, but because they distinguished him from the self-seeking manner of
an impostor.

22. The following verse also confirms this interpretation: Paul says, "For in what
were you less favored than the rest of the churches?" (2 Cor. 12:13). Here
Paul refers to his personal care for them. The fact that they were not lacking in
any of Paul's care and attention would prove to them that the "signs of a true
apostle" were performed among them only if these "signs" included *all* of Paul's
ministry to them. But Paul's care for them would not prove his point if the
"signs of an apostle" were just miracles.

23. The KJV translates verse 4, "God also bearing *them* witness, both with signs and
wonders." This translation suggests that the miracles bore witness to the *people*
who heard Jesus and first preached. But the word "them" is represented by no
word in the Greek text, and this translation is not followed by modern versions.

24. See Walter Chantry, *Signs of the Apostles*, pp. 18-19: "New Testament miracles
are viewed in Scripture itself as God's stamp of approval upon the message of
the apostles, which was an inspired record of the things they had seen and
heard while with Jesus. Recalling these wonders should deepen our respect for
the authority of their words and prompt us to give the more careful heed."

25. It might be objected at this point that speaking in tongues is not speech
empowered by the Holy Spirit, but is speech that comes from the speaker's
own human spirit. But Paul clearly views all these spiritual gifts as generally
empowered by the Holy Spirit, even the ones in which human personality comes
fully into play. This would be true of teachers, helpers and administrators, as
well as those who speak with tongues. In each of these cases the active agent in
performing the activity is the Christian who has the particular gift and uses
it, but all these are nonetheless empowered by the Holy Spirit in their functioning, and that would also be true of the gift of tongues.

26. Also relevant at this point is John's reassurance to his readers, in the context of
demonic spirits that had gone out into the world: "He who is in you is greater
than he who is in the world" (1 John 4:4).

27. See, for example, C. Fred Dickason, *Demon Possession and the Christian*
(Westchester, IL: Crossway, 1987), pp. 126-127; 188-191; 193-197.

28. Dickason, *Demon Possession*, p. 127.

29. We should remember that Dickason has a cessationist view with respect to
speaking in tongues today (see p. 189: "I told her I doubted that there were any
genuine tongues from God today in the New Testament sense"). Therefore,
from his perspective, he is not making Scripture subject to experience, but sees
these experiences as confirming his understanding of Scripture.

30. See this interpretation in O. Palmer Robertson, "Tongues: Sign of Covenantal Curse and Blessing," *Westminster Theological Journal* 38 (1975-1976), 43-53.
31. I have discussed this passage in more detail in Wayne Grudem, "1 Corinthians 14:20-25: Prophecy and Tongues as Signs of God's Attitude," *Westminster Theological Journal* 41:2 (Spring 1979): 381-396; see also Wayne Grudem, *The Gift of Prophecy in the New Testament and Today* (Eastbourne, England: Kingsway, and Westchester, IL: Crossway, 1988), pp. 171-182.
32. This paragraph and the next five paragraphs are taken from Grudem, *Gift of Prophecy*, pp. 177-179.
33. O. Palmer Robertson, "Tongues: Sign of Covenantal Curse and Blessing," *WTJ* 38 (1975-1976), pp. 43-53.
34. Zane Hodges, "The Purpose of Tongues," *Bib Sac* 120 (1963), pp. 226-233.
35. Robertson is followed at this point by Richard B. Gaffin, *Perspectives on Pentecost* (Presbyterian and Reformed 1979), pp. 106-109.
    John F. MacArthur, Jr., *The Charismatics: A Doctrinal Perspective* (Grand Rapids, MI: Zondervan 1978), sees tongues both as a judicial sign of judgment to Israel and as a sign of the transition to a period of gospel proclamation to all nations. But a fundamental flaw in this argument is that here MacArthur also overlooks the fact that in 1 Corinthians 14:20-25 Paul is talking about an *abuse* of tongues (speaking without interpretation), not a *proper* use of tongues (speaking with interpretation, vv. 27,28). MacArthur repeats this argument in *Charismatic Chaos* (Grand Rapids, MI: Zondervan, 1992), p. 232.
36. Carson, *Showing the Spirit*, p. 111, in response to Robertson and Gaffin.
37. Of course, our greatest example of dealing with demonic powers by speaking to them directly and commanding them to leave is the example of Jesus Himself, who frequently did this in the Gospels, and by example and word He taught the disciples to imitate Him (see question 15). But I have mentioned these other examples at this point because someone might object that only Jesus had this kind of authority, and it was not given to other human beings.
38. It is therefore not true (as some assume) that every revelation from God must result in words equal to Scripture in authority as Acts 21:10,11,32,33 suggests.
39. Now it is true that Agabus uses a similar phrase ("Thus says the Holy Spirit") in Acts 21:11, but the same words (Greek *tade legei*) are used by Christian writers just after the time of the New Testament to introduce very general paraphrases or greatly expanded interpretations of what is being reported. (See Ignatius, *Epistle to the Philadelphians* 7:1-2 [about A.D. 108] and *Epistle of Barnabas* 6:8; 9:2,5 [A.D. 70-100]). The phrase can apparently mean, "This is generally (or approximately) what the Holy Spirit is saying to us."
40. John MacArthur, Jr., *Charismatic Chaos*, pp. 60-61.
41. Ibid., p. 70.
42. The canon is the list of books included in the Bible.
43. Michael Harper, *Prophecy: A Gift for the Body of Christ* (Logos, 1964), p. 26.
44. Dennis and Rita Bennett, *The Holy Spirit and You* (Eastbourne, England: Kingsway, 1971), p. 107.
45. Donald Gee, *Spiritual Gifts in the Work of Ministry Today* (Springfield, MO: Gospel Publishing House, 1963), pp. 51-52.

46. Donald Bridge, *Signs and Wonders Today* (Leicester, England: InterVarsity Press, 1985), p. 183.

47. See the extended argument in Wayne Grudem, *The Gift of Prophecy in the New Testament and Today*, pp. 49-51. The same grammatical construction (article-noun-*kai*["and"]-noun) is used in Ephesians 4:11, not to refer to prophets, but to refer to "pastors and teachers" in a phrase that many people translate not "pastors and teachers" (two groups) but "pastor-teachers" (one group). I think the translation "pastor-teachers" is appropriate in this verse.

48. The phrase *tous de prophētas* in Ephesians 4:11 repeats the definite article before the noun "prophets," and so is translated differently, showing that Paul has a different group in mind when he used the word "prophets" in this context—he was referring to Christians in general who had the gift of prophecy, not just to the apostles.

49. D. Martyn Lloyd-Jones, *Prove All Things*, edited by Christopher Catherwood (Eastbourne, England: Kingsway, 1985), pp. 32-33.

50. John Calvin, *The First Epistle of Paul the Apostle to the Corinthians*, trans. by J. W. Fraser, ed. by D. W. Torrance and T. F. Torrance (Grand Rapids, MI: Eerdmans, 1960), p. 281.

51. Compare 1 Corinthians 13:8 ("tongues" and "knowledge") with 12:8,10 (part of a broader list of spiritual gifts) and see G. Fee, *The First Epistle to the Corinthians* (NICNT, ed., F. F. Bruce; Grand Rapids, MI: Eerdmans, 1987), p. 644 and n. 21.

52. I think the office of apostle ended in the first century A.D., after all the books of the Bible were written. See Wayne Grudem, "The Office of Apostle," in *The Gift of Prophecy in the New Testament and Today*, pp. 269-276. However, I do not think of "apostle" as a gift but rather a church office (somewhat like the offices of elder and deacon, which began in the first century and continue today).

53. Some may object that one exception to this may be the vision of the end times in Revelation 13:7, where the beast "was allowed to make war on the saints and to conquer them." But even here there is no indication that the miraculous powers of the beast are greater than the power of the Holy Spirit. This seems to be best understood not as a confrontation of miraculous power but simply as a persecution by military force, for we read later of "those who had been beheaded for their testimony to Jesus and for the word of God, and who had not worshiped the beast or its image and had not received its mark on their foreheads or their hands" (Rev. 20:4).

54. The fact that people who name the name of Christ are able to prophesy and cast out demons and do "many mighty works" in His name (Matt. 7:21-23) does not contradict this, because these are non-Christians. Jesus says to them, "I never knew you; depart from me, you evildoers" (Matt. 7:23). Although it is possible that these are false miracles worked by demonic power, it seems more likely that they are operations of common grace God works through non-Christians, similar to the effectiveness of the gospel God sometimes allows when it is preached by those who have impure motives and do not know Christ in their hearts (cf. Phil. 1:15-18).

55. D. A. Carson, in Horton, ed., *Power Religion*, pp. 100-101.
56. Although Jesus is speaking specifically to the official ("Jesus therefore said *to him*"), the Greek text shows that He uses a plural verb to speak of the Galileans generally ("Unless you (plural) see signs and wonders you (plural) will not believe").
57. Carson in Horton, ed., *Power Religion*, p. 101.
58. Carson, in Horton, ed., *Power Religion*, p. 101; id., *The Gospel According to John* (Leicester, England: InterVarsity, and Grand Rapids, MI: Eerdmans, 1991), p. 238.
59. In order to support the idea that "the welcome the Galileans accorded Jesus was fundamentally flawed, based as it was on too great a focus on miraculous signs" Dr. Carson's commentary (*The Gospel According to John*, p. 238) mentions verse 45 ("So when he came to Galilee, the Galileans welcomed him, having seen all that he had done in Jerusalem at the feast, for they too had gone to the feast"). But this verse talks only about the welcome of the Galileans, and does not mention faith, whether strong or spurious. A more likely interpretation is that many who saw Jesus' miracles were pondering the miracles and gradually growing in their positive assessment of Him, and that day after day more were coming to believe in Him. Their welcome was simply a welcome, as the text says, and no generalization about the nature of their faith at that point should be drawn from it.

Carson's commentary (p. 238) also mentions John 2:23-25, but I doubt that "inadequate faith" is indicated here. It simply says that when people saw the signs He did "many *believed in his name*"—the same expression used in John 3:18 to refer to saving faith. The fact that Jesus "did not trust himself to them" (John 2:24) simply refers to the fact that He did not yet fully disclose His Messiahship and deity to them, not that their faith was inadequate. I doubt that the fact that people "believed in his name" can be made to say that people did not believe in His name. If John had wanted his readers to be warned by these stories of people coming to faith because of miracles, he would not have portrayed the results so positively.
60. Here the word "sign" (*sēmeion*) is not used and "work" (*ergon*) is found instead, but I agree the reference is primarily to Jesus' miracles; cf. K. H. Rengstorf, "*sēmeion*," *TDNT*, vol. 7, pp. 247-248: "Most of the 27 *erga* ['works'] passages in John are clearly related to the *sēmeia* ['signs'] of Jesus....Furthermore they...establish a close connection between the *erga* ['works'] of Jesus as *sēmeia* ['signs'] and the work of God effected in *erga* ['works']....When the Johannine Jesus Himself refers to what John calls *sēmeion* ['sign'] He consistently uses the word *ergon* ['work']."
61. Horton, *Power Religion*, p. 101.
62. Ibid.
63. John 2:24 likewise says nothing about their faith being spurious but simply suggests that many who believed were not yet capable of understanding and committing themselves to Jesus' full messianic mission (John 6:14,15,60-70). This does not demonstrate that their faith was spurious or false.
64. Carson in Horton, ed., *Power Religion*, p. 101.

65. Ibid.
66. Ibid.
67. Ibid., pp. 100, 101.
68. Ibid., p. 92.
69. Ibid., p. 93.
70. Ibid., pp. 125-126, emphasis mine.
71. Ibid., p. 93.
72. Norman Geisler, *Signs and Wonders* (Wheaton, IL: Tyndale House, 1988). His definition of miracles is found on pp. 28-32 and 149-155.
73. I would define a miracle as follows: A miracle is a less common kind of God's activity in which He arouses people's awe and wonder and bears witness to Himself. (See the next question [27] for further discussion of this definition, and other common definitions.)
74. Geisler, *Signs and Wonders*, p. 150.
75. Geisler also has much difficulty explaining Mark 5:8 (where Jesus more than once commanded some demons to leave) and Mark 6:5 (where the text says that Jesus was not able to do any miracles in Nazareth because of their unbelief); see Geisler, *Signs and Wonders*, pp. 149, 152.
76. See also 1 Corinthians 13:1-3 where Paul gives examples of some gifts developed to the highest imaginable degree, examples he uses to show that even such gifts without love would bring no benefit.
77. The present participle of *phero*, "bear, carry" gives the sense of continual activity.
78. For further discussion of God's providence, see Wayne Grudem, *Systematic Theology: An Introductory Course in the Doctrinal Teachings of the Whole Bible* (Leicester, England: InterVarsity, and Grand Rapids, MI: Zondervan, 1993), chap. 16.
79. A study of the biblical terminology for miracles frequently points to this idea of God's power at work to arouse people's wonder and amazement. Primarily three sets of terms are employed: (1) "sign" (Hebrew *'ôt*, Greek *semeion*), which means something that points to or indicates something else, especially (with reference to miracles) God's activity and power; (2) "wonder" (Hebrew *môpēt*, Greek *teras*), an event that causes people to be amazed or astonished; and (3) "miracle" or "mighty work" (Hebrew *gəbûrāh*, Greek *dunamis*), an act displaying great power, especially (with reference to miracles) divine power.

Often "signs and wonders" is used as a stock expression to refer to miracles (Exod. 7:3; Deut. 6:22; Ps. 135:9; Acts 4:30; 5:12; Rom. 15:19, etc.), and sometimes all three terms are combined, "mighty works and signs and wonders" (Acts 2:22) or "signs and wonders and miracles" (2 Cor. 12:12; Heb. 2:4).

In addition to the meanings of the terms used for miracles, another reason supporting our definition is that miracles in Scripture do arouse people's awe and amazement and indicate that God's power is at work. The Bible frequently tells us that God Himself is the one who performs "miracles" or "wondrous things." Psalm 136:4 says that God is the one "who *alone* does great wonders" (cf. Ps. 72:18)." The Song of Moses declares, "Who is like you, O Lord, among the gods? Who is like you, majestic in holiness, terrible in glorious deeds, doing wonders?" (Exod. 15:11). Thus, the miraculous signs Moses did when his staff turned into a snake and back again, or when his hand became leprous and then clean again (Exod. 4:2-8) were given in order that Moses might demonstrate to the people of Israel that God had sent him. Similarly, the miraculous signs God did by the hand of Moses and Aaron through the plagues, far surpassing the false miracles or imitation signs done by the magicians in Pharaoh's court (Exod. 7:12; 8:18,19, 9:11), showed that the people of Israel were those who worshiped the one true God. When Elijah confronted the priests of Baal on Mount Carmel (1 Kings 18:17-40), the fire from heaven demonstrated that the Lord was the one true God.

80. Others may prefer to be more restrictive in their definition of miracles, reserving the term (for example) for events that absolutely *could not* have happened by ordinary means, and that are thoroughly witnessed and documented by several impartial observers. In that case, they will see far fewer miracles, especially in a skeptical, antisupernatural society. But such a definition may not encompass all the kinds of things Paul had in mind when he talked about miracles in the churches of Corinth (1 Cor. 12:10,28,29) and Galatia (Gal. 3:5), and may prevent people from recognizing a gift of miracles when it is given to Christians today. (Of course, Christians who hold such a restrictive definition will still readily thank God for many answers to prayer that they would not call miracles).

81. The appropriateness of such a definition is not lost simply because the same event might be called a miracle by some people and an ordinary event by others, for people's evaluation of an event will vary, depending on their nearness to the event, the assumptions of their worldview and whether or not they are Christians.

82. In this chapter, sections of questions 5, 6, 7, 11, 12, 13, 14, 15, 22, 26 and 27 were taken from Wayne Grudem, *Systematic Theology: An Introductory Course in the Doctrinal Teachings of the Whole Bible* (Leicester, England: InterVarsity, and Grand Rapids, MI: Zondervan, 1993), and are used by permission. Sections of questions 16, 17, 18, 19, 20 and 21 were taken from Wayne Grudem, *The Gift of Prophecy in the New Testament and Today*, and are used by permission.

3

A BIBLICAL VIEW OF THE RELATIONSHIP OF SIN AND THE FRUITS OF SIN:

SICKNESS, DEMONIZATION, DEATH, NATURAL CALAMITY

PETER H. DAVIDS

INTRODUCTION

Christ's death on the cross atones for and cleanses us from all sin, and the atonement of the cross provides the basis for God's work to sanctify us and restore us from the brokenness that sin brought into our lives (Isa. 53:4-6; Mark 10:45; Rom. 3:22-25; 5:8,9; 2 Cor. 5:21; Gal. 3:13; Col. 1:21,22; 1 Tim. 2:6; Heb. 2:14; 9:14,26-28; 10:10; 1 Pet. 1:18-21; 2:24; 3:18; 1 John 2:2; 3:5,8). How is sin related to healing and wholeness in the Bible, and how is personal sin related to praying for someone's healing as prescribed in James 5?

The problem with the human race is, according to Scripture, sin, and the problem with sin is that it has effects. What is more, the effects are not simply the immediate results of the sinful act, but also the long-term consequences of the act, sometimes affecting only the person and at times engulfing the whole of the human race.[1] In this chapter, we want to look at what parts of the human experience are traceable to sin, as well as examine the biblical solution to these consequences.

SIN AND THE FRUIT OF SIN IN THE OLD TESTAMENT

The history of sin in the Old Testament begins with the introduction of sin in Genesis 3. The human beings (both the woman and the man, "who was with her," Gen. 3:6) desired to "be like God," disobeyed and so sinned. The results are portrayed immediately: shame at their nakedness (3:7; perhaps shame is a symbol for their vulnerability); fear of the presence of God (3:8); disorder in the natural world (3:14,17); disruption of human relationships (3:16); disturbance of the generative process (3:16);[2] loss of sovereignty (3:15,18); and death (3:19).

In other words, the original creation in which human beings were sovereign over the world, animals lived at peace with human beings, the earth easily produced food for them, man and woman lived in the equality of mutuality, and death was unknown, is no more after the Fall. Sin has, according to Genesis, forever changed the world. The next three chapters of Genesis work out these consequences with the disruption of human relationships extending to murder and polygamy. Also we see the disruption of man's relationship with the natural world leading one branch of humanity into a total estrangement from the land and thus to building cities and creating technology as a substitute for farming (Gen. 4).[3] The litany of birth and death of Genesis 5 leads to the culmination of violence in Genesis 6, which introduces the Flood narrative.

The Flood narrative itself indicates the pervasiveness of sin. At both ends of the narrative the writer declares, "every thought (or, thing formed in the thought) of a human being was only evil from youth" (Gen. 6:6; cf. 8:21). While on the one end of the narrative this inner evil is the reason for the destruction of the created order, a return to watery chaos, from which only Noah and his family are saved, on the other it results in a type of resigned understanding on the part of God. Yet the next chapter places some limitations on violence in that, unlike the penalty exacted on Cain, now murderers will be executed. Law, then, becomes a result of sin.[4]

The rest of the Old Testament amplifies these positions about the results of sin. That sin can lead to judgment and death is almost a cliché in the Old Testament. The cycle of sin and oppression (which included death in battle and death through oppression) is the theme of Judges. The prophets are concerned about impending judgment, which they speak about in terms of various forms of death (e.g., sword, plague, etc.).

SIN CAN LEAD TO BROKEN RELATIONSHIPS AND POVERTY

Another mark of sin seen in the Old Testament is the destruction of the social fabric of the people. One sees this graphically in the case of Lot in Genesis 19. On the one hand, the sin of Sodom (lack of hospitality to the extent of the abuse of foreigners) leads to the destruction of the city, for it confirms the "outcry against Sodom" (Gen. 18:20). Thus, the sin of Sodom seals its doom, especially since every man in Sodom is involved and Lot has only 4 people with him (thus less than the 10 righteous needed to save the city). On the other hand, the narrative ends with incest by Lot's daughters because society as they knew it was gone. Here is a destroyed social fabric to the extent that the incest taboo is broken. The author of Genesis appears to contrast this fate with that of Abraham; Lot may have been righteous, but he is not as righteous as Abraham.

One could illustrate this fruit of sin in the Psalms and prophets as well, for in these works a result of sin (including Baal worship) is neglecting the widow, orphan and foreigner, failing to release Hebrew slaves, neglecting the Sabbath year (which had important social consequences), and a rise in adultery and violence (including legally sanctioned violence, such as forcing the poor into bankruptcy and slavery). All of these sins are part of a breakdown in social relationships.

A specific fruit of sin that is also a social dislocation in the Old Testament is poverty. In Deuteronomy 15:4,5 we read, "However, there should be no poor among you, for in the land the Lord your God is giving you to possess as your inheritance, he will richly bless you, if only you fully obey the Lord your God." A better translation is, "There will, however, be no one in need among you" (NRSV). In other words, just as in Eden the land supplied the needs of the first human beings, so Palestine will supply the needs of the Israelites. None will suffer want, so long as they obey. The failure to obey God, of course, is sin.

The fruit of sin, poverty, is the abrogation of the promise.[5] One way this is worked out is through injustice, the legal oppression of the weaker Israelites by the more powerful, which Amos speaks out against, (e.g., Amos 2:6-7; cf. 4:1). Another way poverty came about was through famine (i.e., natural disaster), which was often viewed as a direct punishment from God. A third way poverty came about was through personal misfortune, which is the presumed situation of Job, but may form the actual background for the sudden coming of the Lord to judge His people in Malachi 3:8-11 (assuming that this is not simply a collective promise).

SIN CAN LEAD TO SICKNESS

Another specific mark of sin is the presence of disease. On the positive side, Exodus 15:26 states, "If you listen carefully to the voice of the Lord...I will not bring on you any of the diseases I brought on the Egyptians, for I am the Lord who heals you" (cf. Deut. 7:12-16, which expands upon this theme). On the negative side, the other end of the Pentateuch states, "If you do not obey the Lord your God....The Lord will plague you with diseases....The Lord will strike you with wasting disease, with fever and inflammation, with scorching heat and drought, with blight and mildew, which will plague you until you perish" (Deut. 28:15,21,22).[6]

This concept (i.e., sickness as the fruit of sin) is illustrated throughout the Exodus narrative. Miriam develops leprosy when she opposes Moses (Num. 12:10). Those who brought a negative report about Canaan died of a plague (Num. 14:37). The sin at Baal-Peor resulted in a plague in which 24,000 died (Num. 25:9). Such examples continue throughout the Old Testament. While in the Deuteronomic history most of the examples are about sin leading to death through defeat, there are examples of sin leading to sickness, such as the plague in 2 Samuel 24:15, which kills 70,000 because of David's sin. Azariah (Uzziah) contracted leprosy (2 Kings 15:5; cf. 2 Chron 26:16-20, which attributes this to his sin). The Elijah-Elisha cycle also connects sin to illness, at least in the minds of others (1 Kings 17:18).

The significant issue in each of these instances is that the sickness comes prior to the completion of a full life. Presumably everyone in Scripture dies of what we would call sickness or natural death. The desire of the Hebrews, however, was that any final illness come at the end of a full life and not be a type that separated the person from their community (such as leprosy, which could never be considered a normal illness because it made the person taboo[7]). Thus. Hezekiah, when informed that his illness is terminal, implores God for a longer life because he has "walked before [the Lord] in faithfulness with a whole heart," so his premature death would have been inappropriate (2 Kings 20:3, NRSV; repeated in Isa. 38:3). The promise of 15 additional years apparently gave him what he thought was a reasonably long life, so it was received without complaint.

The deathbed scenes of Old Testament folk who are "old and full of days" are relatively peaceful in the sense that they accept death as appropriate and are not asking for a longer life, but instead are passing on instructions to others (e.g., Elisha in 2 Kings 13:14). On the other hand, Ahaziah dies a premature death from injury brought on by sin (2 Kings 1:16) and Abijah, son of Jeroboam I, dies because of his parent's sin (1 Kings 14:1-18; yet God finds "something pleasing to the Lord" (1 Kings 14:13, NRSV) in the child so he receives an honorable death and burial, unlike the rest of the family, which dies violently and without burial).

The latter prophets also give us examples of this perspective. For example, Jeremiah prophesies the death of Hananiah the prophet because of his lying prophecy (Jer. 28:15-17). While his death could have occurred due to an accident or other violence, the simple term "died" most naturally indicates that he became ill and died. In the writings that constitute the third division of the Old Testament (divided into the law, the prophets and the writings), the Psalms picture illness as the result of sin (Ps. 32:3,4; 38:3,5; cf. 31:10, which calls for healing because his illness was not a result of sin). Sin, then, is closely connected with illness, especially with premature illness or illnesses that made a person taboo.

SIN CAN LEAD TO DEMONIZATION

A last result of sin in the Old Testament is demonization. Though references to the demonic in the Old Testament are scarce, there is, however, one example—Saul. That Saul lost the kingdom due to disobedience is clear enough (1 Sam 13:13,14; 15:17-19,22,23,26). It is after this that "an evil spirit from the Lord tormented [Saul]" (1 Sam 16:14, NRSV). While the connection is not developed, the progression in the narrative suggests that the loss of the divine Spirit and the presence of a demonic spirit is a fruit of Saul's sin.[8] The final consequence, of course, is his consultation with the medium in Endor (1 Sam. 28:3-25).

SIN AND THE FRUIT OF SIN IN THE NEW TESTAMENT

Sin is taken no less seriously in the New Testament than in the Old Testament. At the same time, the New Testament provides a more complex picture in that the role of Satan is far more important. Evil and misfortune, which might have been attributed directly to God in the Old Testament, are now attributed to Satan. Likewise, the connection between sin and disease and personal disaster, which only begins to break down in the Old Testament (Job being the chief example), is relativized even more in the New Testament. Still, while one must be more careful in attributing causation to personal sin in a New Testament perspective, the teaching that evil is the result of sin in the world is never challenged.

SIN LEADING TO BROKEN RELATIONSHIPS AND SOCIAL DYSFUNCTION

As in the Old Testament, social dysfunction in the New Testament is the result of sin. Romans 1:18-32 traces this out. Idolatry leads to sexual dysfunction, either heterosexual (assuming that is the point of 1:24) or homosexual. Finally, comes a list of a series of evils, many of which are indicative of social breakdown (e.g., murder, strife, deceit, disobedience to parents),[9] all of which are traced to the original sin of the rejection of God.

SIN LEADING TO NATURAL CALAMITY

Natural disasters are rarely traced directly to sin in the New Testament[10] until one comes to Revelation. There one finds famine (Rev. 6:6) and a series of other natural disasters (Rev. 8:7-10) depicted as judgments of God. The text repeatedly indicates that those not killed by the disasters "did not repent of [idolatry]....And they did not repent of their murders or their sorceries or their fornication or their thefts" (Rev. 9:20,21, NRSV, is only one example). This shows the connection between sin and the result of sin—the disasters sent by God—in the mind of the prophet.

SIN LEADING TO POVERTY

Unlike the Old Testament, poverty is not directly connected to sin in the New Testament. In other words, there is neither a clear promise of sufficiency based on obedience nor a warning of lack as a result of disobedience. Such a warning may be implied in the connection of sowing to reaping in such passages as 2 Corinthians 9:6 and Galatians 6:7, but this is a far less direct connection than in the Old Testament. The New Testament promises of provision appear far more unconditional (e.g., 2 Cor 9:10,11; but cf. Matt. 6:33).

At the same time, the Old Testament point of view is reflected in a number of ways. First, poverty is connected to oppression in places such as James 5:1-6. Second, there is the reflection in some New Testament books of the *Armen-frömigkeit* (intrinsic piety attributed to the poor) of the intertestamental period (the period between the Old and New Testament periods). In Luke, for example, while the poor are blessed, the rich are cursed (Luke 6:20,24). In James, Christians are called "poor," but are never called "rich." Third, the kingdom of God is pictured as a place of plenty, whether the kingdom is the heavenly Kingdom (e.g., Luke 6:21; Rev. 7:16) or the more limited earthly expression (e.g., Mark 10:29,30 and other promises of present provision).[11] In a world without sin (i.e., the Kingdom), poverty would not exist.

SIN LEADING TO SICKNESS

Like poverty, sickness is viewed in the New Testament as a fruit of sin. While this is true in general in that death came into the world through sin (Rom. 5:12), it is also true in specific individual situations. In John 5:14, Jesus meets the man whom He healed at the pool and tells him, "Stop sinning or something worse may happen to you." Certainly in the context the implication is that the "something worse" is an illness.[12]

Less clear is the situation of the paralytic in Mark 2:1-12. In this case, Jesus forgives the sins of the man when He sees the faith of those who brought the man to Him. While this authority to forgive sin may be the reason Mark included the story (since it begins a series of conflicts between Jesus and the interpreters of the law), it does not appear likely that Jesus was simply using the sick man to make a point. (Did Jesus ever use people for His purposes, or did He meet the person's need, which sometimes allowed Him to make a further point?) It is certainly possible—perhaps probable—that the reason for forgiving sins was that sin was the root problem of man and only with sin taken care of could sickness be healed (cf. Jas. 5:16, "Confess your sins to one another and pray for each other so that you may be healed").[13]

A number of places in the New Testament connect sin to specific sicknesses. In 1 Corinthians 11:27-30, Paul connects impropriety at the Lord's Supper to "many" being "weak and sick" and "a number" having died. Although the situation is far more blatant, the sicknesses of Herod Agrippa I (Acts 12:23) and Elymas Bar-Jesus (Acts 13:8-12) are connected to specific sins.[14]

Naturally, personal sin is not the only cause of illness. The New Testament makes this clear. When asked about a blind man in John 9:1-3, Jesus responds that neither the sins of the man nor those of the parents had caused him to be born blind.[15] Notice that He does not deny such sins *could* cause illness in a child, but instead simply states that this was not the situation in this case. This means that no absolute equation is valid that attributes sickness to personal sin in either the sick person or a near relative.

James 5:15 is a similar case in point. James 5:16 states that Christians should confess their sins to one another and pray for one another so that they might be healed, connecting sin to sickness. However, James 5:14,15 states that a person will be healed when the elders pray a prayer of faith and "anyone who has committed sins will be forgiven" (NRSV). The construction is very clear. If sin is a cause of the sickness, it will be forgiven. But the "if" (kan Jas. 5:15) is the important term.[16] Although personal sin is a possible cause of the sickness, it is not the only possibility. If it is present to forgive, it will be forgiven, but one cannot make the simple equation sickness = personal sin. Discernment is needed.

SIN LEADING TO DEMONIZATION

Demonization is another fruit of sin in the New Testament. Although the New Testament does not give a comprehensive discussion on how people get demonized, probably because the issue for New Testament authors was expelling demons rather than a person's previous history, it does give us some illuminating examples of the connection of the demonic with sin. Judas Iscariot is the first example that comes to mind. Although Luke 22:3-6 indicates that Satan had "entered into" Judas (cf. Matt. 26:14-16; Mark 14:10,11, which do not mention the demonic element), it does not give a motive, although a motive is suggested in mentioning the promise of money or the request for money.[17] John 12:6, however, places a reference to Judas being a thief into the earlier account of the anointing at Bethany. John then retains the reference to Satan entering Judas in John 13:27. Is this a suggestion that Judas's sinfulness (greed, thievery) was the basis for Satan's entering him? We cannot be certain, but that would be one possible implication, which could also be latent in Luke's account, where the request for money is underlined.[18]

A second example of demonization connected to sin is in Acts 5:1-3, the story of Ananias and Sapphira. Here it is clear that they sinned (i.e., lied to the Holy Spirit). Yet we must ask what Peter meant by "Satan has filled your heart (v. 3)."[19] The plot to deceive is clearly attributed to Satan, but (1) was this demonization and (2) was this the fruit of sin or the cause of sin? The evidence seems to suggest that it was demonization—Ananias was clearly influenced by Satan who "filled [his] heart."[20]

The evidence also seems to suggest that this demonization was the fruit of sin. Surely it is hard to believe that such a deliberate (attempted) deception was conceived and executed without some previous weakening of their moral fiber.[21] Did that create an opening for this temptation? Since the phrase "Satan has filled your heart" suggests demonization (even if only a mild form), then they (or at least Ananias) were Christians who were demonized as a result of their sin.

Two passages describe Christians being handed over to Satan as a result of sin, 1 Corinthians 5:4,5 and 1 Timothy 1:20. In both cases, the people committed a specific sin. The result of the sin is not automatic, but the Church (or in the case of 1 Timothy, Paul) hands them over to Satan who will be the agent of discipline (and hopefully salvation). Clearly, this is not a willing role Satan plays (why would Satan ever do something that might lead a person to reject sin or even "be saved in the day of the Lord"?), Rather, the author describes the effect of Satan's activities. In this case, we cannot say that demonization is the fruit of sin alone, for the Church assists. What we do observe is that when a person was put outside the protection of the Church, demonization, at least to the extent of physical or some other form of affliction by Satan, was the expected result.[22]

Another set of passages indicates that Satan has designs on Christians: 2 Corinthians 2:10-11; 1 Timothy 3:6,7; 1 Peter 5:8. In the first passage, 2 Corinthians 2:10-11, a repentant person who had been excommunicated (probably for opposition to Paul's authority) is to be forgiven and received again in order to keep him from becoming a prey of Satan, presumably through depression (sorrow). In the second passage, 1 Timothy 3:6,7, elders are not to be conceited but are expected to be experienced Christians of character so that they do not fall into Satan's traps (i.e., he is seeking to "get his hooks into" them). In the third passage, 1 Peter 5:8, Satan is looking for Christians to devour (the context might suggest through pride or through harboring anxiety), so alertness and self-discipline are to be practiced. All of these suggest that a lack of virtue makes a Christian vulnerable to Satan, although the exact nature of his traps or influence is not specified.

A final group of texts speaks of the danger of falling into Satan's trap: 1 Corinthians 7:5 (sexual temptation); Ephesians 4:26,27 (anger); 2 Timothy 2:25,26 (false teaching, opposing the truth). Abstinence from sexual intercourse between married partners, anger or involvement in sin (perhaps those mentioned in 2 Tim 2:21,22) cause one to become Satan's captive or to become trapped by him. Although this may simply mean further involvement in sin as a result of previous sin, it does seem to indicate a level of demonic influence in which at least a person's mind or will is involved.

We conclude that the New Testament does not directly say demonization can be a fruit of sin, but it does imply this connection. It does this in narrative form by connecting sin and demonic (Satanic) influence. It does this in the Epistles by connecting sin to falling under the influence of Satan. In some cases, the demonization might be mild (temptation), in others, more intermediate (having a mind captive to Satan, probably indicating compulsive sin or deception), and in the case of the excommunicated, it may be rather severe (e.g., to the extent of illness, which may destroy their body). Although the data are not as clear as we might desire, the connection is legitimate, according to the New Testament.

REVERSING THE FRUIT OF SIN IN THE OLD TESTAMENT

If the fruits of sin include those things we discussed above, we need to ask if there is a way to reverse them. In other words, if one sins (or if others sin and one is exposed to the results), must he or she simply accept the bitter fruit, or does the Scripture present some other solution?

The Old Testament provides an answer, which is Yahweh himself. "I am the Lord who heals you" (Exod. 15:26, NRSV). How does one appropriate this health? By submission to Yahweh, "If you will listen carefully to the voice of the Lord your God" (Exod. 15:26, NRSV). The essence of sin in Genesis 3 was to seek independence from God, thus the essence of the healing of sin is to return to a relationship of submission to God. Naturally, with the healing of the sin itself comes the healing of the effects of sin, such as sickness. (See also Prov. 3:7,8; 4:22.)

Thus, Psalm 103:3 (NRSV) describes God as the one, "who forgives all your iniquity, who heals all your diseases," and then goes on to describe rescue from death ("the Pit") and promise long life. The psalm continues and describes Yahweh as the one whose nature focuses on forgiving. (See also Isaiah 33:22-24, and in a metaphorical sense of the nation as a whole, Jeremiah 30:17.) In Psalm 103, submission to Yahweh is also presented as protection from the fruit of sin in the world around us (specifically, protection from disease and death in battle).

Although we have chosen specific illustrative texts, this is a consistent picture throughout the Old Testament. Yahweh is the one who announces the penalty for sin; He is also the one who describes Himself as, "The Lord, the Lord, a God merciful and gracious, slow to anger, and abounding in steadfast love and faithfulness" (Exod. 34:6,7, NRSV). Now it is true that the same passage indicates He will "[visit] the iniquity of the parents upon the children...to the third and the fourth generation," but this appears to be more the divine response to continued rebellion than the core of His nature.

Although one can find plenty of examples of severe judgment in the Old Testament, God is also continually pictured as forgiving. We might not be surprised that David (a "man after [God's] own heart") is forgiven when he commits adultery and murder (2 Sam. 12:13).[23] But Jonah pictures God as forgiving the Assyrians, 1 Kings 21:29 as forgiving Ahab, 2 Kings 5 as healing the Aramean commander Naaman (when the latter submits to the directive of God), and Jeremiah 38:17-23 as offering salvation to Zedekiah if the king would only obey Yahweh. None of these latter three people were good folk in any sense of the word. In two of the cases, they were within days of a judgment (a fruit of sin), which had been announced without any "ifs" about it. Yet repentance and submission could still avert the judgment.

A similar picture of God as the deliverer from the fruit of sin appears in Job, in which suffering for other than personal sin is discussed. The pious Job does suffer because of the sin of others (assuming that Satan is viewed as an evil being and the attacks of the various raiders are sinful acts). All of the time Job is suffering, God is not seen on the earthly plane. For some reason never explained, He has accepted Satan's challenge and permitted the evil to happen. When God is seen by Job, He shows up as the deliverer.

Thus, in the Old Testament the answer to the fruit of sin is Yahweh. When one repents and returns to a position of submission to Yahweh, the corporate and individual fruits of sin are removed. The drought ends, the armies are victorious, the plague ceases, and the individual disease is healed. Certainly ambiguities exist in this picture, but the basic picture is clear.

REVERSING THE FRUIT OF SIN IN THE NEW TESTAMENT

In the New Testament, God has already shown up on earth in Jesus. According to the whole witness of the New Testament, the culmination of Jesus' mission was His death on the cross, which atoned for all sins, providing the basis for God's sanctifying, restoring work to reverse the fruits of sin (Matt. 8:16,17 and Isa. 53:4-6; Matt. 20:28; Mark 10:45; John 12:27-33; Rom. 3:22-25; 5:8,9; 2 Cor. 5:21; Gal. 3:13; Col. 1:21,22; 1 Tim. 2:6; Heb. 2:14; 9:14,26-28; 10:10; 1 Pet. 1:18-21; 2:24; 3:18; 1 John 2:2; 3:5,8).

Jesus' ultimate mission in the New Testament's view, then, was to atone for sin and reverse sin's fruits. Accordingly, when Jesus arrives on the scene, the fruits of sin are reversed. Mark presents this paradigm through narrative. In Mark 1:21-28, the presence of Jesus excites a demon (presumably one the people did not know existed in the man it was affecting) who cries out, "Have you come to destroy us?" (Mark 1:24). Jesus' response is affirmative, at least in the sense that He expels the demon. Demonization is an effect of sin, conceivably, *the primary* effect of sin, if we view the whole world as demonized by Satan through the results of the Fall as 1 John 5:19 suggests (cf. John 12:31). Because of this, the presence of Jesus reveals this fruit of sin and then reverses it. This is a consistent pattern in the life of Jesus.

Mark moves directly on to the healing ministry of Jesus (Mark 1:29-31), including the healing of leprosy, a disease that made one ritually taboo (1:40-45). It is in the healing of the paralytic in Mark 2:1-12 that the forgiveness of sins is followed immediately by the healing of the disease. That is, both sin and the fruits of sin are removed.[24]

Luke presents this picture a little differently. It is after a successful confrontation with the devil that Jesus goes to Nazareth and quotes His programmatic passage from Isaiah 61:1,2 (Luke 4:18,19). The goals of Jesus' mission have to do with those suffering the effects of sin: the poor, the prisoners, the blind, the oppressed. Jesus does announce good news to the poor (Luke 6:20) and does heal the blind (Luke 7:21-23; 18:35-43). He does not release any prisoners from human jails, although God does do that in Acts (Acts 12:11, where "the Lord" could be either God the Father or Jesus), but He does release people who have been bound by Satan (Luke 13:10-17). Thus, it is reasonable to view the works of Jesus in Luke as the reversal of or—remedy for—the fruit of sin.

In another narrative, Luke suggests that Jesus reverses death, the ultimate fruit of sin. This is clear in Luke 7:11-17, where He raises the son of the widow in Nain. This is also the case in Luke 8:40-42,49-56, where He raises up Jairus's daughter.[25] Likewise, Luke has three apparent resurrections in Acts—9:36-43; 14:19,20; 20:7-12. Only the first and third narratives clearly state that the person was dead, so the second, 14:19,20, could simply be a remarkable healing. Yet, the statement that the people believed Paul to be dead and the symmetry between the two narratives in the Gospel of Luke and the Acts narratives suggests that it is viewed as a resurrection.[26]

Naturally, none of the writers trace the various deaths to specific sin, certainly not to the sin of the people who died, yet could anyone who was a reader of the Old Testament be unaware that death was the result of sin? And would anyone in the New Testament period, Jew (except such Jews as the Sadducees), Jewish-Christian or gentile-Christian see the resurrection of the dead as anything less than a foretaste of the age to come (cf. Heb. 6:5)? Given this general theological context, it is likely that Luke views these events as examples of the coming great reversal of death in the eschaton.

Although the Johannine tradition also recounts one resurrection of the dead, that of Lazarus in John 11, the culmination of the Book of Signs,[27] it puts the wider issue of the reversal of the fruit of sin somewhat differently than the Synoptics do. When Jesus heals the man at the pool of Bethesda in John 5, He later instructs the man, "Stop sinning or something worse may happen to you" (John 5:14, mēketi hamartane, the negative plus the present imperative indicating the cessation of something ongoing). This not only assumes that sin had been the cause of the illness, but also that the man might continue or already had continued in his sin and needed the exhortation to stop. Here is a case in which the fruit of sin was reversed before the sin itself was dealt with. But that is in line with 1 John 3:8, "The reason the Son of God appeared was to destroy the devil's work." Although the focus of 1 John is on sin itself, the fruit of sin is also the work of the devil. Jesus works in one case from root to fruit and in the other from fruit to root. Both have to be removed.

The fruit of sin is reversed through the work of Jesus in two ways: through His sovereign grace and through the repentance and faith of men and women.

First, there are what we may call the works of sovereign grace. The works of sovereign grace are the invasion of the kingdom of God into this world. Those are the situations in which no one but Jesus appears to have faith and yet significant healing/deliverance results. For example, the demonized man in the synagogue in Capernaum (Mark 1:21-28) does not appear to have come seeking healing nor to have had any expressed faith. The presence of Jesus revealed the demon, and Jesus expelled it. Other activities in this category might include the raising of the son of the widow at Nain (Luke 7:11-17), the stilling of the storm (Mark 4:35-41 and parallels), and perhaps the calling of Levi (Mark 2:13-17). This latter incident deserves some comment.

However honest a tax collector Levi was (if "honest tax collector" was not an oxymoron to first-century Jews), he was experiencing an effect of sin, rejection, and alienation from his community. He does not seek Jesus, but Jesus calls to him as Jesus is passing by. Levi responds to the sovereign action, as does Zacchaeus in Luke 19. The result is a reversal of the alienation caused by sin as the person enters the community of the renewed Israel. In the case of Levi, he becomes one of the Twelve along with Simon the Zealot (Mark 3:18 and parallels). If this reading of the text is accurate,[28] then bitter enemies were reconciled through a sovereign act of Jesus. Similar deeds can be reported for His followers in Acts.

Second there is repentance and faith, which from the human side appear to call forth from Jesus the reversal of the fruit of sin. That Jesus responded to faith is clear from such passages as Matthew 9:1-8 and parallels, the healing of the paralytic: "When Jesus saw their faith." In this case, the faith appears to be in the men carrying the paralytic, not in the paralytic himself, but wherever the faith is located, Jesus responds. He first forgives the paralytic's sins and then heals him. The leper in Mark 1:4 clearly has faith. Mark 6:5 indicates that the lack of faith in Nazareth prevents the reversal of the fruit of sin, (i.e., the working of miracles).

The faith spoken of in the New Testament is basically a confident trust in a person, namely in Jesus and His Father.[29] That is, it is not primarily a belief that something will happen (although because one knows the person it contains the belief that the person could do what is desired). Nor is faith a belief that something has already happened although all evidence is to the contrary (the New Testament is relentlessly reality oriented to the degree that it allows the observable to indicate the reality of the unobservable, cf. Jas. 2:14,17,20,26; no one is ever called to believe that what he or she sees is not real). Rather, faith is trust in a person who can make things happen no matter what the odds are against him.[30]

This nature of faith shows up in James when James speaks of prayer in 1:5 and 4:3. The faith without doubt of James 1:5 is a trust in God as the one who freely gives good gifts, rather than the "faith" of the double-minded who does not really trust God at all, but prays as a last resort or in case it might help (their real sense of security is found not in relationship with God but in the world). Likewise in James 4:3 prayers are not answered because they are prayed out of the motivation of desire, what Paul would call "the flesh." The next verse makes it clear that the person is trying to straddle two stools: he or she wants to have God and also be a friend of the world. In the process, they have become God's enemy. Obviously, someone who has to find security in the world as well as in God cannot be a person who trusts God very much at all.[31] Yet, the elders who are able to pray "the prayer of faith" can expect to see the sick raised and the fruit of sin (whether the specific sin of the person or the fruit of sin in general) reversed (Jas. 5:15).

The idea of faith being a relational trust in God or about faith in God leading to the reversal of the fruit of sin would not be strange to Paul or to other New Testament writers. Since, in Paul, true faith leads to a sense of sonship (e.g., Gal 4:4-7) and an experience of the Spirit that includes the working of miracles (Gal. 3:4,5), it is clearly relational trust that he is talking about. In the Johannine tradition, the one who has true faith will do even greater works than those of Jesus (John 14:12; the works of Jesus cited in the context are His miracles,[32] those works John has cited as "signs" should lead to belief[33]). It is the one who believes who "overcomes the world" (1 John 5:4). This trust in Christ is what overcomes the effects of sin, for whether it is proclamation, loving others or healing the sick (all mentioned in the Johannine corpus), "The reason the Son of God appeared was to destroy the devil's work" (1 John 3:8).

Bound together with faith is repentance. Repentance is the turning from sin, which is logically the preparatory move before faith. Thus, Zacchaeus shows at least curiosity in seeking to see Jesus, but his clear internal motivation in the end (we are not told when it arose) is that of repentance, which is seen in his parting from his money (Luke 19:8). This is certainly mixed with faith in that he recognizes Jesus as an authoritative figure ("Lord"). For Luke, of course, this is a miracle—without such a miracle no rich person can be saved (Luke 18:24-27). Few other clear examples of repentance exist in the teachings of Jesus, but then, many of the followers of Jesus had previously been associated with John the Baptist, whose ministry was a call to repentance.

In the Epistles, James 5:16 clearly connects repentance with the healing of the fruit of sin. Having just mentioned that if the sickness of a person were due to sin and the sin would be forgiven when the elders prayed for healing, James turns from the specific situation of calling the elders to the general principle: "Confess you sins to one another, and pray for one another that you may be healed." The point here is that one should confess sins, where appropriate, then pray for healing, and then healing will follow. In case people object, because they are merely ordinary people and not qualified to pray, James continues with the example of Elijah, an ordinary man who prayed, having great effect.

In all of these situations, whether in the Gospels or in the Epistles, the fruits of sin are reversed through the coming of Jesus and ultimately through His death on the cross to atone for sin. The fruits of sin can be reversed through a sovereign act, which does not presuppose any faith on the part of the recipient. But it is most likely to come when repentance from sin occurs (if personal sin is involved in the situation) and faith in Christ. Negatively, a lack of faith in Jesus appears to block the reception of this reversal, even when Jesus Himself is personally present (Matt. 13:58; Mark 6:5,6). This reversal extends to all classes of the fruit of sin: death, broken relationships, alienation from God, demonization, and physical illness. Yet it is still not the full story.

THE NOT-YET NATURE OF REVERSING THE FRUIT OF SIN

In Jesus and the Early Church, we see some of the fruit of sin reversed. However, the New Testament also acknowledges that the fruits of sin have not yet been totally turned around. Although we could cite examples in all realms of experience, the clearest is death. Death came through sin, but the resurrections of the dead we see in Scripture are only occasional. It is true that Jesus is reported in the various Gospels to have raised two people from the dead. It is also true that part of the Matthean mission charge to the Twelve was "raise the dead" (Matt. 10:8). Yet, Acts reports only two (or possibly three) dead people being raised and, unlike the summary reports in which many sick are said to be healed, no such summaries are given (e.g., "many dead were raised to life") for raising the dead. At the same time, there is a clear expectation in the New Testament of a final resurrection of the dead when all of the dead will be raised ("the redemption of our bodies," Rom. 8:23). Thus, the "not yet" of the present points to the coming fulfillment of human hope, while the "already" of the occasional raising of the dead whets the appetite for the full event.[34]

The same could be said for all of the effects of sin. While in the present some people bow to Jesus (i.e., are evangelized), in the future "every knee will bow" (Phil 2:10). In the present, people are brought together in the Church, where there is reconciliation of the various divisions of humanity (most notably the Jew-gentile division, Eph. 2:14). However, in the coming age there will be one city, "the Holy City, Jerusalem," (Rev. 21:10), which appears to unify many of the themes of Scripture (e.g., the Twelve apostles and the Twelve tribes) and which answers to the search for community (Enoch, Gen. 4:17; Nimrod's cities, Gen. 10:8-11). Although stories are told in Scripture of the present provision of food and protection from the danger of natural disaster, in that age "they will hunger no more, and thirst no more; the sun will not strike them, nor any scorching heat" (Rev. 7:16, NRSV).

Obviously, the same type of "already—not yet" tension is present in the case of disease and the demonic. Paul performs all types of healing miracles, but at least once he must leave a sick coworker behind (2 Tim. 4:20; cf. Phil. 2:26,27; 1 Tim. 5:23; Gal. 4:13,14); yet there is no disease whatsoever in the heavenly city, where every tear is wiped away (Rev. 21:4). In the case of the demonic, Christians expel demons now but may not be able to expel every demon in the world, and there is no indication that Christians will expel the principalities and powers Paul speaks about. Yet in Revelation the demonic has disappeared into the Lake of Fire (Rev. 20:10; cf. Matt. 25:41).

The point that needs to be underlined is that in no area are the effects of sin completely reversed in this age, although in *all areas* some reversal of each of the effects of sin occurs.[35] Some tension always remains, even if there is a significant taste of "the powers of the age to come" (Heb. 6:5).[36] Although this protects the Church against a triumphalism that denies the reality of the present battle, it also points in hope to the coming final victory and the present experience of the partial reversal of the fruits of sin. The "not yet," while inducing a longing for the future, should give faith and hope in the present as we see the "already" and realize that as it happens, as the fruits of sin are reversed, it is not perfection, but simply a down payment on what is coming.

Notes

1. Both of these first two statements would be accepted by all orthodox Christian theologians of whatever stripe. For example, *The Westminster Confession of Faith*'s article VI. "Of the Fall of Man, of Sin, and of the Punishment Thereof" describes the original sin and its effects (G. I. Williamson, ed., *The Westminster Confession of Faith for Study Classes* [Philadelphia, PA: The Presbyterian and Reformed Publishing Company, 1964] pp. 53-61), but so does the popular Mennonite work by Paul Erb, *We Believe* (Scottdale, PA: Herald Press, 1969) pp. 19-22, and *Seventh-day Adventists Believe* (Washington, DC: Ministerial Association, General Conference of Seventh-day Adventists, 1988) pp. 87-91. We could go on and multiply examples, but these scattered ones should be sufficient.
2. The text refers to the multiplication of conceptions and childbirths and the connection of labor with this process, the same type of labor that will be associated with farming (3:17). It appears that the original design was that conceptions would be fewer, for there was no death to be overcome, and pregnancy and delivery would be without difficult labor. Of course, we have no example of this happening through which to compare the before and after, so unlike some of the other consequences, this one is more of an extension from the text.
3. See Jacques Ellul, *The Meaning of the City* (Grand Rapids, MI: Wm. B. Eerdmans, 1970). While the city in Scripture is usually a human attempt to overcome alienation, even Jerusalem becoming the abode of evil so that before the exile and again in Revelation it can be compared to Sodom (Rev. 11:8), the vision of Revelation 21 is of a new Jerusalem in which the idea of the city (or human community) is redeemed, for God is in that city and all sin is outside of it.
4. Like all Old Testament law, one cannot simply assume that this is appropriate for disciples of Jesus Christ. Instead, Christians must carefully examine the implications of the new era that has dawned in the life, death and resurrection of Jesus and from that learn how this law may or may not apply to their behavior now.
5. We can observe this from archaeology when we compare the relative equality of tenth-century Israel (although the living standard was modest) with the stark rich—poor contrasts of eighth-century Israel. See Roland De Vaux,

Ancient Israel, Its Life and Institutions (London, England: Darton, Longman and Todd, 1973) pp. 72-73.

6. The blight and mildew were certainly classed with human sicknesses, for the laws of leprosy (Lev. 13—14) include mildew in houses along with skin diseases under the same general category. Perhaps drought and scorching heat were also seen in this category or it may be that they are included here because they also led to human deaths.

7. I prefer the term "taboo" to "unclean," for the latter in English normally indicates physical uncleanness, which is never intended by the Hebrew term, while the former (at least in its anthropological meaning) means, "prohibited" or "avoided by social custom" or to "exclude or prohibit by authority or social influence" (quotations from J. B. Sykes, ed., *The Concise Oxford Dictionary* [sixth edition] [Oxford, England: Clarendon Press, 1976]). This definition complex would fit both people and animals (e.g., pigs). The alternative is "ritually unfit," which is appropriate for the separation of people from Jewish cultic ritual, but not for their separation from the community nor for the prohibition on certain animals.

8. We should not be surprised that the evil spirit is "from the Lord," for all events are attributed directly to the Lord in the Deuteronomic history. It is only in Chronicles where we discover that some of what was attributed to the Lord should be attributed to Satan (a being not named in preexilic books). Compare 2 Samuel 24:1 with 1 Chronicles 21:1. Progress in revelation occurs within the Old Testament.

9. The disturbance of family relationships was especially significant in the ancient world in which the family was one's security, and submission to parents was a cardinal virtue. This was true not only for the Jewish world, but also for the whole Graeco-Roman world. Thus, an apocalyptic scenario is pictured in terms of family breakdown in Mark 13:12, while the blessing of God was associated with family restoration, as in Malachi 4:6.

10. Other natural disasters, such as the famine and the storm at sea are reported in Acts (Acts 11:28; 27:13ff.). The famine is never connected with any type of sin. In the storm at sea, only the damage to the particular ship Paul is on is connected to sin (i.e., the failure of those responsible to listen to Paul, Acts 27:9-12), not the storm itself.

11. The fact that in Mark the "hundred times as much" is not necessarily owned by the Christian, but simply to supply his or her needs does not mitigate its being a divine provision and a rejection of lack as not being part of the Kingdom. At the same time, it does cause problems for those Christians who would measure their spirituality by the quantity of goods they possess rather than that their needs are being met. See further Gordon D. Fee, *The Disease of the Health and Wealth Gospels* (Costa Mesa, CA: The Word for Today, 1979) and John White, *The Golden Cow* (Downers Grove, IL: InterVarsity Press, 1979). The problem with the positions these men criticize is that they have lost the "already-not yet" tension of the New Testament (Matt. 12:28; Luke 11:20; 17:21; 1 Cor. 13:8-12; 15:24,25; Rev. 11:15-17) and so, among other things, try to live out an overrealized eschatology. Of course this does not excuse the

opposite error of living without faith in either the healing power or the provision of God, even if our experience of both is partial in this age.

12. John 5:14: "Later Jesus found him at the temple and said to him, 'See, you are well again. Stop sinning or something worse (*cheiron...ti*) may happen to you.'" Several scholars have made remarks regarding this passage, like those of H. van der Loos, *The Miracles of Jesus* (Supplements to Novum Testamentum, vol. 8. Leiden, Netherlands: E. J. Brill, 1965), p. 458f.: "One can surmise, but not establish, a relationship between the man's sins and his disease. Something worse might happen to him. This might be taken to mean a 'worse' disease, or some form or the other of chastisement, indeed eternal punishment....It would be a calamity which would form a sharp contrast to the salvation which the man had just been permitted to receive in his healing"; similarly, G. Bertram, "*hamartanō*," *TDNT*, vol. 1, p. 288, n. 58; A. Oepke, "*iaomai*," *TDNT*, vol. 3, p. 204; id., "*nosos*," *TDNT*, vol. 4, p. 1095.

In the Johannine literature, Revelation 2:22 is often cited as an instance of sin resulting in sickness. Yet, although the English phrase "bed of suffering" (NIV) is common for sickness in English, the term *thlipsis* "suffering" in Greek literature indicates persecution rather than illness. "Jezebel" has been involved in adultery, which includes participating in idolatry. The irony is that instead of getting a comfortable bed, she will get a bed of affliction, namely that the pagans with whom she has been compromising will turn on her. See further on this word group, Peter H. Davids, "Sickness and Suffering in the New Testament," in C. Peter Wagner and F. Douglas Pennoyer, eds., *Wrestling with Dark Angels* (Ventura, CA: Regal Books, 1990) pp. 215-237.

13. Compare James 5:15,16: "The prayer offered in faith will make the sick person well; the Lord will raise him up. If he has sinned, he will be forgiven. Therefore confess your sins to each other and pray for each other so that you may be healed." In Rabbinic Judaism, personal sin was viewed as the cause of sickness (A. Oepke, *TDNT*, vol. 3, p. 201, nn. 24-25; A. Richardson, *The Miracle-Stories of the Gospels* [London, England: SCM Press, 1942], pp. 65f.), an assumption at least partly based on the Old Testament's view of sin and sickness (cf. Ps. 103:3 and compare Exod. 15:26; Deut. 7:12-16; 28:15,21,22; Ps. 32:3,4; 38:3,5). Jesus seems to have affirmed such a view in cases such as that of the paralytic in Mark 2:1-12.

14. We could add to this list the deaths of Ananias and Sapphira in Acts 5, in which lying to the Holy Spirit is the cause of their deaths, but as their deaths are not attributed to a disease—they just die—we cannot say for sure that a sickness was involved.

15. It is easy to understand how the sins of parents could lead to illness in a person, for not only is this stated in the Old Testament (Exod. 20:15; Deut 5:9), but we also see it frequently in such diseases as fetal alcohol syndrome. How one's own sins could cause a person to be born blind is less clear. While some parts of prefirst-century Judaism did believe in the preexistence of the soul before conception (see Wisd. Sol. 8:19,20), later rabbinic Judaism spoke of the possibility of sin in the womb (see Gen. Rab. 63 [39c]). See further on this the standard commentaries on John 9:1-3. Although we cannot tell whether the rabbinic

attitude was common in Judaism in Jesus' time, it would certainly explain the comments of the Twelve.

16. The Greek *kan* plus the subjunctive $\bar{e}$ followed by a future tense in the next clause expresses the "if" and shows that this is a conditional sentence in which there is a real possibility but not a certainty that this is the case.

17. In itself, this does not necessarily indicate the primary motive. One could ask whether Judas had another reason to betray Jesus (e.g., disappointment with Jesus' messianic program) and, knowing that the Jewish leaders would pay well for his assistance, chose to get money for what he might have done anyway or whether money was the primary motive.

18. The story of Judas Iscariot, unfortunately, does not settle the issue of whether a Christian may be demonized. The question itself is of relatively recent origin, dating from the end of the last century. For its first 1,800 years the Church simply did not raise the question, but did tell stories about Christians who had been demonized. See, for example, the *Dialogues of Gregory the Great* (Gregory the Great, *Dialogues*, trans. Odo John Zimmerman, New York: Fathers of the Church, 1959). Those who raise the question usually do so on the basis of the idea that demons "possess" a person and could not do so if the Holy Spirit indwelt the person; that is, they do it on the basis of a deductive process rather than on the basis of a scriptural text. The problem is that the Greek term *daimonizomai* simply indicates that a person is in some way influenced by a demon (cf. Foerster, "*daimonizomai*," *TDNT*, vol. 2, pp. 19-20, who translates the term "to suffer from a *daimōn*."). The idea of "possession" is a development of theology in the post-Nicene and later era.

Can the Holy Spirit indwell a person who is also influenced by a demon? Why not? The Holy Spirit certainly indwells people who sin, who are assaulted by temptation, and who fall quite seriously. Still, in seeking biblical substantiation one must ask whether Judas was in fact a believer. Certainly there is no reason to believe he was any less successful than the others in doing the works Jesus sent the disciples out to do, nor do we find any evidence that the other disciples had any suspicions about his character. It is likely that at least initially he believed all that the other disciples believed. At the same time, since the whole of Jesus' ministry was pre-Pentecost, one could argue that none of these people were believers in the modern sense in that they were not necessarily indwelt by the Holy Spirit. Judas was certainly demonized in the end, but the issue of whether or not he was a believer rests on one's definition of what it means to be a believer.

19. The "your" is singular (*tēn kardian sou*), which suggests that only Ananias was directly inspired by Satan, while Sapphira had agreed with Ananias and in that sense had been tempted by him.

20. Demonization is suggested by the language used in the passage; for example, *plē roō* "fill," used in this passage of Satan filling Ananias's heart is the same word used in Ephesians 5:18 of the believer's being filled with the Holy Spirit (see BAGD, pp. 670-671, "*plēroō*" [1a] and [1b]).

21. The alternative would be to believe that Satan totally overwhelmed a pure, upright man. This did happen in the case of Eve, but seems less likely in this

situation, especially since Ananias is presumably filled with the Holy Spirit as the other members of the Church were.

22. For more information on these passages see Gordon D. Fee, 1 Corinthians (NICNT, ed., F. F. Bruce; Grand Rapids, MI: Wm. B. Eerdmans, 1987) or Gordon D. Fee, 1 and 2 Timothy, Titus (NIBC, ed., W. Ward Gasque; Peabody, MA: Hendrickson Publishers, 1988). While the commentary literature takes seriously the idea that "the destruction of the flesh" indicates physical suffering (like Job's?), most writers on church discipline look at it as the destruction of the sinful nature through being in the sphere of Satan (e.g., John White and Ken Blue, Healing the Wounded [Downers Grove, IL: InterVarsity Press, 1985] pp. 104-106; Marlin Jeschke, Discipling in the Church [Scottdale, PA: Herald Press, 1988] pp. 80-83). Either way, results happen due to the influence of Satan, results that it is hoped will lead to repentance and salvation. These results are, then, some form of demonization.

23. David's son by Bathsheba does die (2 Sam. 12:14), so there is some bitter fruit of the sin. There is also the rebellion of Absalom (2 Sam. 12:11,12). Yet, when one realizes that the penalty for either of David's sins was death, there is a real sense in which God does remit the fruit of sin. David himself lives to a ripe old age and sees his son Solomon (by Bathsheba) on the throne. The declaration of forgiveness has more than a spiritual effect.

24. Mark knows of the healing of natural disasters as well in that he reports the stilling of the storm (Mark 4:35-41) and the feeding of the 5,000 (Mark 6:30-44). Although these incidents do reverse what could be said to be the general fruit of sin (i.e., in Eden there was no lack of food nor any indication that there would be natural disasters), there is no specific tracing of these events to sin, although it is possible that Mark sees the demonic behind the storm in that Jesus speaks to the elements using the same words He uses elsewhere to rebuke demons (cf. Mark 4:39 and Mark 1:25). At the same time, the speaking could also be a prophetic declaration without indicating that a personal evil force was involved.

25. This is probably also the situation in Mark 5:21-24,35-43, although in this case one could argue that it was simply a misdiagnosis given Jesus' statement, "The child is not dead but asleep." But Luke makes it clear that she was dead by stating, "Her spirit returned." Matthew also sees it as the raising of the dead in that the "ruler" says, "My daughter has just died" (Matt 9:18).

26. On the symmetry, see Roger Stronstad, The Charismatic Theology of St. Luke (Peabody, MA: Hendrickson, 1984) pp. 33-35, especially the chart on page 34.

27. In our view, the structure of the fourth Gospel is that of a Prologue (ch. 1), the Book of Signs (chaps. 2-12, containing six signs), the Book of Glory (chaps. 13-20, which are divided between the Farewell Discourses and the Passion Narrative) and an Epilogue (chap. 21). Thus, the resurrection of Lazarus at least forms the culmination of the Book of Signs and, if the latter work once existed independently of the rest of the Gospel, it may have formed the conclusion of the book, chapter 12 rounding off the narrative.

28. That the meaning of Judas's surname in Mark is correctly interpreted by Luke

(Luke 6:15; Acts 1:13) as "the Zealot" and that this probably refers to his activity as an extreme nationalist of the type who were called Zealots in the period before the Jewish War of A.D. 66-70 is argued by R. A. Guelich, *Mark 1-8:26* (WBC 34A, Dallas, TX: WORD, Inc., 1989) p. 163; and C. E. B. Cranfield, *The Gospel according to St. Mark* (CGTC; Cambridge, England: Cambridge University Press, 1959) p. 132.

29. Compare the remarks of C. H. Powell, *The Biblical Concept of Power* (London, England: Epworth Press, 1963), pp. 182ff.

30. The classic article on this topic is that of R. Bultmann, *"pisteuō ktl.,"* TDNT, vol. 6, pp. 174-228.

31. For further information on these verses see P. H. Davids, *The Epistle of James* (NIGTC; Grand Rapids, MI: Wm. B. Eerdmans, 1982) on the respective passages, as well as the section on prayer in the introduction.

32. For *erga* denoting "miraculous works" when referring to Jesus and God in the Gospel of John: BAGD, p. 308; G. Bertram, *"ergon,"* TDNT, vol. 2, p. 642; K. H. Rengstorf, *"sēmeion,"* TDNT, vol. 7, pp. 247-248.

33. For miraculous signs functioning to evoke and encourage faith, see John 2:11,23; 7:31; 9:16,35,36,38 [cf. 9:30-32]; 10:37,38; 11:45,47,48; 12:10,11; 14:11; 20:30,31 (cf. Matt. 11:21; Mark 2:10); van der Loos, *The Miracles of Jesus*, p. 245, 265; H. Hendrickx, *The Miracle Stories of the Synoptic Gospels* (San Francisco, CA: HarperSanFrancisco, 1987), p. 17.

34. In using "already—not yet" language we are indicating our dependence on the perspective on New Testament theology pioneered by Oscar Cullmann, *Christ and Time* (London, England: SCM Press, 1951), and developed by George Eldon Ladd, first in *Jesus and the Kingdom* (revised as *The Presence of the Future*) but most fully in *A Theology of the New Testament* (Grand Rapids, MI: Wm. B. Eerdmans, 1974). These works should be consulted for a fuller treatment.

35. We need to underline the "all areas," for results in all areas of ministry are partial. Just as we do not see all people we pray for healed, so we do not see all we preach to converted. Just as we do not see all the dead raised, so we do not yet see the twistedness in human nature, our fallenness, eradicated (cf. Rom. 7 and 1 John 1:6-9). This is important to realize, for some people see the spiritual results of the work of Christ as complete in the present, while the physical results they see as mostly incomplete. As a concordance study would show, salvation in all its aspects has three tenses—those of having been saved, being saved and going to be saved—and these three tenses apply to the spiritual results as much as to the physical results in the New Testament.

36. The tragedy is when the Church allows the fact that we do not yet see all of the effects of sin reversed so to dampen its faith, that it experiences almost none of the effects of sin being reversed (often limiting the ones it has faith for to the invisible, spiritual arena). Whenever this happens, the Church has become like the people of Nazareth among whom Jesus could not do any mighty works (Mark 6:5,6), although the reason for the modern lack of faith may be different from that found in the first-century town.

THE PURPOSE OF SIGNS AND WONDERS IN THE NEW TESTAMENT:

WHAT TERMS FOR MIRACULOUS POWER DENOTE AND THEIR RELATIONSHIP TO THE GOSPEL

GARY S. GREIG

The year is 1906. A young 16-year-old girl named Henrietta Mears, living in Minneapolis, Minnesota, has just had a painful accident. She somehow "jabbed a hat pin into the pupil of an eye. Her doctors could do nothing for the condition and predicted possible blindness for her."[1] Henrietta's family, which attends the First Baptist Church of Minneapolis, asks a close friend named Mr. Ingersoll, an elder in a local Presbyterian church, to come pray for Henrietta's eye in accordance with James 5:14-16. In response to their prayers, God graciously heals Henrietta's vision:

> Henrietta had no doubt that the God who had made her could
> also heal her eye. Specialists who later examined the eye agreed

there was indeed a hole in the pupil and shook their heads in amazement that she could see anything out of it. That she was, in fact, seeing could not be explained except that God had stretched forth His hand and healed her eye—even though the hole remained. Henrietta learned from this experience and from her mother to accept all Scripture at face value. For God to touch her body simply meant taking Him at His word.[2]

Henrietta Mears went on to be greatly used by God as director of Christian Education and college teacher at Hollywood Presbyterian Church, Hollywood, California. She founded Gospel Light Publications and Forest Home Christian Conference Center in the San Bernadino mountains of Southern California. She influenced the ministries and lives of such great evangelical leaders as Bill Bright, who founded Campus Crusade for Christ, and Billy Graham, who called her "one of the greatest Christians I have ever known."[3] Toward the end of her life, Henrietta sought all the gifts of the Spirit for her life and Christian work. "I have enjoyed spiritual gifts,...I have had the Spirit's presence. But now I want everything that He has for me. I want all the gifts."[4]

Can cases of healing through prayer in Christ's name like that of Henrietta Mears be called a "sign" or a "wonder" in the biblical sense? On many occasions my wife, Catherine, and I (and many in our church, a Presbyterian church) have seen God touch and restore people in similar ways through prayer. My wife and I share the following personal accounts, because we wish to avoid the questions of exaggeration and distortion, which third person accounts inevitably pose. We personally witnessed what is recounted in the following paragraphs. We do not wish to suggest that our faith is focused on spiritual gifts and healing. Our focus is on Christ and the work of His cross. We understand the gifts, as 1 Peter 4:10,11 suggests, simply as some of *His tools* available to all believers[5] to do *His work* of evangelism, discipleship, service, and encouragement so that "God may be praised through Jesus Christ" (1 Pet. 4:11).

In the spring of 1991, when our son, Jonathan, was four years old, he underwent two painful and traumatic surgeries to correct a congenital birth defect. That summer the condition had not healed as expected and the specialist who had performed the first two surgeries predicted my son would need a third surgery in the early fall. After persistent prayer by my wife and me and the elders of our church, God touched and healed our son of the condition. The specialist told us that Jonathan's condition had reversed itself and that this was "highly unusual" in cases like my son's. My son never had a third surgery and continues to this day without any further need of medical attention for his former condition.

On many occasions, my wife and I have also seen God give supernatural insight in prayer to accomplish His purposes. In late February 1992, my wife was praying with a woman named Carolyn at a monthly church meeting. Carolyn did not know my wife or me well. At the time, she knew nothing of our personal lives nor that we had a four-year-old son and a one-and-a-half-year-old daughter. Carolyn also did not know that my wife was concerned that she was not spending enough quality time with our son, who at that time had a language-processing deficiency. My wife did not know that Carolyn had been unemployed for six months and had finally gotten a job that very day.

Neither my wife nor Carolyn shared these personal details with each other before they prayed together. As they prayed and asked the Lord to guide their time of prayer, Carolyn saw a picture of a backyard with two children, a boy and a girl, playing on a swing set and in a wooden-sided sandbox (the only two play items which were in our backyard at that time). Carolyn sensed God saying, "Everything is alright with the children because I am watching over them." At the same time, my wife saw a picture of the beach and the ocean, which she did not understand. It just so happened that Carolyn had the job interview that day at a Ventura beach. Carolyn then shared that God had provided her with a job that day "at the beach." My wife and Carolyn thanked the Lord for this encouraging witness of His provision and protection in both their lives (Matt. 6:8; Phil. 4:5-7).

In late September 1992, I took a cab from the Los Angeles International Airport to nearby Santa Monica and was praying for the cab driver, a middle-aged man, and for an opportunity to share Christ with him. Three thoughts flashed through my mind as I prayed: he was Russian, he was Jewish, and he had a daughter whom he dearly loved (I saw a picture in my mind of a young five-year-old girl with him). The first fact I could have inferred from his name, Boris. The last two facts I could not have known naturally (his last name was not typically Jewish but Russian). I shared these insights with him and found out they were all true—he was Jewish and had only one child, a daughter about five years old, whom he loved very much.

Then I told the cab driver about Jesus, who revealed those insights, who knew every detail of his life, and who, as Israel's Messiah, loved him enough to die for his sins. Though he did not receive Christ as Savior at that moment, he was grateful for what I said and for my prayer for him and his family. And I was grateful that the Lord demonstrated His presence and His love for this man in a way I could not have done by myself.

Can "ordinary" healing, words of knowledge[6] (insights from God), or spiritual gifts of these types be called "signs and wonders" in the sense the New Testament uses the phrase? What do signs and wonders refer to in the New Testament and what are their function and purpose? Are ongoing signs and wonders to be expected in evangelism and ministry in the Church today? Some evangelicals say no, claiming to argue from biblical and linguistic grounds.

The following study will focus on "signs, wonders, and miracles" attributed to God in the New Testament and will not consider in detail counterfeit signs and wonders worked by Satan in the last days that are mentioned in Matthew 24:24; Mark 13:22; 2 Thessalonians 2:9; Revelation 13:13; 16:14; 19:20. (For discussion of counterfeit miracles, see Wayne Grudem's chapter [2] in this book, objection number 23, *How do we know that spiritual gifts today aren't just demonic counterfeits designed to lead people astray?*) The fact that there will be "*counterfeit* miracles, signs, and wonders" (2 Thess. 2:9) worked by Satan in the last days suggests that there will also be *genuine* miracles, signs, and wonders worked by God (cf. Rev. 11:3-13).

I. "SIGNS, WONDERS, AND MIRACLES" DENOTE HEALING, DELIVERANCE, AND SPIRITUAL GIFTS IN THE NEW TESTAMENT

A recent study of signs and wonders by D. A. Carson claims that New Testament signs and wonders have little to do with healing and spiritual gifts. But the analysis he offers fails to account for all the relevant evidence in the New Testament. Carson claims in his essay that "in Wimber's predominant usage, signs and wonders include exorcism, healing the sick, and words of knowledge."[7] He also claims that "at the purely *linguistic* [italics his] level, 'signs and wonders' cannot easily be made to align with the kinds of phenomena that interest Wimber"[8] and that it is "against New Testament usage" to "apply the expression 'signs and wonders' to all Christian expressions of the more spectacular *charismata*, or of miracles generally."[9]

However, these statements entirely contradict the linguistic evidence related to the phrase "signs and wonders" (*sēmeia kai terata*) in the New Testament, which largely denotes precisely miraculous healing of the sick, deliverance from demons, and the gifts of the Spirit, including word of knowledge and healing. Long ago in a linguistic study of the evidence, S. V. McCasland noted that the phrase "signs and wonders" in the New Testament largely denotes "ordinary deeds of healing performed by faith" rather than "grandiose phenomena" as it denotes in the Septuagint, the Greek translation of the Old Testament.[10]

The vocabularies of all natural languages are grouped in various semantic fields or lexical fields—groups of words having the same or related meanings and denoting the same or related entities in the outside world.[11] Most languages have lexical fields for color (red, black, yellow, etc.), furniture (bed, chair, lamp, etc.), animals (cat, dog, cow, bull, etc.), and so on.

It is clear from the evidence listed in the paragraphs below that in the New Testament the phrase "signs and wonders" (sēmeia kai terata) is synonymous with other Greek words such as dunamis "miracle" (plural dunameis "miracles") and ergon denoting "miraculous work" in the Gospel of John. In a monograph dealing with the linguistic evidence, R. C. Trench pointed out a century ago that the words "sign" (sēmeion), "wonder" (teras), and "miracle" (dunamis), all belong to a group of Greek words that are "all used to characterize the supernatural works wrought by Christ in the days of his flesh."[12]

Some evangelicals claim for theological reasons, "There is a danger...of equating 'power' with 'miracles'" in various New Testament passages.[13] But such statements simply do not explain well the lexical evidence of Greek dunamis and the concept of God's "power" in the New Testament. The Greek word dunamis denotes both "power" and "miracle, deed of power" in the New Testament.[14] The fact that "power" and "miracle" are related senses of the same word shows the obviously close relationship between the concept of God's "power" and the concept of "miracles" in the New Testament, as several scholars have noted.[15]

"Miracles, works of power (dunameis)" are manifestations of God's power, as Dr. Alan Richardson pointed out half a century ago.[16] Dr. Karl Gatzweiler adds, "While the plural dunameis throughout denotes miracles, the singular dunamis can, on the other hand, mean likewise the power which produces miracles...as well as the power and the Spirit which the miracles reveal."[17]

Together with these words the phrase "signs and wonders" comprises the lexical field of "Power" in New Testament Greek.[18] This lexical field is comprised of dunamis "power" and its synonyms, which include the phrase "signs and wonders (sēmeia kai terata)." Herman Hendrickx cites the following words, which belong to this word group: "power, miracle (dunamis)," "acts of power, miracles (dunameis)," "signs and wonders (sēmeia kai terata)," erga denoting "miraculous works," "wonders (thaumata, thaumasia)," "wonderful thing (paradoxon)."[19] Richardson adds "power in exercise, energy[20] (energeia)," "force, violent power (bia)," "strength, especially physical (ischus)," "might, manifested power (kratos)," and "authority, liberty of action (exousia)."[21]

Within this lexical field, the words and phrases "signs and wonders (sēmeia *kai terata*)," "signs (*sēmeia*)," "miracles (*dunameis*)," and "miraculous works (*erga*)" all denote healing and deliverance from demons[22] (otherwise denoted by *therapeuō* "cure, heal,"*iaomai* "heal," and *sōzō* "save, heal").[23] The phrase "signs and wonders" and the words "sign" and "miracle" are also often associated with and may denote the gifts of the Holy Spirit—including, of course, the gift of "word of knowledge."

The following passages show that "signs, wonders, and miracles" denote healing, deliverance from demons, and spiritual gifts in the New Testament:

IA. "SIGNS"[24] AND "SIGNS AND WONDERS" DENOTE HEALING AND DELIVERANCE

> **Acts 14:3**—Paul and Barnabas preach and work "signs and wonders": "So Paul and Barnabas spent considerable time there, speaking boldly for the Lord, who confirmed the message of his grace by enabling them to do miraculous *signs and wonders [sēmeia kai terata]*." This description of ministry in Iconium parallels the description of Paul preaching and healing in Lystra a few verses later, **Acts 14:8-10:** "In Lystra there sat a man crippled in his feet, who was lame from birth and had never walked. He listened to Paul as he was speaking. Paul looked directly at him, saw that he had faith to be *healed* and called out, 'Stand up on your feet!' At that, the man jumped up and began to walk."

> **Acts 8:6,7,13**—Philip preached and worked "signs and miracles" of healing and deliverance from demons: "When the crowds heard Philip and saw the miraculous *signs [sēmeia]* he did, they all paid close attention to what he said. With shrieks, *evil spirits came out* of many, and many *paralytics and cripples were healed [therapeuō]* ....Simon himself believed and was baptized. And he followed Philip everywhere, astonished by the great *signs and miracles [sē meia kai dunameis]* he saw."

> **Acts 5:12,15,16**—The apostles work "signs and wonders" of healing and deliverance: "The apostles performed many miraculous *signs and wonders [sēmeia kai terata]* among the people....People brought the sick into the streets and laid them on beds and mats so that at least Peter's shadow might fall on some of them as he

passed by. Crowds gathered also from the towns around Jerusalem, bringing their sick and those tormented by evil spirits, and all of them were healed [therapeuō]."

Acts 4:16,22—The healing of the crippled beggar by the Beautiful gate of the Temple (Acts 3:1-8)—"he was healed [sōzō]" (Acts 4:9); "the man who had been healed [therapeuō]" (Acts 4:14)—the healing is called an "obvious sign [gnōston sēmeion]" (Acts 4:16) and "this sign of healing [to sēmeion touto tēs iaseōs]" (Acts 4:22).

John 12:17,18—The raising of Lazarus from the dead is called a "sign [sēmeion]" (John 12:18).

John 9:16—The healing of the blind man (John 9:6,7) is called one of "such miraculous signs [toiauta sēmeia]" (John 9:16).

John 6:2—Speaking of Jesus, this verse mentions "the miraculous signs (ta sēmeia) he had performed on the sick [asthenountōn]," obviously referring to healing of the sick.

John 4:48,54—"Signs and wonders [sēmeia kai terata]" (4:48) and the "sign [sēmeion]" of 4:54 refer to the healing of the royal official's son who had a fever (4:50-52).

Mark 16:17,20[25]—"And these signs [sēmeia] will accompany those who believe....Then the disciples went out and preached everywhere, and the Lord worked with them and confirmed his word by the signs [sēmeiōn] that accompanied it." The "signs" that the Lord worked to confirm the preaching of His word included the gift of "speak[ing] in new tongues" (16:17), deliverance ("they will drive out demons," 16:17), and healing ("they will place their hands on sick people, and they will get well" 16:18).

Ib. "Signs" and "Signs and Wonders" Are Related to and Can Denote the Gifts of the Spirit

Hebrews 2:3,4—"This salvation, which was first announced by the Lord, was confirmed to us by those who heard him. God also testified to it by *signs, wonders [sēmeiois te kai terasin]* and various *miracles [dunamesin]*, and *gifts* of the Holy Spirit distributed *[pneumatos hagiou merismoi]* according to his will." *"Signs and wonders"* in this passage are explicitly related to "miracles" and *"gifts*[26] (or 'distributions') of the Holy Spirit."

1 Corinthians 14:22—*"Tongues*, then, are a *sign [sēmeion]*, not for believers but for unbelievers; *prophecy*, however, is for believers, not for unbelievers."[27]

Mark 16:17,20[28]—"And these *signs [sēmeia]* will accompany those who believe....Then the disciples went out and preached everywhere, and the Lord worked with them and confirmed his word by the *signs [sēmeion]* that accompanied it." The "signs" that the Lord worked to confirm the preaching of His Word included the *gift of "speak[ing] in new tongues"* (16:17) and the *gift of healing* ("they will place their hands on sick people, and they will get well" 16:18).

IC. "MIRACLES" DENOTE HEALING AND DELIVERANCE

Acts 19:11,12—"God did extraordinary *miracles [dunameis]* through Paul, so that even handkerchiefs and aprons that had touched him were taken to the sick, and their *illnesses were cured* and the *evil spirits left them.*"

Acts 8:6,7,13—(quoted above) Philip preached and worked "signs and miracles" of healing and deliverance from demons: "When the crowds heard Philip and saw the miraculous *signs [sē meia]* he did, they all paid close attention to what he said. With shrieks, *evil spirits came out* of many, and many *paralytics and cripples were healed [therapeuō]*....Simon himself believed and was baptized. And he followed Philip everywhere, astonished by the great *signs and miracles [sēmeia kai dunameis]* he saw."

ID. "SIGNS" AND "SIGNS AND WONDERS" ARE SYNONYMOUS WITH "MIRACLES"

Though the word "sign" (*sēmeion*) does not always denote miraculous events (e.g.,

Matt. 26:48; Luke 2:12; Rom. 4:11; 2 Thess. 3:17),[29] the majority of occurrences in the New Testament denote miraculous events of one sort or another.[30]

Hebrews 2:3,4—*"Signs and wonders"* are explicitly related to *"miracles"* and "gifts (or 'distributions') of the Holy Spirit." "This salvation, which was first announced by the Lord, was confirmed to us by those who heard him. God also testified to it by *signs, wonders [sēmeiois te kai terasin]* and various miracles *[dunamesin]* and gifts of the Holy Spirit distributed *[pneumatos hagiou merismois]* according to his will."

2 Corinthians 12:12—"The things that mark an apostle—*signs, wonders* and *miracles [sēmeiois te kai terasin kai dunamesin]*—were done among you with great perseverance."

Acts 8:6,7,13—Philip preached and worked "signs and miracles" of healing and deliverance from demons: "When the crowds heard Philip and saw the miraculous *signs [sēmeia]* he did, they all paid close attention to what he said. With shrieks, *evil spirits came out* of many, and many *paralytics and cripples were healed [therapeuō]* ....Simon himself believed and was baptized. And he followed Philip everywhere, astonished by the great *signs and miracles [sē meia kai dunameis]* he saw."

Acts 2:22—"Jesus of Nazareth was a man accredited by God to you by *miracles, wonders* and *signs,* which God did among you through him."

Ie. "Signs, Wonders, and Miracles" of Healing and Deliverance Are Worked Through the Power of the Holy Spirit (cf. 1 Cor. 2:4,5; 12:9-11; 2 Cor. 12:12)

Galatians 3:5—"Does God give you his *Spirit* and work *miracles [dunameis]* among you because you observe the law, or because you believe what you heard?"

Romans 15:18,19—"I will not venture to speak of anything except what Christ has accomplished through me in leading the Gentiles to obey God by what I have said and done—by the *power* *of signs and wonders [en dunamei sēmeiōn kai teratōn]*, through the *power of the Spirit [en dunamei pneumatos]*. So from Jerusalem all the way around to Illyricum, I have fully proclaimed *[peplērōkenai]* the gospel of Christ."

II. "SIGNS, WONDERS, AND MIRACLES" ARE NOT RESTRICTED TO THE APOSTLES

The claim is also made that "signs and wonders" only relate to the apostles in the New Testament:

> I turn now to the postresurrection period. Once again it proves helpful to begin at the purely linguistic level. It is rather startling to observe that "signs and wonders" (or some minor variation) as a *linguistic category* [italics his] is almost exclusively restricted to the apostles.[31]

These statements seem to show a lack of familiarity with the lexical evidence related to "signs and wonders" in the New Testament. Words and phrases whose semantic properties are being defined do not belong to "linguistic categories" but to "lexical fields" or "semantic fields."[32] The phrase "signs and wonders" in the New Testament does not comprise a "linguistic category" but, as was pointed out above, belongs to a "lexical field," or group of words with the same or related meanings, denoting manifestations of God's power.

Furthermore, the words "signs" and "signs and wonders" and the miracles of healing and deliverance that they denote are not "almost entirely restricted to the apostles." Stephen, Philip, and Ananias were not apostles but laymen:

> **Acts 6:8**—"Now *Stephen*, a man full of God's grace and power, did great *wonders* and miraculous *signs* among the people."

> **Acts 8:5-7,13**—"*Philip* went down to a city of Samaria and proclaimed the Christ there. When the crowds heard Philip and saw the miraculous *signs* he did, they all paid close attention to what he said. With shrieks *evil spirits came out of many* and *many paralytics and cripples were healed*....Simon himself

believed and was baptized. And he followed Philip everywhere, astonished by the great *signs* and *miracles [sēmeia kai dunameis]* he saw."

Acts 9:11,12—"A man...named Saul...is praying. In a vision he has seen a man named *Ananias* come and *place his hands on him to restore his sight.*" **Acts 22:12,13**—"A man named *Ananias*...stood beside me and said, 'Brother Saul, *receive your sight!*' And *at that very moment I was able to see him.*"

Professor G. W. H. Lampe of Cambridge says the following of Stephen, Phillip, and Ananias:[33]

> Stephen's own preaching was accompanied, like that of the apostles, by signs and wonders done publicly (6. 8)....So, too, with Philip at Samaria: the word is associated with works, exorcisms, and the healing of the paralysed and the lame, which recall the acts of Jesus as prophesied in Isaiah 35 [Isa. 35:5-6] and which are described as 'signs' [Acts 8:6, 13]....In the story of the conversion of Saul,...the enemy of the gospel is struck down and blinded by the power of God....He is restored to sight...by Ananias, who, in fulfilling this commission, is acting as the direct agent of Jesus.[34]

"Signs and wonders" are not in any way restricted to the apostles and their immediate associates, because what "signs and wonders" denote—healing, deliverance from demons, and spiritual gifts—were practiced by all believers throughout the Early Church according to the New Testament. Who among the Corinthians (1 Cor. 12-14) with gifts of healing, miraculous powers, tongues, or prophecy—all "signs" according to Mark 16:17,18 and 1 Cor. 14:22 (see above)[35]—was an apostle? Who among the Galatians, among whom God worked miracles (Gal. 3:5), was an apostle? Who among the Ephesians and Thessalonians with gifts of prophetic revelation (Eph. 4:11; 1 Thess. 5:20) was an apostle? Which of Philip's daughters who regularly prophesied in the church of Caesarea (Acts 21:9) was an apostle? How many among the churches in Asia Minor, which 1 Peter 4:10 suggests were fully conversant with all the gifts of the Spirit, were apostles?

Hebrews 6:1-5 includes "the laying on of hands" among the "elementary teachings" of the churches addressed by that letter:

Hebrews 6:1-5—"Therefore let us leave the *elementary teachings* about Christ and go on to maturity, not laying again the *foundation* of repentance from acts that lead to death, and of faith in God, instruction about baptisms, the *laying on of hands*, the resurrection of the dead, and eternal judgment. And God permitting, we will do so. It is impossible for those who have once been enlightened, who have tasted the heavenly gift, who have shared in the Holy Spirit, who have tasted the goodness of the word of God and the *powers [dunameis* lit., "miracles"[36]] *of the coming age....*"

Besides bestowing the Spirit and spiritual gifts,[37] the "laying on of hands," mentioned in the list of elementary teachings, is one of the principle means of prayer for healing in the New Testament (Matt. 9:29; Mark 1:41; 5:23; 6:5; 7:32; 16:18; Luke 4:40; 13:13; Acts 9:17; 28:8; Jas. 5:14, "let them pray over [*epi*] him").[38] It follows that prayer for healing and prayer to convey the power and gifts of the Spirit were included in the "elementary teachings" of the Early Church. Did such "elementary teachings" and experiencing the "powers of the coming age" apply to apostles and their associates only?

Are all the elders apostles through whose prayers James 5:14,15 affirms the Lord will "make the sick person well"? Are the members of the congregations addressed by James 5:16 all apostles: "Therefore confess your sins to each other and pray for each other so that you may be healed"?

Romans 12:6-8, 1 Corinthians 12-14, Galatians 3:5, Ephesians 4:11, 1 Thessalonians 5:20, James 5:14-16, 1 Peter 4:10, and other passages throughout the New Testament suggest that the congregations of the Early Church continued to experience the gifts of the Spirit, miracles, and signs and wonders, quite apart from the apostles. Why should it be any different for churches today?

It is also suggested that the apostles are not examples to Christians in certain areas, presumably in healing ministry and spiritual gifts:

> Thus the apostles and other New Testament writers must be viewed as something more than proto-Christians, models of what all other Christians should enjoy and experience.[39]

But what more should the apostles be viewed as? Where does Scripture teach that the Lord Jesus and the apostles should not be viewed as models for all Christians in *every aspect,* including healing ministry and gift-based ministry? Scripture seems to teach just the opposite:

1 Corinthians 11:1—"Follow my example, as I follow the example of Christ," Paul tells the Corinthians.

Philippians 4:9—"Whatever you have learned or *received* or heard from me, or *seen in me*—put it into practice."

1 Thessalonians 1:5,6—"Our gospel came to you not simply with words, but also with power, with the Holy Spirit and with deep conviction. You know how we lived among you for your sake. *You became imitators of us and of the Lord;* in spite of severe suffering, you welcomed the message with the joy given by the Holy Spirit."

Philippians 4:9 seems rather all-inclusive. Paul does not say, "Whatever you have learned or...seen in me except for signs and wonders, healing and spiritual gifts."[40]

The New Testament evidence shows, then, that Christians throughout the early churches also imitated the way the apostles exercised spiritual gifts, proclaimed the gospel, and preached the Word with healing and gift-based ministry: Acts 6:8; 8:5-7,13; 9:11,12 (22:12,13); 19:5,6; 21:9; Romans 12:6ff.; 1 Corinthians 12:8-10,28 and 14:1,5,13-15,18f.; Galatians 3:5; Ephesians 4:7-11; 1 Thessalonians 5:20; James 5:14-16; and 1 Peter 4:10.

III. SIGNS, WONDERS, AND MIRACLES ARE INTENDED TO ENCOURAGE BELIEF AND DEEPEN FAITH IN CHRIST

It is true that "signs do not in themselves create faith in the hearts of observers and can even harden hearts,"[41] as in the case of the Pharisees. F. F. Bruce noted this as well:

What about the signs he [Jesus] actually performed? Why were they not sufficient to convince his questioners?...If the restoration of bodily and mental health could be dismissed as a work of Satan, no number of healing acts would have established the divine authority by which they were performed....While the healing miracles did serve as signs of the kingdom of God to those who had eyes to see, they did not compel belief in those who were prejudiced in the opposite direction.[42]

But Scripture also shows that one function of signs, wonders, and miracles in the ministry of Jesus and the Early Church was to awaken and encourage faith in the gospel being preached. Why else would the Early Church have prayed prayers like the following, asking God for signs and wonders of healing to accompany its evangelism?

Acts 4:29,30—"Now, Lord, consider their threats and enable your servants to speak your word with great boldness. *Stretch out your hand to heal and perform miraculous signs and wonders through the name of your holy servant Jesus.*"

God obviously granted such requests in the Early Church (e.g., Acts 5:12-16; 6:8; 8:4-8,12,13,26-39; 9:17,18,32-42).

Jesus more than once challenged His listeners to believe His word on the basis of His miraculous works:

John 10:37,38—"Do not believe me unless I do the miraculous works *[ta erga*[43]*]* of my Father. But if I do them, even though you do not believe me, *believe the miraculous works [tois ergois],* that you may know and understand that the Father is in me, and I in the Father."

John 14:11—"Believe me when I say that I am in the Father and the Father is in me; or at least *believe on the evidence of the miraculous works themselves [dia ta erga auta].*"

Mark 2:10—"'But *that you may know* that the Son of Man has authority on earth to forgive sins....' *He said to the paralytic, 'I tell you, get up, take your mat and go home.'*"

In his Gospel, John calls all of Jesus' works of miraculous healing "signs" ($\bar{se}$ *meia*; John 4:54; 6:2; 9:16: 12:17,18)—e.g., John 6:2, "They saw the miraculous signs he had performed on the sick."[44] The miraculous healings of Jesus are also called "works" (*erga*) in John's Gospel.[45] Jesus provided abundant "signs" of miraculous healing to those who were open and seeking God, as every one of the Gospel accounts show. John then said of the signs, "These are written *that you may believe* that Jesus is the Christ, the Son of God" (John 20:31).

In His condemnation of Korazin and Bethsaida's lack of repentance and faith, Jesus indicates that His miraculous works were intended to produce repentance and faith in Him (Matt. 11:21 and Luke 10:13):

> Matthew 11:21—"Woe to you, Korazin! Woe to you, Bethsaida! If the miracles that were performed in you had been performed in Tyre and Sidon, they would have repented long ago in sackcloth and ashes."

Paul expected to proclaim the gospel "in the power of signs and wonders, through the power of the Spirit" (Rom. 15:18,19; 1 Cor. 1:6,7; 2:4,5; 2 Cor. 12:12; 1 Thess. 1:5), and he expected God to continue to distribute spiritual gifts and work miracles among the churches to confirm the gospel and build up and encourage the Church (Rom. 12:6-8; 1 Cor. 1:7; 12:1—14:40; Gal. 3:5; Eph. 4:7-13; 1 Thess. 5:19-22; 1 Tim. 4:14; 2 Tim. 1:6,7). Paul says that the gift of prophecy is a sign "for believers" (1 Cor. 14:22).[46] As a sign, it encourages and builds up the Church in its faith (1 Cor. 14:1-5). Through it, God gives supernatural insight into the secrets of people's hearts ("the secrets of his heart will be laid bare," 1 Cor. 14:25),[47] and thus it demonstrates that "God is really among you!" (1 Cor. 14:24,25).

New Testament scholars have pointed to such evidence showing signs, wonders, and miracles worked by God awakening and deepening faith in Christ:

> The Old Testament repeatedly states that the Israelites were moved to believe or were strengthened in their belief by miraculous deeds (Ex. 4:30, 31; 14:31; Nu. 14:11; I Ki. 17:24; 18:39; 2 Ki. 5:15). We encounter the same idea in the New Testament. Jesus reproached those cities "wherein most of his mighty works were done" with not having "repented" (Mat. 11:20-24; cf. Mk. 5:19, 20; 10:52; Lk. 5:8-11; 17:15, 16; 18:43; Mt. 20:34). The Gospel of John in particular stresses the miraculous sign as a means of arousing faith (Jn. 2:11; 4:53; 6:14; 7:31; 9:30-39; 11:15, 42, 45; 12:11, 17-19; 20:30-31). Paul emphasizes the relation between the proclamation of the word and the might of signs and wonders (Rom. 15:18, 19).[48]

Overwhelmed by the deeds of Jesus, many came to believe: Mt. 14:33 (after the stilling of the storm); Jn. 7:31; 11:45, 48 (the fear of the Jewish council that through Jesus' many miracles "all men" will believe in Him!); 12:11. Cf. also 20:30, 31.[49]

...that purpose [of miracles] being forcibly to startle men from the dull dream of sense-bound existence, and, however it may not be itself an appeal to the spiritual man, yet to act as a summons to him that he now open his eyes to the spiritual appeal which is now about to be addrest to him (Acts 14:8-18).[50]

Jesus looks for a faith that allows itself to be carried further by the sign. His opponents did not have this openness. To them the miracles were not signs. They wanted proofs. Therefore, Jesus said, "no sign shall be given to this generation" (Mk. 8:12).[51]

In the close relationship, always emphasized in this text, which exists between God's Word and God's miraculous deed, it must be assumed from the start that also the miraculous deed will have its chief purpose in awakening faith, establishing and strengthening faith.[52]

IIIA. BOTH CHRIST AND HIS POWER

Despite such evidence from the Bible, the claim is made that one's confidence in faith is *either* a matter of trusting in Christ *or* experiencing Christ's miraculous power and work. Armstrong, for example, seems to assume such a dichotomy:

Wimber insists that "power encounters authenticate conversion experiences in a way that mere intellectual assents do not...." This simply will not do. Every Christian is given confidence and a solid foundation, not because of what he or she has experienced, but because of what (or better yet, whom) he or she has believed and trusted.[53]

The problem with such a conclusion is that no Scripture is cited that shows it is an "either/or" rather than a "both/and" situation—that one's faith is strengthened only by what is believed and not by experiencing God's power and working. Who has not seen the faith of a child strengthened when God has answered a prayer? Or whose faith has not been strengthened when in the face of unanswered prayer God demonstrates His presence and love through the comfort, encouragement, and prayer support of a Christian brother or sister?

It is Paul who affirms that faith in Christ is strengthened in a unique way by demonstrations of His Spirit's power. First Corinthians 2:4,5 clearly shows that it is not a question of *either* trust *or* experiencing God's power, but that both work together. Experiencing God's work and power are an illustration of the Truth and person of Christ in whom we have put our trust. Faith, Paul says, is reinforced when, like young Henrietta Mears, we see Christ doing what His Word says He does:

> **1 Corinthians 2:4,5**—"*My message and my preaching* were not with wise and persuasive words, but *with a demonstration of the Spirit's power [en apodeixei pneumatos kai duameōs],* so that your *faith might not rest on men's wisdom, but on God's power.*"

The use of "Spirit and power" in this passage shows that the "demonstration" referred not only to conveying spiritual gifts (explicitly referred to in 1 Cor. 1:6,7),[54] but also to the signs, wonders, and miracles characteristic of Paul's ministry in Corinth (2 Cor. 12:12 *en pase hupomonē* "with great perseverance") and of his ministry in general (Rom. 15:18,19).[55] Dr. Karl Gatzweiler, whose dissertation (Louvain, 1961) examined the Pauline concept of miracles, says the following of 1 Corinthians 2:4,5 and other related passages:

> As examples...we cite I Thess. 1, 5; 2, 13; I Cor. 2, 4-5; 2 Cor. 6, 7; 13, 3; Col. 1, 29; 2 Tim. 1, 8. In all these places Paul speaks of the proclamation of the gospel which was accompanied by divine power, by the power of the Spirit. The gospel is God's power which is displayed among men. For the reader, who already knows that the apostle worked miracles alongside the proclamation of the gospel (cf. 2 Cor. 12, 12; Rom. 15, 18-19), it suggests miraculous events also be understood as self-evident among the notions of "might" and "power" which accompany the proclamation of the gospel.[56]

The remarks of Dr. E. E. Ellis also suggest that 1 Corinthians 2:4,5 cannot be adequately explained apart from other lexically and thematically related Pauline passages such as Romans 15:18,19; 2 Corinthians 12:12; Galatians 3:5, which clearly show that manifestations of the Spirit's power in signs, wonders, miracles, and spiritual gifts are what are referred to in all such passages:

> "The concept of power is linked indissoluably with that of Spirit."...This is most clearly expressed...in Rom. 15:18f.:..."by the

power of signs and wonders, by the *power of the Spirit.*"...

The same distinction is present in I Cor. 2:4f.:..."in demon-stration of *Spirit and power*: that your faith might not rest in the wisdom of men, but in the *power of God.*" In this passage Origen apparently was the first to identify "Spirit" with (Old Testament) prophecy and "power" with miracles. His interpretation is sup-ported by the literary pattern, by Paul's comment in 2 Cor. 12:12 that his ministry to the Corinthians did include miraculous 'pow-ers' [*dunameis* "miracles"] and by the similar contrast of "Spirit" and "power" elsewhere....

The same distinction probably is present in Gal. 3:5: "the one who supplies the *Spirit* to you and works miracles (*dunameis*) among you." In these texts God's *dunamis* ["power"], manifested in the resurrection of Christ, is operative through the exalted Christ in two distinct ways: in the Spirit (inspired perception and speech) and in power (miracles).[57]

Thus, Paul teaches that *both* the object of one's faith—Christ, the mes-sage of the Truth—*and* God demonstrating the truth by His power in our lives strengthen and reinforce our faith.

This same principle mentioned in 1 Corinthians 2:4,5 is also evi-dent in Paul's own conversion. Paul, himself, was not converted by a pre-sentation of rational evidence (although Acts 9:19,20 suggests this came later) but by a demonstration of God's power through the appearance of Christ to him on the road to Damascus (Acts 9:3ff.,20,22). It was this experience of the manifest power of God that obviously forced him to take another look at the gospel and reevaluate his understanding of Scripture, the Messiah, and the life and work of Jesus of Nazareth (Acts 9:20). His faith was in the *content of the gospel,* but it was born out of his conversion experience of the gospel's power in the risen Christ. When Paul was con-verted, he not only read of Christ in the Scriptures and heard of Christ from the community of believers in Damascus (Acts 9:19), he also *saw* the gospel's power in the risen Christ on the road to Damascus and in being healed of his blindness and filled with the Spirit through Ananias's prayer (Acts 9:10-12,17,18; 22:13).

IIIB. FAITH IN THE GOD WHO ACTS

Many times those who were healed by Jesus or who witnessed His healing works expressed their faith in Him in terms of not only what they were taught or told but also in terms of what they *saw God do for them:*

> **Matthew 11:5 (cf. Luke. 7:22)**—John the Baptist and his disciples were to put their faith in Jesus because of what they *saw and heard:* "Go back and report to John *what you hear and see:* The blind receive sight, the lame walk, those who have leprosy are cured, the deaf hear, the dead are raised, and the good news is preached to the poor."

> **Luke 7:16**—When Jesus raised the widow's son from the dead, the people said, "*God has come to help his people.*"

> **Luke 8:39 (cf. Mark 5:19)**—Jesus said to the Gadarene who was delivered from the demons, "Return home and tell how much *God has done for you.*"

> **Acts 4:20**—Peter and John say to the Council, "For we cannot help speaking about *what we have seen and heard.*"

> **Acts 22:15**—Under the Spirit's guidance, Ananias commissions Paul, "You will be his [Christ's] witness to all men of *what you have seen and heard.*"

> **Acts 26:16**—Jesus appearing on the road to Damascus says to Paul, "I have appeared to you to appoint you as a servant and as a witness of *what you have seen of me and what I will show you.*"

These people *saw* the power of the proclaimed gospel and *saw* God's love in Christ manifested by *what God did.*

Karl Barth speaks of the way the Gospels lead "vom Wunder zum Glauben" (from miracle to faith) and "vom Glauben zum Wunder" (from faith to miracle).[58]

In the final analysis, faith in signs and wonders worked by God cannot be confused with faith in Christ and the gospel, as some critics contend. Faith in Christ's power must necessarily be faith in Christ Himself. Jesus Himself says to the Jewish leaders that to "believe the miraculous works" He does inevitably leads to believing in who He is:

> **John 10:37,38**—"Do not believe me unless I do the miraculous

works *[ta erga]* of my Father. But if I do them, even though you do not believe me, *believe the miraculous works [tois ergois], that you may know and understand that the Father is in me, and I in the Father."*

The centurion, who is praised for his "great faith" by Jesus, believed in Jesus' power because he believed in Jesus' divine identity and authority (Matt. 8:5-13). The two cannot be separated as scholars such as van der Loos and Hendrickx have pointed out:

> Faith in miracles is in the last resort not faith in this or that particular miracle, but in the Lord who reveals himself in and through all these particular events.[59]

> The faith that Jesus asks is not only belief in His power—though He does ask that—but above all faith in who He is, in His coming and actions as the God-given Redeemer and Bringer of salvation.[60]

IV. SIGNS, WONDERS, AND MIRACLES ILLUSTRATE GOD'S GRACE IN THE GOSPEL

Certain evangelicals claim that miraculous healing done in Christ's name somehow detracts from focusing on Christ and His work on the cross. Boice, for example, seems to make such an assumption:

> Christ is everything....Therefore, anything that detracts from Him or His work, even so-called miracles done in His name, is misleading and potentially harmful.[61]

> The working of miracles detracts from faith because it focuses attention, not on Christ, but on the miracle worker.[62]

Such statements seem completely unable to explain all the biblical evidence related to the issue. Scripture nowhere shows that the working of miracles in Christ's name detracts from focusing on Christ. Scripture shows quite the opposite. Romans 15:17-20 shows that both preaching and working signs and wonders were to "glory in Christ" (Rom. 15:17) for Paul. Both word and miraculous deed were to "fully proclaim *[pleroo]* the gospel of Christ" and to "preach the gospel where Christ was not known" (Rom. 15:20):

Romans 15:17-20—"Therefore *I glory in Christ Jesus* in my service to God. I will not venture to speak of anything except what Christ has accomplished through me in leading the Gentiles to obey God by what I have *said* and *done*—by the *power of signs and wonders*, through the *power of the Spirit*. So from Jerusalem all the way around to Illyricum, I have *fully proclaimed [peplērōkenai] the gospel of Christ*. It has always been my ambition to *preach the gospel where Christ was not known*, so that I would not be building on someone else's foundation."

Wasn't Christ everything for Peter when he said to Aeneas, "Jesus Christ heals you. Get up and take care of your mat" (Acts 9:34) and then won the inhabitants of Lydda and Sharon to the Lord? Wasn't Christ everything for Philip when he "proclaimed the Christ" in Samaria (Acts 8:5) by healing the lame and demonized along with his preaching (Acts 8:6,7)? Wasn't Christ everything for Paul when he preached the gospel at Lystra (Acts 14:7,9) and said to the man who had been lame from birth, "Stand up on your feet!" (Acts 14:10)? Or wasn't Christ everything for him when in Corinth he did "the signs of an apostle"[63] with great perseverance along "with signs, wonders and miracles" (2 Cor. 12:12) as part of his ministry there of preaching "nothing...except Jesus Christ and him crucified" (1 Cor. 2:2,4)?

IVa. Bearing Witness to the Risen Christ and His Power to Save Sinners

Miracles worked by the Lord through His people do not detract from the gospel or a focus on Christ. Peter's words in the Temple show that ongoing works of miraculous healing in Christ's name *glorify Christ* and *bear witness to His resurrection* (Acts 2:22; 3:13):

Acts 3:12,13,15,16—"When Peter saw this, he said to them: 'Men of Israel, why does this surprise you? *Why do you stare at us as if by our own power or godliness we had made this man walk?* The God of Abraham, Isaac and Jacob, the God of our fathers, *has glorified his servant Jesus*....You killed the author of life, but *God raised him from the dead. We are witnesses of this*. By faith in the name of Jesus, this man whom you see and know was made strong. *It is Jesus' name and the faith that comes through him that has given this complete healing to him*, as you can all see.'"

Discussing this passage, Dr. Cyril Powell points to the function of healing works to bear witness to the resurrection of Jesus:

> Face to face with a man in need, Peter acts as he knows his Lord would have acted in similar circumstances....His work is clearly being continued by His men....In verse 33 [Acts 4:33] it is stated: "And with great power gave the apostles their witness of the resurrection of the Lord Jesus." By the "power of God manifested in mighty works" (F. F. Bruce), the Apostles went on giving this testimony.[64]

The claim is also made by some that healing and gift-based ministry in Christ's name does not reflect the power of the gospel or the power of God that saves sinners. Boice articulates this view as follows:

> The power of God that saves sinners is *not seen* [italics his] in any contemporary miracle, but only in the death of Christ on the cross.[65]

Such an unfortunate statement can be substantiated nowhere in Scripture. Scripture teaches just the opposite, as attested by New Testament scholars, who have studied the evidence carefully. Dr. Alan Richardson, for example, observes that the power of the gospel *is* seen in miracles:

> The New Testament...sees in the miracles of the Lord a revelation of the power and of the saving purpose of God....The miracle-stories do not constitute a secondary *stratum* of the Gospel tradition which is somehow foreign to the *ethos* of the Gospel in its primary sense.[66]

Professor Walter Grundmann stresses that the power of God, which is the power of salvation in the New Testament's view, is expressed in miraculous healing in Christ's name as well as in proclaiming the gospel:

> In the message of Christ we thus have the power of God which is the power of salvation....The *dunamis Theou* ["power of God"], which is the Gospel, is not an empty word....The risen Lord associates Himself with them [the apostles] and gives them His power, in which they work....The apostles continue the activity of Jesus, both proclaiming the Christian message (...Acts 4:33) and also working miracles (...Acts 4:7...Acts 4:10). Luke gives us a similar picture of

Stephen...in Acts 6:8. This *dunamis* ["power"] is expressed in proclamation on the one side (6:10) and miracles on the other (6:8)."[67]

The fact that *dunamis* is polysemous in Greek—i.e., has several different but related meanings—and denotes both "power" and "miracle" in the New Testament shows, as Grundmann points out, that *miracles* done in Christ's name are an illustration of God's *power* to save sinners through Christ.

IVb. Proclaiming the Gospel in Word and Deed

In Romans 15:18,19, Paul uses the word *plēroo* "fill, fulfill, bring to full expression"[68] to state that he brought the gospel to full expression:[69] *peplērokenai to euaggelion tou christou* literally, "(I) to have fully proclaimed the gospel of Christ." Paul says he proclaimed the gospel not only in word (*logō*) but also in deed (*ergō*). And what were the deeds that proclaimed the gospel? They were "signs and wonders in the power of the Spirit" (*en dunamei sēmeiōn kai teratōn en dunamei pneumatos*, Rom. 15:19). Thus, the gospel is also revealed and given expression through signs and wonders that act as a symbol of God's grace and God's power to save sinners through the gospel.

Similarly, Paul explicitly says the gospel came to the Thessalonians "not simply with words" (*ouk egenēthē eis humas en logō monon*). But the gospel also came to them and was revealed to them "with power *[en dunamei]* and with the Holy Spirit *[en pneumati hagiō]*" (1 Thess. 1:5). The association of "power" (*dunamis*) and "the Spirit" (*pneuma*) with signs, wonders, and miracles of healing and deliverance throughout the New Testament[70] suggests that what is being referred to in this passage are the miraculous deeds of the Spirit's power through which the gospel was manifested alongside Paul's preaching.[71]

Although some evangelicals dissent, suggesting that "there is a danger here [1 Thess. 1:5-6] of equating 'power' with 'miracles,'"[72] mainstream New Testament scholars who have studied the evidence carefully cannot confirm such a view.[73] Although the concept of God's "power" in such passages is not restricted to miracles, it clearly includes them as a basic element of the notion of God's "power." As noted above, Dr. Gatzweiler points out that the concept of "power" cannot be explained in such passages without reference to the lexically related concept of "miracle":

As examples...we cite 1 Thess. 1, 5; 2, 13; 1 Cor. 2, 4-5; 2 Cor. 6, 7; 13, 3; Col. 1, 29; 2 Tim. 1, 8. In all these places Paul speaks of the proclamation of the gospel which was accompanied by divine power, by the power of the Spirit. The gospel is God's power which is displayed among men. For the reader, who already knows that the apostle worked miracles alongside the proclamation of the gospel (cf. 2 Cor. 12, 12; Rom. 15, 18-19), it suggests miraculous events also be understood as self-evident among the notions of "might" and "power" which accompany the proclamation of the gospel.[74]

IVc. SIGNS OF GOD'S FORGIVENESS AND SIGNS OF GOD'S RULE IN CHRIST

Dr. Alan Richardson similarly affirms that the Gospels show miracles of healing to be symbols of God's forgiveness and redemption through Christ:

The connexion between healing and salvation (in the religious sense) is a characteristic feature of the Gospel tradition. Miracles of healing are, as it were, symbolic demonstrations of God's forgiveness in action....

The verb *sōzein* ["save, heal"] is itself ambiguous, meaning, on the one hand, to heal to rescue from danger, to keep safe and sound, and on the other hand, to "save" in the technical biblical-religious sense. The same is true of *iasthai* ["heal, restore"].

The Christian picture of Jesus as the Good Physician, the Saviour of both body and soul, is derived from the miracle-story tradition, which makes use of the healing narratives to convey spiritual teaching concerning salvation. A story recorded by St. Mark culminates in a terse saying of the Lord, which doubtless illustrates the connexion which He Himself perceived between His own healing ministry and His redemptive work: "They that are whole (*hoi ischuontes*) have no need of a physician, but they that are sick: I came not to call the righteous, but sinners" (Mark ii. 17).[75]

In this story [of the healing of the Paralytic, Mk. 2:1-12] Jesus deliberately implies that His healing work authenticates His power to forgive sins....The importance of this story as part of the teaching material of a Church which claimed in the name of its Lord to be able to forgive sins and to heal the sick (cf. Jas. v. 14f.) is obvious.[76]

Many New Testament scholars such as Hunter, Powell, Richardson, and others have pointed out that in the New Testament's view, the miraculous healings in Jesus' ministry, which were continued by the apostles and the Early Church, show the coming of the kingdom of God, God's reign in Christ. They are tokens of God's grace and illustrations of the forgiveness of sin accomplished by Christ's cross:

> The miracles are tokens of the coming of God's Reign in Jesus. They are the Kingdom of God in action—God's sovereign grace and forgiveness operative in Christ.[77]

> If we examine the utterances attributed to Jesus Himself in the Synoptic Gospels on the subject of His own miracles, we find that he regarded them as evidences of the drawing nigh of the Kingdom of God.
>
> This is undoubtedly their significance both in the mind of Jesus and in that of the early Church; The author of Hebrews speaks of Christians as those who have "tasted...the *dunameis* ["powers"] of the Age to Come" (vi.5). That the mighty works of Jesus are the miracles of the Kingdom of God is plainly taught in the account of the Beelzebub Controversy, recorded both in Mark (iii. 22-30) and Q (Matt. xii. 25-37, Luke xi. 17-23).[78]

> Jesus gave a radically new meaning to the "language" of the miracles: they are signs of the kingdom, signs of what God wants to do and is already doing for humankind in Jesus....
>
> If this interrelationship between the miracles of Jesus and his message of the kingdom of God is disregarded, neither the miracles nor the message of the kingdom will be understood correctly. The connection between healings and the kingdom of God is particularly clear: "heal the sick in it and say to them, 'The kingdom of God has come near to you'" (Lk. 10:9)....
>
> Jesus' healing ministry was one aspect of the manifestation of the presence of the kingdom (Mt. 12:28). Since disease was understood to be part of the disobedience of creation against its creator, healing meant that God's plan for the redress of humankind was being activated....The resurrection is the sign *par excellence* which gives meaning to all Jesus' signs.[79]

It seems to be generally agreed that *basileia* means primarily *kingship* rather than *kingdom, reign* rather than *realm*....The working of the *dunamis* ["power"] of God results in the manifestation of His *basileia* ["kingship, reign"]....

The charge which was given by Jesus to his disciples as he sent them forth on their mission is reported four times in the Synoptic Gospels and on each occasion the commission to heal is placed alongside of the commission to preach (Mark vi. 7-13; Matt. ix. 35-x. 23; Luke ix. 1-6, x. 1-20)....From the earliest days the ministry of healing was placed side by side with that of preaching in the missionary labours of the Church.[80]

The working of miracles is a part of the proclamation of the Kingdom of God, not an end in itself. Similarly, the sin of Chorazin and Bethsaida [Lk. 10:13; Mat. 11:21] is spiritual blindness; they do not accept the preaching of the Kingdom of God or understand the miracles which were its inevitable concomitants....Even the heathen, it is implied, would have understood from the preaching the meaning of the mighty works,...and they would have repented....

Because the mighty works of Jesus are the miracles of the Kingdom of God, the appropriate response to them is: "Repent and believe the good news."[81]

The New Testament evidence clearly shows that God desires to heal the sick as a sign of His kingdom reign and His grace toward us in Christ (Matt. 12:28; cf. Isa. 33:22,24). Jesus healed the sick.[82] The apostles and Early Church laity healed the sick (Stephen, Philip, Ananias, the Corinthians, Galatians, Jewish Christian churches, etc.).[83] God gave the Church gifts of healing (1 Cor. 12:9,28,29), and He commands the Church to pray for the sick (Jas. 5:14-16). Some scholars also point out that though God desires to heal as a sign of His kingdom, healing, like the Kingdom, will only be experienced in part in this age:

But just as the kingdom of God has indeed begun but has not yet reached its final fulfilment, so too Christ's healing activity has indeed started but is not yet completed.

Jesus' works are the fully valid (in German: *vollgültig*) confirmation of his message; they are as valid as his word. But they are not the final definitive (in German: *endgültig*) act of God in the bodily realm. The totally new creation which begins with the resurrection will be definitive. The miracles are not just prefigurations of salvation but a real gift of salvation at the present time....The "already" of the salvation offered now is the presupposition and basis of the "not yet" of the definitive, total salvation.[84]

Thus, Scripture shows that in some cases Christians may not experience complete healing in this age.[85] In 1 Corinthians 13, Paul says that in this age the Church will only experience spiritual gifts, which include healing, "in part" (ek merous) until the second coming of Christ: "For we know in part and we prophesy in part" (1 Cor. 13:9; cf. 1 Cor. 1:6,7; 13:8-10,12; 1 John 3:2; Rev. 22:4).[86] With this in mind, James 5:15 nonetheless states the general rule for healing ministry in the Church: "The prayer offered in faith will make the sick person well; the Lord will raise him up."

The scholars quoted above and cited in the notes appear to be unanimous regarding the New Testament evidence. The healings accompanying the preaching of Jesus, the apostles, and the Early Church were symbols, illustrations, and demonstrations of the presence of God's kingdom—God's grace and forgiveness of sin through Christ.

IVd. Cheapening or Illustrating the Gospel?

Despite such evidence, the charge has been leveled by some that miraculous healing somehow "cheapens the gospel." Boice, for example, says the following:

Again, the signs and wonders movement shifts from the sublime to the ridiculous. It cheapens and overshadows the gospel. It cheapens it because it reduces its promises to shrinking goiters, straightening backs, and lengthening legs....Those alleged wonders are next to nothing in comparison to the message of God's redeeming work in Jesus Christ or the true miracle of the new birth.[87]

One can agree that the greatest miracle of all is new birth through faith in Christ, because Jesus Himself explicitly taught this to His disciples in Luke 10:20. But one must ask if simply expecting signs and wonders of healing and deliverance to accompany the proclamation of the gospel, according to the New Testament's consistent model, "cheapens" the gospel?

Was Jesus cheapening God's redeeming work to forgive sin when He healed the paralytic, certainly straightening his back, lengthening and strengthening his legs, by saying, "'So that you may know that the Son of Man has authority on earth to forgive sins....' Then he said to the paralytic, 'Get up, take your mat and go home'" (Matt. 9:6)? Of course not. He was illustrating God's forgiveness through miraculous healing.

Signs and wonders do not cheapen the gospel. They illustrate it. How else could the one word *dunamis* be used to denote God's power to save sinners in such passages as Romans 1:16—"I am not ashamed of the gospel, because it is the power of God for the salvation of everyone who believes"—and simultaneously be used to denote "miracles" throughout the entire New Testament?[88] How else could the one word *sōzō* denote both salvation from sin and healing of illness in the New Testament, unless healing was a symbol of God's power to save sinners?[89]

V. SIGNS AND WONDERS VERSUS "THE SIGN FROM HEAVEN"

Some evangelicals suggest that expecting or asking God for signs and wonders to accompany and confirm the preaching of the gospel and the Word of God is wicked and against God's will. Carson, for example, makes the following case:

> The four gospels preserve many instances where people demanded a sign from Jesus, and he roundly denounced them for it, sometimes dismissing them as 'a wicked and adulterous generation' (Matthew 12:38-45; cf. 16:1-4; Mk. 8:11-12; Lk. 11:16,29). One can understand why: the frequent demands for signs was [sic] in danger of reducing Jesus to the level of clever magician....Such a demand is wicked and adulterous: it makes human beings the center of the universe and reduces God to the level of someone who exists to serve us.[90]

Such statements make it sound as if any expectation, desire, or request for signs and wonders or miraculous healing is wicked. But was the Early Church wicked and adulterous for seeking signs and wonders in Acts 4:29,30?

> **Acts 4:29,30**—"Now, Lord, consider their threats and enable your servants to speak your word with great boldness. *Stretch out your hand to heal and perform miraculous signs and wonders through the name of your holy servant Jesus.*"

God did not seem to consider such requests for signs and wonders to be wicked, since He obviously granted them to the Early Church (e.g., Acts 5:12-16; 6:8; 8:5,6,26-40; 9:17,18; etc.). Was Paul wicked for expecting to proclaim the gospel "in the power of signs and wonders" (Rom. 15:18,19; 2 Cor. 12:12)? Or was he sinful for expecting God to continue to work miracles among the Galatians (Gal. 3:5) and for telling the Corinthians to seek the gift of prophecy, which he said is a "sign" for believers (1 Cor. 14:1,22[91])?

Similarly, one might ask the same about John. Was John misguided in calling all of Jesus' works of miraculous healing "signs" (sēmeia; John 4:54; 6:2; 9:16: 12:17,18)[92]? Or was John misguided for recording Jesus' words suggesting that these "signs" of miraculous healing function to encourage faith and repentance: "Even though you do not believe me, believe the miraculous works [tois ergois[93]], that you may know and understand that the Father is in me, and I in the Father" (John 10:38); "At least believe on the evidence of the miraculous works themselves [dia ta erga auta]" (John 14:11)? Compare Mark 2:10:

Mark 2:10—"'But that you may know that the Son of Man has authority on earth to forgive sins....' He said to the paralytic, 'I tell you, get up, take your mat and go home.'"

Was Jesus misguided in His condemnation of Korazin and Bethsaida's lack of repentance and faith for suggesting that His miraculous works should have produced repentance (Matt. 11:21 and Luke 10:13)? Was Peter unbelieving and wicked when he claimed that God gave testimony to Jesus by signs and wonders (Acts 2:22)? Were the apostles or laymen such as Stephen, Philip, and Ananias sinful and adulterous for working signs and wonders of healing and deliverance (Acts 5:12; 6:8; 8:5-7,13; 9:17,18; 14:3; 15:12; passim)? Or was Luke sinful for describing the miraculous healings of the Early Church as "signs and wonders" in the book of Acts?

The answer to these questions is obviously no. Clearly God provided abundant healing signs and wonders to accompany the proclamation of the gospel in Jesus' ministry and in the Early Church. Why shouldn't the Church today follow the example of the Early Church in Scripture? One looks in vain for statements in Scripture that the Church should ever cease to expect the proclamation of the Word to be accompanied by signs and wonders and spiritual gifts.

The critics have confused the signs and wonders of miraculous healing in the ministry of Jesus and the Early Church with the "sign from heaven" demanded by the Pharisees, which Jesus refused to give. Jesus did not denounce ordinary "people" for seeking signs and wonders (plural) in His healing ministry in

Matthew 12:38-40; 16:1-4; Mark 8:11,12; Luke 11:16; John 6:30f. He denounced *stubborn, unbelieving religious leaders* (Matt. 12:38; 16:1; Mark 8:11) for *demanding* a *"sign* [singular] *from heaven"* (Mark 8:11; Luke 11:16; cf. Matt. 16:1; John 6:30f.). (Even in the so-called "rebuke" of John 4:48, Jesus granted the "sign," healing the royal official's son, and this led to the conversion of the official and his family [John 4:53,54].)

The religious leaders were calling the signs of Jesus' healing ministry demonic (Matt. 12:24; Mark 3:22; Luke 11:15). They were asking for a prophetic sign from heaven beyond those of Jesus' healing ministry like those performed by prophets such as Moses, Elijah, or Isaiah—*manna from heaven* (John 6:30,31); *plagues of the Exodus, which were "signs"* (Exod. 7:3; 8:23; 10:1,2; Num. 14:23; Deut. 6:22; 7:19; 11:3ff.,34; 26:8; 29:3; 34:11; Josh. 24:17); *drought, which was a "sign"* (Deut. 28:22-24,46; cf. 1 Kings 17:1ff.); *the retreating shadow of the sun, which was a "sign"* (2 Kings 20:9). F. F. Bruce points this out:

> According to Mark, the refusal to give a sign was Jesus' response to some Pharisees who, in the course of debate, asked him to supply "a sign from heaven."...
>
> First, what sort of sign would have convinced them? External signs might have been necessary to convince a heathen Egyptian or an apostate king of Israel, but why should they be necessary for custodians and teachers of the law of the true God?...
>
> Secondly, would the kind of sign they had in mind really have validated the truth of Jesus's words?...It may be suspected that it was some...extraordinary but essentially irrelevant sign that was being asked from Jesus....
>
> In the third place, what about the signs he actually performed? Why were they not sufficient to convince his questioners?...If the restoration of bodily and mental health could be dismissed as a work of Satan, no number of healing acts would have established the divine authority by which they were performed....While the healing miracles did serve as signs of the kingdom of God to those who had eyes to see, they did not *compel* belief in those who were prejudiced in the opposite direction....
>
> While the miracles served as signs, they were not performed in order to be signs. They were as much a part and parcel of Jesus's ministry as was his preaching—not...seals affixed to the document to certify its genuiness but an integral element in the very text of the document.[94]

Thus, Scripture is clear that Jesus gave abundant signs of God's kingdom in His healing ministry. But He provided no sensational sign from heaven to those who were unbelieving and remained closed to His teaching and its basis in Scripture (Matt. 5:17-20; cf. John 3:10,11). Such an attitude refused to ask God for guidance about Jesus and His teaching (John 5:39,40; 6:45; 7:17). For such stubborn unbelief God gives no extra sign.

VI. PAST SIGNS AND WONDERS VERSUS ONGOING SIGNS AND WONDERS

Certain evangelicals suggest that Scripture encourages faith on the basis of past signs and wonders but not on the basis of ongoing signs and wonders. Carson and Boice say the following:

> John's readers are called on to reflect on the signs that he reports [Jn. 20:30-31], to think through the significance of those redemptive events, especially Jesus' resurrection, and thereby believe. The mandate to believe here rests on John's reports of God's past, redemptive-historical signs, not on testimonies of present, ongoing ones.[95]

> We do not repeat annual crossings of the Red Sea. Such miraculous events are redemptive events and are not presented as normative for Christian experience. They are to be remembered, not repeated.[96]

But no hint of such a dichotomy between the past and the present can be found in Scripture. First, nowhere does Scripture teach that the miraculous healing ministry and the spiritual gifts exercised by Jesus, the apostles, and the laity of the Early Church are not to be continued today. James 5:14-16 quite clearly suggests the contrary, as well as Romans 12:6-8; 1 Corinthians 12:7-11,28-30; 14:22-39; Galatians 3:5; Philippians 4:9 (and 1 Cor. 11:1); 1 Thessalonians 5:19-21; 2 Timothy 1:6; and 1 Peter 4:10,11. Healing and spiritual gifts accompanied the ministry of the Word as the normal New Testament pattern, as has been adequately demonstrated above. We do not repeat the healing of the lame man at Lystra (Acts 14:8ff.), but we pray for the lame and sick to be healed (Jas. 5:14-16).

Second, the book of Acts and the Epistles show that the Early Church continued to minister with spiritual gifts, healing, miracles, signs and wonders at the same time John wrote in his Gospel, "Jesus did many other miraculous signs....But these are written that you may believe that Jesus is the Christ, the Son of God" (John 20:30,31). In Acts 2:22, Peter points back to the "miracles, wonders and signs" of Jesus and then is said to have performed them himself in Acts 2:43; 4:16,22; 5:12-16 and so on. Stephen, a layman, not only recalls the signs and wonders of the Exodus in Acts 7:36, but he also performed them himself in Jerusalem, according to Acts 6:8.

These facts show a link in the Early Church's understanding between the signs God performed in the past and the ongoing signs and wonders He was performing in the Church.[97] Professor Lampe, for example, remarks:

> These miracles [in the book of Acts]...fulfilled the ancient prophetic hope. Joel had prophesied "wonders" in heaven and earth [Acts 2:17-21]....Joel's prophecy is to find its fulfilment in the signs and wonders done in the name of the exalted Christ through his followers. Soon after the speech in which Peter recalls Joel's words we are told that "many signs and wonders happened through the apostles" (Acts 2:43)....The Spirit that was upon Jesus [Lk. 4:18-19; Acts 10:38] when he was attested by mighty works, signs and wonders is now working through his disciples.[98]

The following passages also show that the Early Church saw the ongoing contemporary occurrence of signs and wonders confirming the proclamation of Christ and the gospel as a continuation of the signs and wonders of God worked in Jesus' ministry: Hebrews 2:3,4; Mark 16:20; Galatians 3:5; Acts 14:3; Romans 15:18,19 (many more passages could be added here).

According to the evidence presented above, the New Testament shows that signs, wonders, and miraculous healing worked by God in Christ's name glorify Christ and testify to His resurrection. They demonstrate in a special way God's rule in Christ and God's presence among His people, the Church. They illustrate the grace and power of God, which saves sinners through the cross of Christ, and they confirm the proclamation of the gospel and the Word of God. Finally, as in Henrietta Mears's case, they show the power of God's Word, Scripture, and teach us the importance of simply "taking Him at His word."[99]

Notes

1. Earl Roe, ed., *Dream Big: The Henrietta Mears Story* (Ventura, CA: Regal Books, 1990), p. 68; citing Barbara Hudson Powers, *The Henrietta Mears Story* (Grand Rapids, MI: Fleming H. Revell, 1957), pp. 100ff.
2. Roe, ed., *Dream Big*, p. 68.
3. Ibid., cited on title page.
4. Ibid., p. 333.
5. John 14:12 (examples of all spiritual gifts, except perhaps tongues and interpretation, can be found in Jesus' ministry and miraculous works according to the Gospels; see scriptural evidence presented by D. Pytches, *Spiritual Gifts in the Local Church* [Minneapolis, MI: Bethany House, 1985], pp. 50-55; J. D. G. Dunn, *Jesus and the Spirit* [Philadelphia, PA: Westminster, 1975], pp. 68-73, 163-170, 172-173, 210-211); 1 Corinthians 12:7; 14:1,5,12,13,24,31; Matthew 7:7-11; James 4:2b. 1 Corinthians 12:28,29 speaks of appointments "in the church"—regular gift-functions in the church—and not of how many gifts one may potentially experience or utilize. Such passages as 1 Corinthians 12:31; 14:1,5,12,13, and Romans 1:14 seem to suggest we can seek and potentially receive from God gifts we do not already have (see also Don Williams' chapter in this book, remarks on 1 Corinthians 12).
6. First Corinthians 12:8; 14:24,25. It is evident that for the Early Church, whose Bible was the Septuagint (the Greek translation of the Hebrew Bible), the "word" (Greek *logos*) in the phrase "word of knowledge" denoted "divine revelation" (hence "*word* of knowledge" = "*divine revelation* of knowledge") as the Hebrew *dābār* "word," which Greek *logos* renders in the Septuagint, frequently denotes (Hebrew *dābār* denoting "divine revelation," 1 Sam. 3:7; 9:27; 2 Sam. 7:4; 1 Kings 17:2,8; 6:11; 13:20; Jer. 1:4,11; 2:1; 13:8; 16:1; 24:4; 28:12; 29:30; Ezek. 3:16; 6:1; 7:1; 12:1; Hos. 1:1; Mic. 1:1; Zeph. 1:1; Isa. 2:1; BDB, p. 182b [meaning III.2]; O. Procksch, "*logos*," *TDNT*, vol. 4, pp. 94-96).
7. D. A. Carson "The Purpose of Signs and Wonders in the New Testament," in *Power Religion: The Selling Out of the Evangelical Church?* edited by Michael Scott Horton (Chicago, IL: Moody, 1992), p. 90.
8. Ibid., p. 92.
9. Ibid., p. 103.
10. S. V. McCasland, "Signs and Wonders," *JBL* 76 (1957): 151.
11. J. Lyons, *Semantics*, vol. I (Cambridge, England: Cambridge University Press, 1977), pp. 250-261; R. H. Robins, *General Linguistics. An Introductory Survey* (White Plains, NY: Longman, 1980), chapter 2; P. Cotterell and M. Turner, *Linguistics and Biblical Interpretation* (Downers Grove, IL: InterVarsity Press, 1989), p. 154f.
12. R. C. Trench, *Synonyms of the New Testament* (London, England: Macmillan, 1894), p. 339.
13. P. G. Hiebert, in J.R. Coggins and P. G. Hiebert, eds., *Wonders and the Word* (Winnipeg, Canada: Kindred Press, 1989), p. 126.
14. BAGD, pp. 207-208.
15. Trench, *Synonyms*, p. 343: "But the miracles are also 'powers' (*dunameis*...),

outcomings of that mighty *power* of God, which was inherent in Christ;...these powers being by Him lent to those who were his witnesses and ambassadors"; id., *Notes on the Miracles of Our Lord* (Fifth ed. revised, London, England, 1856), p. 5: "Here the cause [the 'power' of God] gives its name to the effect ['miracles, works of power']. The 'power' dwells originally in the divine Messenger (Acts vi.8; x.38; Rom. xv.19); is one with which he is himself equipped of God....But then, by an easy transition, the word comes to signify the exertions and separate puttings forth of this power. These are 'powers' [*dunameis*] in the plural, although the same word is now translated...'miracles'"; cf. McCasland's rendering of *dunamis*, "manifestation of divine power," *JBL* 76 (1957): 149; W. Grundmann, *"dunamai/dunamis," TDNT*, vol. 2, pp. 309-311.

16. A. Richardson, *The Miracle-Stories of the Gospels* (London, England: SCM Press, 1941), p. 10: "As in the N.T. generally the miracles *(dunameis)* of Jesus are manifestations of His *dunamis* ['power']."

17. K. Gatzweiler, "Der Paulinische Wunderbegriff," in A. Suhl, ed., *Der Wunderbegriff im Neuen Testament* (Darmstadt, Germany: Wissenschaftliche Buchgesellschaft, 1980), p. 401: "Während der Plural *dunameis* durchweg die Wunder bezeichnet, kann dagegen der Singular *dunamis* ebenso die Kraft bedeuten, die Wunder schafft und die der Geist ist, wie die Kraft und den Geist, den die Wunder offenbaren."

18. Professor C. F. D. Moule of Cambridge referred to the group of words comprising this lexical field in N.T. Greek as "a vocabulary denoting *significant manifestations of power*...signs of God at work" (C. F. D. Moule, "The Vocabulary of Miracle," in Moule, ed., *Miracles. Cambridge Studies in Their Philosophy and History* [London, England: A. R. Mowbray & Co., 1965], p. 238).

19. H. Hendrickx, *The Miracle Stories of the Synoptic Gospels* (San Francisco, CA: HarperSanFrancisco, 1987), p. 10 and nn. 3-4.

20. For translating *energeia* as "energy," see G. Bertram, *"energeō," TDNT*, vol. 2, p. 652; C. H. Powell, *The Biblical Concept of Power* (London, England: Epworth Press, 1963), p. 136.

21. Richardson, *The Miracle-Stories of the Gospels*, pp. 6-7.

22. That the phrase "signs and wonders" and the word "sign" denote healing and deliverance from demons is noted by the German New Testament scholar, Professor Karl H. Rengstorf, *TDNT*, VII, pp. 239-240.

23. The same lexical field (group of words) includes other terms denoting manifestations of God's power in healing and deliverance, such as *hugiēs* "whole," *iasis* "healing," *megaleios* "mighty deed," *endoxos* "glorious deed," *paradoxos* "wonderful thing," *thaumasios* "wonderful thing" according to Trench, *Synonyms*, p. 339.

24. That the word "sign (*sēmeion)*" and the phrase "signs and wonders (*sēmeia kai terata)*" are synonymous and interchangeable was noted in a linguistic study of the Greek terms by McCasland, "Signs and Wonders," *JBL* 76 (1957): 151. The following passages demonstrate this point: John 4:48,54 (*sēmeia kai terata* = *sēmeion)*; Acts 4:16,22,30 (*sēmeion* = *iasis* "healing" = *sēmeia kai terata)*; compare the phrase "signs and miracles (*sēmeia kai dunameis)*" in Acts 8:13 with the phrase "miracles and wonders and signs (*dunamesi kai terasi kai sēmeiois)*" in

Acts 2:22, "signs and wonders and miracles (*sēmeiois te kai terasin kai dunamesin*)" in 2 Corinthians 12:12, and "signs and wonders and...miracles (*sē meiois te kai terasin kai...dunamesin*)" in Hebrews 2:4.

25. The long ending of Mark, Mark 16:9-20, dates from the first half of the second century A.D. (K. Aland and B. Aland, *The Text of the New Testament. An Introduction to the Critical Editions and to the Theory and Practice of Modern Textual Criticism* [Grand Rapids, MI and Leiden, Netherlands: Eerdmans and E. J. Brill, 1989], p. 293) and is therefore a later addition to the Gospel of Mark. Though it is not found in many of the earliest and best Greek manuscripts, the long ending is attested in 99 percent of the extant Greek manuscripts of the New Testament (Aland and Aland, *The Text of the New Testament*, p. 292; W. L. Lane, *Commentary on the Gospel of Mark* [The New International Commentary on the New Testament, Grand Rapids, MI: Eerdmans, 1974], pp. 603-604). This fact suggests that the long ending was widely accepted as authoritative in the Early Church. Lane has suggested the long ending perhaps originated in a second century catechism summarizing post-resurrection events (Lane, *Mark*, p. 604). The wide dissemination of the long ending, seen in the manuscript evidence, suggests that the Early Church readily agreed that Jesus' commission to the disciples did include the expectation that supernatural signs would accompany the preaching of the gospel.

26. BAGD, p. 505.

27. Prophecy and tongues are both signs according to this passage. The grammatical structure of 1 Corinthians 14:22 cannot be understood in any other way, since the elliptical clause *hē de prophēteia ou tois apistois alla tois pisteuousin* depends on the preceding clause for its full grammatical and lexical meaning; see G. Fee, *The First Epistle to the Corinthians* (NICNT, ed., F. F. Bruce; Grand Rapids, MI: Eerdmans, 1987), p. 682 and n. 38; Wayne Grudem, *The Gift of Prophecy in 1 Corinthians* (Washington, DC: University Press of America, 1982), pp. 193-194; id., *The Gift of Prophecy in the New Testament and Today* (Wheaton, IL: Crossway Books, 1988), pp. 173f. and n. 68.

28. See note 25 above.

29. BAGD, pp. 747-748 "*sēmeion*" (1).

30. Ibid., p. 748, "*sēmeion*"(2)

31. Carson in Horton, ed., *Power Religion*, p. 101.

32. Lyons, *Semantics*, vol. I, pp. 250ff. (§8.4); id., *Introduction to Theoretical Linguistics* (Cambridge, England: Cambridge University Press, 1968), pp. 429ff.; Robins, *General Linguistics*, chap. 2; Cotterell and Turner, *Linguistics and Biblical Interpretation*, p. 127, n. 41.

33. See the similar remarks of Powell, *The Biblical Concept of Power*, pp. 139, 143; and E. E. Ellis, *Prophecy and Hermeneutic in Early Christianity: New Testament Essays* (Wissenschaftliche Untersuchungen zum Neuen Testament, vol. 18. Tübingen: J. C. B. Mohr [Paul Siebeck], 1978), p. 130, n. 4.

34. Lampe, in Moule, ed., *Miracles. Cambridge Studies*, pp. 175-176.

35. See notes 27-28 above and also see John 4:48,54 (healing a fever is a "sign"); 6:2 (healing of the sick is called "signs"); 9:6-7,16 (healing blindness is one of "such signs"); 12:17,18 (raising the dead is a "sign"); Acts 4:16,22 (healing a

lame man is an "obvious sign"); 5:12-16 (healing the sick and demonized is called "signs and wonders"); 8:5-7,13 (healing the sick and demonized is called "signs and miracles").

36. BAGD, p. 208; Gatzweiler, "Der Paulinische Wunderbegriff," p. 401; Trench, *Synonyms*, p. 343; id., *Notes on the Miracles of Our Lord*, p. 5.

37. Laying on of hands to bestow the Holy Spirit and spiritual gifts: Acts 8:17; 19:15f.; 1 Timothy 4:14; 5:22; 2 Timothy 1:6. Related to this, laying on of hands to commission for a task: Acts 6:6; 13:3; to bestow blessing: Matthew 19:13-15; Mark 10:16.

38. See E. Lohse, *"cheir,"* *TDNT*, vol. 9, pp. 431-432.

39. Carson in Horton, ed., *Power Religion*, p. 102.

40. Nor does a passage like 2 Corinthians 12:12 suggest that because signs, wonders and miracles were among *"the things that mark an apostle,"* no one else worked them and they were not to be imitated (see discussion in Wayne Grudem's chapter in this book, question number 7); Powell, *The Biblical Concept of Power*, p. 143: "Apostolic power is seen most vividly in Stephen, called by the Church, not to apostolic office at all....Yet in him the Spirit's power was plainly shown." Ellis, *Prophecy and Hermeneutic in Early Christianity: New Testament Essays*, p. 130, n. 4: "Acts...like Paul (2 Cor. 12, 12; cf. Rom. 15, 19), associates signs and miracles with the 'apostle,' but not exclusively so (Acts 6, 8; 8:6f., 13; I Cor. 12, 28f.; 14, 22)." Rather, the passage affirms no more than that anyone who claims to be an apostle would be clearly marked by all the signs of an apostle— not simply signs, wonders, and miracles but primarily Christlike ministry, self-less lifestyle, endurance of hardship, etc. (see Wayne Grudem's chapter in this book, objection number 7).

41. Boice in Horton, ed., *Power Religion*, p.126.

42. F. F. Bruce, *The Hard Sayings of Jesus* (Downers Grove, IL: InterVarsity Press, 1983), p. 96.

43. For *erga* denoting "miraculous works" when referring to Jesus and God in the Gospel of John: BAGD, p. 308; Bertram, *"ergon,"* *TDNT*, vol. 2, p. 642; Rengstorf, *"sēmeion,"* *TDNT*, vol. 7, pp. 247-248; Trench, *Notes on the Miracles of Our Lord*, p. 6: "That his *erga* ['works'] are his miracles, the following passages, v. 36; x. 25, 32, 38; xiv. 10-11; xv. 24;...decisively prove."

44. Rengstorf, *TDNT*, vol. 7, p. 246.

45. For *erga* denoting "miraculous works" when referring to Jesus and God, see references in the previous two notes.

46. The grammatical structure of 1 Corinthians 14:22 cannot be understood any other way: the elliptical clause *hē de prophēteia ou tois apistois alla tois pisteuousin* depends on the preceding clause for its full grammatical and lexical meaning; see Fee, *The First Epistle to the Corinthians*, p. 682 and n. 38; Wayne Grudem, *The Gift of Prophecy in I Corinthians*, pp. 193-194; id., *The Gift of Prophecy in the New Testament and Today*, pp. 173f. and n. 68.

47. See the remarks of Grudem, *The Gift of Prophecy*, pp. 136-137; Oepke, *TDNT*, vol. 3, p. 976 and n. 42.

48. H. van der Loos, *The Miracles of Jesus* (Supplements to Novum Testamentum, vol. 8. (Leiden, Netherlands: E. J. Brill, 1965), p. 245 and nn. 1-4.

49. Ibid., p. 265 and n. 2.
50. Trench, *Notes on the Miracles of Our Lord*, p. 2.
51. Hendrickx, *The Miracle Stories of the Synoptic Gospels*, p. 17.
52. J. Ruprecht, *Das Wunder in der Bibel. Eine Einführung in die Welt der göttlichen Offenbarung und der biblischen Weltanschauung* (Berlin, Germany: 1936), p. 173: "Bei dem engen, in dieser Schrift immer wieder betonten Zusammenhang, der zwischen Gottes Wort und Gottes Wundertat besteht, wird man von vornherein annehmen müssen, dass auch das Tatwunder seinen Hauptzweck darin haben wird, Glauben zu wecken, den Glauben zu befestigen und zu stärken"; cited by van der Loos, *The Miracles of Jesus*, p. 245, n. 7; Similarly, Lépicier, *Le Miracle. Sa nature, ses lois, ses rapports avec l'ordre surnaturel* (Paris, France: 1936), p. 484; cited by van der Loos, *The Miracles of Jesus*, p. 245-246, n. 7.
53. Armstrong, in Horton, ed., *Power Religion*, p. 83.
54. See Fee, *The First Epistle to the Corinthians*, p. 95, n. 2. The context of "weakness" in 1 Corinthians 1—2, which Fee mentions does not make it less likely that 1 Corinthians 2:4 refers to the "signs, wonders, and miracles" of 2 Corinthians 12:12 than the spiritual gifts mentioned in 1 Corinthians 1:6,7, since it is in the very context of mentioning his own weakness that Paul alludes to the signs and wonders of his ministry in 2 Corinthians 12:12 (compare 2 Cor. 12:7-10,21; 13:4,8 and 2 Cor. 12:12).
55. Several facts indicate that the "demonstration of the Spirit's power" in 1 Corinthians 2:4,5 refers to signs, wonders, miracles, and spiritual gifts, as many scholars have interpreted it (Gatzweiler, "Der Paulinische Wunderbegriff," pp. 403-405, n. 52; Ellis, *Prophecy and Hermeneutic in Early Christianity: New Testament Essays*, pp. 64-65; Schweizer, *TDNT*, vol. 6, p. 423 and n. 600; O. Hofius, in C. Brown, ed., *NIDNTT*, vol. II, pp. 632-633; E. Preuschen, *Greichisch-deutsches Wörterbuch zu den Schriften des Neuen Testaments und der übrigen urchristlichen Literatur* [rev. by W. Bauer, Giessen, 1928], sub *apodeixis*; Powell, *The Biblical Concept of Power*, pp. 139-140; J. Ruef, *Paul's First Letter to Corinth* [New York: Penguin, 1971], pp. 16-17):
    a. Elsewhere where Paul couples *pneuma* "Spirit" with *dunamis* "power," *dunamis* denotes "miracle" (e.g., Gal. 3:5) or is explicitly associated with "signs and wonders" (Rom. 15:19).
    b. Paul explicitly states that not only were signs, wonders, and miracles a regular part of his ministry in general, according to Romans 15:18,19, but that they were a regular part of his ministry to the Corinthians according 2 Corinthians 12:12.
    c. Wherever Acts describes the deeds accompanying Paul's preaching, they are clearly signs and wonders of healing and deliverance as well as manifestations of spiritual gifts (Acts 13:7,10,11; 14:3,9,10; 16:14,16-18,26,32; 19:3-6,8-12; 20:7,9,10).
    d. The noun *apodeixis* "demonstration" is paralleled in Acts 2:22 by the related verb from the same root *apodeiknumi*, "attest, show forth, display," which is used of God's attesting to Jesus through the signs, wonders, and miracles of Jesus' healing ministry.
    e. The same noun, *apodeixis* "demonstration," is used of proof

through signs and wonders in contrast to the spoken word (cf. BAGD, p. 89) in Philo's *Life of Moses*, 1, 95, dating from the first half of the first century A.D., just prior to the date of 1 Corinthians: *apodeixesi tais dia sēmeiōn kai teratōn* "by the demonstrations with signs and wonders" in contrast to *ta dia tōn logōn prostattomena* "the orders (given) with words" in Moses and Aaron's confrontations with the Egyptian Pharaoh (F. H. Colson, *Philo*, vol 6 [Loeb Classical Library, Cambridge, MA: Harvard University Press, 1935], p. 324).

56. Gatzweiler, "Der Paulinische Wunderbegriff," pp. 403-405, n. 52: "Als Belege...zitieren wir 1 Thess. 1, 5; 2, 13; I Kor. 2, 4-5; 2 Kor 6, 7; 13, 3; Kol. 1, 29; 2 Tim. 1, 8. An all diesen Stellen spricht Paulus von der Verkündigung des Evangeliums, die von göttlicher Kraft, von der Macht des Geistes begleitet war. Das Evangelium ist Gottes Macht, die sich unter den Menschen entfaltet. Für den Leser, der schon weiss, dass der Apostel bei der Verkündigung des Evangeliums Wunder gewirkt hat (vgl. 2 Kor. 12, 12; Röm. 15, 18-19), liegt es nahe, wie selbstverständlich unter den begriffen 'Macht' und 'Kraft,' die die Verkündigung des Evangeliums begleiten, auch Wunderereignisse zu verstehen."

57. Ellis, *Prophecy and Hermeneutic in Early Christianity: New Testament Essays*, pp. 64-65. Similarly, Schweizer, *TDNT*, vol. 6, p. 423 and n. 600: "In I Cor. 2:4f. the 'demonstration of the Spirit and of power' is differentiated from the 'words of wisdom' and 'the wisdom of men' and indeed from the 'word' generally in I Thes. 1:5....In Rom. 15:19 'the power of the Spirit' is parallel to 'the power of signs and wonders',...and 'Spirit' to 'miracles' in Gal. 3:5. The 'Spirit' is thus everywhere understood as something whose reception may be verified. Paul, e.g., can list glossolalia, gifts of healing and miraculous powers among the works of the Spirit, I Cor. 12:9f., 28-30; 14:18-26...."

58. K. Barth, *Die Kirchliche Dogmatik* (Zollikon-Zurich, 1947-1959), vol 4.2, pp. 263ff.; cited by van der Loos, *The Miracles of Jesus*, p. 270, n. 1.

59. Hendrickx, *The Miracle Stories of the Synoptic Gospels*, p. 18.

60. Van der Loos, *The Miracles of Jesus*, p. 270. Similarly, Oepke, "*iaomai*," *TDNT*, vol. 3, pp. 213-214: "The essential thing for the community [the Early Church in Acts] is never healing alone. The acts of power *(dunamis)* are signs. If they confer benefits on individuals, in this very quality they awaken faith and further the progress of preaching (*sēmeion, teras*, Rom. 15:18f. [I Cor. 2:4f.; I Thes. 1:5?]; 2 Cor. 12:12; also Acts 2:43; 5:12; 6:8; 14:3; 15:12: with *iasis* ["healing"] 4:22,30). The gift of healing is an operation of the name of the exalted Christ (Acts 13:6)....It is an operation of the ascended Lord through the Spirit Acts 9:34; Rom. 15:18f.)."

61. Boice in Horton, ed., *Power Religion*, p. 133.

62. Ibid., p. 134.

63. On the "signs of an apostle" in 2 Corinthians 12:12, including more than miraculous signs and wonders, see Wayne Grudem's chapter in this book, objection number 7.

64. Powell, *The Biblical Concept of Power*, p. 136; Justin Martyr similarly argued in

the second century A.D. that Jesus' healings are a witness of how Jesus would restore the whole body at the resurrection of all those who are in Christ (van der Loos, *The Miracles of Jesus*, p. 248, n. 1).

65. Boice in Horton, ed., *Power Religion*, p. 126.
66. Richardson, *The Miracle-Stories of the Gospels*, p. 17.
67. Grundmann, "*dunamai/dunamis*," *TDNT*, vol. 2, pp. 309-311.
68. BAGD, pp. 670ff.
69. The use of *pleroō* "bring (the gospel) to full expression" in Romans 15:19 cannot mean that Paul *finished* preaching the gospel, because he was still planning to visit Rome and preach the gospel further in Spain (Rom. 1:13, 15; 15:23f.). Nor can it mean that he *said everything* there was to say about the gospel, as Murray points out: "He says he 'fully preached' the gospel. This means that he had 'fulfilled' the gospel (cf. Col. 1:25) and does not reflect on the fulness with which he set forth the gospel (cf. Acts 20:20,27)....Neither does 'fully preached' imply that he had preached the gospel in every locality and to every person in these territories" (J. Murray, *The Epistle to the Romans* [NICNT; Grand Rapids, MI: Eerdmans, 1968], vol. 2, p. 214).

But, as G. Friedrich points out, it means that Paul proclaimed the gospel in the way he described in Romans 15:18,19, "*in word and deed, by the power of signs and wonders, by the power of the Spirit*": "Again, Rom. 15:19...does not mean that Paul has concluded his missionary work, but that the Gospel is fulfilled when it has taken full effect. In the preaching of Paul Christ has shown Himself effective in word and sign and miracle (v. 18). Hence the Gospel has been brought to fulfilment from Jerusalem to Illyricum and Christ is named in the communities (v. 20)" (Friedrich, *TDNT*, vol. 2, p. 732).

70. E.g., Matthew 12:28; Mark 5:30; Luke 5:17; 6:18,19; 8:46; Acts 3:12; 10:38; Romans 15:19; 1 Corinthians 12:4,9,10; Gal. 3:5; Heb. 2:4; etc.; See Grundmann, "*dunamai/dunamis*," *TDNT*, vol. 2, p. 311 and n. 91: "Paul fits the same pattern [of Jesus and the disciples]. His work is done 'in the power of signs and wonders, in the power of the Spirit' (Rom. 15:19)....This power is expressed on the one side in miracles: 'in the power of signs and wonders'. There are many references to these in the epistles: 'the signs of an apostle...signs, wonders, and miracles', II Cor. 12:12; God 'working miracles among you', Gal. 3:5; his activity in Thessalonica did not take place 'in word only, but also in power and in the Holy Spirit', I Thes. 1:5....Alongside the power of miracles is the power of proclamation and edification....Here we see the connexion between Spirit and power, which we have already seen everywhere in Luke. The Spirit is the One who dispenses and mediates power."

See also Schweizer, *TDNT*, vol. 6, p. 398: "The distinctiveness of the saying [Mat. 12:28] lies in the fact that the presence of the Spirit...is interpreted as the presence of the *basileia* ["kingdom"]. Similarly, the promise that God will lay His Spirit on the Servant is seen to be fulfilled in the *healings* [italics his] of Jesus according to Mat. 12:18 [cf. 12:15]. This is in keeping with the view of the [early Christian] community, which perceives the dawn of the last time in the coming of the *miracle-working Spirit* [italics his]."

On the "Spirit" and "power" associated with healing signs, wonders, and miracles in the New Testament, see also Hofius, *NIDNTT*, vol. II, pp. 632-633; Ellis, "Christ and Spirit in I Corinthians," *Prophecy and Hermeneutic in Early Christianity: New Testament Essays*, pp. 63ff.; Oepke, *"iaomai," TDNT*, vol. 3, pp. 213-214; Lampe, in Moule, ed., *Miracles. Cambridge Studies*, p. 171; Gatzweiler, "Der Paulinische Wunderbegriff," p. 401; Powell, *The Biblical Concept of Power*, p. 139; O. Schmitz, *Der Begriff dunamis bei Paulus* (1927), p. 145; E. Sokolewski, *Die Begriffe Geist und Leben bei Paulus* (1903), pp. 1ff.

71. See Gatzweiler, "Der Paulinische Wunderbegriff," p. 403 and n. 52; Grundmann, *TDNT*, vol. 2, p. 311; Ellis, *Prophecy and Hermeneutic in Early Christianity: New Testament Essays*, p. 65; Hofius, *NIDNTT*, vol. II, p. 632.

72. Hiebert, *Wonders and the Word*, p. 126.

73. See references in note 71.

74. Gatzweiler, "Der Paulinische Wunderbegriff," pp. 403-405, n. 52: "Als Belege...zitieren wir 1 Thess. 1, 5; 2, 13; I Kor. 2, 4-5; 2 Kor 6, 7; 13, 3; Kol. 1, 29; 2 Tim. 1, 8. An all diesen Stellen spricht Paulus von der Verkündigung des Evangeliums, die von göttlicher Kraft, von der Macht des Geistes begleitet war. Das Evangelium ist Gottes Macht, die sich unter den Menschen entfaltet. Für den Leser, der schon weiss, dass der Apostel bei der Verkündigung des Evangeliums Wunder gewirkt hat (vgl. 2 Kor. 12, 12; Röm. 15, 18-19), liegt es nahe, wie selbstverständlich unter den begriffen 'Macht' und 'Kraft,' die die Verkündigung des Evangeliums begleiten, auch Wunderereignisse zu verstehen."

75. Richardson, *The Miracle-Stories of the Gospels*, pp. 61-62. For similar remarks about Jesus' healing ministry illustrating the gospel and His victory over Satan, sin, sickness and death, see E. Thurneysen, *Die Lehre von der Seelsorge* (Zürich, Germany: 1946), p. 230: "[Die heilungen] sind...Zeichen, die den Sieg des Christus über Sünde und Tod anzeigen" ([The healings] are...signs which show the victory of Christ over sin and death); Grundmann, *TDNT*, vol. II, p.303; van der Loos, *The Miracles of Jesus*, p. 252: "As evidential power it identifies Jesus as the Messiah-King and reveals His divine mission. As militant power it reveals Jesus as the adversary of all the forces of ruin. For Jesus has come to smash the forces of disease, sin and death, to dethrone Satan. This dual nature of the power function finds striking expression in Jesus' important pronouncement: 'But if I cast out devils by the Spirit of God, then the Kingdom of God is come unto you,' Mt. 12:28, and cf. Lk. 11:20."

76. Ibid., p. 66.

77. A. M. Hunter, *The Work and the Words of Jesus* (London, England: 1950), p. 55; cited by Powell, *The Biblical Concept of Power*, p. 114, n. 35. Similarly, Powell, *The Biblical Concept of Power*, p. 82: "The Kingdom comes chiefly, not as claim and decision, but as saving *dynamis*, as redeeming power, to set free a world lying in the clutches of Satan...."

78. Richardson, *The Miracle-Stories of the Gospels*, p. 38. Similarly, van der Loos, *The Miracles of Jesus*, pp. 223-224; Hendrickx, *The Miracle Stories of the Synoptic Gospels*, p. 12.

79. Hendrickx, *The Miracle Stories of the Synoptic Gospels*, pp. 11-12.

80. Richardson, *The Miracle-Stories of the Gospels*, pp. 41-42.

81. Ibid., pp. 44-45.
82. E.g., **Matthew** 4:23; 9:35,36; 10:1,7,8; 11:5; 12:15,18; 15:30; 19:2 (cf. Mark 10:1); 21:14 (cf. Luke 21:37); **Mark** 1:38,39; 2:2,11; 3:14,15; 6:12,13; 10:1 (cf. Matt. 19:2); **Luke** 4:18; 5:17,24; 6:6-11,17,18; 7:22; 9:1,2; 10:9,13; 13:10-13,22,32; 14:4,7ff.; 21:37 (cf. Matt. 21:14); 16:15-18, 20; **John** 3:2; 7:14,15,21-23,31,38; 10:25,32,38; 12:37,49; 14:10,12; **Acts** 1:1; 2:22; 10:38.
83. E.g., **Acts** 3:6,12; 4:29,30; 5:12-16,20,21,28,42; 6:8,10; 8:4-7,12; 9:17,18 (cf. 22:13),34,35; 14:3,8-10,15ff.; 15:12,36; 18:5,11 (cf. 2 Cor. 12:12; 1 Cor. 2:4,5); 19:8-12; **Romans** 15:18,19; **1 Corinthians** 2:4,5; 11:1; 12:1-11,28-31; **2 Corinthians** 12:12; **Galatians** 3:5; **Philippians** 4:9; **1 Thessalonians** 1:5,6; **Hebrews** 2:3,4; 6:1,2; **James** 5:13-16.
84. Hendrickx, *The Miracle Stories of the Synoptic Gospels*, pp. 14-15.
85. In Ephesians 6:18, Paul commands us to "pray in the Spirit on all occasions with all kinds of prayers and requests" (cf. 1 Thess. 5:17; Col. 4:2). Yet, Paul was ill in Galatia for a long enough period that it "was a trial" to the Galatians (Gal. 4:14); Epaphroditus did not experience immediate healing from illness and almost died according to Philippians 2:27; Timothy had chronic illnesses involving his stomach, which were not completely healed according to 1 Timothy 5:23; and Paul had to leave Trophimus sick in Miletus, apparently seeing no healing in response to prayer (2 Tim. 4:20).
86. On experiencing healing of illness as a "gift of grace" experienced only in part in the Early Church according to the New Testament, see Oepke, *"iaomai,"* TDNT, vol. 3, p. 214; cf. 1 Cor. 12:9,28,29; on experiencing spiritual gifts in this age only "in part (*ek merous* 1 Cor. 13:9)," see Fee, *The First Epistle to the Corinthians*, p. 644 and n. 21; Schneider, TDNT, vol. 4, p. 596.
87. Boice, *Power Religion*, p. 129.
88. BAGD, pp. 207-208; Grundmann, *"dunamai/dunamis,"* TDNT, vol. 2, pp. 309-311; Trench, *Synonyms*, p. 343: "But the miracles are also 'powers' (*dunameis*...), outcomings of that mighty *power* of God, which was inherent in Christ...; these powers being by Him lent to those who were His witnesses and ambassadors"; id., *Notes on the Miracles of Our Lord* (Grand Rapids, MI: Fleming H. Revell, 1953), p. 5; cf. McCasland's rendering of *dunamis*, "manifestation of divine power," JBL 76 (1957): 149.
89. BAGD, pp. 798ff.: *sōzō* "save, heal" denoting salvation from sin (Luke 7:48,50); healing of the woman with hemorraging (Matt. 9:21,22; Mark 5:28,34; Luke 8:48); resuscitation of Jairus's daughter from death (Mark 5:23; Luke 8:50); healing of the sick in marketplaces (Mark 6:56); healing the blind (Mark 10:52; Luke 18:42); healing the demonized Gadarene (Luke 8:36); healing leprosy (Luke 17:19); of Lazarus being restored to health (John 11:12).

Richardson, *The Miracle-Stories of the Gospels*, pp. 61-62: "The connexion between healing and salvation (in the religious sense) is a characteristic feature of the Gospel tradition. Miracles of healing are, as it were, symbolic demonstrations of God's forgiveness in action....The verb *sōzein* ["save, heal"] is itself ambiguous, meaning, on the one hand, to heal to rescue from danger, to keep safe and sound, and on the other hand, to "save" in the technical biblical-religious sense. The same is true of *iasthai* ["heal, restore"]."

90. Carson in Horton, ed., *Power Religion*, p. 97. Similarly, Boice in Horton, ed., *Power Religion*, pp. 125-126, quoting John Woodhouse; Horton, *Power Religion*, p. 332.

91. The grammatical structure of 1 Corinthians 14:22 cannot be understood any other way: the elliptical clause *hē de prophēteia ou tois apistois alla tois pisteuousin* depends on the preceding clause for its full grammatical and lexical meaning; see Fee, *The First Epistle to the Corinthians*, p. 682 and n. 38; Wayne Grudem, *The Gift of Prophecy in I Corinthians*, pp. 193-194; id., *The Gift of Prophecy in the New Testament and Today*, pp. 173f. and n. 68.

92. Rengstorf, *TDNT*, vol. 7, p. 246.

93. For *erga* denoting "miraculous works" when referring to Jesus and God in the Gospel of John: BAGD, p. 308; Bertram, *"ergon,"* *TDNT*, vol. 2, p. 642; Rengstorf, *"sēmeion,"* *TDNT*, vol. 7, pp. 247-248; Trench, *Notes on the Miracles of Our Lord*, p. 6: "That his *erga* ['works'] are his miracles, the following passages, v. 36; x. 25, 32, 38; xiv. 10-11; xv. 24;...decisively prove."

94. Bruce, *The Hard Sayings of Jesus*, pp. 94-97. Similarly, Hendrickx, *The Miracle Stories of the Synoptic Gospels*, p. 17: "Jesus looks for a faith that allows itself to be carried further by the sign. His opponents did not have this openness. To them the miracles were not signs. They wanted proofs. Therefore, Jesus said, 'No sign shall be given to this generation' (Mk. 8:12)"; Richardson, *The Miracle-Stories of the Gospels*, p. 47: "St. Mark leaves us in no doubt that, although He refused to show a sign to the Pharisees, Jesus nevertheless regarded His miracles as 'signs.'"

95. Carson in Horton, ed., *Power Religion*, p. 93.

96. Boice in Horton, ed., *Power Religion*, p. 128; similarly, Ibid., p. 125.

97. A point made by Rengstorf, *TDNT*, vol. 7, p. 241.

98. Lampe, in Moule, ed., *Miracles. Cambridge Studies*, pp. 173-174.

99. Roe, ed., *Dream Big*, p. 68.

FOLLOWING
CHRIST'S EXAMPLE:

A BIBLICAL VIEW OF DISCIPLESHIP

DON WILLIAMS

Is the Church both to bear Jesus' kingdom message and exercise His kingdom ministry by casting out demons and healing the sick? The answer of some is an emphatic no! For them, the time of Christ and the apostles was unique. The claim has been made that "as the age of revelation came to a close, the signs ceased also"[1] and that "Christians who pursue miraculous signs are setting themselves up for satanic deception."[2]

Our answer to whether the Church should bear Jesus' "kingdom message and exercise His kingdom ministry is an emphatic yes! We will fail to see this responsibility if we fail to place the discipling work of Jesus in its historical context and read the Gospels accordingly. How then did people teach and learn in the ancient world? What did discipleship mean?

TEACHING AND LEARNING IN ANTIQUITY

In Israel and her surrounding milieu, learning was based on an intimate relationship between a teacher and his or her pupil. Lindblom notes, "In the Orient teachers have always gathered around themselves disciples...to receive their instruction and pass on their ideas."[3] Even the "writing prophets" of the Old Testament were no loners. Jeremiah had his secretary Baruch and his friends in court (Jer. 26:24; 36:4; 45:1). Isaiah instructs, "Bind up the testimony, seal the teaching among my disciples" (Isa. 8:16, RSV). There are two reasons for this intimate personal relationship between the teacher and his student. First, teaching was largely transmitted orally. Second, this teaching was to be lived out by being with the teacher and imitating his life.

For the Jews, the basic unit of instruction was the family. In the Exodus, the father teaches his son the meaning of the mighty acts of God by answering his questions about Passover (Exod. 10:1,2; 12:26,27). Likewise, in the wisdom literature, a father addresses his son, and a mother her children, guiding them in practical affairs (see Prov. 1:8; 31:1,26).[4] The second century B.C. Jewish educator, Ben Sirach, uses the same father/son form when he speaks to his disciples or pupils (*The Wisdom of Sirach* 2:1; 3:1; 4:1). Likewise, as a father, the apostle Paul trains Timothy and calls him his son in the faith (Phil. 2:22). Down through the generations, this father-son structure communicates both authority and intimacy.

Since learning takes place in personal relationship, Ben Sirach exhorts the prospective student to find a wise man: "Take your stand in the throng of elders: which of them is wise? Attach yourself to him" (6:34). He should hound him: "If you see a man of understanding, go to him early,/ And let your feet wear out his doorstep" (6:36). The Pharisees and their rabbinic leaders agreed. They were "*Torah*-centric" (*Torah* meaning "revelation" written and oral). Rabbi Hillel says, "More Torah, more life" (*Aboth* II.8). Rabbi Shammai advises, "Make thy *Torah* a fixed duty" (*Aboth* I.15) But how is this to be done? Johoshua ben Perahjah answers, "Make to thyself a teacher" (*Aboth* I.6).[5]

Since ancient culture was basically oral, the first vehicle of learning was the spoken word.[6] Plato valued it over the written word because once speech was transcribed it had no life; it could not answer back (*Phaedrus* 275d). The French Old Testament scholar, Roland de Vaux, notes, "Most teaching...was done by word of mouth. The teacher told his story, gave explanations and asked questions; the pupil repeated the story and asked or answered questions. This method of teaching continued under the Rabbis...."[7] Ben Sirach exhorts his student: "Be willing to listen to every godly discourse,/ And do not let any wise proverb escape you" (6:35). Likewise, the Pharisees stressed the importance of hearing *Torah*. Joezer of Zeredah says: "Let thy house be a place of meeting of the wise, and dust thyself with the dust of their feet and drink their words with thirst" (*Aboth* 1.4).

Since their tradition was oral before it was written, the Pharisees also valued memory. Johannan ben Zaccai (second half of the first century A.D.) sums up one of his disciples as "a plastered cistern that loseth not a drop" (*Aboth* 2.11). His input equaled his output. The nature of oral tradition demands this kind of receiver. The Pharisees of Jesus' day mostly studied *Torah* by rote and quoted it from memory, preserving it with precision and accuracy.[8]

Along with the spoken word and an acute memory, the student needed an intimate relationship with his teacher because learning for life demanded the power of a good example. He must observe his teacher and imitate his behavior. As we have seen, according to Ben Sirach, the pupil is to "attach" himself to his teacher (6:34) and virtually live in his house (6:36).[9] He is to learn not only what to say but when to say it: "A proverb on the lips of a fool will be refused,/ For he will not utter it at the proper time" (20:20). Such timing is only mastered by following the teacher's example.

For the Rabbis, *Torah* is not an academic task. This is why Rabbi Shammai says, "Make thy *Torah* a fixed duty. Say little and do much" (*Aboth* I.15). Their disciples saw "living *Torah*" in their teacher's life.[10] Finkelstein gives this example:

> So anxious was [Rabbi] Akiba...to master...the rules of proper behavior that he followed every action of his teachers with the closest scrutiny and recorded their slightest habits,...on one occasion he actually followed Joshua into a privy. "And I learned from him three good habits," he said many years afterward. "How could you be so disrespectful to your teacher?" asked Ben Azzai. "I considered everything part of the *Torah* and I needed to learn."[11]

This pedagogical ideal is given a moral application by Josephus, the first-century Jewish historian. He writes:

> The Law...enjoins sobriety in...[the children's] upbringing from the very first. It orders that they shall be taught to read and shall learn both the laws and the deeds of their forefathers, in order that they may imitate the latter, and being grounded in the former, may neither transgress nor have any excuse for being ignorant of them. (*Against Apion* II. 204.)

Here is education by word and deed. For the Rabbis, even God himself was to be imitated. In *Sotah* 14a walking after the *Shekinah* means clothing the naked as God did, and visiting the sick as God did.[12]

The goal of this intimate education is to reproduce the teacher's life in his pupil. This is true for both Greeks and Jews. Marrou writes of classical education, "For the Greeks, education—*paideia*—meant...a profound and intimate relationship, a personal union between a young man and an elder who was at once his model, his guide and his initiator....Education remained not so much a form of teaching...as an expenditure of loving effort."[13] This ideal continued to operate in Jesus' time. The first-century Stoic philosopher, Seneca, tells Lucilius:

> Of course...the living voice and the intimacy of a common life will help you more than the written word. You must go to the scene of the action, first because men put more faith in their eyes than in their ears, and second, because the way is long if one follows precepts, but short and helpful, if one follows patterns. Cleanthes could not have been the express image of Zeno, if he had merely heard his lectures; he shared his life, saw into his hidden purposes and watched him to see whether he lived according to his own rules....It was not the classroom of Epicurus, but living together under the same roof, that made great men of Metodorus, Hermarchus, and Polyaenus.[14]

Israel shares a similar ideal. Ben Sirach wants to reproduce his life in his pupil. He writes of a student trained in wisdom:

> When his father [teacher] dies,
> It is as though he were not dead.
> For he leaves behind him
> One like himself. (30:4)

Paul carries this same ideal to his ministry. As a father, he brings his converts to Christ. His life is the example they are to imitate. He also disciples Timothy as his son in the faith and reproduces his life and ministry in him. Timothy learns his teaching, follows his ways and is able to communicate them in his absence. As Paul writes to the Corinthians: "I became your father through the gospel. I exhort you therefore, be imitators of me. For this reason I have sent to you Timothy, who is my beloved and faithful child in the Lord, and he will remind you of my ways which are in Christ, just as I teach everywhere in every church" (1 Cor. 4:15-17).*

In the ancient world, then, teaching and learning took place in intimate relationship, father to son, mother to child, teacher to pupil. The teacher's spoken word was learned and his example was imitated. The goal was to reproduce the teacher's life in the life of his student, so that, in the words of Ben Sirach, he would leave behind him "one like himself" (30:4). And this was exactly what Jesus did in discipling "His followers who, in turn, discipled the Church."

JESUS AND DISCIPLESHIP

Jesus came, bearing the authority of the kingdom of God in the power of the Spirit. The Kingdom (the in-breaking of God's dynamic rule) was the center of His *message*. Mark tells us, "Jesus came into Galilee, preaching the gospel of God, and saying, 'The time is fulfilled, and the kingdom of God is at hand; repent and believe in the gospel'" (Mark 1:14,15). The Kingdom was also the center of His *ministry*. In Luke Jesus says, "But if I cast out demons by the finger of God, then the kingdom of God has come upon you" (Luke 11:20). As Grasser notes, this Kingdom "is not something growing within history but is the miracle which is independent of all human history."[15] A. M. Hunter adds, "It is a divine act."[16]

Jesus' message and ministry are one. The presence of the Kingdom dawning in Him is an event that immediately affects the spiritual and social environment around Him. The Kingdom cannot be locked into some "upper story" Platonic ideal or neoorthodox abstraction.[17] Although some, such as John MacArthur, assert that for "Jesus, preaching the Word was more important than performing signs and wonders,"[18] R. H. Fuller sees the unity of his message and ministry. He writes, "...the miracles of Jesus are part and parcel of his kerygmatic activity. In fact, the miracles are part of the proclamation itself, quite as much as the spoken words of Jesus."[19]

Matthew even states that Jesus' healing ministry was *a means of proclamation*: "Jesus withdrew from that place. Many followed him, and he *healed all their sick*, warning them not to tell who he was. *This was to fulfill what was spoken through the prophet Isaiah*: 'Here is my servant whom I have chosen, the one I love, in whom I delight; I will put my Spirit on him, and *he will proclaim justice to the nations*" (Matt. 12:15-18, *NIV*).

Jeremias adds that the Spirit of God always brings both word and deed, "The word is never without its accompanying deed and the deed is never without the word that proclaims it. So too with Jesus: the concluding revelation is manifested in two ways (see Mat. 11:5f.par.) in acts of power and in words of authority."[20]

As we have seen in Luke, Jesus specifically connects the presence of the Kingdom with casting out demons. How are we to understand this? William Barclay frames the first-century worldview, "Men believed that the air and atmosphere were crowded with demons, most of them malignant spirits waiting to work men harm."[21] Guignebert concurs:

> For the Jews of Jesus' day Palestine was a land peopled by good or evil spirits....A man who claimed to speak in God's name and to prepare his ways was known as a true recipient of the *sign of Jahweh* by his intimacy with angels, and still more by his authority over demons.[22]

> As for Jesus himself, there can be no doubt that he was born and bred and lived out his life in the midst of a threatening cloud of hostile spirits, and that belief in their existence and in their activities was one of...[his] formative elements.[23]

This means that since Jesus bears the kingdom of God, He must also cast out the demons who oppose it. MacArthur acknowledges this in part, as he writes, "Jesus encountered Satan and defeated him by his *dunamis*, his power....In every case Jesus' gift of power was used to combat Satan's kingdom."[24] But MacArthur then takes away what he gives by concluding that, "God's intended purpose for miracles: [is] to confirm new scriptural revelation."[25] Which is it? Is Jesus the Warrior-King in battle with the devil, or is He merely using the devil to authenticate Himself as bearing new revelation from God?

Without a real deliverance from evil, Jesus' proclamation is bogus or mythological or docetic—giving us credentialed truth, disconnected from our own fallen history and bondage to Satan. There is no kingdom of God where the ruler of the other kingdom is not put to flight. Jeremias identifies the war that has been declared, "Jesus enters this world enslaved by Satan with the authority of God, not only to exercise mercy, but above all to join the battle with evil."[26] Stauffer agrees and adds, "The kingdom of God is present where the dominion of the adversary is overthrown."[27] With these power-encounters against the enemy, the end, the eschatological climax to all of history has begun. Jeremias notes, "These victories over the power of evil [casting out demons] are not just isolated invasions of Satan's realm. They are more. They are manifestations of the dawn of the time of salvation and of the beginning of the annihilation of Satan."[28] They "are a foretaste of the eschaton [End]."[29] God is making His final move in His Son as He bears the Kingdom come and coming, and this move continues in His Church until the glorious return of her Lord (see 1 Cor. 15:22-25).

Jesus not only drove out demons, He also healed the sick. This, again, was a necessary manifestation of the presence of the Kingdom. While, for MacArthur, Jesus' healings credential the new revelation that He brings, for the Gospel writers they reveal His compassion for the sick (Matt. 9:35,36; 14:14; 20:34; Mark 5:19; Luke 7:13; cf. Acts 4:9) and the restoration of the fallen Creation. The traditional, first-century Jew used the doctrine of retribution far too simplistically by equating sickness with punishment.[30] Jesus, however, saw the demonic in many forms of illness. Hengel comments, "His eschatological struggle was directed against the demonic powers in the light of the sicknesses caused by them....His only weapon in this struggle was the word of authority...."[31] And Hengel concludes:

> The victory which occurs in Jesus' healings, over the power of Satan, which manifests itself in illness and possession, means the signal and visible "dawn" of the rule of God. A heavenly event corresponds to this victory: the fall of Satan, the Accuser before God. Probably Jesus' activity as an "exorcist" and "healer of the sick" awakened among the simple Galilean population at least as much attention and enthusiasm as his preaching. It can be seen that this part of his activity (which we find so hard to understand today) was also given great importance in the early tradition of the community, for in the tradition about the Mission of the disciples the Twelve specifically receive authority to exorcise and to heal the sick....Even an old *baraita* knows of the Jewish Christians of Palestine having authority "to heal" those fallen seriously ill "in the name of Jesus"...and of this being gladly made use of by the non-Christian Jewish population despite the objections of individual rabbis.[32]

It is impossible, therefore, to make the exorcisms and healings of Jesus simply into evidences for His deity, clustered around His historical presence and that of His apostles, as those who oppose the third wave or "Signs and

Wonders" movement tend to do today.[33] A. M. Hunter sees the following serious objections to this position. First, Jesus did not work miracles in order to call attention to His message or Himself. In Mark 8:12, He refused to produce a sign on demand. R. H. Fuller comments, "Like the devil in the temptation, they [the Pharisees] tempt Jesus to perform some striking act to prove who he is. Jesus rejects this kind of a sign *en toto*....Jesus refuses, not to perform signs as such, but signs intended to point to *himself*."[34]

Second, Hunter says that this theory does violence to the close connection between miracles and faith. Jesus does not do His mighty works simply to produce faith ("evidences"). They demand faith. Third, "Worst of all, it portrays Jesus as a sort of 'heavenly bell man.'"[35] To this I would add that the "realized" part of the eschatological Kingdom demands such miracles. Jesus' signs are much more than evidences. They are a real assault on Satan and his demons, delivering people from their power and the debilitating effects they have over their lives.

These miracles are the necessary and substantial events of the Kingdom that is "at hand" (Mark 1:15) and "in your midst" (Luke 17:21). The King is here. Satan's kingdom is now being assaulted and his authority broken (Matt. 12:25-28; Luke 11:17-20). This is the triumphant shout of the New Testament and this is the message and ministry Jesus entrusted to His disciples and through them, to His Church.

Regardless of whether we regard Jesus as a Rabbi,[36] a prophet,[37] a charismatic leader (the Messiah),[38] or all of the above and more, as He really is, the eternal Son of God, it is clear from the Gospels (and the existence of the Church) that He not only bore the message and ministry of the Kingdom, He also called the Twelve and other disciples to bear the same message and ministry on His behalf. In order to accomplish this, like any good teacher in antiquity, He called His followers into an intimate relationship with Himself (Mark 3:14), taught them the message of the Kingdom orally (Mark 4:11), showed them the ministry of the Kingdom in His exorcisms and healings (including His techniques of commanding demons, commanding and touching the sick, etc.)[39] and then sent them with His authority and power to do the same. Mark 3:14,15 tells us, "And He appointed twelve, that they might be with Him, and that He might send them out to preach and to have authority to cast out the demons."

Lest we suppose that this ministry was limited to the Twelve, we must remember that Jesus appointed 70 others, commanding them to heal the sick in the cities they entered and say, "The kingdom of God has come near to you" (Luke 10:9). Later they report with joy, "Lord, even the demons are subject to us in Your name" (Luke 10:17). Jeremias comments, "Authority over the spirits recurs constantly in the mission sayings and is virtually a characteristic of them (Mark 6:7 par.; Matt. 10:7; Luke 10:19....)."[40] In other words, Jesus reproduced His Kingdom ministry in His disciples and through them (and, at Pentecost, through the power of the Spirit as the risen Lord) reproduced His Kingdom ministry in the Church. Jeremias notes:

> They [the Twelve] are to announce the dawn of the time of salvation and to make incursions into the realm of Satan by driving out the demons. That means that they have to make the same announcement as Jesus himself, and they have to do so in the same way as him: in word and action. With them, too, both belong together. The word alone is an empty shell; action alone can be the work of the devil. The reign of God is manifested only in word and action together.[41]

In the context of all that we have seen about teaching and learning in antiquity, Jeremias adds, "...in the person of the messengers, Jesus himself comes. The nature of being a messenger is to represent Jesus."[42] And to represent Jesus, the Messiah, the bearer of the Kingdom, the herald of the End, is to bear His ministry. Hengel writes:

> In what he did, Jesus' aim was not to form tradition or to nurture exegetical or apocalyptic scholarship but to proclaim the nearness of God in word and deed, to call to repentance, and to proclaim the will of God understood radically in the light of the imminent rule of God, which indeed was already dawning in his activity; similarly, "following after" him and "discipleship" were oriented to this one great aim.[43]

While for Hengel Jesus' disciples can be called pupils in a derivative sense, Jesus breaks all the molds with His "unheard of self-confidence [manifested in His messianic self-consciousness, healings, exorcisms, eating with tax gathers and sinners, and actualizing the presence of the kingdom] which cuts across all the analogies in the field of *Religionsgeschichte* (the history of religion) which are known to us from contemporary Judaism."[44]

The one mold that is not broken, however, is Jesus training His disciples to be like Himself in a way similar to other teachers in the ancient world. As He says, "A disciple is not above his teacher, nor a slave above his master. It is enough for the disciple that he become as his teacher, and the slave as his master" (Matt.

10:24,25). Dr. Cyril H. Powell has said of the disciples' training, "In all this, Acts witnesses to the emergence of power in ways comparable to those recounted in the Gospels concerning Jesus. Jesus had said (in Lk only 6:40) 'Every disciple when he is fully equipped (*katertismenos*) shall be as his master.' "[45]

The radical difference in Jesus' discipling is not the form[46] but the content: the presence and power of the Kingdom overcoming the works of the devil (1 John 3:8). Thus, Hengel concludes that Jesus' call to discipleship was a call to participate in His mission and authority "in the eschatological event which taking its beginning in him was moving powerfully towards the complete dawn of the rule of God *en dunamei* [in power] (Mk. 9:1, cf. 13:26 par.)....But this would mean that following Jesus would be comprehensible only as service to the cause of the approaching kingdom of God."[47] Following after Him also meant participation in His sufferings,[48] for His kingdom ministry of power climaxed in the scandal of the Son of Man crucified in weakness (Mark 8:31, par.). On the cross, in humiliation and abandonment, Jesus bore our sins, lifted the curse of the Law, died our death, and defeated the devil. Here, in this final act of sacrifice (and in His glorious resurrection to follow), the enemies of the Kingdom are overcome. Here too, in the Cross, after Pentecost, the kingdom power of God through His Spirit is now released (Gal. 3:1-5).

If Jesus trained His disciples to reproduce His message and ministry of the kingdom, then we should expect that they, in turn, were to train the Church to do the same (1 Cor. 11:1; Phil. 4:9; 1 Thess. 1:6; etc.). This must be the intention of Jesus' commission to make disciples from all the nations "teaching them to observe all that I commanded you" (Matt. 28:20). To eliminate the Kingdom message and ministry from this agenda in favor of Christology or ethics is to cut out its heart. All must be held together to make any sense of the New Testament.

But did Jesus' reproduction of His Kingdom ministry in His apostles end with them? For MacArthur, the answer is yes. He writes, "no miracle ever occurred in the entire New Testament record except in the presence of an apostle or one directly commissioned by an apostle."[49] His attempt to narrow the field of the miraculous fails, however, on the evidence of the 70 who were not apostles (Luke 10:1) and the rest of the New Testament (see especially Gal. 3:5; cf. Acts 9:17,18; 22:13 [Ananias, a nonapostle, lays hands on Paul and heals him]; Rom. 12:6-8; 1 Cor. 12:1-11,28-31; 14:1-31; 1 Thess. 1:5,6; 5:19,20; Heb. 6:2;[50] Jas. 5:14-16; 1 Pet. 4:10,11).

The risen Lord continues to gift His Church with charismatic leaders: apostles, prophets, evangelists, and pastor-teachers, in order to equip the saints, that is, the whole Church, for ministry (Eph. 4:7-12). This is no seasonal (dispensational) gifting, restricted to the Apostolic Age. Acts hints at this when it shows us that the next generation of leadership, men such as Stephen, Philip, Ananias, and Paul, continue to minister with signs and wonders in the power of the Spirit (see Acts 6:5,8; 8:5-7; 9:17,18 [22:13]; 13:8-12, etc.). And, as we have seen, this ministry continues in the life of their churches. How else can we account for the gifts and power-running riot in Corinth, which Paul corrects but does not quench?

Since the charismatic leaders, starting with the apostles, given by the earthly/risen Lord are also to be disciplers, they, in turn, will invest themselves in those who are raised up by the Spirit just as Jesus did in His incarnate ministry. From the whole cultural context of teaching and learning in antiquity, we can be sure that they will continue the chain of Kingdom teaching and training into the next generation. Of necessity, this means that Kingdom ministry will not end with the Apostolic Age, since, starting with the immediate followers of Jesus, each generation will pass on its ministry to the next.

This appears clearly in Paul. Trained as a Pharisee, he transmits the tradition of Jesus[51] and lives out that tradition so that he can be an example to others as he ministers in power. He tells the Romans, "For I will not presume to speak of anything except what Christ has accomplished through me, resulting in the obedience of the Gentiles in word and deed, in the power of signs and wonders, in the power of the Spirit" (Rom. 15:18,19). Paul also expects his converts to minister in the same way: "Be imitators of me, just as I also am of Christ" (1 Cor. 11:1). To restrict this imitation to doctrine or ethics, is to do violence to the New Testament evidence and to miss the point of discipleship in the ancient world.

As Paul manifested the ministry of Jesus, so he expects His Church to manifest that same ministry. He expects a continuing work of signs and wonders among, for example, the Galatians as he asks, rhetorically, "Does He then, who provides you with the Spirit and works miracles among you, do it by the works of the Law, or by hearing with faith?" (Gal. 3:5). Later, when Paul corrects abuses in Corinth, he never suggests that the powerful manifestations of the Spirit are not of God. The exalted Lord continues His ministry there not only through gifted leaders such as Paul, but also through the whole Church, which is His living Body. W.D. Davies writes:

> To use the famous Pauline metaphor...the Church is the Body of Christ, it is the extension of His Being: quite literally Christians are to form the eyes, the feet, the ears, the mind of Christ (the notions of corporate personality, derived from a Semitic background, which lie behind such a conception of an extension of the Being of Christ in His followers, are indispensable to the

understanding of the New Testament doctrine of the Church...). In other words, since the Church is the Body of Christ, it is called upon to perform His work: the Church is the continuation of the life of Jesus, the Messiah.[52]

Thus this self-giving ministry of Christ becomes the norm for the life of the Church, its pattern: the life of the Church is to be the continuation of that ministry, and, in so far as this is actually the case, the Church heals as He healed, and restores as He restored, the brokenness of men.[53]

First Corinthians 12 makes it clear that this ministry includes the works of the Kingdom. Paul describes various gifts of the Spirit such as prophecy, words of wisdom and knowledge, gifts of healings, discernment of spirits, and effecting miracles, which will equip the Church to continue what Jesus did. In MacArthur's attempt to make all of these gifts "sign gifts" (proving revelation rather than affecting ministry), he is forced to define prophecy in the gift list of Romans 12 as preaching, while admitting that prophecy in 1 Corinthians 12 is "revelatory prophecy."[54] We may rightly ask, by what special exegetical insight has one the right to take the same word in the same context of spiritual gifts and give it two separate meanings?

The gifts in 1 Corinthians 12, then, are situationally given by the Holy Spirit (1 Cor. 12:11; cf. 11:18,33,34; 14:23,26) for ministry in the moment (1 Cor. 14:24-26,30). They are also institutionalized in some who are appointed to exercise them regularly in leadership in the Church (1 Cor. 12:28 *appointments* [*tithēmi* "make, appoint"] as opposed to incidental giftings). They are to be actively sought (1 Cor. 14:1) and exercised in love (1 Cor. 13). By giving the gifts of the Spirit, Jesus continues His ministry through His whole Church. Because of this gifting, every Christian has the potential to prophesy or heal the sick (1 Cor. 12:7; 14:1,5,12,13,24,31; John 14:12; Matt. 7:7-11; Jas. 4:2). Here, indeed, is the functional expression of the priesthood of all believers and the ministry of the laity.

The New Testament bears witness to the continuation of the Kingdom ministry of Jesus far beyond the Twelve. His assaults upon Satan's kingdom and the healing of God's fallen creation extend into the next generation (see Heb. 2:3,4 and Luke 10:1; John 6:60—70; 1 Cor. 15:6). But Kingdom ministry did not stop there. Signs and wonders did not cease with the Apostolic Age or become marginal as in the case of the second century A.D. heretic Montanus and his prophetic followers. MacArthur's attempt to make the charismatic movement "the spiritual heir" to Montanus[55] fails on the evidence—the charismatic movement, at its best, instead is the heir of the orthodox Early Church Fathers. Consider their evidence: Justin Martyr writes in the middle of the second century A.D.:

> This Word went out to all nations over which the demons rule, as David testifies, "The gods of the nations are demons." And so it happened that many, powerfully gripped by his Word abandoned the demons whom they served. Now through Jesus they have come to believe in the Almighty God.[56]

But how are these demons expelled? Justin continues, "For every demon is exorcised, conquered, and subdued in the very name of this Son of God."[57] He concludes:

> After all, many of our people have healed a great number of possessed persons who did not receive healing from any other exorcist, sorcerer, or herb doctor. They did this throughout the whole world, and even in your own capital city, by driving out the demons in the name of Jesus Christ.[58]

Irenaeus, Bishop of Lyons, adds his second-century witness to Kingdom ministry as he writes:

> Wherefore, also, those who are in truth, His disciples receiving grace from Him, do in His name perform [miracles], so as to promote the welfare of other men, according to the gift which each one has received from Him. For some do certainly and truly drive out devils, so that those who have thus been cleansed from evil spirits frequently both believe [in Christ], and join themselves to the Church. Others have foreknowledge of things to come; they see visions, and utter prophetic expressions. Others still, heal the sick by laying their hands upon them, and they are made whole. Yea, moreover, as I have said, the dead even have been raised up, and remained among us for many years. And what shall I more say? It is not possible to name the number of gifts which the Church [scattered] throughout the whole world, has received from God, in the name of Jesus Christ....[But] directing her prayers to the Lord, who made all things...and calling upon the name of our

> Lord Jesus Christ, she has been accustomed to work miracles for
> the advantage of mankind.[59]

From these Church Fathers, it is clear that the generations that followed the Apostolic Age experienced the risen Lord continuing His kingdom ministry in the midst of His people, engaging in spiritual warfare against the devil and all his works. This was no diminishing afterglow from the time of the apostles. Fox shows that the battle against the demons, lurking behind the idols and working "wonders and visions," continued for centuries.[60] The church at Rome in A.D. 251 listed among its staff 154 ministers and 52 exorcists.[61] According to Fox, Cyprian, the third-century Bishop of Carthage, "pictures the action of the Spirit on a man's inner demon in terms which are compounded of torture, burning and beating. Ejection, it seems involved a rough combat of powers, with few holds barred."[62] In the fourth century, Jerome reveals that Christians liked to remember their "holy men" having their ways "with demons and miracles."[63] About A.D. 420, Sozoman recounts that Hilarion exorcized a friend of his grandfather and turned the man's family to Christ, "succeeding where Jewish and pagan exorcists had previously failed: Sozoman's grandfather became a Christian too."[64] To identify such ministry as heretical or marginal, as MacArthur attempts to do, is to deny the witness of history in favor of a theological opinion.

IN CONCLUSION

In the book *Ministry and the Miraculous*, several Fuller Theological Seminary professors argue the traditional position that God grants miracles in order to authenticate His Word. David Hubbard, president of Fuller, writes in the foreword, "The theological conclusion to be drawn from the Bible's own use of the miraculous seems clear; the primary motive for divine miracle is not compassion [in manifesting God's kingdom] but revelation."[65] In other words, miracles credential Jesus and His apostles, they are evidences of divine authority and basically end with the Apostolic Age. Out of this study, a vision for ministry at Fuller emerges: "The minister of the gospel should major in the power that enables ordinary people to bear the cross and accept the burdens of suffering for the sake of doing God's will in a world that hungers for forgiveness, reconciliation, justice, peace, the feeding of the hungry, and the relief of the oppressed."[66] This seems to mean that we are to bear with Satan's assaults rather than repulse them. We are to medicate the demonized rather than deliver them. We are to comfort the afflicted rather than heal their affliction.

The Fuller scholars argue their position, first of all, based upon the assumption that foremost among Jesus' works was His "forgiving of people's sins"[67] rather than casting out demons and healing the sick. Forgiveness, however, is never included in the Gospel summaries of His ministry or in His commission to the Twelve and the 70 (Matt. 4:23, etc.). The Fuller position makes a theological judgment rather than a historical observation by placing forgiveness at the top of the list of Jesus' works.[68] Rather, as Matthew 9:6, Mark 2:10,11, and Luke 5:24 (also Jas. 5:15,16) show, healing of sickness and casting out demons are *signs of God's forgiveness of sin*. Richardson notes this when he says "miracles of healing are, as it were, symbolic demonstrations of God's forgiveness in action."[69]

Second, the Fuller scholars warn that Christians should not expect too much worldly benefit (such as healings) because Jesus calls us to suffer.[70] Granted that this is a part of our call, we also live in a kingdom *come* and coming where God's reign is actually breaking in upon us. To stress suffering at the expense of healing is to deny the realized aspect of the Kingdom in our midst (Matt. 10:7,8; Luke 10:9; 17:21; 1 Cor. 4:20; Rom. 14:17).

Third, the Fuller position argues that miracles have a narrow function; they signal that the Kingdom is drawing near in the "unique acts of God in Jesus."[71] But as we have seen, we should expect signs and wonders to continue because they not only reveal the Kingdom, they also *realize* the Kingdom, especially in delivering people from demons as Jesus' own words state in Matthew 12:28 and Luke 11:20. As Acts and 1 Corinthians assert, it is the risen Lord who continues His kingdom ministry in His Body, the Church. He cannot do less than who He is.

Fourth, the Fuller scholars assert that Jesus' mandate to the apostles to preach the Kingdom and heal the sick was a "specific mission" with "limited objectives."[72] Their commission, however, was no more specific and limited than the ministry of Jesus itself. What He did personally and what He did with His disciples hang or fall together.

Fifth, the Fuller scholars claim that there is no healing mandate in the Great Commission. As we have seen, this can be challenged from the form of the Commission in Matthew 28:18-20, where Jesus' disciples are to teach their converts to do everything He commanded them. Must not this include announcing the Kingdom, casting out demons and healing the sick?

The witness of the New Testament shows the Commission must include them. First, in Acts 13:51 Paul and Barnabas obey the command to the Twelve and the seventy-two to *"shake the dust off your feet"* as a testimony against unbelieving towns (Matt. 10:14; Mark 6:11; Luke 9:5; 10:11), showing they still considered the pre-Crucifixion commissions to be binding.[73]

Second, the apostles continued to proclaim the gospel by preaching and healing in the postresurrection period just as they were commanded to do in the pre-Crucifixion commissions to the Twelve and seventy-two (Acts 3:6,12; 4:29,30; 5:12-16,20,21,28,42; 9:34,35; 14:3,8-10,15ff.; 15:12,36; 18:5,11 [cf. 2 Cor. 12:12; 1 Cor. 2:4,5]; 19:8-12; Rom. 15:18,19; 1 Cor. 1:6,7 [cf. 12:9]; 2 Cor. 12:12; 1 Thess. 1:5,6; Heb. 2:3,4).

Finally, the apostles not only proclaimed the gospel by preaching and healing, but they also taught the disciples they made to proclaim the gospel by preaching and healing—nonapostles such as Stephen (Acts 6:8,10), Philip (Acts 8:4-7,12); Ananias (Acts 9:17,18; 22:12-16); congregations such as the Corinthians (1 Cor. 11:1; 12:9); the Galatians (Gal. 3:5), the Philippians (Phil. 4:9); the Thessalonians (1 Thess. 1:5,6); and Jewish Christian congregations (Heb. 6:1,2[74]; Jas. 5:14-16).

To the above points, MacArthur would add that miracles ceased with the apostles and their companions because fresh revelation ceased as well. Apart from his theological position, what concrete evidence does he offer for this assertion? MacArthur answers, "The types of miracles claimed [today] ...are nothing like New Testament miracles. Jesus and the apostles instantly and completely healed people....New Testament miracles were immediate, thorough, and permanent....By contrast, most modern miracles are nearly always partial, gradual, or temporary."[75]

Such a statement seems completely unable to explain modern miracles that are exactly like New Testament miracles—immediate, thorough, and permanent.[76] These miracles are delivering people afflicted with demons by the name of Jesus in the power of the Spirit. Having seen this happen numbers of times, I must simply say that I stand with Justin Martyr and Irenaeus. Jesus has come to break the power of the enemy and He continues to do this today through His Church, just as He did in the early centuries. This will only become real for us as we see demons challenge us as they did Jesus, be silenced by Jesus through us, and then come out, often with physical convulsions or other manifestations just as they did when Jesus sent them packing in His earthly ministry (see Mark 1:21-28).

MacArthur writes, "We are not commissioned to confront satanic power with miracle power. We are commissioned to confront satanic lies with divine truth."[77] But such a statement seems to ignore the fact that we are not only dealing with "lies" but with liars (John 8:44) when we are dealing with real malignant personalities, and they must be driven out. I have seen numbers of witches, drug addicts, sex addicts and others set free from these evil powers by the commanding name of Jesus. This is the core of Kingdom ministry. As quoted above, MacArthur warns, "Indeed, Christians who pursue miraculous signs are setting themselves up for satanic deception." But, in light of our study, may we not warn that Christians who do not pursue miraculous signs according to the biblical model of ministry are setting themselves up for satanic deception? Are they not in danger of "having a form of godliness but denying its power" (2 Tim. 3:5, *NKJV*)?

In conclusion, Jesus the Messiah, the eternal Son of God, bore the Kingdom in His word and work. Like any good first-century teacher, He discipled His followers in order to reproduce not only His life of faith and holiness, but also His ministry in them. When He ascended into heaven, He left behind ones "like himself" (Ben Sirach) who He then filled with Himself by His Spirit. They were like Him in doctrine, character, and ministry. They, in turn, discipled the next generation to be like themselves, as Jesus had done.

The risen Lord, however, is the key to all of this. By His Spirit, He pours His life into His Church and continues His ministry through those who obey His command to preach the Kingdom, cast out demons and heal the sick. In ages of secularization, rationalism, and unbelief, this ministry has grown dim, to be sure. But as God renews His Church, Kingdom ministry breaks forth again. So it is in our generation, across the continents, across ethnic groups, across denominations and across theological traditions. So it is more and more intensively as we approach the end of this age.

Notes

*All Scripture quotations in this chapter are taken from the NASB unless otherwise noted.

1. See, for example, John MacArthur, *Charismatic Chaos* (Grand Rapids, MI: Zondervan, 1992), p. 118.
2. Ibid., p. 120.
3. J. Lindblom, *Prophecy in Ancient Israel* (Philadelphia, PA: Muhlenberg, 1962), p. 160.
4. Similar formulae appear in Egyptian wisdom literature as well. See "The Instruction of King Amen-em-het" (1960 B.C.). "The beginning of the instruction which the majesty of the King...made, when he spoke in a message of truth to his son." James Pritchard, *Ancient Near Eastern Texts Relating to the Old Testament*, 2nd, ed., (Princeton, NJ: Princeton University Press, 1955), p. 418.
5. All Rabbinical citations come from before the fall of Jerusalem (A.D. 70). Unless otherwise noted, they are found in *Pirke Aboth*. See R. H. Charles (ed.), *Apocrypha and Pseudepigrapha*, (Oxford, England: The Clarendon Press, 1913), Vol. II, p. 686.

6. This observation is not intended to depreciate the importance of written texts, from the Old Testament and the legal, mythological, wisdom, and ritual writings of the Ancient Near East, to Homer and the classical Greek philosophers, etc. It is intended to make a point that we who live in a culture dependent upon the written word often minimize or forget.

7. Roland de Vaux, Ancient Israel, Its Life and Institutions (New York: McGraw-Hill, 1961), p. 49.

8. When the Mishnah was published, its original form was not in writing but in a fixed oral text recited by the Tannaim or "repeaters." See Saul Lieberman, Hellenism in Jewish Palestine (New York: Jewish Theological Seminary of America, 1950), p. 88.

9. "Attach" (dābaq), according to Brown, Driver, and Briggs, "starts with the ideal of physical proximity...." Hebrew and English Lexicon of the Old Testament (Oxford, England: The Clarendon Press, 1952), p. 179.

10. Birger Gerhardsson, Memory and Manuscript (Lund, Sweden: C.W.K. Gleerup, 1961), pp. 182ff.

11. Louis Finkelstein, Akiba (New York: Covici Friede Publishers, 1936), p. 181. See B. Berakot 62a; Yer. Berakot 9.8, 14c.

12. Cited in Wolfson, Philo (Cambridge, MA: Harvard University Press, 1947), Vol II, p. 195.

13. Henri Marrou, A History of Education in Antiquity (New York: Sheed and Ward, 1956), p. 31f.

14. Seneca, Ad Lucilium Epistulae Morales, VI.5-7. Cited by Willis De Boer, The Imitation of Paul (Kampen, Netherlands: J.H. Kok, 1962), p.26.

15. Cited in Martin Hengel, The Charismatic Leader and His Followers (New York: Crossroad, 1981), p. 60, n.87.

16. A.M. Hunter, The Works and Words of Jesus (Philadelphia, PA: Westminster, 1975), p. 76.

17. I am indebted to Francis Schaeffer for this thought in Escape from Reason (Downers Grove, IL: InterVarsity Press, 1968), p. 46.

18. MacArthur, op. cit., p. 139.

19. R.H. Fuller, The Mission and Achievement of Jesus (Chicago, IL: Alec. Allenson, 1954), p. 40; Many New Testament scholars have noted the revelatory nature of both word and deed in the ministry of Jesus, the apostles and the Early Church (See also appendix 1 of this book: "Power Evangelism and the New Testament Evidence"): F. F. Bruce, The Hard Sayings of Jesus (Downers Grove, IL: InterVarsity Press, 1983), pp. 96-97; O. Hofius, in C. Brown, ed., NIDNTT, vol. 2, pp. 632-633; K. Tagawa, Miracles et évangile (Études d'histoire et de philosophie religieuses, 62; Paris, France: Presses Universitaires de France, 1966), p. 87 (also see pp. 49-73, espec. pp. 53 and 73); A. Richardson, The Miracle-Stories of the Gospels (London, England: SCM Press, 1941), pp. 17, 35-45; H. van der Loos, The Miracles of Jesus (Supplements to Novum Testamentum, vol. 8. Leiden, Netherlands: E. J. Brill, 1965), pp. 220-224, 252, 284-285; C. H. Powell, The Biblical Concept of Power (London, England: Epworth Press, 1963), p. 131-139; H. Hendrickx, The Miracle Stories of the Synoptic Gospels (San Francisco, CA: Harper & Row, 1987), p. 25; B. Klappert, NIDNTT, vol. 3, p. 1108;

G. Delling, "Botschaft und Wunder im Wirken Jesu," in H. Ristow and K. Matthiae, eds., *Der historische Jesus und der kerygmatische Christus* (Berlin, Germany: Evangelische Verlagsanstalt, 1961), p. 393; G. Friedrich, *"euaggelizomai,"* *TDNT*, vol. 2, p. 720; W. Grundmann, *"dunamis,"* *TDNT*, vol. 2, p. 311.

20. J. Jeremias, *Theology of the New Testament* (New York: Scribner's, 1971), p. 85 (for similar comments, see references in previous note).

21. William Barclay, *The Mind of Jesus* (New York: Harper & Row, 1960), p. 71; cf. T. H. Gaster, "Demon," in *IDB*, vol. 1, pp. 822-823.

22. G. Guignebert, *The Jewish World in the Time of Jesus* (London, England: Routledge and Kegan Paul, 1939), p. 104.

23. Ibid., p. 105.

24. MacArthur, *op. cit.*, pp. 200-201.

25. Ibid., p. 201.

26. J. Jeremias, *op. cit.*, p. 94.

27. E. Stauffer, *New Testament Theology* (New York: MacMillian, 1955), p. 124.

28. Jeremias, *op. cit.*, p. 94.

29. Ibid., p. 95.

30. A. Oepke, *TDNT*, vol. 3, p. 201.

31. Hengel, *op. cit.*, p. 60.

32. Ibid., p. 66.

33. See D.A. Carson, "The Purpose of Signs and Wonders in the New Testament," in Michael Scott Horton, ed., *Power Religion* (Chicago, IL: Moody Press, 1992). It is significant that Carson never relates Jesus' signs and wonders to the presence of the Kingdom or to His battle with Satan. By avoiding this major theme of New Testament theology, Carson makes a linguistic analysis of signs and wonders that is remarkably cut out of its proper context (to say nothing of the other proper context, teaching and learning in antiquity).

34. R.H. Fuller, *op. cit.*, p. 39.

35. A.M. Hunter, *op. cit.*, p. 55.

36. Harald Riesenfeld, *The Gospel Tradition and Its Beginnings* (London, England: Mowbray, 1957), p. 24.

37. Rudolph Bultmann, *Jesus and the Word* (New York: Scribner's, 1958), p. 124.

38. Hengel, *op. cit.*, concludes, "Thus, basically, Jesus stood outside any discoverable uniform teaching tradition of Judaism," p. 49.

39. Compare Mark 1:25; 5:8; 9:25; Luke 4:35 ("come out" *exerchomai*) and Acts 16:18 ("come out" *exerchomai*).
Compare Mark 2:11; 5:41; Luke 5:24; 7:14; 8:54; John 5:8 ("get up" *egeirō*) and Acts 3:6,7 ("get up" *egeirō* majority of texts); 9:34,40; 14:10 ("stand up" *anastēthi*).
Compare John 5:8 ("walk" *peripatei*) and Acts 3:6 ("walk" *peripatei*).
Compare Matthew 8:3,15; 9:25,29; Mark 1:31,41; 5:41; 6:5; 8:23,25; Luke 4:40; 5:13; 8:54; 13:13; 14:4 (laying on of hands) and Acts 8:12; 9:17; 28:8 (laying on of hands).
Compare Luke 18:42 ("see again" *anablepson*) and Acts 22:13 ("see again" *anablepson*).
Compare Matthew 9:25; Mark 5:40 (removing a weeping crowd) and Acts 9:40 (removing a weeping crowd).

40. Jeremias, *op. cit.*, p. 95.
41. Ibid., p. 237.
42. Ibid., p. 238.
43. Hengel, *op. cit.*, p. 53.
44. Ibid., p. 66.
45. Powell, *The Biblical Concept of Power*, p. 138 and n. 36.
46. Although the form was not Rabbinic—Jesus called His disciples, they did not seek Him out. He did not teach with a chain of authoritative tradition, but by His naked word of authority. His methods were not scribal or bookish, etc. Other major differences in form were also the way Jesus preached the urgency of the Kingdom and the "form" of deliverance from demons and healing the sick, for example, by touching them and releasing the power of the Spirit in this way (Mark 1:31, cf. Luke 8:46).
47. Hengel, *op. cit.*, p. 73.
48. Ibid., p. 78.
49. MacArthur, *op. cit.*, p. 121.
50. Besides bestowing the Spirit and spiritual gifts, the *"laying on of hands,"* mentioned in the list of elementary teachings, is one of the principle means of prayer for healing in the New Testament (Matt. 9:29; Mark 1:41; 5:23; 6:5; 7:32; 16:18; Luke 4:40; 13:13; Acts 9:17; 28:8; Jas. 5:14, *"let them pray over [epi] him"*). It follows that prayer for healing and prayer to convey the power and gifts of the Spirit was included in the *"elementary teachings"* of the Early Church.
51. Oscar Cullmann, *The Early Church* (London, England: SCM, 1956), pp. 64-65.
52. W.D. Davies, *Christian Origins and Judaism* (London, England: Darton, Longman & Todd, 1962), p. 234.
53. Ibid., p. 235.
54. MacArthur, *op. cit.*, p. 199.
55. Ibid., p. 75.
56. Eberhard Arnold, *The Early Christians* (Grand Rapids, MI: Baker, 1979), p. 95.
57. *Dialogue with Trypho*, 85.1-2, in Ibid., p. 96.
58. *Second Apology*, 6 in Ibid., p. 138.
59. Irenaeus *Against Heresies*, XXXII.4, in *The Ante-Nicene Fathers* (Grand Rapids, MI: Eerdmans, 1981), Vol. I, p. 409.
60. Robin Lane Fox, *Pagans and Christians* (New York: Harper & Row, 1986), p. 137.
61. Ibid., p. 268.
62. Ibid., p. 328.
63. Ibid., p. 20.
64. Ibid., p. 19.
65. Lewis Smedes (ed.), *Ministry and the Miraculous* (Pasadena, CA: Fuller Theological Seminary, 1987), p. 13.
66. Ibid., pp. 28-29.
67. Ibid., p. 25.
68. I would certainly concur with the Fuller position theologically. There is no tri-

umph of God's kingdom apart from the atoning work of Christ. If Jesus had healed everybody and not died for their sins, they would have all been healthy and gone to hell. We are speaking here of the historical evidence of the Gospels, which gives first place to Jesus' kingdom message and ministry.

69. A. Richardson, *The Miracle-Stories of the Gospels* (London, England: Epworth, 1942), p. 61-62.

70. Smedes, *op. cit.*, p. 26.

71. Ibid., p. 28.

72. Ibid., p. 29.

73. See appendix 3 ("Matt. 28:18-20—The Great Commission and Jesus' Commands to Preach and Heal"); Konrad Weiss (*TDNT*, vol. 6, p. 629 and nn. 47-48) has no trouble relating Paul and Barnabas's obeying the command to shake the dust from their feet in Acts 13:51 to the authority of Christ conveyed to His disciples in the pre-Crucifixion commissions. Dr. van der Loos (*The Miracles of Jesus*, pp. 217-218) also points out that the evidence from the Gospels and Acts suggests a clear relationship between the pre-Crucifixion commissions and the postresurrection ministry of the apostles: "Acts make mention of *many signs* [italics his] performed by the apostles....This miraculous power of the apostles was inseparably bound up with the *instructions and authority* [italics his] which Jesus had given them. The discourse to the disciples before they are sent forth, Mat. 10 and parallel passages, begins with the statement that Jesus called His twelve disciples to Him and gave them power 'against unclean spirits, to cast them out, and to heal all manner of sickness and all manner of disease.' 'Preach, saying, The kingdom of heaven is at hand. Heal the sick, cleanse the lepers, raise the dead, cast out devils: freely ye have received, freely give,' are the direct instructions that Jesus gives His disciples."

74. For the "laying on of hands," mentioned in the list of elementary teachings, as one of the principle means of prayer for healing in the New Testament, see E. Lohse, "*cheir*," *TDNT*, vol. 9, pp. 431-432; cf. Matthew 9:29; Mark 1:41; 5:23; 6:5; 7:32; 16:18; Luke 4:40; 13:13; Acts 9:17; 28:8; James 5:14 "let them pray over [*epi*] him."

75. MacArthur, *op. cit.*, p. 110.

76. See, for example, the tabulated statistics and in-depth analysis of 100 randomly selected cases out of a total of 1,890 cases of healing and other phenomena presented by Dr. David Lewis, a British cultural anthropologist and Cambridge Research Associate (Mongolia and Inner Asian Studies unit) in his book, *Healing: Fiction, Fantasy or Fact? A Comprehensive Analysis of the Healings and Associated Phenomena at John Wimber's Harrogate Conference* (London, England: Hodder & Stoughton, 1989). Dr. Lewis also summarizes his research in his chapter in this book. See also the carefully documented cases of otherwise inexplicable healings associated with prayer in Christ's name, which are investigated by obstetrician and gynecologist, Dr. Rex Gardner, *Healing Miracles: A Doctor Investigates* (London, England: Darton, Longman and Todd, 1986) and Dr. Ann England, ed., *We Believe in Healing* (London, England: Marshall, Morgan & Scott, 1982). Gardner remarks in a 1983 article, which presents detailed accounts of seven contemporary case-histories in the *British Medical*

Journal that "no attempt has been made to prove that miracles have occurred, such proof being probably impossible. The adjective 'miraculous' is, however, permissible as a convenient shorthand for an otherwise almost inexplicable healing which occurs after prayer to God and brings honor to the Lord Jesus Christ" (Gardner, "Miracles of Healing in Anglo-Celtic Northumbria as Recorded by the Venerable Bede and His Contemporaries: A Reappraisal in the Light of Twentieth-Century Experience," *British Medical Journal* 287 [1983], p. 1932).

77. Ibid., p. 135 MacArthur writes, "Today we deal with evil spirits not by finding someone with the gift of powers to cast them out, but by following the instructions of 2 Corinthians 2:10-11; Ephesians 6:11-18; 2 Timothy 2:25-26; James 4:7; and I Peter 5:7-9. All these verses teach us how we can triumph over Satan." Ibid., p. 201. While this is true, MacArthur does not deal with demon possession or demonization. This becomes completely clear if we ask, How do you deal with a demon in a non-Christian? The teaching texts MacArthur cites are for Christians. None of these texts apply to an unbeliever or to one who needs actual deliverance from a demon.

6

POWER MINISTRY IN THE EPISTLES:

A REPLY TO THE EVANGELICAL CESSATIONIST POSITION*

WALTER R. BODINE

In his review of four books favorable to the so-called "signs and wonders" move-ment, Tim Stafford voices an objection that is frequently raised. It is the asser-tion that "the New Testament epistles show such slight interest in miracles."[1] The implication often drawn, though not explicitly by Stafford, is that this indicates the temporary nature of the "sign gifts" (i.e., healing, miracles, prophe-cy, tongues, interpretation of tongues), a view usually known as the "cessation-ist position."[2] Otherwise, as this line of reasoning goes, we would expect more attention to them in the Epistles.

I wish to argue here that this is not the case at all. First of all, I doubt that it is fair to speak of a "slight interest" in miracles in the Epistles. At least five Epistles devote explicit attention to the gifts of the Spirit (Rom. 12:3-8; 1 Cor.

12-14; Eph. 4:1-16; 1 Thess. 5:19-22; 1 Pet. 4:10,11). Wherever the gifts are detailed, those that are regarded from the cessationist viewpoint as temporary are intertwined with those that are regarded as permanent. No distinction is drawn or implied in the New Testament[3], and the space devoted to the subject is hardly insignificant.

I recognize that the emphasis of the Epistles is elsewhere. Their primary concern is with building faith and character. They were written to believers by people who had ministered to them and who deeply cared to see them spiritually established so as to be able to live productively within the Christian community and in society. In other words, the Epistles had a primary focus; and it was other than that of supernatural gifting. The focus was on character development and godly living. This does not call into question the continuance of any of the gifts any more than it questions the ongoing reality of other functions of believers that are likewise not emphasized in the Epistles. Such would include, for example, evangelism, relief to the poor, social action against oppression and so on

Let me amplify, using evangelism as an example. In contrast to frequent exhortations to exercise spiritual gifts (Rom. 12:6-8; 1 Cor. 12:31; 14:1,12,13, 26-39; 1 Thess. 5:19,20[4]; 1 Pet. 4:10,11), I have not yet found one express command to verbal witnessing in the Epistles[5]. Does this mean that the writers of the Epistles viewed personal evangelism as an initiating activity, which would cease once the Church was established, or once the New Testament was complete? The latter could as plausibly be argued as the cessation of certain spiritual gifts at the completion of the canon, and the evidence of the Epistles, if it be interpreted thus, would be stronger for the cessation of evangelism. No evangelical I know would argue that way, nor would I. Neither should such evidence be claimed for a cessationist position regarding certain gifts.

The truth of the matter is that many activities were an integral part of the life of the Early Church and were assumed, although not emphasized, by the writers of the Epistles. Here are some examples of this point with specific reference to the miraculous working of the Holy Spirit in believers' daily lives.

When Paul elaborates on the faith that brings us into relationship with God, he cites the example of Abraham, who fathered a son by faith after he and his wife were both past the age when this was physically possible. In speaking of the God who did this for Abraham, Paul uses present participles, thereby bringing into contact with his and his readers' current experience the God "who gives life to the dead and calls into being that which does not exist" (Rom. 4:17, NASB). In reflecting on his own ministry, Paul made it clear that he saw the manifest work of the Spirit as integral to the full proclamation of the gospel

(Rom. 15:19).[6] A clear focus on the essential message of the gospel and a risk-taking dependence on the Spirit to confirm that message with accompanying demonstrations of God's power were characteristic of his ministry (1 Cor. 2:3-5; 1 Thess. 1:5). Indeed, the operation of the Spirit's power was understood to be a mark of the presence of the Kingdom in the Church (1 Cor. 4:20), even as were righteousness, peace, and joy (Rom. 14:17).

Lengthy instructions were given to believers about how they might properly participate in the communal ministry of the Spirit (1 Cor. 12-14). The release and miracles of the Spirit were an integral part of the life of the church of Galatia, to whom an entire epistle was written to stabilize their faith in Christ, while only one passing reference was made to these miracles (Gal. 3:5). Indeed, the very proclamation of the gospel was a supernatural work of the Spirit through the messengers, so that those who heard were hearing the Lord Himself speak (Eph. 2:17; 4:20,21; 1 Pet. 4:11). The attesting signs that accompanied the message delivered were to the recipients both a confirmation (Heb. 2:3,4) and a foretaste of the coming age (Heb. 6:5).

This pattern of word and deed, preaching and healing, was, after all, what the Lord Jesus had foretold about the ministry of His followers after His ascension. Although the Epistles may not say as much about the miracles of the Spirit as some would like (although the preceding sample could be expanded),[7] the four Gospels and Acts surely say a great deal. Jesus' earthly ministry was marked by the declaration of the Kingdom and by healing miracles, and He indicated that believers would carry on the ministry He had begun (John 17:18; 20:21). Jesus made it a point to say that believers (not just apostles) would do the works He had done and greater (John 14:12). However one may understand what Jesus meant by "greater" works, this must not obscure the plain statement in the first part of the verse.[8] The figure of the Church as the Body of Christ speaks of Him as the head doing His works through His members (1 Cor. 12). Jesus viewed this arrangement (i.e., the Spirit doing His works through believers) as being more advantageous to the Church and her ministry than was His own earthly presence (John 16:7). The same picture of the Church's mission is drawn in Acts, where it is implicitly set forth as a continuation of the ministry of Jesus (Acts 1:1).[9]

It would seem most fitting to read the Epistles in light of this foreview in the Gospels and Acts, and to allow the Epistles to carry their own emphasis. They have a different purpose. I can illustrate by an experience of mine that is similar. John Wimber is an acknowledged advocate of the present operation of all of the gifts of the Spirit. I have heard him expound his understanding at length in conferences. His books, *Power Evangelism* and *Power Healing*, offer a straightforward statement.[10] Yet, when I visited two meetings of his church in November 1985 and heard him preach on both occasions, he did not mention the miraculous in either message. He pastored the people in the morning from 1 Peter about how to respond to suffering, and exhorted them in the evening from Psalm 5 to godly living. Prayer for the sick and looking to God for the gifting of His Spirit were an accepted part of the life of his church, and Wimber's purposes in those services were elsewhere. So it is, I believe, with the Epistles.

In reference to the writers whose works are reviewed by Stafford and to the circles in which they move, I believe that the label "signs and wonders" movement is no longer an adequate description, if it ever was. This is true, at least, of the churches with which I am most familiar, especially those of the Vineyard, in which other emphases have more recently emerged. Healing and other gifts of the Spirit were indeed a prominent emphasis (along with worship), perhaps the most prominent, during the last decade.

It is still a bedrock conviction in the Vineyard and other third wave churches, that the full range of the Spirit's activity described in the New Testament is intended to be operational throughout the Church age (though at His discretion and under His control) and is vital to the ministry that God wants to grant and that we all need. I believe that the affirmation of the gifts of the Spirit during the last decade was a word from God, specifically to His evangelical children to help them catch up in this area with their Pentecostal, charismatic Catholic, and charismatic mainline Protestant brothers and sisters who had already led the way.[11]

I want to acknowledge that there have been excesses and mistakes in these movements both in teaching and in practice.[12] This is characteristic of renewal movements throughout Church history.[13] It has never, however, justified the wholesale rejection of the miraculous gifts of the Spirit; and it does not today.

In conclusion, I will make some final points. One is that the leaders with whom I am familiar of the movement to recover the gifts of the Spirit among evangelicals are sound in their theology, from an evangelical perspective. In addition to Wimber, those whose published works can be consulted include Arnold[14], Blue[15], Foster[16], Green[17], Grudem[18], Kraft[19], Mallone[20], Murphy[21], Pytches[22], Wagner[23], John White[24], Tom White[25], and Williams[26]. These whose word would not be otherwise questioned among evangelicals testify to having witnessed and experienced the miraculous working of the Holy Spirit. Such a testimony demands a fair hearing, not just a rigid, defensive response. I am convinced that it will stand up under open-minded scrutiny. It did for me.

I also recognize that a Christian who opens up to the experiential presence and working of the Holy Spirit does not thereby enter into a life of con-sistent exuberance. The contrary often seems to be the case. The filling of the Spirit can be quite unsettling. Yet the disturbance that comes is a good one, which makes for accelerated sanctification. It is worth far more than the price it exacts to grant the Holy Spirit access to one's entire being.

Second, I want to affirm a higher priority than the recovery of the gifts of the Spirit. I refer to the oneness of the entire Body of Christ. Jesus prayed twice for this in His longest recorded prayer (John 17:21,23), and the answer to that prayer, though it is nowhere near visible on the horizon,[27] is long overdue. The Greek word translated "unity" is used only twice in the New Testament,[28] and these two occurrences, when read back-to-back, underscore that the responsi-bility to maintain a manifested oneness among all true believers in Jesus Christ has never been superseded by any of the lesser issues the Church has found itself addressing.

These passages call on Christians "to preserve the unity of the Spirit in the bond of peace...until we all attain to the unity of the faith and of the knowl-edge of the Son of God" (Eph. 4:3,13, NASB). The entire paragraph in which these verses are embedded (Eph. 4:1-16) makes it eminently clear that the rela-tionship all believers have to one another because of their common relationship to Christ is to be nurtured and demonstrated during the very time they are dealing with differences.

The charismatic question is no exception to this. While I believe that a great deal is at stake in this question, I believe that even more is at stake in the oneness of the Lord's Church. If this is so, at the very least, it would make it incumbent on charismatics to no longer aggressively push their position on others and on noncharismatics to no longer ostracize charismatics. Such behav-ior on both sides is clearly contrary to a text such as Romans 14:3, as well as to all of Romans 14:1—15:7.

It is time for both of these groups to get down to the hard work of "putting up with one another in love" (Eph. 4:2, literal translation).[29] I have no doubt that in such a context, troublesome theological and practical issues will be much more easily resolved. More importantly, even during that process, the Church will have the benefit of its richly varied membership; and those looking on from the outside will finally have an opportunity to catch a glimpse of what the Church was intended to be, something Jesus specifically had in view in His prayer in John 17:21 and 23.

Notes

*I wish to thank John Wimber, who powerfully introduced me to the present work of the Holy Spirit; several friends who gather periodically in my home to talk theology and who critiqued an earlier version of this paper (William Abraham, Rich Milne, David Naugle, and Paul Strube); and Jmel Wilson, who followed my frequent revisions with faithful typing help.

1. Tim Stafford, "Fruit of the Vineyard," *Christianity Today* (November 17, 1989), p. 35.
2. The issues raised here are of concern to evangelical Christians, so I address my remarks to that audience.
3. A more consistent position, if one should wish to exclude certain gifts from the present scene, would be to consign all of them to the first century, though there is no warrant in the New Testament for this either. An example of this approach may be found in Gene A. Getz, *Sharpening the Focus of the Church* (Wheaton, IL: Victor, 1984), pp. 153-65.
4. In 1 Corinthians 14:39 and 1 Thessalonians 5:19,20, Paul specifically enjoins his readers not to suppress the exercise of tongues and prophecy. In contrast to the subtle nuances, which must be coaxed out of the biblical text to marshal a case for cessationism, here are straightforward commands on the other side in the case of two of the disputed gifts. This is significant within evangelicalism, where the Bible is championed as the sole basis upon which theology is to be established. In light of texts such as these, it seems to me that the cessationist position brings upon itself Barr's critique of Protestants who celebrate the Bible's authority but refuse to allow the biblical text to speak in contradiction of a prevailing hermeneutic (James Barr, *Holy Scripture: Canon, Authority, Criticism* [Philadelphia, PA: Westminster, 1983], pp. 31-32).
5. I hasten to say that such passages as Romans 10:13-15; 2 Corinthians 5:18-20; 2 Timothy 4:1-5; and 1 Peter 2:9,10 and 3:15 clearly indicate good news that is to be shared. It could be said that all of these references, except the ones in 1 Peter, refer to leaders and not ordinary Christians. I do not believe they should be read that way, any more than I believe that certain gifts of the Spirit were the sole province of the Apostles. Miraculous gifts did authenticate the apostles (2 Cor. 12:12), but they also accompanied other believers (Acts 6:8; 8:6; 9:17,18 [22:13]; 14:3; 1 Cor. 1:7). My point here is simply that there is no direct command to witness verbally in the Epistles, the purpose clause in 1 Peter 2:9 and the exhortation to readiness in 1 Peter 3:15 being the closest to such, whereas there are several such commands with reference to spiritual gifts.

Another common misunderstanding among evangelicals regarding the gifts of the Spirit is the notion that, when they are present, they always operate to the fullest possible degree, e.g., that someone endowed with the gift of healing could heal anyone at any time. If this were the nature of the gifts, then I would readily agree that they have passed away, for I neither know nor have heard or read of anyone with such ability. I do not believe, however, that this is the way Spirit gifting operates today, or has ever operated in the past (see Rom. 12:6; 2 Tim. 1:6; and Wayne Grudem's chapter in this book, objection number 26). Evangelical professors of homiletics acknowledge this implicitly every time they critique a sermon delivered by a gifted preacher who is in training under them and point out mistakes in the sermon. Again, many courses are in place in evangelical seminaries to teach gifted pastors how to shepherd and help them mature in their gifting. If other gifts operate at less than a perfect level and must be cultivated, then the same should also be granted for healing, prophecy, etc.

6. I do not wish to claim too much on this point. It should not be said that the presence of the miraculous will assure that others will come to faith, for this is not necessarily the case (e.g., John 11:45-53; 12:9-11,17-19,35-40). Also, there is a penchant for signs, which does not go to the level of genuine faith (John 4:48; 1 Cor. 1:22). Nevertheless, the proclamation of the gospel, ever central to the Church's mission, should, from the perspective of the New Testament, be accompanied by the manifestation of the gracious power of God (Matt. 10:7,8; Acts 4:29,30; 1 Cor. 2:1-5). Even as the gifts of the Spirit can be subverted from their ordained purpose, so can the Bible. Jesus made this very point when He spoke to religious leaders about how they diligently scrutinized the Bible, as though it were the source of their lives, instead of using it as an avenue into an experiential relationship with Himself, the one to whom the Bible bore witness (John 5:39,40). Both gifts and Bible were given, not as ends in themselves, but as aids to bring us to Him who is our true and only end. Just as the Church would be impoverished without the Bible, so is the evangelical wing of the Church that has obstructed the work of the Holy Spirit impoverished thereby.

7. As Walter Grundmann's remarks suggest (*"dunamis," TDNT*, vol. 2, p. 311): "Paul fits the same pattern [of Jesus and the disciples]. His work is done 'in the power of signs and wonders, in the power of the Spirit' (Rom. 15:19). In the preceding verse this power is attributed directly to Christ....This power is expressed on the one side in miracles: 'in the power of signs and wonders.' The Epistles contain many references to these: 'the signs of an apostle...signs, wonders, and miracles,' 2 Cor. 12:12; God 'working miracles among you,' Gal. 3:5; his activity in Thessalonica did not take place 'in word only, but also in power and in the Holy Spirit,' 1 Thess. 1:5."

8. In discussing the meaning of the "greater" works in this verse, Carson concludes that the expression has to do with the fuller witness to who Jesus is through the Church after the death, resurrection, and exaltation of the Lord (D. A. Carson, "The Purpose of Signs and Wonders in the New Testament," in *Power Religion: The Selling Out of the Evangelical Church* [Chicago, IL: Moody, 1992], pp. 108-10). I like his explanation. Perhaps Paul had a similar thought in mind when he wrote of the surpassing glory of the Church's ministry in 2 Corinthians 3. The only problem I see with Carson's discussion of John 14:12 is that, in the process of wrestling with the meaning of the word "greater," he omits consideration of the first part of the verse, which plainly states that believers are to carry on the ministry Jesus began, doing the very works He had done (see appendix 2 in this book). I must add that I have never felt "signs

and wonders" was an apt label for the movement under discussion.

9. It should be remembered that many of the Epistles were being written while the events recorded in Acts were going on, i.e., that which was the ongoing experience of the churches did not call for special notice in the Epistles. Karl Gatzweiler noted this fact ("Der Paulinische Wunderbegriff," in A. Suhl, ed., *Der Wunderbegriff im Neuen Testament* [Darmstadt, Germany: Wissenschaftliche Buchgesellschaft, 1980], pp. 403-405, n. 52): "As examples...we cite I Thess. 1, 5; 2, 13; I Cor. 2, 4-5; 2 Cor. 6, 7; 13, 3; Col. 1, 29; 2 Tim. 1, 8. In all these places Paul speaks of the proclamation of the gospel which was accompanied by divine power, by the power of the Spirit. The gospel is God's power which is displayed among men. For the reader, who already knows that the apostle worked miracles alongside the proclamation of the gospel (cf. 2 Cor. 12, 12; Rom. 15, 18-19), it suggests miraculous events also be understood as self-evident among the notions of 'might' and 'power' which accompany the proclamation of the gospel."

10. John Wimber with Kevin Springer, *Power Evangelism* (San Francisco, CA: HarperCollins, 1986); *Power Healing* (San Francisco, CA; HarperCollins, 1987). See also Kevin Springer, ed., with Introduction and Afterword by John Wimber, *Power Encounters Among Christians in the Western World* (San Francisco, CA: HarperCollins, 1988). John Wimber and Kevin Spring, *Power Points* (San Francisco, CA: HarperCollins, 1991) may be consulted for an overview of Wimber's broader theology, with a practical emphasis.

11. Space and time do not allow me to document this statement. I believe it is a fair summary of the progress of this movement, at least in the broadest strokes, in the United States in the present century. In contrast to some evangelicals, I personally have no hesitation in acknowledging the presence of true faith on the part of many Catholics and mainline Protestants. If my statement is fair, then it would be well for evangelical Christians to ponder its implications. My statement would suggest that, in the following order, the poor (who constituted the larger part of the Pentecostal movement, at least initially), Catholics, and liberals (evangelical terminology for mainline Protestants) more readily recognized and made room for the renewing work of the Spirit of Jesus than did evangelicals. If this is true, then it suggests that there is something deeply wrong with the system of evangelical theology. It is unthinkable that a theological system could occasion an error of this magnitude while being otherwise unflawed. I make this observation humbly, for I was a part of the evangelical resistance to the Spirit for 20 years, though with decreasing fervor over that time period. It was only when the Lord granted me a deep emotional healing in 1985 that I was finally able to acknowledge what had already taken place within me gradually over the space of that 20 years, what Kraft has described as a shift in worldview (Charles H. Kraft, *Christianity with Power: Your Worldview and Your Experience of the Supernatural* [Ann Arbor, MI: Servant, 1989], a book that is refreshingly candid about the author's own struggles with the issues he addresses). I have recounted my change of conviction briefly in "Overtaken by Reality," *Ministries Today* (March/April, 1992), p. 8.

12. See my essay "Sickness and Suffering in the New Testament" in *Wrestling with*

Dark Angels: Toward a Deeper Understanding of the Supernatural Forces in Spiritual Warfare, eds. C. Peter Wagner and F. Douglas Pennoyer (Ventura, CA: Regal Books, 1990), pp. 241-42, regarding the unfortunate treatment of tongues in Pentecostal and charismatic circles. That Paul found it necessary in his first letter to the Corinthians to devote significant attention to correcting an overemphasis on tongues (1 Cor. 14) is suggestive that this gift may be especially subject to misuse. Even given this, however, he still concluded his discussion, as already mentioned, with a cautionary command that the gift be allowed to function, thereby indicating that the value of the gift is worth the effort required to keep it within its proper guidelines.

13. This aspect of the history of revivals is treated helpfully and discerningly in John White, *When the Spirit Comes with Power: Signs and Wonders Among God's People* (Downers Grove, IL: InterVarsity, 1988), especially in chapter nine, "How Safe is Spiritual Power?"

14. Clinton Arnold, *Powers of Darkness* (Downers Grove, IL: InterVarsity, 1992).

15. Ken Blue, *Authority to Heal* (Downers Grove, IL: InterVarsity, 1987).

16. Richard Foster, *Prayer: Finding the Heart's True Home* (San Francisco: Harper-Collins, 1992).

17. Michael Green, *I Believe in the Holy Spirit* (Grand Rapids, MI: William B. Eerdmans, 1975).

18. Wayne Grudem, *The Gift of Prophecy in the New Testament and Today* (Wheaton, IL: Crossway, 1988).

19. See note 11 above; Charles H. Kraft, *Defeating Dark Angels* (Ann Arbor, MI: Servant, 1992).

20. George Mallone, *Those Controversial Gifts* (Downers Grove, IL: InterVarsity, 1983); id., *Arming for Spiritual Warfare* (Downers Grove, IL: InterVarsity, 1991).

21. Ed Murphy, *A Handbook of Spiritual Warfare* (Nashville, TN: Thomas Nelson, 1992).

22. David Pytches, *Come, Holy Spirit* (London, England: Hodder & Stoughton, 1985; published in North America as *Spiritual Gifts in the Local Church*, Minneapolis, MN: 1985); id., *Set My People Free* (London, England: Hodder & Stoughton, 1986).

23. Especially C. Peter Wagner, *How to Have a Healing Ministry in Any Church* (Ventura, CA: Regal Books, 1988). See also by Wagner, *Engaging the Enemy: How to Fight and Defeat Territorial Spirits* (Ventura, CA: Regal Books, 1991); *Prayer Shield: How to Intercede for Pastors, Christian Leaders and Others on the Spiritual Frontlines* (Ventura, CA: Regal Books, 1992); *Warfare Prayer: How to Seek God's Power and Protection in the Battle to Build His Kingdom* (Ventura, CA: Regal Books, 1992); *Breaking Strongholds in Your City: How to Use Spiritual Mapping to Make Your Prayers More Strategic, Effective and Targeted* (Ventura, CA: Regal Books, 1993).

24. See note 13 above.

25. Tom White, *The Believer's Guide to Spiritual Warfare* (Ann Arbor, MI: Servant, 1992).

26. Don Williams, *Signs, Wonders, and the Kingdom of God: A Biblical Guide for the Reluctant Skeptic* (Ann Arbor, MI: Servant, 1989).

27. I am aware of stirrings in this direction in New England, on the Northwest coast, and in the Austin area and know there are likely more of which I have not heard. I am hopeful to see such beginnings multiplied and integrated.
28. Apart from an unlikely variant in Colossians 3:14.
29. I am grateful to Howard Hendricks for first calling my attention to the literal meaning of this phrase, as well as for many other valuable practical lessons.

THE EMPOWERED
CHRISTIAN LIFE*

JAMES I. PACKER

It is clear from the New Testament that the power of God is meant to accompany the gospel, and to find expression through its messengers and in the lives of those to whom the message comes.

Each December, *Time* magazine produces a set of lighthearted comments on the previous year. At the end of 1987, the editors were isolating the most overworked word of the year, the one most ready for retirement. The word they chose was "power," as in "power lunch," or "power tie." I confess my mind ran to various uses of the word "power" in Christian circles that seemed similarly overwrought, and I agreed there was a strong case for retiring the word.

But then I thought again.

THE SPIRIT IN ACTION

During the past century, Christians have been very concerned about power. Have they been wrong to be concerned about it? Not altogether. In the middle and late 1800s, there was great concern to find "the path of power." The path of power meant one's ability to perform set tasks and overcome temptations. Was it wrong to seek the power of God for greater self-control and a richer practice of righteousness? Of course not. At the same time, concern focused on being able, through the power of God, to impact others for God through preaching and witness. Was it right to be anxious lest one's witness should be powerless? Of course it was right.

More recently, Christians touched by that movement known variously as Pentecostalism, charismatic renewal, and the third wave, are finding, if they can, the ability to channel supernatural demonstrations of God's power in healings of all sorts: healings of the body, inner healing of the heart, exorcisms where there appears to be something demonic in a person's life. Is it wrong that Christians are concerned about these things? Though I see various pitfalls, I cannot find it in my heart to say this is wrong. In my New Testament, I read a great deal about such manifestations of the power of God—understood simply as "powers of the coming age" (Heb. 6:5) or, in other words, the Holy Spirit in action.

MIRACLES OF NEW CREATION

The coming of Christ the Savior has meant the outpouring of the Spirit on the Church and on the world. And the Holy Spirit comes with power. In the New Testament, we see this power manifested in all the aforementioned modes: the ability to perform set tasks and overcome temptation, the ability to impact others through preaching and witness, and the ability to act as a channel for God's power in miracles, healings, and the like. Let us consider each of these three modes, in reverse order.

First, in the Gospels, we encounter works of power in the physical realm, including miracles of nature and healings of all sorts. The scriptural phrase "signs and wonders" describes them.

These are, to use C.S. Lewis's apt phrase, "miracles of the new creation," in which the power of God that created the world works again to bring something out of nothing, that is, to cause an inexplicable state of affairs in terms of what was there before. Everyone knows you cannot get food for 5,000 out of five loaves and two fishes, but Jesus did it. Everyone knows you cannot bring the dead back to life, but Jesus on three occasions brought the dead back to life.

To be sure, these three "raisings from the dead" were only resuscitations; in each case, the person died again a little further down the line. Jesus, however, rose from the dead never to die again. His resurrection is an even more remarkable miracle of new creation—indeed, the normative one: Christ is the firstfruits, the beginning of the new creation of God, as the New Testament itself says.

WORDS OF POWER

Second, one reads on in the New Testament and finds that words of power in Christian communication are very much a part of the gospel story and of the story of the new church. Luke is particularly interested in the power of God, and several texts in Luke are significant here.

In Luke 4:14 we read that, following the wilderness temptation, "Jesus returned to Galilee in the *power* of the Spirit." This text introduces not only His works of power, but also the words of power that came from His lips. Then, after His resurrection, Jesus told the disciples to wait in Jerusalem until they were endued with "*power* from on high" for the ministry of worldwide evangelism to which He was committing them (see Luke 24:49).

At the beginning of Acts, Luke picks up the same theme. Jesus tells His followers, "You will receive *power* when the Holy Spirit comes on you; and you will be my witnesses...to the ends of the earth" (Acts 1:8). Then later we read, "With great *power* the apostles continued to testify to the resurrection of the Lord Jesus, and much grace was upon them all" (Acts 4:33).

EMPOWERED PREACHING

Paul, likewise, has tremendous things to say about the power of God working through the gospel and through its messengers. "I am not ashamed of the gospel, because it is the *power* of God for the salvation of everyone who believes" (Rom. 1:16). At the end of the lengthy argument that makes up the book of Romans, and speaking of his own ministry, Paul says, "I will not venture to speak of anything except what Christ has accomplished through me in leading the Gentiles to obey God by what I have said and done—by the *power* of signs and miracles, through the *power* of the Spirit" (Rom. 15:18,19).

And again, in his first letter to the Corinthians, "For Christ did not send me to baptize, but to preach the gospel—not with words of human wisdom, lest the cross of Christ be emptied of its *power*. For the message of the cross is foolishness to those who are perishing, but to us who are being saved it is the *power* of God" (1 Cor. 1:17,18).

"I knew what you wanted," Paul says in the opening chapters of 1 Corinthians, "and I was resolved not to give it to you. You wanted me to show off as a philosopher, with dazzling arguments, but I wouldn't do it. And so you thought me a fool." Rather, Paul says, "My message and my preaching were not with wise and persuasive words, but with a demonstration of the Spirit's *power*, so that your faith might not rest on men's wisdom, but on God's *power*" (1 Cor. 2:4,5).

TRANSFORMED LIVES

Third, the New Testament speaks not only of God's power in the miraculous and in the communication of the gospel, but also of God's power at work *in us*, enabling us to understand and to do what we otherwise could not.

In Ephesians 1:17-19, Paul tells the Christians what he prays for God to give them, "I keep asking that the God of our Lord Jesus Christ, the glorious Father, may give you the Spirit of wisdom and revelation, so that you may know him better. I pray also that the eyes of your heart may be enlightened in order that you may know the hope to which he has called you, the riches of his glorious inheritance in the saints, and his incomparably great *power* for us [other translations say, "*in* us"] who believe."

It is not just power in the *message*. It is not just power through the *messenger*. It is power *in and upon those who believe*, making their life utterly different from what it was before. It is resurrection power—a matter of God raising with Christ those who have become willing to die with Christ. Clearly, Paul is expecting tremendous changes in the lives of those who now belong to Christ.

Paul is talking about something radical, in the fullest sense of that word: Something produces a total change. He is praying that through this marvelous inner transformation and enrichment the Ephesians will be utterly different from folk around them—utterly different, indeed, from what they have been so far.

HEIGHTENED EXPECTATIONS

It is clear from the New Testament that God meant His power to accompany the gospel, and to find expression through its messengers and in the lives of those to whom the message comes.

This conviction leads me to five theses about the manifestation of God's power among His people today. May we be more disposed to receive and manifest the power of God in its various forms.

1. It is right to bring the supernatural into prominence and to raise Christians' expectations with regard to it.

Our expectations about seeing the power of God transforming people's lives are not as high as they should be.

When the Reformation broke on the Church in the sixteenth century, there was a tremendous amount of superstition regarding the saints working miracles. I am not denying that God may well have worked many miracles through many saints before the Reformation, as it seems He has worked miracles through His saints since the Reformation. But the reformers looked around and saw a great deal that seemed to them unmistakably superstitious, so they reacted against it.

Packer's Proverb, however, is that the reaction of man worketh not the righteousness of God. If you are walking backward away from something you think is a mistake, you may be right in supposing it is a mistake, but for you to be walking backward is never right. You know what happens to people who walk backward in the physical sense. Eventually they stumble over some obstacle behind them they never saw, because they fixed their minds and eyes on what they were trying to get away from, and then they fall. We are meant to walk forward, not backward, and reaction is always a matter of walking backward.

I believe the reformers' reaction against the supernatural in the lives of God's people in this age of the Holy Spirit was, frankly, more wrong than right—as have been many subsequent attempts to rule out the present-day reality of the supernatural.

It has been necessary to recover this theme in the twentieth century, and we should thank God that expectations of supernatural healing and answer to prayer have risen during this past 30 or 40 years. I would caution that there is a danger in undervaluing the natural and the ordinary. There are people who want every problem solved by an immediate miracle, a display of the supernatural, a wonderful providence that will change everything. That is a sign of immaturity.

Repeatedly, the Lord leads us into painful and difficult situations, and we pray—as Paul prayed regarding his thorn in the flesh—that the Lord will change the situation. We want a miracle! But instead, the Lord chooses to strengthen us to cope with the situation, as He did with Paul, making His strength perfect in our continuing weakness.

Compare it to the training of children, and you will see my point. If difficult situations never demand self-denial and discipline, if there are never any sustained pressures to cope with, if long-term strategies never force you to stick with something for years in order to advance, there will never be any maturity of character. The children will remain spoiled all their lives, because everything has been made too easy for them. The Lord does not allow that to happen in the life of His children.

When one starts thinking in positive terms about the supernatural in one's personal life, one must also remember it may very well please God to leave situations as they are, to decide not to work a miracle, to strengthen us His children who are involved in the situation so we can from it grow.

EMPOWERED MINISTRY

2. It is right to aspire to use one's God-given gifts in powerful and useful ministry.

It is right to want to know what gifts for ministry God has given us. It is right to want to harness them and see them used for the blessing of others as widely as possible.

But there is always a danger that the person who believes God has given him or her a good sprinkling of gifts will fall captive to that old enemy, self-importance. God does not value us according to the number of gifts we have, or by their spectacular quality. God does not value us primarily for what we can do—even what we can do in His strength. He values us primarily for what He makes us, character-wise, conforming us to Christ by His grace.

Jesus was already sounding the warning note when His disciples came back from a preaching tour all gung ho and excited. "Lord," they cried, "even the demons are subject to us in your name!" (Luke 10:17, RSV).

"Very good," says Jesus. "But don't rejoice that the demons are subject to you. That is not the truly important thing. Rejoice, rather, that your names are written in heaven. Rejoice in your salvation. Rejoice in what you *are* by the grace of God, rather than in the way God uses you. Rejoice in being His child and in entering upon your destiny of being transformed into Jesus' image."

Gifts are secondary. Sanctity is primary. Never let anything divert your mind and heart from holding fast to that truth.

MEETING NEEDS

3. It is right to want to be a channel of divine power into other people's lives at their points of need.

Just be careful, however, lest you become one of those people who suffers from the neurosis of needing to be needed—the state of not feeling you are worthwhile unless you are able to feel that others need you. That is not spiritual health. That is *lack* of spiritual health.

One of the disciplines to which the Lord calls us is the willingness, for certain periods of our life, not to be used in significant ministry. Here is a gifted sister, and for quite a long period it may seem the Lord sidelines her so that her ministry is not being used. What is going on? Is this spiritual failure? It likely is not spiritual failure at all, but the Lord teaching her again that her life does not depend on finding people that need her. The source of her joy in life must always be the knowledge of God's love for her—the knowledge that though He did not need her, He has chosen to love her freely and gloriously so she may have the eternal joy of fellowship with Him.

In the spiritual life, what we are is always before what we do. If we lose touch with what we are, and with the reality of God's free mercy as the taproot of our spiritual life, the Lord may have to sideline us until we have learned this lesson again.

EMPOWERED EVANGELISM

4. It is right to want to see God's power manifested in a way that has a significant evangelistic effect.

The line of thought to which I am referring here is the one that says evangelism is not evangelism until it has a particular kind of miracle attached to it. Frankly, I think that is an overstatement, a real error. The danger it gives rise to is that those who practice evangelism will devise ways and means of manipulating people and situations to make it look as if wonderful things are happening through the power of God. Dishonesty and deception at this point must prove disastrous.

Nonetheless, it is not wrong to want to evangelize in a way that impresses and blesses people because it convinces them that all this talk about a new life in Christ through God's power is for real. Moral and spiritual transformation by the Holy Spirit through new birth remains the supreme miracle and should fig-ure prominently in evangelism. Firsthand witness to Christ doing for lost souls what alcohol, rock music, sex, and drugs could not do for them still causes the most fruitful sort of "power encounter" between the sinner and the Savior.

5. It is right to want to be divinely empowered for righteousness, for moral victories, for deliverance from bad habits, and for pleasing God.

The good news is that through the means of grace, all Christians *may* be so empowered. Through the Spirit, you and I may and must mortify the deeds of the Body. Through the Spirit, you and I may and must manifest the new habits, the new Christlike behaviors that constitute the fruit of the Spirit. I trust this thesis presents no problem except for the practical one that confronts our will: Now that we know this is how it ought to be, what are we going to do about it?

THE POWER PATH

I spoke earlier of the "power path." Perhaps it will be clearer now what I mean when I say that *the power path is humble dependence on God to become channels of His power.* First, we are to be channels through which the power of God flows into the depths of our own being as we open ourselves up to the Lord and His grace. Then, by God's grace, we will find that repeatedly we are becoming chan-nels of His power into the lives of others.

God's power is *God's* power, and He exercises it. He does not give us power as a gift. He does not give us power as our possession. The power of God is not something handed over to us for us to use at our discretion. Our relation to the power of God should be one of becoming, by His grace, channels through which He exercises His power. We must never seek to possess the power of God for ourselves to use it at our discretion. If ever you hear Christians talking about using the power of God, I hope red lights flash in your mind. If, however, you hear Christians talking about finding the place where God's power can use them, nod your head.

WEAKNESS AND STRENGTH

Finally, a few words about what I call "the power scenario." The power scenario is that God *perfects His strength in our weakness*. And therefore, I would say, the more conscious we are of that weakness, the better.

Think again of Paul and his thorn in the flesh (2 Cor. 12:7-10). We do not know, of course, exactly what the "thorn" was. But whatever it was, it was surely something painful or he would not have called it a thorn, and it was surely something in his own makeup or he would not have called it a thorn "in his flesh."

Paul went to the Lord Jesus in solemn seasons of prayer three times over. He went to the Lord Jesus because Jesus was the healer, and this was something that needed the healer's touch. He prayed that the thorn might depart from him, but the Lord said no. He said, "I have something better in view for you, Paul." (God always reserves the right to answer our prayers in a better way than we ask them.) "I'll tell you what I'm going to do," the Lord said. "I'm going to make my strength perfect in your continuing weakness so that all the things you fear—the end of your ministry, the diminution of your ministry, the enfeebling of your ministry, the discredit of your ministry—will be avoided. Your ministry will go on in power and in strength as it has done, but it will also go on in weakness. You will carry that thorn in the flesh around with you as long as you live. But my strength will be made perfect in that weakness."

This pattern is likely to be worked out repeatedly in your life and in mine. The Lord first makes us conscious of our weakness, so that our heart cries out, "I can't handle this." We go to the Lord, telling Him, "I can't handle this. Please take it away!" And the Lord replies, "In my strength you *can* handle this, and in answer to your prayer, I will *strengthen you* to handle it." Thus in the end, your testimony, like Paul's, will be, "I can do all things through Christ who strengthens me" (Phil. 4:13, *NKJV*). That, I believe, is the fullest expression of the empowered Christian life.

Note

*This chapter is adapted from a paper that was presented to the 1991 conference of Allies for Faith and Renewal, on "Repentance, Holiness, and Power."

II

PASTORAL REFLECTIONS

A Pastor's View of
Praying for the Sick

and Overcoming the Evil One in the
Power of the Spirit

Roger Barrier

The simple teaching of James 5 had long struck fear into my "Southern Baptist"[1] pastoral heart: "Is any one of you sick? He should call the elders of the church to pray over him and anoint him with oil in the name of the Lord. And the prayer offered in faith will make the sick person well" (Jas. 5:14,15). Sick people read the Bible in hopeful simplicity. It was inevitable that someone would one day sit in my office and ask me to pray this prayer—and expect for it to work!

Part of my fear stemmed from the fact that my denominational upbringing ill-prepared me for this request. Our churches were organized around deacons. We had no elders to pray for the sick. And besides, I had never heard a "prayer of faith" attempted—much less observed one to work. I had never seen anyone anointed with oil. Furthermore, not once was this biblical injunction regarding healing ever addressed in my seminary training.

Some of my fear was produced by the fact that my denominational culture did not sanction this passage as accepted "Southern Baptist" practice. The unwritten but strongly implied rule stated that pastors who ministered in the area of healing were "charismatic" at best, and deluded at worst. They were to be alienated whatever the reason because "good Southern Baptists did not do such things!"

Most of my fear centered around the *risk* and *potential failure* involved. What if I tried James 5:13-17 and it did not work?

Sally[2] sat now at my feet. Some of the nerves in her back had been badly damaged by cancer radiation treatments. The cancer near her spinal cord had been obliterated; but the resulting damage left her in constant pain. "The doctors can do nothing more for me," she said. "My life is painful agony. God is the only hope I have. I was reading through James and saw this passage on healing. Would you please gather the elders and pray for me?" Her plea for help was simple enough. She was just doing what the Bible said.

I responded carefully: "Sally, you are the first person who has ever asked me to pray for their healing according to James 5. I decided long ago that when this request was made, I would ask the person to join me in prayer and fasting to ascertain God's will. Will you join me in praying and fasting for five days. I'll meet you in my office next Friday afternoon, and if God tells us both that we are to follow through with this, we will proceed." Sally readily agreed. She was not a novice in Christianity. She had walked with God for many years.

Five days later Sally was in my office. We both strongly sensed that God was leading in this direction. Since we had no elders, I thought that our deacons were close enough to what God had in mind. We set up the prayer meeting for Sunday afternoon.

During the 30 minutes before Sally arrived, I explained to the deacons Sally's request, the background to her pain problem, and what I knew of James 5. I asked if anyone had participated in a healing service before. No hands lifted. This was a pioneering experience for all of us.

When Sally arrived, we ushered her to a seat and explained that we were going to anoint her with oil and pray for her healing. However, we first thought it important to have her confess any known sin in her life because James mentioned this. When she finished, I took the bottle of olive oil I had purchased at Lucky supermarket and began to pour the oil over her head. One of the deacons quietly whispered to me that he thought it best if we put a drop of oil on our finger and lightly touch her forehead. I agreed. My way would have been a mess. We passed the bottle and each of us prayed and anointed her in turn.

I am not certain what I expected when we finished praying. Would Sally leap up at some point and shout, "Glory to God! I'm healed!" or perhaps announce quietly that the pain had gone away? And then we were finished. And nothing happened. She thanked us for our time and left each of us to our own thoughts. Disappointment was certainly not the word to describe the mood in the room. I suppose we each experienced a quiet contentment that we had done what the Bible instructed.

In the early morning hours, Sally was awakened by a strange sensation over her body. She related later that she instantly knew God was healing her body. By the time she was out of bed, the pain was gone—never to return. As Sally related her healing to me, she provided insight into my unverbalized question: "I have been thinking that the reason God did not heal me yesterday was because the deacons might get proud and think they had done this. I think God waited until I was alone so there would be no doubt that He gets all the glory." I have little doubt that she was right.

From that inauspicious beginning, God has slowly integrated the ministry of physical healing into the fabric of our church family. As I reflect over the years since my encounter with Sally, I see that my theology of healing is fashioned upon a biblical foundation with a solid dose of practical reality.

May I share a few personal pastoral thoughts and principles about healing, which I hope will be of help to you. These insights have been hammered out over the past 20 years of my ministry.

A BIBLICAL UNDERSTANDING OF HEALING CONFIRMS THAT GOD HAS NO INTENTION OF HEALING EVERY ILLNESS

Although the Bible tells us that Jesus healed every disease (Matt. 4:23), we need to put in perspective our role in the process of healing. An examination of the ministry of Paul gives us insight into what we can and cannot expect.

Although the apostle Paul was instrumental in accomplishing some powerful healing and resurrection miracles (Acts 28:9), he could not do it every time. Paul could not help his close friend Epaphroditus, who was so sick that he nearly died (Phil. 2:25-27). Paul failed to encourage Timothy to go to the local faith healers for a cure for his chronic stomach condition. Instead, he told Timothy that a little wine would do wonders (1 Tim. 5:23). Paul left Trophimus sick at Miletus (2 Tim. 4:20). Paul himself was obviously in poor health during much of his ministry (1 Cor. 2:3; 2 Cor. 12:5,7-10; Gal. 4:13). Paul raised others from the dead; but he was unable to find physical relief from the thorn that tormented him relentlessly. God's will for Paul did not include healing from this malady. Instead of sending someone with the gift of healing, the Lord gave him Dr. Luke as a constant companion.

Those who present themselves for healing must understand that it is not always God's will or intention to answer a prayer for healing positively. Other dynamics come into play.

A Prayer for Healing Must Be Exercised in Accordance with God's Will, Plan, Discipline, and Glory

In John 9, Jesus healed a man who was born blind. "His disciples asked him, 'Rabbi, who sinned, this man or his parents, that he was born blind?' 'Neither this man nor his parents sinned,' said Jesus, 'but this happened so that the work of God may be displayed in his life'" (John 9:2,3).

Few gifts in the Church are so trafficked with and commercialized today as healing. Healing is not something anyone can demand in every situation. Although God desires to heal, as James 5:14-16 suggests, sickness is sometimes allowed by God for His purposes. Sickness may be for God's glory, as in John 9, where the man was blind from birth in order that his healing would bring glory to God. On the other hand, it may be the direct result of God's discipline, as with the Corinthian believers who desecrated the Lord's Supper (1 Cor. 11:30).

My first child died in my arms. Jessie was born with all sorts of medical problems. A chromosomal problem had ruined her heart.

At 4:00 A.M. Thursday, several hours after her birth, I was standing in the shower having a discussion with God: "Why me? Why do I get the baby that's going to die? Is this the way You treat Your pastors? I've dedicated my life to serving You. Is this all the thanks I get?"

Then I paused to get control of my thoughts. In the early days of my ministry, I hammered out a basic biblical theology to handle the fact that a loving God could allow sickness, suffering, and tragedies on earth. Mentally, I went through my biblical checklist of three questions.

This checklist is by no means exhaustive. Many sicknesses are the result of our humanity and come to us in the normal course of living. However, this list seems to cover the larger human tragedies that force many to wonder if

God is intervening supernaturally in their lives—or if He exists or if He even cares.

1. Is Jessie's sickness unto death?

Frankly, sometimes it is time to die: "Man is destined to die once, and after that to face judgment" (Heb. 9:27). Was it time for Jessie to die after only so short a life? God never guarantees anyone a set number of years. Some are designed to live to the ripe, old age of 85. Others fulfill their destiny by the age of 2 (Ps. 139).

2. Is Jessie's sickness the result of some sin?

The Bible is very clear in teaching that there are times when we get out of line and God spanks us: "But after Uzziah became powerful, his pride led to his downfall. He was unfaithful to the Lord his God, and entered the temple of God to burn incense....While he was raging at the priests...leprosy broke out on his forehead....the Lord had afflicted him" (2 Chron. 26:16-20; cf. 1 Cor. 11:30). I could think of all kinds of sins I had committed over the years. If God wanted to discipline me with a dying daughter, He had plenty of justification.

3. Is Jessie's affliction for God's glory?

Sometimes God allows trials and experiences to conform us into the image of Christ: "To keep me from becoming conceited because of these surpassingly great revelations, there was given me a thorn in my flesh....Therefore I will boast all the more gladly about my weaknesses, so that Christ's power may rest upon me" (2 Cor. 12:7-9). Perhaps God was intending to get glory out of Jessie's situation.

To be honest, it was not easy to imagine anything good coming from this experience. The sense of agony and despair was overwhelming.

Jessie died in my arms on a Saturday night. She was lying on a little pillow that had been her home and bed for the last eight months. Julie and I were sitting in the hospital room painstakingly watching as her breath became more shallow. Finally, Julie said, "Roger, she's gone." I remember using that age-old method to detect death. I put my cheek down to her little nostrils to see if there was any breath, and there was none. Almost in unison Julie and I found ourselves saying, "Hi, Jessie. We're your Mommy and your Daddy. We love you with all of our hearts." We understood then that she was more alive now than she had ever been before.

Months later, in the midst of my anger and questioning of God, He spoke a very precious word to me. I look back on it now as one of those spiritual markers that refuse to pass unnoticed. The voice was certainly not audible; however, the message was precise: "Roger, Jessie's sickness was not an accident, it was designed for My glory. Do you know how much your heart hurt to have a little baby who could not grow up physically?"

"Yes, Lord," I answered.

Then God spoke in carefully measured words, which have forever shaped my ministry: "I wanted to give to you a taste of how much My heart hurts when one of My newborn Christians refuses to grow up spiritually."

I relate the above story to emphasize that praying for the sick requires an interactive understanding of God's plan and will. This often comes through prayer and careful counseling. For example, James encourages those seeking healing to confess their sins "so that you may be healed" (Jas. 5:16). Our elders encourage those who seek healing to pray for God to search their hearts to see if their illness may be related to unconfessed or unrepented sin.

Whether or not God heals often depends upon whether illness or recovery best contributes to His main purpose of conforming Christians into the image of Christ.[3] A simple study of Paul's prayers reveals Paul's predominant concern for spiritual development. I do not recall one instance where Paul records his prayers for someone to be healed. His greatest concern is for the growth and maturity of the "inner being" (Eph. 1:15-19; 3:14-21; Phil. 1:9-11; Col. 1:9-12). How often God's perspective differs from ours! The angels of heaven are not said to rejoice over bodies that are healed. Angels rejoice over sinners who repent (Luke 15:10). God will sacrifice the body every time—if that is what it takes to mature the inner spirit, which is eternal.

The prayer for healing is not exercised on the basis of the patient's faith, will, or wish, but on the condition of the will and plan of God. The sick need guidance to pray for an acceptance of God's will, whatever He may have in mind.

The importance of an initial acceptance of God's will was deeply impressed upon my mind as a teenage boy. I recall Dr. L. T. Daniel sharing a story about a pastor in rural England during the late nineteenth century. The pastor was called upon late at night to pray with a mother for her dying baby. The mother insisted that they pray immediately for the baby to be healed. The pastor thought it best that they seek God's will in the matter first. The mother was indignant: "Do you mean you are not going to pray with me for my child to live?"

"I did not say that," the pastor replied. "I just want to pray first and see if we can ascertain whether or not God has something else in mind."

"What kind of hard-hearted preacher are you?" she screamed as she escorted him out the door. She then proceeded to pray earnestly for God to intervene and heal her dying son. Her son survived.

I cannot verify the details of this story. As I recall, Dr. Daniel gave neither source nor credit. But, I will never forget the penetrating power of his final statement: "Eighteen years later that mother watched her son mount the steps of the village gallows to be hanged for murdering their next door neighbor."

THE PRAYER OF FAITH CAN ONLY BE EXERCISED IN LIGHT OF GOD'S WILL

I have often wondered what James meant by the "prayer of faith" (Jas. 5:15). I do not delude myself into thinking that I understand the depths of what he had in mind—not even the shallow water of meaning behind this prayer. However, I offer these insights into the "prayer of faith" as a result of my own prayer, practice, and practical experience.

Faith is based upon a word from God. Faith is not positive thinking. It is not a great leap into the unknown. It is not believing something so strongly that we make it come true—or that God must do what we believe will happen. The heroes in Hebrews 11 heard a word from God by one means or another. In every case, their faith was based on what they heard. And God blessed them for their faith. Faith rests on the facts of the Word of God. It must not rest on emotions or feelings.

The prayer of faith can only be prayed when God speaks to reveal His will and intention. When I pray for people who come to the elders, I usually have no idea what God intends to do in their situation. Occasionally, God makes His will known clearly. In those latter cases it is exciting to pray a prayer of faith—and watch God work.

My first experience in praying the prayer of faith came years before I comprehended what happened. Early in my ministry in Tucson, one of the young mothers in our congregation was in the hospital with a brain aneurysm. It was hard to accept. Rhonda was so vibrant and healthy the Sunday before. As I drove to the hospital, I considered what I could say to bring some comfort. I knew she would be as concerned for her two small children as she was for her own health. I stopped outside the door to her room and prayed for God to tell me what to say to her. As I was praying, I had a deep inner impression that she was going to be fine. I asked God if He was trying to tell me something. From my innermost being, I heard God telling me that Rhonda's sickness was not unto death. She would survive with no complications and be able to raise her children. A struggle ensued within my mind: Was God really speaking to me? Was

I just making this up? What if I told her what I heard and she died? I would look like a fool. I could not get over the fact that I had asked God to tell me what to say. I had not, however, really expected Him to answer like this.

Rhonda was awake and conscious. "Surgery is tentatively scheduled for Monday," she told me. "The doctors want to allow the swelling to go down before they operate. There is no guarantee that the artery will hold until then." Rhonda was a strong Christian; but, while the spirit was willing, the flesh was weak. Fear filled her eyes.

Words fail to convey properly the next moments. I looked carefully at her and shared what happened in the hallway. Then I looked straight at her and said, "Rhonda, this sickness is not unto death. Whether the doctors need to operate on Monday or not, you are going to be fine. Be at peace. All is well." Never had I said words like these before. I knew I was taking a risk. I found myself praying for her healing and recovery with no ifs, ands, or buts. I reminded God that she was a young mother with children to raise, and I reasoned with Him that there was no reason why she should not be allowed to raise her children. Now I see that my reasoning served only to bolster my faith, God already had shared His will for Rhonda in direct answer to my seeking. My prayer of faith rested on the facts of a word from God.

Only in the last few years have I begun to understand that God shared a "word of knowledge" (1 Cor. 12:8, NKJV) in the hallway with me. Without a word from God it is not possible to pray the prayer of faith (compare James's use of Elijah as an example in Jas. 5:14-18 and 1 Kings 18:1,41-44).

By the way, Rhonda's surgery was a complete success. Fifteen years have passed since we prayed together in the hospital room. Her daughters are grown and married. She is alive and well.

Usually, I have no idea what God intends to do when I am asked to pray for the sick. It is not that I do not ask. God seldom tells me. I suppose this is because my primary ministries are preaching, pastoring, and training disciples for ministry. I am thankful for enough experiences in the area of healing to be able to help others develop their skills and abilities; but, I feel no call, nor gifting, to do this work full time.

When our elders gather for healing prayer, we always ask God to tell us His intentions. When His will is known, the prayer of faith is easy to pray. When we are not certain, we feel free to tell God what we would like to see happen. On the basis of James 4:2, "You do not have, because you do not ask God," I tell God in prayer what I would like to see happen: I always want them to be healed! I do not want anyone to miss God's blessing because we failed to ask. However, I am careful to acknowledge with an attitude of submission that ultimately I want God's will done:

"Father, you told us we could ask, so we did. Now, since we do not know your will in this case, we submit to what You have in mind. Your will be done."

As I reflect back over the years, when we did not know God's will, some of the people we prayed for got well, some did not. I suppose only eternity will reveal the profitability of the prayers for any particular person. I do not say this with resignation. I am convinced that some of the people prayed for were divinely touched by God just because they followed James 5 and asked the elders to pray.

But there is something more here. As I think back over those times of prayer, the sense of peace and goodwill that pervades the prayer time makes the experience worthwhile—healing or not. On many occasions I have noted with satisfaction that the one who asks for prayer has the calm assurance that he or she has done everything before God that they can. Now more than ever, they are able to leave the outcome in His hands.

THE GIFTS OF HEALINGS
TAKE DIFFERENT FORMS

A simple survey of the Bible reveals that God's healing hand moves in a variety of ways. The literal translation for the spiritual gift mentioned in 1 Corinthians 12:9 is "gifts of healings." The double plural indicates many forms of healings. Occasionally, healing is spoken directly to the sick person. Peter said to the lame man, "Silver or gold I do not have, but what I have I give you. In the name of Jesus Christ of Nazareth, walk" (Acts 3:6). Sometimes hands are laid on the one who is sick: "His father was sick in bed, suffering from fever and dysentery. Paul went in to see him and, after prayer, placed hands on him and healed him" (Acts 28:8).

Sometimes a healing takes place immediately in order to strengthen the sick person's faith. An immediate healing aggressively reveals God's power before a group of people as in the case of the man born blind (John 9:1-41) or the resurrection of Lazarus (John 11:38-45). Many healings do not occur immediately. Once Jesus healed a blind man and the job was only half finished: "I see men like trees, walking" (Mark 8:24, NKJV). He then went on to finish the job.

I wish someone had explained to me earlier in life why "gifts of healings" is a double plural. The disappointment would have been much less when Sally did not jump up immediately healed after our first prayer for healing. On the other hand, seeing God interact with different people in various ways as He processes their diseases has expanded my understanding of God. I now recognize Him far outside the confining little box in my mind, which once set limits on what I perceived He could do and how He could do it.

HEALING DOES NOT NECESSARILY DEPEND ON THE SICK PERSON'S FAITH

The phone rang in my office several years ago. The person said, "Hello. My name is Joe. You don't know me. I visited in your church once. I'm out at Tucson Medical Center, and the doctors tell me I'm dying. I need to talk to you right now."

As I walked into Joe's hospital room, I suddenly recognized him as the golf professional at a country club my parents belonged to when I was a child. I never knew him personally. He moved to Tucson after a short time in Dallas and had worked at a local country club ever since.

Joe was weeping as he said, "I've got to get healed. The doctors tells me I have liver cancer. I have six months or less to live. But I'm going to beat this thing. I'm not going to die. I'm going to think positive about it. I'm not going to die. I'm going to get healed. I've got to get healed. I want you to help me."

After talking several minutes, it was obvious to me that Joe had never received Christ as his personal Savior. We talked for a while and then prayed together. Fortunately, the opportunity was ripe for me to tell him about Christ. He listened respectfully.

I will never forget the words he spoke to me when I left his hospital room. He was weeping again, "Roger, if I only had these 53 years to live over again, there are sure a lot of things I'd do differently." When a person faces death, it is amazing how the things that really matter come to the forefront.

During the next several months, I talked to Joe a number of times. One day he called and said, "Roger, you've got to come over fast. You have to baptize me. I've got to get baptized before I die because I want to go to heaven."

I said, "No, Joe, I'm not going to come over and baptize you because being baptized is not what sends you to heaven." I very carefully explained to him that being baptized is not what saves a person.

"But you have to come and baptize me."

"I'm sorry. I'm not going to come and baptize you. That's not what makes you right with God." I shared with him again the plan of salvation.

About four months after he became ill, I was visiting at Joe's house. Sitting in the chair beside his bed, I explained very simply about Jesus Christ and how He forgives our sins and how we need to receive Him as Lord and Savior.

Quietly he said, "You know, I'd like to receive Jesus Christ as my Savior and Lord." He had spent all these months saying, "I'm not going to die. I can't die. God's got to heal me. My positive thinking will keep me from dying. I know I'm not going to die. I'm not going to die. God's going to heal me."

Joe quietly said, "Roger, I'd like to receive Jesus Christ. And if God chooses to heal me, that'll be all right. And if God chooses to let me die, then that'll be all right, too." A precious prayer time followed.

As I turned to go, I wished I had a tape recorder. Joe looked up at me and said, "Roger, if the whole purpose of this sickness was to bring me to Jesus, then it was worth it."

Healing does not necessarily depend on the sick person's faith. Joe's faith was maturing daily during his sickness. If anyone had "faith" to believe in healing it was Joe. But more issues are involved. I suppose this was the only way God could get Joe's attention long enough to secure him for eternity.

Unfortunately, the perception exists in some circles that lack of healing is the result of faltering personal faith. I have seen this twisted teaching bring untold pain and mental anguish to unwary sufferers.

Faith is often an important component in healing. Think of the Centurion who so impressed Jesus (Matt. 8:5-10). Remember the palsied man whose friends let him down through the roof while Jesus was preaching (Luke 5:17-20). But we must accept the fact that faith is not the only component involved.

As a result of my biblical studies on sickness and of my hearing from God, I was not too unsettled when a woman approached me one Sunday evening and asked to speak quietly with me. "I do not normally attend your church," she said, "but I heard about your baby, Jessie, and I am here to tell you that if you just have enough faith, God has promised to heal your baby."

For the first time, I understood the consternation, confusion, and guilt that often overwhelms people who are told that the real problem is not the sickness, or suffering, but their lack of faith! Fortunately, I had settled the matter about Jessie by careful prayer. Other factors were involved than just my faith.

NOT ALL SUPERNATURAL HEALING IS FROM GOD

In light of the surge of New Age spiritism that is sweeping America, pastors and church leaders need to utilize discernment more than ever before. The growing awareness in our church family to the supernatural workings of God attracts many people. Not all are heaven-sent. I recall several of our single adults excitedly sharing with me the news that a newcomer to their group had verifiable healing powers. I scheduled an interview. He seemed to have powers all right. But a careful examination convinced me that he was calling upon a spirit different from the Holy Spirit.

Not all healing is divine; some is demonic. The powers of darkness enabled the magicians of Egypt to do many unusual feats (Exod. 7:11,12,22; 8:7). First-century believers lived in a world that was filled with demon-energized healers and magic workers (Acts 8:9-11; 13:8-10). The Bible teaches that these same spirits are still in the world today. Test every spirit to see if it is from God (1 John 4:1).

PRAYERS FOR HEALING ARE NOT INTENDED TO REPLACE MEDICAL ATTENTION

In James 5, mention is made of the anointing oil. Evangelicals seem divided about the meaning of the oil. Many anoint with oil as a sacred symbol of the Holy Spirit. Many others believe that the oil represents medical help and attention. It may well be that James had both meanings in mind. Two extremes are to be avoided. One extreme is to pray with "faith" and refuse medical attention. The other extreme is to resort to medical help and never pray.

Earnestly seeking medical help is not a contradiction to earnest prayer and faith. Earnest faith is not invalidated by going to a doctor. After suffering with an intestinal disease for a number of years, I wondered if my taking prescription medicine was a sign of unbelief. After all, I had often prayed for God to heal me; however, my disease grew progressively worse. As a young, searching, seminary student, who was questioning the limits of practical Christianity, I was willing to take a risk. I had no intention of allowing lack of faith to jeopardize my healing. I told God that I was going to put my full faith in Him for healing. I stopped taking my medicine. In less than a month, my disease was out of control. The doctors recommended an ileostomy. I have lived without a colon ever since. Now I understand that what I considered to be lack of faith was good medicine. What I considered to be faith was simple presumption. It is dangerous to put God to the test regarding the issue of healing.

HEALING IS SIMPLY ANOTHER MINISTRY TOOL TO HELP HURTING PEOPLE

The church I pastor is based upon several carefully thought out principles. For example, because the world will always be filled with problems, we believe that we can structure our church to help hurting people in a biblical way. We also believe that God will minister in supernatural ways to help hurting people that far transcend our natural skills and abilities.

Healing is not the focus of our church. Never is it put on ostentatious display. We treat it as just another useful tool in the ministry toolbox of our church. Our goal is not to be known in town as the local healing church. The gift of healing emphasized out of proportion leads to all sorts of abuse. So we try to keep it quietly in proper perspective.

If you were to come to Casas Adobes Baptist Church, you would find that I mention the subject of healing perhaps two or three times a year in the natural course of my preaching ministry. Healing is not our primary focus. However, we want to be in a position to help hurting people. Our Sunday worship bulletin contains a standing announcement that our intercessors meet at 5:00 P.M. for prayer in the counseling center. Anyone who would like special prayer for any need is invited to come.[4]

It is not at all uncommon for someone to ask me after a worship service if an elder can anoint and pray for them before an upcoming surgery. It is not unusual for people to call me at home and ask how to get in touch with the elders for healing prayer. I tell these folks the same thing: "Tom is our elder in charge of arranging a healing service. Call him and he will make arrangements." Within the next few days a number of elders gather with the one who is sick and the prayer time begins.

Recently we have begun what we call "ministry services." After a time of worship and Bible teaching, one of our pastors leads in a time of personal prayer, and then we encourage our people to come to any one of 25 or so prayer stations set up in our worship center for prayer, ministry, and the Lord's Supper. At least one elder and an intercessor or two are stationed at each prayer altar. Families or individuals are welcomed to request prayer. The response to this ministry has been overwhelming. Anointing oil is provided for use at the elder's discretion for anyone who may request prayer for healing.

A young man and an older woman approached me after one of our morning worship services. He introduced himself and his mother-in-law. "I want to encourage you with how God is working here," he began. "My wife is pregnant and having a number of complications. She has gestational diabetes and terrible swelling, among other things. At this point it is questionable whether or not the baby has damage. We were quietly waiting for the service to begin when a woman sat down beside us. The woman said that she noticed my wife was pregnant and wanted to know if she could pray for her and the baby. We agreed. The woman prayed and then suddenly stopped and said, 'I have this strange impression that I need to pray for your blood. May I pray for your blood?' And so she did." The man then looked me squarely in the eye and continued, "You don't know how frightened we have been—and how comforting it is to come to church and have someone we have never seen stop by to minister to us in such a manner. Thanks."

The world is filled with hurting people. Any church can set its heart on helping hurting people. Our supernatural God is delighted to interact with anyone who desires to help those in distress for their profit and for His glory. Healing is just another tool God makes available in the toolbox for helping people in need.

OVERCOMING THE EVIL ONE

Now we must change gears. Another group of hurting people exists in our society who have been largely ignored by the traditional evangelical church: the demonically oppressed. My introduction to spiritual warfare began with a prayer during my college days. I was reading 1 John 2:12-14 about spiritual children, spiritual young men, and spiritual fathers. I set my heart on becoming a spiritual father "who knows him who is from the beginning." I have prayed often since that day for God to make me a spiritual father at any price. As I was reading, I noticed that spiritual young men "have overcome the evil one." I was not certain what that phrase meant. But, it vaguely registered in my mind that learning how to defeat Satan would be part of the training to be a spiritual father. My training began shortly thereafter.

My wife, Julie, and I went to visit in a rural hospital with Harry. He was a member of the little church I pastored in college. A serious heart attack and subsequent loss of oxygen had resulted in a coma. It was lunch time and we encouraged his wife to go to the cafeteria and take a break. We would stay with Harry. She gratefully agreed.

After a while, Julie and I decided to pray for Harry. In the midst of our prayer, Harry opened his eyes, propped himself on his pillow, and said, "Jesus Christ did not come in the flesh." Julie and I were stunned. Harry laid back softly on his pillow. We confirmed what we had heard and remembered 1 John 4:2,3: "Every spirit that acknowledges that Jesus Christ has come in the flesh is from God, but every spirit that does not acknowledge Jesus is not from God. This is the spirit of antichrist." Needless to say, we were shaken. Julie began to cry. Then she asked, "What shall we do?"

Perhaps by divine coincidence we had studied the Gadarene Demoniac in my "Life and Teachings of Christ" class that morning in school. I remembered that the professor had said, "Jesus always found out the demon's name before casting it out." I said to Julie, "Let's pray and ask for a name." So we did.

Much to our surprise, Harry opened his eyes and said, "My name is Clarissus." Then Julie really began to cry. I was more than a little terrified. Of course, when you are young and in college, you are willing to try most anything. So we bowed our heads and began to pray for Clarissus to come forth and leave Harry! We had no idea what we were doing. Nothing happened.

Presently Harry's wife returned. "How did things go?" she asked.

"Just fine," we said. We were not about to tell her what had occurred in that hospital room. We were not certain ourselves.

We were in the parking lot when she came running out the front door of the hospital: "Wait! Wait! What happened in there? Something happened to Harry! He's conscious and smiling. What happened?"

But we said not a word. We were both in shock—and fright.

I never spoke to Harry again. He fully came out of his coma about 10:30 that night. He said to his wife: "I just had the strangest dream. I was climbing the steps to heaven and Saint Peter said, 'You can't come in now.' So I climbed down the ladder and here I am. I guess there are more things God wants me to do on earth."

Ten minutes later he had a massive heart attack and died. I conducted his funeral three days later. I had many questions I wanted to ask him. Fortunately, God has provided some of the answers for me in the 25 years since that intriguing Thursday afternoon in central Texas.

May I share with you a few principles I have found to be helpful in ministering to people who have opened their lives to a spiritual attack from the evil one. Remember, nothing is unusual about fighting the evil one. Overcoming Satan is just another dimension of growing to be a spiritual man or woman.

OVERCOMING THE EVIL ONE MUST NOT BE NEGLECTED JUST BECAUSE SOME EVANGELICAL CHRISTIANS HAVE PROBLEMS WITH THE FACT OF DEMONIZATION

The man from the utility company finished his work at my house, then he said to me, "You're Roger Barrier, aren't you? I listen to your radio program every day. I have a problem; can you help me? My wife and I are both Christians. She's really having some personality problems; in fact, there are times when I wonder what's going on inside of her. Do you believe in demons?"

"Yes," I replied. "Why don't we sit down in the kitchen and you tell me when all of this began."

"Several months ago we went to a spiritualist church. We were invited to pray to receive spirit guides to help direct our lives. I didn't pray for any; but my wife did. She hasn't been the same since. Sometimes it's as if there is a different person inside. Her voice changes; her face contorts; she has an aversion to the things of God. Our marriage is falling apart. She won't go back to our Christian church! It all came to a head last night! We had a big argument. She walked into the hallway and slowly turned. There was a sneer on her face as she almost snarled at me: 'Don't you know who we are?' Her voice rose to a scream as she repeated over and over again, 'Don't you know who we are? Don't you know who we are?' Could she have a demonic problem like they talk about in the Bible? Can you help me?" Fortunately, God gives Christians every tool necessary for complete victory over the evil one and his forces.

The deliverance ministry in our church developed because an increasing number of people came to us seeking help. As we began to make it known that we were helping people who had demonic problems, some in our congregation were quite unsettled! Some were afraid; some were convinced that demons were for the first-century world and no longer existed; others were indignant; most were ignorant. A few went so far as to try to get me fired! But hurting people are hard to ignore. Someone must try to help.

Early in the development of our church deliverance ministry, I determined that I did not want to be a "Lone Ranger." Fortunately, the associate pastors and most of the elders who led our church had a desire to help these people. After a series of "misfires," we agreed that this ministry needed backing by the entire church. Patience and careful biblical teaching are powerful tools in advancing the Kingdom.

I began a series of sermons and teaching classes to share what the Bible has to say about Satan and his activity. The Bible clearly teaches the reality of demons (Mark 1:23,24; 1 Cor. 10:20; Rev. 12:3-9). But it reveals so much more. Over a period of several weeks, I used a concordance for the Old Testament and I read the New Testament to find and underline with a yellow highlighter every verse in my Bible that describes Satan and his devices. I was shocked. My Bible almost drips yellow highlighter! This exercise convinced me more than ever to prepare my congregation to protect themselves in spiritual warfare. Many years have gone by since I began exposing my congregation to what Satan can do to Christians. Many battles occurred in the beginning. But now the deliverance ministry is an accepted part of our church. People in spiritual battle are free to seek and receive help in all sorts of ways.

About a decade ago one of our elders, our associate pastor in charge of counseling, and I were asked to conduct a spiritual warfare conference in

Phoenix for 35 pastors from our denomination. As the morning progressed, the looks of disbelief, and even hostility, increased. At the lunch break, the only two Spanish pastors in the group approached us quietly. One of them spoke volumes with a simple statement: "We have been wondering how long it would take you Anglos to catch up with what we have been dealing with in Mexico for generations." We have too long ignored the reality of the evil one in our churches.

Let's face it, in past generations the United States was gripped in the choking hold of materialism. Satan hardly needed to expose himself to get people into hell. Today, in conjunction with society's disenchantment with materialism and its increasing desire for the spirit realm, the evil one has "upped the ante in our generation." With the advent of the New Age movement, the spirit world is facing us like never before. I believe that the Christians and churches that wise up and get into the battle will be greatly used by God in this next generation. The rest will be left behind.

CHRISTIANS CAN NEVER BE "DEMON POSSESSED" BUT THEY CAN CERTAINLY BE SPIRITUALLY NEUTRALIZED

One of the early questions we dealt with at Casas church in developing a deliverance ministry was, Can a Christian be demon possessed? What an explosive issue this was! Confusion reigned. Some talked about possession; some talked about oppression; others said that Christians cannot be touched by Satan at all. What frightened Christian people the most was the term "demon possession." It implied that Satan might be inside them! But this "baggage laden" terminology sidetracked from the real issue: Christians can be attacked and neutralized by the evil one and his forces.

We are careful never to use the term "demon possessed." In fact, we are careful to teach that the exact term "demon possession" is never found in the Greek Bible. The Greek word *daimonizomenos* literally translated is "demonized" (Matt. 12:22, for example). In Scripture, the term "demonized" seems to denote different degrees of severity.

In order to alleviate fears about being "possessed," today we use a straight-line model instead of a circle model to illustrate how Satan can attack Christians. Visualizing three concentric circles labeled from outside to inside as "body, soul, and spirit," implies that Satan can get inside to harm us. A straight line with the labels "body, soul, and spirit," going from left to right on a straight line indicates that Satan can attack us at any point on the line—except our spirit. A solid vertical line between "soul," and "spirit," models the fact that the Christian's regenerated "spirit" is safe and secure for eternity from satanic attack because it is indwelt by the Holy Spirit: "[We] were sealed with the promised Holy Spirit" (Eph. 1:13, RSV). This statement from Paul is a mark of protection. This straight-line model reduces the negative impression of "possession" while helping our folks understand that they are open to attack in some areas and must take precautions. (By the way, people who are not Christians, and who thus do not have their spirits regenerated by the Holy Spirit, can be totally demonized or fully under the control of Satan. This full domination can never happen to Christians.)

Satan's goal is to spiritually neutralize Christians. Satan cannot completely destroy Christians (John 10:10; Acts 26:17,18; Col. 1:13; 1 John 4:4; 1 Cor. 3:16; 6:19,20; Eph. 4:27). But he can certainly wreak havoc in their lives (2 Tim. 2:24-26; 1 Pet. 5:8,9; Eph. 6:12). From Satan's perspective, it may well be that the next best thing to a damned spirit is a neutralized Christian. If Satan can neutralize Christians by stifling their testimony, taking away their prayer lives, quenching their desire to hear God speak, filling them with fear, crowding out time for Bible study, enticing them to sin, filling them with lies, increasing their doubts, stealing their joy, and making them self-centered, then he has effectively taken them out of the battle of advancing the kingdom of Christ on earth.

In our spiritual warfare classes, we encourage Christians to realize that since the earth is now in the hands of the evil one (Matt. 4:8,9; John 14:30,31; 16:11; 2 Cor. 4:4; Eph. 2:1,2; 1 John 5:19), we Christians are guerrilla soldiers who are behind the enemy's spiritual lines. We must take care not to be taken captive and spiritually neutralized.

SOME PEOPLE'S PROBLEMS CAN ONLY BE UNDERSTOOD IN LIGHT OF SATANIC ACTIVITY

The conflict between God and Satan has been going on since before the Fall of man. Those who have eyes to see (and those who read the Bible) discern that the cosmic spiritual struggle is often manifested on earth with human beings in the middle. Remember Job? His problems were only understood in light of the behind-the-scenes battle between God and Satan. Remember Job's statement after he lost his children and possessions: "The Lord gave, and the Lord has taken away; blessed be the name of the Lord" (Job 1:21, RSV)? We admire Job's faith; but we sympathize with his deception. God had not taken these things away; Satan had! Job was the pawn in an eternal struggle—and at the end of the book he was still struggling to understand what was happening to him. His problem could only be understood in light of satanic activity.

I have watched a marked transformation occur in the ministry of our associate pastor in charge of counseling in our church. He has a solid Christian orientation. He is well trained by every secular standard in counseling. Like many counselors, he has often been frustrated that some people who ought to find victory over their problems never do. He has mentioned with sorrow that many who seek help from the mental health professions are frustrated with the results. Over the years, I have watched him add the spiritual warfare component to his many tools for helping people. The results are gratifying. People who could not find victory in any other way find victory by applying basic biblical guidelines regarding spiritual warfare.

Of course, a demon does not "reside behind every bush." But, when a problem does not yield to medical attention, standard psychological counseling, biblical insight, or the usual prayer requests, it is not unwise to consider the possibility of a spiritual attack.

CHRISTIANS NEED TO BE AWARE OF SATAN'S DEVICES

Shortly before his death, Dr. Walter Martin and I were discussing the issue of satanic attacks against Christians. He said to me: "It is not paranoid for Christians to think that Satan is out to get them!" As a result, while we reassure our people of God's power and protection, we teach them that the areas of our lives that are not under submission to the Holy Spirit are open to attack and harassment by demonic spirits.

Unfortunately, many Christians have trouble recognizing satanic attacks or devices. Christians had trouble in the first century, and they still have trouble today (2 Cor. 2:11).

To begin with, Satan blinds the eyes of unbelievers so that they cannot see the gospel of Christ (2 Cor. 4:3,4). How our evangelism improves when we realize that some refuse Christ, not only because they love their sin, but because they are in an intense spiritual struggle that is intended to damn their souls to hell!

Satan's major tool is deception. Job was deceived (Job 1:21; 2:10). If perfect Eve was deceived (2 Cor. 11:3), how vulnerable must we fallen Christians be? The Bible is filled with warnings for Christians to beware of what Satan can do to harm them (Acts 13:10; 2 Cor. 11:13-15; 2 Thess. 2:9-12; 1 Tim. 4:1; 2 Tim. 3:13). Satan's tools include, but are not limited to: lying (John 8:32,44), anger (Eph. 4:26,27), an unforgiving spirit (2 Cor. 2:10,11), sin (Eph. 2:1,2; 1 John 3:8-10), accusations and insinuations (Rev. 12:10), temptation (1 Cor. 7:5; 1 Thess. 3:5), contact with the occult (Deut. 18:10-13), and drug and alcohol abuse (Gal. 5:20,21). Of course, our "sinful nature" (Rom. 7:1-25; Col. 3:5-10) is able to produce sin in any of these areas. However, careful scrutiny of problems in these areas may reveal a satanic attack.

CARELESS CHRISTIANS OPEN THEIR LIVES TO SATANIC ATTACK IN NUMEROUS WAYS

Pete came to my office late one afternoon for an appointment. Over the years, he slipped away from his childhood devotion to Christ. He responded to the growing spiritual longings in his life by attending a spiritualist church in our city. When the church leaders asked if he wanted a "spirit guide" to help him through life, he responded enthusiastically. But now he looked desperately at me and said, "And I got something that night and I don't like what I got. Please help me." Then he went into a trance. After a while he came back to himself and said simply, "They're back, aren't they?"

I was not quite certain what "they" were, but I agreed, they were back. He then detailed the symptoms of his problem, which ranged from astral projection to demonic visions.

We are surrounded today by the tools of the occult world masquerading as innocent things—and they are not. They are doorways into the spirit world. Christians who enter the occult world are committing spiritual whoredom (Lev. 19:31; 20:6,27). Nevertheless, I never cease to be amazed at the number of unsuspecting Christians who open the door to the occult. We have in our counseling department a checklist of past activities for people to examine. Christians who have been involved with any of the following activities do well to confess, repent, and renounce (2 Cor. 4:2; Prov. 28:13) any involvement with the enemy if they desire to remove every occult influence over their lives:

1. Contact with occult activity (read Deut. 18:19-13 for God's glossary of the occult).
2. Personal invitation for demonic guidance and help (2 Cor. 11:3,4).

3. Drug and alcohol involvement (Gal. 5:20,21).
4. Habitual sin (Eph. 4:27).
5. Transference and/or ancestral sin (Exod. 20:5,6).
6. An undisciplined or out-of-control mind (2 Cor. 10:3-5).
7. Sexual sin or abuse (Rom 1:24,25 and 1 Cor. 10:19-21; Hos. 4:12,13).[5]

The above list is suggestive, not exhaustive. Every area of life not under submission to the Holy Spirit is open to the control and influence of demonic spirits. Christians can never be fully controlled by Satan because they have the Holy Spirit (see 1 Cor. 6:17; 1 John 4:4). But areas held back from submission to God are open to demonic influence!

GOD PROVIDES EVERY CHRISTIAN WITH THE TOOLS NECESSARY FOR COMPLETE VICTORY OVER ANY DEMONIC ATTACK

Many years have passed since I counseled with Pete in my office. This Christian brother opened the door to the occult and wanted to close it. Could I help?

I had recently finished reading *The Adversary*,[6] by Mark Bubeck. I handed the book to Pete and showed him the suggested prayers that dealt with his problem. I said to Pete, "I believe everything you need for victory is in this book. Read it, do what it says, and you will find freedom. If not, let me know and we'll take the next step."

I was running an experiment with Pete. I had previously guided people with prayer and counseling as they dealt with attacks from the evil one. I had used the guidelines in *The Adversary* during several deliverance sessions and seen God's power manifested. I wanted to see if Pete could get victory on his own. Pete took the book, followed the guidelines, prayed the suggested prayers, and found freedom. He has served faithfully in our church for the past 15 years.

After those sessions, I understood for the first time what Jesus meant when He said, "Do not rejoice that the spirits submit to you, but rejoice that your names are written in heaven" (Luke 10:20). Realizing and acting on the truth of our identity in Christ sets us free (John 8:32), as Neil Anderson affirms in his books, *The Bondage Breaker* and *Victory over the Darkness*.[7] Few people can witness a deliverance session without believing in the power of Satan— and the greater power of God.

An attack from the evil one can be repulsed by any Christian by using the tools God reveals in the Bible. Only on rare occasions, for example, when a demonic manifestation is in progress and a person no longer has personal control, have I found it necessary to conduct a deliverance session. We make it a policy at our church to guide those under demonic harassment to utilize the God-given scriptural tools that guarantee victory. I think it is fair to say that a very small percentage of the people who seek counsel in this area need any sort of direct intervention.

Many Christians have areas in their lives that are out of control. One of my personal areas of struggle is worry. I have tried for years to pray it through and get victory. I applied the principles of Romans 6:1-10, and reckoned myself dead unto this sin. But, I found little relief. Finally, I realized I had worried so long that according to Ephesians 4:27, Satan had gained a foothold in my life. I was not just fighting the "flesh." I was experiencing an attack from Satan. I practiced Romans 6, and began praying for protection from Satan and his attacks in the area of worry. The elusive victory began to come.

To make it simple, James 4:7 gives a simple formula for success: "Submit yourselves, then, to God. Resist the devil, and he will flee from you." This formula works with problems ranging from anger to temper, worry, lust, bitterness, envy, and everything in between.

"Submit to God" deals with the "flesh" and the "sinful nature." We are invited here to: (1) confess that the area is out of control and needs help; (2) consciously yield the area to God; and (3) consider ourselves dead to that sin, according to Romans 6.

If the problem is solved, then thank God, it was only a sin of the flesh. If the struggle persists, the second half of James 4:7 comes into play. We may well be experiencing a spiritual attack and will not find freedom until we battle on spiritual grounds.

"Resist the evil one" deals with the spiritual dimension. We are invited here to: (1) renounce the forces attacking us in this area; and (2) petition the Holy Spirit to fill the area and allow us the opportunity to choose freedom in that area. During my pastoral years I have seen James 4:7 bring victory to Christians who could not find relief in any other way.

Proper prior protection from Satan's fiery darts is much better than spending months or years in the spiritual hospital recovering from an attack. Too many Christians are going around spiritually naked. The Christian armor of Ephesians 6:10-17 provides daily protection. In our training classes we encourage our people to pray on the armor daily.

We also teach our people to pray for a hedge of protection. God built a hedge around Job (Job 1:10). I pray daily for that hedge to be around my family, my church, and myself. The hedge is built according to Psalm 91:

1. I make the Lord my habitation and refuge (Ps. 91:1,9,10). David emphasizes this in Psalm 27:3-6.
2. I want to love God with all my heart (Ps. 91:14).
3. I acknowledge His name (Ps. 91:14).

A demonic problem is always a prayer project. Underline that last statement carefully. Prayer is the fundamental tool in overcoming the evil one. Prayer provides prior protection and a place to reaffirm who we are in Christ (John 8:32). Prayer provides offensive weapons to neutralize attacking spiritual forces (Eph. 6:12). Prayer provides healing balm for recovery from inflicted spiritual wounds.

No justifiable reason exists for Christians to be afraid of spiritual warfare. God has given us every tool necessary for overcoming the evil one. And even in our inexperience and ignorance we have the quiet confirmation that: "Greater is He who is in you than he who is in the world" (1 John 4:4, NASB). We win in the end!

DO NOT GO PROUDLY MARCHING IN WHERE ANGELS FEAR TO TREAD—EXPECT COUNTERATTACKS

My experience tells me that Christians can get hurt when they move too quickly into areas they "know not of." As we go to war on behalf of hurting people, we can expect to be attacked. The same forces attacking the one in need will often turn to attack the one who is trying to help. The attacks can take many forms. Marital discord, children's nightmares, spousal depression, physical illness, depression, and hassles at work are just a few of the things that may be manifestations of the evil one at work. The undiscerning will often think of these as unfortunate coincidences. Sometimes they are; but occasionally, a spiritual attack is in progress (cf. Acts 16:16-23 and Eph. 6:12). Do not be afraid. Pray for protection and have the spiritual armor intact.

The only organized opposition I have had against me in almost 20 years at Casas came from people who were dead set against any sort of ministry to those harassed by the occult. The pain of that experience still lingers. Be patient and careful in developing a spiritual warfare ministry within the framework of an established local church. It needs to be done—but, move wisely and slowly. In our established evangelical church, I have worked for almost 20 years for the freedom to preach and implement what the Bible teaches about overcoming the evil one—and about healing, for that matter.

One of my elders shared with me that the Roman Catholics never allow "upper level" priests to do deliverance sessions. They are not expendable. I have no idea if the Roman Catholics follow that guideline or not. The elder provided no verification, but the principle here is important: People can get hurt in this ministry. Those who minister to others in spiritual warfare need to be growing and maturing Christians—not spiritual children. Remember, spiritual young men—not children—are the ones who have overcome the evil one (1 John 2:12-14). Children can get hurt more easily. I look back with sorrow at some of the "casualties" from our earlier learning years. I choose not to tell those stories. Suffice it to say, a war is going on out there. We are called to be soldiers of Christ. We must not be carelessly "shot" in battle as we liberate others for the kingdom of Jesus Christ.

Spiritual Warfare Is Simply Another Ministry Tool to Help Hurting People

Pastors can become so involved in deliverance work that their time and energy is sapped from doing other duties. As I began to make myself available, I discovered that Satan was "delighted" to bring me into contact with demonically attacked people from all over town. I could be busy with these people every day. So I helped "pioneer" the spiritual warfare ministry in our church and then turned it over to others. It gets no more time nor prominence than the other ministries in our church family. It is simply there for those who need it.

Spiritual warfare is not to be out of balance in the ministry of a local church. A church that is unable or unwilling to help people with these problems is as out of balance as a church that overemphasizes them to distraction.

The world is filled with hurting people. No church can minister to everyone. Healing and spiritual deliverance are two of the many tools God has given to help people. As long as we have the available resources, I desire our church to utilize as many tools as God gives us. People are blessed and encouraged by Christians who are willing to discover more tools and learn how to use them.

One of our church members was talking with a fellow school teacher before a teachers' meeting began. The topic of church attendance arose. When our member mentioned Casas, her friend replied, "Oh, I know about that church. That is the church that helps people!" I hope so. Prayer for healing and prayer for spiritual warfare are two of the tools any church can use to help those in need.

Notes

1. Please note that any comments regarding my denominational upbringing are not made with any negative, or disparaging intention. I am trying to portray accurately the circumstances, impressions, and parameters that affected the understanding, development and practice of healing and spiritual warfare related gifts in my ministry.
2. I have taken the liberty to use pseudonyms for the sake of the confidentiality of those involved in the stories I relate.
3. *Principles of Spiritual Growth*, by Miles Stanford, (Lincoln, NE: Back to the Bible, 1979) and *Hind's Feet on High Places*, by Hannah Hurnard, (Greensburg, PA: Barbour and Company, 1985) are simple but profound books. They can be read and understood by any teenager to senior adult. I have used them for years to help people get a grasp on understanding God's purpose for conforming believers into the image of Christ.
4. Over the past several years, we have been quietly building a network of prayer "warriors," whom we call intercessors. They intercede for Casas Adobes Baptist Church and have a running record of God's answers to their prayers. They also strengthen and encourage each other in the development of their spiritual gifts. They make themselves available to pray for those with personal hurts and needs—including healing.
5. Our counselors share that they rarely find cases of sexual sin or sexual abuse without some level of spiritual attack involved.
6. Mark Bubeck, *The Adversary* (Chicago, IL: Moody Press, 1975).
7. In addition to *The Adversary*, we often recommend *Victory over the Darkness* (Ventura, CA: Regal Books, 1990), and *The Bondage Breaker* (Eugene, OR: Harvest House, 1990), both by Neil Anderson, and *The Believer's Guide to Spiritual Warfare* (Ann Arbor, MI: Servant, 1990), by Thomas White, to Christians who need help in overcoming a spiritual attack.

HEALING AND DELIVERANCE—
BECAUSE OF THE CROSS:

SEEING THE POWER OF THE GOSPEL AT WORK
THROUGH PRAYER FOR HEALING
AND DELIVERANCE

LLOYD D. FRETZ

SANDRA—A DEACON'S WIFE

The phone rang on Monday evening—our night to relax. Sandra, one of our deacons' wives, asked if my wife, Marie, and I could come to talk. Sandra had a mild epileptic seizure in the dentist's chair that day and was worried. This had not been the first instance but she had not shared her seizure attacks with anyone except her family. Another evening off was soon to be an exciting night of ministry.

We listened to her story of mounting concern as she explained when and where she had experienced these seizures. Each occurrence found her in a protected place, the hospital with one of her children, the dentist's chair, at home, but never driving the car.

"Do you know of any sin in your lives, in your marriage or family?" I asked Sandra and her husband.

"We can't think of any," they replied.

"What about unforgiveness? or bitterness? Is there any occult involvement in your background?"

They shook their heads.

"Do you know of anyone at work or in the neighborhood who hates you enough to harm you?"

Again their answer was no.

I was drawing a blank. Nothing seemed to point to this present crisis. Were these seizures the onset of an epileptic problem?

By this time, as a pastor and counselor, I had learned to listen to God's "still small voice" while I listened to people's stories. I heard nothing in this case. I prayed and asked the Lord to show me the root of the problem, whether it was spiritual or physical. So that I would be able to listen more quietly, I asked Marie to pray and as she prayed I began to hear the word "ache." I remembered thinking that if I said this word I would sound foolish. How proud we are and slow to trust the Holy Spirit's promptings.

When my wife finished praying, I said that all I heard was the word "...." Instead of saying "ache" I said "Achan," to my great surprise. My next question drove to the root of the problem as I breathed a quick prayer. "What do you have in your house that doesn't belong to you?"

Sandra's head dropped and she whispered, "See Don, I told you!"

Their story began to pour out as Marie and I sat and listened quietly. The Lord once more had helped us to hit the "hot button." I am still amazed each time this happens. A miracle had just happened but everything seemed so normal, just the same as before but the Lord of glory had quietly directed and there was the answer.

Don was a construction-site foreman and one day he brought a vanload of building materials home. He had assured Sandra that these were leftover materials and indicated in a vague way that he had permission to remove them from the job site.

Sandra helped Don carry the various items into their basement to be used to help finish their family room. Soon the room was built and they decorated it beautifully. That was when she had her first seizure. The timing of the first attack was very significant. We were getting closer to the root of the problem.

I glanced at Don and I could see the awful realization beginning to dawn upon him. I felt sorry for him because I understood what it was like to be put on the spot. But God is so gracious and patient with us. The Lord cares and He knows all the sins and weaknesses we think are hidden safely away in our hearts where no one knows or sees. Don admitted to us that he did not have permission to take the building materials and that he had stolen them and lied to Sandra.

How easily we as Christians lie and bury our sins. We deceive ourselves and go on as if nothing has happened. Then when problems begin to arise we are not able or willing to look at ourselves from God's perspective. God loves us so much that problems and trials are allowed in order to get our attention. Often Satan is behind the situation. Scripture makes it clear that we are not to give Satan a foothold by the way we live (Eph. 4:27).

In Sandra's situation, she was left "uncovered" because of her husband's trespass and like Achan's family at Jericho, she was attacked and the enemy gained a foothold (Josh. 7). When Sandra became party to Don's sin, she was vulnerable spiritually. Satan then used a spirit of infirmity (Luke 13:11; see appendix 5: "Spiritual Warfare") that posed as epilepsy to torment her.

I do not believe that all epilepsy is of the devil. But I do know the devil's schemes well enough to realize that he tries to hide his work in situations that seem to indicate the obvious, but the obvious is not always the case. Often his tactics are well covered by our ignorance. We either blame Satan for everything or never recognize his work. This demonstrates the absolute necessity for the gift of discerning of spirits (1 Cor. 12:10). Balance is difficult but essential.

Don repented. He proved that he was sorry for his sin by later paying the company for the material he had taken. Because he was a deacon in the church, he promised at the first opportunity to share with the church what he had done and ask their forgiveness (Jas. 5:16). After Don promised to do these acts of repentance, I was then free to deal with Sandra and her "epileptic" problem.

We prayed and asked the Lord to send His angels to protect us and our families. "The angel of the Lord encamps around those who fear him, and he delivers them" (Ps. 34:7). Next, I led them in a prayer of confession. We stated that Jesus had come and that His death on the cross had destroyed all the devil's work (1 John 3:8). I then commanded the spirit of infirmity to loose itself from Sandra and to go to the place where Jesus would have it go. Sandra immediately gulped as she sensed a sudden pressure released from her throat. She felt the thing go. She was free! We prayed that the Lord would heal her of any damage that had been done; then we praised the Lord for the wonderful miracle.

Sandra has been seizure free from that moment on! Not all encounters with the enemy have been that quick or simple. Most of the people to whom I have ministered deliverance have received freedom. Some have received partial freedom in one area or another, while others have been helped, like Sandra, with one particular problem. Deliverance is not the "quick fix" many people have thought it to be. I have found that this ministry is necessary in many cases to pave the way for other ministries of help such as psychological healing, the healing of past hurts, and physical healing.

If this situation had transpired 10 years earlier, I would have encouraged Don and Sandra to call for the elders to have her anointed with oil for healing. We would have questioned them regarding any sin in their lives as well, according to James 5. Then if she was no better, I would have suggested they go to the doctor. Doctors are given to us in God's plan for our help and healing (see 1 Tim. 5:23; 2 Kings 20:5-7), but there is a clear difference in ministry to hurting people when one's worldview, founded on Scripture, allows for problems to have demonic roots.

Don and Sandra still live in Toronto and are serving the Lord in faithful leadership through their local church. Their experience has given many people courage to believe that healing and deliverance are a significant aspect of Christ's victory over Satan at the cross. This is good news.

MARGUERITE—SUNDAY SCHOOL DIRECTOR

Every pastor prays for faithful, loyal, and gifted persons to be on their team to do the best job. When we moved to Sarnia, Ontario, in 1986 to pastor in the beautiful "Bluewater" border area across the river from Port Huron, Michigan, there was Marguerite. Near retirement age now, Marguerite had served various departments of the church ever since it was just a small struggling congregation. The church had been experiencing difficulties and a number of families left to serve in other churches in the area. But not Marguerite. She was wonderfully dependable and loved her calling to the teachers and students of the Sunday School.

I began to preach the Word in the light of a biblical worldview on deliverance from Satan's power. People seemed hungry for answers and practical ministry so they began to come to me for prayer and spiritual counseling. As people were helped, the word began to get around and of course it was not all positive. People did not understand, had not heard these ideas before, thought I was a "crazy charismatic," and had not gotten the true story in some cases. I believe they all meant well, they just did not want anymore trouble. I did not blame them. I did not want any trouble either. But let me warn you: Satan does not like having his territory invaded.

As many received help with their tremendous problems, the church began to grow. This does not mean all went smoothly, however. Others in the congregation became upset with this ministry of deliverance as they saw many hurting people come for prayer. Not Marguerite. The more she listened, the more she began to think of her own situation.

Since she was a young girl Marguerite had suffered from narcolepsy and cataplexy. The first caused her to go to sleep, almost paralyzing her in whatever she was doing at the moment—whether driving her car, sitting in church, or opening the kitchen cupboard door. She could never stay awake while reading her Bible. Usually it ended up on the floor and sometimes she ended up there as well. Whenever she sensed this coming upon her she would try to prepare herself as quickly as possible. If she was driving her boys to a hockey practice, she would quickly park her car on the shoulder of the road and sleep for five minutes or so. There they waited for mother to get over the spell, while she slept behind the wheel.

Cataplexy affected Marguerite differently. Whenever she showed any strong emotion, she would collapse in a heap wherever she happened to be. Her children often used this problem to their advantage. When she was about to discipline them for some misdemeanor, they would try to make her laugh and down she would go so she could not catch them. These two problems had been in her life for many years. Neither medication from the doctor nor prayer for healing had made any change in her condition. She had wanted to come and talk to me about the problem on at least three occasions but had changed her mind. Now she wondered if her problem was more than just physical. She was afraid to face this possibility.

Finally the day came. As I waited at the front door of the church for someone else to arrive, Marguerite came and stood talking to me. She had been doing a little work in the new church addition and decided to take a short break. She began to share with me what had been happening in relation to her "sleeping problem" and I could see she was quite troubled.

Just that morning Marguerite was getting something out of the cupboard. As she reached to open the door she went to sleep and hit her head on the door. This had happened three times before she was able to open the door. Worse still, the previous week while driving to her daughter's home, she felt herself begin to drop off to sleep. She stopped the car on the shoulder of the highway but could not move her hand from the steering wheel to the gearshift in order to put the car into park. She was terrified because she knew if she fell asleep with the car still in drive, her foot would relax and slip off the brake and the car would go—who knows where. Just as she was slipping away she managed to say, "Jesus!" Immediately she was wide awake!

Why did the name of Jesus have such a dramatic affect? That is when she decided to share her problem with me. So here we were, finally into the story. As we talked, she began to share more incidents about how terrible this whole thing was and how it had hindered her in many ways for a number of years. Lately it was getting much worse and she was obviously very concerned about the future. Could this problem be more than just physical? Perhaps it was spiritual as well.

We moved to the privacy of my church office as I began to question her regarding her difficult childhood and teen years. Marguerite was raised by her grandparents because of problems in her home. I questioned her regarding her relationship with her siblings and peers, her parents' relationship, their background and many other areas. Somewhere during the history taking, we talked about her involvement in anything connected with the occult. People usually say they have not been involved until I ask specific questions about areas that are common in our society. Questions concerning palm reading, card laying, teacup reading, and visiting a fortune-teller usually get the response, "Yes, I've done that, but I wasn't serious!" Many people have played with a Ouija board, read their horoscope, and witched for water without actually connecting these activities to the occult, much less to demons or Satan.

Scripture states very clearly that we are to have nothing to do with anything occultic. "When you enter the land the Lord your God is giving you,...let no one be found among you who sacrifices his son or daughter in the fire, who practices divination or sorcery,...is a medium or spiritist or who consults the dead. Anyone who does these things is detestable to the Lord....You must be blameless before the Lord your God" (Deut. 18:9-11). Deuteronomy 27 and 28 explain without a doubt that if we go to the dark side for information about the future we bring a curse upon ourselves and upon our children's children. One of Satan's best ploys is to get us to seek help from demons without our realizing the nature of the source.

After interviewing hundreds of people and reading numerous accounts regarding the occult, it is clear to me that this affects us in three major ways. First, confusion comes, making it difficult to make good decisions. Second, there seems to be fighting, separation, and family breakdown. And third, lust and perversion usually become a difficult problem.

I have discovered that the persons who are the most opposed to these findings are often those who have been involved quite deeply in the occult themselves. Usually the more occult involvement, the stronger the aversion to asking oneself honest questions about its rightness. Some people have gotten very angry and refused to talk, or have not been remotely willing to consider the possibility that their problems may be connected to this area in their lives.

In Marguerite's situation, she told me her grandmother had taken her to a fortune-teller when she was a young teenager and that she had made another visit when she was around 18. "When did you begin to experience the two problems?" I asked.

Marguerite paused and looked surprised. "You know, it was right after that visit," she said. "I have never thought of that before. Do you suppose that has any connection to my narcolepsy?"

I told her it did not matter what I supposed but only what was actually the truth. In this case only the Lord knew.

The next step was to pray and ask God what had happened. During the short prayer, I had an overwhelming sense that we had found the root of her sickness. It was spiritual. The Lord did not say anything to me but somehow I just knew. I expressed this to her. We talked about her becoming a Christian when she was in her early 20s and her condition not changing at that time. We discussed the times she was anointed with oil for healing but was never healed and how the doctor had prescribed many different drugs that did not help. The more we talked, the more certain I was that this was the answer. We had found the real cause of this scary condition that was slowly closing her down.

After praying for protection, I led her in a prayer to renounce her involvement with the occult and to break the devil's hold in her life and in her body. We broke the curse that was passed down to her by claiming liberty through the matchless name of Jesus and through the blood that was freely given for her at the Cross (Rev. 12:11; 1 John 3:8). The occult and infirmity spirits were bound and commanded to leave her. She did not feel anything. Nor did she react in any outward manner, but I sensed a wonderful release in my spirit. After asking the Lord Jesus to come and heal her I simply trusted that He had. I told her she would know if anything had happened, so she went home.

She was not at church the following Sunday, but on Tuesday she came bouncing into my office. "I haven't felt like this since I was a teenager," she said.

"Naturally not," I replied. "That's when the enemy obtained his foothold and now he is gone!"

Marguerite has never had the problem since that time and I am writing this account almost four years later.

Not everyone in the church was happy about this event. Although Marguerite shared publicly her entire story, many did not believe her. One main reason was that if this really happened, people would have to reexamine their own theology and that is a difficult task. Perhaps many more believe, now that time has passed and more is printed and understood about deliverance ministry, but I am sure some will continue to deny that the occult was the real cause of this dear lady's health problem. Those who know her well know that something miraculous has happened.

VARIOUS MIRACLES OF HEALING AND DELIVERANCE

A YOUNG BOY

Young children, as well, are not always safe from the clutches of Satan. A young boy of five years was brought to me from a neighboring city by his parents and pastor. After questioning the father and mother for more than an hour, we finally discovered that the child's aunt had severely affected her nephew during her six-week stay at her sister's house. The aunt had been involved in occultic activity.

Less than a week after the aunt's arrival, the child's behavior suddenly changed and he became wild and difficult to manage. He especially reacted to religious pictures, artifacts, and to church attendance. His actions became noticeable by all who knew the family, so the parents were desperate for help.

The boy's father brought the child into the office where we were sitting and held him while I explained to the boy what we had discovered. As we shared with the boy, he said there was a "bad man inside him telling him to do and say awful things."

After a prayer of protection and with the father's hand on the little fellow's head, I simply commanded the "bad man" to leave in Jesus' name. As quick as a cat, the boy bounded out of his father's arms and out the door, back to his toys he had just left. Seven months later the father called me to report that his son had no trouble sleeping from that night onward and that his behavior returned to normal just as quickly. Children are easy to minister to. Their faith is simple, and they usually tell the truth about their feelings and what they sense.

A YOUNG MAN

I received a phone call from a friend who was dealing with a troubled young man in his church. They drove the 100 miles to my office to see if we could get to the root of his dilemma. For the last six months, the young man was unable to attend church or read his Bible without hearing foul language in his mind. He could not get near the communion elements without a wave of nausea sweeping over him.

Again, after questioning him, it became apparent that this trouble began with the young man's involvement in pornography. Filthy literature always opens wide the door of the soul, and Satan uses such an opportunity to make his move. Continuing to feed the mind this way soon dulls any desire for the Lord and His Word. Very soon this young man was caught.

The young man confessed his sin and I led him in a prayer to break the bondage of the demon of lust (cf. Hos. 4:12,13,17; Num. 25:1-3; Ps. 106:28,36-39). He was set free, later attended Bible college and is serving the Lord to this day. He has been free from this common trap now for many years.

A WOMAN WHO WAS A SMALL-GROUP LEADER

I saw a lady from another church five times before she was set free. When she first came to see me, she was punishing herself by scratching her face with her fingernails. She was a beautiful woman but she saw herself as ugly. Her urge to commit suicide was overwhelming at times. I attempted to minister deliverance but did not seem to get very far, although she did get professional help regarding the desire to destroy and hurt herself. During the year or more that she came to see me, she spent two sessions in an institution. After the last two-week period of hospitalization, she called me and was desperate.

That day as I talked to her I was desperate, too. I did not know what else to do or say. She now was having terrible fits of rage and was tempted to kill her husband and children. I called out to the Lord for the answer and as I prayed that day the Lord whispered to me that she was bound by a deaf and dumb spirit.

The moment I addressed this spirit she collapsed in a heap on my office carpet. This had never happened to me before, so I thought I should continue to come against this spirit in the strong name of Jesus and by the power of Jesus' blood. I sang about the blood of Christ and prayed for approximately 30 minutes.

All of a sudden I sensed that the demon left her. Her eyelashes began to flutter and she opened her eyes slowly. "What am I doing on the floor?" she whispered.

I told her what had happened during the 30 minutes that had just elapsed. She had not heard or remembered a thing. It took her another 10 minutes to gain enough strength to get up and sit in her chair. After she was strong enough, she got to her feet and left. I did not see her or her husband for almost a year, but when we met again, they joyfully reported she was freed that day and she had been making wonderful progress in her Christian growth ever since her chains were broken. I rejoiced with them that day.

MIRACLES IN MY FAMILY

Early in my ministry, I decided that if what I believed and preached did not work in my life and in my own home, I would not burden others with a theology that was not effective where they live and hurt. I wanted to be honest and real at all costs.

My wife, Marie, and I were called to plant a new church in eastern Toronto, so we moved there and began to meet our neighbors in order to influence them for Christ. We soon started to have Sunday morning services and a few people came. My wife and I became involved in their lives and after two to three years we ran out of ideas and strength. This was too hard. If God did not do something soon, we would be finished.

We searched for answers in Scripture about the source of power the early disciples obviously possessed. After a full year of desperate prayer and longing, we concluded that we needed the release of the Holy Spirit in our lives so that He might minister through us (Acts 1:8). We saw that this kind of gifted ministry could help us be effective, and we gave the Lord the credit because we had proved to ourselves and everyone else that in our own strength we just "didn't have it."

This new release of the Holy Spirit in our lives happened during the summer of 1972. Many people had openly shared with me during counseling times and I wanted desperately to be effective in helping them. So I began to ask the Lord to show me what was wrong. God, the Holy Spirit, began to do this but I was slow in hearing. I did not know how to listen.

Up to this time, I had never had anyone share with me that it was possible to actually hear the Lord speak (1 Sam. 16:6,7; Ps. 16:7; Luke 12:12; John 10:27; 14:26; 16:13,14; Acts 8:29; 9:11; Rom. 8:16; see appendix 7 in this book and Wayne Grudem's chapter, objection numbers 16, 17, 18). I did remember my mother telling us children how she had misplaced her keys, how she had prayed and the Lord told her just where they were. I was determined to learn how to hear. Little by little both my wife and I began to minister with more and more gifting, and people started to come for help. Our children were also watching.

One Saturday evening Alayne, our 15-year-old daughter, came downstairs to my wife who was sitting in the living room and asked her mother to look at her arms. She had just discovered while looking at herself in the mirror that one arm was shorter than the other. Sure enough, the left arm was one inch shorter than the right arm. We had always known that her left foot was almost a full inch shorter than her right foot. After listening to talk in our home about the Lord healing people, she had faith to believe God would heal her. She asked her mother to pray for her foot and arm to be lengthened. Marie felt this was a job for me, so she and Alayne came to where I was watching the Saturday night hockey game. I did not look up but simply told Marie to pray.

How spiritual I was! While I watched my sporting event, my wife sat Alayne in a chair, knelt down in front of her, took her shorter foot in her hands and began to pray. The thing grew right there in her hands! I was no longer interested in the game! Holding a measuring tape on Alayne's short arm, my wife prayed again and it too grew to the length of her right arm. I had missed the wonderful privilege of praying for my daughter because of lack of faith and indifference. I am thankful I was not struck dumb for a period of time as was the father of John the Baptist.

We have experienced many wonderful miracles in our family. Matthew, our oldest son, was healed instantly one night of bronchial asthma at a Katheryn Kuhlman meeting in London, Ontario. He had just turned 12. We had not expected this or asked for this to happen. We made him sleep on a feather pillow that night in order to make sure he was better. He slept soundly all night and has never had an asthma attack from that day to now.

Our youngest daughter's foot was also lengthened more than one-half inch and guess who prayed for Rebecca? My wife did because I figured the odds were in her favor. We originally measured Rebecca's feet and tried to fit the six-year-old with matching shoes and couldn't. Two days later we returned to the same store with two matching feet and bought her new shoes that fit.

When Rebecca was five or six, she developed a planters wart on the instep of one foot. We prayed that the Lord would take it away. It did not go away. The wart finally became a cluster and bothered her walking. One Sunday we told her we were going to pray one more time and if it did not go away we would take her to the doctor who would burn it out. We prayed and she cried. I forgot about it until Friday when I asked her how her wart was. She said she could not feel it, so I had her take off her shoe and stocking. Not a trace of the ugly cluster of warts remained. What a celebration we had as a family—especially Rebecca!

The Lord is real in our family and has shown Himself as the God who answers prayer (1 Cor. 2:4,5). Again, not everyone in the church was happy about these miraculous things that happened. We were excited to share with everyone but not everyone was excited to listen.

During the last 20 years, I have had the privilege of praying and counseling hundreds of people. I know many have been helped by the healing and delivering power of the Holy Spirit. Many times people have approached me after a meeting, saying how well they were doing because I prayed for them. I often could not remember who they were or the circumstances under which they needed prayer. But God is the one who has done it all and we give Him all the credit and the glory for the ministry He has allowed us to share.

I encourage all who long to see the Lord work through them to seek God's fullness, live a clean, holy, and transparent life before Him. It is imperative to understand Satan's power and how he operates. "In order that Satan might not outwit us. For we are not unaware of his schemes" (2 Cor. 2:11). The fact that we have authority over our arch foe needs to be understood in light of the truth of the blood of Jesus and what He accomplished for each believer on the cross. At the cross, Jesus bore our sins (1 Peter 2:24) and overcame Satan for us (Rev. 12:11).

Jesus said to His disciples who were unsuccessful in casting out a demon, "This kind can come out only by prayer" (Mark 9:29). We must understand the necessity of prevailing prayer. The minister's prayer life must be vibrant and strong. Support from others who understand the wiles of the enemy is an absolute must as well. They must be willing to take the time to pray alongside the deliverance team and the pastor as the ministry is in process.

In closing, I am fully convinced by more than 20 years of pastoral ministry that the message of the Cross is truly good news to bound and broken people. Jesus Christ died to break the power of the devil through sin (Heb. 2:14; 1 John 3:4,8; Rev. 12:11; 1 Peter 2:24). He ascended on high in order to give gifts to people (Eph. 4:8). The Lord desires to give us ministries utilizing all spiritual gifts to reach a sin-sick society with the gospel. I encourage all who are hungering to minister under the anointing of the Holy Spirit to ask the Lord to equip them. He will. Then move out with faith, and courage to a waiting, wanting world.

10

COMING OUT
OF THE HANGAR:

CONFESSIONS OF AN EVANGELICAL DEIST

KIRK BOTTOMLY

WAITING FOR THE BREAKTHROUGH

I have never seen a miracle. Not one I recognized. I have prayed for folks who were sick—sick with cancer, disease, or some disability. No one was supernaturally healed when I prayed. I have heard firsthand accounts of people suffering from demonic oppression. That is something I have never seen. I have Christian friends who say they hear audible messages from the Lord; others who receive distinct impressions about how to minister or what to say in a specific situation. This has never happened to me. I have wrestled with destructive patterns and habits of sin in my life, and have asked the Holy Spirit for supernatural resources to give me victory over those habits. And yet, typically, the severity of the temptation and the strength available to me seemed unchanged. When I experienced victory, I do not know if it was anything more than willpower and discipline.

Why is my Christian experience so devoid of supernatural reality? Why this raging disjunction between the faith I profess and the faith I practice?

Maybe this is your story too. You have wondered, *Is this all there is to Christian faith—an experience of God that does not venture beyond my own subjective thoughts and feelings?* Where is the power that was available to Jesus and the Early Church, the power of the Spirit Paul commended to his Christian congregations, and some Christians today continue to testify to? *Is something wrong with me? Is my Christian faith subnormal?*

Those are the questions I want to tackle here—as an evangelical Christian and as a Presbyterian pastor.

I said, I am an evangelical Christian. I believe the Bible is God's Word, Jesus Christ is the Son of God and the Savior God sent for the salvation of the world, Jesus died on the cross for our sins and rose bodily from the dead, and people must repent and put their faith in Him to receive and experience God's forgiveness and eternal life.

I believe God is alive, He created the world and is intimately involved in it today. I believe in supernatural reality. I believe in the miraculous ministry of Jesus and of the Apostolic Church, and I further believe God continues to minister powerfully and miraculously in the world today through the Church and in the name of Jesus.

I have heard and read personal testimonies of healing and deliverance, of supernatural encounters with God and manifestations of His Spirit. Some of these were perhaps psychosomatic healings or psychologically induced experiences. But many of them ring true and most of them I believe. They are often similar to biblical accounts. Why should I believe the Bible but disbelieve similar stories told by reasonable, sober Christians? When these stories came from the mission field in Africa and Latin America, evangelicals had far less trouble believing them than more recently when they came from Christian neighbors in the same suburban tract. Suddenly it is spooky and disturbing.

So far, God has always done these special things when I was out of the room. But when I hear about them now, I rejoice over the power of God manifest in other people's lives and say cheerfully to God, "Maybe next time, Lord, I'll be there."

As I said, I am a Presbyterian pastor. I belong to a denomination that many Bible-believing Christians think has become doctrinally apostate and spiritually dead. The same could be said of other mainline churches—Methodist,

United Church of Christ, Lutheran, Episcopal, and American Baptist. I have to admit that many of the official pronouncements and preoccupations of my denomination appall me. But much life and faith still remain in Presbyterian congregations I know. I love my church's godly heritage and tradition. And although it is sufficiently faithful to its biblical and spiritual roots and sufficiently open to new things God is doing (and new forms in which to express it), it wins my allegiance. All denominational allegiances are provisional. I belong to Christ first and to a Presbyterian church somewhere after that.

Both the mainline denominations and evangelicals have had difficulty dealing with healing and other supernatural ministries—sometimes for different reasons. Let me try to explain those difficulties.

If they knew what a deist was, many Presbyterians would check that box. For them, God has wound up the universe like a great clock and it is more or less ticking away on its own. They say that miracles do not happen, or if they do, they are confined to a special historical or religious situation (such as, the life of Jesus). God intersects people's lives only in a spiritual, subjective dimension (in their "heart," in their "soul," etc.). I do not pretend to defend this position; it is unbiblical and unchristian. But you find it all over the American church scene, especially in mainline churches such as mine, espoused by pastors and laypeople alike. You can understand, then, their difficulty with the notion of supernatural ministry.

There are also Bible-believing Presbyterians, like those I hang out with, who are supernaturalists in principle, but often unconscious deists in practice. In worship we sing *about* God and talk *about* God, but often the style of worship actually distances us from God and prevents us from experiencing His presence and power.

Evangelicals believe in miracles but do not generally experience them. We pray for all manner of divine intervention and wholeness, but do not expect much response. We expect the clock to keep ticking pretty much as it always has. We affirm the reality of the supernatural, but have little firsthand contact.

Pastors are no exception. If they go to orthodox Princeton Seminary (as I did) or Bible-believing Dallas Seminary or evangelical Fuller Seminary, they receive little or no training in Spirit-empowered ministry and submit to a curriculum that is far more academic than spiritual. We are generally trained to know *about* God, but not to know God or to do the work of God.

Among evangelical and mainline pastors and church leaders, there is a fear and distrust of supernatural ministry, an underlying disbelief and a tremendous professional insecurity about it. If you are a pastor, and healing, deliverance, and supernatural gifts are not part of your Christian experience, you seem to be stuck with an awkward choice: either those experiences are sub-Christian (phony or self-induced) or *you* are sub-Christian. Do you see the dilemma?

My own experience of the reality of God has been largely subjective. It has been confined mainly to God's power to change people's hearts and create faith, to console and exhilarate me when I read the Bible and reflect upon the love of Christ, to point me and tug me in the direction of righteousness, and to move me to hope in the coming kingdom of God when Christ returns in glory. There is much spiritual reality and consolation in all of that, and yet for me it is not enough. It is virtually all psychological. I believe in a livelier, more active and robust reality of God in the world. I believe these things not because my intuition or experience insists upon them, but because I read the Bible, and this kind of lively, powerful reality of God is what the Bible teaches me and shows me. My conscience is captive to His Word.

I wish to be as honest and forthright as possible about this peculiar disjunction between my deepest religious convictions and my personal spiritual experience. How do I cope with it? What am I doing about it?

I feel the same prickling uneasiness and frustration about it that I felt when I was a boy wrestling with a difficult mathematical concept and not "getting it"— or trying repeatedly to master some athletic skill or finesse and being repeatedly thwarted. In both of those instances, a breakthrough moment came where the mathematics suddenly made sense and where the skill to hit a ball right was finally "there." The math may have taken a couple of days to coalesce; the ball skills took 10 years. I experienced both breakthroughs as gifts. I had to want them, had to seek them, but in the end they had to be given. I could not make them happen.

Christian life has many breakthrough moments—moments of grace and visitation, of insight and consolation. I am still waiting for this breakthrough in my ministry—courting it, seeking it. And, I confess, I am still retreating from it, hiding, dreading it. My Presbyterian congregation is pretty lively and evangelical, but they would be happy if I stayed away from all this "power ministry" stuff and never brought it up. So would the other pastors on staff. For whole months I let it rest, but afterward the restlessness comes again.

If you are going to seek this kind of ministry from the Lord, these are the tensions you will have to contend with.

A FORM OF GODLINESS, BUT NO POWER—2 TIMOTHY 3:5

How did we get to this place? What accounts for this peculiar schizophrenia where we profess a supernatural faith, but we practice a faith that is really powerless and faithless? I see two reasons.

First, we evangelicals have unconsciously imbibed the antisupernatural and rationalistic assumptions of the culture surrounding us.

Second, the faith of the church's own community (especially our leadership) has been corrupted by religious pride, a powerful spirit of unbelief, a fear of the supernatural, and an unwillingness to be open to the movement and work of the Holy Spirit.

As severe as that indictment sounds, it probably describes the Western Church in most times and places since at least the fourth century when persecution ceased and Christianity gained political ascendancy. A church that is faithful in both proclamation and demonstration is the historic exception. Even the apostles during their years of preparation, living with the Lord and witnessing His wonders firsthand, fell regularly into unbelief. They did not believe God would be there for them or minister through them.

The evangelical church can no longer read the Lord's words—"Why are you so afraid? Do you still have no faith?" (Mark 4:40)—with any smug condescension. We are as timid and powerless as the disciples were. Ours, too, is the "unbelieving generation" (Mark 9:19). How long shall the Lord put up with us before He entrusts His kingdom ministry and the lively presence of His Spirit to others in His Church who will faithfully watch and learn from Him?

It may be too late already. The growth of the North American and European churches went into free-fall years ago. Between them, they are hemorrhaging members to other religions and no religion, roughly 2 million a year in Europe, a million a year in the United States. (Those are net losses after new conversions are counted.)[1]

In the meantime, the Spirit is moving in power in the churches of Africa, South Asia, and Latin America. In Brazil alone, 10,000 new Christians are baptized *every day*. In Africa, the Church of Jesus Christ grew by 6 million members last year and by 35 million in China and Southeast Asia, where conversion is often dramatic and costly. In these places, the Church is not only taking discipleship seriously, but is also ministering confidently in the Spirit. The power of the gospel over rival religions and ideologies is dramatically evident in ministries of healing and deliverance. Sick people are cured by the power of God and demonic powers are broken. This sort of thing not only gets people's attention, but also wins their heart-allegiance.

Anyone aware of the decline of the Christian religion in the West in the face of Christianity's astonishing growth in the Third World must wonder about its vitality there and its paralysis and exhaustion here. Are Third-World people simply more naive and susceptible to faith than more sophisticated and skeptical Westerners? That is certainly one way to see it. Meanwhile, the economic and cultural underclasses of the world are pouring into the kingdom of God while the Christians in the West play church, rearrange deck chairs, and offer no compelling witness to the reality and power of their faith.

Ironically, the evangelical church, while combating the deistic and rationalistic heritage of the Enlightenment, has largely succumbed to a rationalistic spirit in its evangelism and ministry. While rejecting the undue emphasis on subjectivity and religious feelings of nineteenth-century liberalism and more recent religious existentialism, the evangelical church champions a gospel ministry whose manifestation is almost wholly subjective and psychological. While rightly repudiating the nature-grace dualism of medieval scholasticism and the nature-freedom dualism of the Enlightenment, evangelicals have preached a largely "upper-story" salvation: "Christ came into my heart and gave meaning to my life." There is little practical difference between this gospel and the feel-good, self-help therapies so prevalent in the culture around us. In some cases, the occult and New Age religions offer more tangible power.

In the ministry of Jesus and the Apostolic Church, by contrast, the proclamation of the gospel was typically accompanied by extraordinary demonstrations of God's power:

1. Healing the sick and casting out demons (see appendix 1 in this book; Matt. 4:23; 9:35,36; 10:1,7,8; 11:5; 12:15,18; 15:30; 19:2 [cf. Mark 10:1]; 21:14 [cf. Luke 21:37]; Mark 1:38,39; 2:2,11; 3:14,15; 6:12,13; 10:1 [cf. Matt. 19:2]; Luke 4:18; 5:17,24; 6:6-11,17,18; 7:22; 9:1,2; 10:9,13; 13:10-13,22,32; 14:4,7ff.; 21:37 [cf. Matt. 21:14]; 16:15-18,20; John 3:2; 7:14,15,21-23,31,38; 10:25,32,38; 12:37,49; 14:10,12; Acts 1:1; 2:22; 3:6,12; 4:29,30; 5:12-16,20,21,28,42; 6:8,10; 8:4-7,12; 9:17,18 [cf. 22:13],34,35; 10:38; 14:3,8-10,15ff.; 15:12,36; 18:5,11 [cf. 2 Cor. 12:12; 1 Cor. 2:4,5]; 19:8-12; Rom. 15:18,19; 1 Cor. 2:4,5; 11:1; 12:1-11,28-31; 14:22-25; 2 Cor. 12:12; Gal. 3:5; Phil. 4:9; 1 Thess. 1:5,6; Heb. 2:3,4; 6:1,2; Jas. 5:13-16).

2. Speaking words of supernatural insight and knowledge (Matt. 9:4; Mark 2:8; Luke 5:22; 6:8; 7:39,40,47; 9:47; John 1:48-50; 4:17,18; Acts 5:3; 9:11,12; 10:3-6,19; 11:28; 22:17,18; 23:11; 27:24,25; 1 Cor. 14:24,25).

3. Teleporting a person across great distances (John 6:21; Acts 8:39,40; 2 Cor. 12:1-5).

4. Seeing visions (John 1:48-50; Acts 7:55; 9:10-12; 10:3,11-13; 11:5; 16:9,10; 18:9; 22:17,18; 26:19; 2 Cor. 12:1-5; Rev. 1:9ff.).

5. Experiencing extraordinary rescue, protection, and provision (Luke 4:30; Acts 12:3-17; 16:25,26; 23:12-33; 27:13-44; 28:3-6).

6. Witnessing God answer intercessory prayer in powerful and unambiguous ways (Acts 4:29-31 and 5:12-16; 12:3-17).

When we speak of the work of Christ, the Church focuses—rightly—on the Cross and the Resurrection. In doing so, the life and ministry of Jesus leading up to Calvary are often overlooked or ignored. Here Jesus modeled for three years the work He expected His disciples to carry on: the proclamation and demonstration by the power of the Holy Spirit that the kingdom of God has come in Jesus Christ (Matt. 10:1,7,8; 28:20a; Mark 6:7,12,13; Luke 9:1,2; 10:1,9; Acts 1:3; 8:5-7,12; 14:3,22; 19:8-11; 28:31). The rule of God is being reestablished and extended in the midst of a rebel world. By the power of Christ's death and resurrection, God is making creation new and is making a new humanity. That is the gospel—the "good news of the kingdom of God" (Acts 8:12). God's kingdom come...and still coming.

For the most part, the evangelical church preaches, teaches, and practices a gospel that is only half the gospel. It is all proclamation and little or no power (see 1 Thess. 1:5 "our gospel came to you *not simply with words*, but also *with power*"). The *gospel enacted* through signs and wonders has been amputated. We are left with a gospel that hobbles on one foot.

Why are Europeans and North Americans so reluctant to embrace a one-legged gospel? That is not hard to figure out. Men and women long for wholeness. They want to believe in something that has real—not imagined—power to heal their deepest hurt and brokenness. They want more than mind games and good feelings. They experience themselves—rightly—as body-and-soul beings, and they long for power that gives wholeness to their bodies and souls—a salvation that offers hope to them and the whole creation.

That hope and wholeness is the whole gospel of Jesus Christ. The salvation of creation—what Paul described as the liberation and glory of the sons and daughters of God in a world set free forever from its slavery to sin and corruption (Rom. 8:18-39)—that salvation awaits a fullness that will come on the day of Christ, when Jesus returns in glory. But a real concrete measure of salvation already broke upon the world when the Son of God became human, lived among us and conquered sin and Satan, died and conquered death. The Church, as the Body of Christ in the world, living in the power of the Holy Spirit, can expect substantial signs, even now in this in-between time, of the reality, presence, and power of God's kingdom (Rom. 14:17; 1 Cor. 4:20; 12:1—14:40; Gal. 3:5; 1 Thess. 1:5,6; 5:19,20; Heb. 6:5; Jas. 5:14-16). The Lord Jesus inaugurated that Kingdom, and entrusted His kingdom ministry of preaching and power to His Church (Matt. 10:1,7,8; 28:20; Mark 6:7,12,13; Luke 9:1,2; 10:1,9; Acts 1:8; 8:5-7,12; 14:3,22; 19:8-11; Rom. 15:18,19; 1 Cor. 11:1; 12:8-10; 14:24,25; Phil. 4:9; 1 Thess. 1:5,6; on this point, see Don Williams' chapter and appendix 2 and 3 in this book).

So where is the power?

Paul spoke prophetically of a future church retreating from the full truth of the gospel, "holding to the outward form of godliness but denying its power" (2 Tim. 3:5, NRSV). Was the Lord showing him a glimpse of the evangelical church at the beginning of the twenty-first century?

A testimony to God's powerful grace is that even a one-legged myopic church, such as it is, can still do ministry, can still sow the Word and gather to harvest. The Holy Spirit graciously comes alongside this hobbling church and blesses its work. I am a Christian today because of this faithful ministry, and so perhaps are you. And yet the ministry of the evangelical church also fitted me with a pair of distorted spectacles, which kept me from reading and seeing what was plainly in God's Word about life in the Spirit.

RECOVERING THE WHOLE GOSPEL

In the last two decades, a gradual recovery has been occurring in evangelical theology of the wholeness of the gospel. God is Lord of all of creation. Discipleship means being a faithful steward of creation and responsive to the cry of the poor and oppressed as much as being a faithful evangelist. Christ's lordship extends over my vocation and recreation as well as over my worship, Bible study, and personal morality.

This recovery of "gospel wholeness" has yet to reshape our evangelism. Our gospel message is still subjective and individual in its appeal. We are still trying to save souls while ignoring the claim of God upon a person's entire life and the rule of God over the entire creation. It appeals to a person who feels guilty or spiritually empty or religiously incomplete. When I trust Christ as my Savior, I experience forgiveness, spiritual fulfillment, something to live for besides myself and my temporal values. Do you see how spiritualized this salvation package is? Nothing about it is concrete. It speaks only to my soul and my religious feelings.

How far this is from the ministry of Jesus and the apostles can be seen by looking at almost any ministry story in the Gospels or Acts. Peter to the lame man at the Beautiful Gate: "Silver or gold I do not have, but what I have I give you. In the name of Jesus Christ of Nazareth, walk" (Acts 3:6). Or this incident from Acts: "When the crowds heard Philip and saw the miraculous signs he did, they all paid close attention to what he said. With shrieks, evil spirits came out of many, and many paralytics and cripples were healed. So there was great joy in that city" (Acts 8:6-8).

When Jesus sent out the Twelve and afterwards the 70, it was not to save souls, but to "preach the kingdom of God *and* to heal the sick" (Luke 9:2; cf. Matt. 10:7,8; Mark 6:12,13; Luke 10:9)—to demonstrate the power of God to reclaim and heal His kingdom. When the risen Christ gave His disciples their final ministry instructions prior to His ascension, He taught them "things concerning the kingdom of God" (Acts 1:3, NASB). The apostle Paul described his ministry as having "gone about preaching the kingdom" (Acts 20:25) and the book of Acts closes with a picture of the Church faithful to the evangelistic commission of Jesus (Acts 1:8), moving in the power of the Holy Spirit, despite religious and political opposition and persecution, "proclaiming the kingdom of God and teaching about the Lord Jesus Christ with all boldness and without hindrance" (Acts 28:31, NRSV).

Where is the kingdom of God and this bold reliance on the power of the Holy Spirit in our evangelism today? An alertness and sensitivity to the prompting of the Holy Spirit and a readiness to move in supernatural ministry is so foreign to the evangelical church, we are fearful and suspicious of anyone expressing such an idea or wishing to demonstrate such a ministry. The power dimension of the gospel, which is consistently present in New Testament ministry, is lacking in evangelical churches (I think) for at least two reasons—one practical, one theological. In practice, the power is missing in evangelical ministry. We do not expect it; we believe it as biblical truth but not as existential truth. God worked wonders through the apostles; God works supernaturally on the mission field and in extraordinary local situations; but God will not do it in my church or my ministry. And so, a powerful spirit of unbelief has captured our churches.

And then, to rationalize the otherwise embarrassing absence of supernatural ministry, some parts of the evangelical church have constructed an elaborate and ingenious (though hardly biblical) theology explaining why the miraculous works and gifts of the Holy Spirit have ceased in our day. This is an instance of the Church letting its experience, not Scripture, dictate its theology.

Many in the Church say, "We don't experience the supernatural in our ministry. And yet, we are mature Christians. We have the Spirit of God. We conclude therefore that our ministry is normative and that God's normal mode of operation is a nonmiraculous, subjective mode that works mainly through the preaching and teaching of Scripture."

In numerous unspoken ways, the Church promotes a deistic, rationalistic model of ministry. The exercise of gifts clearly commended in Scripture, such as healing, words of knowledge, prophecy, working of miracles, speaking in and interpreting tongues are discouraged, forbidden, and even demonized by these cessationist churches.

The problem with such a theology is that a straightforward reading of Scripture leads overwhelmingly to the opposite conclusion. In addition, cessationism leaks in too many places to be a useful or coherent theology. It admits to many exceptions, most notably the power of intercessory prayer. If we believe God will intervene to supernaturally heal, rescue, give direction, or provide sustenance, we are essentially saying that the supernatural gifts of the Spirit, exercised through prayer, really have not ceased. And then we become quite arbitrary if we declare some supernatural gifts (notably tongues and prophecy) have ceased but not others. What is more, there are just too many credible testimonies of Spirit-empowered supernatural ministry to discount or deny it any longer (see references cited in Dr. David Lewis's chapter in this book).

COMING OUT OF THE HANGAR: WHAT CHANGED MY MIND

I love the Christian life and I know there is more to it than I have experienced so far. It is a great banquet, and perhaps I have hung out too long at the salad bar. I love salads, and the Christian life even as an appetizer has been great. I have experienced it as intellectually exhilarating and have found much joy and triumph in trying to live a life faithful to Jesus Christ and His Word. Still, people are eating some very interesting things at this table, and these items look more like entrees. I believe the Lord is offering me something heartier and more substantial.

In the last few years, God has been expanding my spiritual horizons in a way I never anticipated. I feel as though in the early stages of my faith, the Lord set me free to play in an enormous airplane hangar. An airplane hangar is high and wide—having more room to run and whoop and jump than a kid would need and lots of stuff—airplanes, machinery, tools, ladders, catwalks—to delight and intrigue me. Learning about the supernatural ministry of the Holy Spirit—learning from Scripture and from firsthand accounts—was like one day finding the door of the airplane hangar rolled open. Up to then, I thought that wonderful hangar was the whole spiritual universe. And then I step to the doorway and look out and look up. And there, stretching as far up and wide as I can see is the real playground the Spirit of God intended for me.

I am going to go out there.

I know a score of pastors and many more laypeople who are undergoing this same transformation I am. Many of them are diving into the bracing spiritual waters much more boldly than I am and are having more dramatic results.

It does not seem as difficult for laypeople; they do not have to pretend they have already "arrived" and have all the answers to truth and life.

Recently I attended a conference on spiritual warfare hosted by the Vineyard Christian Fellowship in Anaheim, California. I resisted wearing a false nose and wig. In God's great humor, I ran into half a dozen Presbyterian laypeople I knew, as well as several friends in pastoral ministry who were all unlikely attendees—from the Presbyterian, Conservative Baptist, Southern Baptist, United Church of Christ, and Covenant churches.

The evangelical church is opening up to the supernatural work of the Holy Spirit.

Two things changed my mind. First, Scripture. The charismatic church is often accused of elevating experience above Scripture as a guide for doctrine and life. For me, Scripture pointed me in the direction of power ministry before any personal experience of the Spirit confirmed it. I believe it because the Bible teaches it. And I will pray for this anointing; I will wait for the Lord to bestow it; I will seek it from the Lord's hand—in obedience to the Word. God will give it in His time.

The second reason I changed my mind on this issue was because of the powerlessness I experienced in my own spiritual life and ministry. In wrestling with recurring habits of anger and purity, I felt my spiritual resources—even when I called upon the Holy Spirit—to be inadequate. In sharing my faith, I was often frustrated by the lame sparring between my "truth system" and the other guy's. I was discouraged by a relatively ineffective ministry of intercessory prayer. I long for a stronger, surer, exhilarating sense of God's presence—to look into God's face, catch God's eye.

What I was desiring—and desire now—is more of a supernatural manifestation of God's reality in order to break the grip of false religion and ideology and open a person to the power and truth of the gospel; to deliver us from the bondage of sinful habits and addictions; to show the Church (and the unchurched) what the gospel means, what the forgiveness of sins is like, by healing those who are sick (see, for example, Matt. 9:6; Mark 2:10,11; Luke 5:24; Jas. 5:15,16).

Many people in my church and denomination are watching tentatively and have the same longings and fears. They want very much to plunge into the water, although just to stick their toes in it right now is a terrifying prospect. My colleagues in ministry are cautious for the most part, but supportive. Most Presbyterian pastors in the region stayed away from a recent Presbytery-hosted conference on the Holy Spirit, where Don Williams spoke, a pastor formerly on staff at Hollywood Presbyterian Church, now with the Vineyard in La Jolla near

San Diego (Don also contributed a chapter on biblical discipleship to this book). That was probably too threatening for most of my colleagues. Yet, I am sure if the Holy Spirit were to fall mightily upon me tomorrow, most of them would want to know about it in more than an idly curious way. The very fact that the conference even happened is evidence of a new openness in my church.

CATCHING IT

An institutional training center for this kind of power ministry does not exist in the evangelical community. It is not in the standard curriculum anywhere (except for Fuller Seminary where Professors C. Peter Wagner and Charles H. Kraft teach courses on power ministry and prayer). You have to take risks and venture outside to learn about it. There is a sociology of the Spirit: The people who do this kind of ministry are not uniformly distributed throughout the Church of Jesus Christ. They are concentrated in scattered pockets, like-minded communities where people practice and encourage this ministry. You have to find them and hang out with them. Your initial encounters may be both hilarious and petrifying.

They do not teach you anything about power ministry or the supernatural at most seminaries. At Princeton, they did not teach me anything about prayer either, and it has taken me nearly three years to recover my reverence for Scripture. The deistic spirit, which informs nearly all seminary training (including evangelical seminaries such as Fuller, Dallas, Trinity) succeeds in inoculating most graduating pastors, even evangelical pastors, against any Spirit-anointed, supernatural ministry unless God somehow undoes it or endues it.

Let me make a few modest suggestions, however, to evangelical and mainline Christians like me who are open to the kind of ministry of the Spirit I have described here and who want to know how to "catch" it, learn it, grow in it.

Study the Scriptures. The principal teacher on the subject of power ministry is the Word of God. Do your own Bible study on the kingdom of God, particularly as it relates to the ministry of Jesus and the ministry He taught and commissioned the Church to do. Read Luke and Acts (both written by Luke) and pay attention to the consistent connection between proclamation and miraculous signs. Watch the role that the Holy Spirit plays as the agent of power, not just in the apostles' ministry but in Jesus' ministry.

Try to read Scripture with a second naïveté, divesting yourself of theological presumptions that may distort your interpretation of the Word. Presumptions such as the Apostolic Age was an exceptional period of miraculous activity; the operation of the Spirit in the first century is different from the operation of the Spirit in our age; the miracles of Jesus were the result of His divinity rather than the work of the Holy Spirit through Him (Matt. 12:28 shows Jesus' own view on the matter; also suggested by Luke 4:1,14-18; Acts 2:22; 10:38; etc.).

Do some homework. Read a good theology of Kingdom ministry—the ministry of healing and deliverance from demonic oppression that Jesus linked to preaching the gospel of the kingdom of God. Some excellent works of biblical theology that organize the scriptural material into a coherent whole are available. I suggest a seminal evangelical work such as *Jesus and the Kingdom* or *A Theology of the New Testament*, both by G. E. Ladd. The seminal works of European scholars such as Alan Richardson[2] and H. van der Loos[3] would also be helpful.

In addition, it is important to read the principal works of third wave theologians so that we understand their position, not a caricature of it. These works include:

- *Power Evangelism* (HarperCollins) and *Power Healing* (HarperCollins) by John Wimber and Kevin Springer.[4]
- *Signs, Wonders, and the Kingdom of God* (Servant) by Don Williams. An excellent primer, this is probably the best work of biblical theology on the kingdom of God from a third wave perspective. Williams, now a Vineyard pastor in La Jolla near San Diego, is a respected scholar, popular teacher, and the former college pastor at one of the largest Presbyterian churches in Southern California.
- *When the Spirit Comes with Power* (InterVarsity Press) by John White. White's work is especially interesting because his credentials as an evangelical are impeccable,[5] and he writes from the perspective of a veteran missionary and professional psychiatrist.
- *Christianity with Power* (Servant) by Charles Kraft. Kraft is an anthropologist, a linguist, and a former missionary, now on the faculty of Fuller School of World Mission. His book is addressed to evangelicals like himself.

Go out and investigate. Make contact with churches and attend conferences that teach, model, and advocate power ministry. You cannot conduct an honest investigation without on-site study. Nicodemus was a Bible teacher who, nevertheless, went personally to check out Jesus (John 3:1). And so did Nathanael, despite his reservations; he later became an apostle (John 1:45-50).

An academic fallacy is that we can sit in our study and learn everything God wants us to know. The Spirit of God is on the move in the world. We need to exercise an active, professional humility and go to those places where we hear the Spirit is moving (such as the mission frontiers of Brazil and Argentina or the Vineyard fellowship or some other church just across town). As obedient sons and daughters, we watch what the Father is doing, try to discern His purpose, and cooperate in His work (John 5:19,20; 14:10-13).

Take a Sunday off and visit a church with a reputation both for integrity and Spirit-empowered ministry. Many of these churches also have Sunday evening and midweek worship and teaching. In addition, look around your own denomination for respected advocates of this ministry. Call them and start networking with them. Do not be afraid to express your own reservations and fears and to ask them for counsel and prayer.

Conferences and weekend seminars are some of the best ways to be exposed to first-rate teaching and to witness actual Spirit-empowered ministry. Over the next two years, set a goal of attending two or three of these. Besides the general sessions, sit in on workshops or seminars having topics such as prayer for physical healing, inner healing (which refers mainly to the healing of emotions and memories), and spiritual warfare (which corresponds to the biblical ministry of "casting out demons").

Charismatic churches and conferences will inevitably test your comfort level. To attend them you will have to overcome a hundred or more excuses your mind will conjure. "Not this time." "Schedule's full." "Those guys are weird." "I really need to relax and unwind this weekend." "There's *no* way I could explain this to my congregation." "What if I ran into somebody who recognized me?" "What if I start speaking in tongues?"

Let's also appreciate that the charismatic and third wave churches are no more monolithic than evangelical and mainline churches.[6] There are lots of differences among them. There are good and awful churches, good and bad teachers, Sundays that are great and not-so-great. There is a wide range of biblical integrity among these churches as well as a wide range of charismatic styles. Some are comfortably evangelical; others are pretty wild. Remember, God's call to ministry is not always to the intellectually astute or to the graceful, witty, or dignified. Do we believe that even today the Lord may choose the foolish and weak things as instruments of His wisdom and power (1 Cor. 1:26-29)?

Do biblical ministry. That simply means: Watch what Jesus and His disciples do, and do the same. A disciple, says Jesus, does not try to break new ground. If he can just imitate his Teacher, he has passed the course (Matt. 10:24,25).

Much of our own habit and style of ministry is simply doing what we've seen other professional ministers do. In my pastoral circles, we've mainly conditioned ourselves and our congregations to "safe ministry." We fence our worship and prayer in such a way as to prevent any intrusion of the supernatural or miraculous. We clump all the sick together and ask God to heal them—or else to give them grace to stay sick and be content. Can you hear Jesus praying like that?

The issue for me is this: Is the ministry of Jesus to be the ministry of the Church? I do not think anything could be clearer. And what was Jesus' ministry? He preached the kingdom of God. And He demonstrated the concrete reality of that Kingdom by healing the sick, cleansing lepers, and casting out demons.

I am suggesting that—no matter how weird and scary it feels to us—we try to do what Jesus did. We begin to pray specifically and expectantly for people to be healed and delivered. Healed from physical and emotional brokenness and disease. Delivered from the bondage of guilt, destructive habits, and demonic oppression. These are spiritual works, which require a Christian to be attentive and yielded to the Holy Spirit.

We begin to do these works out of obedience and faith, before we see any results. It may be months or even years before there is a breakthrough in our own powerful unbelief. We begin to do these works before we understand fully what we are doing or have mastered any spiritual technique. Answering prayer is God's job; our job is to pray (Jas. 4:2b). I do not pray because God has promised to do miracles through me; I pray because God says in His Word, Pray! This year, as an act of faith, I told the Lord I would pray whenever someone expressed a need. Now I ask, "Can I pray for you about that?" And right there, we pray. I still have much to learn about prayer, but there is no way to grow in prayer without doing it.

Maturity comes with practice; I doubt if mastery ever comes, because there is no standardized technique.[7] Every ministry situation is unique and personal. God's originality and newness is never exhausted.

"But I don't know how to do this. I don't know what I'm doing." Have you ever seen children imitate their mother or father? It is often comical. They do not know what they are doing either. They just want to be like Daddy or Mommy. They want to do what their parents do. There is a bold fearlessness about a child's ventures. I am a child in ministry, but I am going to try to pray like Jesus prayed. I am going to watch Jesus and do what He did.

I urge you in your day-to-day ministry, do not pass up any opportunity to pray for someone who expresses a need to you. Pray for healing, for provision, for a job. Pray for a blessing, for a fruit or gift of the Spirit. We do not do miracles; God does them, as we pray in faithfulness and obedience.

Seek the Lord. Although much of our discussion here has been about more effective and faithful ministry, the real goal is God. Knowing God in a more intimate way, experiencing a more immediate sense of His presence. For evangelicals, this means a reorientation in the way we typically worship, pray, and do Bible study. We need to consciously, intentionally make room in all our habits of grace for meeting God.

What do we need to do to hear God address us more directly and personally? We may need to be quiet in prayer and listen. We may need periodically to stop *studying* the Bible and start *listening* to it. We may need to worship in a way that we regularly hear God say to us, "I love you"—and allow ourselves to be moved by it. And to say back to God—I mean, really *say* it, "Lord, you are indeed the compassionate and gracious God. Full of love. And I bless you. I praise you. You are my God. You are my glory. Your mercy and goodness overwhelm me. You are worth everything to me. Lord, I love you."

This may involve a major shift in our worship from participating as narrator or spectator, to having a genuine heart-to-heart encounter. Less talking about God and hearing about God, more hearing God and seeing God and meeting God.

As a practical step, I suggest listening to contemporary praise music, especially recordings of live worship and music that addresses God directly in praise and love. To sing these songs in a spirit of worship often facilitates a powerful and intimate encounter with the Spirit of God.[8] The evangelical may object that this is simply giving rein to our emotions, that it is not a spiritual encounter at all. But emotions are an integral part of our humanity and an important piece of equipment, like our intellect, which God has given us to relate and to respond to Him: "Love the Lord your God with *all your heart* and with *all* your soul and with *all* your mind and with *all* your strength" (Mark 12:30). The Psalms are full of expressions of emotional and spiritual exhilaration. It is time evangelicals learned to engage their emotions, and no time seems more appropriate than in worship.

In all of this, we are not seeking an experience of God so much as we are seeking God Himself. Seek Him in prayer and worship by using the same persistence and boldness as the psalmist: "When You said, 'Seek My face' My heart said to You, 'Your face, Lord, I will seek'" (Ps. 27:8, NKJV; see also Pss. 24:6; 27:4; 42:1,2; 63:2; 67:1; 84:7; 105:4).

Pray boldly for the fullness of God's Spirit. Boldly, because it is God's will. "That you may be filled to the measure of all the fullness of God" is Paul's prayer (Eph. 3:19). Ask God to reveal to you, in you, and through you the reality and power of the Holy Spirit. "If you then, though you are evil, know how to give good gifts to your children, how much more will your Father in heaven give the Holy Spirit to those who ask him!" (Luke 11:13).

You are seeking from the Lord's hand the same experience as the Apostolic Church, and you are seeking it as a faithful and obedient response to the word of Jesus who commissioned all His disciples to do power ministry (Luke 9:1,2; 10:1-24; Mark 16:17-20; Acts 1:8). Do not be ashamed to ask for this. The apostles asked boldly not only for the courage to proclaim the gospel but also for power to confirm the preaching by healing and wonders performed in Jesus' name (Acts 4:29,30; see also 1 Cor. 2:4,5).

Keep praying for God's fullness. In my own experience, the Lord has filled me in steps, perhaps in response to my own timidity and tenuity. "Lord, fill me," I'll pray, and in my heart I'll say, "but not too full." Pray continually that God will break through the stubborn spirit of unbelief and fear that grips us and continually urges us to retreat from God and any higher spiritual ground.

Bring your church along gently. Your church and lay leaders need to know your faith has a growing edge, too. Bring them along gently. You know best how various people are going to respond to your explorations and experiments. Find people, especially those in leadership, with whom you can honestly share about what you are learning and how you are growing.

Encourage some of your lay leaders to read a book or attend a conference on power ministry and then report back to you. What did they learn? What new experiences did they have? How did they respond? Your own lay leaders may be used by God to prepare the way for this new orientation in ministry. Laypeople are often more open to the Holy Spirit's doing something new than the pastor is. And congregations can tolerate newer views from laypeople better than from their pastor. When you deputize people to go off and learn something from God, you are empowering them for ministry. They will often return to teach, challenge, and stretch your congregation—and you.

Notes

1. These and the following statistics are reported in David Watson, *Called and Committed: World-Changing Discipleship* (Wheaton, IL: Harold Shaw, 1982), p. 2. They are based on a survey conducted by Center for Study of World Evangelization in 1979.

2. A. Richardson, *The Miracle-Stories of the Gospels* (London, England: SCM Press, 1941.

3. H. van der Loos, *The Miracles of Jesus* (Supplements to Novum Testamentum, vol. 8), (Leiden, Netherlands: E. J. Brill, 1965).

4. An excellent 30-page summary of John Wimber's theology, blending personal testimony and Bible study, is his chapter, "Power Evangelism: Definitions and Directions," in *Wrestling with Dark Angels* (Ventura, CA: Regal Books, 1990), edited by C. Peter Wagner and F. Douglas Pennoyer.

5. White has been published by InterVarsity Press for years.

6. In our community, there are two Presbyterian churches—one that is more contemporary in style, one that is more formal. Can they both be Presbyterian? Yes.

7. There is no standardized technique, but there are good models. There is nothing like hearing and observing a good prayer warrior. Attending workshops on prayer where I could observe effective models of intercessory prayer (especially for healing and deliverance) have been especially beneficial to me.

8. A more ideal arrangement would be to attend a worship service with a first-rate praise team, where 30-40 minutes of the service is dedicated to singing love and praise songs to God and where there is room for some free expression, such as standing, kneeling, lifting up your hands, clapping, and so on.

III

RELATED STUDIES

———————

11

Proclaiming the Gospel with Miraculous Gifts in the Postbiblical Early Church

Stanley M. Burgess

The emergence of the Pentecostal, the neo-Pentecostal or charismatic, and third wave movements in our century has raised a variety of vital questions that demand answers. Among these, is the issue of whether the spiritual gifts enumerated by Saint Paul in 1 Corinthians 12 remained active in the Church after the first century. Equally crucial is the question of whether these gifts, if still active, were vitally related to the proclamation of the gospel in the Church during the formative centuries.

Protestant Cessationism

From the Reformation era onward, leading Protestant theologians have popularized the view that the work of the Holy Spirit in evangelism after the Apostolic Age was limited to dynamic proclamation of the Word of God, rather than the exercise of spiritual gifts. This was the position of Martin Luther, who openly rejected the *schwärmer* or enthusiasts of his day—who claimed gifts of prophecy and gave higher credence to the "inner voice" of the Spirit than to the "external word" or Scriptures.[1]

The dominant strand of Protestant biblicism, which Luther inaugurated, has continued into our own century. It combines an emphasis on proclamation of the Word with the cessationist argument that the power gifts evidenced in the first-century Church were neither necessary nor functional after the New Testament had been completed. Representative of this position is Benjamin Breckinridge Warfield (1851-1921), professor of theology at Princeton. Warfield was especially antagonistic toward defenders of revelational religious experience and those who insisted on special spiritual gifts. He felt that these substituted subjective religiosity for the completeness of Scripture.

Voices of cessationism are still with us, and presently are aimed at the healing and gift-based ministries of Pentecostals, charismatics, and third wave churches. Cessationists argue that miracles had little to do with the gospel or were incidental to the proclamation of the gospel in the New Testament. Further, they insist that gifts of healing as well as the other charismata ceased at or near the end of the first century A.D. For example, the claim has been made that "the Church Fathers, who came almost entirely from the East, believed that the apostolic gifts had ceased."[2] Such a claim is simply not true, as the evidence presented below shows.

To make these claims, the cessationists have had to ignore or deprecate what was going on among Protestant fringe groups since the time of the Reformation. It is well known that a strand of enthusiasm has remained active in Protestantism, although most of the enthusiasts had been purged from the mainstream, and had been forced to function from the Protestant fringe. These include the Melchiorites, Sebastian Franck, Kasper von Schwenckfeld, the Society of Friends (or Quakers), the Prophets of the Cevennes (or Camisards), the Moravians, certain early Methodists, the Shakers, the Irvingites, and most recently, the contemporary Pentecostal movement (twentieth-century charismatics and third wave evangelicals are in part mainstream).

Cessationists also have chosen to overlook the record of both Roman Catholic and Eastern Christian traditions. Any honest inquiry into the history of spirituality in both Roman and Eastern traditions leads the scholar to conclude that the Holy Spirit invested the post-Apostolic Church with the same gifts and charismatic vitality experienced during the first century.[3]

Protestant cessationists have been influenced by the Enlightenment, or Age of Reason, which has led many to deny the validity of anything in Christian history that falls outside accepted categories of rationality. This has resulted in a "cleaning up" of religious history, purging it of any taint of "enthusiasm" or nonrational behavior and all reports of the supernatural. The result has been what I call a "demythologizing" of the saints—an attempt to deny the many stories in the Christian tradition that are filled with charismatic giftings, miracles, signs, and wonders.

In the twentieth century, Pentecostals have unwittingly added to the confusion by teaching that the Holy Spirit was somehow "deistically absent" in the 1,800 years between A.D. 100 and 1900, and that the second coming of the Holy Spirit occurred among them at the very beginning of the current century. This fit into their understanding of Joel's prophecy of a former and a latter rain. In typical restorationist fashion, Pentecostals showed little appreciation for earlier waves of Christian renewal. The result of all this is that we have missed an entire chapter in the history of Christianity—namely, the story of post-Apostolic Christians witnessing with power to the unconverted, having their proclamation accented and given credibility by confirming supernatural events.

SPIRIT-EMPOWERED MINISTRY IN THE POST-APOSTOLIC CHURCH

It is clear that the Holy Spirit's activity in the Christian Church did not change dramatically after A.D. 100. As with any other wave of renewal, the time immediately following that of the apostles saw a modest waning of charismatic vitality. But prophets continued to function openly in the Church in the second century, and in fringe groups, such as the Montanists, from that time onward.

There was no cessation of miracles or signs and wonders in this period either, despite occasional claims to the contrary by a few Church Fathers, including Origen.[4] Both the Roman church and Eastern churches have an entire genre of literature known as hagiography, or lives of the saints, which gives innumerable examples of the dynamic evangelistic outreach of people empowered by the divine Spirit. To be sure, we must treat these accounts with a critical, even skeptical eye, given the tendency of the period not to be critical. The fact remains, however, that miracles, signs and wonders were an expected part of Christian life—at least for the spiritually elite who reached beyond their contemporaries in holy living and devotion to God. To insist that none of these accounts are credible, while at the same time assuming that similar stories from the first-century Church given in Scripture are believable, suggests that we are imposing our own presuppositions on the data.

What seems clear is that the supernatural has accompanied gospel preaching in all periods of Christian history (see the sources cited in note 2 for surveys of the evidence). Yes, there have been ups and downs—but there never seems to have been a total absence of the charismata. To illustrate this, I have chosen to discuss four selected examples of Spirit-empowered ministry—two from both East and West—during the first six centuries of the Christian era.

1. GREGORY THAUMATURGUS ("WONDER-WORKER") (CA. 213-CA. 270)

Gregory was born about 213 at Neocaesarea (in Asia Minor, presently Turkey), the son of wealthy, noble parents. His father was devoted to the worship of pagan dieties. When Gregory was 14 years old, his father died and Gregory became a student of the famous Alexandrian theologian, Origen, under whose tutelage he became a devout Christian.

Origen probed his student with questions and taught him to think critically, investigating philosophy, physics, and ethics. Gregory later praised Origen as one who mediated him through divine charisma, speaking as those who prophesy and interpret mystical and divine words.[5]

Following his schooling (ca. 230), Gregory returned to his native Neocaesarea, where, according to his follower, Gregory of Nyssa, there were but 17 Christians. When Gregory the Wonder-worker died 40 years later, there were only 17 in Neocaesarea who were *not* Christians![6]

How was this mass conversion accomplished? At least four of the Church Fathers speak to this question. One of Gregory's spiritual descendants was Basil of Cappadocia. In Basil's famous work *On the Holy Spirit*, he argues that Gregory should be placed among the apostles and prophets as a person who walked by the same Spirit as they.[7] Specifically, Basil reports that by the "fellow-working of the Spirit" Gregory had tremendous power over demons, and was so spiritually gifted that his evangelism was dramatically successful. Basil lists a few of the miracles credited to Gregory's ministry (including prophecy and the turning of the course of rivers). He concludes:

> By the superabundance of gifts, wrought in him by the Spirit in all power and in signs and in marvels, he was styled a second Moses by the very enemies of the Church. Thus in all that he through grace accomplished, alike by word and deed, a light seemed ever to be shining, token of the heavenly power from the unseen which followed him.

Gregory of Nyssa, another of Gregory the Wonder-worker's followers, wrote an essay on his predecessor, which seeks to explain the evangelistic success of the Wonder-worker. Throughout, it is assumed that miracles and other supernatural phenomena resulted in mass conversions.[8]

In his history of the Early Church, the fourth-century historian, Socrates, reports that pagans were no less attracted to the Christian faith by his marvelous acts, than by his words. He reports many miracles, healing of the sick, and the casting out of devils even by means of his letters.[9]

Jerome, who provides us with the earliest "Who's Who in the Church," tells of reports current in the late fourth and early fifth centuries that Gregory's writings were overshadowed by the "signs and wonders," which accompanied his evangelism, bringing "great glory" to the churches.[10]

Curiously, the greatest Church historian of the period, Eusebius, is silent on matters miraculous in Gregory's ministry.[11] This silence has been seized upon by modern "demythologizers" to suggest that they were merely figments of disciples' imaginations. But such an argument, based on negative evidence—based on the absence of evidence for or against—demonstrates nothing. The same scholars argue, in addition, that Gregory's philosophical and reflective tendencies would have been incompatible with a ministry that evidenced "power evangelism." One can only wonder how, given this reasoning, they could so readily accept the same mix in the life of Saint Paul (cf. Acts 17:28 and Rom. 15:18,19)!

2. BASIL OF CAPPADOCIA (CA. 330-379): THE SPIRIT AND SOCIAL CONCERNS

Of all the Early Church Fathers, no one is more concerned about things of the Spirit than Basil of Cappadocia. His writing *On the Holy Spirit* may be the greatest of all such works ever produced in the Christian Church. He lived in the same section of Asia Minor as Gregory the Wonder-worker. This is not at all surprising, because Gregory's influence is directly referred to in Basil's writings on the Spirit.

Basil understood that the vibrant Christian was a "pneumatophor"—an active receptacle, carrier and distributor of the Holy Spirit and of spiritual gifts. He is remembered first for providing Eastern Christianity's most articulate and powerful description of the person and offices of the divine Third Person of the Trinity.[12] Basil also is remembered for establishing the monastic rule, which is used by monks throughout Eastern Christianity. One of the unique aspects of Basil's concept of the Church is that it is a charismatic body, each person exercising unique and separate gifts, without which the community as a whole would be impoverished. Basil expected that those who exercised leadership and care must be spiritual seniors who have gifts of discernment of spirits and healing the sick. They also must be able to foretell the future (i.e., have prophetic gifting: Acts 11:27,28; 20:22; 21:10,11).

One of the charismata Basil encouraged was empowered Christian preaching. He also stressed the gift of teaching. Basil tended to depend heavily on the leadership of those having obvious spiritual endowment. As a bishop, he would, on occasion, give leadership responsibilities to a lesser monk or a lay brother who was gifted spiritually.

Perhaps the most impressive aspect of Basil's charismatic life and outreach was the combining of preaching and teaching with care. He created an entire community, called "New Town"—later referred to as the Basilead—to deal with social needs, including those of widows, orphans, lepers, the poor, and even travelers.[13] In the process, he guided others into the role of pneumatophore—those led by the Spirit to give of themselves, rather than to be self-seeking.

3. AUGUSTINE OF HIPPO (354-430): MIRACLES ACCOMPANYING SERMONS

Without doubt, Augustine stands as the most influential Church Father in the West. He is responsible for crystallizing much of Western theology, including the traditional Western view of the Holy Spirit's person and work.[14]

What most theologians and church historians do not recognize in Augustine is the dynamic of his ministry and his recognition of the place of the miraculous in successful ministry. Although some scholars argue that he was skeptical of the charismata in his early career, by the time he wrote the City of God (413-426), miracles were a part of his own experience. In this work he reports, "Even now...many miracles are wrought, the same God who wrought those we read of still performing them, by whom He will and as He will...."[15] Again, he declares,

"We cannot listen to those who maintain that the invisible God works no visible miracles...God, who made the visible heaven and earth, does not disdain to work visible miracles in heaven or earth, that he may thereby awaken the soul which is immersed in things visible to worship him, the invisible."[16]

Augustine gives several examples, including a Cappadocian brother and sister, Paulus and Palladia, who were widely known for their horrible cases of palsy. They wandered into Hippo one spring, and attended church, where they were prayed for. On Easter morning, when the largest crowd of the year had gathered, Paulus was praying in the church, when suddenly his shaking ceased. Those around recognized what had happened, and soon the whole church was filled with the voices of those who were shouting praises to God. Augustine then ministered to the people, mediating the eloquence of God's work among them.

At the end of the service, there were more shouts, for the palsied sister, Palladia, who had been trembling at the back of the church, suddenly found herself totally healed. At this point, Augustine reports, "Such a shout of wonder rose from men and women together, that the exclamations and the tears seemed like never to come to an end...they shouted God's praises without words, but with such a noise that our ears could scarcely bear it."[17]

Augustine had a practice of requiring all who had experienced miracles to make both oral and written testimony, so those who had heard would not forget, and those who had never heard would be made aware of God's power. He also took his own advice by reporting a variety of contemporary miracles.

Whenever a miracle occurred, Augustine's practice was to mediate the event to the people. This was so that they would understand completely what had happened, so they would not forget, and so that God would receive the glory, rather than the priest.

Augustine insists that true gifts will bear examination. He even suggests a test to determine whether the spirit is of God: "Therefore by this understand ye the spirit that is from God. Give the earthen vessels a tap, put them to the proof, whether haply they be cracked and give a dull sound; see whether they ring full and clear, see whether charity be there"[18] (cf. Matt. 7:20). Furthermore, Augustine warns against the notion that a spiritual work must be accompanied by external proof: "God forbid that our heart should be tempted by this faithlessness."[19]

Strangely, the same Augustine who provides evidence of the supernatural in the fourth- and fifth-century Church, also denies on at least five occasions that the gift of tongues is for his generation. "In the laying on of hands, now, that persons may receive the Holy Ghost, do we look, that they should speak with tongues? When we laid the hand on these infants, did each one of you look to see whether they would speak with tongues, and, when he saw that they did not speak with tongues, was any of you so wrongminded as to say, 'These have not received the Holy Ghost'? Tongues are no longer needed because 'the Church itself now speaks in the tongues of all nations.'"[20]

One can speculate that, in specifically denying glossolalia, Augustine might have been reacting against contemporary enthusiasts of whom we have no historic record. And it is equally significant that he can point to no scriptural passage that demonstrates his assertion regarding the gift of tongues.

4. GREGORY THE GREAT (540?-604): RECORDER OF CONTEMPORARY MIRACLES

Gregory the Great, the fourth and last of the traditional Latin "Doctors of the Church," became Pope in 590. His *Four Books of Dialogues on the Life and Miracles of the Italian Fathers and on the Immortality of Souls* (593-594) simplified the doctrines expressed in Augustine's *The City of God*, and was highly influential during the Middle Ages. This work was composed for the single purpose of recording miracles performed by Italian saints in his own time. He understood that miracles were necessary in the Early Church to accomplish the work of evangelism. So, too, they were necessary in his own time for the conversion of pagans as well as the Lombard heretics. They also were probably intended to deepen the faith of those who were already baptized Christians. While Gregory admits that miracles, with the exception of visions, were not as frequent as they had been in the first century because the number of the faithful had grown considerably, miracles were still a constant of Christian experience.[21]

To remove any reason for disbelief on the part of his readers, Gregory declares that he will give the authority on which each of his miracle stories is based.[22] By and large, he is faithful in keeping this promise. His sources are usually eyewitnesses or members of the immediate entourage of the saints involved in the miracles. Only 19 episodes among the approximately 200 reported have no source given, and most of these have some kind of explanation. Gregory also connects as many miracles as he can to similar accounts in Scripture.

Among the miracles recorded in the *Dialogues*, the most frequently mentioned involve healings of various ailments, raising of the dead to life, exorcisms of evil spirits, prophetically foretelling the future, and deliverance from danger. Those from the life and ministry of Benedict of Nursia are good examples.

Gregory informs the reader that he learned about Benedict's miracles from four of Benedict's own disciples.[23] Benedict brought deliverance to a young monk who had been crushed under a collapsing wall. He also brought healing for numerous illnesses, including leprosy, and raised the dead back to life.

Benedict manifested a spirit of prophecy by foretelling future events and by describing to those who were with him what they had done in his absence (cf. 1 Cor. 14:2,25 and Acts 5:3).[24] He was also able to know the unspoken thoughts in the minds of his monks. For example, he was forewarned of a poison placed by some evil monks into his drinking water. He discerned the work of evil spirits, and exorcised many such spirits. Gregory asserts that such gifts of prophecy and discernment are directly from the Spirit of God. "To us, then, God has made a revelation of it through his Spirit."[25]

Gregory the Great's own ministry apparently was not graced with miracles. He does, however, refer to one personal experience in which he was the beneficiary of a miracle. He recalls being seriously ill with such severe pain from an intestinal illness that he thought he was near death. He especially grieved that he would not be able to fast on the Saturday before Easter. In his distress, he asked the abbot Eleutherius of Spoleto to pray on his behalf. The prayer was no sooner said, then he found strength returning to his weakened body, and his anxiety banished. Not only was he able to keep the fast, but he could have prolonged it to the next day had he so desired.[26]

While miracle stories are most prominent in the *Dialogues*, Gregory systematically reports and refers to them elsewhere as well. His *Homilies on the Gospels*, preached on public occasions, contain many stories of contemporary miracles.[27] In his *Homilies on Ezechiel*, he insists that miracles as striking as any reported in Scripture are being performed: "Now, generally, we see holy men do wonderful things, perform many miracles, cleanse lepers, cast out demons, dispel bodily sicknesses by touch, predict things to come by the spirit of prophecy."[28] In a letter of July 598 to Eulogius, Bishop of Alexandria, Gregory reports that Augustine of Canterbury and his companions in their missionary work in England had such great miracles accompany their preaching that they seemed to imitate the powers of the apostles.[29] In the *Moralia*, Gregory rejoices over the success with which God had crowned their preaching with miracles, for with the conversion of the Anglo-Saxons, virtually the whole world had been brought to the Christian faith.[30]

OTHER EXAMPLES OF SPIRIT-EMPOWERED MINISTRY IN THE POSTBIBLICAL EARLY CHURCH

The four examples given in this chapter provide but a tip-of-the-iceberg view of evangelism in the postbiblical Early Church, which was accompanied by and made credible by the miraculous. For those who are sufficiently curious, the charismatic ministries of the following people in the postbiblical Early Church could be explored:

A. Tertullian (late second-early third century A.D.), who attempted to prove the validity of his teachings against heretics like Marcion, by pointing to the validation of gifts of the Spirit and ecstasy on his side, and not on the other.[31]

B. Martin of Tours (ca. A.D. 316), whom Sulpicius Severus acclaimed as the virtual equal in gifted ministry, not only of the prophets and apostles, but of Christ Himself.[32]

C. Paulinus of Nola (late fourth-early fifth century A.D.), known to us from Gregory the Great's *Dialogues* book three.[33]

D. Antony of the Desert (late third-early fourth century A.D.), whose biography is provided by Athanasius.[34]

E. Pseudo-Macarius of Egypt (fourth century A.D.), who, according to several ancient historians, exercised gifts of healing, of exorcism, and of forecasting the future.[35]

F. Other Fathers of the desert, whose biographies are found in the *Historia monachorum in Aegypto.*[36]

It should be remembered that some of the writings given above are hagiographic in nature, and must be treated critically. This does not suggest, however, that all of the stories told about these saints are spurious or without historical basis. Certainly, these stories were believed by the ancient and medieval Church, and in many cases the miracles, signs, and wonders described herein were understood to be the cause of unbelievers' conversions.

CONCLUSION

We have seen considerable evidence that many of the Church Fathers recognized the continuance of Apostolic gifts and, in certain cases, practiced Apostolic gifts themselves. In addition, there is sufficient testimony of the connection made in the post-Apostolic Church between the exercise of spiritual gifts and successful evangelistic ministry. Finally, it seems reasonable to conclude that all true evangelism, whether or not it is accompanied by miraculous events, is led and empowered by the Holy Spirit (Rev. 19:10). And, given the historical evidence from virtually all centuries of the Christian era of gifted preaching being accompanied by extraordinary validations, it appears that power evangelism has flourished throughout the Church's history.

Notes

1. See K. S. Latourette, *A History of Christianity*, vol. 2 (New York: Harper & Row, 1975), pp. 725f.; but compare Luther's hymn "Ein' feste Burg ist unser Gott" (A Mighty Fortress Is Our God) composed in 1527 or 1528 (ibid., p. 722), which affirms that "the Spirit and the gifts are ours" (verse 4).
2. John Armstrong in M. S. Horton, ed., *Power Religion. The Selling Out of the Evangelical Church?* (Chicago, IL: Moody Press, 1992), p. 71.
3. See Kilian McDonnell and George T. Montague, *Christian Initiation and Baptism in the Holy Spirit: Evidence from the First Eight Centuries* (Collegeville, MN: Liturgical Press, 1991); Stanley M. Burgess, *The Spirit and the Church: Antiquity* (Peabody, MA: Hendrickson, 1984), and *The Holy Spirit: Eastern Christian Traditions* (Peabody, MA: Hendrickson, 1989); see also Max Turner, "Spiritual Gifts Then and Now," *Vox Evangelica* 15 (1985): 41-43; Donald Bridge, *Signs and Wonders Today* (Downers Grove, IL: InterVarsity Press, 1985), pp. 166-177; and Ronald A. Kydd, *Charismatic Gifts in the Early Church* (Peabody, MA: Hendrickson, 1984).
4. Origen, *Against Celsus* 2.48, ANF 4:449-450, seems to suggest that visible miracles were appropriate only for the nascent church. But he does have a good deal to say about the gift of prophecy. He even goes so far as to suggest that a person has to open the mouth in order to receive the charism of prophecy. (*On Exodus* 4:4, *Sources Chrétiennes* (Paris, France: Cerf, 1942ff), 321:130. Scholars debate whether Augustine of Hippo and Gregory the Great, while young men, also were cessationists (see William D. McCready, *Signs of Sanctity: Miracles in the Thought of Gregory the Great* (Toronto, Canada: Pontifical Institute of Mediaeval Studies, 1989). It is clear that both Augustine and Gregory, in their later careers gave evidence of a variety of contemporary miracles, and linked these with the proclamation of the gospel.
5. Gregory Thaumaturgus, *Oration and Panegyric addressed to Origen*, 15; ANF 6:36.
6. Gregory of Nyssa, *Life of Saint Gregory Thaumaturgus*, *Patrologiae cursus completus. Series Graeca*, ed. J. P. Migne (Paris, France: J. P. Migne, 1857-1866), 46:cols. 893-958 (henceforth PG).
7. Basil of Cappadocia, *On the Holy Spirit* 74, NPF 2nd series 8:46-47.
8. Gregory of Nyssa, *Life of Saint Gregory Thaumaturgus*, PG 46: cols. 893-958.
9. Socrates, *Ecclesiastical History* 27, NPF 2nd series 2:111-112.
10. Jerome, *Lives of Illustrious Men* 65, NPF 2nd series 3: 376.
11. Eusebius, *Ecclesiastical History* 6.30, NPF 2nd series 1: 275-6.

12. *On the Holy Spirit*, NPF 2nd series 8: 1-50.
13. Gregory Nazianzen, *The Panegyric on St. Basil* 63, NPF 2nd series 7: 416.
14. Augustine, *On the Trinity*, NPF 1st series 3: 17-228.
15. Augustine, *City of God* 22.8, NPF 1st series 2: 490.
16. Augustine, *City of God* 10.12, NPF 1st series 2: 188-89.
17. Ibid.
18. Augustine, *The Epistle of St. John* homily 6.13, NPF 1st series 7: 500.
19. Augustine, *On the Gospel of St. John* 32.7, NPF 1st series 7: 195.
20. Augustine, *Homily* 6.10 (on the Epistles of St. John), NPF 1st series 7: 497-498; *On Baptism* 3.16.21, NPF 1st series 4:443; *On the Gospel of St. John* 32.7, NPF 1st series 7:195.
21. Gregory the Great, *Homiliae in Evangelia*, *Patrologia cursus completus*. *Series Latina*, ed. J. P. Migne (Paris, France: J. P. Migne, 1844-1904), p. 76: col. 1091 (henceforth PL).
22. Gregory the Great, *Dialogues*, trans. Odo John Zimmerman (New York: Fathers of the Church, 1959), p. 6.
23. *Dialogues* 2 prologue, Zimmerman, p. 56.
24. That 1 Corinthians 14:24,25 refers to prophetic revelation, which includes supernatural insight into the secrets of people's hearts, is noted by A. Oepke, *TDNT*, vol. 3, p. 976, n. 42; and Wayne Grudem, *The Gift of Prophecy*, pp. 136-137.
25. *Dialogues* 2.13, 15, 16, 26, 30, 32; Zimmerman, pp. 77-78, 80, 81, 83, 95, 98, 101.
26. *Dialogues* 3.33, Zimmerman, pp. 172-73.
27. Gregory the Great, *Homiliae in Evangelia*, PL 76: cols. 1075-1312.
28. Gregory the Great, *Homiliae in Hiezechihelem prophetam*, ed. M. Adriaen, *Corpus Christianorum Series Latina* 142 (Turnhout, Belgium: Brepols, 1971), pp. 254-255 (henceforth CCL).
29. Gregory the Great, Letters 3.61, 8.29, CCL 140 and 140a, ed. D. Norberg, (Turnhout, Belgium: Brepols, 1982), pp. 209-211, 550-553.
30. Gregory the Great, *Moralia in Iob*, ed. M. Adriaen, CCL 143b (Turnhout, Belgium: Brepols, 1979-1985), p. 1346.
31. See Stanley M. Burgess, *The Spirit and the Church: Antiquity* (Peabody, MA: Hendrickson, 1984), pp. 65-68.
32. Sulpicius Severus. *Dialogi* 2.5, 3.10, *Corpus scriptorum ecclesiasticorum latinorum*, ed. C. Halm (Vienna, Austria: 1866), 1:186, 208.
33. *Dialogues* 3 prologue, Zimmerman, pp. 111-114.
34. Athanasius, *Life of Antony*, PG 26: cols. 835-975; NPF 2nd series 4: 188-221.
35. Sources for the life of Pseudo-Macarius are Socrates, *Ecclesiastical History* 4.23, NPF 2nd series 2:107; Sozomen, *Ecclesiastical History* 3.14, NPF 2nd series 2:291; Palladius, *Lausiac History* 17, ed. Robert T. Meyer, *Ancient Christian Writers* (New York: Newman Press, 1965), p. 34; Rufinus, *History of the Monks* 28, PL 21: cols.449-52, and Rufinus, *Apology* 1.19, NPF 2nd series 3:444.
36. *Historia monachorum in Aegypto*, ed. A. J. Festugière, *Subsidia hagiographica* 53 (Brussels, Belgium: Société des Bollandistes, 1971). This work has been translated by Norman Russell (Oxford, England: Mowbray; Kalamazoo, MI: Cistercian Publications, 1981).

12

REVIVAL AND THE SPIRIT'S POWER:

A PSYCHIATRIC VIEW OF BEHAVIORAL PHENOMENA ASSOCIATED WITH HEALING AND GIFT-BASED MINISTRY

JOHN WHITE

Let us settle the fact in our minds that certainly in Scripture, God's power may produce unusual reactions in human beings. Are such things happening today? Some people are said to tremble when the power of the Holy Spirit rests on them. Some weep or cry out. Others may shake violently and yet others fall to the ground. A few display bizarre bodily contortions.

This sort of behavior created problems in the days of Edwards, Whitefield, and the Wesleys. It still does. Many of us feel uneasy in the presence of people

---

who behave strangely. I am a psychiatrist, and even though I have spent years dealing with the bizarre and threatening behavior of psychotic patients, I still do not feel comfortable with it. Nor do I feel totally at ease when unusual behavior breaks out in church. But if God should be behind it, my personal reaction must be laid aside.

What, then, accounts for these strange behaviors? Logically, the explanations could be of four types. We could suggest:

1. People do it to themselves. That is to say, the manifestations have a psychological explanation, or are consciously or unconsciously self-induced.
2. Preachers do it to suggestible listeners—producing a so-called mass hysteria or mass hypnosis.
3. The devil does it—the phenomena representing some form of demonic control.
4. Or else God does it.

One of the four possibilities above must account for the behavioral phenomena seen in revival. For the theist, the possibility must extend to two or three of the factors above in combination.

Of course, we can never be sure of the extent to which we are in control of our own or anyone else's behavior. Alcohol-impaired drivers commonly believe they are in full control. On the other hand, some people pretend not to be in control when they actually are.

In meetings where the power of the Holy Spirit is present, some manifestations are obviously not under the control of the affected person. Others may behave suspiciously like an act. And sometimes a sensitive person may say, "I had the feeling that I could 'break out' of what was happening to me."

To add to the complications, not only can strange behavior be self-induced consciously, but also unconsciously. That is, the behavior is psychological. And if the explanation is psychological it can be: (1) a product of rigorous mental discipline; (2) a cheap attempt to gain attention or sympathy; or (3) an expression of an inner conflict the subject is unaware of.

1. ARE MANIFESTATIONS SELF-INDUCED?

Let us start with mental discipline. You can learn to go into a trance state (a condition of altered consciousness) by following certain steps that usually need to be practiced and may call for personal discipline. Christian as well as oriental mystics have for centuries described how to do it. Charles Tart has edited a book, both examining the techniques and investigating the psychology of it.[1]

While some of the techniques are suspect, not all are evil. For instance, some call for focusing attention for long periods on the person of God or on certain biblical truths. Mildly changed states of consciousness may result. Adepts may give themselves over to rigorous devotional exercises, so that in some sense they achieve the results. But the people whose behavior I shall describe later were not following steps or employing techniques, good or otherwise. In most cases they were taken by surprise. Therefore, I discount mental discipline as an explanation of what we are dealing with.

A second possibility is that the unusual behavior represents an attempt to draw attention to oneself, perhaps to gain sympathy. This happens frequently in times of revival and is not always dealt with sympathetically.

In meetings conducted by the Wesleys, powerful manifestations of the Spirit of God were frequent. Imitations also occurred. From Charles Wesley's journals, Dallimore has extracted the following passage:

> Some stumblingblocks, with the help of God, I have removed, particularly the fits. Many, no doubt, were, at our first preaching, struck down, both body and soul, into the depth of distress. Their outward affections were easy to be imitated....Today, one...was pleased to fall into a fit for my entertainment, and beat himself heartily. I thought it a pity to hinder him; so...left him to recover at his leisure. Another girl, as she began to cry, I ordered to be carried out. Her convulsion was so violent, as to take away the use of her limbs, till they laid and left her without the door. Then immediately she found her legs and walked off.[2]

I have spotted attention-seeking behavior in meetings where the power of the Holy Spirit is also manifest. Previous experience in psychiatry helped. I can understand and even sympathize with people giving way to it. Commonly inadequate and suffering from low self-esteem, such persons yearn for approval and love. They feel left out of the drama around them. They perceive, or think they perceive, that falling to the ground and trembling confer some sort of prestige. Some are fully aware of what they are doing. Others do not set out to deceive anyone unless it is that they deceive themselves. But they begin to believe that they, too, are about to fall. And they fall—or shake or moan or whatever.

Perhaps Charles Wesley's approach was right. It is better to ignore unobtrusive performances and to remove noisy ones. To give loving attention when it is sought in that particular way is to reinforce crazy behavior, and to make it more likely that the person will continue to "put on a performance" in order to gather a group of praying people around themselves. If love is to be shown, it is better shown at other times than as a reward for a demonstration.

DO THEY COME FROM UNCONSCIOUS URGES?

But what about unconscious urges? Few of us are the masters of our bodies and emotions. Our behavior can embarrass and shame us. Psychoanalytic theories tell us we may be driven to behave a certain way because of fears, greeds, and rages within us that we know nothing about. We have buried them deep within our beings, have forgotten them and are now blind and deaf to them. We may think we are fully in control of our actions, whereas we are prompted, at least in part, by unconscious drives.

The question then arises: Do people who shake and fall in religious meetings have an unconscious need to shake and fall? Do psychoanalytic theories explain the people Charles Wesley described as "struck down, both body and soul, into the depths of distress"? In an individual case it would be impossible to be sure. An unconscious urge is like a silent and invisible canary—you can neither prove nor disprove its presence. The critical questions will be: Why did the manifestation take the form it did at the time it did? What symbolic significance did the particular manifestation have? Why was the "unconscious material" released in those particular circumstances?

The question is important. "The heart is deceitful above all things and beyond cure. Who can understand it?" (Jer. 17:9). God can and does. And when the power of His Spirit comes upon us what is hidden and latent may be awakened and stirred-up within us.

While unconscious conflict may indeed influence the form of a manifestation, I could say, not only on the basis of careful observation and history taking, but of my own personal experience, that the timing cannot be explained on such a hypothesis.

On Sunday, February 16, 1986, I listened to a man from Northern Ireland speak at the evening service of the Vineyard Fellowship in Anaheim. In a few brief sentences, he described the dilemma there and expressed the hope that God would awaken and use the church in Northern Ireland to avert tragedy. We broke into groups for a brief time of prayer, after which John Wimber began the expository message for the evening. He had uttered only a few sentences when he paused and said, "I believe the Holy Spirit wants to share God's heart toward Northern Ireland with us." For a few moments, there was silence. Then sounds of broken weeping could be heard all over the auditorium.

I watched and listened with a psychiatrist's interest. Suddenly, and greatly to my surprise, sobs began to rise from deep inside me. I suppressed them, and in my effort to do so my shoulders and chest began to shake. For a moment I was not certain what to think. Then I realized that I ought to stop being psychiatric and start to intercede for Ireland and for God's people there, and soon found myself (amid my stifled sobs) crying out silently to God for His mercy to that unhappy country.

Why did it happen to me just then? I am quite used to hearing people weep. I am also of an analytical turn of mind and somewhat overcontrolled, having a natural horror of letting my emotions be seen in public. I had not expected anything like this to happen to me. I was neither putting on a performance nor releasing unconscious urges. I believe my state represented a spirit of intercession stirred up by the Holy Ghost.

2. Are Manifestations Preacher Induced?

In *The Golden Cow*, I described brainwashing techniques that can be used to change people's beliefs and modify their behavior.[3] In *Flirting with the World*, I also warned of the dangers of certain counseling trends in the '70s and '80s.[4] New Age advocates tell us to seek experiences that will expand our consciousness, enabling us to enter a new stage of being. Once sought through mind-expanding drugs (as people such as Timothy Leary and Aldous Huxley urged), these states are produced by techniques such as Ehrhardt Seminars Training (EST) and more recently Forum. Douglas Groothuis describes a typical session.

> In the est experience several hundred people are brought together for two successive weekends of marathon sessions designed to help them get "it." During the sessions they are confined to their chairs for long hours without note-taking, talking, smoking, clock-watching or sitting next to anyone they know. Minimal food and bathroom breaks are strictly observed. Each of the sixteen-hour sessions is led by a trainer who berates, taunts and humiliates the crowd by insisting that their lives don't work. The sustained intensity leads many to become sick, cry or break down in some other way. That's the goal. Through the agonizing hours of torture the tears turn to insight and the sickness into enlightenment. The

participants are told, "You're part of every atom in the world and every atom is part of you. We are all gods who created our own worlds." Eventually the people—at least some of them—claim to get "it"; they experience enlightenment and oneness.[5]

The Ehrhardt technique, quite apart from the sinister teaching, which is pantheistic and monistic, is similar to the brainwashing techniques used in student meetings in communist China following the revolution. It is "preacher manipulation" par excellence.

Brainwashing techniques major on the following elements: (1) physical exhaustion; (2) changes in perceptual levels; (3) cognitive dissonance; (4) inducing a sense of guilt and/or inadequacy and failure; (5) inducing fear; (6) inducing a sense of hopelessness; and (7) crowd effect.

Let me explain what I mean by changes in perceptual levels. All of us are accustomed to a certain level of perceptual input. Day and night our bodies are bombarded continuously by sights, sounds, sensations, and smells. We get used to certain levels of this ongoing bombardment. We not only tolerate it, we grow uneasy when it stops. Too much or too little makes us anxious. And anxiety, when it reaches intolerable levels, can lead to withdrawal, to rage, and to uncontrolled behavior.

Take noise, for example. Adolescents who like rock music grow accustomed to loud sounds that many older people find hard to tolerate. It is the volume of the sound that becomes the bone of contention, for it is the volume that determines levels of relaxation and of anxiety. Once they have grown accustomed to it, younger people "need" the same input of sound if they are to experience relaxation. Lower levels leave them restless, mildly anxious. But the levels that relax adolescents disturb anyone who has never become accustomed to them, raising their anxiety levels.

So if you want to manipulate people, work on their input levels. Scream the gospel at them for a while. Then to keep them off balance, switch to a quiet, intimate joke or two. Then start shrieking again. Your audience will soon get a high anxiety level and be putty in your hands.

Cognitive dissonance has to do with our expectations, and to some extent with our hopes and fears. We expect the earth to feel solid beneath us. We do not anticipate that when we stand on it, it will weave and shake beneath our feet. Terror arises in an earthquake because of the incongruity between what our lifelong daily experience has taught us (that the walls and the ground are solid) and the new reality of a heaving earth and billowing walls.

To manipulate a large number of people you need to exhaust them, to bombard them with levels of sensation they are not accustomed to, to expose them to concepts that frighten them, to humiliate them and make them feel guilty and hopeless, while still offering a new and magical idea. Crowd effect will be on your side, in that the crowd tends to carry people along with it. Writes Dr. Louis Linn, "Students of mob psychology have observed the elation, the impulsivity, the general emotional regression, and the personality dissociation that can occur in seemingly normal adults when they become part of a mob."[6]

Could brainwashing explain what happened in Edwards's meetings? in Wesley's? in Whitefield's? What about contemporary teachers such as John Wimber? I would say it is unlikely. In the Vineyard meetings and seminars, where the teaching is to my mind biblical, I have noted the people are encouraged to feel free to use bathroom facilities; breaks to stretch and chat or to have coffee are frequent; and while the preaching can at times be intense, it is more usually low key. Crowd effect and preaching technique could not account for the onset of the manifestations, though crowd effect might cause some people to "join in the fun."

Examples of manipulative preaching are not, however, hard to find. Such preaching can and does stir up emotion, and under it both spurious and real decisions are made. But the kind of behavior we are talking about does not occur unless the Holy Spirit has originally started the ball rolling. But while I feel that Wesley, Whitefield, and certainly Edwards can be exonerated from the charge of manipulation, other preachers cannot. Many early nineteenth-century preachers opened themselves to charges of bad management and extreme emotional pressure. In their meetings, behavioral manifestations occurred, along with flagrantly sinful behavior. Even so, I doubt that they were responsible for all the behavioral manifestations.

Charles A. Johnson describes the camp meetings that took place in open fields at the end of the eighteenth and during the early nineteenth centuries as the frontiers advanced westward across North America. Violence, gambling, robbery, drunkenness, and sexual immorality were common in the open societies the advancing frontier created. Preachers sent by God to reach them used colorful languages to describe the terrors of hell and the glories of heaven. Among their congregations would be drunken, ribald scoffers. And from all the camp meetings came reports of many conversions and of the kind of manifestations we are talking about.

Johnson accuses the preachers of extreme emotionalism and by their language of deliberately arousing fear.[7] He describes unusual noise levels in exhausting meetings, which commonly continued until dawn.

Perhaps the most famous of the camp meetings took place in Cane Ridge,

Kentucky, when between 10 and 25 thousand people gathered from August 6-12, 1801. The meetings continued without intermission by day through rain and sunshine, and at night by torch and firelight. The organizer and most of the preachers seem to have been Presbyterian, but every shade of opinion apparently was represented. Several preachers might have been seen preaching simultaneously from different makeshift pulpits. People slept on the ground as the need for rest overcame them.

Johnson describes it as "in all probability, the most disorderly, the most hysterical, and the largest" of such efforts to be held in early America. Cited by critics as typical of revival in general, Johnson points out that the meetings were in fact highly atypical. Alcoholics brought their liquor with them, and drunkenness and sexual promiscuity were not uncommon. One lady of easy virtue set herself up under a preaching stand, until she was discovered there with her male consorts. And the spontaneous excitement created by so unusual an event probably contributed to unguarded conduct in some people.

The association of these and many other manifestations with drunken and immoral conduct leaves a sour taste in our mouths. We instinctively feel that everything at the camp meeting must have been tarred with the same evil brush. On the other hand, a God of mercy seems to have looked down on the meeting, and visited it in compassion and with power. Many people were afflicted with the "falling exercise," presumably what is now called "being slain in the spirit." (At one point a conscientious Presbyterian minister carefully counted 3,000 fallen people.) Other people of all ages and social classes sometimes lay writhing on the ground, weeping, crying out to God for mercy.

Johnson quotes the impressions of James B. Finley, who was at the time a freethinker.

> The noise was like the roar of Niagara. The vast sea of human beings seemed to be agitated as if by a storm....Some of the people were singing, others praying, some crying for mercy in the most piteous accents, while others were shouting vociferously. While witnessing these scenes, a peculiarly-strange sensation, such as I had never felt before, came over me. My heart beat tumultuously, my knees trembled, my lip quivered, and I felt as though I must fall to the ground. A strange supernatural power seemed to pervade the entire mass of mind there collected....Soon after I left and went into the woods, and there I strove to rally and man up my courage.
>
> After some time I returned to the scene of excitement, the

waves of which, if possible, had risen still higher. The same awfulness of feeling came over me. I stepped up on to a log, where I could have a better view of the surging sea of humanity. The scene that then presented itself to my mind was indescribable. At one time I saw at least five hundred, swept down in a moment as if a battery of a thousand guns had been opened upon them, and then immediately followed shrieks and shouts that rent the very heavens....I fled for the woods a second time, and wished I had stayed at home.[8]

Finley's reaction to what he saw is interesting. He had gone to the meetings as a "freethinking" observer, a role that would provide a good deal of protection from manipulation and crowd effect, unless something else made him feel threatened. Even in a disorderly, ill-run meeting where manipulative preaching may have abounded, the grace and the power of God does not seem to have been absent.

To decide if all revival phenomena are the result of manipulation, we will have to examine the preaching under which those phenomena occurred. But both in Scripture and in church history, godly preachers, far from being manipulative, have sought to suppress manifestations, which sometimes persist in spite of the preacher's attempts to stop them.

We may look at the revival that broke out during the fifth century B.C. in Jerusalem. Confronted by a mass reaction of distressed weeping as the Holy Spirit moved on postexilic Jews, Nehemiah, Ezra, and the Levites did all they could to calm the people. They cried, "This day is sacred to the Lord your God. Do not mourn or weep....Go and enjoy choice food and sweet drinks, and send some to those who have nothing prepared....Do not grieve, for the joy of the Lord is your strength" (Neh. 8:9,10).

A simple reading of the passage shows that the instruction preceding the outbreak was far from manipulative (Neh. 8:1-8). The weeping could be attributed only to the Holy Spirit's activity in creating a hunger for truth and in making the people aware of how far they had departed from it. And the reality of the work became evident as a series of godly reforms followed the revival (Neh. 9—10).

Henry Venn gives an interesting account of Whitefield's preaching in a parish churchyard in 1757.

Under Mr. Whitefield's sermon, many of the immense crowd that filled every part of the burial ground, were overcome with fainting. Some sobbed deeply; others wept silently...when he came to impress the injunction in the text...several of the congregation burst into the most piercing bitter cries. Mr. Whitefield, at this juncture, made a pause and then burst into a flood of tears.

During this short interval Mr. Madan and myself stood up, and requested people to restrain themselves as much as possible from making any noise. Twice afterwards we had to repeat the same counsel....When the sermon was ended people seemed chained to the ground. [We] found ample employment in endeavoring to comfort those broken down under a sense of guilt.[9]

We may conclude that Whitefield was emotionally moved on this occasion, but we may not conclude that he was manipulative. Manipulation demands control of oneself and of the situation. The manipulator may act emotional (manipulate his own emotions) but it will be with an innate grasp of the total situation. Underneath, the manipulator is coldly using his or her emotions to achieve an effect. This is not what Whitefield was doing.

And the intervention of Venn and Madan was identical to the intervention of Ezra and Nehemiah in the revival of Nehemiah 8. Clearly, there was no attempt to foster or to prolong the fainting spells or an emotional outbreak.

I described earlier how several thousand people were powerfully moved to intercede for Northern Ireland in the evening service at the Vineyard Christian Fellowship, many with bitter tears. As they wept and prayed, John Wimber made no attempt to milk the situation but remained silent for several minutes. Then he prayed, "Now, Lord, grant your servants a spirit of peace!" In less than a minute the weeping had ceased, and without further comment Wimber proceeded with his exposition of Scripture. Neither the weeping nor the cessation of the weeping had been preacher produced. Wimber had made no mention of weeping and remained silent throughout it. God had briefly shared His heart with His people.

3. DO DEMONS PRODUCE PHYSICAL MANIFESTATIONS?

Once when I was traveling in Southern Brazil, I saw a great shaft of rock rising hundreds of feet into the sky. "What do they call it?" I asked my Brazilian companion.

"They call it the Finger of God," he replied.

I had no idea then that the expression came from the book of Exodus.

Confronted by the sight of God's power through Aaron's rod, Egyptian magicians assumed that Aaron's source of power was similar to their own. They demonstrated as much by reproducing Aaron's ability to transform a rod into a serpent, then by turning water into blood and eventually by conjuring up frogs from Egypt's dust, they found they had met their match. Suddenly they discovered they had been mistaken. Unable to succeed in imitating Moses and Aaron, they went to Pharaoh and said, "This is the finger of God" (Exod. 8:19).

The phrase is a metaphor, an anthropomorphic metaphor if you like. It is a colorful way of referring to the awesome nature of divine power, and it carries with it the reminder that it is unwise to look at what God does and to lightly conclude that another power is responsible.

So far I have tried to answer the questions: Do people produce manifestations themselves? And, do preachers produce them by manipulating people? Having the cautions of the Exodus story clearly in mind, let us now ask whether demons produce the physical manifestations found in revivals.

WHEN HELL'S GATES START TO RATTLE

Many Christians shake their heads in alarm at the notion that the Spirit's presence might cause demons to act up. The idea seems incongruous. They feel the Spirit would cause demons to sneak away in silence and shame. Scripture and history both teach us the opposite. When the Spirit is present in power, demons may flee, but they protest and make their presence known. Their power and kingdom are exposed and menaced.

Following His triumph over temptation, Jesus was ministering in the authority and power of the Holy Spirit when one demon in terror cried out, "Ha! What do you want with us, Jesus of Nazareth? Have you come to destroy us? I know who you are—the Holy One of God!" (Luke 4:34). Other demons cried, "You are the Son of God!" (Luke 4:41). The presence of Jesus provoked demonic outcries.

Even satanic delusions, wrong ideas that creep in to spoil a work of God, far from being an indication that the work itself is satanic, may in fact serve as a proof of the very opposite. Jonathan Edwards wisely comments, "Nor are...delusions of Satan intermixed with the work, any argument that the work in general is not of the Spirit of God."[10] Wherever the Spirit moves powerfully, an enemy not only opposes but seeks to undermine.

John Wesley was not surprised when demons manifested themselves in Christian gatherings. In public and in private, he found himself contending with them.[11] John Cennick, one of his preacher-associates, tells us:

One night more than twenty roared and shrieked together while I was preaching...[some of whom] confessed they were demoniacs. Sally Jones could not read and yet would answer if persons talked to her in Latin or Greek. They could tell who was coming into the house, who would be seized next, what was doing in other places, etc....

I have seen people so foam and violently agitated that six men could not hold one, but he would spring out of their arms or off the ground, and tear himself, as in hellish agonies. Others I have seen sweat uncommonly, and their necks and tongues swell and twist out of all shape. Some prophesied and some uttered the worst of blasphemies against our Saviour.[12]

In areas where witchcraft is practiced overtly, open conflict between the kingdom of God and the rule of darkness is common. Wherever the power of the King is displayed and His glorious banners allowed to stream, the powers of darkness may tremble, but they resist. Demonic manifestations are common and may be physically dangerous.

Ralph Humphries, an associate of the Wesleys and Whitefield, put it this way: "I think the case was often this; the word of God would come with convincing light and power into the hearts and consciences of sinners, whereby they were so far awakened....[that] the peace of the strong man armed would be disturbed; hell within would begin to roar; the devil, that before, being unmolested, lay quiet in their hearts, would now be stirred up."[13]

My own experiences over the past three years confirm this view. However, I must add that only a minority of the manifestations I have observed have been demonic. And when they have occurred, unless the demonic presences can be dismissed immediately, those in charge of ministry teams have usually seen to it that the victims are quietly taken somewhere so they can receive ministry privately, without being exposed to embarrassment.

But how do we distinguish what is of God from what is of Satan?

Over the long haul, there is no problem in making the distinction between something that reflects a demonic presence from something that does not. In any case, experience over at least the past 300 years seems to indicate that here in the West the overwhelming majority of manifestations have not been demonic. The difficulty arises in an immediate situation. How do we decide on the spot what is happening? Experiences may be helpful, but if you have no experience, what then?

To begin, we should rid ourselves of two great enemies of discernment—

idle curiosity and fear. Idle curiosity has no place in the battle with the powers of darkness. As for fear, it is not only inappropriate, it hinders discernment. It is inappropriate because demons have been around a long time and have probably been also affecting the person in whom the manifestation is occurring for a long time. A solution should be sought, but there is no urgency about solving the matter in the next 10 seconds.

Fear impedes discernment since learning to distinguish the spirits grows in the soil of quiet confidence in God the Holy Spirit. The more relaxed and at peace we are in the Lord, the more easily will we discern what is demonic. If we are inexperienced, it is wise to seek the help of someone who is experienced.

Usually when demonic manifestations occur in Christian settings they include such things as blasphemous utterances, voices other than the person's own voice coming from the throat of a person, animal-like movements and gestures (such as snakelike writhing).

MANIFESTATIONS PRODUCED BY THE HOLY SPIRIT

The Holy Spirit produced most of the manifestations we shall be discussing. Many people had no means of anticipating what was going to happen to them. Some (like Saul of Tarsus) were vigorously opposed, feeling it was all fraudulent.

If we doubt the genuineness of the whole thing, we should consider several factors. First, we must examine the teaching under which the manifestations occur (not relying only on gossipy reports since in every revival, critics distort the content of the preaching). Then, we must observe the results in the lives of the people in whom they occur. Finally, we must not forget the element of surprise. People having no previous knowledge of what might happen, who were under no kind of stress, others of whom were resisting what they saw happening around them—all have been affected.

For instance, my wife, Lorrie, and I had unconsciously always entertained a stereotypical idea of what it would be like when the Spirit came with power. The reality differed from our unconscious stereotype. During a quiet lecture given at Fuller Seminary in 1985, neither of us knew the Spirit was powerfully present. And certainly neither of us suspected that Lorrie would tremble at such a time.

At first, Lorrie was puzzled and embarrassed at her shaking. She tried to hide the marked tremor in her hands and arms (a tremor that continued to recur periodically for several weeks). Having observed what was happening to Lorrie, I turned to view the rest of the class (mainly missionaries and noncharismatic pastors). From my front-row seat, I saw several people in a similar predicament to hers. Some of them seemed dazed but at peace. The power of God's Spirit could evidently affect people physically even during a quiet lecture period.

It also occurs in people who not only do not believe in such things but who firmly oppose them. In a journal entry dated May 1, 1769, John Wesley records the bewilderment of an indignant Quaker who was disgusted by the manifestations he saw in one of Wesley's meetings: "A quaker, who stood by, was not a little displeased at the dissimulation of these creatures and was biting his lips and knitting his brows, when he dropped down as thunderstruck. The agony he was in was even terrible to behold. We besought God not to lay folly to his charge. And he soon lifted up his head and cried aloud, 'Now I know thou art a prophet of the Lord!'"[14]

Wesley records an even more dramatic instance in a man who witnessed the above incident and who had spent several days warning people about the errors of Wesley and the danger of what was happening in his meetings. He records the incident in a letter to his brother Samuel, dated May 10, 1739.

A bystander, one John Haydon, was quite enraged at this, and, being unable to deny something supernatural in it, laboured beyond all measure to convince all his acquaintance, that it was a delusion of the devil.

I was met in the street the next day by one who informed me that John Haydon was fallen raving mad. It seems he had sat down to dinner, but wanted first to make an end to a sermon he was reading. At the last page he suddenly changed colour, fell off his chair, and began screaming terribly, beating himself against the ground.

I found him on the floor, the room being full of people, whom his wife would have kept away; but he cried out, "No; let them all come; let all the world see the judgement of God."

Two or three were holding him as well as they could. He immediately fixed his eyes on me, and said, "Aye this is he I said deceived the people; but God hath overtaken me. I said it was a delusion of the devil; but this is no delusion."

Then he roared aloud, "O thou devil! Thou cursed devil! Yea, thou legion of devils! Thou canst not stay in me. Christ will cast thee out. I know his work is begun. Tear me to pieces if thou wilt. But thou canst not hurt me."

He then beat himself again, and groaned again, with violent sweats, and heaving of the breast. We prayed with him, and God put a new song in his mouth. The words were, which he pronounced with a clear, strong voice, "This is the Lord's doing, and it is marvelous in our eyes. This is the day which the Lord hath made: We will rejoice and be glad in it. Blessed be the Lord God of Israel, from this time forth for evermore."[15]

It is foolish to suggest that such opponents of the Great Awakening had secret wishes to be convinced. People of this sort have more in common with Saul of Tarsus on the Damascus road, or with the brief incident in John 18:6, where at Christ's majestic confession, "I am he," his captors fell backward to the ground. (John's meaning is clear. The fall had no natural explanation. In the presence of the I AM, the rabble were knocked down by the power of God.)

Similar incidents occur from time to time in the ministry of John Wimber, the most recent being in Sheffield, England, on November 6, 1985. A pastor who had been invited by a colleague decided with some reluctance to attend. He arrived late, entering the building at a point when Wimber was inviting the Holy Spirit to take charge. Disgusted, his worst fears realized, he turned to leave in protest. But before he could reach the door, he was struck down shaking, and was unable to rise for a prolonged period. Eventually he left the building a profoundly changed man.

At the same meeting was David White. Afterward, he wrote the following letter to John Wimber in which he describes his experience at the meeting in full.

Dear John:

Excuse my familiarity, but I feel I know you personally....I went to Sheffield (having previously worshipped at David Pytches' Church in Chorley Wood), and I feel God has given me a totally new ministry, and a fresh start. And it was badly needed. I work and live in Toxteth, just about one of the worst areas in Liverpool, and at times I have got so discouraged. But since Sheffield my life has undergone a dramatic change.

This is really why I am writing; please, please could you tell me what exactly you proclaimed in your blessing on the Thursday night at Sheffield!

I heard about the first three sentences and then POW!! It was incredible. God fell on me, I was utterly broken, my whole life lay before him on the line. I thought he was going to kill me—so much so, I said goodbye to my wife Ruth. It was awesome, and painful, as what felt like high voltage electricity burned through me.

Friends around me described it like I was being stretched. There appeared to be a force around me. And this lasted about fifteen minutes, and then I thought I had died because my body seemed filled, transparent with light. Then, "That's nice—the angels know 'our God reigns'!!" It seems to me that there is a connection between what you prayed for the pastors and my experience. And I want to know. Since then God has confirmed that experience with similar anointings—what is God wanting to do with me?

I hope you don't mind me writing. Be assured of my prayers and please pray that I may remain humble and close to the Lord. And may the Lord protect you and yours.

Yours, in much thankfulness in our lovely Lord,

David White

To theorize that these men were unconsciously desiring such an experience may be an interesting, intellectual exercise. Certainly, the first man consciously wished the very opposite. But even if they were desiring such an experience, the Holy Spirit was the one whose power and grace brought their unconscious wish to the surface.

About a year after the Sheffield conference, I received permission from David White to publish his letter to John Wimber. Some of his comments are interesting. "I would not wish any to think they have to copy my experience," he wrote, "nor would I wish anyone to make unwarranted conclusions about how 'spiritual' a person I am....Of course, the letter has about it the air of new, fresh enthusiasm—that 'POW' makes me cringe now! Yet it is an accurate and valid description."

But what benefits had accrued to him? "Sheffield marked a turning point in my life. In terms of subsequent growth and usefulness to the Lord it has been one of the most significant experiences since conversion....In my ministry I have a new found authority and a greater expectancy of God to work than ever before." He commented on Lloyd-Jones's book *Joy Unspeakable*, and wondered how to categorize his experience. "In one sense, what to call the experience theologically does not bother me, as long as I do not make extravagant claims for perfection and thus repeat the mistakes made in church history...."

For my part, I am glad that God ignores our petty notions of propriety as He deals with men and women. I want God to be God. But because I suffer from a skeptical disposition, I have to see for myself what is happening, to inquire, to test. For though I want to see God acting as God, I have no wish to find anything less. David White's testimony speaks for itself.

Having therefore seen and examined carefully, I am convinced that while some manifestations represent psychological aberrations, and others demonic fear and protest, many and perhaps most of the manifestations associated with revival evidence the presence in power of the Holy Spirit. But these manifestations, while they may be a blessing, are no guarantee of anything. Their outcome depends on the mysterious traffic between God and our spirits. Your fall and your shaking may be a genuine expression of the power of the Spirit resting on you. But the Spirit may not benefit you in the least if God does not have His way with you, while someone who neither trembles nor falls may profit greatly.

THE ORCHARDS AND THE FRUIT

Surely it is fruit that matters (Matt. 7:15-20). And specific fruits tend to be found in certain kinds of orchards. Earlier I pointed out that by their very nature, dramatic behavioral manifestations arouse strong feelings in onlookers. Critics turn away in disgust. Enthusiasts praise the Lord and long for more. And both may suffer from a wrong way of looking at matters. Each evaluates the manifestations by the wrong criteria, assuming a different, but too simple, explanation. In itself, a given manifestation is no sign that something of spiritual value has been accomplished (see Matt. 7:21-23).

According to Edwards, neither a negative nor a positive judgment should be based on the manifestation alone "because the Scripture nowhere gives us any such rule."[16] How then is a manifestation to be judged? Partly by the orchard—the setting the manifestation occurs in, the kind of preaching the subject has listened to. And partly by the fruit—the effects on the life, the ongoing testimony and the subsequent character of the person in whom the manifestation is observed.

Edwards devotes a good deal of attention to what I have called the orchard, focusing mainly on the kind of preaching under which the manifestations occur. In a paper entitled "The Distinguishing Marks of a Work of the Spirit of God,"[17] he expounds 1 John 4:1, "Dear friends, do not believe every spirit, but test the spirits to see whether they are from God, because many false prophets have gone out into the world."

Edwards asks the question: How can one spot a genuine, as distinct from a false, prophet? And in expounding the whole of 1 John 4 he answers: by noting whether his preaching affirms the historic Jesus as the crucified and risen Messiah; whether it opposes sin and worldly lust; whether it awakens respect for Scripture by affirming its truth and its divine source; whether it awakens an awareness of the shortness of life and the coming of judgment; and finally, whether it awakens genuine love both toward God and one's neighbor.

But the fruit is more important than the orchard. An enemy can plant evil trees in the best regulated orchard. "By their fruit," Jesus tells us, "you will recognize them. Do people pick grapes from thornbushes, or figs from thistles?" (Matt. 7:16).

4. WHEN GOD DOES IT

If you read the history of revivals conscientiously, you will read about some pretty unusual behavior in revival meetings. The behaviors we shall examine in the remainder of this chapter are the more common varieties of the late twentieth century, displayed by people whose background is either pagan or conservatively Christian. Of these, the easiest to understand are expressions of emotion.

Let us begin then by looking at three manifestations of emotion—those of fear, of sorrow, and of joy.

TERROR AND THE NUMINOUS

In Scripture, there seem to be two different types of fear of God. There is the fear of the disobedient servant, and there is also what has been called "numinous fear."

Moses experienced both kinds of fear on different occasions. Exodus 4:24-26 contains a disturbing account of the first kind of fear—the fear of the disobedient servant. Moses and Zipporah are on their way to Egypt with their families. Moses' firstborn son is uncircumcised. In a single shattering sentence, we learn that "at a lodging place on the way, the Lord met Moses and was about to kill him." Only after Zipporah carried out the circumcision, smearing the blood on Moses' foot, did the danger pass.

The incident is as rare as it is disturbing and mysterious. Two conditions seem to be of importance. First, Moses is a servant chosen for a special mission for which absolute obedience and devotedness to God and His word are essential, and second, Moses' attitude has been ambivalent. He has been playing fast and loose with the divine covenant. He has been reluctant, perhaps because of Zipporah's obvious distaste for the custom, to circumcise his son. And in a servant whose role is to be crucial, his ambivalence is not to be tolerated.

During the past two years, I have come across two episodes of such a terror—the terror of persons who, caught up in a mystical experience, thought that God was about to kill them. Both incidents took place when the subjects were fully awake and out-of-doors at night. Both people were also servants of God who were about to back away from His call on their lives. In terror, they both instantly repented.

We shrink from the concept of God this suggests to us. But that is because we have no real understanding of His burning rage against all sin.

But more common and understandable than the fear Moses and Zipporah experienced is the fear felt by finite, sinful men and women in the presence of an infinite and holy God. The reactions of Daniel, who collapsed in terror (Dan. 8:17,18,27), and John the apostle, who collapsed when he was "in the Spirit" and Christ appeared to him (Rev. 1:10,13-18) are such cases.

Dr. Rudolph Otto, theologian and philosopher, in his book, *The Idea of the Holy*, writes about the "'supra rational' in the depths of the divine nature." God's holiness is ultimate moral beauty, moral beauty of such a nature and such power that it transcends human understanding. It is the living God Himself. He can, and at times He actually does, communicate it—and Himself—to us.

According to Otto, a number of elements can be distinguished in men and women who have thus encountered God. He vigorously denies Schleiermacher's assertion that these elements are mere extensions of those feelings devout Jews and Christians experience in their worship, feelings of awe and reverence, even of rapture, seeing these as best as analogies of one to whom God has revealed Himself in a close encounter.[18]

Otto uses, as C. S. Lewis did later, the term "numinous" to describe this quality of the fear. The numinous experience is made up of an overwhelming sense of one's creaturehood, such that one experiences a "submergence into nothingness before an overpowering absolute might."[19] Other elements are what he calls, "Mysterium Tremendum," which is not "that which is hidden and esoteric, [but] that which is beyond conceptual understanding, extraordinary and unfamiliar."[20]

The fear may be mingled with joy, so that people are overcome with wonder and adoration, and like Rat in *The Wind in the Willows* they say, "Afraid? Of Him? Oh, never! And yet...I am afraid."

For Jonathan Edwards the fear was crucial. "The Scriptures place much of religion in godly fear; insomuch that an experience of it is often spoken of as the character of those who are truly religious persons. They tremble at God's word, they fear before him, their flesh trembles because of him, they are afraid of his judgments, his excellency makes them afraid, and his dread falls upon them."[21]

Whether people's fear is fear of God's judgment on sin, or of the ineffability of His person, Christians and non-Christians alike experience His fear during times of revival. In Cambuslang, Scotland, in 1742, Dr. Alexander Webster described meetings there: "Many cry out in the bitterness of their soul. Some...from the stoutest men to the tenderest child, shake and tremble and a few fall down as dead. Nor does this only happen when men of warm address alarm them with the terrors of the law, but when the most deliberate preacher speaks of redeeming love...."[22]

I have felt such a fear. I have trembled, perspired, known my muscles to turn to water. On one occasion, it happened as I prayed with elders and deacons in my home. I had tried to teach them what worship was, but I doubt that on that occasion they understood. We then turned to prayer. Perhaps, partly to be a model to them, I began to express worship, conscious of the poverty of my words. Then, suddenly, I saw in front of me a column of flame about two feet wide. It seemed to arise from beneath the floor and to pass through the ceiling of the room. I knew—without being told—knew by some infallible kind of knowing that transcended the use of my intellect, that I was in the presence of the God of holiness. In stunned amazement, I watched a rising column of flames in our own living room, while my brothers remained with their heads quietly bowed and their eyes closed.

Did they know what was happening? They made no comment afterward and I never asked them. In some obscure fashion, I felt I was in the presence of reality and that my brothers were asleep. For years afterward I never spoke of the incident. The others who were present could not have perceived the blend of stark terror and joy that threatened to sweep me away. How could I live and see what I saw? Garbled words of love and of worship tumbled out of my mouth as I struggled to hang on to my self-control. I was no longer trying to worship. Worship was undoing me, pulling me apart. And to be pulled apart was both terrifying and full of glory.

GRIEF AND MOURNING

Strong emotions are rarely pure. They come (depending on how clearly we see truth) in twos and threes, in jumbled and incongruous liaisons. Fear may be coupled with grief, joy with fear, rage with pity. "The town seemed to be full of the presence of God; it was never so full of love, nor of joy, and yet so full of distress, as it was then,"[23] writes Jonathan Edwards of the 1735 revival in New Hampshire.

Edwards uses the term "melting," when in his journal he describes weeping that took place on Saturday, March 1, 1746, in a catechism class he held in Crossweeksung, New Jersey: "Toward the close of my discourse, divine truths made considerable impressions upon the audience, and produced tears and sobs in some under concern; and more especially a sweet and humble melting in sundry that, I have reason to hope, were truly gracious."[24]

Dr. John Hamilton, in a similar vein, gives his own description of the revival in Cambuslang, Scotland: "I found a good many persons under the deepest exercise of soul, crying out most bitterly of their lost and miserable state, by reason of sin; of their unbelief, in despising Christ and the offers of the Gospel; ...I heard them express great sorrow for these things, and seemingly in the most serious and sincere manner, and this not so much...from fear of punishment as from a sense of the dishonour done to God...."[25]

Two occasions of such weeping in John Wimber's meetings stand out in my memory. In March 1984, in the Vineyard church in Anaheim, Wimber invited the unsaved to come forward for counsel and prayer. His address had been restrained, certainly not emotional. I estimate that about 200 people instantly began to move to the front of the church without any pressure. Many burst into tears as they did so, some stopping on their way to the front and turning to anyone near them with an agonized and totally unsolicited outpouring of confession of sin.

A second manifestation of sorrow over sin took place in a seminar in Vancouver, Canada, 18 months later. Wimber had spoken of pastors who in the face of critical scholarship had watered down the biblical content of their preaching, thus robbing the sheep of truth. He then invited any pastors who felt convicted by God of such sin, and who wished to renounce it and preach the truth, to come forward for prayer. Many responded. Some of these spontaneously began to weep. I stood very close to the group and estimated that about one in seven was affected in this way.

Joy Unspeakable

Some of the emotions that provoked criticism in the Cambuslang revival originated under the ministry of a "humanly ineffectual" minister, William McCullough. Dallimore describes the emotions: "They were of two kinds—the outcrying and trembling among the unconverted and the ecstatic joy among believers....Indeed, such joy was more a part of this work than the sorrow over sin. It appears that many believers found themselves so moved by a sense of the Saviour's love to them and, in turn, by their new love in him, as to be lifted almost into a state of rapture."[26]

Sinners were moved by the Holy Spirit so "as to be lifted almost into a state of rapture." They were moved by what they described as a new sense of "the Saviour's love to them." It was not that they had no previous knowledge of the Savior's love, but that with hearts quickened by the Spirit they perceived it with a new and overwhelming clarity. Joy burst from their hearts and along with joy, praise of an almost ecstatic intensity.

In New Hampshire, as in Scotland, the same joy was born. Edwards writes: "Their joyful surprise has caused their hearts as it were to leap, so that they have been ready to break forth into laughter, tears often at the same time issuing like a flood, and intermingling a loud weeping."[27]

Ready to "break forth into laughter"? Joy is one thing, but laughter is something else (which is not unattested in Scripture: Gen. 17:1,3,17; Ps. 126:2; Prov. 14:13; etc.). Yet I have heard people break into laughter when the Holy Spirit touches them, and they are astonishing to observe. The first time I encountered the phenomenon was in the notorious "Signs and Wonders" class at Fuller Seminary in 1984. Wimber had prayed that the Holy Spirit would equip a number of pastors and missionaries for the work God had called them to do. A South African pastor began to giggle and could not stop.

I might have supposed him to be reacting to something incongruous, either in the prayer or in the situation. It was the kind of giggle you associate with someone whose emotional "funny bone" has been touched. But there was a significant difference. People are embarrassed when they "get the giggles," but this man seemed oblivious to the rest of us. His face was open and he was smiling broadly. He seemed unaware that we did not share his secret. He continued to giggle, I am told, for several hours, waking during the night to do so. We were seeing his personal reaction to being "surprised by joy."

I have observed the same phenomenon several times since. When it is genuine, it follows a similar pattern—irrepressibility, unself-consciousness. Often it continues intermittently for a long time. It seems to be associated with a beginning of release of tension in uptight people.

But there is also an imitation. "Holy laughter" in some circles carries prestige. To get the godly giggles or to produce it in others becomes a mark of spiritual achievement. Under those circumstances, one detects a sense of strain. The laughter can be forced and distasteful.

But we must not shun the true because we fear the false. As Edwards wrote, "Though there are false affections in religion, and in some respects raised high: yet undoubtedly there are true, holy, and solid affections; and the higher these are raised the better. And when they are raised to an exceeding great height, they are not to be suspected merely because of their degree, but on the contrary to be esteemed."[28]

TREMBLING AND SHAKING

So far we have been looking at emotional manifestations, and emotional manifestations seem to be all that eighteenth-century writers ever saw. That is not to say the same manifestations did not occur then that occur now, but eighteenth-century writers seem to assume that what they observed was a reaction to consciously experienced emotion. Tears were from grief, ecstasy from joy, trembling from fear, and fainting or falling also from fear or shock. And in many cases this is how it seems to work. But not always.

Take the relationship between fear and trembling, for example. People in revivals do indeed tremble from fear, but others experience trembling in the absence of fear (see Jer. 23:9). I know a woman who trembles frequently (as with Parkinsonism) when she prays for other people. She is an emotionally stable woman whose testimony I respect. She describes the experience in terms of energy coursing through her. The phenomenon began in a meeting she attended where the Holy Spirit was powerfully present. While she cannot, as it were, produce the trembling or the "energy," when it comes, she has the choice either of resisting it, or else of directing it (into prayer, for example). If she does the latter, she experiences a sensation of pulsating energy extending to her fingertips, along with a slight tremor in her hands. Her impression is of energy flowing through her. "You know those anatomical diagrams of the cardiovascular system? It feels as though the energy is flowing along those channels."

If the energy has something to do with the Holy Spirit (and I believe it has), it is important to note that her own control is limited to accepting or rejecting what God is doing. She does not take the initiative. Nor does she make any effort to enter into a trance state. Even her ability to accept or reject is by no means complete, being more a learning how to respond. She does not see her experience as the norm for other Christians and does not bother herself with trying to explain it.

For others (such as my wife and the people I described earlier), the trembling (over which there is initially no control, though control often develops gradually over time) may continue intermittently for months. With the trembling there seems to be no fear, but more of quiet joy mingled with a strange peace.

Trembling varies in its intensity. At times in public meetings, people are seized with violent shaking. Occasionally I have been astounded at the power and violence of the shaking. Such people do not shake, but are shaken, like rag dolls in the teeth of a terrier, their bodies moving backward and forward or from side to side, and their arms and sometimes even their legs flailing in the wake of their moving bodies. I doubt that any ballet dancer or gymnast could reproduce the movements; for the astounding thing is that while some people collapse and fall, the most violent maintain their equilibria.

More commonly, a man's trunk may remain immobile, while the head may shake backward and forward (banging the wall behind in a regular rhythm if he should happen to be leaning against it). The arms, bent at the elbow, usually with palms facing the ground, flap violently up and down from shoulders, elbows and wrist, the most violent movements being commonly at the wrist joint, while the hands flail so quickly as sometimes to dissolve into a blur. The movements are cyclical in intensity, rising repeatedly in slow waves to a crescendo, then subsiding again. Each cycle may last up to two or three minutes. Commonly, crescendos of activity coincide all over the gathering, though it is certain that affected persons are unaware of what other people are doing.

In frontier camp meetings, this would be referred to as "the jerks."

Sometimes the subject of the jerks would be affected in some one member of the body, and sometimes in the whole system. When the head alone was affected, it would be jerked backward and forward, or from side to side, so quickly that the features of the face could not be distinguished. When the whole system was affected, I have seen the person stand in one place, and jerk backward and forward in quick succession, their hands nearly touching the floor behind and after....

I have inquired of those thus affected. They could not account for it; but some have told me that those were among the happiest seasons of their lives. I have seen some wicked persons thus affected, and all the time cursing the jerks while they were thrown to the ground with a violence. Though so awful to behold I do not remember that any of the thousands I have seen ever sustained an injury in body. This was as strange as the accident itself.[29]

Though people affected by shaking are conscious and know where they are, they seem to be in a dazed and dreamlike state. Their sense of time is commonly impaired, in that they may not have a clear idea of how long their manifestation lasted. When waves of movement subside, they will usually respond briefly to questions, though their ability to describe the experience through which they are passing is often limited to a physical description. ("My arms keep shaking. I can't stop them.") They may experience fear but usually do not. One man told me, "I just felt an enormous compassion...for people."

One variety of shaking that has been described to me, but that I have never seen personally, is called "pogo-sticking." Sometimes the bodily shaking is on a vertical axis, the body leaving the ground in a series of bounces. Since the body remains more or less rigid, it looks like someone bouncing on a pogo stick.

The physical energy used must be considerable, especially when one considers that pogo-sticking is no respecter of persons. Yet no bodily harm seems to have occurred from pogo-sticking. Some years ago, as the Holy Spirit's power fell during prayer in an Anglican church in the north of England, the rector fell forward on his face, and several staid members of the congregation (including the church wardens) began to pogo-stick.

Jonathan Edwards describes what could be pogo-sticking. "Since this time [a visit by Whitefield] there have often been great agitations of body, and an unavoidable leaping for joy....."[30]

FALLING

In almost every church I visited on a recent visit to Argentina, people asked me, "*¿Qué es eso de caerse?*" (Roughly—"What's all this business of falling about?") They were referring to what was happening in the evangelistic crusades of Carlos Annacondia. Newspaper and magazine reports were full of accounts of the many people who fell to the ground during his meetings. More dramatic still, some fell on their way to the meetings, while others were reported to fall from their seats in buses that were passing by the meetings.

At some point in the nineteenth century, this particular phenomenon began to be called "being slain in the spirit." In eighteenth-century accounts it is "being overcome" or "fainting." In the Bible it is, "fell at his feet as though dead" (Rev. 1:17), "drew back and fell to the ground" (John 18:6) and "fell on my face" (Dan. 10:9, RSV). It is not one phenomenon but many. It may occur gently or violently, be associated with great distress or profound calm.

In 1982, in Birmingham, England, during his second visit to Britain, John Wimber was at a prayer meeting in a Baptist church. About 30 people were present, including a small ministry team from the United States. Wimber, who frequently prays with his eyes open, began to pray and had got as far as the word, "Lord—"when he saw (in what seemed to be like slow motion) a black man lifted into the air. The man looked as though he were being lifted and laid briefly on an invisible stretcher, before sailing back to crash heavily into several chairs as he screamed, "Hallelujah!" Wimber was afraid that the violence of the fall would have killed him, but the man was unhurt.

Falls are commonly much less violent and may be backward (common) or forward (less common and in my observation more frequent in pastors and ministers). Falls may be associated with further violent movements, head-banging, tremors, movements suggestive of epilepsy, but commonly with a total absence of movement. Subjects may have no experience beyond a pleasant sense of calm, may experience visions, or may feel that they are being crushed. One man told me he felt as though a massive weight was crushing the life out of him, making it impossible for him to breathe and giving him the feeling that he was "being squeezed out like a tube of toothpaste."

Many people may be affected simultaneously. When this is so, the precise timing suggests supernatural choreography rather than mass hysteria. Crowd effect may sometimes be postulated when, for example, the phenomenon has become known in a country or locality. But many times, no one anticipated what would happen and people had no opportunity to see or be influenced by what others were doing. Everyone fell together.

John Strazosich is a Fuller graduate with a charismatic background. He had previously experienced the "baptism of the Spirit" and had spoken in tongues. In January 1985, he attended the Vineyard Christian Fellowship in Los Osos, and during the ministry time asked for "more power." Slowly, beginning with one arm, a shaking took possession of his whole body. Soon he was shaking violently and continued to shake for two hours.

John had the feeling that at any time he could have stopped what was happening, though he was sure he was not producing the shaking himself. However, believing God was ministering to him, he prayed that God would enable him to minister in different ways. Each request caused the shaking to increase in violence. Finally, he could stand no more, and asked God to stop. His muscles ached for three days afterward.

"After that, every time I prayed for someone they would fall down. It went on for some months. When God spoke to me it was very clear. It's not that clear anymore, not as clear as it was—but it was real clear then."

Some days later at a Christian camp John began to "bounce up and down" from a standing position. "God told him" to start praying for some of the young men around him. It was difficult to speak, and he had difficulty in explaining his intentions, it not being easy to speak coherently when bouncing. He prayed for three young men, barely touching them before they fell to the ground. A fourth boy shook, "but was not receiving anything." He was "resistant" because of his desire to heed the lyrics of certain rock songs. A fifth fellow was affected by laughter. Eventually John himself was no longer able to remain standing, and fell to the ground.

The unusual effects of John's praying led to a very embarrassing situation. One Sunday after church John and two friends went to the Marriott Hotel in Anaheim to have supper at the La Plaza restaurant. They were told they would have a 20-minute wait. In the lobby, John proceeded to tell his friends what had been happening in his life. He noticed a man in the lobby and thought he sensed God telling him to pray for the man, but he was uncertain. Eventually the man approached him, having overheard the conversation. He was a Canadian. "That was interesting to listen to." It turned out that the man was attending a conference led by Pentecostal preacher and healer Maurice Cerillo. John asked him whether he wanted John to pray for him.

The man agreed, and John, fearful of a scene in the lobby, suggested they go outside. Outside on the sidewalk by some bushes John prayed, and the man fell backward into the bushes, his legs protruding onto the sidewalk. John was uncertain what he should do next. In church at the Vineyard, there would be an appropriate way of handling the situation. But not here.

So he did what he had done before. He bent down and began to "bless whatever God was doing." As he did so, he heard footsteps approaching and turned to see two security agents bearing down on him, "Stop! Security."

John stood and took a couple of paces toward the men, realizing they thought he had been mugging the man on the ground. "I wasn't mugging the guy! I was praying for him—and God did that." Slowly and semistuporous, the man on the ground had begun to get up. "Tell them I was praying for you!"

The man complied, "Yes—he was just praying..."

"Well, we don't allow that around here!"

John protested. "But I can't stop God..."

"What are you doing here anyway?"

"I'm waiting to eat in the restaurant."

The security agent turned to the Canadian. "And what are you doing?"

"I'm a guest at the hotel."

The agents stared at each other and shook their heads. After a further admonition to the two men, they turned and left them.

Most people who fall are at least partially aware of their surroundings and have a sense of the passage of time. But their sense of time (like Rip Van Winkle's) is impaired. I have received reports such as, "I thought I had been 'out' about 15 minutes—but it was nearer 2 hours," or, "It felt like just a few minutes, but when I came to I was still real groggy, and I'd been on the floor for 4 hours. Nearly everyone had gone home. I was real surprised."

VISIONS

Not infrequently, people who fall report visions. Skepticism about the validity of these is understandable, and caution should be exercised in attaching significance to every reported vision. But some are undoubtedly from God.

At a prayer meeting in New York at the beginning of the last decade, participants were interceding for the city when a young man received a vision, the details of which he later revealed. He saw hands offering him a bowl or cup to drink. Into the bowl had been poured the vileness of the sins of New York. The young man cried out, "No, no!" turning his head away and attempting to push the cup from him.

Instantly he was struck to the ground. A heaviness fell on all the approximately 75 participants, who without exception also fell to the ground. John Wimber, who was present, remembers a sense of heaviness he was unable to support, that made him slump to the ground, where he remained sobbing, along with many others, as he prayed for the city.

The young man has for several years now been walking the streets of New York, ministering powerfully to the homeless, alcoholics, drug addicts, prostitutes, and others. The genuineness of the vision is attested in this case by its results. A young man was thrust into an effective gospel ministry of a kind that few of us would choose. The ministry has brought no personal glory or prestige to him. The vision he received also had a profound moral significance. It had to do with a horror of the vile sins of a city, and the call of the evangelist or prophet to know that horror in experience.

It was the moral and ethical quality as well as the emphasis on a divine solution to the moral dilemma that distinguished John's visions in Revelation from the mass of spurious visions in the apocalyptic literature of his day. The imagery was very similar, much of it being drawn from Daniel's prophetic writings. But unlike the book of Revelation, the rest of the literature is merely predictive. There is a notable absence of any concern about sin and righteousness or a need for redemption. This precise note in the young man's vision (in New York) also suggests the vision's authenticity.

DEMONIC IMITATIONS AND MANIFESTATIONS

As discussed earlier, the powers of darkness may imitate many divine supernatural acts. As we shall see again later, this became evident long ago when Moses found himself face-to-face with the magicians of Egypt (Exod. 7:8-13,20-22; 8:5-7). Therefore, the form the manifestation takes is not a reliable guide to what is taking place.

Shaking has been seen when the Holy Spirit comes on people (Jer. 23:9, RSV). It is also a recognized sign of a demonic trance. "Doc Anderson" collaborates with certain oil-well drillers. His hands shake, stigmata appear and where the blood drips, oil is found. I have seen his performances on TV, and of course it could be faked (except there is the little matter of productive oil wells dug where experts had declared no oil could be found).

I can think of many other instances that could cause confusion. For instance, consider the rapid side-to-side movement of the head that makes the face a blur. I have only seen this once. It was in a Singapore church. At the name of Jesus, a demonized man was flung several feet, landing on his hands and knees before what I believe was a communion table. His nose must have been no more than a millimeter from a sharp corner of the table, and his head was thrashing with frightening violence from side to side, having a range of movement that seemed to exceed what is normal and at a speed that made his features a blur.

At the time, I assumed those particular movements must be characteristic of demonization; that is, wherever they might appear would be a sure sign a demon was around. I am more cautious now. Having seen some of the strange ways people react to the power of the Holy Spirit, the man's movements could have been a demonic imitation of something produced by the Holy Spirit.

Demons do, however, have certain characteristic ways of manifesting themselves. The most obvious are verbal expressions of defiance and hostility (commonly in a changed voice). I remember sitting in the pastor's office of a Baptist church counseling a woman, when from the other side of the church I heard a man's voice roaring in rage. When I went out to see what was happening, I saw my wife and a colleague ministering to a lady who at that point was huddled in a pew. The defiance had come from a demon they had just cast out of the woman.

Not infrequently when I pray for someone in a meeting, the person will immediately go into a trance-like state. Eyes may roll back, the person may fall, may begin to make epileptiform movements—may even foam and dribble mucus from his or her mouth. The signs are not necessarily a proof of a demon (the person may be having a grand mal seizure). Usually, at that point I demand in the name of Jesus that any demon who might be present give me its name. Once the demon does so, I know where I am and can act accordingly.

On one occasion when I addressed a demon I suspected was present in a woman, the woman (she herself was shocked by what happened) suddenly writhed toward me feet first, reared up and hissed in my face. I would say that the manifestation, symbolically serpentine, was characteristically demonic. But there is room for more careful research in this area.

Sometimes in Wimber's meetings a scream or a commotion will occur, either during the message or else when people are praying for someone present. Often this is an indication of demonic activity. An experienced team usually tries to conduct the victim to a quiet, secluded area where he or she may be appropriately helped.

DRUNK WITH THE SPIRIT

In meetings where the Holy Spirit's power is strongly manifest, some people may seem a little drunk. However, I have never seen them noisy or obstreperous in this state. They may describe a "heaviness" that is on them. Their speech may be slightly slurred, their movements uncoordinated. They may need support to walk. They show little concern about what anyone will think of their condition and are usually a little dazed. The condition may endure several hours.

Is it possible that Paul's words in Ephesians 5:18 refer to such a state, "Do not get drunk on wine....Instead, be filled with the Spirit"? Obviously, being filled with the Spirit is preferable to being drunk, however one understands the verse. But it is possible that two kinds of "drunkenness" are being compared.

If so, I would like to have seen what happened at Pentecost (Acts 2). The apostles were certainly speaking in recognizable languages, and evidently without any Galilean accent. But did some of them seem a little drunk? People do not usually accuse others of being drunk unless something about the performance suggests it. If you see an uneducated man whose eye is clear and whose movements are well controlled talking in a recognizable language, drunkenness is not the first explanation that comes into your head. It is possible that what happened to some of them at Pentecost was what I have observed in many other people on whom the Spirit rests.

THE CENTRAL QUESTION

A reading of the history of revivals will bring to light many other forms of manifestation. Anyone interested in traveling widely and recording what is currently taking place will undoubtedly add much to what I have recorded above. How worthwhile such research would be is debatable. The central question has to do with whether God is active or not, and on whether revival could be beginning.

If I am right, what are the implications for each one of us personally? My aim is not to promote manifestations so much as to encourage us all to be open to what God is doing and to what I believe He wants to do in sending revival. I do not want you to close your mind to what God may be doing or to go chasing after unusual experiences under a misapprehension that you need to be "zapped" to be revived. Unusual experiences are by definition not part of normal discipleship. If God should have an unusual experience in store for you, and if that should help your relationship with God, well and good. But the experience itself is neither here nor there, except for being an evidence that God is moving in revival. It is your relationship with God that matters.

Revivals make people holy. Your goal and mine must be to pursue God Himself and to let Him make us holy. It must be to inquire whether further steps of obedience are called for in some area of our lives where we may have been closed to Him. It must also be to collaborate with His purposes by praying according to His will. And to pray such prayers means we must know what God wants to do in our time.

Notes

1. Charles T. Tart, *Altered States of Consciousness* (Garden City, NY: Anchor, 1969).
2. Charles Wesley, as quoted in Arnold A. Dallimore, *George Whitefield*, vol. 1 (Westchester, IL: Crossway, 1980), p. 326.
3. John White, *The Golden Cow* (Downers Grove, IL: InterVarsity Press, 1979).
4. John White, *Flirting with the World* (Wheaton, IL: Harold Shaw, 1982), pp. 113-25.
5. Douglas R. Groothuis, *Unmasking the New Age* (Downers Grove, IL: InterVarsity Press, 1985), p. 24.
6. Louis Linn, M.D., as quoted in Harold A. Kaplan and Benjamin J. Sadock, eds., *Comprehensive Textbook of Psychiatry*, 4th ed. (Baltimore, MD: Williams and Wilkins, 1985), p. 567.
7. Charles A. Johnson, *The Frontier Camp Meeting* (Dallas, TX: Southern Methodist University Press, 1955), p. 55.

8. James B. Finley, as quoted in Johnson, pp. 64-65.
9. Henry Venn, as quoted in Dallimore, vol. 2, pp. 392-393.
10. Jonathan Edwards, *The Works of Jonathan Edwards*, vol. 2 (Edinburgh, Scotland: The Banner of Truth, 1974), p. 265.
11. John Wesley, *The Works of John Wesley*, vol. 1 (Peabody, MA: Hendrickson, 1872; rpt. 1984), pp. 234, 236.
12. John Cennick, as quoted in Arnold A. Dallimore, *George Whitefield*, vol. 1 (Westchester, IL: Crossway, 1980), p. 327.
13. Ralph Humphries, as quoted in Dallimore, vol. 1, p. 326.
14. Wesley, vol. 1, p. 190.
15. Ibid., pp. 36-37.
16. Edwards, vol. 2, p. 261.
17. Ibid., pp. 257-277.
18. Rudolph Otto, *The Idea of the Holy* (New York: Oxford University Press, 1950), pp. 8-9.
19. Ibid., p. 10.
20. Ibid., p. 13.
21. Edwards, vol. 1, p. 238.
22. Alexander Webster, as quoted in Dallimore, vol. 2, p. 128.
23. Edwards, p. 348.
24. Ibid., vol. 2, p. 407.
25. John Hamilton, as quoted in Dallimore, vol. 1, p. 123.
26. Dallimore, vol. 2, pp. 129-130.
27. Edwards, vol. 1, p. 354.
28. Ibid., p. 367.
29. Johnson, *The Frontier Camp Meeting*, p. 60.
30. Edwards, vol. 1, p. 376.

13

A SOCIAL ANTHROPOLIGIST'S ANALYSIS OF CONTEMPORARY HEALING

DAVID C. LEWIS

What kinds of healings are associated with contemporary Christian healing ministries, conferences for training Christians in praying for healing, and such ministry in many evangelical churches? How do medical doctors perceive the healings? How do healings relate to the revelations known as "words of knowledge" (1 Cor. 12:8; 14:24,25)?[1] Can associated physical phenomena be explained by psychological mechanisms? Why does God appear to heal some kinds of people more often than others?

These are important questions, which for the most part have been ignored by critics of healing ministries, who have tended to concentrate on theological and historical questions rather than medical, sociological, or psychological aspects.[2] These are the dimensions to healing I wish to examine in this chapter, since the theological issues have been addressed by other contributors to this book. In particular, I shall present some of the detailed findings from my comprehensive follow-up study of one of John Wimber's conferences as an example of contemporary cases of healing.

In 1986, a detailed questionnaire was given to all those who attended John Wimber's *Signs and Wonders (Part II)* conference in Harrogate, England. The questionnaires were collected just before the final session of the conference. Out of the 2,470 people registered for the conference, 1,890 returned usable forms, producing a response rate of 76.5 percent (which is very high in comparison with most sociological surveys). These were processed through a computer at Nottingham University.

Using a random number table, I then selected from these 1,890 respondents a random sample of 100 people, whom I followed up between 6 and 10 months after the conference. I was able to conduct in-depth personal interviews with 93 of them, involving my traveling almost literally throughout the length and breadth of Britain. Another 7 people had to be interviewed by telephone or by mail because they lived outside Britain or were unavailable for other reasons. My research combined the breadth of the questionnaire with the depth of the interviews. Some other potentially interesting cases outside the random sample were also followed up by telephone, mail, or personal interview. Where appropriate, specialist medical opinions were sought regarding various cases of healing. Although each patient signed a form consenting to the release of confidential medical information, the doctors varied considerably in the extent to which they were willing to cooperate.

Much criticism of evangelical healing ministries and, in particular, of John Wimber and the Vineyard Christian Fellowship has been expressed in print recently. The research described above followed the preliminary study I had undertaken in 1985 of John Wimber's *Signs and Wonders (Part I)* conference in Sheffield. My report on that conference was published as an appendix to Wimber's book *Power Healing*.[3] The report was apparently available to Donald Lewis, who later wrote that his intention was, "to reflect upon my own experience of John Wimber's conferences, rather than to critique what he has written (although I have read his books). My aim is to evaluate one such gathering from the vantage point of an observer-participant."[4]

Although participant observation is a standard research method among cultural anthropologists like myself, it is almost always supplemented by indepth interviews and attempts to understand the perspectives of the participants themselves. Unfortunately, almost all of Lewis's evaluation was of Wimber's theology. He gave no evidence of any interviews with other participants, assessments of the accuracy of "words of knowledge," evaluations of the kinds of healings which took place or analyses of other aspects of the ministry.

What sounds more impressive is the so-called "medical evaluation of a Wimber meeting" presented by Verna Wright, FRCS, Professor of Rheumatology at Leeds University, when addressing a conference in London on 15 November 1986. Wright's so-called "medical evaluation" is based on the second-hand opinions of five unnamed doctors whose description gives no indication of any attempt to interview other participants.[5] As is the case with other observers, many of the comments tend to be more of the nature of *opinion* than *fact*, largely because of the absence of systematic data collection.

MEDICAL VIEWS OF HEALING

It is not surprising that Wright should have come across cases of people who were not healed after receiving prayer at one of John Wimber's conferences, because these are the very people who are likely to go back again to their doctors afterwards for further treatment. By contrast, many of those who had received healing after prayer had seen no need to consult their doctors again. This process means that some medical doctors are likely to hear a disproportionate number of "negative" cases.

Other doctors, however, confirm that they have come across cases of apparently inexplicable recovery following Christian prayer. "More and more Christian doctors, cautious by nature and training, are beginning to expect the unexpected. In ways that defy medical explanation they sometimes see instantaneous, sometimes gradual, reversals of the disease process. 'It's an answer to prayer,' they confess."[6]

Some of the most thorough investigations in this area have been conducted by Dr. Rex Gardner, a Consultant Obstetrician and Gynecologist. His presidential address to the Newcastle and Northern Counties Medical Society was published in the prestigious *British Medical Journal* and contained half a dozen medically documented cases of otherwise inexplicable healings associated with prayer in Christ's name.[7] Following his article in the *British Medical Journal*, Gardner wrote a book containing many more well-documented contemporary cases of Christian healings, which could appropriately be described as "miraculous."[8]

One of the cases, for example, concerns Rebecca, a nine-year-old girl whose audiograms and tympanograms showed a hearing loss of 70 decibels in her right ear and 40 in her left. "The consultant confirmed that she was nerve deaf

in both ears and that there was no cure, no operation, nothing he could do."
However, Rebecca and others among her family and friends began to pray for
God's healing. On 8 March 1983, Rebecca had to visit the audiologist to obtain
a new hearing aid. The following night, at 9:30 P.M. she came running down
from bed to say, "Mummy, I can hear!" Her parents tested her and found she
could hear even their whispers.

When her parents telephoned the consultant, he replied, "I don't believe
you. It's not possible. All right, if some miracle has happened I am delighted.
Have the audiograms done." Rebecca's audiograms and tympanograms were
normal on the 10th March 1983—48 hours after the audiologist had seen her
and knew she was deaf. Both the audiologist and the consultant were unable to
give any kind of known medical explanation for the healing.[9]

In my follow-up study of John Wimber's Harrogate conference, I found
a number of cases which were similarly difficult or impossible to explain
away by reference to known medical processes. One of those I followed up
told me how in 1983 she had received many injuries to her neck, back, arms,
and right knee when she had been involved in a "severe car crash." She had
prolonged treatment, including frequent physiotherapy sessions, but continued to have pain in her right knee. In 1986, a consultant diagnosed her as
having contracted Hoffa's disease in her knee. This is "post-traumatic intra-
pattellar fat pad syndrome," but once the condition is established it is "virtually incapable of cure other than by surgical excision [i.e., cutting out] of
the painful piece of fat."

However, at the Harrogate conference this same woman received prayer
for her knee and discovered a very significant improvement: "Now it's so much
better that the only time I feel it is if I've been for a long walk or bang it against
something...[such as] when I knocked it against some steel railings and knocked
the knee badly." She therefore said it was "90 percent to 95 percent healed."
Some people, however, might say it was actually 100 percent healed, if these isolated incidents were due not to the Hoffa's disease but to natural bruising or
other factors.

In this case, the woman's doctor, in reply to my inquiry, could only repeat
the consultant's opinion that it is "virtually incapable of cure" except through
surgery. He then commented, "I gather she is now very much better and she
regards herself as cured."[10]

This kind of case certainly does not fit the superficial opinion (unsupported by any objective evidence) that the healings which occur at such conferences "are not real miracles at all but are only self-induced 'mind cures' for relatively innocuous and unverifiable ailments."[11] In an appendix to my book

Healing: Fiction, Fantasy or Fact? I list all the different types of physical complaints for which people received prayer at Harrogate.[12]

I also give the maximum, minimum, and mean (average) degrees of healing for each condition on a nine-point scale from no healing (point one) through to total healing (point nine). The 68 cases reported of total healing included conditions as diverse as arthritis in the neck, hand or leg; severe bone malformation due to injury; painful and swollen lymph glands; inability to hear in the higher register; eye squint; hernia; prolapse of the womb; cystitis; allergic reactions; vaginal bleeding (which had been continuing for 25 days); sleeping sickness; endometriosis; urinary problems; fever; breathing difficulties; and pain behind the eyes.

Among the 1,890 people who filled in a questionnaire, 621 had received prayer for some kind of physical healing. As some of these had prayer for more than one condition, there were a total of 867 cases. By the end of the conference, some noticeable improvement was reported in 58 percent of these cases. It is significant that, when I followed up the random sample of 100 people between six months and a year later, virtually the same percentage (57 percent) reported a sustained and noticeable improvement since the conference.

Although healings did take place at the conference itself, the primary intention of the conference was to train Christians to pray for healing in their own local situations. I therefore asked those I interviewed to what extent they had put the teachings into practice, and what results they had obtained. Though many had prayed for other Christians, with varying results, some of the most interesting cases came from the minority who had been willing to try praying in this way for non-Christians. Often they saw signs of God's power in unexpected ways. For instance, the following account was related to me by a young woman in a northern English city:

> We'd been doing a scheme of door-to-door visitation...but I started off on the wrong street. I knocked on the door and then realized that we'd already done that street—but in fact no one had visited that house. I explained who we were and asked if there was anything she needed. She then said, "My baby's got cancer."
>
> ...I'd only been a Christian eight months, and it was a first in everything. I spoke to [my vicar] and he encouraged me to pray for the baby....I'd been to Harrogate with him—just for the last day, and then I went to the team visit at the Grammar school—and he told me to do what I'd seen them doing.
>
> I saw stage by stage, week by week, [the baby's] recovery....One

day...I prayed all day....I couldn't get him out of my mind....Even by
bedtime I was still praying. I was about to give up because I felt
God wouldn't heal unless [the mother] made a commitment [to
Christ]. The next day [the baby] was pronounced healed.

From the hospital consultant who treated the baby, I was able to obtain
copies of the baby's records. They confirmed this account in detail, and showed
that the tumor did suddenly disappear in between two of the hospital examinations. It was also at the time when this young Christian woman had been
praying.[13]

The consultant claimed that this was a case of "spontaneous remission."
However, the available medical literature on this particular type of tumor—
called infantile fibrosarcoma—contains no reference to any other case of "spontaneous remission." A detailed follow-up study of 48 cases showed that 8 patients
had died and the others had been treated by surgery, sometimes followed by
chemotherapy or radiotherapy. The more severe cases had required amputation
of the limb. There were no recorded cases of "spontaneous remission."[14]

The case detailed above, in which the tumor disappeared after persistent prayer and without any medical treatment, was in fact a severe case. It
involved a malignant tumor which had grown around the nerves and arteries.
Treatment of it would normally have necessitated amputation of the baby's
arm. The consultant had no other explanation but the rather unlikely one of so-
called "spontaneous remission."[15]

"Spontaneous remission" is in itself a loose, catch-all term, which does
not explain anything but simply admits that an explanation for the recovery is
beyond the present bounds of medical knowledge. Christians who have been
praying interpret the events as a divine intervention, but the doctor has no
other medical term than the rather hollow one of "spontaneous remission." In
a case of this kind, to speak in terms of probabilities and statistics seems a more
fruitful approach than arguing about whether or not the healing can be
"explained away" by calling it "spontaneous remission." Such arguments involve
the well-known problems of the "God of the gaps" theories, and seem to involve
a rather mechanistic, nineteenth-century view of the universe.

Nowadays, scientific progress in fields as diverse as genetics and nuclear
physics makes much more use of probability and statistics. In medicine, too, new
drugs are tested and the results analyzed according to whether or not they are
associated with a statistically significant difference among a sample of patients:
they do not necessarily produce cures in everyone. Similarly, in examining
cases of miraculous healing, a more fruitful approach is to ask how likely it is

that particular results would have been produced by known medical treatments. Often, we find that prayer is associated with outcomes which would have been very unlikely from a medical point of view.

WORDS OF KNOWLEDGE

A statistical approach is also useful in analyzing the revelations commonly referred to as "words of knowledge."[16] Certainly some of these seem to be "general" and could be expected to apply to at least one or two people in a congregation. More specific ones, however, are less easily dismissed, as I demonstrated in my report on Wimber's Sheffield conference.[17] A good example of a highly specific word of knowledge occurred at the Harrogate conference, when John Wimber announced the following revelation:

> There's a woman named Janet who at eleven years of age had a minor accident that's proven to be a problem throughout her adult life. It had something to do with an injury to her tailbone but now it's caused other kinds of problems and so there's radiating pain that comes down over her—er—lower back and down over her backside and down her legs. It has something to do with damage to a nerve but it also has to do with some sort of a functional problem with the—um—I think it's called the sacroiliac.

Indeed, someone who matched this description exactly was in attendance. She was in the overflow hall down the road, where she received prayer for healing. More than a year later she wrote to me, "My back appears healed and I am not receiving any discomfort from it." Elsewhere I have analyzed this example and worked out the statistical probabilities of correctly guessing all these features by chance alone. I found that, even with very conservative figures, the chances against accurately diagnosing *all* these various details by chance alone were at least 3 million to 1.[18]

Moreover, those responding to such highly specific words of knowledge also tended to report higher degrees of associated healing than those responding to less specific revelations. This process is obscured in the overall percentages of people receiving healing because at the Harrogate conference many more people responded to a less specific word of knowledge for anyone with skeletal problems (including arthritis) to receive prayer. Their degrees of healing ranged from "a great deal" or "total" healing through to "little" or none. It was only in the subsequent statistical analysis that I discovered the tendency for more specific words of knowledge to be associated with greater degrees of healing.[19]

One of Wimber's critics—Dr. Peter Masters of the Metropolitan Tabernacle in London—regards supernatural revelations in the Bible as divinely inspired but classifies contemporary revelations such as those given to Wimber as examples of occult "clairvoyance," which he describes as "disobedient to God's word and highly dangerous."[20] He is right about the dangers of occultism, but may be mistaken in classifying all modern revelations, including those occurring in Christian contexts, as "occult".[21]

Certainly I have found that the revelations associated with Wimber and some of his associates are far more specific and accurate than comparable data available from scientific studies of "extrasensory perception" or of the revelations attributed to psychics and mediums.[22] There is also evidence of fraud involving a well-known British medium named Doris Stokes.[23] However, in my studies of Wimber's conferences I have been able to rule out the likelihood of fraud on the grounds that those registering for the conference had no previous contact with the American visitors. The conferences were advertised in popular Christian magazines and organized by various groups of local Christians who had no control over those who might apply to attend. Moreover, through their exposure to the training received at Wimber's conferences, many "ordinary" Christians have also begun to receive similar kinds of divine revelations in the course of their own ministries.[24]

INNER HEALING

Another area of controversy concerns what is variously called "inner healing," "healing of the memories" or "emotional healing." Often this approach to healing is concerned with overcoming the effects of past hurts which can affect attitudes and behavior in the present. Matzat argues, however, that the main founders of "inner healing," especially Agnes Sanford and Morton Kelsey, took their ideas from secular psychology. In particular, the ideas behind ministering to childhood hurts buried in the subconscious are said to be taken from Sigmund Freud's "depth psychology."[25]

To a large extent, it is possible to accept this general criticism of Sanford and Kelsey even if one might quibble with some of the details. However, influential practitioners of inner healing are aware of some of these difficulties and they warn against the uncritical use of certain kinds of inner healing. For example, John Wimber writes:

I am using the term "inner healing" sparingly...because different authors use it to mean so many different things, many of which I do not agree with. In many instances inner healing is based on secular psychological views of how our personalities are formed and influenced. But where these views contradict the biblical teaching, they must be firmly rejected.[26]

Matzat further claims that methods of "visualizing" Jesus in various scenes from the past (as advocated by Agnes Sanford or Rita Bennett) were borrowed from Carl Jung, another major founder of modern psychology.[27] However, although I came across many cases of inner healing in my study of John Wimber's Harrogate conference, very few of them involved a person receiving a visual picture of Jesus. Wimber says they do not encourage such visualization. Instead, most instances of inner healing were dealt with by *forgiveness, repentance, confession,* and other widely recognized biblical principles, without recourse to "visualization."[28]

Nevertheless, there *are* cases in which Jesus *does* appear to people and minister appropriately to their inner hurts. One of the most dramatic instances concerns Jill, a 17-year-old girl who had come to live with her pastor's family. The pastor's wife told me the following story:

Her parents divorced when Jill was four years old. Her mother was anti-Christian and would have nothing in the house which was Christian. Jill became a Christian when she was ten and had to carry her Bible with her and sleep with it under her mattress or else it would be destroyed....Her mother's boyfriend subjected her to all forms of abuse—everything. Jill's sister who is two years younger had everything lavished upon her but Jill was totally deprived....

After she came to live here, she woke every night screaming with nightmares from what her mother's boyfriend had done to her. No man could go near, only I could....

[One night we] heard her rattling the door in her nightdress. We took her back to bed and as we were doing so we were aware she was talking—in a very childish voice....She talked as a four year old....It was the time of the divorce and she relived it: horror and horror. ([Her mother's boyfriend] sexually handled her, burned her, choked her—she was literally going red in the face and not breathing: we couldn't believe what we were experiencing.) She would even say what she had for dinner—but at the end of the day said, "My Jesus is coming. He's so *big.*" It was so delightful. She gave a full description of how he was dressed: "Long, white and shiny, and a shiny thing round his waist. Gold varnish on feet and hands, a pretty sticky-up thing on his head—and his *eyes,* his *eyes...*"—four year old language. The first one was "Mummy's friend" but "My friend is big—my friend is bigger than your friend. Mind your head, Jesus, don't bump your head on the door." Then he'd come and minister to her. He had pockets on his robe: "I wonder what he's got for me?" Cream to soothe bruises or beating, plasters to put on. Something to eat—she was starved as well. She would go through the motions—a big strawberry milkshake....

There is no way in which I could attribute this girl's experience to the influence of suggestion. In fact, Jill's pastor and his wife recorded her later experiences and were able to confirm the accuracy of her memories from her own diaries. On successive nights, they took turns to be present in Jill's room when they began to hear her talking. On two occasions, while Jill was being ministered to by Jesus, they saw a mist or cloud filling part of the room. It was so dense on the second occasion that it "covered half a chair, blotted out the dressing table and just a bit of the mirror was poking out of the mist." They later identified it with the Shekhinah cloud of God's presence and glory, which is mentioned in the Bible (e.g., Exod. 33:9; 2 Chron. 5:13,14; Matt. 17:5).

One other detail further highlights the divine character of Jill's visions. On one occasion, Jesus brought her a "knickerbocker glory" ice cream with a large strawberry at the bottom. Later, when she went on holiday with her pastor's family, they all decided to have knickerbocker glories—Jill's first taste of a "material" one. Hers alone turned out to have a large strawberry at its base!

Jill's experiences continued for a few months and were punctuated by a recurring vision of a house, the rooms of which symbolized various areas of her past life. As these were dealt with, the doors were shut on them. Finally, Jesus took her outside the front door and across the lawn to where her pastor and his wife were standing. He handed her over to them, indicating that her treatment was over. After this, her visions of Jesus ceased.

The extent of her healing is shown by the fact that she has now been accepted for training as a psychiatric nurse. During her interview for the course, she was asked how she felt about dealing with sexually abused children. Jill replied that she could handle it because she had been through that experience herself. When asked if she needed counseling for it, she said she did not need it and told the interviewers about her own experiences of healing. The fact that they recognized her healing and accepted her for training as a psychiatric nurse testifies to the effectiveness of what Jesus had done for her. Moreover, because of her own experiences she now seems to have a special rapport with children who have been sexually abused, who instinctively seem to know they can trust Jill.

We have to ask, therefore, whether God can make use of *methods* at certain times which appear to parallel those of secular psychology. Essentially, we have to ask whether the one who created humanity and designed human psychology in the first place also knows the kinds of techniques which are most appropriate for healing it. Are these methods ones which God has made available because He knows that sometimes they might be necessary?

Confusion has arisen because of a failure to distinguish between *sources* and *methods*.[29] For physical healing, it is clear that God makes use of a variety of *methods*, so why should the same not be true of emotional or psychological healing? The Gospels record that Jesus used many different *methods* for healing conditions, which are all described as "blindness" (though the causes in each case are not specified). On one occasion, Jesus gave a word of command (Mark 10:52), on another occasion, spat in the blind man's eyes and then laid hands on them (Mark 8:23-25), and another time rebuked a demonic spirit causing the blindness (Matt. 12:22). On yet another occasion, He spat on the ground and mixed His saliva with mud before applying it to the blind man's eyes and telling him to wash it off in the pool of Siloam (John 9:6,7).

It seems that Jesus may not have been the first to use spit in healing contexts but that He made use of an existing practice. In the same way, there are no scriptural precedents for the divine filling of dental cavities, but such miracles have been well attested in recent decades from both North and South America.[30] If God can make use of *methods* which are widely used by dentists of all religious persuasions, or none, can He also make use of techniques for psychological or emotional healing which were humanly pioneered in other contexts?

Most biblical passages relating to forgiveness and Christian attitudes are addressed to groups rather than to individuals. Their focus is more on *preventing* the need for inner healing than on giving directions how to go about it. However, in actual practice, the Holy Spirit appears to make use of a wide repertoire of *methods*, which in themselves might be neutral but can be used for either positive or negative ends.[31]

PHYSICAL AND SPIRITUAL PHENOMENA

Since John White has contributed a chapter to this book concerning the physical manifestations which sometimes seem to accompany the working of the Holy Spirit, here I shall confine myself to a few brief remarks arising out of my own investigations.[32]

When some people at a Baptist church in Leeds began to display behavior such as shaking, weeping or falling over (Jer. 23:9; Dan. 10:10; Neh. 8:6,9; John 18:6; Rev. 1:10,17,18)[33] during a healing service led by some of Wimber's team, a critic later described the events as a case of mass hysteria. This opinion was expressed by a theologian having no training in psychology or psychiatry. However, it led me to include in my follow-up interviews a simple psychological test, which gives a preliminary indication of the plausibility of this explanation.

A retrospective study of a case of mass hysteria among some English schoolgirls confirmed the hypothesis of Professor Eysenck that more hysterical individuals tend to rank high on scales of both extroversion and neuroticism.[34] However, only 12 out of the 100 people in my random sample ranked high on both these scales, and all but 2 of them were only just over the border into the "high" category on only one of the two scales. Nevertheless, virtually all of these 100 people had themselves experienced at least some of the physical phenomena. I found that reports of these experiences were spread across all the different psychological categories of people and were by no means confined to any one psychological "type." This argues against any theory that these physical phenomena can be explained away by a theory of mass hysteria.

Another theory is that these phenomena can be explained away as a form of learned behavior. A number of experts agree that some form of autosuggestion can influence such behavior in at least certain cases. In my questionnaire at John Wimber's Harrogate conference, I asked people to indicate whether or not they had experienced such phenomena in the past or for the first time at Harrogate. The question then arose how to interpret the statistics. For instance, among those who had fallen over (referred to by some as "being slain in the Spirit") in the past, 69 percent (499 out of 725) did not repeat the behavior again at the Harrogate conference. It might therefore be argued that this was not "learned behavior." On the other hand, the fact that 31 percent did fall over again might be regarded either as "learned behavior" or else as further genuine ministry from God which necessitated this kind of phenomenon.

However, it was clear that "milder" phenomena such as the tingling or shaking of hands, weeping or changes in breathing were much more likely to be repeated or else to be manifested for the first time than were more "dramatic" forms of behavior such as falling over, screaming or shouting. These "milder" phenomena are often associated with ministry to others (including weeping in the context of intercessory prayer) and are likely to be repeated, whereas phenomena connected with receiving ministry tend to recur less often and usually cease once the ministry is completed.

For well-known phenomena such as falling over, it was more difficult to test for the influence of suggestion because many of those present at the Harrogate conference had attended other Wimber conferences or heard about them. This was particularly the case for a dozen commonly occurring phenomena publicly mentioned on the third day of the 1985 Sheffield conference during a workshop on physical healing—by which time the participants had already witnessed most of these forms of behavior.

However, when I later tried to classify all the different kinds of phenomena actually reported on their questionnaires by participants at the Harrogate conference, I found that I needed *over two hundred different categories*. Most of these were difficult or else impossible to explain away as due to "suggestion." They included sensations of something like "electricity" or a "force field...like something out of *Star Wars*."[35] A few people spoke not of heat (which could be due to suggestion) but of "cold sensations" or "severe chilling."[36]

Several people mentioned experiences of a heavy weight or pressure upon parts of their bodies, particularly the head or chest.[37] Others felt what they variously described as like a "mantle," a "blanket" or a "heavy sheepskin coat" over them. A few found themselves unexpectedly outside their physical bodies, in one case looking down on her own body receiving ministry while "resting in the Spirit" on the floor.[38] Two people mentioned smelling fragrances of flowers. One of them afterward asked the young German man next to her if he had smelt them too. At first he replied "No," but then he "reluctantly" told her that during that session he had "walked in the garden with the Lord."[39]

It is difficult, and in several cases probably impossible, to explain away these and other kinds of experiences as due merely to "suggestion." There are also many other accounts of people with no prior exposure to this kind of ministry, or teaching about it, who have nevertheless experienced some of these phenomena. A clear example occurred in 1992 at my own church in England. In my message on being "open to God," I had not mentioned these kinds of phenomena at all, but when the Holy Spirit was invited to minister to people, the first person to display any kind of "unusual" behavior—and the only one to "rest in the Spirit"—was a Ukrainian girl who was visiting us at the time. I knew she had definitely not come across such phenomena previously in her limited contacts with Orthodox or Catholic churches in the Ukraine.

WHOM DOES GOD HEAL?

We do not know why God seems to heal some people but not others. Why did Jesus heal one man at the pool of Bethesda and apparently leave other invalids alone? Wimber suggests that a clue is given in John 5:19, when Jesus says the Son can do nothing by Himself but only what He sees the Father doing, but this still leaves unanswered the question of why some are healed when others are not.

The fact that some 57 percent of my sample reported a sustained and noticeable physical improvement following prayer has been regarded by some as a surprisingly high percentage. Others, however, ask why the remaining 43 percent did not receive such healing.

John Wimber himself only prayed with a small number of these people because the primary focus of the conference was on training other Christians how to pray for healing. The ones who prayed were usually members of Wimber's team, often in conjunction with ordinary delegates to the conference who later began to assume more leading roles in praying for others. Since the intention was to provide opportunities for "learning by doing," many of those praying for others were relatively inexperienced in this kind of ministry.

I have heard of one instance in which a woman who did not receive healing at a Wimber conference in Brighton was subsequently healed through the ministry of Andy Arbuthnot of the London Healing Mission.[40] Arbuthnot comments that in this case God wanted to first deal with the effects of certain emotional traumas in the woman's past, which were affecting her physical health. Presumably these other kinds of needs were not discerned by those ministering to her at Brighton.

Another comment on my statistic of 57 percent receiving noticeable and sustained physical healing comes from the director of Ellel Grange, a healing center in the north of England, who assumed that some of those ministering had not discerned the need for rebuking evil spirits associated with certain illnesses. He presumed that the rate of healing would have been higher if more of those praying for others had discerned the need for a ministry of deliverance from demons.[41]

Such ideas may account for some but by no means all cases in which no healing was received. A good example is that of Jennifer Rees-Larcombe, who between 1982 and 1987 had five serious and life-threatening attacks of encephalitis, an inflammation of the brain and meninges, further complicated by inflamed nerves. Between these acute episodes of illness, the inflammation of the brain, meninges, nerves, and muscles seemed to remain in a chronic form and was labeled by the neurologists as Myalgic Encephalomyelitis. Her continual pain, loss of balance, muscular weakness, and fatigue meant that she had to use a wheelchair when she needed to go more than a few yards. Doctors had recognized their inability to provide a cure, and their ability to only alleviate some of the symptoms.

Jennifer was receiving the highest level of State disability allowance and was told that her condition had deteriorated to the point where regular assessments would no longer be necessary—that is, they did not expect her to recover. She had also been to many Christian healing meetings but had not been healed. In fact, she wrote a book entitled Beyond Healing, and the Lord gave her a ministry of encouraging those who were suffering. However, when the Lord eventually did heal her, He chose to use not a well-known person such as John Wimber but a recently converted young black woman who, on account of her own past sins, had felt she was "not good enough" to pray for Jennifer. When she did pray, it was a simple and sincere prayer of faith through which God healed Jennifer.[42]

Jennifer's healing was publicized on the front page of the local free newspaper in her hometown of Tunbridge Wells, and became a well-known sign of God's power. In John's Gospel, Christ's miracles are often called "signs," and helped people to come to faith—but also provoked opposition from the religious establishment. Anecdotal evidence from those I interviewed who had prayed for God to heal non-Christians indicates that often noticeable signs of God's power were at work. It was not always the case, however, but even those who did not receive healing appreciated the concern shown by those who were willing to pray for them.

God's ways are above our ways, and His thoughts above our thoughts (Isa. 55:8,9). Nevertheless, I did find some further interesting clues about why certain categories of people appear to be healed more often than others. What was particularly interesting to me was to note the patterns which emerged from analyzing my results according to sociological variables, such as age and social class, which might give some clues toward understanding why God seems to heal some people but not others.

I found that younger people reported significantly greater degrees of healing than older people.[43] It should be stressed that this is a statistical finding and not an absolute rule: there are always exceptions. For example, a retired missionary told me how before the conference she had been unable to hear her watch tick with her right ear, but since then had been able to do so, and had ceased using a hearing aid.

To some extent, this tendency for higher rates of physical healing to be concentrated among younger people is linked to the fact that more specific words of knowledge tend to identify younger people. At the Harrogate conference, those under 40 constituted 85 percent of those responding to highly specific public words of knowledge. The percentage of those under 40 years old dropped to 60 percent for those responding to revelations of "medium" specificity and 46 percent for those responding to very general "words of knowledge." This correlation was a surprise to John Wimber when I told him about it. It is also statistically significant.[44]

My statistical findings nevertheless raise questions about God's priorities. We do not know the ages of most of the people whom Jesus healed, but we do know that five of the seven biblical accounts of a dead person being raised to life in response to specific prayer involve younger people. Though raising the dead may seem highly unusual to us today, the same correlation with younger people is found in most reports in our own century of raising the dead.[45] Certainly raising the dead is one instance in which a "psychosomatic" component to the healing can be ruled out.

One suggestion which tries to account for my statistical findings regarding physical healing is the idea that younger people have more "vitality" and heal quicker than older people, whose illnesses are often of a degenerative kind. However, the consistency between my statistical findings and the biblical accounts of raising the dead seems to indicate a wider theological explanation. I suggest that these statistical links with the age of the person healed relate to the fact that all healing is, in one sense, "temporary," insofar as we are healed into bodies which eventually die. Presumably there is a purpose if God does grant physical healing in this life. Might it be in order that the person healed might fulfill a particular role on this earth, for which the healing is necessary?

By contrast, I found no statistical links with age for what is variously known as "inner healing," "emotional healing," or "healing of the memories." Often this involves repentance from particular sins or the forgiveness of people against whom one has harbored resentments. Older people are as likely as younger people to report high degrees of inner healing. The result is often a purer life-style—which one might see as a preparation also for heaven. God desires this of all Christians, regardless of how old they are.

Another finding of mine was that those from the highest social class, who are also better educated, report significantly lesser degrees of physical healing.[46] This again ties in with what we read in the ministry of Jesus; He came to bring good news to the poor (Luke 4:18). Two of those from the higher social classes whom He did heal—Jairus's daughter and the nobleman's son—were actually younger people. Today, it might be that somehow the higher education of some people is itself a barrier to their receiving divine healing with a child-like faith.

A disproportionately high proportion of those attending Wimber's Harrogate conference were professional and better-educated people, such as doctors and clergy. Among those in my random sample who received physical healing, some of the more "dramatic" cases were reported by those from the "working class." For instance, one man had almost died after falling 50 feet from a crane. One of the bones in his leg had not grown back straight and "came out sideways as a spur," but the subsequent operation left his leg one-and-one-half inches shorter than the other. At Harrogate, "we prayed for my leg: I watched the leg come level with my right leg and even heard it grow—like breaking wood. I could not walk right for twenty years but now I can go walking with our vicar. I didn't wear a built-up shoe, just limped. I'd learnt to walk with my hip displaced but...my stature had got a wobble on....For the first time in twenty-one years I can walk without discomfort or pain, it seems level to me. People used to ask what was wrong with my leg but now they don't mention it."[47]

Another working-class person in my random sample told me how all her life she had suffered from hypersensitive teeth. Since childhood she had been unable to bite on ice cream, and in winter she had to keep her mouth closed or covered over while outside or else her teeth would throb. Even if she had kept her mouth shut, she could not have a warm drink for half an hour after coming indoors. I have been advised by a dentist that a healing of this degree of hypersensitivity is not the kind which could be attributed to a "normal" reduction of sensitivity over time.

However, after prayer at the Harrogate conference, this woman received complete healing. There was a slight recurrence later that evening, but the following day she was able to walk around outside in the cold and then immediately drink a cup of tea without any of the old sensation at all. Since then she had gone through a whole winter without any pain and without having to take any extra precautions while outside. Her dentist was aware of her hypersensitivity and sent me details from her record card, which confirmed the presence of persistent sensitivity over the previous 4 years and 10 months while she had been receiving treatment from him. At her next routine check-up after the Harrogate conference, the dentist wrote, "patient no longer complains of sensitive teeth."[48]

These examples of healings among "working class" people in Britain may not seem so dramatic when compared with the miraculous filling of dental cavities among very poor people, or cases of raising the dead in parts of Asia, Africa, and Latin America.[49] On a worldwide scale, we in the affluent West all belong to the richer social classes. Might it be for this reason that apparently more dramatic cases of healing seem to occur more often among Christians in Africa,

Latin America, and Asia? Or is it that we tend to rely on divinely ordained medicines and drugs, whereas God specially heals those deprived of access to such treatments?

DIVINE HEALING: FICTION OR FACT?

It is hard to escape the conclusion that many people have received through Christian prayer remarkable healings which bring glory to Christ and which are difficult or impossible to explain away in conventional medical terms. The available medical evidence and case histories indicate that the healings themselves have to be regarded as *facts*. Although some people might attempt to *interpret* those facts in a variety of ways, mounting evidence indicates that prayer in Christ's name seems to be an important factor in many medically inexplicable recoveries.

Moreover, the more specific public "words of knowledge" cannot be explained away as due to "coincidence" or human manipulation, but seem to indicate a source of knowledge beyond that of the person receiving the revelation. In the examples discussed in this chapter, the words of knowledge are associated with healings, but in other cases they can be of a moral nature, intended to lead a person to repentance.[50] This seems to indicate that the source of the revelations possesses consciousness and not only cares about healing and wholeness but is also *morally concerned* to move a person toward godly, biblical norms.

Similar kinds of difficulties arise in trying to explain away associated physical phenomena by reference to known psychological processes. In each case, known medical, psychological, or sociological explanations might account for a limited part of the available facts, but are unable to account for all of them.

A more fruitful approach seems to be a statistical one, which assesses the probability of specific outcomes occurring by "chance." Where these turn out to be highly unlikely, we have to ask if another factor needs to be taken into account. In the case under discussion, the participants attribute these "unexpected" outcomes to the power of God.

What is particularly interesting and unexpected is that the healings and words of knowledge discussed above indicate a significant "bias" in favor of the young and those from the lower social classes. This pattern is even clearer if we consider miraculous healings in a global perspective. The same pattern can also be discerned in the earthly ministry of Jesus. Therefore, the *underlying val-*

ues behind the manner in which God grants physical healing to certain people continue to be the same today as they were in the earthly ministry of the Lord Jesus Christ.

Notes

1. It is evident that for the Early Church, whose Bible was the Septuagint (the Greek translation of the Hebrew Bible), the "word" (Greek *logos*) in the phrase "word of knowledge" denoted "divine revelation" (hence *"word* of knowledge" = *"divine revelation* of knowledge") as the Hebrew *dābār* "word," which Greek *logos* renders in the Septuagint, frequently denotes (Hebrew *dābār* denoting "divine revelation," 1 Sam. 3:7; 9:27; 2 Sam. 7:4; 1 Kings 17:2,8; 6:11; 13:20; Isa. 2:1; Jer. 1:4,11; 2:1; 13:8; 16:1; 24:4; 28:12; 29:30; Ezek. 3:16; 6:1; 7:1; 12:1; Hos. 1:1; Mic. 1:1; Zeph. 1:1; *BDB*, p. 182b [meaning III.2]; O. Procksch, *"logos," TDNT*, vol. 4, pp. 94-96).

2. This certainly applies to two books which specifically purport to be examinations of the ministry of John Wimber, namely James R. Coggins and Paul G. Hiebert (eds.) *Wonders and the Word* (Winnipeg, Canada: Kindred Press, 1989) and R. Doyle (ed.) *Signs & Wonders and Evangelicals* (Randburg: Fabel, 1987).

3. David C. Lewis "Signs and Wonders in Sheffield," in John Wimber and Kevin Springer, *Power Healing* (San Francisco, CA: HarperSanFrancisco, 1987). Wimber adds a note on page 285 stating that during the October 1985 Sheffield conference he was not aware that I was conducting a study and had neither personally met nor heard of me. In fact, my article reached him only through a circuitous route (involving Bishop David Pytches and Dr. John White) and I did not expect the request for permission to publish it in *Power Healing*.

4. Donald M. Lewis "An Historian's Assessment," in Coggins and Hiebert (eds.) *Wonders and the Word*, p. 53.

5. Verna Wright "A Medical View of Miraculous Healing" in *Sword and Trowel* 1987, No.1, pp. 8ff.

6. Dr. Ann England (herself a medical doctor) in Ann England (ed.) *We Believe in Healing* (London, England: Marshall, Morgan & Scott, 1982), p. 15.

7. Rex Gardner, "Miracles of Healing in Anglo-Celtic Northumbria as Recorded by the Venerable Bede and his Contemporaries: A Reappraisal in the Light of Twentieth-Century Experience," *British Medical Journal*, 287, 24-31 December 1983, pp. 1927-1933. Gardner compared the contemporary accounts with similar ones recorded in seventh-century northern Britain by the Venerable Bede, arguing that the modern cases lend credence to Bede's account of similar miracles.

8. Rex Gardner *Healing Miracles: A Doctor Investigates* (London, England: Darton, Longman and Todd, 1986).

9. Gardner *Healing Miracles*, pp. 202-205. He also quotes from the medical report of the consultant ENT surgeon, who confirmed these details and concluded, "I can think of no rational explanation as to why her hearing returned to normal, there being a severe bilateral sensorineural loss."

10. David C. Lewis *Healing: Fiction, Fantasy or Fact?* (London, England: Hodder & Stoughton, 1989), pp. 28-30. (The consultant's remarks are also confirmed by the authoritative text in the U.K. on Hoffa's disease, Smillie's *Diseases of the Knee Joint*.)

11. James M. Boice, "A Better Way: The Power of the Word and Spirit," in Michael S. Horton (ed.) *Power Religion: The Selling out of the Evangelical Church?* (Chicago, IL: Moody Press, 1992), p. 127.

12. Lewis, *Healing: Fiction, Fantasy or Fact?*, op.cit., pp. 276-283.

13. For further medical details, see pages 221-228 of my book *Healing: Fiction, Fantasy or Fact?*, op.cit.

14. E. B. Chung and F. M. Enzinger "Infantile Fibrosarcoma," *Cancer*, 38 (1976), pp. 729-739.

15. He cited an article by P. W. Allen entitled "The fibromatoses: A clinicopathologic classification based on 140 cases," *American Journal of Surgical Pathology* (1977), pp. 255-270, 305-321, which mentioned the possibility of remission among the "fibromatoses." However, Allen recorded no cases of "spontaneous remission" among the tumors of the type which this baby had. In his article, he classified them as "congenital fibrosarcoma-like fibromatosis" but after his article was submitted for publication, Allen read Chung and Enzinger's article (cited above, note 14) and then added a footnote to his own article stating that the tumor should now be reclassified as an "infantile fibrosarcoma" rather than as a fibromatosis. Therefore Allen's remark about the possibility of "spontaneous remission" in the "fibromatoses," which this baby's consultant quoted to me, is not in fact applicable to this case.

16. See note 1 above.

17. David C. Lewis, "Signs and Wonders in Sheffield," in John Wimber with Kevin Springer *Power Healing*, op.cit., pp. 248, 250-259.

18. Lewis, *Healing: Fiction, Fantasy or Fact?*, op.cit., pp. 132-135.

19. Lewis, *Healing: Fiction, Fantasy or Fact?*, op.cit., pp. 155-157. Owing to the relatively small numbers who received prayer in response to highly specific words of knowledge, the correlation is statistically "noticeable"—meaning that it is almost statistically significant but would need a larger sample to confirm if this is the case.

20. Peter Masters, "The Texts all say No!" in *Sword & Trowel*, 1987 No.1, p.21 and *passim*.

21. Differences in psychological and other characteristics associated with Christian and occult involvements are shown by my research among a random sample of 108 nurses in Leeds: those nurses whose principal spiritual experience was the "presence of God" ranked higher than average, and those who had consulted spiritualist mediums ranked lower than average, on scales of psychological well-being, satisfaction with life, and two different measures of altruism. Using a statistical technique known as the analysis of variance, this

difference turned out to be statistically significant. Details are given in my chapter on "Spiritual Powers—Genuine and Counterfeit," in Michael Cole, Jim Graham, Tony Higton and David Lewis, *What Is the New Age?* (London, England: Hodder & Stoughton, 1990), pp. 112-120.

22. Lewis, *Healing: Fiction, Fantasy or Fact?*, op.cit., pp. 140-142; id., "Signs and Wonders in Sheffield," op.cit., pp. 251-259; id., "Is 'Renewal' Really 'New Age' in Disguise?" in Michael Cole, Jim Graham, Tony Higton and David Lewis, *What Is the New Age?*, op.cit., pp. 127-133.

23. See David C. Lewis, "Spiritual Powers—Genuine and Counterfeit," in Michael Cole, Jim Graham, Tony Higton and David Lewis, *What Is the New Age?*, op.cit., pp. 122-123. (Stokes sent free tickets to a woman who had consulted her over the telephone. At the meeting Stokes then announced details of the row in which the woman was sitting, the name of her dead son—with whom Stokes claimed to be in contact—and other previously ascertained details. Although the woman in question was asked to stand up, she was unable to say in public that she had already told Stokes these facts over the telephone.)

24. Examples are given in Lewis, *Healing: Fiction, Fantasy or Fact?*, op.cit., pp. 139-140, 148-149, 351.

25. Don Matzat *Inner Healing: Deliverance or Deception?* (Eugene, OR: Harvest House, 1987), pp. 48-57.

26. John Wimber with Kevin Springer *Power Healing* op.cit., p. 276.

27. Matzat, *Inner Healing: Deliverance or Deception?*, op.cit., pp. 63-75.

28. However, John 5:19 suggests that in all His ministry activity Jesus *looked for* and *saw* what God the Father was doing: "The Son can do nothing by himself; he can do only *what he sees (ti blepei)* his Father doing, because whatever the Father does the Son also does" (cf. John 3:34; 7:16; 8:28; 12:49,50; 14:10,24,31; see W. Grundmann, *TDNT*, vol. 2, p. 304; W. Michaelis, *TDNT*, vol. 5, p. 343 and n. 152; C. H. Dodd, *The Historical Tradition in the Fourth Gospel* [Cambridge, England: Cambridge University Press, 1963], p. 386, n. 2). Jesus also tells His disciples in John 14:19, "Before long, the world will not see me anymore; but *you will see me (theoreite me)*. Because I live, you also will live" (cf. John 14:23; Heb. 12:12; 13:5; Matt. 28:20; Rev. 1:10,13-18; cf. W. Michaelis, *TDNT*, vol. 5, pp. 362-363).

29. The same confusion has arisen concerning words of knowledge and prophecies, because the *methods* (visions and strong "intuitions") can be used both in spiritualism and in Christian contexts. In the same way, apparently similar *methods* for healing hurts from the past can be documented from both Christian and secular sources.

30. See Gardner, *Healing Miracles: A Doctor Investigates*, op.cit., pp. 175-184; Francis MacNutt, *Healing* (Notre Dame, IN: Ave Maria Press, 1974), pp. 327-333.

31. For further discussion of these issues, see chapter two of my book *Healing: Fiction, Fantasy or Fact?*, op.cit., or pages 133-141 of my chapter "Is 'Renewal' Really 'New Age' in Disguise?" in Michael Cole, Jim Graham, Tony Higton and David Lewis *What Is the New Age?*, op.cit., from which most of the above material has been reproduced.

32. This section summarizes some of the material in chapter 4 (pp. 162-202) of

my book *Healing: Fiction, Fantasy or Fact?*, op.cit., to which the reader should refer for further supporting evidence and documentation.

33. See appendix 6 in this book: "Models of Prayer for Healing and Related Phenomena."

34. Peter D. Moss and Colin P. McEvedy, "An Epidemic of Overbreathing Among Schoolgirls," *British Medical Journal*, November 1966, pp. 1295-1300.

35. See appendix 6 in this book: "Models of Prayer for Healing and Related Phenomena"; Dr. Cyril H. Powell, the British New Testament scholar, points to occasions when Jesus said He felt "power had gone out from him" to heal people (Mark 5:30; Luke 5:17; 6:19; 8:46). Some scholars, points out Dr. Powell, have viewed "the *dunamis* [power] mentioned here as something automatic and quasi-physical, like a fluid or operating like an electric current" (C. H. Powell, *The Biblical Concept of Power* [London, England: Epworth Press, 1963], p. 109); cf. the descriptions of others regarding the power of God in these passages—"material substance (stoffliche Substanz)," F. Fenner, *Die Krankheit im Neuen Testament* (Leipzig, Germany: 1930), p. 83; "a power-substance (eine Kraftsubstanz)," W. Grundmann, *Der Begriff der Kraft in der neutestamentlichen Gedankenwelt* (Stuttgart, Germany: 1932), pp. 62ff.

36. The possibility that these cold sensations are sometimes indicative of demonic activity is suggested by a different report of cold sensations which were felt in the context of ministry, at a church in Sheffield, to a non-Christian Japanese man belonging to a Shinto-derived religion named Tenriky.

37. In a footnote to my report on the Sheffield conference (Wimber and Springer, *Power Healing*, p. 286) I mentioned that the Hebrew word for "glory" (*kābod*) is derived from a root with a primary meaning of "weight" or "substance" (*BDB*, pp. 457ff.) and might be related to experiences of the "falling phenomenon." There might be a hint of this in 2 Chronicles 5:13,14 (and 1 Kings 8:10,11), when the priests "could not stand to minister because of the cloud; for the glory of the Lord filled the house of God" (*RSV*). Compare also Ezekiel 3:14,15,22,23; Isa. 8:11; Ps. 32:4.

38. Some Christians are suspicious of "out-of-the-body" experiences because in occult circles they are sometimes artificially induced. However, Dr. Richard Turner, a Christian psychiatrist, informs me that such experiences are also not uncommon "when an individual is experiencing a good deal of emotion," and that in some ways "it can be seen as protective to the individual." Biblical accounts of visions like those mentioned in Ezekiel 3:14,15; 2 Corinthians 12:3,4; or Revelation 1:10 are ambiguous about whether the person was within or outside his physical body, but Daniel 8:2 states that it occurred *in a vision* (which left him exhausted).

39. Fragance associated with Christ is referred to in 2 Corinthians 2:14,16 (see G. Delling, *TDNT*, vol. 5, p. 495; cf. A. Stumpff, *TDNT*, vol. 2, p. 810) and fragance as a sign of the Spirit of God's presence is attested in postbiblical Christian tradition (related to 2 Cor. 2:14,16 by the well-known New Testament scholar, E. Nestle, "Der süsse Geruch als Erweis des Geistes," *ZNW* 4 [1903]: 272; *ZNW* 7 [1906]: 95-96; see S. M. Burgess, *The Holy Spirit: Eastern Christian Traditions* [Peabody, MA: Hendrickson, 1989], pp. 3-4).

40. Mentioned by Arbuthnot in part VI, on "How We Minister" in the video series *Christian Prayer and Healing* (Ashford, Kent, England: Anchor Recordings).
41. Peter Horrobin, personal communication.
42. Jennifer Rees-Larcombe, *Unexpected Healing* (London, England: Hodder & Stoughton, 1991).
43. $p = <0.001$. (This means that the likelihood of this result being due to chance is less than one in a thousand. It is therefore highly significant, considering that a result with a one in twenty likelihood of being due to chance is normally regarded as statistically significant.)
44. $p = <0.05$ (and is virtually at the $p = 0.025$ level).
45. See pages 64-65 of my book *Healing: Fiction, Fantasy or Fact?*, op.cit.; Gardner, *Healing Miracles: A Doctor Investigates*, pp. 84-85, 138-140; David Pytches, *Come, Holy Spirit: Learning to Minister in Power* (London, England: Hodder & Stoughton, 1985; published in North America as *Spiritual Gifts in the Local Church* (Minneapolis, MN: Bethany House, 1985), pp. 232-239; C. P. Wagner, *How to Have a Healing Ministry in Any Church* (Ventura, CA: Regal Books, 1988), pp. 172-178; Mel Tari, *Like a Mighty Wind* (Carol Stream, IL: Creation House, 1971), pp. 66f.; Kurt Koch, *The Revival in Indonesia* (Grand Rapids, MI: Kregal, 1972), pp. 130ff.; Don Crawford, *Miracles in Indonesia* (Wheaton, IL: Tyndale House, 1972), p. 84.
46. $p = <0.01$.
47. Lewis, *Healing: Fiction, Fantasy or Fact?*, op.cit., pp. 37-38. When I interviewed this man, I also could see no noticeable limp. However, one of the frustrating sides to this kind of research was that he was afraid lest my pursuing the medical evidence might affect his legal claim to compensation from his former employers if they learned that he had been healed!
48. Lewis, *Healing: Fiction, Fantasy or Fact?*, op.cit., pp. 38-40.
49. For details, see, for instance, Gardner, *Healing Miracles: A Doctor Investigates*, op.cit., pp. 137-141, 175-184; Pytches, *Come, Holy Spirit: Learning to Minister in Power*, pp. 232-239; Lewis, *Healing: Fiction, Fantasy or Fact?*, op.cit., pp. 331-332; C. P. Wagner, *How to Have a Healing Ministry in Any Church* (Ventura, CA: Regal Books, 1988), pp. 172-178; Mel Tari, *Like a Mighty Wind* (Carol Stream, IL: Creation House, 1971), pp. 66f.; Kurt Koch, *The Revival in Indonesia* (Grand Rapids, MI: Kregal, 1972), pp. 130ff.; Don Crawford, *Miracles in Indonesia* (Wheaton, IL: Tyndale House, 1972), p. 84.
50. An example is given on page 248 of my appendix to Wimber's *Power Healing*.

14

COMMUNICATING AND MINISTERING THE POWER OF THE GOSPEL CROSS-CULTURALLY:

THE POWER OF GOD FOR CHRISTIANS WHO RIDE TWO HORSES

CHARLES H. KRAFT
MARGUERITE G. KRAFT

"Man of God, we will beat you," the demon said, "because your people ride two horses." This statement was made to Tanzanian Christian priest Felician Nkwere as he was breaking the power of a demon. The two horses referred to are the "horse" of allegiance to Jesus and the "horse" of a continued dependence on the power of Satan to fill in gaps not provided for by the Christianity brought to Tanzania by Western missionaries.

What these Tanzanians had experienced was a Christianity without the Bible's full vision of God's power working in and through His people, strong on the need for a commitment to Christ for salvation and strong on truth as understood intellectually. That Christianity was and is weak, however, in the area of greatest concern to peoples like these—the ability to deal with the evil powers that are continually pummeling them with misfortune, disease, infertility, and other ills. Since no answers are provided in these areas by most of the traditional brands of Western Christianity, Tanzanians and a majority of the rest of the peoples of the world who have been converted to such powerless Christianity continue to make use of their traditional power sources. In doing so, they inadvertently are trying to ride a second "horse," a satanic horse, at the same time that they seek to follow Christ.

The Scriptures are clear that we are not to worship any God but the true God for, God says, "I am the Lord your God and I tolerate no rivals" (Exod. 20:3,5, GNB). For most of the world, however, including the Western world, traditional Christianity has presented an incomplete God, a God who created and redeemed but whose current activity is difficult to validate. We have a Christianity with a wonderful past and an exciting future, but the present is for many very disappointing. Though large numbers of Westerners seem relatively satisfied with this God, who is less than the God we see in Scripture, most of the rest of the world is not. They, like biblical peoples, expect God to be a God of the here and now, a God who provides enough spiritual power for daily living, power to ward off the evil powers that torment them.

Perhaps Christianity would not be so disappointing for non-Westerners if a God of present power were not promised in the Christian Scriptures. If all they saw in the Bible was a God as puzzled about and unable to deal with spirit things as we Westerners, this area would not be such a problem. But in the Bible they see a God of miracles, one who stands up to Satan and defeats him, not one who ignores the evil powers. Non-Western peoples know about these powers and spend lots of their time, energy, and resources appeasing the spirits to avoid or repair the damage they bring. And biblical Christianity promises, but usually is hindered by Westerners from delivering to such peoples, a superior power to enable them to be more successful in their attempts.

When Jesus came to earth, He came to people whose expectations were very much like those of the majority of non-Western peoples today. First-century Jews looked for power demonstrations, not simply intellectual arguments, to prove God's presence. Knowing this, Jesus provided power proof (e.g., Matt. 9:6-8; Mark 2:10-12; Luke 5:24-26). And He did this in spite of the risks involved—risks that people would be more interested in power than in the relationship with God He advocated and demonstrated. He was not swayed by the armchair theologians and biblical scholars of His day who, because they refused to believe that God was still doing miracles, even went to the extent of trying to talk a former blind man out of his healing (John 9:13-34)! They, like their successors today, believed God had worked in the past but somehow He had changed and no longer did things like that today. So they asserted to the very person who had been healed:

We know that God spoke to Moses; as for that fellow, however, we do not even know where he comes from! (John 9:29, GNB).

Jesus presented a whole gospel. This involved good news concerning salvation from sin. And *through salvation from sin* it also involved good news concerning God's ability and willingness to release people from present problems (cf. Matt. 9:2,6; Mark 2:5,10,11; Luke 5:20,24; Jas. 5:15,16; see Peter H. Davids' chapter in this book). Prominent among these problems are the need for physical and emotional healing and the need to be released from demons. Much of the world is still looking for a God who is concerned about all of these needs, a God who keeps Jesus' promise to set captives completely free (Luke 4:18).

OUR TESTIMONY

We went to Nigeria as missionaries 35 years ago with all the good news an evangelical background could provide. And many Nigerians responded to the Lord. But, except for recommending the cursory kind of praying over current needs that we practiced ourselves, we and our colleagues could only offer secular means to deal with their physical ills. The people we worked with could read the Scriptures about a wonderful Miracle Worker who used to live and used to do powerful things under the anointing of God. But that was all in the past. We, and presumably He, offered nothing like that now. If they needed healing, they had two choices—the medicine man/woman or the Western clinic/hospital.

Ten years ago, though, God used John Wimber to challenge us to try claiming the power of God to do the same things God used to do through Jesus. In a very unemotional, unweird way, then, we learned to do what Jesus did. As Jesus promised, we discovered that we could learn new truth through experience: "You will know the truth, and the truth will set you free" (John 8:32, GNB; cf. 3:21).[1] We got out of our armchairs, stopped debating whether or not healing was for today and discovered that when we did what Jesus did, God frequently (not always) healed.

Now, when we go back to Nigeria or to the dozens of other places we go to around the world, the Christianity we present has a new kind of credibility because it is more like what Jesus demonstrated. We have not left the commit-ment to the scriptural Christianity we carefully learned as evangelicals. Our message has simply come to make more sense (and be more attractive) because Christ is seen and experienced in a biblical way as being relevant to daily needs in a world full of evil supernatural powers.

"TWO HORSES" CHRISTIANITY

To illustrate what we mean by "two horses" Christianity, let's look at a few typical expressions of Christian faith in various parts of the world. In Taiwan, a Christian mother has a baby. The non-Christian grandparents carefully write down the exact date and time of the baby's birth and take the information to a priest at a Buddhist temple to seek protection against evil spirits and the blessing of good spirits in the life of the child. The parents, faithful members of an evangelical church, are not really sure whether as Christians they should allow this, but every child needs all the protection and blessing possible. So they go along with it.

In Nigeria, a Christian man develops severe swelling and pain in his right leg. He goes to the medicine man who diagnoses the problem as the result of retaliation by his deceased father for not burying him properly, according to custom. To appease his father's angry spirit, the man must conduct an elaborate ceremony in which he sacrifices five goats to his father's spirit. The Christian man believes the medicine man and carries out the ceremony.

Among the Navaho, it is common to see Christians carrying packets of sacred corn pollen in their pickup trucks to protect them against accidents. Again, the view is that people need as much power as possible. So why not use this traditional technique as well as Christian prayer?

In the United States, sizable numbers of Christians regularly consult horo-scopes, go to fortune-tellers, belong to occult organizations such as Freemason-ry, and dabble in New Age or Eastern Mysticism. We have heard of openly New Age Christian churches. Americans are becoming aware that there is more to life than the physical universe and are experimenting with supernatural power sources.

In southern Mexico, a woman brings her sick daughter to the Roman Catholic cathedral to be treated by a *curandero*. She regularly attends mass at that cathedral and is considered a good Catholic. But the ritual her daughter undergoes is not Christian, nor Roman Catholic. It comes from the pre-Catholic substratum of Indian society and demonstrates a belief in spirits, powers, magic, and ritual not endorsed by the Bible or any other Catholic literature or tradition.

Because the Christianity this woman's ancestors embraced provided no effective way to deal with illness, they simply continued their centuries old practices, though they now perform their rituals in the Catholic cathedral.

As evangelicals, we are rightly quite critical of Roman Catholic Christianity in Latin America (and elsewhere) for allowing such syncretism. As we travel the world, however, we are disturbed to find the same kind of thing in abundance (though often less blatantly) among evangelical Protestants as well.

In these and countless other ways, Christians the world over demonstrate that, though they have pledged allegiance to Jesus, they still maintain an allegiance to other powers. This powerless Christianity they are experiencing has not, however, come from liberals. It has come from committed, born-again, Bible-believing Christians who have most of the Christian message right but have, because of worldview blindness,[2] missed the spiritual power dimension of biblical Christianity.

As we travel around the world, talking to Christian leaders, we have come to believe that the most serious problem in worldwide Christianity is what we call "dual allegiance" or "bifurcated Christianity." It happens either:

1. When people come to Jesus but continue to depend on other spiritual powers for protection, healing and guidance (e.g., the continuance of dependence on shamans and pagan, Buddhist or Hindu priests, amulets, sacrifices and pagan, Buddhist or Hindu rituals), or
2. When people add to their Christian commitment a dependence on occult powers (e.g., Freemasonry, New Age, Eastern Martial Arts, fortune-telling, astrology, horoscopes, psychic healing).

Many who have left non-Christian allegiances to embrace Christianity have found themselves without the power to handle life's crises. Christianity has been presented as the answer to the quest for eternal life but offers little to provide protection, healing, and guidance for the present. This contrasts with the great concern for such things in the people's pre-Christian faith, leaving voids in areas of great importance to them.

The need for spiritual power to handle events and problems deemed beyond human control is common to mankind. Most of the world perceives a variety of spiritual beings affecting everyday life. And this perception is affirmed by the Bible (see discussion in appendix 5 in this book: "Spiritual Warfare"). Marriage problems, barrenness, sickness, business or crop failure, accidents, broken relationships are all seen as involving spirit activity. In addition, success, health, fertility of fields, animals and people, protection from danger, and the like are seen as requiring supernatural activity.[3] In such societies, Christianity to be relevant must deal with all aspects of life. Often great voids have been left when Western forms of Christianity have been adopted.

Many of the independent varieties of Christianity in Africa and other places have arisen in reaction to the contrast between what they see in the Bible concerning dealing with spiritual reality and what they have received from the Western advocates of Christianity.[4] Christian preachers talk a lot about a wonderful Miracle Worker who lived long ago. But they usually show little or none of that miracle-working power themselves. The promise of Christianity has not been fulfilled for the preachers and they have become disillusioned.

Many who have been brought up in Christian churches have, likewise, become disillusioned because of the lack of power in the churches. They, therefore, have become vulnerable to contemporary movements (e.g., New Age) that promise and demonstrate spiritual power. A Christianity that talks about and promises spiritual power but leaves out the experiencing in this area that Jesus demonstrated and promised His followers (Matt. 10:1,7,8; 28:20; Luke 9:1,2; 10:1,9; John 14:12; Acts 1:8) is a great disappointment to many. Such Christianity leaves itself open to the problem of dual allegiance.

THE HISTORY

Historically, evangelical Christianity has committed enormous resources to the task of evangelizing the world. Countless missionaries have gone out, supported by countless hours of prayer and countless dollars, pounds, and other currencies.

The vast majority of these missionaries came from the Western world. And they came at a time in history after the Western world had largely ceased to believe in spiritual beings and powers. Even within the church, then, the intellectualism of Reformation Christianity combined with the antisupernaturalism of secular society to produce a brand of Christianity that found more power in reason than in prayer. Medical advances came to be depended on more than prayer for healing, psychology more than deliverance for emotional problems, what humans do in the visible world more than what God does in the invisible. Church meetings came to be centered around sermonizing rather than worship.

From these kinds of churches, then, came the missionaries. In preparation, the missionaries were sent to seminaries and Bible schools where they received more training in rational approaches to theology than in learning the kind of faith-centered behavior of the early Christians (e.g., the book of Acts). Furthermore, they usually received no training to enable them to understand such things as the cultures of the peoples to whom they went or the way these peoples understand reality or the needs that motivate them to act.

Enduring incredible hardships, these missionaries brought with them what, in comparison to the Christianity of the Bible, looks distressingly unsupernaturalistic. They brought this Western brand of Christianity to peoples who, by and large, lived with a very high consciousness of the spirit world. Indeed, those to whom the missionaries came often spent considerable amounts of time and money tending to their relationships with the unseen world of spirits—a world that was strange and incomprehensible to the missionaries. Little in the missionaries' background prepared them to accept, much less deal with the reality of the spirit world.

Many missionaries did, however, take pagan practices relating to the spirit world seriously enough that they were either (or both) frightened by them or committed to reasoning people out of them. Many saw non-Christian societies as so infested with such beliefs and practices that they waged an all-out war against their cultures, on the assumption that Satan was so in control of these cultures that virtually nothing was rescuable.

The amazing drive of many missionaries to replace traditional cultures with Western ways was often rooted in this belief that their customs, but not ours, are the product of satanic influence. Fear that satanic customs would come into the church provided strong motivation to condemn what the missionaries considered strange, infected, and dangerous. In its place, they advocated what to them was familiar, and "Christian"—rationalistic Christianity in league with secular approaches to most of life.

Largely through Western schools, evangelical missionary organizations secularized sizable segments of non-Western societies (as they had done in Western societies) in the process of introducing them to Christ. Though large numbers came to genuine faith in Christ, their traditional supernaturalistic view of life was condemned and taught against. In spite of this, however, many Christians retained their belief in spirit beings and powers and went underground with at least certain of their traditional practices related to them.

The fact that missionized peoples learned to read the Bible and to see the contrasts in this area between biblical Christianity and Western Christianity led many to split off into independent forms of Christianity in which they could openly express their supernaturalism. These forms of Christianity, divorced as they usually were from the guidance and training provided by the missionary churches, often moved into seriously unbiblical practices. Had they been able to receive guidance from missionary sources, though, these missionized people probably would not have been helped much in regard to spiritual power. This is so, because the Western advocates of Christianity and those whom they trained were seriously deficient in the area of spiritual power and, usually, fearful of getting into it.

From early in the twentieth century, Western Pentecostal Christianity began to be introduced. This approach to Christianity was much more intelligible to many of the peoples of the world, because what they assumed in regard to spirit beings and powers was also assumed by Pentecostals. Furthermore, Pentecostals demonstrated that the power of God is greater than the power of evil spirit beings and offered Christian answers that work in the crises of life.

Pentecostal missionaries were, however, still Westerners. Though they made more sense to most of the peoples of the world than traditional evangelical missionaries did, their supernaturalism was often not as developed as that of the people to whom they came. Nor was it as well integrated with biblical supernaturalism as it ought to be. For example, Pentecostals often were nearly as fearful of evil spirits as were the people they came to. In dealing with them, therefore, some Pentecostals tended to give the impression that the satanic kingdom is more powerful than it really is and that only those with special knowledge and gifting can deal with it. Contributing to this aura, others were given to unnecessary loudness and emotionalism in dealing with demons.

Worse, Pentecostals, like other Western missionaries, generally held an anticulture bias and a very Western approach to such things as church organization, music, and communication (largely preaching and a rationalistic approach to witness). Their clergy-centered leadership style often appealed to non-Western peoples but promoted (as it has in the West) groups splitting off and following different leaders. This often disrupted both church and community life and gave a wrong impression of Christianity.

Nevertheless, the much greater success of Pentecostal missions speaks eloquently for the fact that they have been much more on the wavelength of traditional peoples than have evangelicals. Furthermore, it is likely that converts to Pentecostal Christianity have less of a problem with dual allegiance than do those converted to other brands of Christianity.

THE ANSWER

As Westerners, we have a lot to learn about Christianity. We have done well with understanding and promoting Christian allegiance. Salvation by grace through faith has, since the Reformation, been in clear focus. Though we have often intellectualized faith too much and often missed the fact that biblical faith included *faithfulness*, we have done quite well on this aspect of Christianity.

We have also done fairly well with the truth dimension of biblical Christianity. Though, in keeping with our cultural biases, we have tended to overemphasize intellectual truth to the detriment of experiential truth—learning the truth by practicing it—we have been solidly concerned with true understandings of biblical doctrine. We have largely conformed our teaching to what can easily be done in the classroom—conveying information. We have, therefore, tended to ignore the considerable body of truth that only comes through launching out in faith—dependence on God, truth that cannot be reduced to information (John 3:21). We fail to see that it is experiential truth that is in focus in verses such as John 3:21 and 8:32: "You will know [=experience] the truth, and the truth will set you free" (John 8:32, GNB); "The one who practices the truth comes into the light, so that it may be seen that what he has done has been done through God" (John 3:21).

Had we not narrowed our understanding of truth to the informational and intellectual aspects of it, we might well have gone further in understanding and participating in the more supernaturalistic dimensions of our relationship with God.[5] For experiencing a life of faith (fullness) gets one well beyond that which can be rationally understood and explained.

What we have lacked, however, is the experience and understanding of spiritual power that fill the pages of the Bible. We could talk often about how the people of God lived by faith and how they lived in the authority God gave them over the invisible powers of evil. But, with the exception of Pentecostals and charismatics (comparative latecomers in the missionary enterprise), most evangelicals either ignored or explained away the possibility of our living that way today. Thus, the part of the Christian message most attractive to non-Western peoples, and increasingly to Westerners, was not a part of the experience of most of the Western missionaries who carried the gospel to them.

Now, however, many of us are a part of a movement within noncharismatic evangelicalism—a movement called "the third wave" by some—which is embracing the spiritual power dimension of biblical Christianity. This is, of course, a threat to the traditionalists who have theologized God (and, often, Satan as well) out of His ability to do today what He did in New Testament times. How like the Pharisees who also believed that God is only a God of the past and the future (John 9:29)! Beyond the worldview blockage, traditional evangelicals have good reason to fear the emotionalism, experience-orientation and, in some cases, weirdness both of practice and theology that characterize some high-visibility Pentecostals and charismatics. Wimber and others have, however, pioneered for us a way of moving in spiritual power without such extremes. They are teaching us that this dimension of Christianity is a dimension Jesus expected to be normal for us.

There is, therefore, the possibility for things to change today among evangelicals such as the two of us who were once just as skeptical as many of our detractors. Though an incredible amount of damage has already been done, resulting in large numbers of Christians worldwide riding two horses by practicing dual allegiance and nominal Christianity, we could mount a strategy to correct the situation. Elements of the strategy might be as follows:

1. Many of us former missionaries who presented a deficient (powerless) Christianity but have now experienced the missing dimension can do seminars leading people into that missing dimension in non-Western areas, including the places we once served. We can repent and return to a fully biblical view of ministry in God's power. We can teach, demonstrate, and lead our people out of the need for dual allegiance into a powerful, biblical Christianity.

We need to instruct both national and expatriate leaders in biblical models of healing and power encounter in a culturally sensitive way. In doing this, we need to resist any tendency to simply export another Western approach to Christian experience and doctrine. If the problem of dual allegiance is to be counteracted, the understanding and practice of spiritual power by such leaders needs to be firmly rooted in both the Bible and their own cultural foundations.

In most places, this will not be difficult with the nationals, because many of them have simply submerged their traditional supernaturalism. They often are immediately opened up to deal with these issues as soon as they receive our permission to do so. We have experienced this in doing seminars on spiritual power in places such as Nigeria, Kenya, Chuuk, Taiwan, Hong Kong, and Japan among the nationals of these countries. We found, in fact, that many of the pastors in these areas have been practicing healing and deliverance surreptitiously, in spite of the fact that such activities were condemned by church leaders. As we teach the biblical validity of such ministry and demonstrate the willingness of God to move in healing power today, these pastors often gain new freedom to practice these things openly.

Such retraining is often not difficult among missionaries either, because many of them have come to realize the difficulties we have been outlining here. Though some have hardened their traditional categories, those closest to the people usually are searching for ways to use indigenous power consciousness as a bridge to Christianity.

2. We can introduce both leaders from non-Western churches studying in this country and missionaries to a sound, balanced biblical approach to this aspect of Christianity. We are seeing leaders and missionaries who have moved through

this "paradigm shift"[6] return to much more effective ministry. In one case, the people who had noted the difference between the missionaries' approach and what Jesus had promised remarked, "At last you've become real Christians!"

3. Bridges need to be built between noncharismatic and charismatic church leaders worldwide. We have much more in common than we have differences. We evangelicals need to learn more from what charismatics have learned. And they need to learn some things from us. This learning is happening in exciting ways in many parts of the world (e.g., Singapore, United States) but needs to be encouraged elsewhere (e.g., Japan, Germany).

4. One of the things that will be very important to noncharismatics in dealing with spiritual power will be what they perceive as biblical balance and freedom from excesses. They will probably not open themselves up to approaches that encourage the following: a lot of emotion, either in worship or in receiving the infilling of the Holy Spirit; shouting; elitism (e.g., with regard to gifting); an emphasis on tongues as more important than other gifts; "name it, claim it" approaches to healing; mysticism (e.g., "what I understand of God and His works comes directly from Him, not indirectly through others or the Bible"); prophecy (e.g., "God spoke directly to me and told me to tell you..."); and the like. Evangelicals need to be taught by those who know and guard against what evangelicals regard as the excesses of Pentecostal and charismatic Christianity— even when being taught to practice some of those things.

5. Pentecostals and charismatics have a golden opportunity to teach and influence noncharismatics if they will learn to tone down some practices and ministry styles that may be perceived as unnecessarily extreme. Are the Scriptures as strong as many charismatics are on such things as tongues, high emotion (e.g., in worship and receiving the Holy Spirit), shouting in prayer, and dogmatically (and, often, unlovingly) stated prophecies and words of knowledge? A reconsideration and modification of excesses in such areas could contribute greatly to bridge building between charismatics and noncharismatics. And we noncharismatics need all the help we can get from charismatics in overcoming those deficiencies in our Christianity that contribute to the dual allegiance problem.

CONCLUSION

Jesus gave all Christians the Holy Spirit (Acts 1:8; 1 Cor. 12:13) and with Him power and authority over all demons and all diseases (Matt. 10:1; Luke 9:1; 10:17-19). He promised, furthermore, that we would do all that He did and more (John 14:12). The greatest spiritual power in the universe is available to

Christians through the indwelling Holy Spirit. Unfortunately, large numbers of Christians worldwide have not entered into this aspect of Christianity—an aspect that speaks strongly to socially inculcated felt needs. Most of the world's peoples are keenly aware of the spiritual world. And for most of the peoples of the world, the quest for enough spiritual power to live their lives with a minimum of disruption is one of their top priorities.

Failing to find Christianity providing the answers they seek in the area of spiritual power, many Christians have either retained their previous allegiance to powers other than the Holy Spirit or sought new power outside of Christianity to meet their felt needs in this area. This ought not to be. And it need continue no further if we develop biblical strategies to deal with it. May God enable us to do so.

Notes

1. The truth is to be *done*, not just intellectually known according to John 3:21, "The one who *practices* [*poieo* "do, practice"] the truth comes into the light, so that it may be seen that what he has done has been done through God."
2. Charles H. Kraft, *Christianity with Power* (Ann Arbor, MI: Vine [Servant Publications], 1989); cf. Marguerite G. Kraft, *Worldview and the Communication of the Gospel* (Pasadena, CA: Wm Carey, 1978).
3. Marguerite G. Kraft, *Reaching Out for Spiritual Power* (Ph.D. dissertation), (Pasadena, CA: Fuller Seminary, 1990); id., *Worldview and the Communication of the Gospel* (Pasadena, CA: Wm Carey, 1978).
4. David Barrett, *Schism and Renewal* (London, England: Oxford University Press, 1968).
5. See Kraft, *Christianity with Power*.
6. Ibid.

APPENDICES

1

POWER EVANGELISM AND THE NEW TESTAMENT EVIDENCE

The claim is made by some evangelicals that "the New Testament does not teach that evangelism is to be done by cultivating miracles"[1] and that "we are never told that they are God's means for converting unbelievers or that we should seek to perform them."[2]

But such statements seem to completely contradict all the New Testament evidence. Countless New Testament scholars have noted over the last century (see references below) that power evangelism is the normative form of evangelism seen in the New Testament. The New Testament evidence shows, these scholars point out, that miraculous healing, signs, wonders, and manifestations of miraculous spiritual gifts regularly accompanied preaching as the standard form of evangelism practiced by our Lord and by the apostles and Early Church laity (Stephen, Philip, Ananias, the Corinthians, Galatians, Jewish Christian churches, etc.): **Matthew 4:23; 9:35,36; 10:1,7,8; 11:5; 12:15,18;**

15:30; 19:2 (cf. Mark 10:1); 21:14 (cf. Luke 21:37); **Mark** 1:38,39; 2:2,11; 3:14,15; 6:12,13; 10:1 (cf. Matt. 19:2); **Luke** 4:18; 5:17,24; 6:6-11,17,18; 7:22; 9:1,2; 10:9,13; 13:10-13,22,32; 14:4,7ff.; 21:37 (cf. Matt. 21:14); 16:15-18,20; **John** 3:2; 7:14,15,21-23,31,38; 10:25,32,38; 12:37,49; 14:10,12; **Acts** 1:1; 2:22; 3:6,12; 4:29,30; 5:12-16,20,21,28,42; 6:8,10; 8:4-7,12; 9:17,18 (cf. 22:13),34,35; 10:38; 14:3,8-10,15ff.; 15:12,36; 18:5,11 (cf. 2 Cor. 12:12; 1 Cor. 2:4,5); 19:8-12; **Romans** 15:18,19; **1 Corinthians** 2:4,5; 11:1; 12:1-11,28-31; 14:22-25; **2 Corinthians** 12:12; **Galatians** 3:5; **Philippians** 4:9; **1 Thessalonians** 1:5,6; **Hebrews** 2:3,4; 6:1,2; **James** 5:13-16.

Such biblical evidence has been cited and laid out at length already by Wimber and Springer in their seminal works on power evangelism and healing ministry.[3] But critics of power evangelism seem largely to ignore the evidence.

THE BIBLICAL EVIDENCE

The following passages, selected from the list of passages cited above, illustrate how the power of Christ demonstrated through healing and gift-based ministry is, according to Scripture, an integral part of the proclamation of the gospel and a manifestation of the power of Christ and His cross to save sinners. When Jesus preached, "The kingdom of God is near. Repent and believe the good news!" (Mark 1:14,15; Matt. 4:17; Luke 4:14,15), His preaching was inseparably linked to His healing sickness and driving out demons. The same is also true of the apostles and the Early Church:

> **Matthew 4:23**—"Jesus went throughout Galilee, *teaching* in their synagogues, *preaching* the good news of the kingdom, and *healing* every disease and sickness among the people."

> **Mark 1:39**—"So he traveled throughout Galilee, *preaching* in their synagogues and *driving out demons*."

> **Luke 4:40-43**—"The people brought to Jesus all who had various kinds of sickness, and laying his hands on each one, he *healed* them. Moreover, *demons came out* of many people....They tried to keep him from leaving them. But he said, 'I must *preach* the good news of the kingdom of God to the other towns also, because that is why I was sent.'"

Luke 5:15—"Crowds of people came to *hear him* and to *be healed* of their sicknesses."

Luke 5:17 (Matt. 9:1ff.; Mark 2:1ff.)—"He was *teaching*....And the *power of the Lord* was present for him to *heal the sick*."

Matthew 9:6-8 (Mark 2:10-12; Luke 5:24-26)—"'But so *that you may know* that the Son of Man has authority on earth to forgive sins....' Then *he said to the paralytic*, 'Get up, take your mat and go home.' And *the man got up and went home*. When the crowd saw this, they were filled with awe; and they praised God, who had given such authority to men."

Luke 6:17,18—"A great number of people...who had come to *hear him* and to *be healed* of their diseases."

Matthew 9:35—"Jesus went through all the towns and villages, *teaching* in their synagogues, *preaching* the good news of the kingdom and *healing* every disease and sickness."

Luke 9:1,2—"When Jesus had called the Twelve together, he gave them power and authority to drive out all demons and to cure diseases, and he sent them out to *preach* the kingdom of God and to *heal* the sick."

Matthew 10:1,7,8—"He called his twelve disciples to him and gave them authority to drive out evil spirits and to heal every disease and sickness....As you go, *preach* this message: 'The kingdom of heaven is near.' *Heal* the sick, raise the dead, cleanse those who have leprosy, drive out demons. Freely you have received, freely give."

Matthew 13:54—"Where did this man get this *wisdom* and these *miraculous powers?*"

Luke 9:6—"So they set out and went from village to village, *preaching the gospel* and *healing* people everywhere."

Mark 6:7,12,13—"Calling the Twelve to him, he sent them out two by two and gave them authority over evil spirits....They went out and *preached* that people should repent. They *drove out many demons* and anointed many sick people with oil and *healed* them."

John 7:17,23—"If anyone chooses to do God's will, he will find out whether my *teaching* comes from God....Why are you angry with me for *healing* the whole man on the Sabbath?"

Luke 10:9—Jesus says to 70 of His followers, obviously including many more than the twelve apostles: *"Heal* the sick who are there and *tell them,* 'The kingdom of God is near you.'"

Luke 13:22,32—"Jesus went through the towns and villages, *teaching....*'I will *drive out demons* and *heal* people today and tomorrow, and on the third day I will reach my goal.'"

Matthew 21:14—"The blind and the lame came to him at the temple, and he *healed* them"; and **Luke 21:37**—"Each day Jesus was *teaching* at the temple."

Acts 3:6-8—Peter *heals* the crippled beggar, and in **3:11-26**, he *preaches the gospel* to the crowd.

Acts 4:2,10—"The apostles were *teaching* the people and *proclaiming* in Jesus the resurrection of the dead....'It is by the name of Jesus Christ of Nazareth, whom you crucified but whom God raised from the dead, that this man stands before you completely *healed.*'"

Acts 4:29,30—"Now, Lord, consider their threats and enable your servants to *speak your word* with great boldness. Stretch out your hand to *heal and perform miraculous signs and wonders* through the name of your holy servant Jesus."

Acts 4:33—"With *great power* the apostles continued to *testify* to the resurrection of the Lord Jesus, and much grace was upon them all."

Acts 5:12,15,16,20,21—"The apostles performed *many miraculous signs and wonders* among the people. And all the believers used to meet together in Solomon's Colonnade....People brought the sick into the streets and laid them on beds and mats so that at least Peter's shadow might fall on some of them as he passed by. Crowds gathered also from the towns around Jerusalem, bringing their sick and those tormented by evil spirits and all of them *were healed*....'Go, stand in the temple courts,' he [the angel of the Lord] said, 'and *tell the people the full message of this new life*.' At daybreak they entered the temple courts, as they had been told, and began to *teach* the people."

Act 6:8-10—"Now Stephen, a man full of God's grace and power, did *great wonders and miraculous signs* among the people....These men began to argue with Stephen, but they could not stand up against his *wisdom or the Spirit by whom he spoke*."

Acts 8:4-7,12,13—"Those who had been scattered *preached the word* wherever they went. Philip went down to a city in Samaria and *proclaimed the Christ* there. When the crowds *heard Philip* and *saw the miraculous signs he did*, they all paid close attention to *what he said*. With shrieks, *evil spirits came out* of many, and many *paralytics and cripples were healed*....But when they believed Philip as he *preached the good news* of the kingdom of God and the name of Jesus Christ, they were baptized, both men and women. Simon himself believed and was baptized. And he followed Philip everywhere, astonished by the *great signs and miracles*."

Acts 14:3—"So Paul and Barnabas spent considerable time there, *speaking* boldly for the Lord, who confirmed the *message of his grace* by enabling them to do miraculous *signs and wonders*."

Acts 14:7-10—"They continued to *preach* the good news. In Lystra there sat a man crippled in his feet, who was lame from birth and had never walked. He listened to Paul as he was *speaking*. Paul looked directly at him, saw that he had faith to be *healed* and called out, 'Stand up on your feet!' At that, the man jumped up and began to walk."

Acts 18:1,5—"After this Paul left Athens and went to Corinth....When Silas and Timothy came from Macedonia, Paul devoted himself exclusively to *preaching, testifying* to the Jews that Jesus was the Christ"; and **2 Corinthians 12:12**—Paul speaks to the Corinthians, characterizing his ministry in Corinth as follows: "The things that mark an apostle—*signs, wonders* and *miracles*— were done among you *with great perseverance.*"

Acts 19:8,9,11,12—"Paul entered the synagogue and *spoke* boldly there for three months, arguing persuasively about the kingdom of God....He took the disciples with him and had *discussions* daily in the lecture hall of Tyrannus....God did *extraordinary miracles* through Paul, so that even handkerchiefs and aprons that had touched him were taken to the sick, and their *illnesses were cured* and the *evil spirits left them.*"

Romans 15:18-20—"I will not venture to speak of anything except what Christ has accomplished through me in leading the Gentiles to obey God by what I have *said* and *done*—by the *power of signs and wonders*, through the *power of the Spirit.* So from Jerusalem all the way around to Illyricum, I have *fully proclaimed the gospel of Christ.* It has always been my ambition to *preach the gospel where Christ was not known*, so that I would not be building on someone else's foundation."

1 Corinthians 1:6,7—"Our *testimony* about Christ was *confirmed in you.* Therefore *you do not lack any spiritual gift* as you eagerly wait for our Lord Jesus Christ to be revealed."

1 Corinthians 2:4,5—"My *message* and my *preaching* were not with wise and persuasive words, but with *a demonstration of the Spirit's power*, so that your faith might not rest on men's wisdom, but on God's power."

2 Corinthians 12:12 (RSV)—"The signs of a true apostle were performed among you in all patience, with signs and wonders and mighty works."

Galatians 3:5—"Does God give you his Spirit and work *miracles* among you because you observe the law, or because you believe what you *heard?*"

1 Thessalonians 1:5—"Our gospel came to you not simply with *words*, but also with *power*, with the Holy Spirit and with deep conviction."

Hebrews 2:3,4—"This salvation, which was first *announced* by the Lord, was confirmed to us by those who heard him. God also testified to it by *signs, wonders and various miracles, and gifts of the Holy Spirit* distributed according to his will."

1 Peter 4:10,11—"Each one should use whatever gift he has received to serve others, faithfully administering God's grace in its various forms. If anyone speaks, he should do it as one speaking the very *words of God*. If anyone serves, he should do it with the *strength God provides*, so that in all things God may be praised through Jesus Christ. To him be the glory and the power for ever and ever. Amen."

The New Testament evidence is quite clear, then, that preaching and healing were the standard form of evangelism practiced by Jesus, the apostles, and the Early Church. And New Testament scholars around the world have recognized this fact about the evidence.

NEW TESTAMENT SCHOLARS AND THE EVIDENCE

Scholars, publishing in English, German, and French, have recognized for at least a century that the New Testament view of the power and compassion of God in healing and gift-based ministry is integrally related to the New Testament view of proclaiming the gospel and ministering the Word of God (see also references cited and quoted in the introduction above).[4] The German New Testament scholar, Professor Otfried Hofius, summarized the New Testament evidence concerning the integral relationship of healing and gift-based ministry to the proclamation of the gospel and the Word of God:

> According to the witness of the Synoptic Gospels, Jesus sent out his disciples to preach and to perform miracles (Mat. 10:7f.; Mk. 3:14f.; Lk. 9:1f.; 10:9; cf. Mk. 6:7ff.; Lk. 9:6)....
> Similarly, Acts mentions many times the correlation of apostolic proclamation and apostolic miracle-working (2:2f.; 4:29f.; cf.

3:1ff.; 4:16, 22; 5:12; 6:8; 8:5ff.; 9:32ff.; 15:12; 20:7ff.). The miracles are co-ordinated with the preaching—they are "accompanying signs," by which Christ confirms the word of the witnesses (Acts 14:3; cf. Mk. 16:20). As in the authoritative word (Acts 6:10) so in the signs is manifested the power of the Holy Spirit promised to the disciples (Acts 1:8)....

For Paul, too, "word and deed," preaching and signs belong together; in both Christ is at work in the power of the Spirit (Rom. 15:18f.). Signs and wonders accompany the proclamation which takes place "in demonstration of the Spirit and power" (I Cor. 2:4; cf. I Thes. 1:5)....

To the hearers of the preaching also the Holy Spirit mediates miraculous powers (Gal. 3:5). That is why alongside the gifts of proclamation the charisma of healing and the power to perform miracles belong to the living gifts of the Spirit in the church (I Cor. 12:8ff., 28; cf. Jas. 5:14f.).

Finally Hebrews also bears witness that God confirms the preaching of salvation, which proclaims the dawn of the age of salvation, by signs and wonders (2:3ff.), which, as "powers of the world to come" (6:5), foreshadow the completion of salvation....

Preaching and miracles thus belong essentially together according to the New Testament. In both Jesus Christ proves himself to be the living Lord, present in his church in the Holy Spirit.[5]

Professor F. F. Bruce, the well-known evangelical British New Testament scholar, considered Jesus' healing ministry an integral part of the message Jesus preached:

While the miracles served as signs, they were not performed in order to be signs. They were as much a part and parcel of Jesus's ministry as was his preaching—not...seals affixed to the document to certify its genuiness but an integral element in the very text of the document.[6]

The Dutch New Testament scholar, Dr. H. van der Loos, similarly points out:

The miracles were therefore not works or signs which happened for the sake of the apostles, but originated in the point at issue, viz. the proclamation of salvation by Jesus Christ and the coming of His Kingdom. They did not accompany the preaching of the gospel as incidentals, but formed an integral part of it; in the healing, as a visible function of the Kingdom of God, something that could be experienced, God's will to heal the whole of man was manifested.[7]

A. Feuillet, a French New Testament scholar, points out that just as Jesus' preaching was regularly accompanied by healing and gift-based ministry, so was that of His disciples:

> In Mark ii.2 and iv.33 Jesus is seen "to proclaim the Word"....In Mk. xvi.19-20, once Jesus ascended to heaven, the apostles in their turn "proclaim the Word." And as the Word proclaimed by Jesus was accompanied by works of power, it was exactly the same according to Mark xvi.20 for the Word proclaimed by the apostles....What Jesus began to say (the Word) and to do (the miracles), all that is continued after the Ascension by the apostles.
>   Moved by the Spirit, the apostles take up the call of Jesus for repentance ([Acts] ii.38, iii.26, v.31, xviii.30) and his announcement of the "Kingdom of God" ([Acts] viii.12, xix.8, xx.25, xxvii.31)....They bear witness to the resurrection of Jesus: cf. [Acts] i.22, ii.32, iii.15, iv.33, v.32, x.39, 41, xiii.31. They depend on the invocation of the Name of Jesus....It is for this Name that the apostles suffer ([Acts] v.21, xxi.13; cf. I Pet. iv.14); it is this Name that they preach ([Acts] iv.10-12, 17-18; v.28-40). And the invocation of this Name puts into action the divine power kept by Jesus. The result is that, by this invocation, the apostles accomplish miraculous wonders like those of Jesus' public ministry, heal the sick, drive out demons and even raise the dead: [Acts] iii.1-10, viii.6-7, ix.32-43, xiv.8-18, xx.7-12...v.16...xix.12.[8]

C. H. Powell, a British scholar, pointed out the same. The ministry of preaching and healing initiated by Jesus through the power of the Spirit was continued by His disciples who were empowered by the same Spirit:

> They are then the Lord's *shelichim*, receiving from Him power and authority to do the two things distinctive of His ministry: to preach and heal. After the Resurrection, having become His *shelichim* indeed, empowered by the same Spirit that came upon Him at His

Baptism, they carry forward His work, as "witnesses" and "Apostles," "in His Name."[9]

The German New Testament scholar, Professor Gerhard Delling, points out that the message of the gospel preached by Jesus is demonstrated in the mighty works of His healing ministry:

> The healings of Jesus are expressly determined for the general public, for the general public of the Jewish people. That is because the healings and demon expulsions specifically have the task of confirming the message of Jesus in a signifying way. More exactly: to confirm the proclamation of the invading rule of God.
>
> This confirmation is not perchance only a formal one. It proves not only the full power of Jesus in general, but it stands in an intrinsic relationship with the proclamation of the rule of God. The mighty works of Jesus confirm the content of the message of Jesus—because this (message) signifies: God is beginning decisively to bring about his rule; the time of salvation is breaking in. And this is demonstrated in the mighty works themselves, even if only in an anticipatory way and in indications which are veiled to the one who does not believe the message.[10]

Professor Gerhard Friedrich, also a German New Testament scholar, points out that the New Testament concept of preaching the gospel is more than verbally communicating the rational content of the gospel and that it includes demonstrating the power of the gospel through healing ministry:

> *Euaggelizesthai* ["to preach the gospel"] is not just speaking and preaching; it is proclamation with full authority and power. Signs and wonders accompany the evangelical message. They belong together, for the Word is powerful and effective. The proclamation of the age of grace, of the rule of God, creates a healthy state in every respect. Bodily disorders are healed and man's relationship to God is set right (Mt. 4:23; 9:35; 11:5; Lk. 9:6; Acts 8:4-8; 10:36ff.; 14:8-18; 16:17ff.; Rom. 15:16-20; II Cor. 12:12; Gal. 3:5). Joy reigns where this Word is proclaimed (Acts 8:8). It brings *sotēria* ["salvation"] (I Cor. 15:1f.)...Hence, *euaggelizesthai* ["to preach the gospel"] is to offer salvation. It is the powerful proclamation the good news, the impartation of *sotēria* ["salvation"]. This would

be missed if *euaggelizesthai* ["to preach the gospel"] were to take place in human fashion *en sophia logou* ["(merely) in the wisdom of words"] (I Cor. 1:17).[11]

A LIMITED ROLE FOR MIRACLES IN BRINGING PEOPLE TO FAITH?

One recent handbook of theology seems to suggest that the role of miracles is limited in bringing people to faith in the New Testament: "After Jesus' ascension, there were few miracles recorded in Scripture, and those involved a very few disciples."[12] Others make similar claims: "The fact is that few who were healed [by Jesus, the apostles, and the Early Church] became disciples";[13] "Peter and John healed the lame man at the temple gate, and Stephen, full of grace and power, did many signs and wonders among the people. These demonstrations, however, were not followed by mass conversions."[14]

It is noteworthy that none of these statements are substantiated with biblical references. The fact is that such claims cannot be substantiated in Scripture, because they flatly contradict the New Testament evidence. Acts chapters 3 to 5 make it clear that the preaching *and* healing signs and wonders of Peter and the apostles led to explosive growth in the Jerusalem church. People "came running to [Peter and John] in the place called Solomon's Colonnade" (Acts 3:11) not because Peter was a good preacher but because the paralytic had just been healed. The healing of the man became the opening theme of Peter's sermon about the resurrected Jesus, whom God glorified by healing the paralytic. The healing of the man demonstrated the presence and power of the risen Lord Jesus to "wipe out" their sins (Acts 3:19):

> Acts 3:12,13,15,16,18,19—"When Peter saw this, he said to them: 'Men of Israel, why does this surprise you? *Why do you stare at us as if by our own power or godliness we had made this man walk?* The God of Abraham, Isaac and Jacob, the God of our fathers, *has glorified his servant Jesus....*You killed the author of life, but *God raised him from the dead. We are witnesses of this.* By faith in the name of Jesus, this man whom you see and know was made strong. *It is Jesus' name and the faith that comes through him that has given this complete healing to him,* as you all can see....This is how God fulfilled what he had foretold through all the prophets, saying that his *Christ would suffer. Repent then, and turn to God, so that your sins may be wiped out.*'"

As Professor Bruce has noted, the result of only the one healing and Peter's preaching was that at least *five thousand men* put their faith in Christ (Acts 4:4).[15]

The fact that the Jerusalem believers were "highly regarded by the people" (Acts 5:13) and that "more and more men and women believed in the Lord and were added to their number" (Acts 5:14) is couched between accounts of the miraculous signs and wonders that accompanied the apostles' preaching:

> **Acts 5:12-16**—"The apostles performed many miraculous signs and wonders among the people. And all the believers used to meet together in Solomon's Colonnade. No one else dared join them, even though they were highly regarded by the people. Nevertheless, more and more men and women believed in the Lord and were added to their number. As a result, people brought the sick into the streets and laid them on beds and mats so that at least Peter's shadow might fall on some of them as he passed by. Crowds gathered also from the towns around Jerusalem, bringing their sick and those tormented by evil spirits, and all of them were healed."

Again, Bruce notes the connection between the preaching and healing of the apostles and the growth of the Church:

> Again we are told of the "signs and wonders" performed through the agency of the apostles; the general atmosphere is like that of the earlier days of our Lord's Galilaean ministry (Mark 1:32-34 par. Luke 4:40-41)....No wonder that...the number of believers increased.[16]

Similarly, Acts 9:35 states that when Peter healed Aeneas, the paralytic in Lydda, "All those who lived in Lydda and Sharon saw him and turned to the Lord." Passages like these hardly show that "these demonstrations...were not followed by mass conversions." Why else would preaching and healing be the normal pattern of evangelism practiced by the apostles and the Early Church: **Acts** 3:6,12; 4:29,30; 5:12-16,20,21,28,42; 6:8,10; 8:4-7,12; 9:17,18 (cf. 22:13),34,35; 14:3,8-10,15ff.; 15:12,36; 18:5,11 (cf. 2 Cor. 12:12; 1 Cor. 2:4,5); 19:8-12. **Romans** 15:18,19; **1 Corinthians** 2:4,5; 11:1; 12:1-11,28-31; 14:24,25; **2 Corinthians** 12:12; **Galatians** 3:5; **Philippians** 4:9; **1 Thessalonians** 1:5,6; **Hebrews** 2:3,4? One gets precisely the same impression of the passages describing Jesus' preaching and healing: **Matthew** 4:23; 9:35,36; 10:1,7,8; 11:5; 12:15,18; 15:30; 19:2 (cf. Mark 10:1); 21:14 (cf. Luke 21:37); **Mark** 1:38,39; 2:2,11; 3:14,15; 6:12-13; 10:1 (cf. Matt. 19:2); **Luke** 4:18; 5:17,24; 6:6-11,17,18; 7:22; 9:1,2; 10:9,13; 13:10-13,22,32; 14:4,7ff.; 21:37 (cf. Matt. 21:14); 16:15-18,20; **John** 3:2; 7:14,15,21-23,31,38; 10:25,32,38; 12:37,49; 14:10,12; **Acts** 1:1; 2:22; 10:38. Passages such as John 7:31 explicitly state that "many in the crowd put their faith in him. They said, 'When the Christ comes, will he do more miraculous signs than this man?'" And the lament of the Jewish leaders in John 11:47,48 also suggests that Jesus' miraculous signs were causing great numbers of people to believe in Him:

> **John 11:47,48**—"Here is this man performing many miraculous signs. If we let him go on like this, *everyone will believe in him*, and then the Romans will come and take away both our place and our nation."

Some have cited the fact that Jesus did not entrust Himself to those who believed in Him through His miraculous signs in John 2:23,24 in order to suggest that the faith of those who believe in Christ through His miraculous works is spurious or inferior.[17] But nothing in the language of John 2:23,24 suggests that the faith of the crowds is not true faith. That Jesus did not entrust Himself to people with such faith demonstrates nothing more than that their faith was uninformed, as shown by the parallel passage John 6:14,15, and, therefore, that their faith was not yet capable of enduring (John 6:60-66) or bearing fruit by "holding to [Jesus'] teaching" (John 8:31).

However, these facts do not demonstrate that the faith of the crowds in John 2:23,24 was spurious or false. Their faith was, on the contrary, true saving faith, since the phrase *pisteuein eis* ("to believe in"), which is used to describe the faith of the crowds in John 2:23, is used elsewhere in John of *saving faith*— John 1:12; 3:15,16,18,36; 4:39 (cf. 4:42); 6:29,35,40,47; 7:38,39; 8:30; 10:42; 11:25,26; 12:42,44,46; 14:1,12; 17:20—saving faith that often comes precisely from witnessing Jesus' miraculous works—John 2:11; 7:31; 9:16,35,36,38 (cf. 9:30-32); 11:45,47,48; 12:10,11.

After all, one of the greatest examples of faith Jesus pointed to was the faith of the centurion in Matthew 8:5-13 and Luke 7:1-10. The centurion believed in Jesus' miraculous power by virtue of believing in Jesus' person and authority (Matt. 8:8,9; Luke 7:7,8). And to such faith Jesus replied, "I tell you the truth, I have not found anyone in Israel with *such great faith*. I say to you that many will come from the east and the west, and will take their places at the feast with Abraham, Isaac and Jacob in the kingdom of heaven" (Matt. 8:10,11; Luke 7:9). Such words make it clear that Jesus considered faith in His miraculous power and in His person and identity like that of the centurion to be saving faith.[18]

These facts along with the preaching and healing pattern of the ministry of Jesus, the apostles, and the Early Church suggest that miraculous healing was used regularly and fruitfully alongside preaching to bring people to saving faith in Christ.

SIGNS, WONDERS, AND MIRACLES VERSUS THE GOSPEL?

Yet, in spite of such evidence in the New Testament, the claim is still made that signs and wonders of healing are somehow at odds with proclaiming the message of the gospel:

> "Faith comes from hearing the message, and the message is heard through the word of Christ" (v. 17 [Rom. 10:17]). One wrong way of doing religion is by proclaiming signs rather than the *message* through which, as Paul states, faith comes to us.[19]

But how did Paul himself characteristically bring this message? He brought it along with working signs and wonders of healing and deliverance (Acts 13:7-12 [blinding of a sorcerer]; 14:3 [signs and wonders]; 14:9,10 [healing a lame man]; 15:12 [signs and wonders]; 16:16-18 [casting out a demon]; 16:26-32 [earthquake]; 19:4-6 [conveying the Spirit and gifts on disciples]; 19:8-12 ["extraordinary miracles" of healing and deliverance]; 20:7-10 [raising the dead]; 28:8,9 [healing fever and dysentery]):

> **2 Corinthians 12:12**—"The things that mark an apostle—*signs, wonders* and *miracles*—were done among you with great perseverance."

> **Romans 15:18,19**—"I will not venture to speak of anything except what Christ has accomplished through me in leading the Gentiles to obey God by what I have said and done—by the *power of signs and wonders [sēmeiōn kai teratōn]*, through the *power of the Spirit*. So from Jerusalem all the way around to Illyricum, I have *fully proclaimed [plēroō]* the gospel of Christ."

1 Corinthians 2:4,5—"My message and my preaching were not with wise and persuasive words, but *with a demonstration of the Spirit's power*, so that your faith might not rest on men's wisdom, but on *God's power.*"

1 Thessalonians 1:5—"Our gospel came to you *not simply with words [en logō monon]*, but also *with power, with the Holy Spirit* and with deep conviction."

The German scholar, Professor Walter Grundmann, says of Paul's proclaiming the message of the gospel:

Paul fits the same pattern [of Jesus and the disciples]. His work is done "in the power of signs and wonders, in the power of the Spirit" (Rom. 15:19). In the preceding verse this power is attributed directly to Christ....

This power is expressed on the one side in miracles: "in the power of signs and wonders." There are many references to these in the epistles: "the signs of an apostle...signs, wonders, and miracles," II Cor. 12:12; God "working miracles among you," Gal. 3:5; his activity in Thessalonica did not take place "in word only, but also in power and in the Holy Spirit," I Thes. 1:5....

Alongside the power of miracles is the power of proclamation and edification: "in the power of the Spirit." Here we see the connexion between Spirit and power, which we have already seen...in Luke. The Spirit is the One who dispenses and mediates power.[20]

Dr. Cyril H. Powell adds:

In the Spirit, in the power of Christ, and in this personal relationship with Him, Paul carries forward his Gospel, and follows his Lord, as one of His Apostles, in healing and preaching.[21]

PREACHING VERSUS MIRACULOUS HEALING?

Certain evangelicals seem to assume that a dichotomy exists between preaching and healing, claiming that in the New Testament preaching has little connection with miraculous healing:

It is why the apostles, who were able to perform miracles, nevertheless were sent into the world to be "witnesses" (Acts 1:8) and "teachers" (Matthew 28:20). And it is why even Jesus, when urged to return to Capernaum to perform miracles there as he had done before, replied, "Let us go somewhere else—to the nearby villages—so I can preach there also. That is why I have come" (Mark 1:38).[22]

Such an assumption fails to explain the New Testament evidence recognized by scholars such as those quoted above. The remarks made a half century ago by Dr. Alan Richardson, the British New Testament scholar, concerning the integral role of miraculous healing in New Testament preaching indict such a false dichotomy:

> So far have we departed from the biblical standpoint that the miracle-stories have come to be regarded as a sort of detrimental offshoot to the preaching of the Christian message, like a sucker which must be pruned off the rose-tree before it saps the vitality of the flower-bearing stem. We must retrace our steps and ask whether we cannot reach some more convincing explanation of the prominence which the miracle-stories came to receive in the Gospel tradition....The task of the biblical theologian is to ask, first of all, the reason why the miracle-stories were included in the Gospel as an integral and not an accidental part of it.[23]

Healing ministry was an integral component of Jesus' preaching and teaching. This is suggested by the fact that Jesus can describe His purpose as that of preaching—"I must preach...that is why I was sent" (Luke 4:43)—and at the same time characterize His ministry largely or entirely in terms of healing:

> **Luke 13:32**—"I will drive out demons and heal people today and tomorrow, and on the third day I will reach my goal."

> **Matthew 11:1-5**—"He went on from there to *teach and preach* in the towns of Galilee....'Go back and report to John what you *hear* and *see*: The blind receive sight, the lame walk, those who have leprosy are cured, the deaf hear, the dead are raised, and the good news is preached to the poor.'"

In Matthew 11:20-30 and Luke 10:13-15, Jesus condemned Korazin and

Bethsaida, mentioning only the miracles He worked there (not His verbal teaching) as that which should have produced repentance in those towns:

Matthew 11:21—"Woe to you, Korazin! Woe to you, Bethsaida! If the miracles that were performed in you had been performed in Tyre and Sidon, they would have repented long ago in sackcloth and ashes."

Richardson remarks about this saying in Matthew 11:21 and Luke 10:13:

The working of miracles is a part of the proclamation of the Kingdom of God, not an end in itself. Similarly, the sin of Chorazin and Bethsaida [Lk. 10:13; Mat. 11:21] is spiritual blindness; they do not accept the preaching of the Kingdom of God or understand the miracles which were its inevitable concomitants....Even the heathen, it is implied, would have understood from the preaching the meaning of the mighty works,...and they would have repented.

Can we interpret the remarkable connexion which this Q saying establishes between the miracles and repentance in any other way than by understanding the miracles as the necessary concomitants of the preaching of the Kingdom of God?...

Because the mighty works of Jesus are the miracles of the Kingdom of God, the appropriate response to them is: "Repent and believe the good news."[24]

In recounting Jesus' preaching ministry in the Temple during Passion Week, Luke describes Jesus' *teaching*—"Each day Jesus was *teaching* at the temple," Luke 21:37—and Matthew describes Jesus' *healing*—"The blind and the lame came to him at the temple, and he *healed* them," Matthew 21:14.

Philip, a layman, proclaimed Christ in Samaria. His preaching is described as verbal teaching and doing miraculous signs of healing and deliverance:

Acts 8:5-7,12,13—"Philip went down to a city in Samaria and *proclaimed the Christ* there. When the crowds *heard Philip* and *saw the miraculous signs he did*, they all paid close attention to *what he said*. With shrieks, *evil spirits came out* of many, and many *paralytics and cripples were healed*....But when they believed Philip as *he preached the good news* of the kingdom of God and the name of Jesus Christ, they were baptized, both men and women. Simon himself believed and was baptized. And he followed Philip every-where, astonished by the *great signs and miracles*."

Even when Paul "devoted himself exclusively to preaching [*suneicheto tō logō*]" in Corinth (Acts 18:5), his preaching consistently included signs, won-ders, and miracles of healing and deliverance, as 2 Corinthians 12:12 demon-strates (cf. 1 Cor. 2:4,5):

> **2 Corinthians 12:12**—"The things that mark an apostle—*signs, wonders* and *miracles*—were done among you *with great persever-ance*."

As pointed out above, Paul's idea "preaching the gospel where Christ was not known" (Rom. 15:20) and "fully proclaiming the gospel of Christ" (Rom. 15:19) explicitly included deeds consisting of signs and wonders in the power of the Spirit according to Romans 15:18-20:

> **Romans 15:18-20**—"I will not venture to speak of anything except what Christ has accomplished through me in leading the Gentiles to obey God by what I have *said* and *done*—by the *power of signs and wonders*, through the *power of the Spirit*. So from Jerusalem all the way around to Illyricum, I have *fully proclaimed* [*peplērōkenai*)] *the gospel of Christ*. It has always been my ambition to *preach the gospel where Christ was not known*, so that I would not be building on someone else's foundation."

JESUS' HEALING MINISTRY SUBSIDIARY TO HIS PREACHING?

Some even suggest that there was an opposition between Jesus' healing ministry and His preaching in which healing ministry was secondary and, seemingly, less important than His preaching and teaching:

> Even within the ministry of Jesus, healings and exorcisms are clear-ly in a subsidiary role to Jesus' teaching and preaching....There is no record of Jesus going somewhere in order to hold a healing meeting, or of Jesus issuing a general invitation to be healed, or of Jesus offer-ing generalized prayers for healing. Where Jesus does undertake to

heal an individual, the procedure is never prefaced by some generalizing announcement (there is no "I have a word from the Lord: there is someone here with a back pain, and God wants to heal you"), and the result is never ambiguous.[25]

These statements do not explain at all well the evidence from the Gospels. Healing ministry was not in "subsidiary" opposition to teaching and preaching in Jesus' ministry. That healing and deliverance were as important a part of Jesus' ministry of proclaiming the gospel as verbal preaching and teaching is shown by passages where Jesus describes His ministry entirely or largely in terms of healing (as the apostle Peter also described Jesus' ministry in Acts 10:38):

Luke 13:32—"I will drive out demons and heal people today and tomorrow, and on the third day I will reach my goal."

Matthew 11:1-5—"He went on from there to *teach and preach* in the towns of Galilee....'Go back and report to John what you *hear* and *see*: The blind receive sight, the lame walk, those who have leprosy are cured, the deaf hear, the dead are raised, and the good news is preached to the poor.'"

Matthew 11:21—"Woe to you, Korazin! Woe to you, Bethsaida! If the miracles that were performed in you had been performed in Tyre and Sidon, they would have repented long ago in sackcloth and ashes."

Matthew 21:14—"The blind and the lame came to him at the temple and he healed them," versus **Luke 21:37**—"Each day Jesus was teaching at the temple."

That healing and deliverance were as important as verbal preaching in the ministry of Jesus is also shown by the numerous passages that describe only Jesus' healings in a certain place. It is simply not true that there is "no record of Jesus going somewhere in order to hold a healing meeting." The following passages would make no sense at all if the New Testament's view was that Jesus' verbal preaching was more important than His healing ministry:

Matthew 8:16,17 (Mark 1:32-34; Luke 4:40,41)—Jesus heals *all the sick in a crowd* gathered at Peter's home in Capernaum *without mention of preaching or teaching:* "When evening came, *many* who were demon-possessed were brought to him, and he drove out the spirits with a word and *healed all the sick.*"

The following sounds very much like a "healing meeting": **Mark 1:32-34**—"That evening after sunset the *people brought to Jesus all the sick and demon-possessed.* The whole town gathered at the door, and Jesus *healed many* who had various diseases. He also *drove out many demons.*"

Matthew 8:2-4 (Mark 1:40-45; Luke 5:12-16)—Jesus heals a leper without mention of preaching or teaching.

Matthew 8:14,15 (Mark 1:29-31; Luke 4:38,39)—Jesus heals Peter's mother-in-law without mention of preaching or teaching.

Matthew 12:15-21 (Mark 3:7-12)—Jesus heals *all the sick of a crowd* following Him by the Sea of Galilee without mention of preaching or teaching: "*he healed all their sick*" (Matt. 12:15); "*he had healed many*" (Mark 3:10).

Matthew states that Jesus' healing "*all their sick*" was *a means of proclaiming* the gospel: **Matthew 12:15-18**—"Jesus withdrew from that place. Many followed him, and *he healed all their sick,* warning them not to tell who he was. *This was to fulfill what was spoken through the prophet Isaiah:* 'Here is my servant whom I have chosen, the one I love, in whom I delight; I will put my Spirit on him, and *he will proclaim justice* to the nations.'"

Matthew 8:5-13 (Luke 7:1-10)—Jesus heals the centurion's servant without mention of preaching or teaching.

Luke 7:11-17—Jesus raises the widow of Nain's son from the dead without mention of preaching or teaching.

Matthew 8:28-34 (Mark 5:1-20; Luke 8:26-39)—Jesus heals the demonized Gerasene man without mention of preaching or teaching. Jesus does not tell the man "Go tell your family what I preached to you" but "Tell them how much *the Lord has done for you, and how he has had mercy on you*" (Mark 5:19).

Matthew 9:18-26 (Mark 5:21-43; Luke 8:40-56)—Jesus heals the woman with the issue of blood and raises Jairus's daughter without mention of preaching or teaching.

Matthew 9:27-30—Jesus heals two blind men without mention of preaching or teaching.

Matthew 9:32-34—Jesus heals a demonized mute man without mention of preaching or teaching.

Matthew 14:34-36 (Mark 6:53-56)—Jesus heals the sick in *a crowd* at Gennesaret and *"all who touched him* were healed" (14:36; 6:56) without mention of preaching or teaching.

Matthew 15:21-28 (Mark 7:24-30)—Jesus heals the Canaanite woman's daughter without mention of preaching or teaching.

Matthew 15:29-31—Jesus heals the lame, the blind, the crippled, and the mute *in a crowd* by the Sea of Galilee without mention of preaching or teaching: *"Great crowds* came to him, bringing the lame, the blind, the crippled, the mute and many others, and laid them at his feet; and *he healed them*" (Matt. 15:30).

Mark 8:22-26—Jesus heals a blind man in Bethsaida without mention of preaching or teaching.

Matthew 17:14-20 (Mark 9:14-29; Luke 9:37-43)—Jesus heals a demonized mute boy without mention of preaching or teaching.

Mark 10:46-52 (Matthew 20:29-34; Luke 18:35-43)—Jesus heals blind Bartimaeus without mention of preaching or teaching.

It will not do to say that Jesus did not initiate the occasions of healing the crowds and that He was passively responding to the crowds, since, as was pointed out above, Jesus describes healing as central to His ministry in Matthew 11:4,5,20-30; (cf. 21:14; Luke 21:37); Luke 4:18,19; 7:22; 10:13-15;

13:32. And Peter, Jesus' chief apostle, also described Jesus' ministry largely in terms of healing:

> **Acts 10:37-39**—"You know what has happened throughout Judea, beginning in Galilee after the baptism that John preached—how *God anointed Jesus of Nazareth with the Holy Spirit and power,* and how he went around doing good and *healing all who were under the power of the devil,* because God was with him. We are witnesses of everything he did in the country of the Jews and in Jerusalem."

Professor Lampe of Cambridge remarked about this passage: "God had anointed Jesus with the Holy Spirit and power. This meant that God was with him and that his ministry could therefore be summed up in terms of beneficence, and of healing those who were under the tyranny of the devil (Acts 10. 38). This reference to the anointing of Jesus looks back to his proclamation in the synagogue at Nazareth...."[26]

The Gospels give no evidence that Jesus *did* or *did not* use "general invitations" to be healed, "generalized prayers for healing" or "generalizing announcements"[27] or words of knowledge. The lack of evidence—negative evidence—demonstrates nothing about whether or not Jesus used such methods. No evidence shows that He *did not* or *could not* have used such methods. All we are told is that Jesus often healed *all the sick in a crowd,* which is the obvious procedural intent of methods such as general invitations, prayers, and announcements.

Finally, it is simply not true that when Jesus heals the sick "the result is never ambiguous."[28] (See also the discussion in Wayne Grudem's chapter in this book, objection number 26, *"Weren't miracles in the Bible always successful, instantaneous, and irreversible?"*) In Mark 5:8, Jesus had to command demons more than once before they left a demonized man: "Jesus had been saying [*elegen*] to him, 'Come out of this man, you evil spirit!'" The result of Jesus' healing is also ambiguous on another recorded occasion when He healed a blind man at Bethsaida (Mark 8:22-26). When Jesus first laid hands on him, the man's sight was only partially healed:[29]

> **Mark 8:23,24**—"When he had spit on the man's eyes and put his hands on him, Jesus asked, 'Do you see anything?' He looked up and said, 'I see people; they look like trees walking around.'"

Jesus had to lay hands on him once more before the man's sight was fully restored. If the Son of God ministered healing in stages characterized by ambi-guity as in this case, we should not be surprised if we see more of the same as we pray for healing in the Church today:

> **Mark 8:25**—"Once more Jesus put his hands on the man's eyes. Then his eyes were opened, his sight was restored, and he saw everything clearly."

Further, in John 5:14 Jesus expressly warned the man whom He had healed of lameness in 5:8,9 that a condition worse than the first could come back upon him if he persisted in sin:

> **John 5:14**—"Later Jesus found him at the temple and said to him, 'See, you are well [*hugies* "healed, sound"[30]] again. Stop sinning or something worse [*cheiron...ti*] may happen to you.'"

"Something worse" [*cheiron...ti*] not only foresees eternal punishment, which is what sin ultimately leads to, according to the broader context of the Gospel of John (John 3:18; 5:24; 8:21,24).[31] The immediate cotext suggests that "something worse" primarily refers to a condition worse than that of which Jesus healed the man.[32] The cotextual referent of *cheiron...ti* ("something worse")—the previous element in the story to which the comparative "some-thing worse" refers—is the man's previous condition of lameness (John 5:3-6), which is in contrast to his subsequent state of physical wholeness (John 5:14, *hugies*, "healthy, sound, healed"[33]). What the comparative adjective *cheiron* "worse" refers to in each of the New Testament passages in which it occurs depends entirely on its cotext in each passage,[34] and it does refer to worse con-ditions of physical illness in three other passages: Mark 5:26 (a worse condi-tion of hemorrhaging); Matthew 12:45 and Luke 11:26 (a worse condition of demonization).

Thus, Jesus' warning to the man healed at the pool of Bethesda suggests that just as a worse state of demonization may ensue through unrepentance after cast-ing a demon out of a person (Matt. 12:43-45; Luke 11:24-26), so, after one has been healed of illness, a worse condition of illness or suffering than that which has been healed may return through persisting in sin and unrepentance. The ambi-guity surrounding the wholeness of the man healed at the pool of Bethesda depended on his own resolve to turn away from sin and put his faith in Jesus.

The evidence set forth above shows that healing was not always unam-biguous and was not subsidiary to preaching in Jesus' ministry. On the contrary, healing had an *integral indispensable role* in Jesus' proclaiming the gospel, as has been recognized by scholars the world over who have studied the evidence carefully.

HEALING AND PREACHING SIDE-BY-SIDE

Several scholars have noted that accounts of Jesus' healings are given equal prominence in the Gospels alongside accounts of His preaching and teaching. An example may be found in the study of miracles in the Gospel of Mark by the Japanese New Testament scholar, Dr. Kenzo Tagawa, who published his doctoral dissertation (University of Strasbourg, France) on the Gospel of Mark in French. Apparently the earliest of the Synoptic Gospels, Mark is based on the account of Jesus' ministry given by Peter, Jesus' chief apostle, and therefore it offers an early view of the role healing had in Jesus' preaching:

> The two other motifs are very important. The juxtaposition of the teaching and of the healing shows that the evangelist attaches an equal importance to the one and to the other moment of the activity of Jesus. The acclamation of the crowd in v. 27 [verse 27, i.e., Mark 1:27] shows that the evangelist considers these two particulars of the tradition on Jesus from the same point of view....It may be concluded that one same importance is accorded to teaching and to miracle.[35]

Dr. Alan Richardson speaks of the high proportion of narrative in the Gospels devoted to Jesus' healing ministry:

> The stories of the mighty deeds of Jesus became an original and essential part of the preaching of the Gospel message. It is perhaps worth while to call attention at this point to the high proportion of the Gospel tradition that is devoted to the subject of miracle. Sometimes the miraculous element of the tradition is spoken of as though it represented a merely negligible fraction of the total. In St. Mark's Gospel some 209 verses out of a total of 667 (to xvi. 8) deal directly or indirectly with miracle (*i.e.* over 31 per cent.)....In the first ten chapters of the Gospel (*i.e.* omitting the whole Passion narrative), 200 out of 425 verses deal directly or indirectly with miracle (*i.e.* about 47 per cent).[36]

As was pointed out above, the New Testament does not distinguish Jesus' teaching from His healing in describing His preaching ministry, as some evangelicals do. Dr. H. van der Loos mentions the "side-by-sideness" of preaching and healing in the Synoptic Gospels:

> Now preaching, then healing comes to the fore, whilst sometimes they are mentioned side by side. The effect on the people of both Jesus' words and His deeds is also portrayed in a strongly parallel fashion. This parallelism is further to be found in the instructions to the disciples (Mt. 10:1ff.; Mk. 3:14, 15; 6:12, 13; Lk. 9:1ff). Jesus thus operates through two gifts,...viz. through the word and through the miracle: the first proclaims that the Kingdom of God is nigh, the second shows its force.[37]

THE GOSPEL MAY BE SEEN AS WELL AS HEARD

The passages cited above obviously do not show that verbal preaching was sometimes unimportant in Jesus' ministry. However they also show that healing ministry was not in any way "subsidiary" to Jesus' preaching but that healing was an integral component of His proclaiming the gospel. As was noted above, Matthew 12:15-18 shows that Jesus' healing ministry was *a means of proclamation:*

> **Matthew 12:15-18**—"Jesus withdrew from that place. Many followed him, and *he healed all their sick*, warning them not to tell who he was. *This was to fulfill what was spoken through the prophet Isaiah:* 'Here is my servant whom I have chosen, the one I love, in whom I delight; I will put my Spirit on him, and *he will proclaim justice* to the nations.'"

As Dr. Herman Hendrickx has said, "Jesus proclaimed the good news to the poor not only in words but also in mighty deeds, in healings and exorcisms. The latter indicated the end of Satan's rule."[38]

Dr. Bertold Klappert, a German New Testament scholar, similarly describes the unity of word and deed in Jesus' proclamation:

> The healings are part of Jesus' word and are not to be detached from his proclamation. According to Lk. 4:18, Jesus related the prophetic word of Isa. 61:1f. to his own mission. God sent him to

bring good news to the poor and sight to the blind. This denotes the unity of word and deed in Jesus' proclamation....The proclamation of the kingdom of God takes place by means of Jesus' word, and Jesus' healings are the physical expression of his word.[39]

Jesus' description of His own ministry in Luke 4:18,19 suggests that the gospel He preached was not only to *be heard* but could also *be seen* in "freedom for the prisoners," "recovery of sight for the blind" and in "releasing the oppressed":

Luke 4:18,19—"The Spirit of the Lord is on me, because he has anointed me to *preach good news* to the poor. He has sent me to *proclaim freedom for the prisoners* and *recovery of sight for the blind*, to *release the oppressed*, to proclaim the year of the Lord's favor."

The same is suggested in Jesus' description of His ministry to John's disciples three chapters later in Luke. The gospel is not only *heard* but is also *seen* in Jesus' ministry:

Luke 7:22 (Matt. 11:4)—"Go back and report to John what you have *seen* and *heard*: The blind receive sight, the lame walk, those who have leprosy are cured, the deaf hear, the dead are raised, and the *good news is preached to the poor*."

Similarly, Paul's description of preaching the gospel in Romans 15:18-21 explicitly states that the gospel is not simply a message one hears verbally proclaimed but that it is also something one can *"see"* (Rom. 15:21), according to Paul, *"in deed"* (Rom. 15:18) *"by the power of signs and wonders, by the power of the Holy Spirit"* (Rom. 15:19):

Romans 15:18-21—"I will not venture to speak of anything except what Christ has accomplished through me in leading the Gentiles to obey God by *what I have said* and *done*—by the *power of signs and wonders [sēmeiōn kai teratōn]*, through the *power of the Spirit*. So from Jerusalem all the way around to Illyricum, I have *fully proclaimed [plēroō]* the gospel of Christ. It has always been my ambition to *preach the gospel where Christ was not known*, so that I would not be building on someone else's foundation. Rather it is written: 'Those who were not told about him will *see*, and those who have not *heard* will understand.'"

Thus, "fully proclaiming the gospel," according to Paul means not just talking about it but also showing it in deed. Paul also told the Thessalonians and the Corinthians that the gospel came to them in works of power, not just in the verbally proclaimed word:

1 Thessalonians 1:5—"Our gospel came to you *not simply in word* [ouk egenēthē eis humas en logō monon], but also *in power* [en dunamei], in the Holy Spirit and in deep conviction."

1 Corinthians 2:4,5—"My message and my preaching were *not with wise and persuasive words, but with a demonstration of the Spirit's power*, so that your faith might not rest on men's wisdom, but on God's power."

2 Corinthians 12:12—"The things that mark an apostle—signs, wonders and miracles— were done among you with great perseverance."

How else could Paul speak of himself as a witness of the gospel (Acts 20: 24) and elsewhere as a witness of what he had "*seen* and *heard*" (Acts 22:15; 26:16):

Acts 20:24—"I consider my life worth nothing to me, if only I may finish the race and complete *the task the Lord Jesus has given me*—the task of *testifying to the gospel of God's grace*."

Acts 22:14,15—"'The God of our Fathers has chosen you to know his will and to see the Righteous One and to hear words from his mouth. *You will be his witness* to all men of what you have *seen* and *heard*.'"

Acts 26:15-18—"'I am Jesus, whom you are persecuting,' the Lord replied. 'Now get up and stand on your feet. I have appeared to you to appoint you as a servant and as *a witness of what you have seen of me* and *what I will show you*. I will rescue you from your own people and from the Gentiles. I am sending you to them to open their eyes and turn them from darkness to light, and from the power of Satan to God, so that they may receive *forgiveness of sins* and a place among those who are *sanctified by faith in me.*'"

POWER EVANGELISM VERSUS EVANGELISM WITHOUT MIRACLES?

Certain evangelicals set up another false dichotomy when they suggest that power evangelism—evangelism utilizing miraculous spiritual gifts and healing—is at odds with programmatic evangelism or verbal proclamation of the gospel alone:

> The signs and wonders movement has a realized eschatology in the sense that it considers any form of evangelism not accompanied by miracles as not being true evangelism.[40]

However, John Wimber himself has affirmed just the opposite:

> My contention is not that programmatic evangelism has been wrong. After all, power evangelism employs the heart of programmatic evangelism, a simple presentation of the gospel. Programmatic evangelism has been responsible for bringing millions of people to a personal relationship with Christ. I encourage the practice and development of new kinds of programmatic evangelism. Power evangelism is a catalyst in the programmatic task. My point is that programmatic evangelism is often incomplete, lacking demonstration of the kingdom of God in signs and wonders— but this in no way invalidates the gospel presentation.[41]

Carson rightly emphasizes that evangelism without signs and wonders is not substandard:

> Occasional causes of faith include any number of personal experiences: personal tragedies, a kind deed performed by a friend, a good argument, a deep friendship, a sudden bereavement, some Christian music, an exorcism. But biblical evangelism is not substandard when any one of these phenomena is lacking—and it is not substandard when no genuine sign or wonder is performed.[42]

The fact that Paul preached the gospel without any signs and wonders at the Areopagus in Athens (Acts 17:16-34) is enough to show that biblical evangelism is not substandard "when no genuine sign or wonder is performed."

However, it is biblically abnormal to ignore or resist the way Jesus, the apostles, and the Early Church laity evangelized by preaching accompanied with the use of spiritual gifts and healing.

SIGNS AND WONDERS CONFUSING ONE'S FOCUS ON THE GOSPEL?

The claim is made by some that power evangelism is something other than the proclamation of the gospel and will confuse one's understanding of the gospel:

> If "power evangelism" is something other than the proclamation of the truth of the gospel of God's grace, then is it not something more, by definition?...When the focus is on the unusual phenomena of signs and wonders rather than on the rational content of the gospel itself, confusion as to the main features of that message is bound to arise.[43]

As shown above, in the Gospels, Acts, and the Epistles, signs and wonders are *a part of* the proclamation of the gospel and are not separate from it. Romans 15:19 explicitly describes the full proclamation of the gospel as including signs and wonders:

> **Romans 15:18,19**—"I will not venture to speak of anything except what Christ has accomplished through me in leading the Gentiles to obey God by what I have said and done—by the *power of signs and wonders*, through the *power of the Spirit*. So from Jerusalem all the way around to Illyricum, I have *fully proclaimed* [*pleroo*][44] the gospel of Christ."

One might also ask if Jesus' focus was confused by the fact that healing had a central role in His ministry of proclaiming the gospel of the Kingdom according to Matthew 11:1-5,21; 12:15-18; 21:14 (and Luke 21:37); Luke 4:18,19; 7:22; 10:13-15; 13:32. Or was Peter's focus on the gospel confused when he described Jesus' ministry largely in terms of healing in Acts 10:38 (cf. 2:22)?

Was the apostles' focus on the gospel confused when they did "many wonders and signs" in Jerusalem (Acts 2:43; 5:12)? Was Stephen's focus on the gospel confused when he "did great wonders and miraculous signs among the people" (Acts 6:8)? Was Philip's focus on the gospel confused when he proclaimed Christ in Samaria and also did "miraculous signs," healing the lame and driving out evil spirits (Acts 8:6,7)?

Was Paul's focus on the gospel confused when, in describing his proclamation of the gospel to the Gentiles, he devotes the majority of his description to the signs and wonders that were part of the full proclamation and expression of the gospel in Romans 15:18,19? Or was Paul and Barnabas's focus on the gospel confused when they did "miraculous signs and wonders" to confirm the "message of [God's] grace" in Iconium (Acts 14:3,9,10)? Was their focus on the gospel confused when they characterized the work of God through them among the Gentiles by telling about "the signs and wonders God had done among the Gentiles through them" (Acts 15:12)?

Was God Himself confused about the gospel in Ephesus when He "did extraordinary miracles through Paul, so that even handkerchiefs and aprons that had touched him were taken to the sick, and their illnesses were cured and evil spirits left them" (Acts 19:11,12)? Or was God confused about the message of salvation when He "also testified to it by signs, wonders and various miracles, and gifts of the Holy Spirit distributed according to his will" (Heb. 2:3,4)?

The answer is obviously no. The New Testament evidence shows that signs and wonders, healing and spiritual gifts do not confuse one's understanding of the gospel, they reveal the grace of God through the gospel.[45] It is for this reason that they regularly accompany the proclamation of the gospel in Jesus' ministry as well as that of the apostles and the early churches scattered throughout the Roman Empire. Why should the way the Church evangelizes today be any different?

Notes

1. J. M. Boice in Michael Horton, ed., *Power Religion* (Chicago, IL: Moody Press, 1992) p. 128.
2. Ibid., p. 127.
3. Wimber and Springer, *Power Evangelism*, 1st ed. (San Francisco, CA: Harper-SanFrancisco, 1986) pp. 191-192 (chap. 7, note 2), 2nd ed. (San Francisco, CA: HarperSanFrancisco, 1992), pp. 257 (chap. 12, note 1), 262-263 (chap. 31, notes 1-5); id., *Power Healing* (San Francisco, CA: HarperSanFrancisco, 1987), pp. 245-247; id., *Power Points* (San Francisco, CA: HarperSanFrancisco, 1991), pp. 166-172; 206-207; Wimber in C. P. Wagner and F. D. Pennoyer, eds. *Wrestling with Dark Angels* (Ventura, CA: Regal Books, 1990), pp. 25-26.
4. Compare references cited in notes below and also J. Becker, "Wunder und Christologie," NTS 16 (1969-1970): 138-140; G. Delling, "Das Verständnis des Wunders im Neuen Testament," ZSTh 24 (1955): 265-280; J. Hempel, *Heilung als Symbol und Wirklichkeit im biblischen Schrifttum* (Nachrichten der Gesellschaft der Wissenschaften zu Göttingen, Philosophisch-historische Klasse, 3) 1958; B. Klappert, "Die Wunder Jesu im Neuen Testament," *Das Ungewöhnliche, Aussaat-Bücherei* 45 (1969): 25ff.; G. Mensching, W. Vollborn, E. Lohse, and E. Käsemann, "Wunder," in K. Galling et al., eds., *Die Religion in Geschichte und Gegenwart* (3rd ed., 1957-1965), vol. 6, pp. 1831ff.; R. Renner, *Die Wunder Jesu in Theologie und Unterricht*, 1966; G. Siegmund, "Theologie des Wunders," *Theologische Revue* 58 (1962): 289ff.; R. E. Brown, *The Gospel According to John*, vol. 1 (1967), pp. 525-532 ("Signs and Works"); id., "The Gospel Miracles," *New Testament Essays* (1965), pp. 168-191; A. B. Bruce, *The Miraculous Elements in the Gospels*, 1886; R. H. Fuller, *Interpreting the Miracles*, 1963; A. de Groot, *The Bible on Miracles* (St. Norbert Abbey Series 19), 1966; J. Kallas, *The Significance of the Synoptic Miracles*, 1961; K. Tagawa, *Miracles et évangile: La pensée personnelle de l'évangéliste Marc* (Études d'histoire et de philosophie religieuses, vol. 62 (Paris, France: Presses Universitaires de France, 1966), pp. 75-80; J. S. Lawton, *Miracles and Revelation*, 1959; H. van der Loos, *The Miracles of Jesus* (Supplements to Novum Testamentum, vol. 8, Leiden, Netherlands: E. J. Brill, 1965); L. Monden, *Le miracle, signe de salut*, Desclée, 1960; A. Richardson, *The Miracle-Stories of the Gospels* (London, England: SCM Press, 1941).
5. O. Hofius, *NIDNTT*, vol. II, pp. 632-633.
6. F. F. Bruce, *The Hard Sayings of Jesus* (Downers Grove, IL: InterVarsity Press, 1983), pp. 96-97.
7. H. van der Loos, *The Miracles of Jesus* (Supplements to Novum Testamentum, vol. 8, Leiden, Netherlands: E. J. Brill, 1965), p. 220.
8. A. Feuillet, "Le 'Commencement' de l'Economie Chrétienne d'après Heb. ii.3-4, Mar. i.1 et Acts 1.1-2," NTS 24 (1978): 171-173: "En Marc ii.2 et iv.33 on voit Jésus 'proclamer la Parole'....En Mc. xvi.19-20, une fois Jésus monté au ciel, les apôtres à leur tour 'proclament la Parole.' Et comme la Parole proclamée par Jésus était accompagnée d'oeuvres de puissance, il en va exactement de même d'après Marc xvi.20 pour la Parole proclamée par les apôtres....ce que

Jésus a commencé à dire (la Parole) et à faire (les miracles), tout cela est continué après l'Ascension par les apôtres....Mus par l'Esprit, les apôtres reprennent l'appel de Jésus à la repentance (ii. 38, iii.26, v.31, xviii.30) et son annonce du 'Royaume de Dieu' (viii.12, xix.8, xx.25, xxviii.31)....ils attestent la résurrection de Jésus....Ils s'appuient sur l'invocation du Nom de Jésus....C'est pour ce Nom que les apôtres souffrent (v.21, xxi.13; cf. I Pet. iv.14); c'est ce Nom qu'ils prêchent (iv.10-12, 17-18; v.28-40). Et l'invocation de ce Nom met en action la puissance divine détenue par Jésus. Il en résulte que, par cette invocation, les apôtres accomplissent des prodiges semblables à ceux du ministère public de Jésus, guérissent les malades, chassent les démons et même ressuscitent des morts: iii.1-10, viii.6-7, ix.32-43, xiv.8-18, xx.7-12...v.16...xix.12."

9. C. H. Powell, *The Biblical Concept of Power* (London, England: Epworth Press, 1963), p. 131.
10. G. Delling, "Botschaft und Wunder im Wirken Jesu," in H. Ristow and K. Matthiae, eds., *Der historische Jesus und der kerygmatische Christus* (Berlin, Germany: Evangelische Verlagsanstalt, 1961), p. 393: "Die Heilungen Jesu sind ausgesprochen für die Öffentlichkeit bestimmt, für die Öffentlichkeit des jüdischen Volkes. Und zwar deshalb, weil die Heilungen und Dämonenaustreibungen speziell die Aufgabe haben, die Botschaft Jesu zeichenhaft zu bestätigen. Genauer: die Proklamation der anbrechenden Gottesherrschaft zu bestätigen. Diese bestätigung ist nicht etwa nur eine formale, sie erweist nicht nur die Vollmacht Jesu überhaupt, sondern sie steht in einem inhaltlichen Zusammenhang mit der Ankündigung der Gottesherrschaft. Die Machttaten Jesu bestätigen den Inhalt der Botschaft Jesu—denn diese besagt: Gott beginnt seine Herrschaft entscheidend durchzusetzen, die Heilszeit bricht an. Und das erweist sich, wenn auch nur vorwegnehmend und in für den, der der Botschaft nicht glaubt, verhüllten Hinweisen, in den Machttaten selbst."
11. G. Friedrich, *TDNT*, vol. II, p. 720.
12. David L. Smith, *A Handbook of Contemporary Theology* (Wheaton, IL: Victor, 1992), p. 237. This book is a highly helpful overview of contemporary theological trends, which contains an interesting but occasionally inaccurate survey of third wave sources. Its discussion of the relevant scriptural evidence fails, unfortunately, to account for all the relevant biblical evidence on the issues.
13. P. G. Hiebert, in J. R. Coggins and P. G. Hiebert, eds. *Wonders and the Word* (Winnipeg, Canada: Kindred Press, 1989), p. 126.
14. Ibid., p. 133.
15. Noted by F. F. Bruce, *The Book of Acts* (*NICNT*, ed., F. F. Bruce. Grand Rapids, MI: Eerdmans, 1988), p. 90.
16. Ibid., p. 109.
17. Carson in Horton, ed., *Power Religion*, p. 101.
18. Van der Loos, *The Miracles of Jesus*, p. 270 and n. 1; Oepke, "*iaomai,*" *TDNT*, vol. 3, p. 211; Powell, *The Biblical Concept of Power*, p. 156 and n. 13; A. Richardson, *The Miracle-Stories of the Gospels* (London, England: SCM Press, 1941), p. 19; H. Hendrickx, *The Miracle Stories of the Synoptic Gospels* (San Francisco, CA: HarperSanFrancisco, 1987), pp. 15-17, 26; Jesus often said to

those who came to Him to be healed and forgiven, "Your faith has saved (sōzō) you" (Matt. 9:22; Mark 5:34; 10:52; Luke 7:50; 8:48; 17:19; 18:42).

19. Boice in Horton, ed., *Power Religion*, p. 119-120.
20. Grundmann, *"dunamis," TDNT*, vol. 2, p. 311.
21. Powell, *The Biblical Concept of Power*, p. 139.
22. Boice in Horton, ed., *Power Religion*, p. 132.
23. Richardson, *The Miracle-Stories of the Gospels*, p. 35.
24. Ibid., pp. 44-45.
25. Carson in Horton, ed., *Power Religion*, pp. 98-99.
26. G. W. H. Lampe, "Miracles in the Acts of the Apostles," in C. F. D. Moule, ed., *Miracles. Cambridge Studies in Their Philosophy and History* (London, England: A. R. Mowbray & Co., 1965), p. 167.
27. Carson in Horton, ed., *Power Religion*, p. 99.
28. Ibid.
29. Van der Loos, *The Miracles of Jesus*, p. 419-421 who also cites Calvin's remarks, *Commentary on the Four Gospels*, re. Mark 8:23, that the grace of Christ flowed to this man as it were "drop by drop"; S. Eitrem, *Some Notes on the Demonology in the New Testament* (Symbolae Osloenses Fasc. Supplet., 12, Osloae, 1950), p. 45: "Apparently this cure is a difficult one, being completed in two stages"; cited by van der Loos, p. 419, n. 5.
30. BAGD, p. 832.
31. G. Bertram, *"hamartano," TDNT*, vol. 1, p. 307, n. 151.
32. Van der Loos, *The Miracles of Jesus*, p. 458f.: "One can surmise, but not establish, a relationship between the man's sins and his disease. Something worse might happen to him. This might be taken to mean a 'worse' disease, or some form or the other of chastisement, indeed eternal punishment....It would be a calamity which would form a sharp contrast to the salvation which the man had just been permitted to receive in his healing." For "something worse" referring to the immediate condition of illness from which the man was healed, see Bertram, *"hamartano," TDNT*, vol. I, p. 288, n. 58; Oepke, *"iaomai," TDNT*, vol. III, p. 204; id., *"nosos," TDNT*, vol. IV, p. 1095.
33. BAGD, p. 832.
34. *cheiron* "worse": Mattew 9:16 (a worse tear in a garment); 12:45 (a worse condition of demonization); 27:64 (a worse deception); Mark 2:21 (a worse tear in a garment); 5:26 (a worse condition of hemorrhaging); Luke 11:26 (a worse case of demonization); 1 Timothy 5:8 (a person worse than an unbeliever); 2 Timothy 3:13 (worse evil men and imposters); Hebrews 10:29 (worse punishment); 2 Peter 2:20 (a worse condition of corruption).
35. K. Tagawa, *Miracles et évangile* (*Études d'histoire et de philosophie religieuses*, 62; Paris, France: Presses Universitaires de France, 1966), p. 87 (also see pp. 49-73, espec. pp. 53 and 73): "Les deux autres motifs sont plus importants. La juxtaposition de l'enseignement et de la guérison montre que l'évangéliste attache une importance égale à l'un et à l'autre moment de l'activité de Jésus. L'acclamation de la foule au v.27 montre que l'évangéliste considère ces deux données de la tradition sur Jésus du même point de vue....On peut conclure qu'une même importance est acordée à l'enseignement et au miracle."

36. Richardson, *The Miracle-Stories of the Gospels*, pp. 35-36.
37. Van der Loos, *The Miracles of Jesus*, pp. 284-285.
38. Hendrickx, *The Miracle Stories of the Synoptic Gospels*, p. 25.
39. B. Klappert, *NIDNTT*, vol. 3, p. 1108.
40. Horton, *Power Religion*, p. 348.
41. John Wimber and Kevin Springer, *Power Evangelism*, 1st ed. (San Francisco, CA: HarperSanFrancisco, 1986), p. 47.
42. Carson in Horton, ed., *Power Religion*, p. 117.
43. Armstrong in Horton, ed., *Power Religion*, p. 81.
44. *BAGD*, pp. 670ff. The use of *pleroō* "bring (the gospel) to full expression" in Romans 15:19 cannot mean that Paul *finished* preaching the gospel, because he was still planning to visit Rome and preach the gospel further in Spain (Rom. 1:13,15; 15:23f.). Nor can it mean that he *said everything* there was to say about the gospel, as Murray points out: "He says he 'fully preached' the gospel. This means that he had 'fulfilled' the gospel (cf. Col. 1:25) and does not reflect on the fulness with which he set forth the gospel (cf. Acts 20:20, 27)....Neither does 'fully preached' imply that he had preached the gospel in every locality and to every person in these territories" (J. Murray, *The Epistle to the Romans* [The New International Commentary on the New Testament; Grand Rapids, MI: Eerdmans, 1968], p. 214).

   But, as G. Friedrich points out, it means that Paul proclaimed the gospel in the way he described in Romans 15:18,19, (RSV) "*by word and deed, by the power of signs and wonders, by the power of the Holy Spirit*": "Again, Rom. 15:19...does not mean that Paul has concluded his missionary work, but that the Gospel is fulfilled when it has taken full effect. In the preaching of Paul Christ has shown Himself effective in word and sign and miracle (v. 18). Hence the Gospel has been brought to fulfilment from Jerusalem to Illyricum and Christ is named in the communities (v. 20)" (Friedrich, *TDNT*, vol. 2, p. 732).
45. "Miracles of healing are, as it were, symbolic demonstrations of God's forgiveness in action." Richardson, *The Miracle-Stories of the Gospels*, p. 61-62.

APPENDIX

2

JOHN 14:12–THE COMMISSION TO ALL BELIEVERS TO DO THE MIRACULOUS WORKS OF JESUS

In John 14:12, Jesus linked the miraculous works He did with the ongoing miraculous works He would do through anyone who believes in Him in the postresurrection period:

> **John 14:12,13**—"I tell you the truth, anyone who believes in me will do the works that I am doing *[ta erga ha egō poiō]*. He will do greater (works) than these *[meizona toutōn]*, because I am going to the Father. And I will do whatever you ask in my name, so that the Father may be glorified in the Son."

The clear grammatical and lexical meaning of this passage has unfortunately been obscured by some evangelicals. Carson suggests concerning John 14:12:

Jesus' followers perform "greater things" (the expression is ambiguous enough to include more than miracles)....Doubtless they may include miracles, but there is not a scrap of evidence to restrict those "greater things" to miracles....[1]

Such a statement does not explain at all well the grammatical and lexical evidence in the verse. Scholars who have studied the evidence in an unbiased way agree that what the passage is speaking of is not "greater *things*" but "greater *works*"—the works the Father is doing through Jesus of which Jesus is speaking in the immediately preceding cotext (John 14:10-12). The "scrap of evidence" indicating that *meizona toutōn* "greater ones than these" refers to the miraculous works of Jesus are:

1. The anaphoric function of the phrase *meizona toutōn*, pointing back to its antecedent, *ta erga* "the works" of 14:12a.[2] The demonstrative pronoun *toutōn* (plural genitive), literally "of these," is certainly anaphoric[3] and can only refer to the neuter plural *erga* "works" of 14:12a. The neuter plural comparative adjective *meizona* "greater ones" means nothing by itself without reference to the noun to which comparison is being made.[4] The fact that *meizona* is a comparative links it to its antecedent with which it constitutes a comparison—the only possible antecedent in the cotext being *ta erga* "the works" of the previous clause in 14:12a. Therefore, *meizona* cannot mean anything unrelated to *ta erga* "the works" of God through Christ.

2. The fact that *erga* "works," when referring to Jesus and God the Father in the Gospel of John, denote miraculous works[5] and are closely related to the *sēmeia*, "signs," of Jesus.[6] So, for example, the healing of the man born blind in John 9 is referred to as "*the works of God [ta erga tou Theou]*" in John 9:3 and as one of "*such signs [toiauta sēmeia]*" in John 9:16.

Professor C. H. Dodd of Cambridge, for example, in his study of the Gospel of John, *The Interpretation of the Fourth Gospel*, translated John 14:12 as follows: "I assure you, he who has faith in me will do the works I am doing; and because I am going to the Father, he will do greater works still."[7] Dodd then points out that the "works" in question are the miraculous works of Christ: "Christ will continue His mighty works in His disciples (xiv. 12)."[8]

In an article devoted to John 14:12 and surveying scholarly study of the passage, C. Dietzfelbinger never even questions whether *meizona* "greater ones" refers to *ta erga* "the works" of Jesus and the Father, but he identifies them, as the majority of scholars have, as the miraculous works done by Christ through His disciples like those the Father worked through Christ:

> What is promised to the disciples in 14. 12 is identical with that which the Father will give Jesus according to 5. 20f. From the *disciples*, then, raising of the dead and judgment will go forth; in the being and speaking of the *disciples* will men be granted the gift of eschatological life....The actual activity of Jesus, which only has its prelude and sign in His miracles, is realized through the disciples.[9]

Dietzfelbinger concludes concerning the promise of John 14:12 that it refers to all those who are a part of "the believing community":

> It does not suffice, then, according to John to adhere to and at times to actualize the old Jesus-tradition, just as it does not suffice to tell of the past deeds of Jesus and to represent them in missionary recruiting talk. As Jesus is to be spoken of anew, so His present works are to spoken of, the works which He accomplishes through the Existence of the believing community as the One who has gone to the Father, and these are the greater works than those which occurred earlier.[10]

Countless other scholars have also identified the "greater works" primarily as the miraculous works of Christ through His disciples in the postresurrection period.[11] Thus, nothing restricts the "greater works" of John 14:12 to the miraculous works of Christ alone, but the plain grammatical and lexical meaning of the passage and related passages in the Gospel of John all show that the "greater works" are *primarily* the miraculous works of Jesus, which He promises to work through anyone who believes in Him.

Notes

1. D. A. Carson in Michael Horton, ed., *Power Religion* (Chicago, IL: Moody Press, 1992), pp. 109-110.

2. *Meizona touton*, literally "greater ones than these," of John 14:12b refers anaphorically to its antecedent in 14:12a, *ta erga ha ego poiō* "the works which I do," as pointed out by a number of scholars: Eduard Schweizer, *TDNT*, vol. 8, p. 385: "In Jn. 14:12 one may detect the eschatological prospect of *meizona* (*erga*) to the glorifying of the Father in the Son"; C. H. Dodd, *The Interpretation of the Fourth Gospel* (Cambridge: Cambridge University Press, 1968), pp. 195 and n. 2; 395; C. K. Barrett, *The Gospel According to St. John* (London, England: 1955), sub 14:12; Powell, *The Biblical Concept of Power*, pp. 148, 185; van der Loos, *The Miracles of Jesus*, pp. 218-220.

3. F. Blass and A. Debrunner, *A Greek Grammar of the New Testament and Other Early Christian Literature* (Chicago, IL: University of Chicago Press, 1961), § 290 (2); A. T. Robertson, *A Grammar of the Greek New Testament in the Light of Historical Research* (Nashville, TN: Broadman Press, 1934) p. 289 (e), 697 (f).

4. Wherever the comparative adjective *meizōn* "greater" occurs, what it refers to is textually bound and can be derived only from its cotext: Mattew 18:4 (a person); 23:11 (a person); 23:17 (the temple); 23:19 (the altar); Mark 4:32 (a plant); 9:34 (a person); 12:31 (a commandment); Luke 7:28 (a person); 9:46 (a person); 12:18 (barns); John 1:50 (demonstration of miraculous knowledge); 4:12 (a person); 5:20 (healings such as the healing of the lame man at the pool of Bethesda); 8:53 (a person); 13:16 (a person); 14:28 (God the Father); 15:20 (a person); Romans 9:12 (a person); 1 Corinthians 13:13 (virtues); 14:5 (a person); 2 Peter 2:11 (angels); 1 John 5:9 (God's testimony); 3:20 (God).

5. "The deeds of God and Jesus, specifically the miracles" (*BAGD*, p. 308); "That *ergon* ['work'] in the singular may, and here [Jn. 17:4] does, signify his [Jesus'] whole work and task, is beyond all doubt; but that his *erga* ['works'] are his miracles, the following passages, v. 36; x. 25, 32, 38; xiv. 10-11; xv. 24; to which others might be added, decisively prove" (Trench, *Notes on the Miracles of Our Lord*, p. 6); "The concept of God's saving acts [*erga*] through Christ is common in John's Gospel: 5:20, 36; 7:3, 21; 9:3, 4; 10:25, 32, 37, 38; 14:10, 11, 12; 15:24. These statements relate to individual works done by Jesus. As miracles, they bear witness to Jesus and to the salvation which he brings" (Bertram, "*ergon*," *TDNT*, vol. 2, p. 642).

6. "Most of the 27 *erga* ['works'] passages in John are clearly related to the *sēmeia* ['signs'] of Jesus....Furthermore they...establish a close connection between the *erga* ['works'] of Jesus as *sēmeia* ['signs'] and the work of God effected in *erga* ['works']....When the Johannine Jesus Himself refers to what John calls *sēmeion* ['sign'] He consistently uses the word *ergon* ['work']" (Rengstorf, "*sēmeion*," *TDNT*, vol. 7, pp. 247-248).

7. Dodd, *The Interpretation of the Fourth Gospel*, p. 195 and n. 2.

8. Ibid., p. 395.

9. Chr. Dietzfelbinger, "Die grösseren Werke (Joh 14. 12f.)," *NTS* 35 (1989): 31: "Was den Jüngern in 14. 12 verheissen wird, ist identisch mit dem, was der

Vater Jesus laut 5. 20f. geben wird. Von den *Jüngern* also wird Auferweckung der Toten und Gericht ausgehen; im Sein und Reden der *Jünger* wird den Menschen die Gabe eschatologischen Lebens gewährt,...Das eigentliche Tun Jesu, das in seinen Wundern nur sein Vorspiel und Zeichen hat, wird durch die Jünger verwirklicht."

10. Ibid., pp. 44-45: "Es reicht also laut Johannes nicht, die alte Jesustradition festzuhalten und jeweils zu aktualisieren, ebenso wie es nicht reicht, von den vergangenen Taten Jesu zu erzählen und sie in missionarischer Werberede zu vergegenwärtigen. Wie Jesus jetzt neu zur Sprache zu bringen ist, so ist auch von seinen jetzigen Werken zu reden, von den Werken, die er als der zum Vater Gegangene durch die Existenz der glaubenden Gemeinde vollbringt, und das sind grössere Werke als die früher geschehenen."

11. See references cited by Dietzfelbinger, "Die grösseren Werke (Joh 14. 12f.)," *NTS* 35 (1989): 27ff.; and e.g., W. Bauer, *Das Johannesevangelium* (Tübingen, Germany: 1933), p. 181: missions successes (Missionserfolge), numerous miracles (zahlreiche Wunder), and unusual manifestations of the Spirit (seltsame Manifestationen des Geistes); Powell, *The Biblical Concept of Power*, pp. 148, 185: miracles and "exceptional gifts of the Spirit," works of power, "prophetic preaching" and "healing"; Lampe in Moule, ed., *Miracles. Cambridge Studies*, p. 170: miraculous works; Grundmann, *TDNT*, vol. 4, p. 537: miraculous works; Bertram, *TDNT*, vol. 2, p. 642: "miracles"; Rengstorf, *TDNT*, vol. 7, pp. 248-249: miraculous works functioning as signs; van der Loos, *The Miracles of Jesus*, p. 220: "signs, miracles and proclamation of the gospel to Jews and heathens"; Dodd, *The Interpretation of the Fourth Gospel*, p.395: "Christ will continue His mighty works in His disciples (xiv. 12)."

3

MATTHEW 28:18-20—THE GREAT COMMISSION AND JESUS' COMMANDS TO PREACH AND HEAL

The claim has been made by certain evangelicals that Jesus' command to the 12 apostles and to many other disciples of His to preach the kingdom of God and heal the sick in their missionary journeys in Israel (Matt. 10:1f.,5-8; Mark 6:7,12,13; Luke 9:1-2; 10:1,9) is not a part of what Jesus told the apostles in the Great Commission passage to teach their disciples, Matthew 28:20 (cf. the parallel commission passages Mark 16:15-20; Luke 24:46-49; John 20:21-23; Acts 1:8), *"teaching them to obey everything I have commanded you"*:

> Matthew 28:18-20—"Then Jesus came to them and said, 'All authority in heaven and on earth has been given to me. Therefore go and make disciples of all nations, baptizing them in the name of the Father and of the Son and of the Holy Spirit, and *teaching them*

to obey everything I have commanded you. And surely I am with you always, to the very end of the age.'"

It has been suggested that earlier commissions to preach and heal are not contained in Jesus' final commission to His disciples:

> It will not do to cite Matthew 28:20, "teaching them to obey *everything* I have commanded you," as if that authorizes the automatic applicability of those passages to all believers: after all, the same commissions to the twelve and the seventy-two also included prohibitions against going to the Gentiles or the Samaritans, and commands to take no bag for the journey, and so forth.[1]

Several facts show that Jesus' earlier command to His disciples to preach and heal is part of what is referred to by the phrase "everything I have commanded you" in the Great Commission of Matthew 28 and that all disciples were to be taught to evangelize as Jesus Himself taught His own disciples to do—with preaching and healing:

1. There is no evidence in Matthew 28:18-20 and its parallels, Mark 16:15-20; Luke 24:46-49; John 20:21-23; Acts 1:8, that the phrase "teaching them to obey everything I have commanded you" excludes the commission of the Twelve and the seventy-two to proclaim the gospel with preaching and healing just as Jesus had done.

2. Only two items, at the most, in the commission to the Twelve and the seventy-two were changed in the Great Commission of Matthew 28:18-20 and its parallels, Mark 16:15-20; Luke 24:46-49; John 20:21-23; Acts 1:8.

    a. First, the prohibition against going to the Gentiles was explicitly reversed: "make disciples of all nations" (Matt. 28:19); "go into all the world" (Mark 16:15); "to all nations" (Luke 24:47); "to the ends of the earth" (Acts 1:8).

    b. Second, the prohibition against taking extra provisions (Matt. 10:9; Mark 6:8,9; Luke 9:3; 10:4) was merely incidental to the precrucifixion missions Jesus' disciples carried out. Jesus' words in Luke 22:35,36, which reversed this command, are enough to show this point: "Then Jesus asked them, 'When I sent you without purse, bag or sandals, did you lack anything?' 'Nothing,' they answered. He said to them, 'But now if you have a purse, take it, and also a bag; and if you don't have a sword, sell your cloak and buy one.'"

3. The following facts show that all the other commands of the commission to the Twelve and the seventy-two, including the command to preach and heal, were considered still to be in force in the postresurrection period by the Early Church:

a. In Acts 13:51, Paul and Barnabas obey the command to the Twelve and the seventy-two to "shake the dust off your feet" as a testimony against unbelieving towns (Matt. 10:14; Mark 6:11; Luke 9:5; 10:11), showing they still considered the precrucifixion commissions to be binding.[2] That they preached and healed (e.g., Acts 14:3,8; 15:12; etc.) also complied with the same commissions, as Richardson suggests.[3]

b. The apostles continued to proclaim the gospel with preaching and healing in the postresurrection period just as they were commanded to do in the precrucifixion commissions to the Twelve and seventy-two (Acts 3:6,12; 4:29,30; 5:12-16,20,21, 28,42; 9:34,35; 14:3,8-10,15ff.; 15:12,36; 18:5,11 [cf. 2 Cor. 12:12; 1 Cor. 2:4,5]; 19:8-12; Rom. 15:18,19; 1 Cor. 1:6,7 [cf. 12:9]; 2 Cor. 12:12; 1 Thess. 1:5,6; Heb. 2:3,4).

c. The apostles not only proclaimed the gospel with preaching and healing, but they also taught the disciples they made to proclaim the gospel with preaching and healing—nonapostles such as Stephen (Acts 6:8,10), Philip (Acts 8:4-7,12); Ananias (Acts 9:17,18; 22:12-16); congregations such as the Corinthians (1 Cor. 11:1; 12:9); the Galatians (Gal. 3:5),[4] the Philippians (Phil. 4:9); the Thessalonians (1 Thess. 1:5,6); and Jewish Christian congregations (Heb. 6:1,2;[5] Jas. 5:14-16).

d. The longer ending of Mark 16:9-20 dates from circa the first half of the second century A.D. and is therefore a later addition to the Gospel of Mark.[6] Though it is not found in many of the earliest and best Greek manuscripts (e.g., Vaticanus, Siniaticus, etc.), the long ending is nevertheless attested in 99 percent of the extant Greek manuscripts of the New Testament.[7]

It, therefore, reflects an early postbiblical understanding of Jesus' postresurrection commission to His disciples and to all "those who believe" (Mark 16:17), which, as the manuscript evidence suggests, was widely accepted in the Early Church.[8]

The wide dissemination of the long ending, seen in the manuscript evidence, suggests that the Early Church readily agreed that Jesus' commission did have preaching and healing in mind, like that which Jesus commanded the Twelve and the seventy-two to do, and did include the expectation that supernatural signs would accompany the preaching of the gospel.

Dr. van der Loos points out that the evidence from the Gospels and Acts suggests a clear relationship between the precrucifixion commissions and the postresurrection ministry of the apostles recorded in Acts:

Acts make mention of *many signs* [italics his] performed by the apostles....This miraculous power of the apostles was inseparably bound up with the *instructions and authority* [italics his] which Jesus had given them. The discourse to the disciples before they are sent forth, Mat. 10 and parallel passages, begins with the statement that Jesus called His twelve disciples to Him and gave them power "against unclean spirits, to cast them out, and to heal all manner of sickness and all manner of disease." "Preach, saying, The kingdom of heaven is at hand. Heal the sick, cleanse the lepers, raise the dead, cast out devils: freely ye have received, freely give," are the direct instructions that Jesus gives His disciples.[9]

These facts suggest that the Church is still commissioned by Jesus to proclaim the gospel through verbal witness as well as through praying for healing and using all spiritual gifts. This conclusion is also suggested by the fact that Scripture shows preaching accompanied by healing and gift-based ministry to be the normative pattern of evangelism practiced by Jesus, His disciples, and the Early Church, as was demonstrated in appendix 1.

Notes

1. D. A. Carson in Michael Horton, ed., *Power Religion* (Chicago, IL: Moody Press, 1992), p. 103.
2. Konrad Weiss (*TDNT*, vol. 6, p. 629 and nn. 47-48) has no trouble relating

Paul and Barnabas's obeying the command to shake the dust from their feet in Acts 13:51 to the authority of Christ conveyed to His disciples in the precrucifixion commissions.

3. A. Richardson, *The Miracle-Stories of the Gospels* (London, England: SCM Press, 1941), pp. 41-42: "The charge which was given by Jesus to his disciples as he sent them forth on their mission is reported four times in the Synoptic Gospels and on each occasion the commission to heal is placed alongside of the commission to preach (Mark vi. 7-13; Matt. ix. 35-x. 23; Luke ix. 1-6, x. 1-20)....From the earliest days the ministry of healing was placed side by side with that of preaching in the missionary labours of the Church."

4. *Dunameis* "miracles" primarily refer to miraculous healing and deliverance from demons in the New Testament: compare Acts 2:22 and 10:38 (*dunameis* = *iaomai*), and see passages cited in *BAGD*, p. 208, column a, no. 4; cf. van der Loos, *The Miracles of Jesus*, pp. 252ff.; Grundmann, "*dunamai/dunamis*," *TDNT*, vol. 2, pp. 301-302.

5. Besides bestowing the Spirit and spiritual gifts, the "laying on of hands," mentioned in the list of elementary teachings, is one of the principle means of prayer for healing in the New Testament (Matt. 9:29; Mark 1:41; 5:23; 6:5; 7:32; 16:18; Luke 4:40; 13:13; Acts 9:17; 28:8; Jas. 5:14 "let them pray over [*epi*] him"; E. Lohse, "*cheir*," *TDNT*, vol 9, pp. 431-432). It follows that prayer for healing and prayer to convey the power and gifts of the Spirit was included in the "elementary teachings" of the Early Church.

6. K. Aland and B. Aland, *The Text of the New Testament. An Introduction to the Critical Editions and to the Theory and Practice of Modern Textual Criticism* (Grand Rapids, MI and Leiden, Netherlands: Eerdmans and E. J. Brill, 1989) p. 293; W. L. Lane, *Commentary on the Gospel of Mark* (NICNT, ed., F. F. Bruce. Grand Rapids, MI: Eerdmans, 1974), p. 605.

7. Aland and Aland, *The Text of the New Testament*, p. 292 ; Lane, *Mark*, pp. 602-605.

8. Lane has suggested the long ending perhaps originated in a second-century catechism summarizing postresurrection events (Lane, *Mark*, p. 604).

9. Van der Loos, *The Miracles of Jesus*, pp. 217-218.

4

SPIRITUAL GIFTS–A WONDER-WORKING GOD VERSUS A WONDER-WORKING CHURCH?

The claim is made by some evangelicals that God working miracles is something other than God's people working miracles:

> We can be open to the claim that God can and does perform miracles....Warfield exposes many bogus claims of miracles from the patristic age to the twentieth century....Warfield began from the perspective that miracles were given by God to authenticate the office of the apostles and ceased with them....He nevertheless believed, as do Christians everywhere, that God answers prayer and sometimes heals...."We believe in a wonder-working God," he wrote, "but not in a wonder-working church."[1]

Such reasoning is problematic because not a shred of evidence in the

New Testament demonstrates or even suggests that any gift of the Spirit should or would cease in the Church until the second coming of Christ.[2] To say that the gift of healing ceased, and in the next breath, "God...sometimes heals in answer to prayer" is a logical contradiction. Such a statement as, "God...heals in answer to prayer" is merely a description of the way the gift of healing works. Those so gifted do the praying, and God does the healing (Jas. 5:15). This is illustrated in the description of Paul, who certainly had the gift of healing, in Acts 28:8: "Paul went in to see him and, after prayer, placed his hands on him and healed him."

Further, believing in a "wonder-working God...but not in a wonder-working church" directly contradicts the clear teaching of Scripture. There is no such dichotomy in Scripture. The New Testament clearly shows that it is God who works wonders through His people who are bearers of His Spirit's gifts. Even the miraculous works of Christ, according to Scripture, were worked by God through Christ:

> **John 5:19**—"Jesus gave them this answer: 'I tell you the truth, the Son can do nothing by himself; *he can do only what he sees his Father doing, because whatever the Father does the Son also does.*'"

> **John 14:10**—"The words I say to you are not just my own. Rather, *it is the Father, living in me, who is doing his work.*"

> **Acts 2:22**—"Jesus of Nazareth was a man accredited by God to you by miracles, wonders and signs, which *God did among you through him.*"

First Corinthians 12:4-11 clearly states the different gifts, services, and workings, including "gifts of healing" and "miraculous powers," that "the same God works all of them *in all men*" (*ho de autos Theos, ho energōn ta panta en pasin*, 1 Cor. 12:6). Galatians 3:5 clearly shows that the miracles worked in the Galatian congregation are worked by God:

> **Galatians 3:5**—"Does God give you his Spirit and *work miracles among you [en humin]* because you observe the law, or because you believe what you heard?"

Dr. Karl Gatzweiler, whose doctoral dissertation (Louvain, Belgium, 1961) is a study of the Pauline conception of miracles says the following about Galatians 3:5:

The apostles are certainly not mentioned in the text [Galatians 3:5], and the Spirit is given to all without distinction. The best interpretation seems to us to be "among you and through you." In Galatia there were in fact charismatics who worked miracles (cf. I Cor. 12, 10. 28. 29). The subject of the participles like that of the main verb, which is to be supplied, is God Himself.[3]

It was not Peter who healed Aeneas in Acts 9, but Peter said to Aeneas, "Aeneas...*Jesus Christ heals you*. Get up and take care of your mat" (Acts 9:34). Paul and Barnabas did not tell the apostles and elders of the church in Jerusalem all the miraculous signs and wonders they had done on their first missionary journey, but they told about "the miraculous signs and wonders God *had done* among the Gentiles *through them*" (*di' autōn*, Acts 15:12).

Acts 19:11 does not say Paul by himself did extraordinary miracles in Ephesus, it says, "*God did* extraordinary miracles *through Paul [dia tōn cheirōn Paulou]*." In Romans 15:18,19, Paul does not say that he accomplished the obedience of the Gentiles through signs and wonders accompanying the preached word. He speaks of "what Christ accomplished *through me [di' emou]*."

It is because of evidence such as this that scholars point out there is no dichotomy in Scripture between a wonder-working God and a wonder-working church or the works God did through Christ and the works God does through the Church:

The works of God performed through Christ and those performed through believers cannot be separated from one another. They are the one work of God.[4]

The healing work of the early Church is a continuation of the same ministry [as that of Jesus], carried on in the name of Jesus and in the power of his presence. Particularly significant are the words of Peter to Aeneas: "Jesus Christ heals you" (Acts 9:34).[5]

The significance of the description of the Church as the "Body of Christ" is best understood in this way. This is the community empowered by the Spirit to witness for Him, and to proclaim the Gospel of the "Christ-event." It should experience the reality of the "Lord in the midst," and, feeling His continual inspiration, continue His double work of preaching and healing....

The earliest of the passages describing the Church as the Body of Christ (I Cor. 12) is one detailing the various *charismata* given by the Spirit to individuals....The use of the verb *energein* is noticeable throughout this passage....It stresses the effective working out of God's power through the gifts poured out upon members of the Church: "the word of wisdom," "the word of knowledge," "faith," "gifts of healing," "workings of miracles," "prophecy," "discernings of spirits," "kinds of tongues," "the interpretation of tongues."[6]

Certain evangelicals also suggest that it is acceptable for Christians to be indifferent about spiritual gifts:

We can be open to the claim that God can and does perform miracles. There is a difference of opinion on this point among evangelicals, and we ought to be very careful to maintain a certain liberty of conviction in the matter of spiritual gifts.[7]

But one thing evangelicals cannot afford to do is to "maintain a certain liberty" about unbiblical ideas. As mentioned above, not a shred of evidence in Scripture shows that spiritual gifts would cease before the return of Christ.[8] And Paul did not leave us with any such liberty of conviction regarding spiritual gifts. The Word of God commands us to eagerly desire spiritual gifts and to pray for and excel in the gifts that build up the Church:

1 Corinthians 12:31—"But *eagerly desire [zēloō, "show zeal for, strive, desire, exert oneself earnestly for"][9] the greater gifts.*"

1 Corinthians 14:1—"Follow the way of love and *eagerly desire [zē loō] spiritual gifts, especially the gift of prophecy.*"

1 Corinthians 14:5—"I would *like every one of you to speak in tongues,* but I would *rather have you prophesy.*"

1 Corinthians 14:12,13—"*Try to excel in gifts that build up the church.* For this reason anyone who speaks in a tongue *should pray that he may interpret* what he says."

1 Corinthians 14:39,40—"Therefore, my brothers, *be eager to prophesy,* and *do not forbid speaking in tongues.* But everything should be done in a fitting and orderly way."

1 Thessalonians 5:19-21—*"Do not put out the Spirit's fire; do not treat prophecies with contempt. Test everything. Hold on to the good."*

2 Timothy 1:6—*"Fan into flame the gift of God, which is in you."*

The claim has been made that Scripture is somehow unconcerned about an indifferent attitude toward the gifts:

> All these passages that assume the presence of miraculous gifts outside apostolic ranks focus...not on the justification of miracles but on their purpose or limitation or control in some way....I Corinthians 12 insists that not all Christians have the same gifts....James 5:13-16 focuses on personal holiness. In no passage are readers berated because they have been insufficiently concerned with gifts of healing and exorcisms.[10]

A simple reading of James 5 shows that James 5:13-16 does not focus on personal holiness but focuses on not being indifferent about illness but praying expectantly for healing. Sin is confessed in order *"that you may be healed"* (Jas. 5:16). The passage clearly commands Christians not to sit passively by when someone is ill but to pray for healing in the sick person's presence again and again (Jas. 5:17,18 and 1 Kings 18:43) and to confess any sin that may hinder God's work in the course of that prayer.

Furthermore, the passages cited above—1 Corinthians 12:31; 14:1,5, 12,13,39,40; 1 Thessalonians 5:19-21; 2 Timothy 1:6; and James 5:14-16—do not "berate" readers but clearly *encourage* them not to neglect or suppress the exercise of spiritual gifts but to pursue and develop the use of the gifts in service to the Body of Christ (1 Pet. 4:10,11).

Similarly, the claim has been made that in Paul there is a dichotomy between the Spirit's association with miracles, on the one hand, and the Spirit's association with sanctification, on the other:

> The burden of the associations with the Spirit in Paul is not on miracles but on sanctification, ethics, revelation, transformation of character....[11]

But the connection between the "Spirit" and "power" in Paul is sufficient to show that it is not a matter of either "miracles" or "sanctification" but a matter of *both* "miracles" *and* "sanctification":

Here [in Rom. 15:19; II Cor. 12:12; Gal. 3:5; I Thes. 1:5] we see the connexion between Spirit and power, which we have already seen everywhere in Luke. The Spirit is the One who dispenses and mediates power...."Spirit and power" I Cor. 2:4; "power of the Spirit" Rom. 15:19; "Spirit of power" II Tim. 1:7. We thus have all three possible connexions.[12]

In Rom. 15:19 "the power of the Spirit" is parallel to "the power of signs and wonders," and "Spirit" to "power" in Gal. 3:5.[13]

It is obviously the same Spirit who works miracles regularly through faith (Gal. 3:5) that also sanctifies the believer (Gal. 5:16-26) and causes His fruit to grow in the believer's life (Gal. 5:22). Since first-century believers assumed and experienced the Spirit's miraculous work, as Gatzweiler points out, the miraculous work of the Spirit did not have to receive special mention in Paul's letters:

As examples...we cite I Thess. 1, 5; 2, 13; I Cor. 2, 4-5; 2 Cor. 6, 7; 13, 3; Col. 1, 29; 2 Tim. 1, 8. In all these places Paul speaks of the proclamation of the Gospel which was accompanied by divine power, by the power of the Spirit. The Gospel is God's power which is displayed among men. For the reader, who already knows that the apostle worked miracles alongside the proclamation of the Gospel (cf. 2 Cor. 12, 12; Rom. 15, 18-19), it suggests miraculous events also be understood as self-evident among the notions of "might" and "power" which accompany the proclamation of the Gospel.[14]

Thus, the fact that Paul says much in his letters about the sanctifying work of the Spirit does not mean that the miraculous work of the Spirit was less important to Paul, as the passages quoted by Gatzweiler and those quoted above demonstrate. Quite the reverse of today, the miraculous work of the Spirit was *assumed* in the Early Church, while the sanctifying work of the Spirit needed Paul's attention.

Notes

1. James M. Boice in Michael Horton, ed., *Power Religion* (Chicago, IL: Moody Press, 1992), p. 124.
2. See Professor Gordon Fee's comments on 1 Corinthians 13:9,10 in his commentary, *The First Epistle to the Corinthians*, pp. 644-645, n. 23; 646 and nn. 30-31; F. F. Bruce, *1 and 2 Corinthians*, (The New Century Bible, London, England: Marshall, Morgan and Scott, 1971), p. 122; see also Wayne Grudem's chapter in this book, objection number 21.
3. Gatzweiler, "Der Paulinische Wunderbegriff," p. 383: "Die Apostel werden ja im Text nicht erwähnt, und der Geist wird allen ohne Unterschied geschenkt. Die beste Interpretation scheint uns 'unter euch und durch euch' zu sein. In Galatien gab es in der Tat Charismatiker, die Wunder wirkten (vgl. I Kor. 12, 10. 28. 29). Das subjekt der Partizipien wie des zu ergänzenden Hauptverbums ist Gott selbst."
4. Bertram, "*ergon*," *TDNT*, vol. 2, p. 643.
5. Powell, *The Biblical Concept of Power*, p. 136, n. 28; see also G. B. Caird, *The Apostolic Age* (1955), p. 65.
6. Powell, *The Biblical Concept of Power*, p. 147.
7. Boice in Horton, ed., *Power Religion*, p. 124.
8. See note 2 above.
9. *BAGD*, p. 338.
10. D. A. Carson in Horton, ed., *Power Religion*, pp. 104-105.
11. Ibid., p. 106.
12. Grundmann, *TDNT*, vol. 2, p. 311 and n. 91; cf. O. Schmitz, *Der Begriff dunamis bei Paulus* (1927), p. 145; E. Sokolewski, *Die Begriffe Geist und Leben bei Paulus* (1903), pp. 1ff.
13. Schweizer, *TDNT*, vol. 6, p. 423.
14. Gatzweiler, "Der Paulinische Wunderbegriff," pp. 403-405, n. 52: "Als Belege...zitieren wir 1 Thess. 1, 5; 2, 13; I Kor. 2, 4-5; 2 Kor 6, 7; 13, 3; Kol. 1, 29; 2 Tim. 1, 8. An all diesen Stellen spricht Paulus von der Verkündigung des Evangeliums, die von göttlicher Kraft, von der Macht des Geistes begleitet war. Das Evangelium ist Gottes Macht, die sich unter den Menschen entfaltet. Für den Leser, der schon weiss, dass der Apostel bei der Verkündigung des Evangeliums Wunder gewirkt hat (vgl. 2 Kor. 12, 12; Röm. 15, 18-19), liegt es nahe, wie selbstverständlich unter den begriffen 'Macht' und 'Kraft,' die die Verkündigung des Evangeliums begleiten, auch Wunderereignisse zu verstehen."

APPENDIX

5

SPIRITUAL WARFARE–A BIBLICAL VIEW OF DEMONS AND GOD–DIRECTED WEAPONS

Certain evangelicals find it difficult to believe that demons can have specific functions and they seem to deride any such suggestion:

> Those accounts quickly slide over into descriptions of demoniza-
> tion and exorcism of a very different order, descriptions involving
> "demons" of bondage, temptation, fear, pain, and even physical
> ailments like itching....But that trivializes and cheapens the reali-
> ty of spiritual warfare. It reduces the seriousness of our war with the
> heavenly rulers to the silly.[1]

> Wagner even called together a conference at the seminary in an
> effort to get Christian leaders to bind the various demons (includ-
> ing the demon of homelessness, the demon of sickness, and the
> demon of the Bermuda Triangle).[2]

What such remarks do show is an apparent lack of awareness regarding what Scripture shows about evil spirits. One might ask if the attribution of the deformed condition of the woman in Luke 13:11 to a *"spirit of sickness [pneuma astheneias]"* was also "trivial" and "silly"? But Scripture clearly shows that demons have specific functions and assignments:

1 Timothy 4:1—"deceiving spirits" (*pneumasin planois*)
1 John 4:6—"spirit of error" (*to pneuma tēs planēs*)[3]
2 Timothy 1:7—"spirit of fear" (*pneuma deilias*)[4]
Romans 11:8—"spirit of stupor" (*pneuma katanuxeōs*)[5]
Romans 8:15—"spirit of bondage to fear" (*pneuma douleias...eis phobon*)[6]
Acts 16:16—"spirit of divination" (*pneuma puthōna*)
Luke 13:11—"spirit of sickness" (*pneuma...astheneias*)
Luke 11:14—"demon of muteness" (*daimonion...kōphon*)
Mark 9:17,25—"deaf and mute spirit" (*pneuma alalon/to alalon kai kōphon pneuma*)
Matthew 12:22—*blindness* and *muteness* caused by a demon (*daimonizomenos tuphlos kai kōphos*), which Jesus healed by driving out the demon (Matt. 12:24,28)
Matthew 9:33—*muteness* caused by a demon (*anthrōpon kōphon daimonizomenon*)
Zechariah 13:2—"spirit of impurity" (*rûaḥ haṭṭumʾāh*), a lying spirit inspiring false prophecy (13:3)
Hosea 4:12—"spirit of prostitution" (*rûaḥ zənûnîm*), which leads Israel astray; associated with idols (4:12,17) and leading to literal prostitution and adultery (4:13)[7]
Job 4:15—The spirit (*rûaḥ*) that Eliphaz encountered in Job 4:12-17 and that inspired Eliphaz's message to Job was apparently a lying spirit according to Job 42:7,8
1 Kings 22:22 (2 Chron. 18:21)—"spirit of deception" (*rûaḥ šeqer*) a personal evil spirit who speaks through prophets and inspires false prophecy (1 Kings 22:21-23).

References also show evil spirits related to specific vices in the Dead Sea Scrolls and other early Jewish and Christian apocryphal literature.[8] Professor Eduard Schweizer cites references to "spirit(s) of ambition," "spirit(s) of fornication," and "spirit(s) of wrath."[9] Professor Foerster adds "spirit(s) of blindness," "spirits of sickness," "seducing spirits," as well as spirits of "witchcraft," "war," "strife," and "bloodshed."[10] Such a worldview in first-century Palestine was not contradicted by Jesus and the apostles but was affirmed and assumed to be true, as the New Testament references cited above show:

> The New Testament conception of demons is, in general, identical with that which obtains in the apocryphal and pseudepigraphic literature, the Dead sea Scrolls, and the earlier strata of the Talmud. The existence of demons, as agents of all manner of ills, is taken for granted. They continue to be regarded as the ministers of Satan....
>
> More commonly, the term *daimonia* ["demons"] is used to denote "unclean spirits" (*pneumata akatharta*; cf. Lk. 8:29; Acts 5:16; 8:7; etc.)—analogous to the Talmudic "spirit of catalepsy" (*rûaḥ ṣərādāh*; Pes. 111b), "spirit of delirium" (*rûaḥ ḥăzāzît*; J. T. Yom. 45b), or "spirit of melancholy" (*rûaḥ qardiyāqôs*...; J. T. Git. 48c)— which "enter into" a man (Lk. 8:30;...), "trouble" (*ochlein*; Acts 5:16) or "overtake" him (*katalambanein*; Mk. 9:18), or which a man "possesses" (*echein*; Lk. 4:33), and which produce in him disorders either physical (Mat. 4:24; 8:16, 28; 9:32; 12:22; Mk. 9:18; Lk. 11:14; 13:11) or psychic (Mat. 11:18; Lk. 4:33; Jn. 10:19-21).[11]

The notion that demons desire to inhabit human bodies is apparently thought worthy of scorn by certain critics:

> Wimber adds a few experiences of his own. For instance, his experience with demons taught him that "there are many demons that don't have a body....Having a body...is like having a car. They want to have a car so they can get around...."[12]

The alleged quotation of John Wimber is quite dubious, since the reference cited as the source of the quotation is obscure and not easily verifiable. What these remarks show is lack of familiarity with Scripture's teaching about demons. Of course, the idea that demons desire to inhabit bodies did not originate with John Wimber but with Jesus. Is Jesus also suspect because He taught that demons desire to inhabit human bodies?

Matthew 12:43-45 (Luke 11:24-26)—*"When an evil spirit comes out of a man*, it goes through arid places seeking rest and does not find it. *Then it says, 'I will return to the house I left.'* When it arrives, it finds the house unoccupied, swept clean and put in order. Then it goes and takes with it seven other spirits more wicked than itself, and *they go in and live there.* And the final condition of that man is worse than the first."

Are New Testament scholars who discuss such passages also worthy of suspicion and scorn? Dr. Alan Richardson says of the concept of demonization in first-century Jewish thought and in the New Testament:

The daemons must inhabit the body of someone—even swine, if the worst came to the worst—or perish, since they had no body of their own (cf. Matt. xii. 43 = Luke xi. 24; and Mark v. 10, 12); and the choice of a victim was quite fortuitous and irrational.[13]

The claim has also been made that the instructions about spiritual warfare in Ephesians 6:10-18 have nothing to do with "binding" evil spirits with specific functions:

No weapon is offered here for the saint's use that compares with the sort of "spiritual warfare" one often sees in rallies in which the demon of this or the spirit of that is "bound."[14]

Such a statement, once again, shows only a lack of familiarity with the New Testament and with its first-century Jewish background. It has been adequately demonstrated that the New Testament assumes demons have functions ("the demon of this or the spirit of that"). It is also clear that Jesus did speak of "binding" Satan and demons in relation to His demon expulsions:

Matthew 12:29 (Mark 3:27)—"How can anyone enter a strong man's house and carry off his possessions unless he first *ties up [deō* "bind, tie up"] *the strong man?* Then he can rob his house."

Luke 11:21,22—"When a strong man, fully armed, guards his own house, his possessions are safe. But when *someone stronger attacks and overpowers him,* he takes away the armor in which the man trusted and divides up the spoils."

It is also obvious in the Gospels that the way Jesus bound or tied up "the strong man"—Satan and his demons—was with a Spirit-directed word of command:

Matthew 4:4,7,10; Luke 4:4,8,12—"It is written..." Jesus resisted Satan by speaking the written Word of God.

Matthew 4:10—"Away from me, Satan!" Jesus sent Satan away with an immediate word of command under the guidance of the Spirit (Matt. 4:1,4b; Mark 1:12; Luke 4:1; John 5:19; 8:28; 12:49; 14:24).

Matthew 8:16—"When evening came, many who were demon-possessed were brought to him, and *he drove out the spirits with a word* and healed all the sick."

New Testament scholars who have studied the evidence carefully have recognized this fact:

> While the pagans and Jews...tried to drive out the demons by magic, exorcisms and other magical practices, Jesus needed only his word of command (Mat. 8:16)....Because Jesus with the authority of God showed himself the stronger (Mk. 1:24 par.), the demon had to yield to him and bow to his power. In his majesty Jesus also gave his disciples authority to cast out demons (Mat. 10:1, 8). His dominion over these powers was a sign that the kingdom of God had come in his person (Mat. 12:22-28).[15]

> The casting out of demons reveals that the devil has been bound by one stronger than he (Mat. 12:29; Mk. 3:27; Lk. 11:21).[16]

> Jesus is conscious that He now breaks the power of the devil and his angels because He is the One in whom the dominion of God is present on behalf of humanity (Mt. 12:28 and par.)....The crucial thing is that demons are expelled by a word of command issued in the power of God....[17]

> Satan exercises his dominion in the different forms of sin and sickness and possession and death. The demons are his agents....The saying of Jesus [Mat. 12:29]...speaks of Satan as an *ischuros*, a strong man who exercises rule. The *skeue* ["possessions"] (Mat. 12:29 and Mk. 3:27) or *ta huparchonta* ["the possessions"] (Lk. 11:21) and *ta skula* ["the spoils"] (v. 22) are the men whom he rules.

The mission of Christ means that the *ischuroteros* ["the stronger one"] comes, that He overcomes and binds the *ischuros* ["the strong man"] when He has entered his house, and that He robs him of his spoil. This is how the exorcisms are to be understood....The mighty power of Jesus, displayed in His proclamation and miracles, is the power of the kingdom of God, and it has vanquished the might of Satan.[18]

What was "the sword of the Spirit, which is the Word of God" (Eph. 6:17) in Jesus' confrontations with Satan and demons? Jesus said nothing except what God the Father guided Him to say, according to John 8:28; 12:49; 14:24. Thus the word of command Jesus used to resist Satan in the wilderness and to cast out demons were God-directed words of command. These included speaking the written Word of God, on the one hand ("It is written..." Matt. 4:4,7,10; Luke 4:4,8,12), and, on the other hand, immediate words from God, applying scriptural truth to the situation at hand ("Away from me Satan! For it is written...." Matt. 4:10; "Be quiet!...Come out of him!" Mark 1:25; Luke 4:35; "Come out of this man, you evil spirit!" Mark 5:8; "Go!" Matt. 8:32; "You deaf and mute spirit,...I command you, come out of him and never enter him again" Mark 9:25; expelling a "spirit of sickness" afflicting a woman, "Woman, you are set free from your infirmity" Luke 13:12).

What was "the sword of the Spirit, which is the Word of God" in the ministry of the apostles and the Early Church? Jesus promised the disciples that in their missionary witness His Spirit would direct and guide what they would say (Matt. 10:19; Luke 12:11) and do (John 14:26; 15:1-5). Acts shows, for example, the Spirit speaking to and guiding Stephen, Philip, and Ananias, all nonapostles (Acts 6:10; 8:26; 9:15), and Paul (Acts 16:6ff). What was the "sword of the Spirit" Peter used in confronting the satanically inspired deception perpetrated by Ananias and Sapphira? The only possibility is the rebuke of Acts 5:4,9: "You have not lied to men but to God....The feet of the men who buried your husband are at the door, and they will carry you out also." What was the "sword of the Spirit" Stephen used when he confronted the satanic opposition of the Sanhedrin to Christ? Possibilities include first, the Spirit-inspired exposition of Scripture of Acts 7:2-53 (see 6:10), and then the rebuke and vision of Acts 7:51,56: "You always resist the Holy Spirit!.....I see heaven open and the Son of Man standing at the right hand of God."

What was the "sword of the Spirit" Paul used in confronting the Jewish sorcerer on Cyprus? The only possibility is the rebuke of Acts 13:10,11: "You are a child of the devil....The hand of the Lord is against you. You are going to be blind." What was the "sword of the Spirit" Paul used in confronting the spirit of divination in the slave girl at Philippi? The only possibility is the word of command of Acts 16:18: "In the name of Jesus Christ I command you to come out of her!"

It is clear, then, that Ephesians 6:10-18 *does* refer to a weapon with which demons can be bound—the Word of God, Scripture (obviously including the proclamation of the gospel, Eph. 6:15, 19ff.; 1 Pet. 1:23-25) and the immediate God-directed word of command applying scriptural truth to the situation at hand.[19] This does not suggest that immediate prophetic words from God are *the Word of God* or that they are to be put on the same level as the Word of God, Scripture. On the contrary, they are to be *under* the authority of Scripture and *tested by* Scripture (1 Thess. 5:19-22; 1 John 4:1; 1 Cor. 14:29; see Wayne Grudem's chapter, objection numbers 16, 17, 18 and appendix 7 following).

Notes

1. James M. Boice in Horton, ed., *Power Religion* (Chicago, IL: Moody Press, 1992), p. 129.
2. John H. Armstrong in Horton, ed., *Power Religion*, p. 64.
3. 1 John 4:1-3 makes it clear that this is a personal demonic spirit.
4. That the second "spirit"—the Spirit of love, power, and discipline—is personal suggests the first "spirit" is personal, too.
5. That this refers to demonic agency and not just an inner attitude is suggested by 2 Corinthians 4:4, which is part of a discussion by Paul of the veil over Israel's heart (2 Cor. 3:15) similar to the discussion of Israel's unbelief in Romans 11.
6. Personal demonic agency here is suggested by Hebrews 2:14,15 (cf. Eph. 2:2).
7. Hardly just an inner attitude, since the theme of spiritual prostitution elsewhere clearly refers to involvement with personal evil spirits and demonic deities (Lev. 17:7; 20:5,6; Num. 25:1-3; Ps. 106:28,36-39).
8. See following notes and cf. the discussion of Dr. Clinton Arnold, *Powers of Darkness: Principalities and Powers in Paul's Letters* (Downers Grove, IL: InterVarsity Press, 1992), pp. 67-69.
9. E. Schweizer, *TDNT*, vol. 6, pp. 390 and n. 329; 391 and n. 339.
10. W. Foerster, *TDNT*, vol. 2, pp. 13, nn. 99-100; 15.
11. T. H. Gaster, "Demon," in *IDB*, vol. 1, pp. 822-823.
12. Armstrong in Horton, ed., *Power Religion*, p. 77.
13. A. Richardson, *The Miracle-Stories of the Gospels*, p. 71.

14. Horton, *Power Religion*, p. 17.
15. H. Bietenhard, *NIDNTT*, vol. 1, pp. 453-454.
16. B. Klappert, *NIDNTT*, vol. 2, p. 382.
17. Foerster, *TDNT*, vol. 2, p. 19.
18. W. Grundmann, *TDNT*, vol. 3, p. 401; Similarly, van der Loos, *The Miracles of Jesus*, p. 182, and n. 2.
19. Dr. Edward F. Murphy, *The Handbook for Spiritual Warfare* (Nashville, TN: Nelson, 1992), pp. 35-36, 266, 411-412; cf. Arnold, *Powers of Darkness*, pp. 76-78, 157-158.

APPENDIX

6

MODELS OF PRAYER FOR HEALING AND RELATED PHENOMENA

Certain evangelicals contend that third wave models of prayer for healing and related phenomena are questionable and inconsistent with Scripture:

> Peter Wagner appears to be embarrassed by the petition in the Lord's Prayer, "Thy will be done." That is a "passive approach," Wagner argues. "The active approach does seem to release more healing power."[1]

Unfortunately, Dr. Wagner's position on prayer is misrepresented by such statements. First, Wagner *does not* equate the Lord's Prayer affirmation "Thy will be done" with passivity. He calls *lack of faith and discernment* passive:

> More timid souls, in order to cover their bases and create a fail-safe

situation, will pray, "God I don't know what your will is, but if it is your will, please heal this person." The basic principle is sound, namely, that we want nothing other than God's will to be done. But frequently this type of prayer reflects not only submission to God's will, which is good, but also lack of faith and lack of discernment, which are not.[2]

Second, God has made His will regarding healing of sickness clear to the Church in James 5:14-16—we are to pray expectantly for healing of the sick. "The prayer offered in faith will make the sick person well; the Lord will raise him up" is the general principle according to James 5:15. This suggests (along with many other passages) that God desires to heal the sick. Jesus healed the sick.[3] The apostles and Early Church laity healed the sick (Stephen, Philip, Ananias, the Corinthians, Galatians, Jewish Christian churches, etc.).[4] God gave the Church gifts of healing (1 Cor. 12:9,28,29), and He commands the Church to pray for the sick on an ongoing basis (Jas. 5:14-16). All this also suggests God desires to heal the sick.

And, although God desires to heal, Scripture also makes it clear that in some cases we may not experience complete healing in this age.[5] In 1 Corinthians 13, Paul says that in this age the church will only experience spiritual gifts, which include healing, "in part" (ek merous) until the second coming of Christ: "For we know in part and we prophesy in part" (1 Cor. 13:9; cf. 1 Cor. 1:6,7 and 13:8-10,12; 1 John 3:2; Rev. 22:4).[6]

Third, it is simply not true that Wagner is embarrassed by the prayer, "Thy will be done":

> I continue to pray daily "Thy will be done on earth as it is in heaven." Because I am a front-line representative of the kingdom of God, I will continue to oppose the works of Satan. In the power of the Holy Spirit I will witness to the lost and pray for the sick, knowing ahead of time that not all will be saved and not all will be healed. But some will, and that constitutes abundant reward for labors invested.[7]

Fourth, it is Jesus who, alongside His teaching on the Lord's Prayer, teaches active prayer that is bold and persistent. There is no inherent contradiction between bold, active prayer and the prayer, "Thy will be done":

Luke 11:8,9—"Though he will not get up and give him the

bread because he is his friend, yet *because of the man's boldness* [*anaideia*, "persistence, shamelessness, impudence"],[8] he will get up and give him as much as he needs. So I say to you: *ask* and it will be given to you; *seek* and you will find; *knock* and the door will be opened to you."

Luke 18:7—"Will not God bring about justice for his chosen ones, who *cry out* to him *day and night*? Will he keep putting them off?"

The charge has also been leveled that methods used in third wave prayer models are somehow inconsistent with Scripture:

A tendency toward spiritual technology, though subtle, is apparent in the Vineyard movement. For instance, Wimber says concerning his healing practices: "At the same time I'm gathering information with my five senses I'm sending up my antenna into the cosmic reality." Is this what our Lord and his apostles did when they engaged in healing?[9]

It is unfortunate that a dubious third-party quotation of Wimber was used as a source of John Wimber's teaching in these remarks rather than a first-hand source published by Wimber himself.[10] It is difficult to take seriously such impressionistic, potentially inaccurate research.

It is clear from Wimber's own words what he does when he prays for healing:

While I am interviewing the person, on a supernatural level I ask God for insight into the ultimate cause of the condition. These insights usually come to me through words of knowledge, words of wisdom, and distinguishing of spirits.[11]

It is also clear from Scripture that asking God for insight and direction is precisely what Jesus and the apostles did when they healed the sick. After healing the lame man at the pool of Bethesda (John 5:1ff.), Jesus explicitly told the Jewish leaders who criticized this healing that He could "do only what he sees his Father doing, because whatever the Father does the Son also does" (John 5:19) and "I judge only as I hear,...for I seek not to please myself but him who sent me" (John 5:30). Both statements show that Jesus looked and listened for insight and guidance from God the Father when He healed the sick.

How else can one explain Jesus rebuking not only a mute spirit in the demonized boy of Mark 9, but a *deaf* and mute spirit: "You deaf and mute spirit,...I command you, come out of him" (Mark 9:25). The boy's father had only told Jesus that his son had a *mute spirit* (*pneuma alalon*, Mark 9:17). Jesus, obviously, supernaturally discerned from God the Father that the spirit also caused deafness in the boy. Jesus also obviously received this insight and guidance from God the Father while He was interviewing the boy's father with questions such as, "How long has he been like this?" (Mark 9:21).

How else could Peter be so presumptuous as to claim to speak for the Lord when he told Aeneas, the paralytic of Lydda, "Aeneas, Jesus Christ heals you," (Acts 9:34) unless the Lord had specifically guided Peter to do so? Even Philip, a layman, listened for and followed the Spirit's guidance when he evangelized the Ethiopian eunuch (Acts 8:29). Why should we act any differently when we pray for the sick and evangelize today?

The charge of "spiritual technology" aimed at coercing God's power has also been leveled at Wimber's idea of training Christians to pray effectively for the sick, based on scriptural principles:

> Spiritual technology must be created to harness power...rendering a picture of God as more of a power source, impersonal force, or dispenser, than as a sovereign, personal deity.[12]

But this charge is absolutely false. God is not treated as an impersonal power source by Wimber at all:

> Frequently I encounter people who want a method for healing, a formula they can follow that guarantees them automatic healings. But divine healing is neither automatic nor dependent on our right actions; it is rooted in a relationship with God and the power of his Spirit.[13]

> The Holy Spirit is the doctor and the cure; he does not need our technical knowledge to heal.[14]

> I always ask God about how I should intercede for a sick person.[15]

The accusation of spiritual technology used to coerce God's power is false. Dependence on God and His guidance is what Scripture[16] and, accordingly, third wave leaders such as Wimber and Wagner have taught.

Such charges also ignore the fact that biblical discipleship involves learning how Jesus healed the sick (see discussion in Don Williams' chapter in this book). That Jesus' ministry methods became a model for the disciples is shown by the fact that under the Spirit's guidance they healed the sick, using many of the same words and methods Jesus Himself had used:

> **Compare** Mark 2:11; 5:41; Luke 5:24; 7:14; 8:54; John 5:8 ("get up" *egeirō*) **and** Acts 3:6,7 ("get up" *egeirō* majority of texts[17]); 9:34,40; 14:10 ("stand up" *anastēthi*).
>
> **Compare** Luke 13:12 (eye contact) **and** Acts 3:4; 14:9 (eye contact).
>
> **Compare** John 5:8 ("walk" *peripatei*) **and** Acts 3:6 ("walk" *peripatei*).
>
> **Compare** Luke 18:42 ("see again" *anablepson*) **and** Acts 22:13 ("see again" *anablepson*).
>
> **Compare** Matthew 9:25; Mark 5:40 (putting away a weeping crowd) **and** Acts 9:40 (putting away a weeping crowd).
>
> **Compare** Mark 1:25; 5:8; 9:25; Luke 4:35 ("come out" *exerchomai*) **and** Acts 16:18 ("come out" *exerchomai*).
>
> **Compare** Matthew 8:3,15; 9:25,29; Mark 1:31,41; 5:41; 6:5; 8:23,25; Luke 4:40; 5:13; 8:54; 13:13; 14:4 (laying on of hands) **and** Acts 8:12; 9:17; 28:8 (laying on of hands).

Referring to such parallels between the ministry methods of Jesus and those of the disciples, Dr. Cyril H. Powell has said, "In all this, Acts witnesses to the emergence of power in ways comparable to those recounted in the Gospels concerning Jesus. Jesus had said (in Lk only 6[40]) 'Every disciple when he is fully equipped (*katērtismenos*) shall be as his master.'..."[18] How else does one explain the answer given by the man healed of blindness in John 9:27 when the Jewish leaders repeatedly asked him *what methods* Jesus used to heal him:

> **Compare John 9:15**—"The Pharisees also asked him *how [pōs]* he had received his sight. '*He put mud on my eyes*,' the man replied, '*and I washed*, and now I see.'"
>
> **and John 9:26,27**—"Then they asked him, '*What [ti]* did he do to you? *How (pōs)* did he open your eyes?' He answered, '...Why do you want to hear it again? Do you want to *become his disciples, too?*'"

If it is considered illegitimate to look to the Gospels and Acts for exemplary methods to use in praying for healing, as some critics seem to suggest, how does one explain Paul resuscitating Eutychus, using the methods described in the Old Testament of Elijah and Elisha? In Acts 20:10, Paul throws himself on the body, just as Elijah and Elisha did respectively in 1 Kings 17:21 and 2 Kings 4:34,35. Paul's example shows that it is entirely legitimate to use scriptural descriptions as examples in praying for healing (cf. 1 Cor. 11:1; Phil. 4:9; 1 Thess. 1:6).

Specific objections have been raised against the five-step prayer model[19] pioneered by Wimber and adapted by Wagner and other evangelicals:

> Peter Wagner insists, "There is no secret formula, ritual, or pro-
> cedure, which when used correctly, makes the healing [...sic] and
> we cannot write the [sic] script" for God. And yet, amazingly, only
> a few pages later Wagner offers "a five step process" to be followed
> in obtaining the miracle of healing.[20]

Not only do these remarks cite the wrong page number from Wagner's publication,[21] Wagner's words are distorted in the above quote by omitting certain crucial words. What Wagner actually says is (the omitted words are in bold face italics):

> There is no secret formula, ritual or procedure, which, when used
> correctly, makes the healing **happen. God does the healing,** and
> we cannot write **His** script **for Him.**[22]

Obviously, "God does the healing," not our methods, as Wagner affirms.

The remarks of both Wagner and Wimber about some of the steps in the five-step prayer model show that there is no contradiction with God's sovereign role in using the five-step model. Rather, the five-step model primarily helps one listen to God and follow His direction in how to pray for a person:

STEP 1: THE INTERVIEW

> **Wimber:** "Divine healing is a gift from God, an act of his mercy
> and grace. Our part is to listen to him and carry out his
> word....There are many ways in which we practice being open to
> God's presence and grow in hearing his word—Scripture study,
> worship, prayer, and meditation being foremost.[23]

"I ask [the person], 'What do you want me to pray for?' Then I listen to the answer on two levels: the natural and the supernatural."[24]

Wagner: "It is necessary to listen, not only to the sick person, but also to God, for sometimes God will reveal special information during the interview."[25]

STEP 2: DIAGNOSTIC DECISION

Wimber: "While I am interviewing the person, on a supernatural level I ask God for insight into the ultimate cause of the condition."[26]

Wagner: "While the interview is taking place, try to discern what is the underlying cause of the symptoms....I do try to keep my spiritual antenna tuned to what God wants to say to me."[27]

STEP 3: PRAYER SELECTION

Wimber: "This step answers the question, 'What kind of prayer is needed to help this person?' What lies behind this question is an even more fundamental question. What does God want to do at this particular time for this person? While I assume God wants to heal, I do not assume that God wants to heal at the exact instant in which I am praying for someone. So I ask, 'Lord, do you want to heal right now?'"[28]

"I always ask God about how I should intercede for a sick person."[29]

Wagner: "Sometimes I anoint the person with it [oil], sometimes I don't, depending on how I feel God is leading during the prayer selection phase."[30]

STEP 4: PRAYER ENGAGEMENT

Wimber: "After laying on hands, I pray aloud that the Holy Spirit will come and minister to the person. My prayers are quite simple:

'Holy Spirit, I invite you to come on this person and release your healing power,' or 'Holy Spirit, come and show us how to pray.'"[31]

Wagner: "As we gain experience in listening to God as well as talking to Him, we will, in many cases, be able to know what His will is by the time we get through the first three steps. This enables us to pray with a degree of boldness that otherwise we could not have."[32]

The charge has also been leveled that certain unusual phenomena accompanying prayer and the presence of God's Spirit are somehow inconsistent with Scripture:

The phenomena third wave proponents hold forth as normative for believers today (include shaking, falling down, jumping up and down in place, heavy breathing) were not even normative...in the apostolic church.[33]

The recurring images of the testimonies (electricity, a Jell-O-like substance applied for the healing of memories [referring to Fr. Mike Flynn in prayer seeing Jesus replace darkness with light in a woman's heart who was emotionally broken and seeking prayer], and so on) appear to borrow more from popular science fiction than from Scripture.[34]

In the fourth stage of this five-stage process, "Sometimes there is a fluttering of eyelids or a kind of aura that surrounds the person. Sometimes there are other manifestations." [citing Wagner, *How to Have a Healing Ministry*, p. 228] Such a statement, of course, goes beyond the question of whether the gifts are still in use in our day, for even if they are, surely nothing like the phenomena Wimber [*sic*] mentions appears in all Scripture. Where in Scripture does one find such a sophisticated technology for miracles, complete with auras to let the person know when something is happening?[35]

First, such statements seem to be unaware that Scripture clearly associates certain phenomena with the presence of God in power. Scripture may not describe every detail we may wish to know, but it does show some basic facts about the issue. Scripture promises that the Holy Spirit would teach believers all things (John 14:26; 1 John 2:27), obviously including details Scripture does not set forth systematically but are nonetheless attested to and implied by clear scriptural evidence.

Second, third wave proponents do not claim that such unusual phenemona are "normative." They simply observe them happen from time to time when God is at work:

> When I travel I am frequently asked if the weekly meetings of the Anaheim Vineyard Christian Fellowship are a cocophony of bizarre physical manifestations [i.e., shaking, falling over, etc.] of the Holy Spirit. My answer is "No, though there is some of this from time to time, as we have visitors in need of healing."[36]

Third, no evidence from the New Testament demonstrates the claim that such unusual phenomena did not occur in the Early Church. No direct discussion in the New Testament shows that such phenomena were or were not "normative" or that they did or did not occur in the Early Church.

But much evidence in Scripture relates some of the phenomena to occasions when God was present in power. One may ask if it was normative for Ezekiel to fall over in the Lord's presence (Ezek. 1:28; 3:23) or for Daniel to fall over and tremble in the presence of the angel of the Lord (Dan. 10:8-11). One might ask if the following passages suggest it was normative to tremble in the Lord's presence.

Psalm 114:7—"Tremble, O earth, at the presence of the Lord."

Jeremiah 5:22—"Should you not tremble in my presence?"

Or was it normative for Jeremiah's bones to tremble[37] and for him to swagger in a drunken state, "because of the Lord and his holy words" (Jer. 23:9)? Was it normative for John to fall over "in the Spirit" when Christ appeared to him (Rev. 1:10,17) or for Paul (Acts 9:4; 26:11) and the soldiers and officials (John 18:6) to do the same? Was it normative for believers to stagger about intoxicated by the Spirit's presence in power in Acts 2 (Acts 2:4,13,15)? The answer is obviously no, but such phenomena clearly happened in the Lord's presence, according to Scripture.

One may also ask if Jesus borrowed from "popular science fiction" on occasions when He said He felt *"power* had *gone out* from him" to heal people (Mark 5:30; Luke 5:17; 6:19; 8:46). Such "power" going out of him healed a woman instantly (Mark. 5:30; Luke 8:46), caused a paralytic to walk (Luke

5:17ff.) and healed all the sick and demonized of crowds that touched Him (Luke 6:19). Greek *energeia* denoting "energy, working"[38] is a synonym of *dunamis* "power," the word used in these passages of Jesus' healing power.[39] Was Paul in Colossians 1:29 and Philippians 3:21 mystifying otherwise sound thinking when he associates God's "power (*dunamis*)" with God's "energy (*energeia*)"? All these references in modern English would obviously approximate the description of electricity as scholars have pointed out:

> Some of Luke's references to healing *dunamis* ["power"] call for closer examination. They seem strangely "physical." There is, for instance, the reference already noted in 5:17f.: "And it came to pass on one of those days, that he was teaching...and the power of the Lord was with him to heal." "In other words," comments Otto, "the charismatic power had its particular hours, when it was present for healing, and manifestly also those when it was not present...."
>
> The picture conveyed by Luke 5:17, several commentators have suggested, is similar to that of being filled with an electric potential....The fact that so many of Jesus's miracles involve the use of touch heightens this impression....Mark's comment (5:30) leaves little doubt that he understood that this touch was felt by Jesus in such a way that He knew that *dunamis* ["power"] had gone from Him....Luke 6:19 is in the same vein: "for power came forth from him, and healed all."[40]

Some scholars, points out Dr. Powell, have viewed "the *dunamis* [power] mentioned here as something automatic and quasi-physical, like a fluid or operating like an electric current."[41]

Is "popular science fiction" responsible for people seeking healing by Peter's shadow falling on them (Acts 5:15) or the sick and demonized being healed by handkerchiefs and aprons that Paul had touched (Acts 19:12)? Is science fiction responsible for peculiar actions and events in Scripture that represent spiritual transactions?

> **Genesis 15:17,18**—God makes a smoking pot with a blazing torch float through the air and pass between sacrificial animal parts to signify a covenant.

> **Isaiah 6:7**—A burning coal singes a man's lips to cleanse him of sin and guilt.

Jeremiah 1:9—God's hand touches a man's lips to give him God's words.

Ezekiel 36:26—God speaks of taking a heart of stone out of a person's body and replacing it with a heart of flesh to give them a "new spirit."

Mark 9:7—A man says a cloud spoke as God the Father to him.

John 1:48—Jesus' seeing a man under a fig tree leads to the man's conversion and faith.

Acts 8:39,40—A man suddenly disappears and then reappears miles away, claiming that God's Spirit transported him from one location to the other to do more evangelism.

Acts 9:3-8—A man and his friends fall over and are blinded by a brilliant shining figure in the sky speaking Aramaic, leading to the man's conversion.

Acts 10:9-17—A man prays and falls into a trance, seeing a sheet full of camels, rabbits, pigs, eels, vultures, bats, rats, and lizards and hearing a voice say "kill and eat" (Acts 10:11,13; Lev. 11; Deut. 14). He claims that the vision means God wants him to redirect evangelistic work to non-Jews.

Revelation 10:9-11—A man eats a scroll that tastes sweet but turns his stomach sour to signify what he is to prophesy about.

Saying that something is peculiar in someone's testimony, obviously does not in itself demonstrate any inconsistency with Scripture or with the work of the God of Scripture. What the testimony leads to—the fruit—in terms of what is taught and in terms of how one lives is the more crucial issue to test in the light of Scripture (Matt. 7:20-23).

The phenomena Wimber and Wagner mention accompanying the Holy Spirit's work through prayer do appear in Scripture. The presence of God working by His Spirit may be marked in Scripture by the following:

1. Trembling, falling over, and intoxication-like behavior which was

mentioned above (Ps. 114:7; Jer. 5:22; 23:9; Ezek. 1:28; 3:23; Dan. 8:18; 10:9,10; John 18:6; Acts 2:4,13; 26:14; Rev. 1:17);[42]

2. Exuberant joy and weeping (Neh. 8:6,9 [weeping in the midst of worship and praise]; Luke 1:41,42,67; 10:21; Acts 13:52);[43]

3. Light, radiance or prophetic vision (Acts 2:3,4 [tongues of fire]; 6:9,10,15 and 7:55 [Stephen, filled with the Spirit had a radiant face][44]; 2 Cor. 3:7,13,17,18 [the radiance of Moses' face is from the "Lord who is the Spirit"]).

These phenomena that may accompany the presence of God's Spirit are attested in early Judaism[45] and postbiblical early Christian tradition.[46]

Many accounts of Jesus, the apostles, and the Early Church healing in Scripture do not give details of just what happened when someone was prayed for and healed. But certain accounts, which recount some details, show that attention was paid to signs that showed the Spirit's work and that showed healing was taking place:

> **Mark 5:29,30 (cf. Matt. 9:22; Luke 8:44,46,47)**—The woman with the hemorrhage is said to have "felt in her body" (*egnō tō sōmati*) that the bleeding had stopped. Jesus also felt the power or energy (*dunamis = energeia*)[47] of God leave His body to heal her.

> **Luke 6:19**—Healing power (*dunamis*) was felt coming out of Jesus into the crowd, healing the sick and demonized (*dunamis par' autou exērcheto kai iato pantas* "power was coming from him and healing them all").

> **Mark 8:23,24**—When Jesus laid hands on the blind man of Bethsaida to restore his sight, Jesus asked him if anything was happening, "Do you see anything?" (8:23). Because the man was only partially healed and saw "people...like trees" (8:24), Jesus laid hands on him again to fully restore his sight.

> **Acts 9:17,18**—When Ananias laid hands on Paul and prayed for him to be healed of his blindness (9:17), the text describes "something like scales" falling from Paul's eyes (Acts 9:18).

These passages suggest that Jesus and the Early Church did watch for signs of God's work and healing when they prayed for and ministered to the sick and demonized.

It has been suggested that "the distinction of the Vineyard movement does not lie in its prayers for the sick but in its insistence that signs and wonders *must* be a part of normal Christianity."[48] But the discussion above has illustrated that one of the unique contributions the Vineyard and third wave movement has made to evangelicalism *is* in pioneering an effective, biblical model of praying for the sick, which can be used in any church or tradition, within a biblical framework of lay ministry and evangelism, encouraging use of all the gifts of the Spirit. John Wimber and the Vineyard do not "insist" that signs and wonders be a part of normal Christianity. They simply have a biblical expectation of them.

On the contrary, it is *Jesus Himself* who said that we should expect His miraculous works to be a normal part of the Christian faith. It is *Jesus Himself* who said that everyone who believes in Him would be empowered to do His miraculous works (John 14:12; see appendix 2).

Notes

1. John H. Armstrong in Michael Horton, ed., *Power Religion* (Chicago, IL: Moody Press, 1992), p. 75.
2. C. Peter Wagner, *How to Have a Healing Ministry in Any Church* (Ventura, CA: Regal Books, 1988), p. 229.
3. E.g., **Matthew** 4:23; 9:35,36; 10:1,7,8; 11:5; 12:15,18; 15:30; 19:2 (cf. **Mark** 10:1); 21:14 (cf. **Luke** 21:37); **Mark** 1:38,39; 2:2,11; 3:14,15; 6:12,13; 10:1 (cf. Matt. 19:2); **Luke** 4:18; 5:17,24; 6:6-11,17,18; 7:22; 9:1,2; 10:9,13; 13:10-13,22,32; 14:4, ff.; 21:37 (cf. Matt. 21:14); 16:15-18,20; **John** 3:2; 7:14,15,21-23,31,38; 10:25,32,38; 12:37,49; 14:10,12; **Acts** 1:1; 2:22; 10:38.
4. E.g., **Acts** 3:6,12; 4:29,30; 5:12-16,20,21,28,42; 6:8,10; 8:4-7,12; 9:17,18 (cf. 22:13),34,35; 14:3,8-10,15ff.; 15:12,36; 18:5,11 (cf. 2 Cor. 12:12; 1 Cor. 2:4,5); 19:8-12; **Romans** 15:18,19; **1 Corinthians** 2:4,5; 11:1; 12:1-11,28-31; **2 Corinthians** 12:12; **Galatians** 3:5; **Philippians** 4:9; **1 Thessalonians** 1:5-6; **Hebrews** 2:3,4; 6:1-2; **James** 5:13-16.
5. In Ephesians 6:18, Paul commands us to "pray in the Spirit on all occasions with all kinds of prayers and requests" (cf. 1 Thess. 5:17; Col. 4:2). Yet, Paul was ill in Galatia for a long enough period that it "was a trial" to the Galatians (Gal. 4:14); Epaphroditus did not experience immediate healing from illness and almost died according to Philippians 2:27; Timothy had chronic illnesses

involving his stomach, which were not completely healed according to 1 Timothy 5:23; and Paul had to leave Trophimus sick in Miletus, apparently seeing no healing in response to prayer (2 Tim. 4:20).

6. On experiencing healing of illness as a "gift of grace," (1 Cor. 12:9,28,29) experienced only in part in the Early Church according to the New Testament, see Oepke, *"iaomai,"* TDNT, vol. 3, p. 214; on experiencing spiritual gifts in this age only "in part (*ek merous* 1 Cor. 13:9)," see Fee, *The First Epistle to the Corinthians*, p. 644 and n. 21; Schneider, TDNT, vol. 4, p. 596.

7. Wagner, *How to Have a Healing Ministry*, p. 112.

8. BAGD, p. 55.

9. Armstrong in Horton, ed., *Power Religion*, p. 73.

10. See ibid., p. 87, n. 43 citing a source critical of Wimber, which in turns cites a nonspecific series of cassette tapes. This sort of impressionistic, poorly researched criticism is sadly typical of certain critics.

11. Wimber and Springer, *Power Healing*, p. 200.

12. Armstrong in Horton, ed., *Power Religion*, p. 73.

13. Wimber and Springer, *Power Healing*, p. 180.

14. Ibid., p. 199.

15. Ibid., p. 207.

16. John 5:19,15; cf. John 3:34; 7:16; 8:28; 12:49,50; 14:10,24,31; Acts 8:29; 10:13ff.,19; Galatians 5:16,18,25; 6:8; Romans 8:5-9; 12:1; Hebrews 3:7ff.

17. Though it is not found in the best Greek manuscripts: see Bruce M. Metzger, *A Textual Commentary on the Greek New Testament* (United Bible Societies, 1971), p. 307.

18. Powell, *The Biblical Concept of Power*, p. 138 and n. 36.

19. For other models of prayer for healing that are not based on the five-step approach but that similarly stress listening to the person being prayed for as well as listening to God for direction, see Richard Foster, *Prayer: Finding the Heart's True Home* (San Francisco, CA: HarperSanFrancisco, 1992), pp. 210-215; Francis MacNutt, *Healing* (Alamonte Springs, FL: Creation House, 1988), pp. 201-213.

20. Armstrong in Horton, ed., *Power Religion*, p. 74 and n. 46, which incorrectly cites page 228 of Wagner's *How to Have a Healing Ministry*. The quote actually comes from page 224 of *How to Have a Healing Ministry*.

21. See previous note. The five-step procedure for praying for the sick is not "a few pages later" as Armstrong states (*Power Religion*, p. 74) but on the same page (p. 224 of Wagner, *How to Have a Healing Ministry*), showing carelessness in Armstrong's research.

22. Wagner, *How to Have a Healing Ministry*, p. 224.

23. Wimber and Springer, *Power Healing*, pp. 180-181.

24. Ibid., p. 199.

25. Wagner, *How to Have a Healing Ministry*, p. 225.

26. Wimber and Springer, *Power Healing*, p. 200.

27. Wagner, *How to Have a Healing Ministry*, p. 226.

28. Wimber and Springer, *Power Healing*, p. 204.

29. Ibid., p. 207.

30. Wagner, *How to Have a Healing Ministry*, p. 228.
31. Wimber and Springer, *Power Healing*, p. 212.
32. Wagner, *How to Have a Healing Ministry*, p. 229.
33. Armstrong in Horton, ed., *Power Religion*, p. 72.
34. Ibid., p. 73.
35. Ibid., p. 74.
36. Wimber and Springer, *Power Healing*, p. 215.
37. Hebrew, *rāḥăpû*, qal-perfect, 3rd plural, of *rāḥap* meaning "flutter, tremble, shake" as the RSV ("shake"), KJV ("shake"), and NIV ("tremble") render it (see E. Lohse, *TDNT*, vol. 9, pp. 623-624; Bertram, "*saleuō*," *TDNT*, vol. 7, p. 66). This meaning is suggested by Mishnaic Hebrew *rāḥap* "move, vibrate" (Jastrow, *Dictionary* s.v., which knows no attestations of this root meaning "grow soft, relax" against BDB's suggestion that *rāḥap* only here in the Hebrew Bible means "grow soft, relax" for which there is no demonstrative evidence in the text itself); by piel forms meaning "hover (of an eagle)" in Genesis 1:2; Deuteronomy 32:11; by Semitic cognates: Ugaritic *rḥp* "fly, flutter"; Syriac *raḥḥēf* "extend the wing" (J. Aistleitner, *Wörterbuch der ugaritischen Sprache* [Berlin, Germany: Akademie Verlag, 1974], pp. 292-293); and by the Septuagint's rendering the word with Greek *saleuō* "shake."
38. BAGD, p. 265; for the meaning "energy," see Colossians 1:29 (RSV, NIV); Philippians 3:21; Bertram, "*energeō*," *TDNT*, vol. 2, p. 652; Powell, *The Biblical Concept of Power*, p. 136.
39. Richardson, *The Miracle-Stories of the Gospels*, p. 6.
40. Powell, *The Biblical Concept of Power*, pp. 108-109.
41. Ibid., p. 109; cf. the descriptions of others—"material substance (stoffliche Substanz)" (F. Fenner, *Die Krankheit im Neuen Testament* [Leipzig, Germany: 1930], p. 83); "a power-substance (eine Kraftsubstanz)" (W. Grundmann, *Der Begriff der Kraft in der neutestamentlichen Gedankenwelt* [Stuttgart, Germany: 1932], pp. 62ff.).
42. On trembling, falling over, and intoxication-like behavior, cf. Exodus 19:16; 1 Chronicles 16:30; Ezra 9:4; Psalm 2:11; 96:9; Isaiah 66:2,5; Matthew 28:4; 1 Corinthians 14:25; Ephesians 5:18; etc.
43. On joy and exuberant praise, cf. Luke 1:46-55,64,68-79; 5:25; 17:15; Acts 3:8-10; Romans 14:17.
44. "Like the face of an angel," Acts 6:15; cf. Acts 12:7; Ezekiel 40:3; Daniel 10:6; Luke 2:9; Matthew 28:2,3.
45. Early Judaism: The presence of God's Spirit marked by light and radiance, radiant face (E. Sjöberg, *TDNT*, vol. 6: 381-382 and nn. 250, 259); prophetic vision, knowledge, sudden inspiration (Ibid., pp. 382, n. 263; 384, n. 284; 386; cf. p. 408, n. 489).
46. Postbiblical Christian tradition: The presence of God's Spirit marked by seeing light and radiance, inner joy, tears, contrition for sin (S. M. Burgess, *The Holy Spirit: Eastern Christian Traditions* [Peabody, MA: Hendrickson, 1989], pp. 3-4) and fragrant scents (Ibid.; fragance associated with Christ is referred to 2 Cor. 2:14,16, and fragance as a sign of the Spirit of Christ's presence in the postbiblical Early Church is related to 2 Cor. 2:14,16 by the well-known New Tes-

tament scholar, E. Nestle, "Der süsse Geruch als Erweis des Geistes," ZNW 4 [1903]: 272; ZNW 7 [1906]: 95-96; see also G. Delling, *TDNT*, vol. 5, p. 495; cf. A. Stumpff, *TDNT*, vol. 2, p. 810).

47. References above, nn. 38-39.
48. Carson in Horton, ed., *Power Religion*, p. 111.

7

THE SUFFICIENCY OF SCRIPTURE AND DISTORTION OF WHAT SCRIPTURE TEACHES ABOUT ITSELF

Certain evangelicals rightly claim that Scripture is sufficient to reveal all that Christians need to know about God, a point Scripture supports everywhere (e.g., 2 Tim. 3:15,16; Acts 17:11; Isa. 8:20; etc.). But in doing so they distort what Scripture itself teaches about the work of Christ and the Holy Spirit in conjunction with Scripture (see also Wayne Grudem's chapter in this book, objection numbers 16, 17, 18):

> "What I am commanding you today is not too difficult for you or beyond your reach. It is not up in heaven....Nor is it beyond the sea....The word is very near you; it is in your mouth and in your heart so you may obey it." [Deut. 30:12-14] Moses' point was that Israel had the Word of God, the law, and that the law was all they

needed. They were not to seek an additional revelation but were to busy themselves with obeying what they had.[1]

On the contrary, Deuteronomy 30:12-14 says nothing about not seeking additional revelation or an additional word from God. The point of the passage was that the message of God—the Law—was *near and accessible* not far and inaccessible. This did not mean that additional revelation besides the Law was not needed. On the contrary, Deuteronomy 18:15,20-22 assumes true prophets with additional revelation from God would arise in Israel, requiring standards by which to distinguish true prophets from false prophets.

Furthermore, if Israel did not need an additional revelation from God, how does one explain God sending prophetic words and revelations to Israel *in conjunction with* the written Law, which Deuteronomy 31:9ff. suggests they possessed: Judges 2:1-5 (angel of the Lord); 4:4 (Deborah, the prophetess); 6:7,8 (an unnamed prophet); 13:1-3 (angel of the Lord); 1 Samuel 2:27ff. (an unnamed prophet); 3:19-21 (Samuel, the prophet); 9:9 (unnamed prophets); 10:11 (Saul prophesies with the prophets); 2 Samuel 7:2 (Nathan, the prophet); 15:27 (Zadok, the priest, a seer); 24:11 (Gad, the prophet, David's seer); 1 Kings 18:4 (Jezebel kills the Lord's prophets); 20:35 (unnamed prophet); 11:29 (Ahijah, a prophet); 16:7 (Jehu the prophet); 18:36 (Elijah); 19:16 (Elisha); 22:8 (Micaiah the prophet); 2 Kings 2:5; 4:38; 6:1 ("the company of the prophets"); 14:25 (Jonah, the prophet); 19:2 (Isaiah, the prophet); Amos 1:1; Habakkuk 1:1; Hosea 1:1; Jeremiah 1:5; Micah 1:1; Nahum 1:1; Obadiah 1:1; Zephaniah 1:1; etc.

The same claim is made of the Church and the New Testament by certain evangelicals:

> As far as Christians are concerned, the same meaning holds. For neither do Christians need an additional word from God. They have what they need already, and it is the gospel message being proclaimed by the apostles.[2]

> But God has determined that we derive all of our knowledge of Him, not through direct encounters, but through the written Word, the Bible and in the Person and work of His incarnate Son.[3]

But such claims are only half-truths at best.

How do such statements explain numerous passages in the New Testament that show continuing revelation alongside and consistent with the written Word of God (Isa. 8:20; Acts 17:11; 1 Cor. 12:3; 1 Thess. 5:19-21), as is the case in the Old Testament? The following passages are only representative examples:

John 10:27—"My sheep *listen to my voice*; I know them, and they follow me."

John 14:26—"But the Counselor, the Holy Spirit, whom the Father will send in my name, *will teach you all things* and *will remind you of everything I have said to you.*"

John 16:13,14—"But when he, the Spirit of truth, comes, he will guide you into all truth. He will not speak on his own; *he will speak [laleō]* only what he hears, and *he will tell [anaggelō] you* what is yet to come. He will bring glory to me by taking from what is mine and *making it known to you.*"

Romans 8:16—"*The Spirit himself testifies [summarturei*, whose verb base is *martureō* 'bear witness, testify, speak'] *with our spirit* that we are God's children."

1 Corinthians 14:29,30—"Two or three prophets should speak, and the others should weigh carefully what is said. And *if a revelation comes to someone* who is sitting down, the first speaker should stop. For *you can all prophesy in turn.*"

Ephesians 1:17—"I keep asking that the God of our Lord Jesus Christ, the glorious Father, may give you the Spirit of wisdom and *revelation, so that you may know him better.*"

1 John 2:27—"As for you, the anointing you received from him remains in you, and you do not need anyone to teach you. But as *his anointing teaches you about all things* and as that anointing is real, not counterfeit—*just as it has taught you, remain in him.*"

How do claims of no continuing revelation in the Church explain the ongoing work of God through prophetic revelation in the Church according to Romans 12:6; 1 Corinthians 12:10,28; 14:1,4,5,22,24,29-31,39; Ephesians 4:11; 1 Thessalonians 5:19-21; etc.? Did Stephen, a layman, not need an additional prophetic vision of Jesus in heaven in Acts 7:55? Did Philip, a layman, not need an additional word from God through the angel of the Lord or from the Holy Spirit in Acts 8:26,29? Did Ananias, a layman, not need an additional revelation from God about praying for Saul in Acts 9:10-12? Did Peter not need the additional revelation from God through a vision and a direct word from the Spirit in Acts 10:9-19?

Did the church at Antioch not need an additional word from the Lord about Paul and Barnabas in Acts 13:1-3? Did the Early Church not need an additional word from God through Agabus about the imminent famine in Acts 11:27,28? Did Paul not need the additional revelation in the vision of the Macedonian man in Acts 16:9,10 or in the vision at Corinth in Acts 18:9? Did the Ephesian disciples not need the additional prophetic words God put in their mouths when Paul prayed for them in Acts 19:5,6? Did the church of Caesarea not need the additional revelation God gave it through Philip's daughters (Acts 21:8,9)? Did the believers in the Early Church not need "the fellowship of the Holy Spirit" (2 Cor. 13:14),[5] which certainly involves the Spirit speaking and communicating with believers, as the following passages show: Matthew 10:19,20; Luke 2:25-29; 12:11; John 16:13,14; Acts 8:29; 10:13-19; 11:7-12; Romans 8:16.

One could go on and on—Acts 20:23 (prophetic messages to Paul "in every city"); 21:10,11 (prophecy of Agabus to Paul); 21:17,18 and 23:11 (words from the Lord to Paul); 27:23,24 (angel of the Lord to Paul); Romans 12:6; 1 Corinthians 12:10,28; 14:1,4,5,22,24,29-31,39; Ephesians 4:11; 1 Thessalonians 5:19,20 (ongoing prophetic revelation in the church); etc.

The references cited above show that Jesus, the apostles, and the laity of the Early Church expected to hear God speak in a variety of ways alongside Scripture. The biblical model of hearing God shows that Scripture is the primary means of hearing God's voice and is to be used to test all other means (2 Tim. 3:16; 2 Pet. 1:19,20; 3:16; Acts 17:11; Isa. 8:20; see Wayne Grudem's chapter in this book, objection numbers 16, 17, 18). Scripture itself is also quite clear that the written Word of God *does not* exhaust the various ways God may communicate with His people. Scholars have commented on passages such as those quoted above, pointing out the Spirit's function of speaking and teaching all believers[6]—not only apostles,[7] but also the laity of the Early Church:[8]

> [In John 16:13] it cannot be contested that the task of instruction can here be ascribed to the Spirit. As may be seen from what follows, He exercises "leading" as a "speaking" and "reporting" (cf.

also the "telling" of 16:12), and there is indeed a direct parallel in [John] 14:26: "He will teach you all things." This instructing or teaching of the Spirit continues, supplements and completes the proclamation of Jesus (16:12).[9]

Especially strongly emphasised as the work of the Spirit is insight into the will of God which is otherwise concealed, the more so when this yields immediate directions for concrete action: Acts 8:29 [Philip]; 10:19 [Peter]; 11:12 [Peter]; 13:2, 4 [believers at Antioch]; 16:6f. [Paul and companions]; 20:22 is also to be taken thus...; the reference, then, is to the direction of the Spirit given to Paul himself, while v. 23 [Acts 20:23] mentions directions given to other members of the community ("from city to city")....It might be that this is also the point in [Acts] 7:51 [Stephen], but not in 7:55, where the Spirit gives a vision of the heavenly world in the hour of death, though this also leads to "witnessing" in word and deed.[10]

Scripture cannot be sufficient if what it teaches about itself is distorted. Scripture is only sufficient in conjunction with the ministry of Christ and the Holy Spirit in our lives, as Scripture itself attests:

John 5:39,40—"You diligently study the Scriptures because you think that by them you possess eternal life. These are the Scriptures that testify about me, yet you refuse to come to me to have life."

James 1:5,6—"If any of you lacks wisdom, he should ask God, who gives generously to all without finding fault, and it will be given him. But when he asks, he must believe and not doubt."

1 Thessalonians 5:19-22—"Do not put out the Spirit's fire; do not treat prophecies with contempt. Test everything. Hold on to the good. Avoid every kind of evil."

Notes

1. James M. Boice in Michael Horton, ed., *Power Religion* (Chicago, IL: Moody Press, 1992), p. 120.
2. Ibid., p. 121.
3. Horton, *Power Religion*, p. 337.
4. BAGD, pp. 492-493.
5. Professor Eduard Schweizer points out that parallel passages such as 1 Corinthians 1:9 and Philippians 3:10 show that 2 Corinthians 13:14 (Greek text, 13:13) refers to fellowship and communion *with* the Holy Spirit Himself (Schweizer, *TDNT*, vol. 6, p. 434).
6. W. Michaelis, *TDNT*, vol. 5 pp., 100-101; E. Schweizer, *TDNT*, vol. 6, pp. 408 and n. 491; 442-443.
7. E. Schweizer, *TDNT*, vol. 6, pp. 442-443.
8. E. Schweizer, *TDNT*, vol. 6, p. 408 and n. 491.
9. W. Michaelis, *TDNT*, vol. 5, pp. 100-101.
10. E. Schweizer, *TDNT*, vol. 6, p. 408 and n. 491.

ABBREVIATIONS

ANF	*Ante-Nicene Fathers*, New York: Christian Literature Company, 1890-97. Reprint, Grand Rapids, Michigan: Eerdmans, 1980-82.
BAGD	Bauer, W., W. F. Arndt, W. F. Gingrich, and F. W. Danker, *A Greek-English Lexicon of the New Testament and Other Early Christian Literature*, Chicago: University of Chicago Press, 1979.
BDB	Brown, F., S. R. Driver, and C. A. Briggs, *A Hebrew and English Lexicon of the Old Testament*, Oxford: The Clarendon Press, 1951.
CCL	*Corpus Christianorum Series Latina*
CGTC	*Cambridge Greek Testament Commentary*
EBC	*Expositor's Bible Commentary*
Gen. Rab.	*Genesis Rabbah (Midrash—Rabbinic commentary)*
GNB	*Good News Bible, Today's English Version (TEV)*
ICC	*International Critical Commentary*
IDB	*Interpreters Dictionary of the Bible*, ed., G. Buttrick et al.
JBL	*Journal of Biblical Literature*
NIBC	*New International Biblical Commentary*
NIC	*New International Commentary*
NICNT	*New International Commentary on the New Testament*
NIDNTT	*New International Dictionary of New Testament Theology*, ed., C. Brown
NIGTC	*New International Greek Text Commentary*
NPF	*Nicene and Post-Nicene Fathers*, 1st Series. New York: Christian Literature Company, 1887-94. Reprint, Grand Rapids, Michigan: Eerdmans, 1971-80.
NTS	*New Testament Studies*
PG	*Patrologia cursus completus. Series Graeca*, Jacques Paul Migne, ed., Paris, J. P. Migne, 1859-87.`
TDNT	*Theological Dictionary of the New Testament*, ed., G. Kittel
ThZ	*Theologische Zeitschrift...Universität Basel*
TNTC	*Tyndale New Testament Commentary*
WBC	*Word Biblical Commentary*
	Wisd. Sol. Wisdom of Solomon (Apocrypha)
WTJ	*Westminster Theological Journal*
ZNW	*Zeitschrift für die neutestamentliche Wissenschaft und die Kunde der älteren Kirche*
ZSTh	*Zeitschrift für systematische Theologie*

SELECT BIBLIOGRAPHY

Aland, K. and B. Aland. *The Text of the New Testament. An Introduction to the Critical Editions and to the Theory and Practice of Modern Textual Criticism.* Grand Rapids, MI: and Leiden, Netherlands: Eerdmans and E. J. Brill, 1989.

Anderson, Neil. *Victory over the Darkness.* Ventura, CA: Regal, 1990.

_____. *The Bondage Breaker.* Eugene, OR: Harvest House, 1990.

Arnold, C. *Ephesians: Power and Magic.* Cambridge, England: Cambridge University Press, 1989.

_____. *Powers of Darkness: Principalities and Powers in Paul's Letters.* Downers Grove, IL: InterVarsity Press, 1992.

Bauer, W., W. F. Arndt, W. F. Gingrich, and F. W. Danker. *A Greek-English Lexicon of the New Testament and Other Early Christian Literature.* Translation and adaptation of W. Bauer, *Greichisch-deutsches Wörterbuch zu den Schriften des Neuen Testaments usw.* (4th edition, Berlin, Germany: 1949-52). Chicago, IL: University of Chicago Press, 1979.

Bertram, G. "ergon." In G. Kittel, ed., *TDNT*, vol. 2, pp. 635-652.

Blass, F. and A. Debrunner. *A Greek Grammar of the New Testament and Other Early Christian Literature.* Chicago, IL: University of Chicago Press, 1961.

Blue, Ken. *Authority to Heal.* Downers Grove, IL: InterVarsity Press, 1987.

Bridge, Donald. *Signs and Wonders Today.* Downers Grove, IL: InterVarsity Press, 1985.

Brown, C., ed. *The New International Dictionary of New Testament Theology.* Four vols. Grand Rapids, MI: Eerdmans, 1986.

_____. *That You May Believe: Miracles and Faith Then and Now.* Grand Rapids, MI: Eerdmans, 1985.

Bruce, F. F. *The Hard Sayings of Jesus.* Downers Grove, IL: InterVarsity Press, 1983.

Bruner, F. D. *A Theology of the Holy Spirit: The Pentecostal Experience and the New Testament Witness.* Grand Rapids, MI: Eerdmans, 1970.

Bubeck, Mark. *The Adversary.* Chicago, IL: Moody Press, 1975.

_____. *Overcoming the Adversary.* Chicago, IL: Moody Press, 1984.

Burgess, S. M. *The Holy Spirit: Eastern Christian Traditions.* Peabody, MA: Hendrickson, 1989.

_____. *The Spirit and the Church: Antiquity.* Peabody, MA: Hendrickson, 1984.

Burgess, S. M., G. B. McGee, and P. H. Alexander. *Dictionary of Pentecostal and Charismatic Movements.* Grand Rapids, MI: Zondervan, 1988.

Buttrick, G. A. et al., eds. *The Interpreters Dictionary of the Bible.* Four vols. Nashville, TN: Abingdon, 1962. Supplementary Volume, 1976.

Carson, D. A. *The Gospel According to John.* Leicester, England: InterVarsity, and Grand Rapids, MI: Eerdmans, 1991.

Coggins, J. R. and P. G. Hiebert, eds. *Wonders and the Word.* Winnipeg, Canada: Kindred Press, 1989.

Colson, F. H. *Philo*, vol. 6. Loeb Classical Library. Cambridge, MA: Harvard University Press, 1935.

Cotterell, P. and M. Turner. *Linguistics and Biblical Interpretation.* Downers Grove, IL: InterVarsity Press, 1989.

Cullmann, O. *Christ and Time.* London, England: SCM Press, 1951.

_____. *The Early Church.* London, England: SCM Press, 1956.

Davids, Peter H. *The Epistle of James. NIGTC.* Grand Rapids, MI: Wm. B. Eerdmans, 1982.

Delling, G. "Botschaft und Wunder im Wirken Jesu." In H. Ristow and K. Matthiae, eds. *Der historische Jesus und der kerygmatische Christus,* pp. 389-402. Berlin, Germany: Evangelische Verlagsanstalt, 1961.

De Vaux, R. *Ancient Israel, Its Life and Institutions.* New York: McGraw, Hill and London, England: Darton, Longman and Todd, 1961.

Dietzfelbinger, Chr. "Die grösseren Werke (Joh 14. 12f.)." *NTS* 35 (1989): 27-47.

Dodd, C. H. *The Interpretation of the Fourth Gospel.* Cambridge, England: Cambridge University Press, 1968.

Dunn, J. D. G. *Jesus and the Spirit: A Study of the Religious and Charismatic Experience of Jesus and the First Christians as Reflected in the New Testament.* Philadelphia, PA: The Westminster Press, 1975.

_____. *Baptism in the Holy Spirit: A Re-examination of the New Testament Teaching on the Gift of the Spirit in Relation to Pentecostalism Today.* Studies in Biblical Theology, 2nd series, no. 15. London, England: SCM Press, 1970.

Edwards, Jonathan. *The Works of Jonathan Edwards.* 2 vols. Edinburgh, Scotland: The Banner of Truth, 1974.

Ellis, E. E. *Prophecy and Hermeneutic in Early Christianity: New Testament Essays.* Wissenschaftliche Untersuchungen zum Neuen Testament, vol. 18. Tübingen, Germany: J. C. B. Mohr (Paul Siebeck), 1978.

Fee, Gordon D. *The Disease of the Health and Wealth Gospels.* Costa Mesa, CA: Word for Today, 1979.

_____. *The First Epistle to the Corinthians.* The New International Commentary on the New Testament, ed., F. F. Bruce. Grand Rapids, MI: Eerdmans, 1987.

Feuillet, A. "Le 'Commencement' de l'Economie Chrétienne d'après Heb. ii.3-4, Mar. i.1 et Acts 1.1-2." *NTS* 24 (1978): 163-174.

Foster, Richard. *Prayer: Finding the Heart's True Home.* San Francisco, CA: HarperSanFrancisco, 1992.

Friedrich, G. "*Euaggelizomai, euaggelion.*" In G. Kittel, ed., *TDNT,* vol. 2, pp. 707-737.

Fuller, R. H. *The Mission and Achievement of Jesus.* Chicago, IL: Alec Allenson, 1954.

Gatzweiler, K. "Der Paulinische Wunderbegriff." In A. Suhl, ed., *Der Wunderbegriff im Neuen Testament.* Darmstadt, Germany: Wissenschaftliche Buchgesellschaft, 1980.

Green, Michael. *I Believe in the Holy Spirit.* Grand Rapids, MI: Eerdmans, 1985.

Groothuis, Douglas R. *Unmasking the New Age.* Downers Grove, IL: InterVarsity Press, 1986.

Grudem, W. *The Gift of Prophecy in 1 Corinthians.* Washington, DC: University Press of America, 1982.

_____. *The Gift of Prophecy in the New Testament and Today.* Westchester, IL: Crossway Books, 1988.

_____. *Systematic Theology: An Introductory Course in the Doctrinal Teachings of the Whole Bible.* Leicester, England: InterVarsity, and Grand Rapids, MI: Zondervan, 1993.

Grundmann, W. "Dunamai/ dunamis." In G. Kittel, ed., *TDNT*, vol. 2, pp. 284-317.

Hendrickx, H. *The Miracle Stories of the Synoptic Gospels*. San Francisco, CA: HarperSanFrancisco, 1987.

Hengel, M. *The Charismatic Leader and His Followers*. New York: Crossroad, 1981.

Hofius, O. "Miracle (sēmeion, teras)." In C. Brown, ed. *The New International Dictionary of New Testament Theology*, vol. 2, pp. 626-635. Grand Rapids, MI: Eerdmans, 1986.

Horton, M. S. *Power Religion: The Selling Out of the Evangelical Church?* Chicago, IL: Moody Press, 1992.

Hunter, A. M. *The Works and Words of Jesus*. Philadelphia, PA: Westminster, 1975.

Jeremias, J. *Theology of the New Testament*. New York: Scribner's, 1971.

Kelsey, Morton T. *Healing and Christianity*. New York: HarperCollins, 1976 (revised and expanded, *Psychology, Medicine, & Christian Healing*, HarperCollins, 1988).

Kittel, G., ed. *Theological Dictionary of the New Testament*. Ten vols. Grand Rapids, MI: Eerdmans, 1964-74.

Knoch, O. *Der Geist Gottes und der neue Mensch: Der Heilige Geist als Grundkraft und Norm des christlichen Lebens in Kirche und Welt nach dem Zeugnis des Apostels Paulus*. Stuttgart, Germany: Verlag Katholisches Bibelwerk, 1975.

Kraft, Charles H. *Christianity with Power: Your Worldview and Your Experience of the Supernatural*. Ann Arbor, MI: Vine Books, 1989.

_____. *Defeating Dark Angels*. Ann Arbor, MI: Servant, 1992.

Ladd, G. E. *The Gospel of the Kingdom*. Grand Rapids, MI: Eerdmans, 1959.

_____. *A Theology of the New Testament*. Grand Rapids, MI: Wm. B. Eerdmans, 1974.

Lampe, G. W. H. "Miracles in the Acts of the Apostles." In C. F. D. Moule, ed. *Miracles. Cambridge Studies in Their Philosophy and History*, pp. 165-178. London, England: A. R. Mowbray & Co., 1965.

Lane, W. L. *Commentary on the Gospel of Mark*. The New International Commentary on the New Testament, ed., F. F. Bruce. Grand Rapids, MI: Eerdmans, 1974.

Lewis, David. *Healing: Fiction, Fantasy or Fact? A Comprehensive Analysis of the Healings and Associated Phenomena at John Wimber's Harrogate Conference*. London, England: Hodder & Stoughton, 1989.

Liddell, H. G. and R. Scott. *A Greek-English Lexicon*. Oxford, England: Clarendon, 1968.

Linn, Dennis and Matthew Linn. *Deliverance Prayer*. New York: Paulist Press, 1981.

Lyons, J. *Introduction to Theoretical Linguistics*. Cambridge, England: Cambridge University Press, 1968.

_____. *Semantics*. Two vols. Cambridge, England: Cambridge University Press, 1977.

MacArthur, J. F. *Charismatic Chaos*. Grand Rapids, MI: Zondervan, 1992.

MacNutt, Francis. *Healing*. Notre Dame, IN: Ave Maria Press, 1974.

Mallone, George. *Those Controversial Gifts*. Downers Grove, IL: InterVarsity Press, 1983.

Martyn Lloyd-Jones, D. *Prove All Things*. Edited by C. Catherwood. Eastbourne, England: Kingsway, 1985.

McCasland, S. V. "Signs and Wonders." *JBL* 76 (1957): 149-152.

McDonnell, K. and G. T. Montague. *Christian Initiation and Baptism in the Holy Spirit*. Collegeville, MN: Liturgical Press, 1991.

Monden, L. *Le Miracle, Signe de Salut*. Bruges, Belgium: Desclée, 1960. English transl.: *Signs and Wonders: A Study of the Miraculous Element in Religion*. New York: Desclée, 1966.

Moriarty, M. G. *The New Charismatics. A Concerned Voice Responds to Dangerous New Trends*. Grand Rapids, MI: Zondervan, 1992.

Moule, C. F. D., ed. *Miracles. Cambridge Studies in Their Philosophy and History*. London, England: A. R. Mowbray & Co., 1965.

Murphy, E. F. *The Handbook for Spiritual Warfare*. Nashville, TN: Nelson, 1992.

Murray, J. *The Epistle to the Romans*. The New International Commentary on the New Testament, ed., F. F. Bruce. Grand Rapids, MI: Eerdmans, 1968.

Oepke, A. *"Iaomai."* In G. Kittel, ed. *TDNT*, vol. 3, pp. 194-215.

Powell, C. H. *The Biblical Concept of Power*. London, England: Epworth Press, 1963.

Pritchard, J. *Ancient Near Eastern Texts Relating to the Old Testament*. Third ed. Princeton, NJ: Princeton University Press, 1969.

Pytches, David. *Come, Holy Spirit: Learning to Minister in Power*. London, England: Hodder & Stoughton, 1985. Published in North America as *Spiritual Gifts in the Local Church*, Minneapolis, MN: Bethany House, 1985.

Rengstorf, K. H. *"Semeion."* In G. Kittel, ed. *TDNT*, vol. 7, pp. 200-269.

Richardson, A. *An Introduction to the Theology of the New Testament*. New York: Harper and Row, 1958.

_____. *The Miracle-Stories of the Gospels*. London, England: SCM Press, 1941.

Robertson, A. T. *A Grammar of the Greek New Testament in the Light of Historical Research*. Nashville, TN: Broadman Press, 1934.

Robins, R. H. *General Linguistics. An Introductory Survey*. White Plains, NY: Longman, 1980.

Roe, Earl. *Dream Big: The Henrietta Mears Story*. Ventura, CA: Regal Books, 1990.

Ruef, J. *Paul's First Letter to Corinth*. New York: Penguin, 1971.

Schweizer, E. et al. *"Pneuma."* In G. Kittel, ed. *TDNT*, vol. 6, pp. 332-455.

Smedes, Lewis, ed. *Ministry and the Miraculous*. Pasadena, CA: Fuller Theological Seminary, 1987.

Smith, D. L. *A Handbook of Contemporary Theology*. Wheaton, IL: Victor, 1992.

Springer, Kevin, ed. *Power Encounters among Christians in the Western World*. San Francisco, CA: HarperSanFrancisco, 1988.

Stauffer, E. *New Testament Theology*. New York: MacMillian, 1955.

Strack, H. L. and P. Billerbeck. *Kommentar zum neuen Testament aus Talmud und Midrasch*. Six vols. München, Germany: Becksche Verlagsbuchhandlung, 1922-1961.

Tagawa, K. *Miracles et évangile. La pensée personnelle de l'évangéliste Marc. Études d'histoire et de philosophie religieuses*, vol. 62. Paris, France: Presses Universitaires de France, 1966.

Trench, R. C. *Synonyms of the New Testament*. London, England: Macmillan, 1894.

_____. *Notes on the Miracles of Our Lord*. Fifth ed. revised. London, England: Macmillan, 1856.

van der Loos, H. *The Miracles of Jesus*. Supplements to Novum Testamentum, vol. 8. Leiden, Netherlands: E. J. Brill, 1965.

Wagner, C. P. *How to Have a Healing Ministry in Any Church*. Ventura, CA: Regal Books, 1988.

_____. *The Third Wave of the Holy Spirit*. Ann Arbor, MI: Vine, 1988.

Wagner, C. P. and F. D. Pennoyer, eds. *Wrestling with Dark Angels*. Ventura, CA: Regal Books, 1990.

Warner, Timothy M. *Spiritual Warfare*. Wheaton, IL: Crossway, 1991.

Wesley, John. *The Works of John Wesley*. Peabody, MA: Hendrickson, 1984; orig. published 1872.

White, John. *When the Spirit Comes with Power: Signs and Wonders among God's People*. Downers Grove, IL: InterVarsity Press, 1988.

White, Thomas B. *The Believer's Guide to Spiritual Warfare*. Ann Arbor, MI: Servant, 1990.

Williams, Don. *Signs, Wonders, and the Kingdom of God*. Ann Arbor, MI: Servant, 1989.

Wimber J. and K. Springer. *Power Evangelism*. 2nd revised and expanded edition, San Francisco, CA: HarperSanFrancisco, 1992 (first edition, 1986).

_____. *Power Healing*. San Francisco, CA: HarperSanFrancisco, 1987.

SUBJECT INDEX

Abraham 42
Agabus 78
Ahab 121
Akiba 177
Ananias 60, 66, 190, 401
Anderson, N. 239
Apostle-prophets 86
Apostles 142, 144, 190, 198 (see note 5), 199, 279, 280, 285, 286
Augustine 282
Barclay, W. 180
Barth, K. 151
Basil of Cappadocia 280
Ben Sirach 176, 178
Bennett, Dennis and Rita 84
Body of Christ 185
Brainwashing technique 293
Bridge, D. 85
Bright, B. 134
Bruce, F. F. 24, 162, 366, 370
Cairns, D. S. 26
Carson, D. A. 91, 136, 199 (see note 8), 386
Centurion's faith 371
Cessationism 18, 64, 85, 87, 98, 197; no evidence for cessation of gifts in the New Testament 405, 406 and note 2
Church Fathers 187, 188, 278
Compassion in healing (see healing, compassion)
Cyprian 188
David, king 46
Davies, W. D. 185
de Vaux, R. 176
Dead Sea Scrolls 414
Deistic and rationalistic heritage of the Enlightenment 262
Delling, G. 368
Demonization 115, 122; demonization and sin 118; overcoming the evil one and doubts about demonization 233
Demons: commanding demons in the name of Christ 75, 76;
demons, manifesting in Christian gatherings 299
Desiring the gifts of the Spirit: scriptural command to eagerly seek spiritual gifts 96
Dietzfelbinger, C. 395
Discipleship and the healing ministry of Jesus 182; witnessing in word and deed 25, 179, 180, 183, 281, 383
Distinguishing marks of a work of the Spirit of God 305
Dodd, C. H. 394
Dunamis "power, miracle" 69, 137
Early Church Fathers (see Church Fathers)
Edwards, Jonathan 289, 305, 309
Ehrhardt Seminars Training (EST) 293
Elijah 162
Elijah and Elisha 43
Ellis, E. E. 149
Endor 115
Enlightenment 262
Epaphroditus 63, 98
Erga "works" 394; denoting miraculous works in John 146
EST (see Ehrhardt Seminars Training)
Eusebius 281
Evangelism (see also Witnessing): evangelism with or without miracles 213; witnessing in word and deed 25, 179, 180, 183, 281, 383
Faith (see also Prayer of Faith): coming to faith in Christ through miraculous signs 94; "inferior" faith and miracles 93; faith as relational trust in Jesus 124; saving faith related to miracles in John 371
Falling under the Spirit's power (see Spirit)
False miracles (see Miracle)
False prophets 56

Fathers, Church (see Church Fathers)
Fear and the Spirit's power 308
Feuillet, A. 24, 367
Finkelstein, L. 177
Foster, R. 32
Fox, R. L. 188
Friedrich, G. 25, 368
Fruit: testing the fruit of a work purporting to be from God 57, 71, 305
Fuller Theological Seminary 188
Fuller, R. H. 179, 182
Gatzweiler, K. 137, 149, 155, 406
Gee, D. 84
Geisler, N. 97
Gentile inclusion revealed to the apostles 86
Gifts of the Spirit: gifts and empowerment in ministry 212; gifts may vary in strength 99, 198 (see note 5); miraculous gifts used to edify 63; gifts, situationally given (I Cor. 12-14) 186; spiritual gifts and demonic counterfeits 70, 90; Stephen, Philip, Ananias, the Corinthians, Galatians, Jewish Christian churches ministering with miraculous spiritual gifts and healing 30, 60, 66, 142, 143, 161, 164, 190, 401, 418, 422
Glory given to Christ (Rom. 15:17) through preaching with signs and wonders 152 (see also Healing; Preaching and healing)
Glory given to God through healing 63
Gospel: seeing and hearing the gospel 151, 384; "gospel of the kingdom of God" (Acts 8:12) 263; gospel and forgiveness of sins illustrated in healing and deliverance 160, 383, 384; Paul brings the gospel to full expression with signs and wonders 155; witnessing in word and deed 25, 179, 180, 183, 281, 383
Graham, Billy 28, 134
Great Awakening 303
Green, M. 32
Gregory Thaumaturgus ("Wonderworker") 280
Groothuis, D. 293
Grundmann, W. 26, 154, 373
Harper, M. 84
Healing: compassion in healing 63; glory to God through healing 63; Glory given to Christ (Rom. 15:17) through preaching with signs and wonders 152; healing and the atonement 22, 49; central role of healing in Jesus' ministry of proclaiming the gospel of the Kingdom 387; healing "signs" (John 4:54; 6:2; 9:16; 12:17-18) 161; healing as an illustration of God's forgiveness of sin 156; God's desire to heal 158; sickness and experiencing healing in part 30; sickness as a fruit of sin 117; _sozo_ "save, heal" denoting both salvation from sin and healing of illness in the Gospels 156, 160; Stephen, Philip, Ananias, the Corinthians, Galatians, Jewish Christian churches proclaiming the gospel with miraculous spiritual gifts and healing 30, 60, 66, 142, 143, 161, 164, 190, 401, 418, 422
Hendrickx, H. 137, 383
Hengel, M. 181, 183, 184
Hillel 176
Hofius, O. 27, 365
Holy Spirit (see Spirit, Holy)
Hunter, A. M. 179, 182
Irenaeus, Bishop of Lyons 187, 190
Jeremias, J. 180, 181
Jerome 188, 281

Jesus and Moses 42
Josephus 177
Job 114, 121, 236
Jonah 121
Joy and the Holy Spirit 309, 432
Judas Iscariot 118
Justin Martyr 187, 190
Kingdom ministry (see Ministry of
    the Kingdom)
Kingdom of God 263; "already—
    not yet" nature of the Kingdom
    126
Klappert, B. 25, 383
Kuhlman, K. 255
Ladd, G. E. 269
Lampe, G. W. H. 143, 380
Laughter and the Spirit's power 310
    (see Spirit, Holy; Joy)
Laying on of hands 144
Levi 123
Lewis, C. S. 307
Lexical fields 137
Lindblom, J. 176
MacArthur, J. 80, 179, 184, 186
Manipulative preaching 294, 295
Martin, W. 237
Martyrdom 31
McCasland, S. V. 136
Mears, H. 133
Ministry of the Kingdom, disciples
    learned from Jesus 182; wit-
    nessing in word and deed 25,
    179, 180, 183, 281, 383
Miracle: definition of miracle 100;
    false miracles 90; true vs. false
    miracles 58; greatest miracle of
    all is new birth 159, 214; mira-
    cles and "inferior" faith 91;
    miracles not restricted to the
    apostles 59, 67, 198 (see note
    5); Stephen, Philip, Ananias,
    the Corinthians, Galatians,
    Jewish Christian churches min-
    istering with miraculous spiri-
    tual gifts and healing 30, 60,
    66, 142, 143, 161, 164, 190,

401, 418, 422; present day mir-
    acles 95; miraculous healing in
    Christ's name glorifying Christ
    and bearing witness to His res-
    urrection 153; miraculous heal-
    ing in Jesus' ministry continued
    by the apostles and the Early
    Church 157; miraculous heal-
    ing showing the coming of the
    kingdom of God 157; the
    Reformation and the rejection
    of miracles 211
Montanists 279
Montanus 187
Moses 162
Moses and Jesus 42
Naaman 121
Natural disaster and sin 113, 116
New Age spiritism and counterfeit
    healing 229
New Testament Scholars and the
    Evidence for preaching and
    healing in the NT 365
Origen 280
Otto, R. 307
Overcoming the evil one and
    doubts about demonization 233
Pagan religion 45
Paul's conversion (Acts 9) 150
Paul and proclaiming the gospel
    with preaching and healing
    372
Persecution 31
Pharisees 56
Philip 60, 66, 190, 401
Philip's daughters 143
Plagues 42
Pleroo "fill, fulfill, bring to full
    expression": Paul brings the
    gospel to full expression with
    signs and wonders 155
Poverty and sin 113, 116
Powell, C. H. 184, 367, 373, 425,
    430
Power evangelism, miraculous gifts
    and healing accompanying the

gospel 57, 58, 69, 213

Power for righteousness 214

Power and the Spirit (see Spirit and power)

Power in weakness 212, 215

Power of God, expecting the power of God 211

Power of God and ministering at people's point of need 213

Power through humble dependence on God 214

Prayer of faith (Jas. 5:15) 225, 226

Preaching and healing: preaching and healing 373, 376, 382, 400, 401; Jesus' preaching inseperably linked to His healing sickness 360; preaching and healing side-by-sideness in the Gospels 383; glory to God through healing 63; glory given to Christ (Rom. 15:17) through preaching with signs and wonders 152; Paul and proclaiming the gospel with preaching and healing 372; preaching and healing in the postresurrection period 190; witnessing in word and deed 25, 179, 180, 183, 281, 383

Prophecy: contemporary congregational prophecy and Scripture 77; revelation and hearing from the Lord 83; new revelation and Scripture 80; prophetic revelation in the Church according to the NT 439

Prophets (see also Apostle-prophets): prophets in the OT 42; parallels between the miracles of OT prophets and those of Jesus and apostles 43

Raising the dead 336; resurrections in Acts 122

Rationalism and deism 262

Reformation and the rejection of miracles 211

Richardson, A. 25, 27, 137, 154, 156, 189, 269, 374, 375, 382, 401, 416

Sanctification 30; priority of sanctification 212

Satanic delusions 299

Saul, king 45

Saving faith, related to miracles in John 371 (see Faith)

Schweizer, E. 414

Scripture, prophecies, and additional revelation 77

Scripture, sufficiency of and prophetic revelation 81

Seeing and hearing the gospel 151 (see Gospel)

Seneca 178

Sēmeia, "signs," 136ff., 394

Shammai 177

Sickness and healing in part 30

Sickness and sin 117

"Sign from heaven" 160, 161

Signs and Wonders, 136ff.; healing "signs" (John 4:54; 6:2; 9:16; 12:17-18) 161; signs 146; signs and wonders and proclaiming the gospel 199 (see note 6); signs and wonders showing God's grace in the gospel 388; ongoing signs and wonders 95, 163; seeking signs and wonders 146; "signs of an apostle" 65; "signs" of miraculous healing leading to faith in Christ and repentance 124, 161

Sōzo "save, heal" denoting both salvation from sin and healing of illness 156, 160

Spirit, Holy: distinguishing marks of a work of the Spirit of God 305; falling under the Spirit's power 313; Fear and the Spirit's power 308; Holy Spirit, attention given to in worship and prayer 88; Spirit speaking to believers in the NT 418

Spirit and power 373, 410; power in weakness 212, 215; expecting the power of God 211; ministering in God's power at people's point of need 213; power through humble dependence on God 214; association of "power" (*dunamis*) and "the Spirit" (*pneuma*) with signs, wonders, and miracles in the NT 155; trembling and the Spirit's power 301, 429f.; fear and the Spirit's power 308; weeping and the Spirit's power 309, 429f.; joy and the Spirit's power 309, 429f.; laughter and the Spirit's power 310

Spiritual Warfare: overcoming the evil one and doubts about demonization 233, 413

Stafford, Tim 197

Stephen 60, 66, 164, 190, 401

Stephen, Philip, and Ananias 142, 143, 161, 418, 422; Stephen, Philip, Ananias, the Corinthians, Galatians, Jewish Christian churches ministering with miraculous spiritual gifts and healing 30

Suffering 30

Tagawa, K. 382

Thomas 93

Thurneysen, E. 26

Tongues and demonic counterfeit 70 (see Gifts)

Trembling and the Spirit's presence 301

Trench, R. C. 137

van der Loos, H. 26, 27, 269, 366, 383, 402

Visualization and inner healing 329

Wagner, C. P. 413, 421, 422, 424, 426, 431

Weakness 30

Weeping and the Spirit's power 309

Wesleys 289

Whitefield 289

Wimber, J. 31, 200, 322, 386, 415, 424, 426, 431

Witnessing (see also Evangelism): Paul as witness of what he had "seen and heard" 385; powerless witness 208; witnessing in the epistles 198 (see note 5); witnessing in word and deed 25, 179, 180, 183, 281, 383

Woodhouse, John 95

Word and deed 25, 179, 180, 183, 281, 383; education by word and deed 178

Words of knowledge 321

Works (*erga*), denoting miraculous works in John 146, 394

Zaccai, Johannan ben 177

Zacchaeus 123, 125

Zedekiah 121

SCRIPTURE INDEX

Genesis **chap. 3** 112; **6:6** 112;
    15:17-18 430; **17:1,3,17** 310;
    18:20 113; **chap. 19** 113; **20:7**
    43; **20:17** 43
Exodus **4:24-26** 306; **7:3** 42; **7:11-
    12,22** 230; **8:7** 230; **8:19** 299;
    10:1-2 176; **12:26-27** 176;
    15:26 114, 120; **20:3, 5** 346;
    20:5-6 239; **33:9** 330; **34:6-7**
    120
Leviticus **19:31** 238; **20:6,27** 238
Numbers **11:25** 47; **11:26** 47;
    11:29 47; **25:1-3** 253
Deuteronomy **15:4-5** 113; **18:9-11**
    250; **18:10-13** 238; **18:15**
    438; **18:19-13** 238; **18:20-22**
    438; **chaps. 27-28** 250; **28:15,
    21-22** 114; **30:12-14** 437;
    chap. 32 45
Joshua **7** 247
1 Samuel **15:23** 45; **16:6-7** 254;
    16:13,23 46; **16:14** 45, 115
1 Kings **17:18** 114; **17:19-24** 43;
    17:21 426; **17:24** 44; **18:43** 31,
    409; **22:19-28** 46; **22:22** 414
2 Kings **4:32-37** 43; **4:34-35** 426;
    5:15,17 44; **20:3** 114; **20:5-7**
    248
2 Chronicles **5:13-14** 330; **18:21**
    414; **26:16-29** 223
Nehemiah **8:1-8** 297; **8:6,9** 332,
    432; **8:9-10** 297
Job **1:10** 241; **1:21** 237; **2:10** 237;
    4:15 414
Psalms **16:7** 254; **27:8** 272; **32:3-4**
    115; **34:7** 247; **38:3,5** 115; **91**
    241; **103:3** 120; **106:28,36-39**
    253; **106:37-38** 45; **114:7**
    429; **126:2** 310; **139** 223
Proverbs **1:18** 176; **3:7-8** 120; **14:13**
    310; **28:13** 238; **31:1** 176
Isaiah **6:7** 430; **8:16** 176; **8:20** 437,

    439, 440; **28:11** 71; **33:22-24**
    120; **chap. 53** 48; **55:8-9** 335;
    61:1-2 122
Jeremiah **1:9** 431; **5:22** 429; **23:9**
    332, 429, 432; **26:24** 176;
    36:4 176; **45:1** 176
Ezekiel **1:28** 429, 432; **2:23** 429;
    3:23 432; **36:26** 431
Daniel **8:17-18,27** 307; **8:18** 432;
    10:8-11 429; **10:9** 313, 432;
    10:10 332, 432
Hosea **4:12** 414; **4:12-13** 239, 253
Joel **2:28-29** 47
Amos **2:6-7** 113
Zechariah **13:2** 414
Malachi **3:8-11** 114
Matthew **4:4,7,10** 417, 418; **4:8-9**
    236; **4:10** 417; **4:17** 360; **4:23**
    26, 262, 359, 360, 368, 371;
    7:7-11 186; **7:16** 57, 306;
    7:20-23 431; **8:2-4** 378; **8:5-
    10** 229; **8:5-13** 152, 371, 378;
    8:14-15 378; **8:16** 417; **8:16-
    17** 49, 377; **8:28-34** 378; **8:32**
    418; **9:1ff.** 361; **9:1-8** 124;
    9:2,6 347; **9:4** 262; **9:6** 160,
    267; **9:6-8** 346, 361; **9:18-26**
    379; **9:22** 432; **9:27-30** 379;
    9:32-34 379; **9:33** 414; **9:35**
    361; **9:35-36** 181; **10:1** 355;
    10:1f.,5-8 399; **10:1,7-8** 263,
    361; **10:7** 183; **10:7-8** 62, 265,
    365; **10:8** 126; **10:19** 418;
    10:19-20 440; **11:1-5** 374,
    377, 387; **11:4** 384; **11:4-5,
    20-30** 379; **11:5** 151, 262,
    359, 371; **11:5f.** 180; **11:20-
    30** 374; **11:21** 25, 147, 158,
    161, 375, 377; **12:15-18** 179,
    359, 378, 383, 387; **12:15-21**
    378; **12:22** 331, 414; **12:25-
    28** 182; **12:28** 62, 189, 269;

12:29 416; 12:38-40 162; 12:43-45 381, 415; 12:45 381; 13:54 361; 13:58 125; 14:14 181; 14:34-36 379; 15:21-28 379; 15:29-31 379; 16:1-4 162; 16:4 55; 17:5 330; 17:14-20 379; 17:20 98; 20:29-34 379; 20:34 181; 21:14 362, 375, 377, 387; 24:24 136; 28:18-20 189, 399; 28:20 184, 263

Mark 1:14-15 179, 360; 1:15 182; 1:21-28 122, 123, 190; 1:23-24 234; 1:25 77, 418; 1:29-31 122, 378; 1:32-34 370, 377, 378; 1:38-39 262, 360, 371; 1:39 360; 1:40 124; 1:40-45 378; 2:1ff. 361; 2:1-12 117, 122; 2:5,10-11 347; 2:8 262; 2:10 146, 161; 2:10-11 267; 2:10-12 346, 361; 3:7-12 378; 3:14-15 182; 3:27 416; 5:1-20 378; 5:8 418; 5:19 151, 181; 5:21-43 379; 5:26 381; 5:29-30 432; 5:30 429; 6:5 124; 6:5-6 125; 6:7 183; 6:7,12f. 263, 361, 399; 6:12-13 262, 263, 265, 360, 361, 371, 399; 6:53-56 379; 7:24-30 379; 8:11-12 162; 8:12 182; 8:22-26 379; 8:23-24 380, 432; 8:23-25 331; 8:24 227; 8:24-25 98; 8:25 381; 8:31 184; 9:1 184; 9:7 431; 9:14-29 379; 9:17 424; 9:17, 25 414; 9:21 424; 9:25 418; 9:29 256; 10:45 121; 10:46-52 379; 10:52 331; 12:30 272; 13:22 56, 136; 16:9-20 401; 16:15-20 399; 16:17-18 143; 16:17-20 139, 140, 273; 16:20 164, 366

Luke 2:25-29 440; 4:1 269; 4:4, 8,12 417, 418; 4:14 209; 4:14ff. 269, 360; 4:18 62, 262, 336, 347, 360, 371; 4:18-19 122, 384, 387; 4:30 262; 4:34 299; 4:35 418; 4:38-39 378; 4:40ff. 360, 370, 377; 4:41 299; 4:43 374; 5:12-16 378; 5:15 361; 5:17 361, 429; 5:17-20 229; 5:20 347; 5:22 262; 5:24 267, 347; 5:24-26 346, 361; 6:17-18 361; 6:19 430, 432; 6:40 184, 425; 7:1-10 371, 378; 7:11-17 122, 123, 378; 7:13 181; 7:16 151; 7:22 151, 262, 360, 371, 384, 387; 8:26-39 378; 8:39 151; 8:40-56 122, 379; 8:44 432; 8:46 429; 8:46-47 432; 9:1f. 62, 76, 262, 263, 273, 355, 360, 361, 365, 371, 399; 9:2 265; 9:6 361; 9:37-43 379; 10:1 184, 263, 399; 10:1, 9 263, 399; 10:1-24 273; 10:9 182; 189, 262, 263, 265, 360, 362, 365, 371, 399; 10:13 25, 147, 158, 161, 182, 262, 360, 371, 375; 10:13-15 374, 387; 10:17 76; 10:17-19 355; 10:19 183; 10:20 159, 239; 10:21 432; 11:8-9 422; 11:13 273; 11:14 414; 11:16 162; 11:17-20 182; 11:20 179, 189; 11:21-22 416; 11:24-26 381, 415; 11:26 381; 12:11 418, 440; 12:12 254; 13:10-17 122; 13:11 247, 414; 13:12 418; 13:22 362; 13:32 362, 374, 377, 387; 15:10 224; 17:21 182, 189; 18:7 423; 18:35-43 379; 19:8 125; 21:37 362, 375, 377, 387; 22:35-36 400; 24:46-49 399; 24:49 209

John **1:45-50** 269; **1:48** 431; **1:48-50** 262; **2:11** 94, 371; **2:23-24** 371; **2:23-25** 92; **3:1** 269; **3:2** 94, 262, 360, 371; **3:21** 353; **4:17-18** 262; **4:48** 91, 139, 162; **4:54** 139; **5:1ff.** 423; **5:3-6** 381; **5:14** 117, 123, 381; **5:19** 406, 423; **5:19-20** 270; **5:30** 423; **5:39-40** 163, 441; **6:2** 94, 139; **6:14-15** 371; **6:21b** 262; **6:30f.** 162; **6:45** 163; **6:60-66** 371; **7:14-15, 21-23,31,38** 262, 360, 371; **7:17** 163; **7:17-23** 362; **8:28** 418; **8:31** 371; **8:32** 238, 347, 353; **8:44** 190, 238; **9:1-3** 117; **9:1-41** 227; **9:2-3** 222; **9:3** 394; **9:6-7** 331; **9:13-34** 347; **9:15** 425; **9:16** 139, 371, 394; **9:26-27** 425; **9:27** 425; **9:29** 347, 353; **9:35,36,38** 371; **10:10** 236; **10:25** 262, 360, 371; **10:27** 57, 254, 439; **10:32** 262, 360, 371; **10:37-38** 91, 146, 151; **10:38** 161, 262, 360, 371; **10:47-48** 371; **chap. 11** 123; **11:38-45** 227; **11:45** 371; **11:47-48** 371; **11:48** 95; **12:17-18** 139; **12:49** 418; **14:1** 371; **14:10** 406; **14:10-13** 270; **14:11** 146, 161; **14:12** 124, 186, 199, 355, 371; **14:12-13** 393; **14:24** 418; **14:26** 254, 418, 428, 439; **14:30-31** 236; **15:1-5** 418; **16:11** 236; **16:13-14** 254, 439, 440; **16:14** 88; **17:18** 199; **17:21** 201; **17:23** 201; **18:6** 303, 313, 332, 429, 432; **20:21** 199; **20:21-23** 399; **20:29-31** 93; **20:30-31** 164; **20:31** 94, 146

Acts **1:1** 199; **1:3** 263, 265; **1:8** 47, 69, 70, 209, 254, 263, 265, 273, 355, 366, 399; **chap. 2** 318; **2:3-4** 432; **2:4,13** 432; **2:4,13,15** 429; **2:17-18** 47, 83; **2:22** 97, 141, 153, 161, 164, 269, 371, 406; **2:43** 388; **3:6** 227, 264; **3:6-8** 362; **3:6,12** 262, 360, 370, 401; **3:11** 369; **3:12-13** 153, 369; **3:13** 153; **3:15-16** 153, 369; **3:19** 369; **4:2,10** 362; **4:9** 181; **4:16,22** 139; **4:20** 151; **4:29-30** 146, 160, 262, 273, 360, 362, 370, 401; **4:29-31** 262; **4:30** 96; **4:33** 209, 362; **5:1-3** 118; **5:3** 262; **5:12-16** 60, 138, 161, 262, 360, 362, 370, 388, 401; **5:13** 370; **5:14** 370; **5:15** 430; **5:20-21** 262, 360, 362, 370, 401; **5:28** 262, 360, 370, 401; **5:42** 262, 360, 370, 401; **6:8** 60, 66, 142, 145, 161, 164, 190, 388; **6:8-10** 262, 360, 363, 370, 401; **6:9-10,15** 432; **6:10** 366, 418; **7:51** 418; **7:2-53** 418; **7:55** 262, 432, 440; **7:56** 418; **8:4-7,12f.** 190, 262, 360, 363, 370, 401; **8:4-8** 26, 368; **8:5** 153; **8:5-6** 161; **8:5-7** 142, 263; **8:6ff.** 60, 62, 66, 138, 140, 141, 153, 264, 388; **8:9-11** 90, 230; **8:12f.** 190, 262, 263, 360, 363, 370, 375, 401; **8:13** 138, 140, 141, 142, 145; **8:26** 418, 440; **8:29** 254, 424, 440; **8:26-40** 161; **8:39-40** 262, 431; **9:3** 370; **9:3ff.** 150, 431; **9:4** 429; **9:10-12** 440; **9:11** 254; **9:11-12** 143, 145, 262; **9:15** 418; **9:17-18** 60, 66, 161, 184, 190, 262, 360,

370 401, 432; **9:19b-20** 150; **9:20,22** 150; **9:34** 153, 407, 424; **9:34-35** 370, 401; **9:36-42** 60; **9:40-41** 63; **10:9-17** 431; **10:9-19** 440; **10:9-36** 86; **10:13-19** 440; **10:37-39** 380; **10:38** 371, 377, 387; **11:7-12** 440; **11:27-28** 440; **12:3-17** 31, 262; **13:1-3** 440; **13:7-12** 372; **13:8-10** 230; **13:10** 238; **13:10-11** 418; **13:51** 189, 401; **13:52** 432; **14:3** 138, 164, 263, 363, 366, 370, 372, 388, 401; **14:7,9** 153; **14:8-10,15ff.** 370, 372, 388, 401; **14:10** 153; **14:22** 263; **15:12** 370, 372, 388, 401, 407; **15:6-18** 86; **15:36** 370, 401; **16:9-10** 440; **16:16** 414; **16:16-18** 372, 418; **16:18** 76, 90, 419; **17:11** 437, 439, 440; **17:16-34** 387; **17:28** 281; **18:1,5** 363; **18:5** 376; **18:9** 440; **19:4-6** 372; **19:5-6** 145, 440; **19: 8-12** 263, 364, 370, 372, 401; **19:11** 407; **19:11-12** 60, 140, 364, 388; **19:12** 430; **20:7-10** 372; **20:10** 43, 426; **21:10-11** 78, 440; **20:23** 440; **20:24** 385; **20:25** 265; **21:8-9** 440; **21:9** 143, 145; **22:12-13** 143; **22:12-13** 145; **22:12-16** 401; **22:13** 60, 66, 184, 262, 360, 370; **26:14** 432; **22:14-15** 385; **22:15** 151, 385; **26:11** 429; **26:15-18** 385; **26:16** 151, 385; **26:17-18** 236; **28:3-6** 262; **28:8** 227, 406; **28:8-9** 372; **28:9** 221; **28:31** 265
Romans **1:16** 69, 160, 209; **1:18-32** 116; **1:24-25** 239; **4:17** 198; **6:1-10** 240; **7:1-25** 238; **8:4-**

16 30; **8:15** 414; **8:16** 254, 439, 440; **8:17** 30; **8:18-39** 263; **11:8** 414; chap. **12** 186; **12:3-8** 197; **12:6** 99, 439; **12:6ff.** 144, 145, 163, 184; **14:1-15:7** 201; **14:3** 201; **14:17** 189, 199, 263; **15:16-20** 26, 368; **15:17-20** 153; **15:18-19** 29, 58, 59, 68, 141, 147, 149, 155, 161, 164, 185, 209, 262, 263, 281, 360, 370, 372, 366, 387, 388, 401, 407; **15:18-20** 364, 376; **15:18-21** 384; **15:19** 60, 69, 98, 199, 373, 410; **15:31** 31
1 Corinthians **1:5** 199; **1:6-7** 31, 50, 147, 149, 159, 364, 401, 422; **1:7** 147; **1:17** 26, 369; **1:17-18** 29, 210; **1:22-23** 68; **1:26-29** 270; **2:2,4** 153; **2:3** 222; **2:3-5** 199; **2:4** 366, 410; **2:4-5** 29, 147, 149, 210, 255, 262, 273, 360, 364, 370, 373, 376, 385, 401; **3:16** 236; **4:15b-17** 179; **4:20** 29, 189, 199, 263; **5:4-5** 119; **6:11-19** 30; **6:19-20** 236; **7:5** 238; **10:19-20** 45; **10:19-21** 239; **10:20** 234; **11:1** 145, 163, 184, 185, 190, 263, 426; **11:27-30** 117; **11:30** 222; chap. **12** 186, 199; chaps. **12-14** 143, 144, 147, 198, 199, 263; **12:1-11, 28-31** 184; **12:3** 70, 439; **12:4-11** 60, 406; **12:6** 406; **12:7** 186; **12:7-11,28-30** 163; **12:8** 226; **12:8-10** 145, 263, 366; **12:9** 30, 158, 190, 227, 401, 422; **12:10** 69, 247, 439; **12:11** 99, 186; **12:13** 355; **12:28** 60, 66, 145, 158, 186, 366, 422, 439; **12:31** 408, 409; chap. **13** 186; **13:8** 87; **13:9**

31, 50, 159, 422; **13:9-10** 406;
14:1 186, 408, 439; **14:1ff.**
145, 161, 184, 186, 409; **14:1-
5** 147; **14:2** 75; **14:4** 71, 74;
14:4-5 439; **14:5** 70, 408;
14:12-13 408; **14:18** 99;
14:22 71, 140, 143, 147, 439;
14:22-25 262, 360; **14:22-39**
163; **14:24** 439; **14:24-25**
147, 262, 263, 285, 370; **14:25**
147; **14:29** 78; **14:29-30** 439;
14:29-31,39 439; **14:39-40**
408; **15:22-25** 181
2 *Corinthians* **1:8-11** 31; **2:10-11**
119, 238; **2:11** 237, 256; **3:7,
13,17-18** 432; **4:2** 238; **4:3-4**
237; **4:4** 236; **4:7-11** 30;
chaps. 10-13 65; **10:3-4** 76;
10:3-5 239; **11:3** 237; **11:3-4**
238; **11:13-15** 238; **12:1-5**
262; **12:5** 222; **12:7-10** 30, 31,
215, 222, 223; **12:12** 26, 63,
68, 69, 141, 147, 149, 153, 161,
262, 360, 363, 364, 368, 370,
372, 373, 376, 385, 401, 410;
13:14 440
Galatians **2:1-2,7-9** 86; **3:1-5** 184;
3:4-5 124; **3:5** 26, 60, 69, 141,
143, 144, 145, 147, 149, 161,
163, 164, 184, 185, 190, 199,
262, 263, 360, 364, 366, 368,
370, 373, 401, 406, 410; **4:4-7**
124; **4:13** 222; **4:13-14** 30,
126; **5:16-26** 410; **5:16-6:10**
30; **5:20-21** 238, 239; **5:22**
410
Ephesians **1:13** 236; **1:15-19** 224;
1:17 439; **1:17-19** 210; **1:18-
20** 29; **2:1-2** 236, 238; **2:14**
126; **2:20** 85; **3:14-21** 224;
3:16-17 29; **3:19** 272; **4:1-16**
198, 201; **4:2** 201; **4:3,13** 201;

4:7ff. 145, 147, 184; **4:8** 256;
4:11 86, 143, 144, 439; **4:26-
27** 236, 238, 239, 240, 247;
5:18 318; **6:10** 29; **6:10-11**
29; **6:10-17** 240; **6:10-18** 76,
416, 419; **6:12** 236, 241; **6:17**
418
Philippians **1:9-11** 224; **2:10** 126;
2:25-27 221; **2:26-27** 126;
2:27 63, 98; **3:21** 430; **4:9**
145, 163, 184, 190, 263, 401;
4:13 215
Colossians **1:9-12** 224; **1:13** 236;
1:29 430; **3:5-10** 238
1 *Thessalonians* **1:5** 30, 147, 155,
364, 366, 373, 385, 410; **1:5-6**
145, 184, 190, 262, 263, 360,
370, 401; **1:6** 184, 426; **3:5**
238; **5:19ff.** 147, 163, 184,
198, 263, 409, 439, 441; **5:20**
143, 144, 145; **5:20-21** 78
2 *Thessalonians* **2:9** 136; **2:9-10** 90;
2:9-12 238; **3:2** 31
1 *Timothy* **1:20** 119; **3:13** 238; **4:1**
238, 414; **4:14** 99, 147; **5:23**
126, 221, 248; **10:38** 269
2 *Timothy* **1:6** 99, 163, 409; **1:6-7**
147; **1:7** 410, 414; **1:8** 30;
2:15 80; **2:24-26** 236; **3:5**
191, 260, 264; **3:11** 31; **3:12**
30; **3:15-16** 437; **3:16** 80, 440;
4:17 31; **4:20** 126, 221
Hebrews **2:3-4** 67, 139, 199, 141,
164, 186, 262, 360, 365, 366,
370, 388, 401; **2:4** 94; **2:14**
121; **6:1-2** 190, 401; **6:2** 184;
6:5 126, 199, 208, 263, 366;
9:27 223
James **1:5** 124; **1:5-6** 441; **4:2** 186,
226, 271; **4:3** 124; **4:7** 76, 240;
5:13-16 262, 360, 409; **5:13-
17** 219; **5:14** 144; **5:14-15**

144, 366; **5:14-16** 18, 30, 31,
97, 133, 144, 145, 163, 184,
190, 222, 263, 401, 422; **5:15**
118, 124, 159, 225, 406; **5:15-
16** 267, 347; **5:16** 117, 125,
144, 224; **5:17-18** 31, 409

1 Peter **2:24** 50, 121, 256; **4:10** 143,
144, 145; **4:10-11** 32, 163,
184, 198, 365, 409; **5:8** 119;
5:8-9 236; **5:9** 76

2 Peter **1:19-20** 440; **1:19-20** 440;
2:1-22 57, 65; **3:16** 440

1 John **2:2** 121; **2:12-14** 232, 242;
2:27 42, 439; **3:2** 87, 159; **3:8**
121, 125, 247, 251; **3:8-10** 238;
chap. 4 306; **4:1** 230; **4:1-3**
232; **4:1-6** 57; **4:4** 236, 241;
4:6 414; **5:4** 124; **5:19** 236

Jude **9** 75

Revelation **1:10** 17, 307, 332, 429;
1:13-18 307; **1:17** 313, 429,
432; **1:17-18** 332; **7:16** 126;
10:9-11 431; **11:3-13** 136;
12:3-9 234; **12:10** 238; **12:11**
251, 256; **13:11-14** 90; **13:13**
136; **16:14** 136; **19:10** 47, 48,
51, 286; **19:20** 136; **21:10** 126;
22:4 87, 159